D0072269

The Music and Dance of
the World's Religions

The Music and Dance of the World's Religions

A Comprehensive, Annotated Bibliography of Materials in the English Language

E. GARDNER RUST

Music Reference Collection, *Number 54*

Greenwood Press
Westport, Connecticut • London

Library of Congress Cataloging-in-Publication Data

Rust, Ezra Gardner.
  The music and dance of the world's religions : a comprehensive,
  annotated bibliography of materials in the English language / E.
  Gardner Rust.
      p.   cm.—(Music reference collection, ISSN 0736–7740 ; no.
  54)
  Includes bibliographical references (p.   ) and index.
  ISBN 0–313–29561–1 (alk. paper)
  1. Sacred vocal music—Bibliography.   2. Music—Bibliography.
  3. Dance—Bibliography.   4. Music—Religious aspects—Bibliography.
  5. Dance—Religious aspects—Bibliography.   I. Title.   II. Series.
  ML128.S17R87   1996
  016.7817—dc20   96–18212

British Library Cataloguing in Publication Data is available.

Copyright © 1996 by E. Gardner Rust

All rights reserved. No portion of this book may be
reproduced, by any process or technique, without the
express written consent of the publisher.

Library of Congress Catalog Card Number: 96–18212
ISBN: 0–313–29561–1
ISSN: 0736–7740

First published in 1996

Greenwood Press, 88 Post Road West, Westport, CT 06881
An imprint of Greenwood Publishing Group, Inc.

Printed in the United States of America

The paper used in this book complies with the
Permanent Paper Standard issued by the National
Information Standards Organization (Z39.48–1984).

10 9 8 7 6 5 4 3 2 1

Contents

Preface and Acknowledgments

The function of music in human society, what music ultimately does, is to control humanity's relationship to the supernatural, mediating between people and other beings....Music functions for all societies as a force for religion. [1]

Throughout human history, music and dance have been inseparable adjuncts to religious observance. Peoples of every society and of every era have addressed the sacred through the mediums of music and dance. So close is this relationship, that neither music, dance, nor the practice of religion would resemble what they are today were it not for the influence each has had on the other. Religion has provided subject matter for the creative imagination to focus on. It has been a laboratory in which composers developed, and continue to develop, the music and dance styles peculiar to their culture. Chant, song, and dance have thereby become vehicles of expression for mankind's most deeply felt fears, needs, and aspirations. Without psalms and hymns, the Protestant church service would lack its most typical occasions for communal praise. Without chant, a Hindu or Jewish temple ritual would not exist. Without dance, little would remain of a Navaho or Mevlevi ceremony.

In spite of the intimate relationship between music, dance, and religion, there is not a single full-length study of this subject from a global perspective. There is only one survey of any length, a series of entries in the Macmillan *Encyclopedia of Religion* (see this Bibliography, nos. 5, 6). A few collections of essays exist on the music of different religions (nos. 2, 3, 4, 8). The literature on specific aspects of religious music or dance, though plentiful, is distributed among hundreds of books, journal articles and essays, and dissertations. There has been

---

[1] Nettl, Bruno. *The Study of Ethnomusicology. Twenty-nine Issues and Concepts.* Chicago, IL: University of Illinois Press. 1983. 159, 161.

no easy way to find this literature. Bibliographical references to the materials are as scattered as the materials themselves; they appear in hundreds of reference works, monographs, articles, and databases. Clearly the need exists for a comprehensive study of this compelling subject. Such a study would require a knowledge of the available materials. It is my hope that in compiling these 3800 references to the music and dance of all of the world's religions and in presenting them in an easy-to-find manner, I will have contributed in some way to a future *Religious Music and Dance of the Whole Earth*.[2]

The present work is comprehensive in two respects. It includes references to religions from every region of the world, to those with scriptures and to those without, to religions that are local, regional, and global. It also brings to the subject a wide variety of approaches. Analysis, description, direct experience, observation, and speculation are all to be found in these references. Authors draw from a variety of disciplines, including sociology, anthropology, history, linguistics, musicology, ethnomusicology, theology, and medicine. The newer fields of semiology and computer-aided scholarship are also represented.

Approximately 80 percent of the references are annotated. The annotations range from brief descriptions to full summaries of contents, in the case of complex or novel works. Some materials were not available to annotate, but were included because of a relevance suggested by their title and author. Histories, dictionaries, encyclopedias, and bibliographies were included without commentary because their scope and subject matter were obvious from their title.

The following factors were considered in the selection of references for this book: 1) subject matter, 2) type of reference, 3) date of publication, 4) quantity of material available on a given subject, and 5) the mode in which the subject matter was transmitted.

1. *Subject matter.* Music and dance in a religious context are the subjects of this bibliography. Under the heading of religion are included all of the topics covered in the essays referred to above and in texts by such authors as Noss and Noss,[3] and Ninian Smart.[4] Most of the topics covered by the bibliography fall easily under this heading. Two topics, shamanism and the relationship between

---

[2] The reference here is to David Reck's magnificent and sadly out-of-print study of the world's music, *Music of the Whole Earth*. New York: Charles Scribner's Sons. 1977

[3] Noss and Noss. *A History of the World's Religions*. Ninth Edition. New York: Macmillan College Publishing Company. 1994

[4] Smart, Ninian & Richard D. Hecht. *Sacred Texts of the World. A Universal Anthology.* New York: Crossroad. 1982

music, mathematics and mysticism, may require some explanation. Shamanism is considered by many scholars to be the earliest form of religious expression. It is a vital component of the religious life of all east and central Asian cultures, as well as of Eskimo and Native American religions. It is also found under other names as an aspect of almost all other indigenous religions. Sound and movement, often of extraordinary intensity, are essential tools in shamanic trance. Because of its religious and musical elements, shamanism has been included in the bibliography.

At least from the time of Pythagoras, music has been thought both to embody and to reveal the mathematical order of the cosmos. The idea of a correspondence between a mathematically structured universe and the intervals of music has stimulated much speculative thought from Greek times to the present. The contemplation of mathematically ordered sound has also played a role in experiences described as mystical. Chapter 26, Music, Mathematics, and Mysticism, provides references to both types of literature, the speculative and the experiential. (For related material, see pp. 80-81, Modern Speculations on Indian Music, as well as references in Chapter 1, General References and Studies.)

2. *Types of references.* The types of references that constitute this bibliography are books, book sections (or essays), journal articles, doctoral dissertations, and entries in dictionaries and encyclopedias. Editions of music, magazine articles (as opposed to journal articles) and most of the articles that appear in the monthly periodicals devoted to the music of specific Christian denominations have been excluded. Such articles are usually very short and are too numerous to include. Biographies of specific European composers and LP and CD album notes have also been excluded, though both can be very informative.

3. *Date of publication.* One of my highest priorities for this book has been the inclusion of the most recent materials on every subject. Where numerous recent writings exist, such as on the music of Medieval Europe and African America, I have chosen the mid-1970s as the cut-off date for the earliest entries. The bibliographies for the *New Grove Dictionary of Music and Musicians* (no. 9) were prepared during this period. Any literature of importance published prior to the mid-'70s would probably be listed there or in other more recent publications. References to older literature have been included where recent publications are scant—as on the music of various Euro-American denominations—or where an important aspect of a subject has not been covered since the 1970s.

4. *The number of references on a given topic.* The bibliography contains noticeable, but nevertheless unavoidable, inequalities in coverage between one religion and another and between music and dance. The literature on Christian music of both the past and the present is inexhaustible. Hundreds of articles appear yearly in more than a dozen scholarly journals and popular magazines that are devoted to the subject. The literature on Hinduism and Judaism is moderately abundant. That on Buddhism, Islam, Taoism, and Confucianism, though not entirely lacking, is by comparison rather spotty. Of indigenous

religious practices, the ceremonials of the Native Americans are relatively well represented. Of the ceremonies of the native peoples of the Pacific, by way of contrast, Christian missionary activity during the 19th century was so thorough that little remains to document.

There are several reasons for the inequalities mentioned above. The first has already been alluded to. Christian music of both the past and the present is the most fully documented of all religious music. It has existed in notated form for more than 1000 years. Thousands of works in hundreds of manuscripts from both Eastern and Western Europe date from the 11th through the 15th centuries alone. These have given scholars ample material to investigate and convey to interested readers. The recent expansion of scholarly interest into non-European and popular forms of Christian music has opened additional areas to explore.

A second reason for the inequalities is that of the language in which scholars of specific religious traditions write. The scholarly language of each culture area is also the dominant written language of that area. Materials on Japanese Buddhist music, for instance, are primarily in Japanese. Those on Byzantine chant are in Slavic languages. Those on the shamanism of Eurasia and Central Asia are in Russian. Research on the music of colonized cultures tends to be written in the tongue of the colonizing power. Most of the literature concerning the Indians of Central and South America, for example, is in Spanish. Thus, in a bibliography restricted to references in English, the topics that are covered most fully are those to which English-language scholars are primarily devoted—the Christian religion and the geographic areas of Western Europe and North America .

The disparity between the materials on religious music and those on religious dance is due to differences in the means of notating the two arts. Duration and pitch (or melodic direction) are relatively easy to symbolize. Methods of notation have existed for more than 1500 years. No satisfactory system of notating dance existed, on the other hand, until the invention of the motion picture. The literature on dance is thus confined to general descriptions of dances, to discussions of history, function, and context, or to suggestions for motions and themes appropriate to contemporary liturgy. This contrasts with the detailed analyses of music and the histories of genres, styles, and forms—all of which are full of references to specific compositions—that are commonly found in scholarly music writings. Such writings have been possible only because music has been preserved in notated form.

5. *Mode of transmission.* The topic of notation brings us to the last major factor to bear on the contents of this bibliography. Broadly speaking, the literature on religious music and dance either deals with historical documents—primarily written documents—or consists of eyewitness accounts of particular events. Stated differently, the subject matter of this work's references is the product either of literate transmission or of oral transmission. Neither notated music nor a live ritual escapes the filter of the scholar's or observer's point of view. Writings on both involve acts of interpretation. But written documents,

especially those of centuries and cultures long past, are of many types and require special kinds of interpretive skills and knowledge.

The types of documents that scholars comb for information concerning religious performance are scriptures, histories, commentaries and chronicles, letters, polemics and theologies, books of rites and liturgies, and music-theory texts and treatises. Visual representations of dance, instruments, and religious ritual are also sources of valuable information. Service books, account books, and other archival materials have recently been added to this list. Notated music in particular presents issues not relevant to music in oral tradition. These issues center on the interpretation of the notation, a study of compositions and repertories, and a recreation of their musical and cultural context.

Clearly, the range of issues related to written documents is broad. The range of competencies required of scholars to deal with these issues has increased dramatically in recent years. Because of these two factors, I have given priority, with respect to the study of written documents, to the most recent research, particularly that since the mid-1970s. This has been done even at the risk of omitting titles long familiar to knowledgeable readers.

A different basis for inclusion has been applied to references to oral traditions. A detailed account of a religious ritual or ceremonial contains useful material, no matter when it was written. With respect to the Native Americans, for instance, some of the most richly detailed descriptions of the Sun and Ghost Dance ceremonials date from the end of the 19th century and the beginning of the 20th. The same is true of Eskimo ceremonies involving shamans. In order to present as complete a picture as possible of the practice of tribal or indigenous cultures, I have included references to literature that is full of detail, regardless of its date.

Some of the most exciting literature on indigenous religious culture has emerged quite recently, however. A new breed of scholars is applying sound scholarship to what they experience and observe as accepted members of a host community. This type of literature, by those who live and participate in a culture for an extended period, conveys more than musical or anthropological data. It gives the context—the sense of time, place, ritual occasion, text, and meaning—as understood and created by the native peoples themselves.[5]

Organization. The bibliography has been organized to make references as easy to find as possible. For the sake of consistency, I have maintained a geographic

---

[5] Authors of such literature include Roseman on the Malay Temiar (nos. 378-381), Harnish in Lombok, (nos. 476-480), Shelemay among the Falasha of Ethiopia (nos. 970-978), Basso (nos. 3450, 3451), Hill (nos. 3470-3476) and Seeger (nos. 3495-3500) among the Kalapalo, Wakuénai and Suya of South America, and Feld among the Kaluli of New Guinea (nos. 3650-3652).

orientation throughout, first by major geographic area, then by region or country, and lastly by religion. The table of contents is given in expanded form to direct a reader to an area of interest without having to resort to an index. The headings and subheadings were dictated by categories found within the country or religion itself and the quantity of literature on a given topic.

Sources. In addition to the bibliographies in the types of literature already cited, the sources for the references contained herein are such hard-copy publications as *Books in Print*, *RILM*, *Music Index*, and *Bibliography Index*. The cumulative bibliography that appears in each issue of the journal *Ethnomusicology* was particularly useful. The many computerized databases available in libraries and on-line were essential sources of references. Both *Melvyl*, the on-line data-base for the entire University of California library system as well as the library of the Graduate Theological Union in Berkeley, and *First Search*, perhaps the largest of all book data-bases, were consulted extensively. For journal articles, *Alta Religion*, *Current Contents*, *First-Search*, *Expanded Academic Index*, and *Articles and Periodicals* were all consulted. The last named was particularly valuable because it includes abstracts of many articles and sometimes the full text as well. *Dissertation Abstracts* is available in both hard-copy and on-line. Most of the references that are annotated are located in the libraries of the University of California, Berkeley, and the Graduate Theological Union.

Acknowledgments. I cannot conclude this Preface without expressing appreciation for those whose labors have found their way into this bibliography and without giving thanks to those who helped me in specific ways. First, I would like to thank the librarians at the Graduate Theological Union and Berkeley libraries for their helpfulness and patience. Special thanks must go to Richard Crocker of the University of California, Berkeley, for his valuable suggestions concerning new research in early Christian liturgy, to Ellen Sinatra of UCLA for her materials on trance, and to Ter Ellingson for his references on Tibetan Buddhism. Lastly, I am especially indebted to my two research assistants, Sabine Henrie, who has a M.A. in religious dance from the Pacific School of Religion in Berkeley, and Kevin Stoll, a major in both Music and English at Sonoma State University.

Please address comments or additional references to

Prof. Gardner Rust
Department of Music
Sonoma State University
Rohnert Park, CA 94928

or to my e-mail address at <gardner.rust@sonoma.edu>

Abbreviations

Grove 5	Grove's Dictionary of Music and Musicians. 1954
Grove 6	New Grove Dictionary of Music and Musicians. 1980
HUCA	Hebrew Union College Annual
ICTM	International Council for Traditional Music
IMS12	International Musicological Society. Report of the Twelfth Congress Berkeley 1977. Bärenreiter-Verlag Kassel. 1981
JAMS	Jounal of the American Musicological Society
JIFMC	Journal of the International Folk Music Council
JPMMS	Journal of the Plainsong and Mediaeval Music Society
JRAS	Journal of the Royal Asian Society
JRMA	Journal of the Royal Music Association
MQ	The Musical Quarterly
NGDAM	New Grove Dictionary of American Music
NOHM II	New Oxford History of Music.
PRMA	Proceedings of the Royal Music Association
YIFMC	Yearbook of the International Folk Music Council
YTM	Yearbook for Traditional Music

1

General References and Studies

SHORT LIST OF SELECTED REFERENCES

1.   Blom, Eric, ed. *Grove's Dictionary of Music and Musicians*. 5th ed., 9 vols. London: Macmillan; New York: St. Martin's Press, 1954.   Contains substantial articles by mid-century scholars.

2.   Collins, Mary, David Powell, and Mellonee Burnim, ed. *Music and the Experience of God*. Concilium: Religion in the Eighties, Vol. 202. Edinburgh: T & T Clark Ltd, 1989.   Twelve articles on Christian and Jewish traditions in Europe and Africa and on ritual.

3.   Daniélou, Alain, ed. *The World of Music: Sacred Music Issue*. 24, 3. 1982.   Articles on Gregorian, Vedic, and Sephardic chant, and Falasha, Islamic and Tibetan Buddhist music.

4.   Daniélou, Alain, ed. *The World of Music: Sacred Music Issue II*. 26, 3. 1984.   Two articles on Buddhist music; articles on musical symbol and on sacred music and sacred time.

5.   Eliade, Mircea, ed. *The Encyclopedia of Religion*. 16 vols. New York: Macmillan, 1987.   The most comprehensive modern encyclopedia of religion in the English language.   See entries on Music, Dance, Drama, Chanting, Drums, and Percussion and Noise, and on any aspect of religious practice and belief. Under "Music," a survey of music and religion from a global perspective is followed by articles on the religious music of ten major geographical areas.   The section "Dance" includes articles on dance and religion, and on theatrical and liturgical dance.   Each article is listed below.

6.   Ellingson, Ter. "Music and Religion." In *The Encyclopedia of Religion*, Mircea Eliade, ed. Vol. 10. 1987. 163-172. One of the very few surveys of religious music from a global perspective.

7.   Hastings, James, ed. *Encyclopedia of Religion and Ethics*. Edinburgh, Scotland: T & T Clark; New York, NY: Scribner's, 1908-1927/repr. 1961. Contains articles on the music of numerous religions and cults. Valuable as a resource for what scholars knew and thought about religious music during the early decades of this century.

8.   Irwin, Joyce, ed. *Sacred Sound: Music in Religious Thought and Practice*. Vol. 50, #1. Journal of the American Academy of Religion Studies, ed. Chico, CA: Scholars Press, 1983. Seven essays on specific aspects of the music of Christianity, Judaism, Sufism, Ga (Ghana), Theravadan Buddhism, and Hinduism, preceded by two essays on issues relating to a theology of music (primarily Christian). Each essay is listed below.

9.   Sadie, Stanley, ed. *The New Grove Dictionary of Music and Musicians*. 20 vols. London: Macmillan; Washington, DC: Grove's Dictionaries of Music, 1980. Contains articles on the music of every culture and religion. Covers the music of every early Christian rite and all forms and styles of music in Christian liturgies. Identified hereafter as "Grove 6."

GENERAL REFERENCES AND BIBLIOGRAPHIES

10.   *Ethnomusicology: Journal of the Society for Ethnomusicology*. Bloomington, IN: Society for Ethnomusicology; Indiana University Press, 1953 to present. Each issue contains a listing of current bibliography, discography, and filmography in the field of ethnomusicology, as well as reviews of books and records in the field. Each Winter issue contains a listing of recently completed dissertations and theses.

11.   Forbes, Fred. *Dance: An Annotated Bibliography, 1965-1982*. New York: Garland Publications, 1986. See chapter on Anthropology.

12.   Grimes, Ronald L. *Research in Ritual Studies: A Programmatic Essay and Bibliography*. American Theological Library Association Bibliography Series 14, Metuchen, NJ: Scarecrow Press, 1985. A useful guide. All materials in English.

13.   Randel, Don, ed. *The New Harvard Dictionary of Music*. Cambridge: Harvard University Press, 1986.

14.   Smart and Hecht. *Sacred Texts of the World: A Universal Anthology*. New York: Crossroad Publishing Co., 1982. Texts from ten major religions, as well as from small-scale traditional religions, new religions, and secular world

views. Many texts were or are sung when performed. Several references to song and dance are contained in the chapter on small-scale traditional religions.

15.   Strayer, Joseph R., ed. *Dictionary of the Middle Ages*. New York: Charles Scribner's Sons, 1982. The *Dictionary* contains useful summaries of all aspects of music in the Middle Ages in largely non-technical language. It includes entries on Jewish, Christian and Islamic as well as indigenous music cultures. Covers the period between 500 and 1500.

16.   Strunk, Oliver. *Source Readings in Music History from Classical Antiquity through the Romantic Era*. New York: W. W. Norton, 1950. Eighty-seven selections from Greek and Western sources, through the 19th century.

17.   Weiss, Piero and Richard Taruskin, ed. *Music in the Western World. A History in Documents*. New York: G. Schirmer Books, 1984. One-hundred-fifty-five documents from Greek and Western sources, through 1983.

MUSIC AND RELIGION

18.   Abell, Arthur M. *Talks with Great Composers*. Garmisch-Partenkirchen: G.E. Schroeder-Verlag, 1964. Comments by 19th and early 20th century European composers about the divine source of their musical inspiration.

19.   al-Faruqi, Lois Ibsen. "What Makes 'Religious Music' Religious?" In *Sacred Sound*, Joyce Irwin, ed. Chico: Scholars Press, 1983. 21-34. Because of their transcendent and non-phenomenal aspects, Christian plainchant and the Qur'anic chant of Islam are ideal forms of religious music.

20.   Andrews, Ted. *Sacred Sounds: Transformation Through Music and Word*. St. Paul, MN: Llewellyn Publications, 1992. On the relationship of music to magic.

21.   Berendt, Joachim-Ernst. *Nada Brahma: The World is Sound. Music and the Landscape of Consciousness*. Helmut Bredigkeit, transl. Rochester, VT: Destiny Books, 1987. First published as *Nada Brahma: Die Welt ist Klang*. Frankfurt am Main, West Germany: Insel Verlag, 1983. Berendt proposes that all the world is sound, rhythm, and vibration, and supports his idea through physical experimentations and religious cosmologies, from Christianity to Zen, Islam to Confucianism, that proclaim a sound-related existence. His final position is that harmony is the ultimate goal of evolution.

22.   Bloch, Maurice. "Symbols, Song, Dance and Features of Articulation: Is Religion an Extreme Form of Traditional Authority?" *Archives Européennes Sociologiques [de Sociologie]* 15, 1 (1974): 55-81.

23.   Boilès, Charles. *Man, Magic, and Musical Occasions*. Columbus, OH: Collegiate Publishing, 1978. A study of music used in magical situations that are

described as actions or words used to invoke or coerce the non-physical power believed to reside in things, conditions and times.

24.   Brame, Grace Adolphsen. "The Relationship between the Mystical and the Artistic." In *Mysticism, Creativity and Psi*, M. Rose, ed. 1984. 38-46.

25.   Cole, Basil. *Music and Morals: A Theological Appraisal of the Moral and Psychological Effects of Music*. New York, NY: Alba House, 1993.

26.   Daniélou, Alain. "Popular Religious Music in the Twentieth Century." *Cultures* 1, 3 (1974): 227-36. In spite of the strength of notated music, secular music, and court and church-controlled music, the Dionysian spirit still survives in popular religious music of Georgian, Coptic, Cyprian, Celtic and similar religious traditions.

27.   Drinker, Sophie. "The Origins of Music: Women's Goddess Worship." In *The Politics of Women's Spirituality: Essays on the Rise of Spiritual Power with the Feminist Movement*, Charlene Spretnak, ed. Garden City, NY: Anchor Books, 1982. 39-48. On the origins and development of music throughout the world from a feminist perspective. Cites evidence of woman-centered sacred music as an on-going cross cultural phenomenon. Reprint from 1948.

28.   Edappilly, John. "Divine and Devotion in the Music of East and West." *Journal of Dharma* 15, July (1990): 245-258.

29.   El Din, Hamza. "The Gnosis Interview with Hamza El Din." *Gnosis* #27/Spring (1993): 47-49. The famous *oud* and *tar* player muses on the sacred in music and on the links between Islam and music.

30.   Fried, Martha N. and Morton Fried. *Transitions: Four Rituals in Eight Cultures*. New York: W.W. Norton & Co., 1980. Birth, Puberty, Marriage, and Death as observed by the Tikopia, Tlinget, !Kung, Hausa, Taiwanese, Mainland Chinese, Cubans and Russians.

31.   Gerson-Kiwi, Edith. "Religious Chant: A Pan-Asiatic Conception of Music." *Journal of the International Folk Music Council* 13 (1961): 64-67. Reprinted in *Migrations and Mutations of the Music in East and West*. Tel Aviv: Tel Aviv University. 1980: 50-53.

32.   Gerson-Kiwi, Edith. "The Birth of Musical Sound and Melody." *Orbis Musicae* 10 (1990/91): 272-277. The birth of melody as a biological act lies in the alternation of tension and release found in the inhalation and exhalation of breathing. Its social origin lies in the use of vocal sounds by shamans—the mediators between a people and their deities—for magical purposes, best illustrated by the music of American Indians, Mongolian tribes, and Pacific Islanders.

33.   Godwin, Joscelyn. *Music, Mysticism and Magic. A Sourcebook*. London: Routledge and Kegan Paul, 1986. A collection of writings of 61 authors from Plato to Stockhausen concerning the relationship between music and various expressions of religious and metaphysical thought.

34.   Govinda, Lama Anagarika. *Creative Meditation and Multi-Dimensional Consciousness*. Wheaton, IL: Theosophical Publishing House, 1976. Includes chapters on the use of sound (mantra) to change consciousness.

35.   Hammerstein, Reinhold. "Music as a Divine Art." In *The Dictionary of the History of Ideas*, Philip Wiener, ed. Vol. 3. 1973. 267-272. Metaphysical notions of music as an invention of or influencing the divine in primitive peoples, civilized cultures, Greek culture, the Christian Middle Ages, the Reformation, the Baroque, and the Post-Baroque.

36.   Hammerstein, Reinhold. "Music as a Demonic Art." In *The Dictionary of the History of Ideas*, Philip Wiener, ed. Vol. 3. 1973. 264-267. Metaphysical notions of demonic influence over music in primitive peoples, civilized cultures, Christian Middle Ages, and the Post-Medieval period.

37.   Harrison, Frank Ll. "Music and Cult: The Functions of Music in Social and Religious Systems." In *Perspectives in Musicology*, B.S. Brook, E.O.D. Downes, and S. Van Solkema, ed. New York: W.W. Norton, 1972. 307-34. Topics include attitudes towards liturgy from the 16th century, editions of liturgical books, and the value of examining all documents from the most ancient to the modern. Argues for anthropomusicology: the study of music behavior in the context of total behavior.

38.   Herbert, Steven G. "Music: Universal Language, Universal Religion." *Journal of Religion and Psychical Research* 13, Oct. (1990): 187-191. Draws on Hindu, Judaic, and shamanic traditions to show the transcendent and healing powers of music.

39.   Herndon, Marcia and Norma McLeod. *Music as Culture*. 2nd ed., Darby, PA: Norwood Editions, 1982. See Chapter 4: The Relationship of Music to Social Institutions: Religion (114-134).

40.   Herndon, Marcia and Susanne Ziegler, ed. *Music, Gender, and Culture*. International Council for Traditional Music Study Group on Music and Gender, New York: C.F. Peters Corp., 1990. Includes several articles on the role of women in ritual, and on women, spirituality and music.

41.   Jackson, Anthony. "Sound and Ritual." *Man* 3 (new series) (1968): 293-99. A friendly response to Needham (see #116). Distinguishes between human speech and music on the one hand and accidental bodily sounds and work-a-day noises on the other. Because the former are socially ordered and ordering sounds designed to facilite communication, they are preferable in ritual.

42.   Kaufmann, Walter. "Parallel Trends of Musical Liturgies and Notations in Eastern & Western Asia." *Orbis Musicae* 3-4. A comparison of Jewish and Tibetan Buddhist liturgical music with respect to use of instruments, unison choral singing, use of meaningless syllables, and the development of notation, with additional references to Chinese, Japanese and Indian practices.

43.   Koskoff, Ellen. "Both In and Between: Women's Musical Roles in Ritual Life." In *Music and the Experience of God*, Collins, Power, and Burnim, ed. Edinburgh, Scotland: T. & T. Clark Ltd, 1989. 73-81. Compares women's roles in Jewish, Korean shamanic, and Iroquois religious-societal practices with special attention to ceremonial song and dance and positions of power or power structures within which the society operates.

44.   Merriam, Alan P. "Music—Bridge to the Supernatural." *Tomorrow* 5 (1957): 61 ff.

45.   Nadel, S.F. "The Origins of Music." *Musical Quarterly* 16 (1930): 531-546. After rejecting sexual selection (Darwin), emotional outcry (Rousseau, Spencer), and human activity such as the work-call (Bücher, Stumpf) as the origins of music (i.e., vocal melody), and after noting the world-wide connection between music and religious vocalization, Nadel locates the 'artificiality' of vocal melody, i.e., its differentness from everyday speech, as well as of art in general, in the necessity to communicate about and with the non-natural, the extra-ordinary in human experience. (Reprinted in *Readings in Ethnomusicology*, David P. McAllester, ed. New York, Johnson Reprint Corporation, 1971: 277-291.

46.   Perris, Arnold. *Music as Propaganda: Art to Persuade, Art to Control.* Westport, CT: Greenwood Press, 1985. See Chapter 6, "Sacred or Profane: Music in Religion: Propaganda"—the conscious plan to pursuade or control—as used in Jewish, Christian, Muslim, and Hindu worship.

47.   Roberts, Phyllis B. "Mysticism in Music." In *The Silent Encounter: Reflections on Mysticism*, Virginia Hanson, ed. 1974. 163-170.

48.   Rowell, Lewis. "Time in the Musical Consciousness of Old High Civilizations—East and West." In *The Study of Time*, J.T. Fraser, N. Lawrence, and D. Park, ed. Vol. 3. New York: Springer-Verlag, 1978. 578-611. An investigation of time and rhythmic systems in music as cosmological statements, with examples from ancient Greece, India, and China.

49.   Rowell, Lewis. "Paradigms for a Comparative Mythology of Music." In *Music and Myth. A Collection of Essays*, Bombay: Indian Musicological Society, 1989. 14-29. A survey of world mythologies reveals diverse answers to questions relating to the source and discoverer/giver of music, its effects and that of instruments, how music is grasped and perceived, the relationship of music, man, and cosmos, etc.

50.   Rudhyar, Dane. *The Magic of Tone and the Art of Music*. Boulder: Shambhala, 1982 (reprint).

51.   Rycenga, Jennifer Joanne. *The Composer as a Religious Person in the Context of Pluralism*. Ph.D. diss., Graduate Theological Union, 1993. The study of music from an immanentalist religious perspective locates the sacrality of music in its inner workings, rather than in symbolic or theological explorations of musical creativity. Exx. include Tyagaraja, Sun Ra, John Cage, and Jon Anderson; Pauline Oliveros; Ornette Colemen; The Beatles and Yes; and Charles Ives—all of whom, in different ways, create relationship, ethics and ontology through their music itself. Close musical analysis, philosophic hermeneutics, and feminist theory form the basis of this study.

52.   Schechner, Richard. "Ritual and Performance." In *Companion Encyclopedia of Anthropology: Humanity, Humanity, Culture, and Social Life*, Tim Ingold, ed. London; New York: Routledge, 1994.

53.   Schechner, Richard and Willa Appel, ed. *By Means of Performance: Intercultural Studies of Theatre and Ritual*. Cambridge: Cambridge University Press, 1990.

54.   Schneider, Marius. "Primitive Music." In *New Oxford History of Music, 1: Ancient and Oriental Music*, Egon Wellesz, ed. London: Oxford University Press, 1957. 1-82. Primitive music is intimately bound up with the psychological, sociological, religious, symbolic, and linguistic factors of everyday life. Totemistic music: Every object and person has its indestructible sound, and vocal imitation is the strongest form of mystic participation in the surrounding world. Describes the spiritual culture in which music functions.

55.   Schneider, Marius. "The Birth of the Symbol in Music." *The World of Music* 26, 3 (1984): 3-19. Music is symbolic when it allows the creating principle behind it to be intuitively perceived. Hindu scriptures point to the transcendent, primordial plane, the cosmic rhythm, that is attainable through the properly rhythmic use of sound. Ancient man intuitively grasped this connection; Western music, however, is largely the product of rational thought.

56.   Seeger, Anthony. "Music and Dance." In *Companion Encyclopedia of Anthropology: Humanity, Culture, and Social Life*, Tim Ingold, ed. London; New York: Routledge, 1994.

57.   Serjak, Cynthia. *Music and the Cosmic Dance*. Washington, DC: The Pastoral Press, 1987. On the role of music in the creating of human unity and the rediscovering of our religious roots.

58.   Shipp, John Arthur. *A Study of Metaphysical Techniques and Principles as Used by Selected Musicians*. Ed.D., University of Houston, 1986.

59.   Spector, Johanna. "Chant and Cantillation." *Musica Judaica* 9, 1 (1986-87 [1988]): 1-21. A comparison of Byzantine, Gregorian, Armenian, Qur'anic, Vedic and Tibetan Buddhist chant styles with Jewish cantillation.

60.   Spector, Johanna. "Chanting." In *Encyclopedia of Religion*, Mircea Eliade, ed. Vol. 3. 1987. 204-213.

61.   Spencer, Jon Michael. *Theological Music: Introduction to Theomusicology*. Contributions to the Study of Music and Dance, No. 23, New York: Greenwood Press, 1991. Theomusicology—theologically informed musicology —is a multi-disciplinary view of civilization's three domains: the sacred (the religious), the secular (the unreligious), and the profane (the irreligious). Provides methods and models and applies these to Afro-American literary works.

62.   Stockmann, Doris. "Music and Dance Behaviour in Anthropogenesis." *Yearbook of Traditional Music* 17 (1985): 16-30. The study of biocommunication, tool production, and language development and the discipline of archaeology combine to give a picture of early rituals: the audio-visual presentation of symbols for totemistic and fertility beliefs.

63.   Sullivan, Lawrence E. "Sacred Music and Sacred Time." *The World of Music* 26, 3 (1984): 33-52. A study of the relationship between sacred music and cosmogenic, cosmological, cultural, and eschatological times. Sacred music is considered a symbolic way of describing and dealing with time and notions of change. Native South American sacred music is used to illustrate this relationship.

64.   Tambiah, S. J. "The Magical Power of Words." *Man* 3, n.s., 2 (1968): 175-208. A study of language used in ritual forms such as songs, prayers, spells, blessings, etc. Rituals examined include Sinhalese healing rituals, Ndembu hunters' cult songs, Northeast Thailand Buddhist chants and rituals, Lao 'calling the spirit essence' ritual, Sinhalese mantra, and sacred languages of the occidental Catholic church, Jews, Hindus, and Muslims.

65.   Tame, David. *The Secret Power of Music*. Rochester, VT: Destiny Books, 1984.

66.   Tanner, Michael. "Metaphysics and Music. (The Impulse to Philosophise)." *Philosophy* 67, July 15 (1992): 181-200. Because classical music combines emotional expressiveness with a form of compositional development that resembles an argument and is also capable of conveying a sense of transcendence, it satisfies in a way that metaphysics, with its reliance on reason alone, does not.

MUSICAL INSTRUMENTS AND RELIGION

67.   DeVale, Sue Carole. "Musical Instruments and Ritual: A Systematic Approach." *Journal of the American Musical Instrument Society* 14 (1988): 126-160. On the music instrument (or the spirit within it) treated either as an object of ritual or as an agent in ritual performed for someone or something else; in the latter case, both its voice and body participate.

68.   DeVale, Sue Carole. "Power and Meaning in Musical Instruments." In *Music and the Experience of God*, Collins, Power, and Burnim, ed. 1989. 94-110. On the symbolic and spiritual roles granted to certain instruments. Power and spiritual presence are invested in instruments according to religious culture in an attempt to bring together the physical and spiritual worlds.

69.   Ellingson, Ter. "Drums." In *Encyclopedia of Religion*, Mircea Eliade, ed. Vol. 4. 1987. 494-503.

70.   Howard, Joseph H. *Drums in the Americas*. New York: Oak Publications, 1967. A study of drums of Amerindian, European, African, Asiatic and Oceanic origin. References to use in religious contexts occur throughout.

71.   Kartomi, Margaret, ed. *On Concepts and Classifications of Musical Instruments*. Chicago: University of Chicago Press, 1990. A brilliant, detailed study of a variety of classification systems and their underlying cultural structures from around the world. Includes references to the sacred origin, power, and use of instruments.

72.   Sadie, Stanley, ed. *The New Grove Dictionary of Musical Instruments*. 3 vols. New York: Macmillan, 1984.

DANCE AND RELIGION

73.   Backman, L. *Religious Dances*. London: George Allen and Unwin, Ltd., 1972.

74.   Boas, Franz, ed. *The Function of Dance in Human Society: A Seminar Directed by Franz Boas*. 2nd ed., New York: Dance Horizons, 1972. First ed., 1944. Includes descriptions of religious dances among the Kwakiutl, several West African Tribes, Haitians and Balinese.

75.   Davis, Charles. *Body as Spirit. The Nature of Religious Feeling*. London: Hodder & Stoughton; New York: Seabury Press, 1976.

76.   Dooling, Dorothea M., ed. *Sacred Dance*. Parabola, 4, No. 2. 1979. 95 pp. A collection of short articles on Greek, early Christian, Navaho, Balinese, Indian, and Chinese religious dance, as well on non-denominational but related topics.

77.   Ginn, Victoria. *The Spirited Earth: Dance, Myth, and Ritual from South Asia to the South Pacific*. New York: Rizzoli, 1990.

78.   Hanaway, William L., Jr. "Performance and Ritual." In *Encyclopedia of Religion*, Mircea Eliade, ed. Vol. 4. 1987. 436-446.

79.   Hanna, Judith Lynne. "Dance: Dance and Religion." In *Encyclopedia of Religion*, Mircea Eliade, ed. Vol. 4. 1987. 203-212. A survey of religious dance throughout the world, organized in terms of eight categories or roles, including worship, supernatural beneficence, effecting change, personal possession, masquerade, etc.

80.   Hanna, Judith Lynne. *To Dance is Human: A Theory of Nonverbal Communication*. Chicago, IL: University of Chicago Press, 1987. A scholarly study of the communicative power of dance. Employs anthropology, semiotics, sociology, communications, folklore, religion and other disciplines to discover the ways in which dance communicates.

81.   Hanna, Judith Lynne. "The Representation and Reality of Divinity in Dance." *Journal of the American Adacemy of Religion* 56, 2 (1988): 281-306. The author shows how dance, by embodying different types of images of the divine, is able to bring the divine into the human world.

82.   Hanna, Judith Lynne. *Dance, Sex, and Gender: Signs of Identity, Dominance, Defiance, and Desire*. Chicago, IL: University of Chicago Press, 1988. Religious dance educates its public to religious precepts and attitudes toward gender and sexuality.

83.   Hanna, Judith Lynne. "Dance and Ritual." *Journal of Physical Education, Recreation and Dance* 59, 9 (Nov-Dec) (1988): 40-43. A study of how ritual dance influences attitudes and actions.

84.   Highwater, J. *Dance, Rituals of Experience*. 3rd ed., Pennington, NJ: Pennington Book Co., 1992. 1st ed., 1978; 2nd, rev. ed., 1985. Ritual dance, whether tribal or modern, unselfconscious or idiosyncratic, is experience symbolically represented through body movement. The book begins with ritual dance in tribal cultures, particularly Native American.

85.   Kealiinohomoku, Joann. "Dance as a Rite of Transformation." In *Discourse in Ethnomusicology II: A Tribute to Alan P. Merriam*, C. Card et al., ed. Bloomington: Indiana University: Ethnomusicology Publications Group, 1981. 131-152.

86.   Lorimer, David, ed. *The Circle of Sacred Dance: Peter Deunov's Paneurythmy*. Shaftesbury: Element Books, Inc., 1991.

87.   Meerloo, Joost Abraham Mauritis. *Dance Craze and Sacred Dance*. London: P. Owen, 1962. An examination of the role of dance rhythms in

creating religious experience. After a brief introductory text, dance rituals and styles from across the world's religions are illustrated and explained.

88.   Oesterley, W.O.E. *The Sacred Dance; A Study in Comparative Folklore.* Brooklyn: Dance Horizons, 1923/repr. 1968. A pioneering attempt to gage the role played by sacred dance among ancient Mediterranean peoples as well as among tribal peoples of the 1920s, to account for its origin, and describe the occasions and purposes of its performance.

89.   Poplawski, Thomas. "Eurythmy." *Gnosis* #27/Spring (1993): 41-45. A description of Rudolf Steiner's view of dance as originating in nature and the sacred and of his attempt to revive the spirit of the ancient temple dances.

90.   Snyder, Allegra Fuller. "Dance in a Ritual Context: A Dance Ethnologist's Point of View." In *Dance—A Multicultural Perspective: Report of the Third Study of Dance Conference, University of Surrey, 5-9 April 1985*, 2nd ed. Janet Adshead, ed. Guildford, Surrey, Eng.: National Resource Centre for Dance, University of Surrey, 1986. 22-32.

91.   Sorrell, Walter. *The Dance Through the Ages.* New York: Grosset and Dunlap; London: Thames & Hudson, 1967. Sorell presents a general overview of the history of dance in Eastern and Western religious life. Stress is placed on what Sorell describes as the fundamentally religio-spiritual nature of all "true" dance.

92.   Welsh, Deborah Jane. *Symbolic Expression in Dance Experience: Individuation and the Sacred in Three Forms of Dance.* Ed.D. diss., Syracuse University, 1984. A study of the dimension of grace, or the unification of the dancer's energies, in dance. Investigates the struggle toward wholeness (from Jung) and the sacred (from Eliade). Includes examples of shamanic dance, particularly that of African Kung Bushmen and Native American (Black Elk).

93.   Wosien, M.-G. *Sacred Dance. Encounter with the Gods.* London: Thames & Hudson, 1974. In sections entitled "Cosmos and Man," "Ritual and the Gods," "Life, Death, Rebirth," "The Spirit as Ancestor," "Sacred Space," "Mystery," and "Symbol and Worship," the author looks at the different contexts in which dance was and is used in connection with religious practice or alluded to through religious texts. Draws on dance traditions from around the world. Beautifully illustrated.

MUSIC AND TRANCE, SHAMANISM, AND HEALING

94.   Barton, George A. "Semitic and Christian Possession." In *Hastings' Encyclopedia of Religions and Ethics*, James Hastings, ed. Vol. 10. 1918. 133-139.

95.   Becker, Judith. "Music and Trance." *Leonardo Music Journal* 4 (1994): 41-52. An application of recent research in brain topography and neuro-chemistry to the world-wide association of trance with music and to Bali's trance dance in particular. Topics include connectionism, physiological metonyms, the noetics of trance, rhythmic entrainment, and endorphins.

96.   Béhague, Gerard. "Percussion and Noise." In *Encyclopedia of Religion*, Mircea Eliade, ed. Vol. 11. 1987. 235-239.

97.   Bourguignon, Erika. *Possession*. San Francisco: Chandler and Sharp, 1976. A general study of possession trance, with particular emphasis on Haiti. Bourguignon describes different types of trance, dealing with only those cultures where a belief system concerning spirit possession is widely held.

98.   Campbell, Don, ed. *Music: Physician for Times to Come: An Anthology*. Wheaton, IL: Quest Books. The Theosophical Publishing House, 1991.   An anthology of writings based on the idea of the healing powers of the vibratory properties of music.

99.   Christman, Brian. *Power Music: Music and Trance in the Shamanic Universe*. Redwood City: Redwood City Seed Company, 1993.

100.   Edsman, Carl-Martin, ed. *Studies in Shamanism: Based on Papers read at the Symposium on Shamanism held at Åbo on the 6th-8th of September, 1962*. Stockholm: Almqvist and Wiksell, 1967.   Two articles on research in shamanism, eight articles on the shamanism of the Eskimo and North America, Central Asia, Europe, and the Old Testament.

101.   Eliade, Mircea. *Shamanism: Archaic Techniques of Ecstasy*. rev. and enl. ed., Willard R. Trask, transl. Bollingen Series, Princeton: Princeton University Press, 1964/1972. A classic study of shamanic phenomena and their place in the history of religion. Details and examples are drawn from all over the world.

102.   Garrett, Clarke. *Spirit Possession and Popular Religion: From the Camisards to the Shakers*. Baltimore and London: The Johns Hopkpins University Press, 1987.

103.   Halifax, Joan. *Shamanic Voices: A Survey of Visionary Narratives*. New York: Dutton, 1979. A superb collection of shaman stories from around the world told in the first person.

104.   Hammerschlag, Carl A. *The Dancing Healers*. San Francisco/New York: Harper & Row, 1988.

105.   Harner, Michael. *The Way of the Shaman: A Guide to Power and Healing*. San Francisco: Harper and Row, 1980/repr. 1990. A detailed 'how-to' book on Shamanic healing, *The Way...* covers such topics as shamanism and

states of consciousness, power and power animals, and extracting harmful intrusions. Includes exercises and illustrative stories from many cultures.

106.   Heinze, Ruth-Inge, ed. *Proceedings of the [nth] International Conference on the Study of Shamanism and Alternate Modes of Healing.* 9 vols. International Conference on the Study of Shamanism and Alternate Modes of Healing, Berkeley: Independent Scholars of Asia, 1984-1992. Proceedings of nine conferences held yearly in St. Sabina Center, San Rafael, CA, between 1984 and 1992 on shamanism and healing. Contains many articles on song and dance as used in shamanic healing rituals in various cultures, particularly among the Native Americans and east Asians.

107.   Hoppál, Mihály. *Shamanism: Past and Present.* 2 vols. Budapest: Hungarian Academy of Science, 1989. A collection of 39 articles covering many aspects of shamanism in Eurasia, Siberia and North America.

108.   Horwitz, Jonathan. "On Experiential Shamanic Journeying." In *Shamanism Past and Present: Part 2.* Hoppál and Sadovszky, ed. Budapest: Hungarian Academy of Science, 1989. 373-376.

109.   Horwitz, Jonathan. "Shamanic Rites Seen from a Shamanic Perspective." In *The Problem of Ritual*, Tore Ahlbäck, ed. Åbo, Finland: The Donner Institute for Research in Religious and Cultural History, 1993. 39-51. An illuminating examination of the differences between describing shamanic practices from the outside—as ritual or performance—and from the inside, from the standpoint of what a shaman actually experiences when in shamanic trance.

110.   Hultkrantz, Åke. *Shamanic Healing and Ritual Drama.* New York: The Crossroad Publishing Company, 1992.

111.   Kovach, Ada Mae Stein. "Shamanism and Guided Imagery and Music: A Comparison." *Journal of Music Therapy* 22, 3 (1985): 154-65.

112.   Lewis, I.M. *Ecstatic Religion: A Study of Shamanism and Spirit Possession.* 2nd ed., London: Routledge, 1989. A multi-disciplinary approach to shamanism and possession in all cultures and among all religions. Distinguishes between cults dominated by men and those in which women play central roles.

113.   Lex, Barbara. "Physiological Aspects of Ritual Trance." *Journal of Altered States of Consciousness* 2, 2 (1975): 117-151.

114.   Lex, Barbara. "The Neurobiology of Ritual Trance." In *The Spectrum of Ritual*, E. d'Aquili, C. Laughlin, and J. McManus, ed. New York: Columbia University Press, 1979.

115.   McClellan, Randall, MD. *The Healing Forces of Music: History, Theory and Practice.* New York: Amity House, 1988. The first comprehensive cross-cultural study of the philosophy and methodology of sound and music for

therapeutic purposes in the English language. See Chap. 5 on mantra, Chap. 8 on shamanism, Chap. 9 on music cosmologies, and Chap. 11 on trance and meditational music.

116.   Needham, Rodney. "Percussion and Transition." Lessa and Vogt, ed. *Reader in Comparative Religion*. New York: Harper and Row, 1972. 311-317. Asks why percussive sound is used within such a wide range of religious traditions to invoke, contact and communicate with the supernatural, then questions the relationship between percussive sound and transition in human experience. Hypothesizes that percussive sounds are meaningful in expressing transformation. Leaves it to social anthropologists to supply answers. First appeared in *Man* Vol.2, 1967: 606-614.

117.   Neher, Andrew. "A Physiological Explanation of Unusual Behavior in Ceremonies Involving Drums." *Human Biology* 34, February (1962): 151-160. Controlled laboratory experiments support empirical evidence that the behavior observed in ceremonies that involve drums is due to the effects of drumming on the central nervous system and is thus physiological in nature, not just the result of conditioning.

118.   Porter, James et al. "Trance, Music and Music/Trance Relations: A Symposium: UCLA, June 3, 1987." *Pacific Review of Ethnomusicology* 4 (1987): 1-38. Scholars from the disciplines of African Studies, Anthropology, and Music debate the positions taken by Rouget (see #121). With examples taken from the Warao of Venezuela, Nubians in southern Egypt, the Hanea Bori of Nigeria, Vodun in Haiti, and the Sufis, the specialists agreed with Rouget that possession is a learned behavior but maintained that it functions on two levels: symbolic and physiological and that music plays a role on both levels.

119.   Reinhard, Johan. "Shamanism and Spirit Possession." In *Spirit Possession in the Nepal Himalayas*, John Hitchcock and Rex Jones, ed. Warminster: Aris and Phillips; New Delhi: Vikas Publishing House, 1976. 12-20.

120.   Riches, David. "Shamanism: The Key to Religion." *Man* 29, 2 (1994): 381-405.

121.   Rouget, Gilbert. *Music and Trance: A Theory of the Relations between Music and Possession*. Brunhilde Biebuyck, transl. Chicago: University of Chicago Press, 1985 (French ed., 1980). The most thorough, and most controversial, study of the relationship between music and trance. Distinguishes sharply between shamanism, a state in which the shaman remains aware of himself during trance, and possession, in which the personality of the possessed is taken over completely by the possessing spirit. Also suggests that the function of music is to socialize, rather than trigger, the trance state.

122. *Shamans and Shamanisms: On the Threshold of the Next Millennium.* Summer: 1992. Diogenes. No. 158. An entire issued devoted to shamanism.

123.   Swan, James A. "The Shaman's Song: Its Process and Work." In *Proceedings of the Fifth International Conference on the Study of Shamanism*, Ruth-Inge Heinze, ed. Berkeley, CA: Independent Scholars of Asia, 1988. 198-207. Essay on use of rhythmic instruments, chanting, words as power and lyric songs, spiritual power, and 'pneumata' manner of singing. Includes a recount of a shamanic lecture/demonstration and a story of a medicineman's boyhood.

124.   Thorpe, Shirley Ann Daum. *Communication with the Divine: Shamanism in Siberian, Zulu and Shona Religions*. D.Th. diss., University of South Africa, 1988. The Siberian shaman, Zulu and Shona doctor-diviner, and prophet-healers in the Independent Churches of Africa are similar in their position as mediums or religious communicators whose role is to maintain a "holistic stance" in relation to both visible and invisible realms.

125.   Walsh, R. "What is a Shaman: Definition, Origin and Distribution." *Journal of Transpersonal Psychology* 21, 1 (1989): 1-11.

126.   Wavell, Stewart, Audrey Butt, and Nina Epton. *Trances*. London: Allen and Unwin, 1966. A detailed account of a wide range of trance and shamanic behaviors and observations from around the world.

127.   Winkelman, Michael James. "Shamans and Other Magico-Religious Healers: A Cross-Cultural Study of their Origins, Nature, and Social Transformations." *Ethos* 18, 3 (1990): 308-352.

128.   Winkelman, Michael James. *Shamans, Priests and Witches: A Cross-Cultural Study of Magico-Religious Practitioners*. Tempe, AZ: Arizona State University, 1992.

2

Asia: General References

GENERAL REFERENCES AND BIBLIOGRAPHIES

129. Danielou, Alain. "Symbolism in the Musical Theories of the Orient." *The World of Music* 20, 3 (1978): 24-37. On the symbolic value assigned to certain intervals in Hindu and Chinese music systems, to the concept of raga and shruti along with the symbolic significance of the associated scales, and to melodies, rhythmic formulas, instruments, and instrumental timbres in various cultures.

130. Ellingson, Ter. "Music and Consciousness-Transformation Rituals in Three Asian Cultures." *Proceedings of the XXXI International Congress of Human Sciences in Asia and North Africa* (1984): 680-682. Tokyo: Toho Gakkai. A comparison of Newar Vajrayanacarya dances, Tamang Bonpo Shamanism, and the Tibetan State Oracle. All use music in rituals to transform individual consciousness into a state of identification with a deity. They differ in details in performance and in observable aspects of cause and effect.

131. Karpati, Janos. "Mythic and Ritual Correlations of Instrument Symbolism in Asian Cultures." In *Tradition and Its Future in Music: Report of SIMS Osaka*, Tokumaru Yoshiko et al., ed. Tokyo: Mita Press, 1991. 229-36. Three approaches to the question of instrument symbolism: materials, shape and structure (as reflection of the world), and functions (who uses the instrument and how).

132. Kaufmann, Walter. *Musical Notations of the Orient: Notational Systems of East, South, and Central Asia.* Bloomington: 1967.

133. Wong, Isobel. "Music and Religion in China, Korea and Tibet." In *Encyclopedia of Religion*, Mircea Eliade, ed. Vol. 10. 1987. 195-203.

ASIAN DANCE AND THEATRE

134.   Bowers, Faubion. *Theatre in the East: A Survey of Asian Dance and Drama.* New York: Grove Press, 1956/repr. 1960. A survey of theatre and dance including sections of dance with religious background and/or significance. Covers fourteen countries or areas from South Asia, Southeast Asia, China and Japan.

135.   Brandon, James R. "East Asian Dance and Theater." In *Encyclopedia of Religion*, Mircea Eliade, ed. Vol. 4. 1987. 459-462.

136.   Koizumi Fumio, et al. *Dance and Music in South Asian Drama: Cchau, Mahakali Pyakhan and Yakshagana.* Report of Asian Traditional Performing Arts 1981, Tokyo: Academia Music, 1983.

137.   Marasinghe, E. Walter. "Asian Drama." In *Report of the Asian Workshop on Liturgy and Music*, Manila, Philippines: Asian Institute for Liturgy and Music, 1987. On the religious origins and structural form of Asian drama. Formal elements include a disregard for realism, never offending the audience with an unhappy ending, and spectator identification with the protagonist. Music and dance are dominant elements.

138.   Yasuji, Honda. "Reflections on Dance, its Origins, and the Value of Comparative Studies." In *Dance as Cultural Heritage*, Betty True Jones, ed. Vol. 1. 1983. 99-102. The gestures used in Japanese dance range from meaning-less (in early shamanic and ritual dance) to symbolic (in Kagura) to mime (in recited narrative). The same range may be found in Indian dance: Kathak and Bharat Natyam employ both decorative and symbolic gestures, and Kathakali employs mime. Studies of other Asian dance and puppet genres should be undertaken along these lines.

139.   Zarina, Xenia. *Classic Dances of the Orient.* New York: Crown, 1967. A survey of classic religious dance including those from the Natya Shastra in India, the Siva cult in the Royal Thai Ballet and Royal Cambodian Dance, Hinduism, animism and other cults in Javanese and Balinese dance, and the various religious influences in the dances constituting Japanese Nihon Buyo. Includes personal observations on the cultures and information on masks and makeup, dance rehearsal and performance, and dance technique and exercises.

BUDDHISM: GENERAL REFERENCES

140.   Blofeld, John. *Mantras: Sacred Words of Power.* New York: Dutton Books, 1977. An exploration of the use and efficacy of mantras in Buddhism.

141.   Demiéville, Paul. "Notes on Buddhist Hymnology." In *Buddhist Studies in Honour of Walpola Rahula*, London & Sri Lanka 1980. 44-61.

142.   Ellingson, Ter. "Buddhist Musical Notations." In *The Oral and the Literate in Music*, Tokumaru and Yamaguti, ed. Tokyo 1986. 302-341. A study of various Buddhist musical notational systems. Indian, Nepalese, and Tibetan systems seem to have a direct relationship; Japanese systems may have a tantric connection.

143.   Khe Tran Van. "Buddhist Music in Eastern Asia." *The World of Music* 26, 3 (1984): 22-30. An overview of the music of the three main divisions of Buddhism: Mahayana, Hinayana, and Lamaism. Surveys genres and styles, and common and special characteristc in the liturgies.

144.   Mabbett, Ian W. "Buddhism." *Asian Music* 25, 1-2 (1993/1994): 9-28. A study of Buddhist music in metaphysical thought and in functional application: as notation and chant, as evangelical technique in mystery plays, as cosmological symbolism in shakuhachi and meditation, as ritual framework in mantra and mudra, as ritual offering in chanting of the Buddha's name, as dissolving the one into the many in mystery plays, and as inducing altered states of consciousness. Surveys Buddhist music in Japan, Tibet, Sri Lanka, China, Korea, Viet Nam and India.

145.   Mott, David. "Music as Transformation and New Buddhist Music." *Spring Wind* 5, 3 (Fall, 1985): 85-90.

CHRISTIANITY: GENERAL REFERENCES

146.   Asian Workshop on Liturgy and Music. *Report of the 1987 Asian Workshop on Liturgy and Music*. Manila, Philippines: Asian Institute for Liturgy and Music, 1987.

147.   McCredie, A.D. "Transplanted and Emergent Indigenous Liturgical Musics in East Asia, Australasia and Canada." In *Musica indigena: einheimische Musik und ihre mögliche Verwendung in Liturgie und Verkündigung:* Musik-ethnologisches *Symposion*, Rome, Italy 1975. 117-40.

148.   Steenbrink, Karel A. "Music in African and Asian Churches." *Exchange* 20, Apr. (1991): 1-45. Church music, liturgy and culture. Includes reprints from 2nd National Liturgical Conference, Jogjakarta, 1983.

3

North Asia and Lapland: Shamanism

149.   Ahlbäck, Tore and Jan Bergman. *The Saami Shaman Drum: Based on Papers Read at the Symposium on the Saami Shaman Drum Held at Åbo, Finland, on the 19th-20th of August 1988.* Vol. 14. Åbo, Finland: Donner Institute for Research in Religious and Cultural History; Almqvist & Wiksell/Coronet Books, 1991. A collection of nine articles on shamanism and the shaman's drum among the Saami (Lapps).

150.   Balzer, Marjorie Mandelstam, ed. *Shamanism: Soviet Studies of Traditional Religion in Siberia and Central Asia.* Armonk, NY: M. E. Sharpe, 1990. Nine articles including studies of a Turkic shamanic seance, Northern Siberian shamanic ritual, and the structure and function of Buryat shamanism.

151.   Diószegi, Vilmos, ed. *Popular Beliefs and Folklore Tradition in Siberia.* Bloomington: University of Indiana Press, 1968. Includes essays that deal with shaman's drums, songs, rites, and methods of trance induction.

152.   Diószegi, Vilmos and Mihály Hoppál, ed. *Shamanism in Siberia.* Budapest: 1978. See Sec. 3 for essays on rituals, Sec. 4 on analyses of Nenet shaman songs, and the Index for numerous references to drums.

153.   Emsheimer, Ernst. "On the Symbolism on the Lapp Magic Drum." *The World of Music* 19, 3/4 (1977): 45-53. A description and explanation of the symbols on the Lapp Magic Drum. With illustrations.

154.   Graceva, G.N. "Shaman Songs and Worldview." In *Shamanism in Eurasia*, Mihály Hoppál, ed. Vol. 1. Göttingen: Edition Herodot, 1984. 193-200. A given piece of music may of itself be a spirit, or may communicate, independently of its text, the ritual message of the text.

155. Grim, John A. *The Shaman: Patterns of Siberian and Ojibway Healing.* Civilization of the American Indian Ser., Norman, OK: University of Oklahoma Press, 1983.

156. Helimsky, Evgeny A. and Nadezhda T. Kosterkina. "Small Seances with a Great Nganasan Shaman." *Diogenes: Shamans and Shamanism: On the Threshold of the Next Millennium,* 158 (1992): 39-55. Tubiaku Kosterkin, a great Nganasan shaman of Siberia, held two seances in 1989 before his death. Two spirits spoke through Tubiaku, directing specific remarks to those present.

157. Hoppál, Mihály. *Shamanism in Eurasia.* 2 vols. Göttingen: Edition Herodot, 1984. Thirty-six essays on all aspects of Eurasian and East Asian shamanism. See especially the articles on shaman's songs, drums, and mediational abilities.

158. Hoppál, Mihály and J. Pentikainen, ed. *Northern Religions and Shamanism.* Ethnologica Uralica, Vol. 3. Budapest: Akademiai Kiado; Helsinki: Finnish Literature Society, 1992. From the Regional Conference of the International Association of the History of Religions. On the shamanism of the Uralic and Arctic peoples.

159. Jankovics, M. "Cosmic Models and Siberian Shaman Drums." In *Shamanism in Eurasia,* Mihály Hoppál, ed. Vol. 1. Göttingen: Edition Herodot, 1984. 149-73.

160. Jochelson, W. *The Yakut.* New York: American Museum of Natural History, 1933. See esp. 188-122 for description of drum and performance to heal a sick man.

161. Kristoffersson, Rolf. "The Sound Picture of the Saami Shamanic Drum." In *The Saami Shaman Drum,* Tore Ahlback and Jan Bergman, ed. Abo, Finland: Donner Institute for Research in Religious and Cultural History; Stockholm, Sweden: Almqvist & Wiksell International, 1991. 169-182.

162. Li Lisha. "The Symbolization Process of the Shamanic Drums Used by the Manchus and Other Peoples in North Asia." *Yearbook for Traditional Music* 24 (1992): 52-80. The shaman's drum communicates symbolically in several ways: aurally, through timbre, rhythm, volume and tempo; visually, through its materials, shape, decorations, attachments, etc.; by touching the drum or by its being touched by the shaman; by odor; by mystical numbers; by its life cycle; and by the way it is played.

163. Lopatin, Ivan A. "A Shamanistic Performance to Regain the Favor of the Spirit." *Anthropos* 35-36 (1922): 352-55. A detailed description of a ritual conducted by a shaman in order to regain the healing powers that she had lost.

164. Michael, Henry N. *Studies in Siberian Shamanism.* Anthropology of the North, Translations from Russian Sources no. 4. Arctic Institute of North

America, Toronto: University of Toronto Press, 1963. Five lengthy essays on different aspects of Siberian shamanism, including two by A.F. Anisimov, on Siberian cosmology and on the paraphernalia of a shaman and its symbolism.

165.   Novik, E. S. "Ritual and Folklore in Siberian Shamanism: Experiment in a Comparison of Structures." *Soviet Anthropology and Archeology* 28, 2 (1989): 20-84.

166.   Pentikäinen, J. "The Sámi Shaman—Mediator between Man and Universe." In *Shamanism in Eurasia*, Mihály Hoppál, ed. Göttingen: Edition Herodot, 1984. 125-141. Introductory article on Scandinavian shamans with sections on chants, 'word-doctors' who cure with special chants, and the shaman's drum, which is used to induce trance and is a totemic symbol.

167.   Siikala, Anna-Leena. *The Rite Technique of the Siberian Shaman*. Folklore Fellows Communication, Vol. 220. Helsinki: Soumalainen Tiedeskaremia Academia, 1978.

168.   Siikala, Anna-Leena and Mihály Hoppál. *Studies on Shamanism*. Ethnologica Uralica, Vol. 2. Budapest: Akademiai Kiado; Helsinki: Finnish Anthropological Society, 1992. On shamanism in Siberia and Hungary.

169.   Siikala, Anna-Leena and Mihály Hoppál.. "Two Types of Shamanizing and Categories of Shamanic Songs: A Chukchi Case." In *Studies on Shamanism*, Anna-Leena Siikala and Mihaly Hoppal, ed. Helsinki: Finnish Anthropological Society, 1992. 41-55.

170.   Siikala, Anna-Leena and Mihály Hoppál.. "Singing of Incantation of Nordic Tradition." In *Studies on Shamanism*, Anna-Leena Siikala and Mihály Hoppál., ed. Helsinki: Finnish Anthropological Society, 1992. 68-78.

171.   Simoncsics, P. "The Structure of Nenets Magic Chant." In *Shamanism in Siberia*, V. Dicszegi and M. Hoppal, ed. Budapest, Hungary: Akademiai Kiado, 1978. 387-402. A lengthy and detailed musical analysis of a magic song recorded in 1842, the first ever recorded.

172.   Sommarström, B. "The Sami Shaman's Drum and the Holographic Paradigm Discussion." In *Shamanism Past and Present: Part 1*, Hoppál and Sadovsky, ed. Budapest: Hungarian Academy of Science, 1989. 125-144.

173.   Strömback, D. "The Realm of the Dead on the Lappish Magic Drums." *Studia Ethnographica Uppsaliensia* 11 (1956): 216.

174.   Tolbert, Elizabeth Dawn. *The Musical Means of Sorrow: The Karelian Lament Tradition*. Ph.D. diss., UCLA, 1988. Ecstatic manner of performance, musical obfuscation of the text, and improvisatory musical form signal the presence of spiritual power in the performance of Karelian lament and symbolize the essence of Karelian folk cosmology.

4

China/Taiwan

GENERAL REFERENCES, ORIGINAL SOURCES, AND BIBLIOGRAPHIES

175. Crossley-Holland, P. "Chinese Music." In *Grove 5*, Vol. 2. 1954. 219-248.

176. de Bary, William Theodore, ed. *Sources of Chinese Tradition.* 2 vols. New York: Columbia University Press, 1960. Consult index of Vol. 1 under Li (rites) and Yüeh (music).

177. DeWoskin, K. "Sources for the Study of Early Chinese Music." *Archaeologia Musicalis* 2 (1988): 70-97. A valuable essay on the primary materials and both traditional and modern scholarship concerning Chinese music. Includes an extensive bibliography (pp. 86-97).

178. Fung Yu-Lan. *A History of Chinese Philosophy.* 2nd ed., 2 vols. Princeton: 1937/repr.1983. Consult index of each vol. under *li* (ceremony), music, and religion.

179. Kaufmann, Walter. *Musical References in the Chinese Classics.* Detroit Monographs in Musicology, Detroit: Information Coordinators, 1976. trans. of *Yueji* [Record of Music].

180. Picken, Laurence. "The Music of Far Eastern Asia. I. China." In *New Oxford History of Music I: Ancient and Oriental Music*, 1957. 83-134.

181. Thompson, Laurence. *Chinese Religion Publications in Western Languages, 1981-1990.* Los Angeles, CA: Ethnographic Press, USC, 1993. Pp. 12-14, on religious music, incorporates material from 1985 edition.

TAOISM AND CONFUCIANISM

182.   Blacking, John. "Problems in the Documentation and Analysis of Ritual." *Studies in Taoist Rituals and Music of Today* (1989): 10-14.

183.   Chee, Wai-Ling Maria. "References to Dance in the Shih Ching and Other Early Chinese Texts." In *Dance as Cultural Heritage*, Betty True Jones, ed. Vol. 1. New York: Congress on Research Dance, 1983. 126-144. Dance played a major role in the ancestor worship and nature worship of the Chou (Zhou) Dynasty (11th century BC.-222 BC).

184.   Chen Fu-yen. *Confucian Ceremonial Music in Taiwan with Comparative References to Its Source*. Ph.D. diss., Wesleyan University, 1975. The mainland Chinese sources for Confucian ritual in Taiwan.

185.   Falkenhausen, Lothar Alexander. *Ritual Music in Bronze Age China: An Archaeological Perspective*. Ph.D. diss., Harvard University, 1988. On the use of bronze bells in ancient Chinese ritual music.

186.   Falkenhausen, Lothar von. "Music in the Life of the Marquis Yi's Court." *Archaeology* 47, 1 (1994): 47. A set of music instruments found in the tomb of Marquis Yi of Zeng (5th-century BC China) were probably used to play traditional liturgical music and accompany ritual hymns.

187.   Ishida Hidemi. "An Introduction to Musical Thought In Ancient China: Sound, Order, Emotion." *Contemporary Music Review* 1, 2 (1987): 75-84.

188.   Keupers, John. "A Description of the *Fa-ch'ang* Ritual as Practiced by the *Lü Shan* Taoists of Northern Taiwan." In *Buddhist and Taoist Studies I*, Michael Saso and David W. Chappell, ed. Honolulu: University Press of Hawaii, 1977. 79-94.

189.   Kornfeld, F. "Twelve Ritual Melodies of the T'ang Dynasty." In *Studia Memoriae Bela Bartok Sacra*, Budapest 1956. 147. A transcription of 12 ritual melodies of the 12th century from pitch pipe and flute notations.

190.   Lam, Joseph Sui Ching. *Creativity within Bounds: State Sacrificial Songs from the Ming Dynasty (1368-1644)*. Ph.D. diss., Harvard University, 1987. On the guidelines according to which composers composed sacred songs for Confucian ritual.

191.   Lu Ping-Chuan and Tsao Pen-Yeh. "The Ritual Music of Taoist "Chiao"—Studies Made in Lin-cheung and P'eng-hu." *Proceedings of the 31st International Congress of Historians and Sociologists* Vol. 2 (1984): 656-657. This brief article on the most important Taoist ceremony, a ritual expression to the Gods, includes a description of instruments and formal sections, and a suggestion that in the 'chiao' may lie the origin of Chinese opera.

192.   Moule, G.E. "Notes on the Ting-Chi, or Half-Yearly Sacrifice to Confucius (with an appendix on the music by A.C. Moule)." *Journal of the North China Branch of the Royal Asiatic Society* 33 (1899-1900): 120-156. Shanghai. Includes translation of six hymn texts and much excellent musical information. Consult index for numerous references to music and music instruments.

193.   Nakaseko Kazu. "Symbolism in Ancient Chinese Music Theory." *Journal of Music Theory* 1, 2 (1957): 147-180. A demonstration from early Chinese writings of how the numerical symbolism of ancient Chinese music theory (pitch and scale systems) is inextricably related to the symbolism of the two principal philosophical systems of the time: the yin-yang doctrine and the doctrine of the five elements.

194.   Picken, Laurence. "Twelve Ritual Melodies of the T'ang Dynasty." In *Studia Memoriae Belae Bartok Sacra*, Zoltan Kodaly et al., ed. Budapest 1956. 145-172. A transcription and intervallic analysis of twelve 12th-century melodies and a discussion of their history in print.

195.   Pirazzoli-T'Serstevens, Michele. "The Bronze Drums of Shizhai Shan, their Social and Ritual Significance." In *Early South East Asia: Essays in Archaeology, History, and Historical Geography*, R.B. Smith and W. Walton, ed. New York: Oxford University Press, 1979. Some 50 tombs excavated between 1955 and 1960 reveal that, during the Western Han period (206 BCE-CE 9), the bronze drum was important at every level of social organization.

196.   Saso, Michael. "The Structure of Taoist Liturgy in Taiwan." *Studies in Taoist Rituals and Music Today* (1989): 36-65.

197.   Schipper, Kristofer. "Mu-lien Plays in Taoist Liturgical Context." In *Ritual Opera Operatic Ritual: "Mu-Lien Rescues His Mother' in Chinese Popular Culture*, David Johnson, ed. Publications of the Chinese Popular Culture Project, no. 1, Berkeley: University of California Press, 1989. 126-54. Distributed by IEAS Publications. Taoist funeral ceremonies and the Mu-Lien funeral plays share elements found in shamanism (trips to the underworld), Taoism (immortality of the soul) and Buddhism (offerings to the priest class). This article examines the history and structure of the plays and the relationship between them and their religious sources.

198.   Tong Kin-Woon. *Shang Musical Instruments*. Ph.D. diss., Wesleyan University, 1983. The excavation of four types of instruments and of bones with oracular pictographs indicates that the main function of performances in Shang times (16th-11th century BC) was religious. Other uses were entertainment, military and signaling.

199.   Tsao Pen-Yeh. "Variation Technique in the Formal Structure of Music of Taoist Jiao-shi in Hong Kong." *Journal of Hong Kong Branch of the Royal Asiatic Society* (1983): 172-181.

200.   Tsao Pen-Yeh. *Taoist Ritual Music of the Yu-lan Pen-hui (Feeding the Hungry Ghost Festival) in a Hong Kong Taoist Temple: A Repertoire Study.* Ph.D. diss., University of Pittsburgh, 1989.

201.   Tsao Pen-Yeh and Daniel P.L. Law, ed. *Studies of Taoist Rituals and Music of Today.* Hong Kong: Chinese University of Hong Kong, 1989. Includes 8 English-language articles on various aspects of Taoist ritual, music and dance. From a 1985 conference.

202.   Tsao Pen-Yeh and Shi Hinming. "Current Research of Taoist Ritual Music in Mainland China and Hong Kong." *Yearbook for Traditional Music* 24 (1992): 118-25. Describes attempts to collect, compile, and analyze region-specific Taoist ritual music traditions at a time when many of these traditions are on the verge of extinction.

BUDDHISM

203.   Chou Ta-fu. "Three Buddhist Hymns." *Sino-Indian Studies* 1 (1944): 85-98.

204.   Humphreys, Paul. "Time, Rhythm, and Silence: A Phenomenology of the Buddhist Accelerating Roll." In *Tradition and Its Future in Music: Report of SIMS Osaka*, Yosihiko Tokumaru, ed. Tokyo: Mita Press, 1991. 287-93. On the contexts for the accelerating roll, its origin in Chan Buddhism, and its focusing effect. The application of Husserlian phenomenology points to the roll's effect on our perception of time through the changing relationship between sound and silence.

205.   Kouwenhoven, Frank. "The Tianjin Buddhist Music Ensembles' European Tour." *Chime* 7 (1993): 104-113. In October and November of 1993, the Buddhist Music Ensemble of Tianjin performed in Europe a type of Buddhist ritual music never heard before in the West. The ensemble of six played cymbals, a large drum, gongs, mouth organ, and a double reed. The music, which even for funerals was described as 'swinging' and vital, embodied aspects of a Buddhist vision of life: from darkness to light.

206.   Li Ch'un-jen. "The Study of Buddhist Music from Ancient Records." *Journal of Buddhist Culture* 2 (1973): 89. On the importance of painting and sculpture in studying the influence of Buddhism on the music of T'ang Dynasty in China.

207.   Li Ch'un-jen. "An Outline of the History of Chinese Buddhist Music." *Journal of Buddhist Culture* 1 (1972): 123-130. A very brief outline of the development of Chinese Buddhist chant from the Three Kingdoms period through the Pure Land school, the Suei and T'ang dynasties, and up to the Ch'an school which effectively confined Buddhist chant to monasteries. Specific instruments and ceremonies are also discussed.

208.   Li Wei. "The Duality of the Sacred and the Secular in Chinese Buddhist Music: An Introduction." *Yearbook for Traditional Music* 24 (1992): 81-90. An essay on the specifically religious conception of traditional Buddhist musical practices and categorizations juxtaposed against present-day notions in Buddhism which embrace global modernization. Discusses doctrinal contexts and actual practices.

209.   Liu Chun-jo. "Five Major Chant Types of the Buddhist Service, Gong-tian." *Chinoperl Papers* 8 (1978): 130-160. Essay on the celebration of an approaching lunar new year (1977), its place within the Buddhist chant repertory, and a systematic categorization of chant styles into five major types.

210.   Lü Ping-Chuan. "Buddhist Chant in Taiwan." *Shih Chien Journal* 11 (1980): 1-7. Taipei: Shih Chien College

211.   Perris, Arnold. "Feeding the Hungry Ghosts: Some Observations on Buddhist Music and Buddhism from Both Sides of the Taiwan Strait." *Ethnomusicology* 30, 3 (1986): 428-48. A description of the effect different social, economic and political changes in Taiwan and mainland China have had on traditional Buddhist practices c. 1983-4.

212.   Whitaker, K.P.K. "Tsaur Jyr and the Introduction of Fannbay into China." *Bulletin of the School of Oriental and African Studies* 20 (1957): 585-597. On the sources and musical characteristics of a type of Buddhist chanting.

213.   Zheng Ruzhong. "Musical Instruments in the Wall Paintings of Dunhuang." *Chime* 7 (1993): 4-57. The musical instruments depicted in murals in the Buddhist caves testify to nearly one thousand years of musical life in China. The wall paintings in the more than 200 caves contain over 500 large and small music ensembles, more than 4000 music instruments, and some 3000 musicians and dancers. The performers are primarily celestial beings.

SHAMANISM

214.   Ching, Julia. *The Dragon in Early Imperial China.* Ph.D., University of Toronto, 1993. Among the many roles of the dragon in ancient Chinese religious traditions was that of rain-maker. Shamans played the main role in summoning the dragon spirit through dance and other coercive means.

215.   Hopkins, L.C. "The Shaman or Chinese Wu: His Inspired Dancing and Versatile Character." *Journal of the Royal Asiatic Society, Parts I-II* 3, 16 (1945).

216.   Lawton, Thomas. *New Perspectives on Chu Culture During the Eastern Zhou Period.* Washington, DC: Smithsonian Institution: distr. by Princeton University Press, Princeton, NJ, 1991. Four essays and discussion that include reference to ritual music and shamanism.

217.   Shi Kun. "Shamanic Practices among the Minorities of South-West China." In *Shamanism: Past and Present, Part 2*. M. Hoppal and O. J. von Sadovszky, ed. Budapest, Los Angeles: ISTOR Books, 1989. 241-251. On healers, diviners, prophets, magicians and psychopomps among the Jingpo, Drung, Zhuang, and 11th-century Chinese shamans, and the music instruments they use.

218.   Yuan Ch'u. *The Nine Songs: A Study of Shamanism in Ancient China*. 2nd ed., Arthur Waley, transl. San Francisco, CA: City Lights Books, 1973. Reprint of 1955 ed.

CHRISTIANITY

219.   Barker, James H. *The Use of Indigenous Chinese Hymnody in Baptist Churches of Taiwan*. D.M.A. thesis, Southwestern Baptist Theological Seminary, 1992.

220.   Cheung Samuel Sai-Ming. *A Study of Christian Music in the People's Republic of China, 1949-1983*. DMA, Southwestern Baptist Theological Seminary, 1989. A history of Christian music in China, from the multi-denomi-national hymnal and the independent hymnal, through political patriotic hymns and destruction of all Bibles and hymnals, to secret home-based worship and finally the still politically controlled Hymns of Praise.

221.   Sheng, David Shuan-en. *A Study of the Indigenous Elements in Chinese Christian Hymnody*. D.M.A. thesis, University of Southern California, 1964. A lengthy work, weak on musical analysis, stronger on textual analysis. Excellent survey of hymnology in China.

222.   Yeh Wen Chang. *The Role of Music in Taiwan Christian Churches*. M.A. Miss, Fuller Theological Seminary, School of World Mission, 1990. This study of music's role in Taiwan Presbyterian Mission and church development advocates "the courageous use of an indigenous church style and the brave innovative incorporation of indigenous Christian music."

5

Tibet

223. *Asian Music: Tibet Issue*. 10. Society for Asian Music, 1979. An issue devoted entirely to Tibetan music.

224. Amaladoss, M. "Music as Sadhana." *Journal of Dharma* 7, Apr/June (1982): 181-188.

225. Canzio, Richard (Ricardo). "On the Way of Playing the Drums and Cymbals among the Sakyas." In *Tibetan Studies in Honour of Hugh Richardson: Proceedings of the International Seminar on Tibetan Studies*, Michael Aris and Aung San Suu Kyi, ed. Warminster, England; Forest Grove, OR: Aris and Phillips, 1979. 67-72. On the ritual use of drums and cymbals.

226. Chang Garma C.C. *The Hundred Thousand Songs of Milarepa*. 2 vols. New Hyde Park, NY: University Books, 1962. The biography of the great Tibetan saint. Song as the spontaneous expression of enlightenment.

227. Crossley-Holland, Peter. "Tibetan Music." In *Grove 5*, Vol. 8. 1954. 456-464.

228. Crossley-Holland, Peter. "The Religious Music of Tibet and its Cultural Background." In *Proceedings of the Centennial Workshop on Ethnomusicology*, Peter Crossley-Holland, ed. 3rd ed. Vancouver: Government of British Columbia, 1975. 79-91. Revision of 1968 article. A discussion of the origins, instruments, and forms and styles of chant of Tibetan ritual and of the religious significance of ritual music. Includes an appendix on the similarities between Tibetan ritual music and ritual occasion and those of the American Indians of the Canadian West Coast [*see* Addendum to this volume, #3759].

229. Crossley-Holland, Peter. "rGya-gLing Hymns of the Kamu-Kagyu: The Rhythmitonal Architecture of Some Tibetan Instrumental Arts." *Selected Reports in Ethnomusicology* 1, 3 (1970): 79-114. A transcription and descriptive analysis, with historical setting, of two ritual melodies for shawms.

230. Crossley-Holland, Peter. "Tibet." In *Grove 6*, Vol. 18. 1980. 799-811.

231. Crossley-Holland, Peter. *Musical Instruments in Tibetan Legend and Folklore*. Los Angeles: University of California, 1982.

232. Egyed, Alice. "Note on the Origin of Tibetan Religious Music." In *Tibetan and Buddhist Studies Commemorating the 20th Anniversary of the Birth of A. Csöma de Korös*, György Ligeti, ed. Vol. 1. Budapest: Akademiai Kiado, 1984. 191-198.

233. Ellingson, Ter. "Some Techniques of Choral Chanting in the Tibetan Style." *American Anthropologist* 72 (1970): 826-830. A preliminary study.

234. Ellingson, Ter. "'Don rta dbyangs gsum: Tibetan Chant and Melodic Categories." *Asian Music* 10, 2 (1979): 112-156. The first published study of the systems of classification used by performers of Tibetan chant to simplify their vast repertory. Categories include text, tradition, the object and deity addressed by the chant, and function.

235. Ellingson, Ter. "The Mathematics of Tibetan *Rol Mo*." *Ethnomusicology* 23, 2 (1979): 225-243. A structural, rather than symbolically-oriented, analysis and explanation of the complex mathematical organization of the music of the Tibetan monastery ensemble.

236. Ellingson, Ter. *The Mandala of Sound: Concepts and Sound Structure in Tibetan Ritual Music*. Ph.D. diss., University of Wisconsin, 1979. The most complete study of Tibetan religious music available.

237. Ellingson, Ter. "Ancient Indian Drum Syllables and Buston's *Sham pa ta Ritual*." *Ethnomusicology* 24, 3 (1980): 431-452. On Indian drum syllables and their possible relation to a lost 'drum language.' Examines Buddhist and tantric music and ritual.

238. Ellingson, Ter. "Indian Influences in Tibetan Music." *The World of Music* 24, 3 (1982): 85-91. Illustrates Tibetan Buddhist preservation of music and musical styles that originated in Indian Buddhism: instruments made of body parts, *lha mo* (musical theatre), *dbyangs* (chant) deriving from *svarasvasti*, and ritual dance performance.

239. Goldblatt, Elizabeth Ann. *Vajrayana Buddhism as Viewed through a Tibetan Ritual, the Padmasambhava Ceremony*. Ph.D. diss., UCLA, 1993. A musicological study of a Tibetan ritual that employs pure sound—the Dbyangs style of chant—to affect the practitioner's state of mind and being.

240.   Govinda, Anagarika. *Foundations of Tibetan Mysticism, According to the Esoteric Teachings of the Great Mantra OM MANI PADME HUM.* York Beach, ME: Samuel Weiser, Inc, 1969. Original, 1956.

241.   Helffer, Mireille. "An Overview of Western Work on Ritual Music of Tibetan Buddhism (1960-1990)." In *European Studies in Ethnomusicology: Historical Developments and Recent Trends.* Max Peter Baumann, Artur Simon, and Ulrich Wegner, ed. Wilhelmshaven: Florian Noetzel Verlag, 1992. 87-101. A survey of museum collections, recordings, publication of Tibetan sources, and completed works and work in progress. In spite of Chinese domination of Tibet and the destruction of Tibetan monasteries and culture, work on Tibetan Buddhism during the last three decades has progressed spectacularly. Many sources are available, but collective effort needs to be made to create archives and to increase the number of those who are trained sufficiently to conduct research.

242.   Jigten Sumgon. *Bri-gun Chos-rje 'Jeg-rten-mgon-po: Prayer Flags: The Life and Spiritual Songs of Jigten Sumgon.* Khenpo Rinpoche K'onghog Gyaltsen, transl. Washington, DC: Tibetan Meditation Center, 1984.

243.   Kartomi, Margaret J. "The Priority of Musical over Religious Characters in Grouping Tibetan Monastic Instruments." In *On Concepts and Classifications of Musical Instruments*, Margaret J. Kartomi, ed. Chicago and London: The University of Chicago Press, 1990. 75-83. The Tibetan Buddhist classification of musical instruments, though possessing powerful religious associations, is based on performance technique and characteristics of shape and material, and is related to the broad classification of music as an aspect of scientific knowledge.

244.   Kaufmann, Walter. *Tibetan Buddhist Chant: Musical Notations and Interpretations of a Song Book by the Bkah Brgyud Pa and Sa Skya Pa Sects.* Thubten Jigme Norbu, transl. Bloomington: Indiana University Press, 1975. Translation, transcription, and analysis of a chant manuscript from the Tibetan by Thubten Jigme Norbu. Review by Ter Ellingson (*Asian Music* 8, 2, 1977: 64-81) highlights flaws in the text and serves as a preface to the work.

245.   Laufer, Berthold. *Use of Human Skulls and Bones in Tibet.* Anthropology Leaflet No. 10, Chicago: Field Museum of Natural History, 1923. An informative though outdated approach to the study of the uses of human bones in religious contexts. Describes skulls and thighbones used as musical instruments.

246.   Lerner, Lin. "Two Tibetan Ritual Dances: A Comparative Study." *Tibetan Journal* 8, Winter (1983): 50-57. A comparison of *Cham*, a monastic dance for men only, with *Ling Dro Dechen Rolmo*, a ritual folk dance for men and women.

247.   Lerner, Lin. "Lingdro Dechen Rolmo: A Tibetan Ritual Dance in Mandalic Form." In *A Spectrum of World Dance: Tradition, Transition, and Innovation*, Wallen and Acocella, ed. New York: Congress on Research in Dance, 1987. 31-35.

248. McCormac, James. *Tibetan Ritual Chant: A Preliminary Study of Vocal Style*. M.A. thesis, UCLA, 1978.

249. Nebesky-Wojkowitz, Rene de. *Tibetan Religious Dances: Tibetan Text and Annotated Translation of the 'chams yig*. Religion and Society, No. 2, Christoph von Fürer-Haimendorf, ed. Hawthorne, NY; The Hague: Mouton de Gruyter, 1976. This posthumous compilation includes a translation of detailed instructions on the performance of temple dances. The existence of the manual explains the uniformity and persistence of the dances over time and in widely separated areas. Also includes an essay from 1961 by Walter Graf, on the materials collected by Nebesky-Wojkowitz. See extended review and essay 'Dancers in the Marketplace' by Ter Ellingson in *Asian Music*, 10, 2, 1979: 159-178.

250. Nebesky-Woykowitz, René von. "Tibetan Drum Divination 'Ngamo.'" *Ethnos* 1, 4 (1952). Stockholm: Bökforlags aktiebolaget Thule. An excellent study of Bon/Buddhist ritual use of drums.

251. Norbu, Jamyang, ed. *Zlos-Gar: Performing Traditions in Tibet*. Dharmsala, India: Library of Tibetan Works & Archives, 1986. A survey of court, folk, and religious performing arts. Includes articles on Bon and Buddhist sacred dance.

252. Perris, Arnold. "Padmasambhava's Paradise: Iconographical and Organological Remarks on a Tibetan Ritual Painting." *Imago Musicae* 1 (1984): 175-187. Of the 71 persons represented in a *thanka* depicting the paradise of the founder of Tibetan Buddhism, 29, both gods and mortals, play a total of 35 ritual instruments, the same that are used today in Tantric monastic services.

253. Pertl, Brian. "Some Observations on the Dung Chen of the Nechung Monastery." *Asian Music* 23, 2 (1992): 89-96. A study of the pedagogy, notation, and aesthetics of *dung chen* of the Buddhist ritual orchestra.

254. Rinjing Dorje and Ter Ellingson. "'Explanation of the Secret Gcod Da Ma Ru': An Exploration of Musical Instrument Symbolism." *Asian Music* 10, 2 (1979): 63-91. A discussion of a short treatise concerning the profound symbolism of the small hour-glass shaped drum used in Tibetan Buddhist ritual. A thorough examination of the drum, which is said to be a microcosmic embodiment of the basic structure of the universe and of sentient life, encompasses the entire scope of Buddhist philosophy and meditation.

255. Samuel, Geoffrey. "Music and Shamanic Power in the Gesar Epic." In *Metaphor: A Musical Dimension*, Jamie C. Kassler, ed. Australian Studies in the History, Philosophy and Social Studies of Music, Vol. 1. Sydney: Currency Press, 1991. 89-108. In Tibet, the epic is a vehicle for the shaman/bard to manipulate the reality of the listeners and, in this case, involve the powers of the Buddhist tantric deities, of whom Gesar is the earthly representative.

256.   Scheidegger, D.A. *Tibetan Ritual Music: A General Survey with Special Reference to the Mindroling Tradition.* Opuscula Tibetana, 19, Rikon/ZH: Tibet Institut, 1988.

257.   Smith, Huston. "Tibetan Chant: Inducing the Spirit." In *Huston Smith Essays on World Religion*, New York: Paragon House, 1992. 166-175. A recollection of experiencing Tibetan overtone singing, a physical description of how the effect is produced, supplementary observations on Tibetan Buddhism, and a discussion of the hermeneutics of Tibetan Buddhist chant. Includes a spectrum analysis of Rgyud skad. Appeared originally as "Unique Vocal Abilities of Certain Tibetan Lamas" in *American Anthropologist* 69, 2 (April, 1967): 209-212. See also "On an Unusual Mode of Chanting by Certain Tibetan Lamas" in *Journal of the Acoustical Society of America* 41, 5 (1967): 1262-1264.

258.   Tethong, Rakra. "Conversations on Tibetan Musical Traditions." *Asian Music* 10, 2 (1979): 5-22. An excellent introduction to various aspects of Tibetan religious music, including monastic traditions, instrumental training, vocal music, and dance.

259.   Tsukamoto Atsuko. "The Music of Tibetan Buddhism in Ladakh: The Musical Structure of Tibetan Buddhist Chant in the Ritual *Bskan-gso* of the *Dge-Lugs-pa* Sect." *YTM* 15 (1983): 126. An analysis of the Bskan-Gso ritual of Tibetan Buddhist monks in Ladakh. Discusses instrumentation, notation, chant, rhythmic structure, text and rhythm, and melodic structure including scales and patterns, using exclusively Western terminology.

260.   Tucci, Giuseppi. *The Religions of Tibet.* Geoffrey Samuel, transl. Berkeley and Los Angeles, CA: UC Press, 1980. A basic text on the history, characteristics, doctrines, monasticism, and ceremonies of Tibetan Buddhism and Tibetan folk religions. Original, 1970.

261.   Vandor, Ivan. "Tibetan Musical Notation." *The World of Music* 17, 2 (1975): 3-7. A description, with examples, of a notation whose chief function is mnemonic, that is unlike any other, and whose origin is unknown. It has both vocal and instrumental forms.

262.   Vandor, Ivan. "Aesthetics and Ritual Music. Some Remarks with Reference to Tibetan Music." *The World of Music* 18, 2 (1976): 29-32. Aesthetics plays no role at all in the three interdependent aspects of Tibetan ritual music: origin (from those of high spiritual development), function (the revelation of true reality), and symbolism (of the instruments and the music itself).

263.   Wangdu, Konchok. "Chanted Blessings in Disguise." *Parabola* 14, Sum. (1989): 36-41. An interview with the abbot of the Gyüto monastery in India concerning the religious chanting of Tibetan Buddhism in terms of both musical theory and spiritual practice.

6

Korea

GENERAL REFERENCES AND BIBLIOGRAPHIES

264.   Chong-Hwa, Park, ed. *Survey of Korean Arts: Traditional Music*. Seoul: National Academy of Arts, 1973. See for essays on Confucian temple music and shamanistic music.

265.   Condit, Jonathan. *Sources for Korean Music, 1450-1600*. Ph.D. dissertation, University of Cambridge, 1976.

266.   Hahn Man-Yong. "Religious Origins of Korean Music." *Korea Journal* 15, 7 (1975): 17-22. Traditional sources of Korean folk, court, and religious and ceremonial music are shamanism, Buddhism and Confucianism.

267.   Lee Hye-Ku. *An Introduction to Korean Music and Dance*. Seoul, Korea: Royal Asiatic Society, Korea Branch, 1977.

268.   Lee Hye-Ku, ed. *Essays on Traditional Korean Music*. 2nd ed., Robert C. Provine, transl. Seoul: The Royal Asiatic Society, Korea Branch, 1983.

269.   Pratt, Keith L. *Korean Music: Its History and Its Performance*. Seoul and London: Faber Music (in association with Jun Eum Sa Pub. Corp., Seoul, Republic of Korea), 1987. A study of 1500 years of Korean music. Chap. 4, Religious Music, provides commentary on 40 plates of religious music.

270.   Song Bang-Song. "Supplement to an Annotated Bibliography of Korean Music." *Korea Journal* 14, 12 (1974): 59; 15, 1 (1975): 59; 15, 2 (1975): 58; 15, 3 (1975): 64; 15, 4 (1975): 69. See *Asian Music*, 9, 2 (1978): 65-112 for "Korean Music: An Annotated Bibliography (Second Supplement)."

271.   Song Bang-Song, transl. *Source Readings in Korean Music*. Seoul: Korean National Commission for UNESCO, 1980. See Chap. 7: Religious and Ritual Traditions.

272.   Suhr Moon Ja Minh. *A History of Korean Dance*. Ph.D. diss., Texas Woman's University, 1988.

273.   UNESCO. *Traditional Korean Music*. Falcon Cove, OR: Pace International Research, 1983. See articles on Religious Origins of Korean Music, Chinese Ritual Melodies and Ritual Music, and Korean Buddhist Chant.

CONFUCIAN CEREMONIAL MUSIC

274. *The Court Ritual Music of Korea*. Journal of Asian Culture,1980. Originally introduced from China c. 1116 CE, Munmyoje, of Confucian Temple Ritual, is performed today according to 15th century reforms. The order and type of rituals (heavenly, earthly, or human), the selection and arrangement of instruments, and the music itself, are governed by an elaborate complex of symbolic systems including *um* and *yang* (*yin* and *yang*), the five elements, and number symbolism, as well as systems relating to color, direction, position, and times of performance.

275.   Provine, Robert C., Jr. "Sejong and the Preservation of Chinese Ritual Melodies." *Korea Journal* 14, 2 (1974): 34-39. Even with the aid of other mss., restoring *Treatise on Ceremonial Music* (1430) to its original contents proved beyond today's knowledge.

276.   Provine, Robert C., Jr. "The Sacrifice to Confucius in Korea and Its Music." *Transactions of the Korea Branch of the Royal Asiatic Society* 50 (1975): 43-69.

277.   Provine, Robert C., Jr. "Chinese Ritual Music in Korea: The Origins, Codification, and Cultural Role of Aak." *Korean Journal* 20, February (1980): 16-25.

278.   Provine, Robert C., Jr. "Chinese Ritual Music in Korea." In *Traditional Korean Music*, Korean National Commission of UNESCO, ed. Arch Cape, OR 1983. A study of A'ak, Confucian ceremonial music. Elegant music arrived from China in the 12th century, was thoroughly modified by the 15th century, and is today almost purely Korean in the stateliness of its melodic style.

279.   Provine, Robert C., Jr. "State Sacrificial Rites and Ritual Music in Early Choson." *Kugagwon nonmunjip [Journal of the Korean Traditional Performing Arts Centre]* 1 (1989): 239-307.

280.   Provine, Robert C., Jr. "The Korean Courtyard Ensemble for Ritual Music." *YTM* 24 (1992): 91-117. A study of ritual music of a sacrifice to

Confucius as it existed in its most grandiose form in the 12th-century, in a somewhat reduced form in the 15th century, and in its present constrained form which is nevertheless attempting to restore aspects of its former existence.

281.   Song Pang-Song. "Ritual Tradition of Korea." *Asian Music* 8, 2 (1977): 26-46. A description of Confucian ritual orchestras and their alternation during ritual performances.

BUDDHISM

282.   Hahn Man-Young. "Buddhist Chant." In *Survey of Korean Arts: Traditional Music*, Park Chong-Hwa, ed. Seoul: National Academy of Arts, 1973. 161-174. With Transcriptions of *hossori* and *chissori*.

283.   Hahn Man-Young. *Studies in Korean Buddhist Chant.* Seoul: Seoul National University, 1981.

284.   Hahn Man-Young. "The Four Musical Types of Buddhist Chant in Korea." *Yearbook for Traditional Music* 15 (1983): 45-58. A description of the four types of Korean-style Buddhist chant and the three types of dance performed with the chant.

285.   Kim Eung-Suk. "Creating Sacred Sound of Drum." *Koreana* 3, 2 (1989): 38-44.

286.   Lee Byong-Won. *Hossori and Chissori Pomp'ae: An Analysis of Two Major Styles of Korean Buddhist Ritual Chant.* Master's thesis, University of Washington, 1971. Based on personal observation, interviews with Buddhist musicians, private instruction, and analysis of tape recordings, this thesis provides a history of Buddhist ritual performing arts, an introduction to Buddhist rites, ritual music and dance, and a thorough study of *hossori* and *chissori* pomp'ae.

287.   Lee Byong-Won. *An Analytical Study of Sacred Buddhist Chant of Korea.* Ph.D. diss., University of Washington, 1974.

288.   Lee Byong-Won. "Structural Formulae of Melodies in the Two Sacred Buddhist Chant Styles of Korea." *Korean Studies, USA (U. of Hawaii)* 1 (1977): 111-196.

289.   Lee Byong-Won. "Micro- and Macro-Structure of Melody and Rhythm in Korean Buddhist Music." In *Traditional Korean Music*, UNESCO, ed. Falcone Cove, OR: Pace International Research, Inc., 1983. 152-160. In *pomp'ae*, Korea's most ancient and revered form of Buddhist chant, the effect of rhythmic acceleration is achieved by the shortening of successive phrases.

290.   Lee Byong-Won. "The Features of the Mahayana Buddhist Ritual Performing Arts of Korea." *The World of Music* 27, 2 (1985): 49-62. This study provides the historical background and a description of the main forms of Korean Buddhist performance: sutra style chant, folk style chant, solemn chant (*pomp'ae*), outdoor band, and ritual dance.

291.   Lee Byong-Won. *Buddhist Music of Korea*. Traditional Korean Music Series, Vol. 3, Seoul, Korea: Jungeumsa, 1987.

292.   Provine, Robert C. "Korea: Buddhist Ritual Music." In *Grove 6*, Vol. 10. 1980. 204-207.

SHAMANISM

293.   Hahn Man-Yong. *Kugak: Studies in Korean Traditional Music*. Inok Paek and Keith Howard, transl. Seoul: Tamgu Dang, 1990. See Chap. 9: Shaman music of Chiju Island.

294.   Howard, K. *Bands, Songs, and Shamanistic Rituals: Folk Music in Korean Society*. 2nd ed., Seoul: Royal Asiatic Society, Korea Branch, 1990.

295.   Kendall, Laurel. "Mugam: The Dance in Shaman's Clothing." *Korea Journal* 17, 12 (1977): 38-44. A description and analysis of mugam, a dance performed by women during the interlude in a healing ritual, as to whether it is an expression of 'ecstatic religion' or a way women compensate for social deprivation in daily life, or both. Also examines the role of mugam in shamanic cures and the shaman's perception of possession and possessing spirits.

296.   Kendell, Laurel. "Giving Rise to Dancing Spirits: Muqam in Korean Shaman Ritual." In *Dance as Cultural Heritage*, Betty True Jones, ed. Vol. 1. New York: CORD, 1983. 224-232. A description of a woman's dance in the *kut*, the Korean shaman's most elaborate ritual. The author muses on the cathartic effect, expression of ecstatic state, and healing powers, as well as describes the dance and includes participants' reflections.

297.   Kim Kwang-lei. "Shamanist Healing Ceremonies in Korea." *Korea Journal* 13 (1973): 41-47.

298.   Kim Seong-Nae. *Chronicle of Violence, Ritual of Mourning: Cheju Shamanism in Korea*. Ph.D. diss., University of Michigan, 1989. Shaman's divination dreams, spirit possession, and ritual lamentations of the dead recall past historical violence and aid in healing suppressed memories.

299.   Kim Seong-Nae. "Dances of 'Toch'aebi' and Songs of Exorcism in Cheju Shamanism." *Diogenes: Shamans and Shamanisms: On the Threshold of the Next Millennium*, 158/Summer (1992): 57-68. The many social and economic

oppositions within society (rich/poor, island/mainland) and the transcendence of them are symbolized in a dance ritual that exorcises the stranger deity 'toch'aebi'.

300.   Kim T'ae-Gon. "Shaman Chant." In *Survey of Korean Arts: Folk Arts*, Seoul: National Academy of Arts, 1974. 115-133. A discussion of the character, kinds, form, and composition of shamanistic chant.

301.   Kim T'ae-Gon. "The Realities of Korean Shamanism." In *Shamanism: Past and Present*, M. Hoppal and O. J. von Sadovszky, ed. Budapest, Los Angeles: ISTOR Books, 1989. A description of the four regional types of shaman in Korea, a case study of a shaman's mysterious experience, and a section on chant-epic, lyric, narrative, theatrical, and ritual.

302.   Kim Theresa Ki-ja. *The Relationship between Shamanic Ritual and the Korean Masked Dance-Drama: The Journey Motif to Chaos/Darkness/Void*. Ph.D. diss., New York University, 1988.

303.   King, Eleanor. "Dionysius in Seoul: Notes from the Field on a Shaman Ritual in Korea." In *Dance as Cultural Heritage*, Betty True Jones, ed. Vol. 1. New York: CORD, 1983. 213-23. A first-hand, detailed account of a ritual involving an aging, well-known shamaness in her final appearance as a shaman.

304.   Lee Jung Y. *Korean Shamanistic Rituals*. Religion and Society, Hawthorne, NY: Mouton de Gruyter, 1980.

305.   Park Il-Young. "Communion Feast in Korean Shamanism." *Korea Journal* 31, 1 (1991): 73-86.

306.   Park, Mikyung. *Music and Shamanism in Korea: A Study of Selected 'Ssikkum-gut' Rituals for the Dead*. Ph.D. diss., University of California, Los Angeles, 1985. A study of the most important shamanistic ritual performed in contemporary Korea. Music unifies dancing, poetry, drama, magic and possession in rites designed to bring good luck to the family and to ward off evil spirits. The ritual is an intricate combination of learned and improvised elements expertly performed by musicians individually and collectively.

307.   Walraven, Boudewijn. *Muga: The Songs of Korean Shamanism*. Ph.D. diss., Rijksuniversiteit te Leiden, 1985.

308.   Walraven, Boudewijin. *Songs of the Shaman: The Ritual Chants of the Korean Mudang*. London; New York: Kegan Paul International, 1994.

309.   Yang Jong-Sung. "Korean Shamanism: The Training Process of Charismatic 'Mungang.'" *Folklore Forum* 21, 1 (1988): 20-40.

7

Japan

GENERAL REFERENCES AND BIBLIOGRAPHIES

310.   de Bary, William Theodore, ed. *Sources of Japanese Tradition.* 2 vols. New York: Columbia University Press, 1958. See esp. Chapter 14: "The Vocabulary of Japanese Aesthetics II" (on *No* Drama and Buddhist influence thereon), 277-297.

311.   Harich-Schneider, Eta. *A History of Japanese Music.* London: Oxford University Press, 1973.

312.   Kishibe Shigeo. "Music and Religion in Japan." In *Encyclopedia of Religion*, Mircea Eliade, ed. Vol. 10. 1987. 203-204.

313.   Malm, William P. *Japanese Music and Musical Instruments.* Rutland, VT: Tutle, 1959. The standard survey of Japanese music. See pp. 64-74 on Buddhist chant, as well as references to Buddhist influence on No, shakuhachi and biwa music.

314.   Nelson, Steven G. *Documentary Sources of Japanese Music.* Tokyo: Research Archives for Japanese Music, Ueno Gakuen College, 1986.

315.   Tsuge, G. *Japanese Music: An Annotated Bibliography.* Garland Bibliographies in Ethnomusicology, ii; Garland Reference Library of the Humanities, no. 472, New York: Garland, 1986. Consult index under Ritual and Festival Music, Shinto Music, and Shomyo as well as occasional references under Gagaku, No and Kyogen, and Shakuhachi Music.

316.   Waterhouse, D.B. "Japan: II. Religious Music." In *Grove 6*, Vol. 9. 1980. 506-510.

NOH THEATRE

317.　Asai, Susan Miyo. *Music and Drama in Nomai of Northern Japan*. Ph.D. diss., UCLA, 1988. Originally introduced by an eclectic, ascetic religious order to proselytize, Nomai became an art form in which music, dance, and drama united in ritual to become a communal expression of the world view of Northern Japanese villagers.

318.　Bethe, Monica and Karen Brazell. *Dance in the No Theater*. Cornell University East Asia papers 29, Ithaca, NY: China-Japan Program, Cornell University, 1982.

319.　Itaya Toru. "The Torimono Dance: The Re-enactment of Possession and the Genesis of a No-type Performance." *Current Anthropology* 28, 4 (1987): 49-58.

320.　Komparu K. *The Noh Theater: Principles and Perspectives*. New York: Weatherhill/Tankosha, 1983.

321.　Nogami Toyoichiro. *Zeami and His Theories on Noh*. Ryozo Matsumoto, transl. Tokyo: Hinoki Shoten, 1955. Includes an extended discussion of the term 'yugen' as well as other aspects of the Buddhist influence on the aesthetic of No as developed by Zeami (1363-1443). An abridged translation of the Japanese original.

322.　Ortolani, Benito. "Spirituality for the Dancer-Actor in Zeami's and Zenchiku's Writing on the Nô." In *Dance as Cultural Heritage*, Betty True Jones, ed. Vol. 1. New York: CORD, 1983. 147-58. An article on the Shinto, shamanic, and Buddhist roots of Nô drama, and of its religious purposes: fulfillment of divine duties and the rigorous disciplining of the performers.

323.　Ortolani, Benito. "Shamanism in the Origins of the Nô Theatre." *Asian Theatre Journal* 1, 2 (1984): 166-90.

324.　Quinn, S.F. "Dance and Chant in Zeami Dramaturgy: Building Blocks for a Theater of Tone." *Asian Theater Journal* 9, 2 (1992): 201-214.

325.　Suzuki, Beatrice L. *Nogaku: Japanese No Plays*. New York: E. P. Dutton, 1932. See pp. 39-47 in particular for Buddhist influences on No.

326.　Wolz, Carl. "The Spirit of Zen in Noh Dance." In *Asian and Pacific Dance*, Adrienne L. Kaeppler, ed. New York, NY: Committee on Research in Dance, 1977. 55-64. On Noh dance-drama and the influence Zen Buddhism on Noh dance.

SHINTO

327.   Averbuch, Irit. *Yamabushi Kagura: A Study of a Traditional Ritual Dance in Contemporary Japan*. Ph.D. diss., Harvard University, 1990. Originally performed by *yamabushi* (mountain ascetics), the *kagura* still evokes and manipulates powerful symbols to exercise shamanic and magical efficacy, for the benefit of both its human and divine audiences. A study of dance as 'religious text'.

328.   Garfias, Robert. "The Sacred Mi-kagura of the Japanese Imperial Court." *Selected Reports in Ethnomusicology* 1, 2 (1968): 150-78. A description and partial transcription, with historical setting, of the 11th-century Shinto ritual songs and dance performed solely for the entertainment of the gods, and with only the royalty in attendance.

329.   Harich-Schneider, Eta. "Dances and Songs of the Japanese Shinto Cult." *The World of Music* 25, 1 (1983): 16-27. Describes various Shinto dances and songs, translates songs and parts of sacred texts, and discusses rituals and beliefs.

330.   King, Eleanor. "Kagura: The Search." In *Dance Research Monography One: 1971-1972*, Patricia Rowe, ed. New York, NY: CORD, 1973. 77-112. An attempt to discover in the 1200 year-old dance ceremonials of the Kasuga Shrine the ancient dance of the sorceress Miko (Kagura).

BUDDHISM

331.   Emmert, Richard. "The Japanese Shakuhachi and Some Compositions with Several Flutes of Southeast Asia." In *Asian Musics in an Asian Perspective: Report of Asian Traditional Performing Arts, 1976*, Tokyo, Japan: Heibonsha, 1977. 115-124. Includes a description of the use of the shakuhachi in Zen Buddhism.

332.   Garner, Edwin C. *Mode: Three Modes of Shingi Shingon Shomyo as Analysed by ECG*. Ph.D. diss., Wesleyan University, 1976. A description, comparison and analysis of melismatic chants from the Nika No Hoyo service. The term "mode" here does not seem to mean scale-type; the author uses to it to refer to the before, during, and after stages of satori and to the totality of elements that constitute the state of affairs at any given moment, of which the analyst, the reader, and the examination process are all parts.

333.   Gutzwiller, Andreas. "The Shakuhachi of the Fuke-Sect: Instrument of Zen." *The World of Music* 26, 3 (1984): 53-65. Through the use of the shakuhachi as an instrument of meditation, the mendicant monks of the Fuke sect of Zen Buddhism (17th-century through 1871) strove to play in a 'state of freedom from the rational mind' that would eventuate in the Absolute Tone, satori achieved through musical means.

334.   Gutzwiller, Andreas and Gerald Bennett. "The World of the Single Sound: Basic Structure of the Music of the Japanese Flute Shakuhachi." *Musica Asiatica* 6 (1991): 36-59. On the shakuhachi and its music's structuralization in 'tone cells.' Musical analysis is combined with acoustical analysis mirroring the hypothesis that the 'tone cell' stands between the phrase (musical analysis) and the tone (acoustical analysis).

335.   Hill, Jackson. "Ritual Music in Japanese Esoteric Buddhism: Shingon Shômyô." *Ethnomusicology* 26, 1/Jan. (1982): 27-39. A study of the Shingon sect of Japanese Buddhism and their practice of Shômyô (esoteric ritual chant). Covers the metaphysical aspects, the ritual, and the music.

336.   Howard, Gregg W. "Musico-religious Implications of Some Buddhist Views of Sound and Music in the Surangama Sutra." *Musica Asiatica* 6 (1991): 95-101. On the relevance and influence of the 17th-century Chinese Surangama Sutra on Japanese Fuke Zen practice of shakuhachi playing. Discusses the Sutra's origins, identification with Zen, and the concept of meditation on sound.

337.   Kárpáti, Janos. "Divergency of Theory and Practice in Japanese Buddhist Chant." *Orbis Musicae* 8 (1982/83): 23-28. A hypothesis that medieval shomyo chant, rather than being based on the anhemitonic scales of Chinese court music as stated by medieval textbooks, in fact shared with Japanese folk music the use of hemitonic pentatony.

338.   Miyata Taisen. *A Study of the Ritual Mudras in the Shingon Tradition: A Phenomenological Study of the Eighteen Ways of Esoteric Recitation in the Koyasan Tradition.* Sacramento, CA: s.n., 1984.

339.   Payne, Richard Karl. *The Tantric Ritual of Japan: Feeding the Gods; the Shingon Fire Ritual.* Delhi, India: Pradeep Kumar Goel for Aditya Prakshan, 1991.

340.   Sanford, J. "Shakuhachi Zen: The *Fukeshu* and *Komuso*." *Monumentica Nipponica* 32 (1977): 411.

341.   Sawada Atsuko. "Transformation of Melody in the Buddhist Chant of the Shingi School of the Shingon Sect." In *Festschrift..*, Tokyo: Ongaku no Tomo, 1990. 37-48.

342.   Tanabe Hisao. *Japanese Music.* Tokyo: Kokusai Bunka Shinkokai, 1959. See pp. 21-31 for descriptions of Buddhist chant (shomyo) and other music influenced by Buddhism.

343.   Yoshida Tsuenzo. "An Introduction to the Shomyo of the Tendai School." *Journal of the Society for Research in Asiatic Music* 12-13, Sept. (1954).

SHAMANISM

344.   Blacker, Carmen. *The Catalpa Bow: A Study of Shamanistic Practices in Japan*. London: George Allen and Unwin, 1986. First ed., 1975. A study of the various forms of shamanism in Japan. A Japanese shamaness, as mediator between spirits of both the living and the dead and humans, beats a drum and twangs a bow made of catalpa wood as she delivers her spell.

345.   Drake, C. "A Separate Perspective: Shamanic Songs of the Ryukyu Kingdom: Review Article." *Harvard Journal of Asiatic Studies* 50, 1 (1990): 283-333.

346.   Gilday, Edmund T. "Dancing with Spirit(s): Another View of the Other World in Japan." *History of Religions* 32, Fall (1993): 273-300.

347.   Kárpáti, Janos. "*Azuma Asobi*, Entertainment or Ritual? Remarks on the Interpretation of a Japanese Court Genre." *Orbis Musicae* 10 (1990/91): 241-47. An inquiry into whether *Azuma Asobi* was part of aristocratic court music tradition (*mi kagura*) exclusively or whether it was also performed by shamanesses in the traditional ritual dance preserved in provincial shrines (*sato kaguna*).

348.   Miller, Alan L. "Myth and Gender in Japanese Shamanism: The 'Itako' of Tohoku." *History of Religions* 32, 4 (May, 1993): 343-67. Blind 'itako' shamans of Tohoku, Japan, sing ritual songs whose metaphors suggest that the shamans' sacred power derives from their social marginality.

349.   Miura Teeji. "Itako and the Azusayumi." In *Asian Musics in an Asian Perspective: Report of Asian Traditional Performing Arts, 1976*, Tokyo, Japan: Heibonsha, 1977. 83-85, 320-322. A study of the training and rituals of blind women who become shamans (itako) in northern Hunshu Island. The Azusayumi is the musical bow the shaman uses during ritual.

8

Mongolia

350. Aalto, Pentti. "The Music of the Mongols: An Introduction." In *Aspects of Altaic Civilization: Proceedings of the Fifth Meeting of the Permanent International Altaistic Conference*, D. Sinor, ed. Denis Sinor, Westport, CT: Greenwood Press (reprint); Bloomington, IN: University of Indiana, 1963/repr. 1981. An inventory of the instruments used in shamanistic and lamaistic services and a reference to literature by Rudnev on their song types.

351. Emsheimer, Ernst. "Music of Eastern Mongolia." In *The Music of the Mongols, 1*, Stockholm 1943. 1-97.

352. Emsheimer, Ernst. "Earliest Reports About the Music of the Mongols." *Asian Music* 18, 1 (1986): 1-19. Begins with a description by 13th-century travelers of shamanistic rituals.

353. Hamayon, Roberte. "Mongol Music." In *Grove 6*, Vol. 12. 1980. 482-485.

354. Heissig, Walther. *The Religions of Mongolia*. Geoffrey Samuel, transl. Berkeley, CA: University of California Press; London: Routledge & K. Paul, 1980. German original, 1970. A study of Mongolian shamanism and Lamaism. Describes the shaman's drum and other implements. Includes translations of many prayers and invocations.

355. Heissig, W. "New Material on East Mongolian Shamanism." *Asian Folklore Studies* 49, 2 (1990): 223-244.

356. Vähi, Peeter. "Buddhist Music of Mongolia." *Leonardo Music Journal* 2, 1 (1992): 49-53. On musical and dance practices in contemporary Mongolian Lamaist monasteries. Discusses rituals, instruments, song styles, and texts.

9

Central Asia

357.   Basilov, Vladimir N. "Islamic Shamanism among Central Asian Peoples." *Diogenes: Shamans and Shamanisms: On the Threshold of the Next Millennuim*, 158/Summer (1992): 5-18. Islam has affected two forms of Central Asian shamanism—Turkish (pastoral) and Tazhik (agricultural)—as to both ideology and the instruments and invocations used.

358.   Chadwick, Nora K. "Shamanism Among the Tatars of Central Asia." *Journal of the Royal Anthropological Institute of Great Britain and Ireland* 66 (1936): 75-112.

359.   Crossley-Holland, Peter. "Central Asia, Eastern (Music of)." In *Grove 6*, Vol. 4. 1980. 61-67.

360.   Diószegi, Vilmos. "Tuva Shamanism: Intraethnic Differences and Inter-ethnic Analogies." *Acta Etnographica* 11 (1962): 143-190. Includes detailed description of Shaman drums.

361.   Emsheimer, Ernst. "On the Ergology and Symbolism of a Shaman Drum of the Khakass." *Imago Musicae* 5 (1989): 145-66. On the drum of the Khakass shaman of Southwestern Siberia: how it is communally made, the ceremony and ritual surrounding the 'bringing to life' of the drum, and the importance of the drum as a shamanistic symbol.

362.   Siiger, Halfdan. "Shamanistic Ecstasy and Supernatural Beings. A Study Based on Field-Work among the Kalash Kafirs of Chitral." In *Studies in Shamanism*, Carl-Martin Edsman, ed. Stockholm: Almqvist and Wiksell, 1967. 69-81.

10

Southeast Asia

GENERAL REFERENCES

363.   Brandon, James R. *Theatre in Southeast Asia*. Cambridge: Harvard University Press, 1967. A study of theatre and dance including religious influences from animism, Hinduism, Buddhism, and Islam.

364.   Hatch, Martin. "Music and Religion in Southeast Asia." In *Encyclopedia of Religion*, Mircea Eliade, ed. Vol. 10. 1987. 191-194.

365.   Kempers, A.J. Bernet. "The Kettledrums of Southeast Asia: A Bronze Age World and Its Aftermath." In *Modern Quarternery Research in Southeast Asia*, 10. Rotterdam and Brookfield: A.A. Balkema, 1988.

366.   Osman, Mohd. Taib, ed. *Traditional Drama and Music of Southeast Asia*. Kuala Lumpur: Dewan Bahasa dan Pustaka/Kementerian Pelajaran Malaysia, 1974. A collection of papers presented at the International Conference on Traditional Drama and Music of Southeast Asia divided into three sections: The Shadow Play, Traditional Theatre, and Music and Musical Instruments.

BURMA

367.   Cooler, Richard. *The Karen Bronze Drums of Burma: The Magic Pond*. Ph.D. diss., Cornell University, 1979.

368.   Cooler, Richard. "The Use of Karen Bronze Drums in the Royal Courts and Buddhist Temples of Burma and Thailand: A Continuing Mon Tradition?" In *Papers from a Conference on Thai Studies in Honor of William J. Gedney*, Robert J. Bickner, Thomas J. Hudak, and Patcharin Peysantiwong, ed. Ann

Arbor: Center for South and Southeast Asian Studies, University of Michigan, 1986.

CAMBODIA

369.   Blumenthal, Eileen. "Cambodia's Royal Dance." *Natural History*, April (1989): 55-63.

370.   Brunet, J. "Music and Rituals in Traditional Cambodia." In *Traditional Drama and Music of Southeast Asia*, M.T. Osman, ed. Kuala Lumpur: Dewan Bahasa dan Pustaka/Kementerian Pelajaran Malaysia, 1974. 219-222. Music is sacred in origin and in its capacity to please the invisible powers. Through purification and offerings, instrument makers must treat their trade as a religious act. Musicians must regard the drum, the dwelling place of the spirits of music, with particular respect. Through ceremonial invocations, dancers become vehicles of the Gods when wearing the masks of the Royal Ballet.

371.   Cravath, Paul. "The Ritual Origins of the Classical Dance Drama of Cambodia." *Asian Theatre Journal* 3 (1986): 179.

372.   Cravath, Paul. "Khmer Classical Dance: Performance Rites of the Goddess in the Context of a Feminine Mythology." In *Text, Context, and Performance in Cambodia, Laos and Vietnam*, A. Catlin, ed. Selected Reports in Ethnomusicology. Vol. 9. Los Angeles: University of California, 1992. Study of Khmer dance reveals four archetypes of the Great Goddess: primordial consort, beneficent warrior, contested wife, and celestial dancer. Also examines ritual functions of the dance in a traditional context.

LAOS

373.   Archaimbault, C. "Temple Drums." In *Kingdom of Laos: The Land of the Million Elephants and of the White Parasol*, Rene de Berval, ed. Saigon: France-Asia, 1959. 185. Music instruments have souls. The making of a drum is therefore as much a religious act as it is one of craftsmanship.

MALAYSIA

374.   al-Faruqi, Lois I. "Qur'an Reciters in Competition in Kuala Lumpur." *Ethnomusicology* 31, 2 (1987): 221-228. Contestants from throughout the Muslim world compete in the artful recitation of the Koran. Contestants are judged on correct recitation (*tajwid*), vocal quality, intonation, and eloquence.

375.   Blasdell, R.A. "The Use of the Drum for Mosque Services." *Moslem World* 30 (1940): 41. The author briefly describes the musical and theological

evolution that led to the use of two types of drums in Islamic religious services in the Malay Peninsula.

376.   Laderman, Carol. *Taming the Winds of Desire: Psychology, Medicine and Aesthetics in Malay Shamanistic Performance*. Berkeley, CA: University of California Press, 1991.

377.   Malm, William P. "Music in Malaysia." *The World of Music* 21, 3 (1979): 6-16. A survey of jungle, agricultural, coastal, and courtly traditions. Emphasis is on shamanism and theater pieces.

378.   Roseman, Marina. *Sound in Ceremony: Power and Performance in Temiar Curing Rituals*. Ph.D. diss., Cornell University, 1986. During healing ceremonies filled with sound, movement and odor, spirits are coaxed to act through an entranced medium to counter the agents of illness.

379.   Roseman, Marina. "Head, Heart, Odor, and Shadow: The Structure of the Self, the Emotional World, and Ritual Performance among Senoi Temiar." *Ethos* 18, 3/Sep. (1990): 227-50. A study of detachable selves (the heart self, the head self, and the odor self), spirit-longing in dreams, the disintegrative effect of sudden emotion, and the reintegrative role of ritual—singing, the beating of bamboo tubes, and dancing.

380.   Roseman, Marina. *Healing Sounds from the Malaysian Rainforest: Temiar Music and Medicine*. Comparative Studies of Health Systems and Medical Care, Berkeley: University of California Press, 1991. A study of healing rituals and songs as reframing and transformative devices utilizing metaphor to restore individual, social, and cosmological worlds to harmony. Combines performance theory, medical anthropology, and ethnomusicology.

381.   Roseman, Marina. "Inversion and Conjuncture: Male and Female Performance among the Temiar of Peninsular Malaysia." In *Gender, Genre, and Power*, Arjun Appadurai, Frank J. Korom, and Margaret A. Mills, ed. Philadelphia: University of Pennsylvania Press, 1991. Normal gender categories and roles are reversed and upended in rituals involving spirit entities and trance-dancing, without upsetting day-to-day relations among the sexes.

PHILIPPINES

382.   Baes, Jonas. "*Marayaw* and the Changing Context of Power among the Iraya of Mindoro, Philippines." *International Review of the Aesthetics and Sociology of Music* 19, 2 (Dec) (1988): 259-67. A ritualistic power song (*marayaw*), employed to heal the sick and cast magical skills, is used to study the changing context of power among the Iraya.

383.   Catalyo, Vilma May Chavez. *Musical Works Built on the Native Language To Bring About Musical Knowledge and Cultural Development*. EdD,

Columbia University Teachers College, 1986. The anthem based on Bible texts has been used by the Visayan-speaking United Church of Christ in the southern Philippines as a way to bring Visayan congregations into fuller participation in church liturgy.

384.   Goemanne, Noel. "Liturgical Music in the Philippines." *Sacred Music* 98, 4 (1971): 11-16. On Roman Catholic music in the Philippines.

385.   Maceda, José. "Chants from Sagada Mountain Province [Part I]." *Ethnomusicology* 2, 2 (1958): 45-55. Part II appears in *Ethnomusicology*, 2, 3: 96-107. Textual and musical analysis of seven songs from Sagada, four of which have ritual or ceremonial significance.

386.   Maceda, José. *The Music of the Magindanao in the Philippines*. Ph.D. diss., University of California, 1963.

387.   Maceda, José. *A Manual of a Field Music Research with Special Reference to Southeast Asia*. Quezon City: University of the Philippines, 1981. In the section "Music in Rituals," Maceda describes the life-cycle and other rituals of the Kalinga of northern Luzon—childbirth, courting, marriage, peace pacts, victory, harvesting of rice, etc.—that are performed by a medium.

388.   Maceda, José. "A Cure of the Sick *Bpagipat* in Dulawan, Cotabato." *Acta Musicologica* 56, 1 (1984): 92-105. A detailed description of a healing ceremony (*bpagipat*) involving a female medium, with music provided by the *tambul* and *kulintang*.

389.   Mora, Manolete. "The Sounding Pantheon of Nature: T'boli Instrumental Music in the Making of an Ancestral Symbol." *Acta Musicologica* 59 (1987): 187-212. According to T'boli mythology, all animals, birds, and insects were once humans, and their 'voices' are interpreted as omens. Through its imitation of natural sounds, music of the wooden percussion beam *bogul k'lutang* associates itself with mythology, the natural world, and the dualism of male-female polarity and complementarity.

390.   Ness, Sally Ann. "Dance in the Philippines: A Semiotic Analysis of the Commercialization of a Ritual." In *Educating the Dancer and Scholar for the 21st Century: Refereed Papers, Congress in Research in Dance, 1986 Conference, University of Washington, Seattle, Washington*, Seattle, WA (?): s.n., 1986. 61-67.

391.   Pfeiffer, William. *Filipino Music: Indigenous, Folk, Modern*. Dumaguete City, Philippines: Silliman Music Foundation, 1976. Includes descriptions of indigenous and Muslim ceremonies.

392.   Raats, Pieter Jan. "Mandarangan: A Bagobo Spirit of the Sky and Heat." *Philippine Quarterly of Culture and Society* 1, 2 (1973). Cebu City: University of San Carlos.

393.   Raymundo, Graciana, Sr. *Sacred Music in the Philippines*. General Educational Education Journal, Quezon City: University of the Philippines, 1970.

394.   Rice, Delbert. "Developing Indigenous Church Music in Kalahan Society." *Silliman University Journal* 16, 4 (1969). Western hymn tunes have long been associated with Christianity. By using Kalahan instruments, musical forms, and poetic forms, the author has successfully expressed Christian concepts through the use of indigenous materials.

395.   Vista, Salvador B. "Notes on a Subanon Ritual." *Silliman Journal* 26, 3 (1974). A funeral rite of the Subanon group of Zamboanga del Norte, the *gukas* is performed only for a village headman, within nine days of his burial. It is conducted by a shaman to insure that the soul of the departed proceeds successfully to the land of the dead.

396.   Walcott, Ronald H. *The Mountains Ring out their Joy (Christian Music from the Cordilleras of Northern Philippines)*. AILM Collection of Asian Church Music, no. 7, Manila, Philippines: Asian Institute for Liturgy and Music, 1987.

THAILAND

397.   Durrenberger, E. Paul. "A Soul's Journey: A Lisu Song from Northern Thailand." *Asian Folklore Studies (Nagoya)* 34, 1 (1977): 35-50.

398.   Grow, Mary Louise. *Laughter for Spirits, a Vow Fulfilled: The Comic Performance of Thailand's Lakhon Chatri Dance-Drama*. Ph.D. diss., University of Wisconsin, Madison, 1991. *Lakhon chatri* is a comic dance-drama performed at religious rituals in which spirits are honored and placated primarily to gain economic assistance for the patrons and performers.

399.   Miller, Terry E. "A Melody Not Sung: The Performance of Lao Buddhist Texts in Northeast Thailand." In *Text, Context, and Performance in Cambodia, Laos, and Vietnam*, Selected Reports in Ethnomusicology, Vol. 9. Los Angeles: University of California, 1992. 161-188. A variety of Buddhist 'sung' genres (chant, sermon, spirit ceremony, etc.) are described and are used to address the issue that all that sounds like music or song to persons of one culture may not be so considered by those in another.

400.   Miller, Terry E. *Traditional Music of the Lao: Kaen Playing and Mawlum Singing in Northeast Thailand*. Westport, CT: Greenwood Press, 1985. Includes a description of religious song categories and ritual.

401.   *Pali Chanting, with Translations*. Bangkok, Thailand: Mahamakut Rajavidyalaya Press, 1974, 1983. Chanting in Pali, the language of Theravadan Buddhist scriptures.

402.   Schwörer-Kohl, Gretel. "Mouth Organ and Drum: The Symbols of Death among the Hmong in Northern Thailand." In *Tradition and Its Future in Music: Report of SIMS Osaka*, Tokumaru Yoshiko et al., ed. Tokyo: Mita Press, 1991. 249-53. By following the tones of the spoken language, melodies on instruments contain coded histories of ritual and legend and communicate with souls of deceased persons and sacrificed animals. By this means, the mouth organ, together with the drum, can guide spirits of the deceased to the land of the ancestors.

403.   Tambiah, Stanley J. *Buddhism and the Spirit Cults in Northeast Thailand.* Cambridge: Cambridge University Press, 1970. An excellent discussion of the spirit world and its ritualists, ceremonies, and meaning.

404.   Terwiel, B.J. *Monks and Magic: An Analysis of Religious Ceremonies in Central Thailand.* Scandinavian Institute of Asian Studies Monograph Series, No. 24, Lund, Sweden: Studentlitteratur, 1975.

405.   Textor, Robert Bayard. *Patterns of Worship: A Formal Analysis of the Supernatural in a Thai Village.* New Haven, CT: Human Relations Area Files, 1973.

406.   Wells, Kenneth Elmer. *Thai Buddhism, its Rites and Activities.* New York: AMS Press, 1939/repr. 1960, 1982. A detailed description of both the daily and the occasional temple and public rites by monks and laity. See chapters entitled 'Services of Worship at Temples', 'Temple-centered Ceremonial', 'The Rites and Duties of the Monks', 'Home and Funeral Ceremonies', and 'State Ceremonies.'

407.   Wong, Deborah and René T.A. Lysloff. "Threshold to the Sacred: The Overture in Thai and Javanese Ritual Performance." *Ethnomusicology* 35, 3 (1991): 315-48. In both Javanese shadow puppet theater and in Thai Hindu-Buddhist ritual, the overture establishes the atmosphere for what is to follow: ritual time and space for the theater audience, and for the ritual participants, an invocation to the gods for their presence.

408.   Young, Ernest. *The Kingdom of the Yellow Robe: Being Sketches of the Domestic and Religious Rites and Ceremonies of the Siamese.* 2nd ed., Kuala Lumpur and New York: Oxford University Press, 1900/repr. 1982.

VIETNAM

409.   Addiss, Stephen. "Music of the Cham Peoples." *Asian Music* 2, 1 (1971): 32-38. A historical look at Cham music followed by a description of surviving music including religious/ceremonial music.

410.   Hinh, Nguyen Duy. "Bronze Drums in Vietnam." *Vietnam Forum* 9, Winter-Spring (1987): 1-22.

411.   Kpa Ylang. "Gong Music in the Water Buffalo Sacrifice Ritual." *Nhac Viet: The Journal of Vietnamese Music* 1, 1 (1992): 7-19.

412.   Nguyen Phong. "Text, Context, and Performance: A Case Study of the Vietnamese Buddhist Liturgy." In *Text, Context, and Performance in Cambodia, Laos, and Vietnam*, Selected Reports in Ethnomusicology, Vol. 9. Los Angeles: University of California, 1992. 225-232. An overview of the types and linguistic origins of Vietnamese Buddhist texts, variations in services, different styles of melody and chanting, and instruments used in services.

413.   Tuyen T. Ton-nu. "Selected Bibliography (1890-1990)." *Nhac Viet Newsletter* 4 (1990): 11-14. Vietnamese music.

INDONESIA: GENERAL REFERENCES

414.   Crawford, M. "Indonesia." In *Grove 6*, Vol. 9. 1980. 167-219.

415.   Knapp, Bettina L. "Indonesian Theatre: A Journal." *Anima* 11, Fall (1984): 47-61. A study of the religious symbols, images, and ideations contained in Indonesia theatre—Wayang Golek, Wayang Kulit, Barong Dance Drama, Kecak or Monkey Dance, and the Ramayana Ballet—with emphasis on the performances themselves.

416.   Pacholczyk, Jósef M. "Music and Islam in Indonesia." *The World of Music* 28, 3 (1986): 3-12. Influences of Islam on the musical practices of Indonesia include instruments such as the shawm and rebab, the Call to Prayer and Qur'anic recitation, Islamic stories that were made into forms of theatre, and the *gamelan sekati* of the mosque.

JAVA

417.   Becker, Judith. "Hindu-Buddhist Time in Javanese Gamelan Music." In *The Study of Time IV: Papers from the Fourth Conference of the International Society for the Study of Time, Alpbach-Austria [1979]*, J.T. Fraser, N. Lawrence, and D. Park, ed. Berlin, New York: Springer-Verlag, 1981. In this study, the sense of the timeless that characterizes the archaic gamelan piece *Langen Bronto*, with its endlessly, evenly repeated 32-beat cycles, is used to compare various concepts of time, and particularly the Hindu-Buddhist concept of cyclic or timeless time with Islamic eschatological time. Also discussed is the importance of the number four in both the construction of gamelan cycles and Hindu-Buddhist structures and cosmology.

418.   Becker, Judith. "Earth, Fire, *Sakti*, and the Javanese Gamelan." *Ethnomusicology* 32, 3 (1988): 385-91. An essay on the Javanese gamelan as representing the sacred in terms of creation and power and as a metaphor of sexuality and gender structures.

419.   Becker, Judith. "The Javanese Court Bedhaya Dance as a Tantric Analogy." In *Metaphor: A Musical Dimension*, Jamie C. Kassler, ed. Australian Studies in the History, Philosophy and Social Studies of Music, Vol. 1. Sydney: Currency Press, 1991. 109-120. The Bedhaya dance, performed in commemoration of the succession of the ruler to the throne, communicates on two levels, the exoteric and the esoteric. The story (the exoteric level) re-enacts the origin-myth of the dance, the union of the Goddess of the South Sea and Sulta Agung, and signifies the sexual union of opposites. The dance formations (the esoteric aspect) portray a person's spiritual progress for a state of desire through conflict and integration to perfection. Thus the sexual and the sacred are joined.

420.   Becker, Judith and A. Feinstein. *Karawitan: Source Readings in Javanese Gamelan and Vocal Music, I, II, III*. Michigan Papers on South and Southeast Asia, Ann Arbor: University of Michigan, 1984, 1987, 1988. Invaluable source material written by Javanese musicians and scholars, translated into English. Vol. 2, in particular, contains stories of the miraculous associated with certain dances, gamelans, and composers or performers.

421.   Brakel-Papenhuijzen, Clara. *The Bedhaya Court Dances of Central Java*. Leiden: E.J. Brill, 1992. An important study concerning the most sacred dances of the major royal courts of central Java. Includes examination of historical sources, song texts, choreography, and notation, and observations about the differences between the modernist renewal in Jogyakarta and the reconstructionist renewal in Surakarta.

422.   DeVale, Sue Carole. "Cosmological Symbolism in the Design and Morphology of Gamelan in Java." In *Essays in Southeast Asian Performance*, K. Foley, ed. Berkeley: Center for South and Southeast Asian Studies, University of California, 1991.

423.   Foley, Kathy. "The Dancer and the Danced: Trance Dance and Theatrical Performance in West Java." *Asian Theatre Journal* 2, 1 (1985): 28-49.

424.   Geertz, Clifford. *The Religion of Java*. Chicago and London: University of Chicago Press, 1960/repr. 1976. A masterly study of Javanese culture according to 'abangan,' 'santri,' and 'prijaji'—the village (folk element, animism), the network of domestic trade relationships (Islam), and the hereditary aristocracy and the bureaucracy (Hindu). Spirit beliefs and life-cycle events are considered under *abangan*, the arts under *prijaji*.

425.   Hatley, Barbara. "Indonesian Ritual Javanese Drama—Celebrating Tujuh-belasan." *Indonesia* 34 (1982): 55-64.

426.   Heins, Ernst, comp. *Music in Java: Current Bibliography 1973-1989*. Amsterdam: Universiteit van Amsterdam, Ethnomusicologisch Centrum 'Jaap Kunst', 1989.

427.   Hood, Mantle. *The Evolution of Javanese Gamelan.* 3 vols. Wilhelms-haven, Germany: Edition Heinrichshofen; New York: C.F. Peters Corporation, 1980. Books I and II deal with the history of the gamelan based on archaeological evidence; Book III deals with theory and methods of improvisation. See Bk. II in particular for frequent references to sacred gamelans.

428.   Hood, Mantle. "Javanese Gamelan Sekati: Its Sanctity and Age." *Acta Musicologica* 57, 1 (1985): 33-37. Only the impressive and unique Gamelan Sekati, first constructed between the 12th and 14th centuries, is allowed to play during the Muslim holy week.

429.   Hood, Mantle and Hardja Susilo. *Music of the Venerable Dark Cloud: Introduction, Commentary, and Analysis.* Los Angeles: University of California Press, 1967. Provides thorough historical background filled with mythological and religious references as an introduction to the commentary and analysis of the pieces on the recording which this text accompanies.

430.   Hostetler, Jan. "Bedhaya Semang: The Sacred Dance of Yogyakarta." *Archipel* 24 (1984): 127-142.

431.   Hostetler, Jan. "'Bedhaya Semang': Problems in a Reconstruction Project." In *Dance as Cultural Heritage,* Betty True Jones, ed. Vol. 2. New York: Congress of Research in Dance, 1985. 22-46. This ancient, sacred dance has not been performed since 1920 at the latest, and is recorded only in a notation system that is coordinated to cues from the music and song text but is incomplete in many respects concerning the dance. The essay describes the problems encountered in the attempt to reconstruct the dance.

432.   Kartomi, Margaret J. "Conflict in Javanese Music." *Studies in Music* 4 (1970): 62-80. A description of how conflict that manifests in the social and religious realms is expressed in gamelan music.

433.   Kartomi, Margaret J. "Music and Trance in Central Java." *Ethnomusicology* 17, May (1973): 163-208. A description of the musical style and type of ensemble associated with each of several types of folk trance performances.

434.   Kartomi, Margaret J. "Performance, Music and Meaning of Reyog Ponorogo." *Indonesia* 22 (1976): 85-130.

435.   Keeler, Ward. *Javanese Shadow Plays, Javanese Selves.* Princeton, NJ: Princeton University Press, 1987. Shadow-play performances retain their fascination for the Javanese because of the concerns of both about potency, status, and speech. Includes a chapter on ritual celebrations.

436.   Kunst, Jaap. *Music in Java: Its History, Its Theory, and Its Technique.* 3rd ed., 2 vols. Ernst L. Heins, ed. The Hague: Martinus Nijhoff, 1973. The most comprehensive of studies on Javanese gamelan.

437.   Mangkunagara VII, K.G.P.A.A., of Surakarta. *On the Wajang Kulit (Purwa) and Its Symbolic and Mystical Elements.* Claire Holt, transl. Southeast Asia Program, Data Paper no. 27, Ithaca, NY: Cornell University, 1957. Original text published in *Djawa*, 13, 1933. A sensitive examination of the mystical and philosophical implications of the *Wayang Kulit*.

438.   Morrison, Miriam. "The Expression of Emotion in Court Dances of Yogjakarta." *Asian Music* 7, 1 (1975): 33-38. A discussion of Javanese dance and restrained facial expression. Relates to religious dance and spiritual edification through dance.

439.   Peacock, James L. "Javanese Wayang." In *Encyclopedia of Religion*, Mircea Eliade, ed. Vol. 4. 1987. 457-458.

440.   Suhardjo Parto, F. X. "A Scenario for the History of Javanese Music." In *The Oral and the Literate in Music*, Tokumaru and Yamaguti, ed. Tokyo: Academia Music, 1986. 428-39.

441.   Suharto, Ben. "Transformation and Mystical Aspects of Javanese Dance." *UCLA Journal of Dance Ethnology* 14 (1990): 22-25.

442.   Sumarsam. "The Meaning of Gamelan Performance." *Progress Reports in Ethnomusicology* 2, 3 (1987-88): 1-11.

443.   Tirtaamidjaja, Musjirwan. "A Bedaja Ketawong Performed at the Court of Surakarta." *Indonesia* 3 (1967): 31-61. On the mythological background and religious implications of the dance of the Goddess of the South Sea, one of Java's most ancient and sacred dances.

444.   Vetter, Roger. "Animism, Hinduism, Islam, and the West: Fusion in Musical and Visual Symbolism in a Javanese Ceremony." *Progress Reports in Ethnomusicology* 2, 4-7 (1989): 1-12. On the history and current practice of *grebeg*, a ceremonial procession held on major Muslim holy days.

445.   Wolbers, Paul Arthur. "Transvestism, Eroticism, and Religion: In Search of a Contextual Background for the Gandrung and Seblang Traditions of Banyuwangi, East Java." *Progress Reports in Ethnomusicology* 2, 4-7 [#6] (1989): [31]-[51]. A study of the *seblang* ritual as the ritualistic counterpart and model for the *gandrung*, the most popular form of traditional entertainment.

446.   Wolbers, Paul Arthur. *Maintaining Using Identity Through Musical Performance: Seblang and Gandrung of Banyuwangi, East Java.* Ph.D. diss., University of Ill. at Urbana-Champaign, 1992. An investigation of *seblang* and other shamanistic trance rituals to determine the Javanese, Balinese and Dutch influence on *seblang* and its role in the development of *gandrung*, the female dance/singer for which this region is known.

BALI

447.   Bandem, I. Made. "Baris Dance." *Ethnomusicology* 19, May (1975): 259-265. This ritual trance-dance from Bali is designed to demonstrate physical maturity through the use of weapons.

448.   Bandem, Made and Fredrik de Boer. *Kaja and Kelod: Balinese Drama in Transition*. Kuala Lumpur and New York: Oxford University Press, 1981. A study of sacred, secular, and demonic dance.

449.   Bali, *Further Studies in Life, Thought, and Ritual*. The Hague: Van Hoeve; Vancouver, BC: University of British Columbia, 1970/repr. 1993. "...a Supplement to and Continuation of...Bali: Studies in Life, Thought, and Ritual." Roelof Goris et al., edd. Dordrecht, Netherlands; Cinnaminson, NJ. Foris Publications. 1960/repr. 1984. Selected Studies on Indonesia by Dutch Scholars, Vol. 8.

450.   Belo, Jane. *Bali: Rangda and Barong*. Monographs of the American Ethnological Society, Vol. 17. New York: J. J. Augustin, 1949. The polarity and unity of Rangda, a gray-haired but insatiable and dangerous old woman, and the fierce and boisterous Barong, are examined against Balinese history and culture.

451.   Belo, Jane. *The Balinese Barong*. New York: J. J. Augustin, 1950.

452.   Belo, Jane. *Bali: The Temple Festival*. Monographs of the American Ethnological Society, Vol. 22. New York: J. J. Augustin, 1953. A detailed description of *odalan*, the major calendrical feast of a temple in Sajan village, as celebrated in 1937 and 1938. The role of trance is emphasized.

453.   Belo, Jane. *Trance in Bali*. New York: Columbia University Press, 1960. An investigation of trance in four districts in Bali. It appears among mediums, in dance, in folk forms and divination, and for healing.

454.   Belo, Jane, ed. *Traditional Balinese Culture*. New York: Columbia University Press, 1970. Essays on Balinese myth, religion, modes of performance, ritual and social organization.

455.   Boon, James A. "Balinese Dance and Dance Drama." In *Encyclopedia of Religion*, Mircea Eliade, ed. Vol. 4. 1987. 455-457.

456.   Eiseman, Fred B., Jr. *Bali: Sekala and Niskala. Volume I: Essays on Religion, Ritual, and Art*. Berkeley, Singapore: Periplus Editions, 1989. A collection of richly detailed essays on a variety of aspects pertaining to religious dance and music.

457.   Eiseman, Fred B., Jr. *Bali: Sekala and Niskala. Vol. II: Essays on Society, Tradition, and Craft*. Berkeley, CA: Periplus Editions, 1990. See Chap. 16.

'Mask Making: Magic and Craftsmanship' (pp. 207-219). On the powers of masks and wayang kulit shadow puppets.

458.   Fowler, John. "The Balinese Theatre: Dance and Drama." *Arts in Asia* 18, 1 (Jan-Feb) (1988): 86-93.

459.   Hiss, Philip Hanson. *Bali.* New York: Duell, Sloan and Pearce, 1941. An excellent introduction to pre-WWII Balinese culture, beautifully illustrated with 8 1/2 x 11 b.w. photographs.

460.   Hobart, Angela. *Dancing Shadows of Bali: Theatre and Myth.* London and New York: KPI, 1987.

461.   Holt, Claire and Gregory Bateson. "Form and Function of the Dance in Bali." In *Traditional Balinese Culture*, Jane Belo, ed. New York: Columbia University Press, 1970. 322-330. Includes a description of trance dance for men (Barong) and for young girls.

462.   I Made Bandem. "The Evolution of Legong from Sacred to Secular Dance of Bali." In *Dance as Cultural Heritage*, Betty True Jones, ed. Vol. 1. 1983. 113-19.

463.   Lange, Roderyk. "Galungan in Bali: A Religious Event." *Dance Studies* 15 (1991): 9-67.

464.   McKean, Philip F. "From Purity to Pollution? The Balinese Ketjak (Monkey Dance) as Symbolic Form in Transition." In *The Imagination of Reality: Essays in Southeast Asian Coherence Systems*, Aram A. Yengoyan and A. L. Becker, ed. Norwood, NJ: ABLEX Publishing Company, 1979. 293-302. Ketchak dances performed as ritual exorcism and purification and Ketchak danced as tourist attraction coexist in modern Bali. Often performed by the same performers, the two have different significance for the Balinese.

465.   McPhee, Colin. *Music in Bali: A Study in Form and Instrumental Organization in Balinese Orchestral Music.* New Haven: Yale University Press, 1966/repr. 1976. Primarily a detailed description of a variety of traditional and modern gamelans on Bali, this classic study includes sections on temple music and sacred ensembles as well as discussions on dance and ritual.

466.   McPhee, Colin. "Dance In Bali." In *Traditional Balinese Culture*, Jane Belo, ed. New York, NY: Columbia University Press, 1970. 290-321. An overview of Balinese dance, past and present, from many angles, including ritual significance, ritual dance, and trance-dance.

467.   Moerdowo, R.M. *Reflections on Balinese Traditional and Modern Arts.* Jakarta, Indonesia: Balai Pustaka, 1980/repr. 1983.

468.   Thompson, Brian James. *'Ngrobah': Ritual Process and Cultural Transformation as Reflected in the Balinese Wayan Kulit*. Ph.D. diss., University of Oregon, 1992.

469.   Zoete, Beryl de and Walter Spies. *Dance and Drama in Bali*. Kuala Lumpur: Oxford University Press, 1938/repr. 1952, 1973. An invaluable, detailed guide to the major forms of Balinese dance and drama.

OTHER AREAS

470.   Atkinson, Jane M. *The Art and Politics of Wana Shamanship*. Berkeley: University of California Press, 1989. A thorough study of the political and cosmic significances of the Magolong, the major shamanic ritual of the Wana of Sulawesi, Indonesia.

471.   George, Kenneth M. *The Singing from the Headwaters: Song and Tradition in the Headhunting Rituals of an Upland Sulawesi Community*. Ph.D. diss., University of Michigan, 1989.

472.   George, Kenneth M. "Felling a Song with a New Ax: Writing and the Reshaping of Ritual Song in Upland Sulawesi." *Journal of American Folklore* 103, 407 (Jan-Mar) (1990): 3-23.

473.   George, Kenneth M. "Music-Making, Ritual, and Gender in a Southeast Asian Hill Society." *Ethnomusicology* 37, 1 (1993): 1-28. A study of the complementarity of gender roles in the *mappurondo* community of South Sulawesi, Indonesia, and of the dominant role men play in ritual, even in this generally egalitarian society.

474.   Goldsworthy, David. "Honey-collecting Ceremonies on the East Coast of North Sumatra." In *Studies in Indonesian Music*, M. Kartomi, ed. Clayton, Australia: Centre of Southeast Asian Studies, Monash University, 1978. Shaman-specialists are required to pacify the spirit of a hive-bearing tree, before climbing can begin to gather honey.

475.   Goldsworthy, David. "The Dancing Fish Trap (lukeh menari): A Spirit-Invocation Song and a Spirit-Possession 'Dance' from North Sumatra." *Musicology Australia/Journal of the Musicological Society of Australia* 9 (1986): 12-28. Two shamans combine ritualistic, linguistic, and musical procedures to induce a spirit to enter and possess a fish trap, causing it to move from side to side of its own accord. Includes notated melody and text with translation.

476.   Harnish, David. "Religion and Music: Syncretism, Orthodox Islam, and Musical Change in Lombok." *Selected Reports in Ethnomusicology* 7 (1988): 123-138. Different types of gamelan and gamelan music are seen as metaphors of the conflict between traditional, syncretic Islam that is rural and Javanese/

Balinese in style and ritual-centeredness, and orthodox Islam that is more modern, urban and Arab-centered in outlook.

477.   Harnish, David. "The Preret of the Lombok Balinese: Transformation and Continuity Within a Sacred Tradition." *Selected Reports in Ethnomusicology: Issues in Organology* 8 (1990): 201-220. An essay on the sacred art of solo *preret*, or shawm, performance on the island of Lombok. Focus is placed on the substitution of the *preret* for the voice in *kidung*, or sacred choral singing.

478.   Harnish, David. *Music at the Lingsar Temple Festival: The Encapsulation of Meaning in the Balinese/Sasak Interface in Lombok, Indonesia.* Ph.D. diss., UCLA, 1991. Traditionally, both minority Hindus and majority Muslims have participated at the major festival at Lingsar temple. A different musical ensemble accompanies each of the festival's rites. By reinterpreting the symbols associated with the cosmos and mythic past, both groups are now redefining their cultural identities. Music continues, however, to encapsulate the festival experience and to present in a vivid way the cosmos, mythic past, and evolving cultural identities. Forthcoming as a book: *Music at the Lingsar Temple: The Balinese and Sasak Intersection of Religion and Politics in Lombok, Indonesia.*

479.   Harnish, David. "The Performance, Context, and Meaning of Balinese Music in Lombok." In *Balinese Music in Context: A Sixty-fifth Birthday Tribute to Hans Oesch*, Danker Schaareman, ed. Winterthur, Germany: Amadeus, 1992.

480.   Harnish, David. "The Future Meets the Past in the Present: Music and Buddhism in Lombok." *Asian Music* 25, 1-2 (1993/1994): 29-50. In order to preserve their indigenous Sasak beliefs, the Boda registered as Buddhists, one of four acknowledged religious faiths. They have modified their festivals and the music of their gamelan *jerujeng* to adapt to their new religion. The rites and music are described.

481.   Kartomi, Margaret J. "Dualism in Unity: The Ceremonial Music of the Mandailing Raja Tradition." *Asian Music* 12, 2 (1981): 74-108. The unity and duality of existence is the basis of the 18th/19th-century, pre-Islamic Mandailing musical practice and is symbolized by the ceremonial orchestra's composition. Mandailing music exemplified how conflicting elements could be resolved into a state of order and unity.

482.   Kartomi, Margaret J. "His Skyward Path the Rainbow Is: Funeral Music of the Sa'dan Toraja." *Hemisphere* 25, 5 (1981): 303.

483.   Kartomi, Margaret J. "Tabut—a Shi'a Ritual Transplanted from India to Sumatra." In *Nineteenth and Twentieth Century Indonesia: Essays in Honour of Professor J.D. Legge*, David P. Chandler and M.C. Ricklefs, ed. Victoria, Australia: Monash University, 1986. 141-62.

484.   Kartomi, Margaret J. "Muslim Music in West Sumatran Culture." *The World of Music* 28, 3 (1986): 13-32. The culture of Minangkabau mixes a

matrilineal social system and customs and local animist, Hindu and Buddhist beliefs with Sufism. Islam introduced Qur'anic chant and a variety of devotional group song-forms performed outside the mosque.

485.   Kartomi, Margaret J. "Experience-Near and Experience-Distant Perception of the Dabôih Ritual in Aceh, Sumatra." In *Von der Vielfalt Musikalischer Kultur: Festschrift für Josef Kuckertz*, R. Schumacher, ed. Salzburg: Verlag Ursula Müller-Speiser, 1992. 247-260. Kartomi uses a pre-battle religious ritual engaged in by two groups of men in trance to distinguish between a description of the experience by someone from the culture and that of someone who is not. A researcher's detailed conceptual understanding of a music may not equal in intensity a native's unselfconscious experience, but it can lead to a perception of the essence of a music and a penetration into the modes of thought and structural principles on which it is based.

486.   Metcalf, Peter. *A Borneo Journey into Death. Berawan Eschatology from its Rituals*. Philidelphia, PA: University of Pennsylvania Press, 1982. Death Songs are the sacred core of Berawan religion. A detailed examination of attitudes and rites regarding death.

487.   Simon, Artur. "Types and Functions of Music in the Eastern Highlands of West Irian." *Ethnomusicology* 22, 3 (1978): 441-55. A primarily musical study, with transcriptions, of four types of vocal music of the Eipo pygmies. The last of these consists of recitals at curing ceremonies.

488.   Simon, Artur. "Functional Changes in Batak Traditional Music and its Role in Modern Indonesian Society." *Asian Music* 15, 2 (1984): 58-66. In spite of attempts by the dominant local Christian institutions to suppress *gondang*, or ceremonial music, and ancestor worship, they have been held on to amid social upheaval for the purpose of ethnic identity.

489.   Simon, Artur. "Gondang, Gods and Ancestors: Religious Implications of Batak Ceremonial Music." *Yearbook for Traditional Music* 25 (1993): 81-88. Among the Batak of Northern Sumatra, music for the gondang ensemble is rapidly vanishing, as are, with the arrival of Christianity and Islam, the complex cosmology and ritual—ancestor worship, possession, and possession dance—associated with it.

490.   Traube, Elizabeth. *Cosmology and Social Life: Ritual Exchange among the Mambat of East Timor*. Chicago: University of Chicago Press, 1986.

491.   Turner, Ashley. "Belian as a Symbol of Cosmic Reunification." In *Metaphor: A Musical Dimension*, Jamie C. Kassler, ed. Australian Studies in the History, Philosophy and Social Studies of Music, Vol. 1. Sydney: Currency Press, 1991. 121-146. With the aid of drum rhythms that operate simultaneously on two planes—the seen world of his community and the unseen world of spirits—the shaman obtains protection and healing for members of his com-

munity and temporarily unifies the two worlds through music and ritual. (Sumatra)

11

South Asia: India, Nepal, Sri Lanka, and Pakistan

INDIA: MUSIC HISTORIES, PHILOSOPHIES, AND BIBLIOGRAPHIES

492. Ayyangar, R. Rangaramanuja. *History of South Indian (Carnatic) Music: From Vedic Times to the Present.* Madras: [the author], 1972.

493. Bake, Arnold. "The Music of India." In *New Oxford History of Music I: Ancient and Oriental Music,* 1957. 195-227, 448. See pp. 196-204 for philosophical importance of music in general and Vedic music in particular.

494. Bandyopadhyaya, Shripada. *Indian Music Through the Ages: 2400 B.C. to the Present Era.* New Delhi: B.R. Publishing Corp., 1949/repr. 1985.

495. Basham, A.L., ed. *A Cultural History of India.* Oxford: Oxford University Press, 1975. Thirty-five essays on as many aspects of Indian culture and society, arranged historically.

496. Bhatkhande, Vishnu Narayan. "A Comparative Study of Some of the Leading Music Systems of the 15th, 16th, 17th, and 18th Centuries." *Sangîta* (1930-31). An attempt to connect Sanskrit treatises of the 15th to 18th centuries to the earlier Nâtya Sastra and Sangita Ratnâkara.

497. Daniélou, Alain. *Northern Indian Music.* New York: Frederick Praeger, 1968. A revised and abridged version of *Northern Indian Music,* 1942. Published in Great Britain by Barrie & Rockliff as *The Raga-s of Northern Indian Music.* Largely a catalog of raga patterns and associated meanings, the book begins with an informative summary of the records and names upon which a history of early Indian music is based.

498. Gautam, M.R. *The Musical Heritage of India.* New Delhi: Abhinav Publications, 1980.

499.   Holroyde, Peggy. *The Music of India*. New York: Praeger Publishers, 1972. 58-71. Chapter 2 (pp. 58-71) contains a discussion of the Philosophy of Pure Sound and its metaphysical implications.

500.   Jairazbhoy, N.A. "Music." In *A Cultural History of India*, A.L.Basham, ed. Oxford 1975. 217-48, 485-6. Chap. 16. This largely technical discussion includes discussion of Vedic chant and other forms of religious song.

501.   Kendadamath, G.C. *Indian Music and Dance: A Select Bibliography*. Varanasi, Indian Bibliographic Centre: 1986.

502.   Neuman, Daniel M. *The Life of Music in North India: The Organization of an Artistic Tradition*. Detroit: Wayne State University Press, 1980. See pp. 60-68: "Music as Divine Expression".

503.   Nijenhuis, Emmie Te. *Indian Music: History and Structure*. Handbuch der Orientalistik, Vol. 6, 2nd series. Leiden: Brill, 1974.

504.   Powers, Harold S. et al. "India." In *Grove 6*, Vol. 9. 1980. 69-166. See especially §I, 3, i: Ritual and ceremonial music, iii: Devotional songs and musical form, 4: Music history to the mid-16th century, 4, i: Sources for music history in the ancient period and 4, ii: Treatises and traditions in the medieval period.

505.   Prajñânânanda, Swâmi. *Historical Development of Indian Music: A Critical Study*. Calcutta: Mukhopadhyay, 1973. Indian music from historical, philosophical, aesthetic, religious, and technical standpoints. Full of references to both Indian and Western authors.

506.   Prajñânânanda, Swâmi. *Music of the South-Asian Peoples: A Historical Study of Music of India, Kashmere, Ceylon, and Bangladesh, and Pakistan*. Calcutta: Ramakrishna Vedanta Math, 1979.

507.   Prajñânânanda, Swâmi. *A Historical Study of Indian Music*. 2nd rev. and enl. ed., New Delhi: Munshiram Manoharlal, 1981. A historical study of Indian music, with chapters on the main genres, the music of Bengal, dance, acoustics, iconography, aesthetics, and philosophy, and a final assertion that music, regarded with purity, helps us to reach the goal of Self-realization.

508.   Ray, Sukumar. *Music of Eastern India*. Calcutta: Mukhopadhyay, 1973. Chapters 1 and 2 deal with the earliest preserved accounts of music in Bengal: Buddhist song of about 1,000 years ago, devotional songs of praise to Krishna (*padavali kirtan*) and songs of the cult of the goddess Sakti.

509.   Ries, Raymond E. "The Cultural Setting of South Indian Music." *Asian Music* 1, 2 (1969): 22-31. On the ties between music and the socio-cultural setting in which it flourishes and how the latter specifically relates to South

Indian music. Special attention is given to *bhakti* and its music, *bhajana*, holding the religious act as their essence.

510.   Sambamoorthy, P. *History of Indian Music*. 2nd ed., Madras: Indian Music Publishing House, 1982.

511.   Sanyal, Ritwik. *Philosophy of Music*. Bombay: Somaiya Publ. 1987.

512.   Sathyanarayana, R. "Indian Music: Myth and Legend." *Journal of the Indian Musicological Society* 18, 1 (Jun) (1987): 1-49.

513.   Singh, Jaidev. "Nada in Indian Tradition." *Journal of the Indian Musicological Society* 11, 1 (March), 2 (June) (1980): 37-43. A study of the metaphysics of *nada, nada* in Yoga, *nada* as described in the philosophy of Grammar, and *nada* in music. This last and most important use is defined as "the consciousness-power of the Divine which unfolds itself as the phenomenal world".

514.   Tagore, Sourindro Mohun. *Universal History of Music, Compiled from Divers Sources; Together with Various Original Notes on Hindu Music.* 2nd ed., Varanasi, India: Chowkhamba Sanskrit Series Office, 1963. Includes a discussion of the role of Buddhist music in the development of Indian music.

515.   Tarlekar, Ganesh Hari and Nalini Tarlekar. *Musical Instruments in Indian Sculpture*. Pune: Pune Vidyarthi Griha Prakashan, 1972.

516.   Veer, Ram Avtar. *The Music of India*. New Delhi: Pankaj, 1986. Vol. 1: 6000 B.C. to 1000 A.D.; Vol. 2: 1001 A.D. to 1986 A.D.

INDIA: SANSKRIT TEXTS IN TRANSLATION

517.   *Dattila [Dattilam: A Compendium of Ancient Indian Music]*. Leiden, Netherlands: E.J. Brill, 1970. Introduction, translation and commentary by Emmie Te Nijenhuis.

518.   de Bary, William Theodore, ed. *Sources of Indian Tradition*. 2 vols. New York: Columbia University Press., 1958. Consult index to Vol. 1 for references to hymns, mantra, music, and vedas.

519.   *The Grihya-sutras: Rules of Vedic Domestic Ceremonies*. Hermann Oldenberg, transl. Delhi: Motilal Banarsidass, 1879, 1886-92/repr. 1964, 1967. Orig. ed., Oxford: The Clarendon Press.

520.   Gupt, Bharat. "Music in the Natya Sastra." *Journal of the Music Academy Madras* 57 (1986): 172-81. 58 (1987): 91-109. 59 (1988): 60-82. A translation of *Natyasastra* with *Sanjivanam*, a Sanskrit commentary by 20th-

century Acharya Kailash Chandra Brhaspati, transl. by Bharat Gupt.   A commentary on the 28th chapter of Bharata's *Natyasastra*, on music.

521.   *Hymns of the Atharva-Veda: Together with Extracts from the Ritual Books and the Commentaries.* Maurice Bloomfield, transl. Vol. 42. New York: Greenwood Press, 1897/repr. 1969. 1897 ed., Oxford: The Clarendon Press; 1964 and 1967 ed., Delhi: Motilal Banarsidass.

522.   Howard, Wayne. *Matralaksanam: Text, Translation, Extracts from the Commentary, and Notes, Including References to Two Oral Traditions of South India.* New Delhi: Indira Gandhi National Centre for the Arts, 1988. A translation from the Sanskrit of portions of the Samaveda, with commentary on the accents and musical structure of chanting Samavedic hymns.

523.   Narada. *Naradiya-Siksa.* Calcutta: Rabindra Bharati University, 1983. Translated and edited by Sures Chandra Banerji. A short, phonetic guide to the chanting of the Samaveda, c.500 A.D.

524.   Narada. *Naradiya Siksa, with the Commentary of Bhatta Sobhakara.* Poona: Bhandarkar Oriental Research Institute, 1986. Translated and edited by Usha R. Bhise.

525.   Sarngadeva. *Sangita-Ratnakara of Sarngadeva.* R.K. Shringy and Prem Lata Sharma, transl. Vol. 1, Treatment of Svara. Varanasi: Motilal Banarsidass, 1978. c. 1240 A.D. A comprehensive synthesis of all previous musical learning in India.

526.   *The Satapatha-Brahmana: According to the Text of the Madhyandina School.* Julius Eggeling, transl. Vol. 12, 26, 41, 43, 44. Delhi: Motilal Banarsidass, 1882-1900/repr. 1963, 1972. "Sattha Brahmanic discourses of a hundred paths" is a detailed explanation and expansion of the sacrificial formulas contained in the Yajur Veda and of the priestly duties connected with them.

527.   *The Samaveda Samhita.* Ralph T.H. Griffith, transl. Delhi: Nag Publishers, 1991. Text, translation, commentary & notes in English, mantra index & name index, mantras not found in the Rgveda, by Ralph Griffith, enlarged by Nag Sharan Singh & Surendra Pratap. 1st ed., 1895.

528.   *Sangitasiromani: A Medieval Handbook of Indian Music.* Brill's Indological Library, Vol. 5, Leiden and New York: E. J. Brill, 1992. Edited with introduction and translation by Emmie te Nijenhuis of *Crest Jewel of Music* of 1428.   A valuable summary of Medieval North Indian musicology.   With Parallel Sanskrit transliteration and English translation.

529. *Vedic Hymns.* 2 vols. Max Müller, transl. Vol. 32, 46. Delhi: Motilal Banarsidass, 1891-97/repr. 1964. Orig. ed., Oxford: Clarendon Press.

INDIA: STUDIES OF SANSKRIT TEXTS

530.   Apte, V. M. "Vedic Rituals." In *The Cultural Heritage of India*, Vol. 1: The Early Phases. Calcutta: The Ramakrishna Mission, 1958. 234-263.

531.   Bhattacharya, Arun. *A Treatise on Ancient Hindu Music*. Calcutta: K.P. Bagchi, 1978.

532.   Brown, W. Norman. "Agni, Sun, Sacrifice, and Vac: A Sacerdotal Ode by Dirghatamas (Rig Veda I.164)." *Journal of the American Oriental Society* 88 (1968): 199-218.

533.   Drury, Naama. *The Sacrificial Ritual in the Satapatha Brahmana*. Delhi: Motilal Banarsidass, 1981.

534.   Findly, Ellison Banks. *"Mantra kavis'asta': Speech as Performative in the Rgveda." Understanding Mantra*. Albany, NY: State University of New York Press, c1982.

535.   Gonda, Jan. *Mantra Interpretation in the Satapatha-Brahmana*. Leiden & New York: E.J. Brill, 1988.

536.   Gray, J. E. B. "An Analysis of Nambudiri Rgvedic Recitations and the Nature of the Vedic Accent." *Bulletin of the School of Oriental and African Studies* 22 (1959): 500-530.

537.   Howard, Wayne. *Sâmavedic Chant*. New Haven: Yale University Press, 1977. A study of Samavedic chant with transcriptions of performances from the Kauthuma, Ranayaniya, and Jaiminiya Schools of Samavedic Chant.

538.   Howard, Wayne. "Music and Accentuation in Vedic Literature." *The World of Music* 24, 3 (1982): 23-32. A general examination of how Brahmanic religious texts or Vedas are passed on through oral tradition and the medium of music.

539.   Howard, Wayne. *Veda Recitation in Varanasi*. Delhi: Motilal Banarsidas, 1986. A study of surviving Vedic ritual traditions in Varanasi, the Hindu pilgrimage city. Offers historical perspective and descriptive analysis of four Vedic chants (Rg, Atharva, Yajur, and Sama) and an undercurrent postulate that the chant today is essentially the same as it was millennia ago.

540.   Howard, Wayne. "The Body of the Bodiless Gayatra." *Indo-Iranian Journal* 30, Jul. (1987): 161-173. On Vedic ritual and chant.

541.   Howard, Wayne. *The Decipherment of the Samavedic Notation of the Jaiminîyas*. Studia Orientalia 63, Helsinki: Finnish Oriental Society, 1988.

542.   Jairazbhoy, N.A. "An Interpretation of the 22 Srutis." *Asian Music* 6 (1975): 38-59. An inquiry into the workings of the sruti scale system, according to comments in the Natyasastra and to the method of Vedic recitation in the style of Tamil Brahmans.

543.   Kaufmann, Walter. "Some Reflections on the Notations of Vedic Chant." In *Essays in Musicology: A Birthday Offering for Willi Apel*, Hans Tischler, ed. Bloomington, IN: Indiana University Press, 1968. 1-18.

544.   Lath, Mukund. "Ancient Indian Music and the Concept of Man." *National Centre for the Performing Arts Quarterly Journal* 12, 2-3 (1983): 1-8. Although the author finds no correlation between Renaissance music and Renaissance/Greek ideals, or between the development of European polyphony and concurrent European world views, he does see correlations between Sama-vedic mantras, the position of music in Buddhism and Jainism, and sacred de-votional music (Gandharva) and the religious philosophies associated with them—the Jaiminiya Upanisad Brahmana, the Sanyasi ideal of world renunci-ation, and the theistic cults of Vaishnavism and Shaivism.

545.   Lath, Mukund. *A Study of Dattilam: A Treatise on the Sacred Music of Ancient India*. rev. ed., Kalamulasastra Series, Indira Gandhi National Centre for the Arts, c1992. A concise manual of ritual music, c. 200 A.D.

546.   Nijenhuis, Emmie Te. *Musicological Literature*. A History of Indian Literature, Vol. 6, Jan Gonda, ed. Wiesbaden: Otto Harrassowitz, 1977. An introduction to early musical treatises.

547.   Prajñânânanda, Swâmi. "Music of Hindu and Buddhist India." Entally Cultural Conference, 8th Annual Session. Calcutta: 1955, Jan.

548.   Raghavan, V. "Some Names in Early Sangita Literature." *Journal of the Music Academy, Madras* 3, 1-2 (1932): 11-32. An introduction to Indian music treatises after the Vedic period up to and including Sarngedeva, c. 1200. Revised reprint in *SNA Bulletin,* 1956 and 1957.

549.   Raghavan, V. "Some More Names in Early Sangita Literature." *Journal of the Music Academy, Madras* 3, 3-4 (1932): 94-102. Dance, vocal, and instrumental music from Bharata to Sarngedeva.

550.   Raghavan, V. "Later Sangita Literature." *Journal of the Music Academy, Madras* 4 (1933): 16-26. Revised reprint in *Sangeet Natak Akademi Bulletin*, 17, July (1960): 1-24 and 18, April (1961): 1-18. Treatises from the time of Sarngedeva to recent times.

551.   Raghavan, V. "Music in the Brhaddharma-Purana." *Journal of the Music Academy, Madras* 9 (1938): 37-39. In a work composed later that Sarngedeva, Narada equates music with the imperishable Brahman. Vishnu describes the

appearance of Nada in different points in the body and equates these with different ragas and raginis.

552.   Raghavan, V. "Music in the Adbhuta-Ramayana." *Journal of the Music Academy, Madras* 16 (1945): 65-72. A product of the Rama cult; important as background for the school of Rama-bhakti (devotions) in South India to which Tyagaraja belonged.

553.   Raghavan, V. "Present Position of Vedic Chanting and its Future." *Bulletin of the Institute of Traditional Cultures* 1 (1957): 48-69.

554.   Raghavan, V. "Samaveda and Music." *Journal of the Music Academy* 33 (1962): 127-133.

555.   Rajagopalam, T.K. "The Music of the Sama-Veda Chants." *Journal of the Music Academy, Madras* 20 (1949): 144-151. An interpretation of the Sama Veda with respect to references in the Chandogya and other Upanishads.

556.   Rajagopalan, L.S. and Wayne Howard. "A Report on the Pracheena Kauthuma Samaveda of Palghat." *Journal of the Indian Musicological Society* 20, 1-2 (1989): 5-16. A sacred text of Kerala.

557.   Ranade, G.H. "The Indian Music of the Vedic and the Classical Period." *The Journal of the Music Academy, Madras* 19 (1948): 71 ff. Renade's translation/summary of Erwin Felber's 1912 study of the history of recitation according to phonogram plates in the archives of the Royal Academy in Vienna. The study revealed three stages: 1) speech; 2) art music; and 3) speech-music or recitation as mid-way between speech and art music. Rg Vedic chant is recitation. Samavedic chant is song, perhaps folk song. The Yajur Veda is chanted on a single tone.

558.   Rowell, Lewis. "Abhinavagupta, Augustine, Time, and Music." *Journal of the Indian Musicological Society* 13, 2 (December) (1982): 18-36. A comparison of both the empirical and philosophical conceptions of time by Abhinavagupta, the 11th-century Kashmiri Shaivite philosopher, and Augustine, the 4th to 5th century north African Christian theologian. Time is conceived as both transient and cosmic though measurable. Time is ultimately a metaphor for the graduated union with the divine, as differently conceived by the two philosophers.

559.   Rowell, Lewis. *Music and Musical Thought in Early India.* Chicago and London: University of Chicago Press, 1992. An excellent current study of the theory and practice of music from the Vedas to c1000 CE.

560.   Sharma, Hriday R. "The Spirituality of the Vedic Sacrifice." In *Hindu Spirituality I. Vedas through Vedanta*, Krishna Sivaraman, ed. New York: Crossroad, 1989. 29-39. On the various three-fold symbolic meanings of Vedic sacrifice, with a section on the form of the Vedic ritual.

561.   Staal, Frits. *Agni, the Vedic Ritual of the Fire Altar*. 2 vols. Berkeley, CA: Asian Humanities Press, 1983. In collaboration with C.V. Somayajipad and M. Itti Ravi Nambudiri; with tapes. A systematic, detailed, definitive study of this ritual.

562.   Staal, Frits. "Vedic Mantras." In *Understanding Mantras*, Harvey P. Alper, ed. Albany, NY: SUNY Press, 1989. 48-95.

563.   Tarlekar, Ganesh Hari. *The Saman Chants: A Review of Research*. Bombay and Baroda: Indian Musicological Society, 1985. A review of 47 works on Samavedic Chant, followed by a retrospect. Also published in *Journal of the Indian Musicological Society*, Vols. 14 and 15 (1983-1984).

564.   Tarlekar, Ganesh Hari. "Some Puranic Legends Relating to Music." *Journal of the Indian Musicological Society* 18, 2/Dec. (1987): 47-51.

565.   Thite, G.U. "Gandharvas and Apsaras in the Vedas." *Journal of the Indian Musicological Society* 18, 2/Dec. (1987): 52-63.

566.   Trikha, J.K. *Rig Veda: A Scientific and Intellectual Analysis of the Hymns*. Bombay: Somaiya Publications, 1981-91.

567.   Varadarajan, Brinda. "Music in the Sama Veda." *Journal of the Music Academy, Madras* 58 (1987): 169-80. The Samaveda is studied as texts of the Rg Veda that are extended and altered to suit the samavedic method of chanting. Includes a description of this method.

568.   Wayman, Alex. "The Significance of Mantra-s, from the Veda down to Buddhist Tantric Practice." *Adyar Library Bulletin* 39 (1975): 65-89.

INDIA: RELIGIOUS MUSIC AND MUSICIANS

569.   Acharya, B.T. *Haridasa Sahitya, the Karnatic Mystics and their Songs*. Bangalore, India: Indian Institute of Culture, Basavangudi, 1953.

570.   Aiyar, M.S. Ramaswami. *Thiagaraja, a Great Musician Saint: With Sargam Notation*. New Delhi: Asian Education Services, 1986.

571.   Appadurai, Arjun, Frank J. Korom, and Margaret A. Mills, ed. *Gender, Genre, and Power in South Asian Expressive Traditions*. South Asia Seminar Series; Publications of the American Folklore Society, new series, Philadelphia, PA: University of Pennsylvania Press, 1991.

572.   Banerji, Sures Chandra. "Influence of Tantra on Indian Music and Dance." *Journal of the Indian Musicological Society* 10, 3-4/Sept.-Dec. (1979): 20-22.

573. Bharati, Agehananda, Swami. *The Tantric Tradition*. rev. ed., Westport, CT: Greenwood Press, 1977.

574. Bharati, Srirama. "Reviving Temple Music." *Indian Music Journal* 13 (1984): 49-59. On the psychological and spiritual values of the devotional aspect of temple music and on temples and villages as sources of temple music.

575. Callewaert, Winand M. "The 'Earliest' Song of Mira (1503-1546)." *Orientalia Lovaniensia Periodica* 22 (1991): 201-214. A review of the first manuscripts of songs assumed to have been composed by Mira. Includes a select bibliography of songs by Mira.

576. Chawla, Rupika. "The Legend of Thyagaraja: Invoking God through Music." *India Magazine* 4, 6 (1984): 42-51.

577. Durga, S.A.K. "Symbolism in Indian Music." In *Tradition and its Future in Music. Report of SIMS 1990 Osaka*, Osaka, Japan: Mita Press, 1990. 197-201. On music's origin in Sama Veda, symbolic shapes of instruments, the connection of drums and drum syllables to Shiva, nâda (sound) and yoga, 22 srutis (divisions of the octave) and tantric worship, singing and 'om' prayer, râga as a spiritual being, religious texts, and the significance of tâla (circle) in Hindu ritual.

578. Hawley, John S. "The Music of Faith and Morality." *Journal of the American Academy of Religion* 52, June (1984): 243-262. A study of poetry and music of Mira Bai, Narasi Mehta, and Pipa Das to show that in devotional Hinduism, music is not a sphere separate from that of morality and faith, as they are often considered to be in Protestant Christianity.

579. Henry, Edward O. "The Mother Goddess Cult and Interaction between Little and Great Religious Traditions." In *Religion in Modern India*, Giri Raj Gupta, ed. New Delhi: Vikas Publishing House, 1983. On "the ideology and ritual context of mother goddess songs".

580. Henry, Edward O. "The Vitality of the *Nirgun* Bhajan: Sampling the Contemporary Tradition." In *Bhakti Religion in North India: Community, Identity, and Political Action*, David Lorenzen, ed. Albany, NY: State University of New York Press, 1994.

581. Iyer, P.R. Rajagopala. "The Greatness of the Compositions of Saint Arunagirinatha." *Journal of the Music Academy, Madras* 60 (1989): 140-67. A study of the unique poetry and song of a famous 15th-century Tamil saint.

582. Jackson, William J. "The Bhakta and External Worship: Sri Tyâgarâja's Utsava Sampradaya Songs." *Journal of the Music Academy, Madras* 60 (1989): 65-91. Tyagaraja was a saint who cherished spiritual solitude and devotion but who also exhorted others to the spiritual life through invoking Rama and other figures of Hindu mythology and participating in communal ritual.

583.   Jackson, William J. *Tyagaraja: Life and Lyrics*. Delhi and New York: Oxford University Press, 1992. A study that places the most celebrated musician-saint of South India in the historical, cultural and social framework in which he lived.

584.   Marcotty, Thomas. *The Way-Music. How to Conjure with Sounds. Rudra Veena: The Theory and Technique of Tantric Music*. Lugano, Switzerland: Decisio Editrice, 1980. A study, based on interviews, of the theory and technique of playing the *rudra-veena*, a stringed instrument used in magic rituals of 'music of the path' (*sangeet marg*). Includes a 90-min. cassette.

585.   Nijenhuis, Emmie Te. "Historical Development of the Musical Forms in India with Reference to the Religious History." In *Von der Vielfalt Musikalischer Kulture: Festschrift for Josef Kuckertz*, R. Schumacher, ed. Salzburg: Verlag Ursula Müller-Speiser, 1992. 377-384. The author traces two types of *bhakti* poetry from the 9th through the 16th centuries. One was esoteric and philosophical and was sung, often as solos, by or for the courtly elite. The other was emotional and devotional and was sung communally by the less educated either in call and response or in stanza-refrain form.

586.   Owens, Naomi. "The Dagar Gharânâ: A Case Study of Performing Artists." In *Performing Arts in India*, Bonnie C. Wade, ed. Lanham, New York: University Press of America, 1983. 158-195. A study of the Dagar family, specialists in the performance of Dhrupad, the most revered form of Indian classical vocal music.

587.   Parichha, Bhaskar. "Samkha, the Sacred Conch." *India Magazine* 8, 3 (Feb) (1988): 46-51.

588.   Raghavan, V. *The Great Integrators: The Saint-Singers of India*. Patel memorial lectures, 1964, Delhi: Publications Division, Ministry of Information and Broadcasting, 1966/repr. 1969.

589.   Raghavan, V. *Tyagaraja*. New Delhi: Sahitya Akademi, 1983.

590.   Ranade, Ashok D. "Devotional Music in India." *Sangeet Natak* 85-86, Jul-Dec (1987): 40-48. After distinguishing between religiosity, mysticism, and devotion, Renade describes the long history, social circumstances, and philosophical content of the *Bhakti* movement as background for a description of the features of devotional music.

591.   Roche, David. "Music and Religion in India." In *Encyclopedia of Religion*, Mircea Eliade, ed. Vol. 10. 1987. 185-191.

592.   Sambamurti, P. *A History of Sacred Music in India*. K.V. Rangaswami Aiyangar Commemoration Volume, Madras: Indian Music Publishing House, 1940.

593.   Shankar, Ravi. *My Music, My Life*. New York: Simon and Schuster, 1968. A personal perspective on music, the religious in music, and the quest for the sublime.

594.   Simon, Robert Leopold. "India: Hindu Popular Religious Music." In *Grove 6*, Vol. 9. 1980. 144-145.

595.   Simon, Robert Leopold. *Spiritual Aspects of Indian Music*. Delhi, India: Sundeep/South Asia Books, 1985.

596.   Simon, Robert Leopold. "Tyagaraja and the South Indian Bhajana Sampradaya." *Asian Music* 20, 1 (Fall-winter) (1988): 114-27. A historical look at South Indian bhajan ritual and Tyagaraja's important role in its formation.

597.   Sivananda, Swami. "Indian Music—Music and Other Arts: The Finest Art of Spiritual Experience." *Journal of the Andhra Historical Research Society* 27 (1961-62): 50-55.

598.   Strickland-Anderson, Lily. "The Mythological Background of Hindu Music." *The Musical Quarterly* 17 (1931): 330-340. On the various deities connected with music and music instruments.

599.   Sudhi, Padma. "The Spiritual Influence of Yoga Activity on Indian Music." *Journal of the Indian Musicological Society* 18, 2 (Dec) (1987): 84-89.

600.   Vyas, R.T. "Sarasvati: A Study in Symbolism with Special Reference to the Motif in Vina." *Journal of the Indian Musicological Society* 18, 2/Dec. (1987): 64-72.

601.   Wulff, Donna Marie. "On Practicing Religiously: Music as Sacred in India." In *Sacred Sound*, Joyce Irwin, ed. Chico, CA: Scholars Press, 1983. 149-172. On *nada* (divine sound), *bhakti* (the devotional tradition), and their beginnings in Vedic literature and its descriptions of the power of sound.

INDIA: RELIGIOUS MUSIC OF SPECIFIC AREAS AND GROUPS

602.   Bargit Research (Preliminary) Committee. "A Scientific Study of the Vaishnava Music of Assam." *Sangeet Natak Akademi Bulletin* 10 (1958): 38-42.

603.   Bhattacharya, D. *Songs of the Bards of Bengal*. Bhattacharya, Deben, transl. New York and London: Grove Press, 1969. A collection of song lyrics of the Bauls (religious nomads) of Bengal. Introduction includes historical background, categorization of songs and instruments, and a discussion of the Baul faith as evidenced through the poetry. Includes a large collection of poems translated into English.

604.   Capwell, Charles. *Music of the Bauls of Bengal*. Kent, OH: Kent State University Press, 1986. A study of the belief system and customs, analysis of music and texts, and description of the types of instruments used and the context of performances.

605.   Capwell, Charles. "The Popular Expression of Religious Syncretism: The Bauls of Bengal as Apostles of Brotherhood." *Popular Music* 7, 2 (May) (1988): 123-32.

606.   Catlin, Amy. "Vatapi Ganapatim: Sculptural, Poetic, and Musical Texts in a Hymn to Ganesa." In *Ganesh: Studies of an Asian God*, Robert L. Brown, ed. Albany, NY: SUNY Press, 1991. 141-169.

607.   Citaristi, Ileana. "Devadasis of the Jagannath Temple: Precursors of Odissi Music & Dance." *Sruti* 33-34, Jun-Jul (1987): 51-57.

608.   Dasgupta, Alokeranjan and Mary Ann Dasgupta transl. *Roots in the Void: Baul Songs of Bengal*. Calcutta: KP Bagchi, India/South Asia Books, 1983. On the possible connection between Tantra and music, through their mutual veneration of Siva, and between Tantra and dance, through similar mudras or hand poses.

609.   Devi, S. "The Musico-Religious Traditions of Assam." *Journal of the Music Academy, Madras* 39 (1968): 63.

610.   Erndl, Kathleen M. "Fire and Wakefulness: The Devi Jagrata in Contemporary Panjabi Hinduism." *Journal of the American Academy of Religion* 59, 2/Summer (1991): 339-360. An all-night vigil dedicated to the Goddess Devi, *Devi jagrata* includes devotional songs and the recitation of the story of Queen Tara, a story that teaches that devotion to the Goddess overcomes ritual pollution. Film music and loudspeakers have been found to enhance worship.

611.   Gomati, Viswanathan. "The Temple Music of South India." *Journal of the Music Academy, Madras* 52 (1981): 217-227. The study of paintings, temple carvings and sculpture, treatises on temple music and ritual, and the actual practice of the many South Indian temples attest to a long, rich, and varied involvement of music in temple life.

612.   Hansadutta, Swami. *Kirtan: Ancient Medicine for Modern Man*. Hopland, CA: Hansa Publications, 1985. The therapeutic value of group chant, from the standpoint of the International Society for Krishna Consciousness.

613.   Henry, Edward O. *Chant the Names of God: Music and Culture in Bhojpuri-Speaking India*. San Diego: San Diego State University Press, 1988. A study of musical life in northern rural India, including explication of song texts, religious ideology and ritual, occasions of performance, and social organization.

614.   Henry, Edward O. *"Jogis* and *Nirgun Bhajans* in Bhojpuri-Speaking India: Intra-Genre Heterogeneity, Adaptation, and Functional Shift." *Ethnomusicology* 35, 2 (Spring-Summer) (1991): 221-42. A study of variant renditions of Hindu devotional songs dedicated to the formless divine (nirgun bhajans) by Muslim mendicant musicians (jogis).

615.   Hooper, J.S.M. *Hymns of the Alvars*. Heritage of India series, Calcutta, India: Association Press; New York, etc.: Oxford University Press, 1929. Pt. 1 is a historical and cultural account of the Alvars, an 1800-year old devotional sect of South India; Pt. 2 contains translations of Alvar devotional hymns, with commentary.

616.   Kuckertz, Josef. "Songs of Brahmans in South Karnataka, India." In *Tradition and Its Future in Music: Report of SIMS Osaka*, Tokumaru Yoshiko et al., ed. Tokyo: Mita Press, 1991. 187-96.

617.   Modak, H.V. "Musical Curiosities in the Temples of India." *National Centre for the Performing Arts Quarterly Journal* 14, 4 (1985): 32-43.

618.   Murase, Satoru. *Patchwork Jacket and Loincloth: An Ethnographic Study of the Bauls of Bengal*. Ph.D. diss., University of Illinois at Urbana-Champaign, 1991. An "empirical investigation" of the Bauls as people: it is a renunciatory, anti-structural element in a social system in whose maintenance it nevertheless plays an essential contributing role.

619.   Neog, Maheshwar. "The Vaishnava Music of Assam." *The Journal of the Music Academy* 30 (1959): 138-145.

620.   Peterson, Indira Viswanathan. "Sanskrit in Carnatic Music: The Songs of Muttusvami Diksita." *Indo-Iranian Journal* 29, Jul. (1986): 183-199.

621.   Reck, Carol and David Reck. "Naga Kalem: A Musical Trance Ceremonial of Kerala (India)." *Asian Music* 13, 1 (1981): 84-98. Songs are an important part of the worship of snake deities in ceremonies conducted in Kerala by castes of wandering minstrels.

622.   Sandra, Green. "The Sacred Dances of Ladakh." In *A Spectrum of World Dance: Tradition, Transition, and Innovation*, Wallen and Acocella, ed. New York: Congress on Research in Dance, 1987. 18-30.

623.   Sarabhai, Malsika, ed. *Performing Arts of Kerala*. Seattle, WA: University of Washington Press, 1992.

624.   Sathyanarayana, R. *Music of Madhva Monks of Karnataka*. Bangalore, India: Gnana Jyothi Kala Mandir, 1988. A study of the devotional songs of five 15th to 17th century south Indian monks: Sripadaraya, Vadiraja, Vyasaraya, Vijayindratirtha, and Raghavendratirtha.

625.   Sharma, Sadashiv Rath. "Musical Instruments in Orissi Dance and Temple Sculpture." *Marg* 13, 2 (1960): 39-43.

626.   Simon, Robert Leopold. *Bhakti Ritual Music in South India*. Ph.D. diss., University of California, 1975.

627.   Slawek, Stephen Matthew. *Kirtan: A Study of the Sonic Manifestations of the Divine in the Popular Hindu Culture of Banaras*. Ph.D. diss., University of Illinois at Urbana-Champaign, 1986. A study of the variety of types of kirtan (congregational devotional song) in India and their interconnections, and a description of the organization, musical content and performance of kirtan-s by devotional associations found in Varanasi. The author finds that "musical style, meaning and significance in these religious gatherings are to a large part contextually determined".

628.   Sontheimer, Günther D. "Bhakti in the Khandoba Cult." In *Devotion Divine: Bhakti Traditions from the Regions of India: Studies in Honour of Charlotte Vaudeville*, D. L. Eck and F. Mallison, ed. Groningen: E. Forsten, 1991. 231-253.

629.   Strickland-Anderson, Lily. "Aboriginal and Animistic Influences in Indian Music." *The Musical Quarterly* 15 (1929): 371-387. On the polytheism, animistic beliefs, and 'orgiastic' dances of the Nagas, Assamese and Oreans that survived in the Vedas and in Buddhism.

630.   Wade, Bonnie. "Songs of Brahmans in South Karnataka, India." In *Tradition and its Future in Music*, Tokumaru, ed. 1991. 187-196. A study of traditional songs of South Indian Brahmans, with translations and transcriptions.

631.   Zide, Norman H. and Ram Dayal Munda. "Structural Influence of Bangali Vaisnava Songs on Traditional Mundari Songs." *Journal of Social Research* 13, 1 (1970): 36-48.

INDIA: MUSIC OF BUDDHISM, JAINISM, AND SIKHISM

632.   Bisht, Krishna. *The Sacred Symphony: A Study of Buddhistic and Vaishnav Music of Bengal in Relation to Hindustani Classical Music*. Ghaziabad, India: Bhagirath Sewa Sansthan, 1986. The Buddhist *caryagiti* of a dissident Buddhist sect active until the mid-17th century and the Vaisnava *kirtan* were musical assemblies whose purpose was to assist participants attain a "direct mystical communication with God via a madding trance and dazed ecstasy." Like Indian classical music, both had clearly formulated sets of rules, regulations and techniques.

633.   I-Ching. *Record of the Buddhist Religion as Practiced in India and the Malay Archipelago, A.D. 671-695*. J. Takakuso, transl. New Delhi, India:

Munshiram Manoharlal, 1966. Includes a description of the monks' rituals and comments on their style of chanting.

634.   Raghavan, V. "Music in Jain Works." *Journal of the Music Academy, Madras* 9 (1938): 40-41. A description of both the defects and the excellences of singing. The defects are trembling, rushing, crowing, and nasality; the excellences are proper projection and emotion, sweetness, etc.

635.   *Sikh Sacred Music.* New Delhi: Sikh Sacred Music Society, 1967.

636.   Singh, Kanwar M. "Guru Nanak and Divine Music." In *Guru Nanak, His Life*, G. N. Singh, ed. 1969. 249-260.

INDIAN DANCE AND DRAMA: ORIGINAL TEXTS IN TRANSLATION

637.   Bharata. *The Natyasastra.* 2 vols. Manomohan Ghosh, transl. Calcutta: Royal Asiatic Society of Bengal, 1961-67. Attributed to Bharatamuni, c. 200 A.D., with a commentary by the editor and translator. Considered to be the most elaborate treatise on drama and its production ever written. The six chapters on music are the earliest source on Indian music theory and practice, and provide detailed descriptions of the music employed in the preliminary rituals and incidental music to plays.

638.   Masson, J.L. and M.V. Patwardhan. *Aesthetic Rapture: The Rasadhyaya of the Natyasastra.* 2 vols. Poona: Deccan College, 1970.

639.   Sarngadeva. *The Samgitaratnakara of Sarngadeva.* K. Kunjunni Raja and Radha Burnier, transl. Vol. 4, on Dancing. Madras: Adyar Library, 1976.

INDIAN DANCE AND DRAMA: STUDIES

640.   Arden, John. "The Chhau Dancers of Purulia." *The Drama Review* 15 (1971): 65-75. Based on Hindu mythology, these recently discovered ritual dances are performed in the village of Purulia in Bangal.

641.   Bali, Vyjayantimala. "Rare Forms of Bharata Natyam." *Journal of the Music Academy Madras* 59 (1988): 140-43.

642.   Bose, Mandakranta. *Movement and Mimesis: The Idea of Dance in the Sanskritic Tradition.* Studies of Classical India, Vol. 12, Dordrecht; Boston: Kluwer Academic Publishers, 1991.

643.   Brhaspati, Acharya. "Music in the Natya Sastra." *Journal of the Music Academy, Madras* 56 (1985): 165-75.

644.   Chaitanya, Krishna. "Kathakali: The Dance-Drama of Kerala." *Canzona* 7, 24/June (1986): 14-23.

645.   Coomaraswamy, Ananda K. *The Dance of Shiva: Fourteen Indian Essays*. New York: Noonday Press, 1947/repr. 1957. See Chap. entitled 'The Dance of Shiva,' on the meanings of dance in Hindu mythology and religion.

646.   Devi, Ragini. *Dances of India*. Calcutta, India: Susil Gupta, 1962. Covers four main dance schools—Bharat Natyam, Kathakali, Kathak, and Manipuri—their background, philosophy, and religious connections.

647.   Dhananjayan, V.P. "Sringara & Bhakti in Dance." *Journal of the Music Academy, Madras* 54 (1983): 203-09. On love as the all-embracing and fundamental state, its maturation into Bhakti—devotional love—and its expression in dance.

648.   Doshi, Saryu, ed. *Dances of Manipur: The Classical Tradition*. Bombay: Marg Publications, 1989.

649.   Gentes, Mary Josephine. *Hinduism through Village Dance Drama: Narrative Image and Ritual Process in South India's Terukkuttu and Yaksagana Ritual Theaters*. Ph.D. diss., University of Virginia, 1987. Two village dance drama traditions, Terukkuttu in Tamilnadu state and Yaksagana in Karnataka, give voice, in their contributions to village ritual celebrations, to the concerns of their communities through material drawn from the Mahabharata. Focus is on indigenous views of the relationship of aesthetic and religious experience.

650.   Govindarajan, Hema. "Ritualism and Dance in Ancient Karnataka—A Historical Survey." *Shanmukha* 11, 3 (1985): 21-26. Prehistoric rock painting, classical treatises, dance in ancient Hindu and Jain temples, and many other evidences point to the ritual origins of dance.

651.   Hema, Govindarajan. *The Natyasastra and Bharata Natya*. New Delhi: Harman Publishing House, 1992.

652.   Iyer, K. Bharatha. *Kathakali, the Sacred Dance-Drama of Malabar*. New Delhi: Oriental Books Reprint Corp., 1955/repr. 1983. Orig. ed., London: Luzac.

653.   Jhaveri, Angana. *The Raslila Performance Tradition of Manipur in Northeast India*. Ph.D. diss., Michigan State University, 1987. The inherent cosmic principles found in this 200-year-old dance-drama based on the devotional worship of Lord Krishna are studied from the time, space and action structures of the performance.

654.   Jones, Betty True. "Kathakali Dance-Drama: An Historical Perspective." In *Performing Arts in India: Essays on Music, Dance, and Drama*, Bonnie C. Wade, ed. Lanham, New York: University Press of America, 1983. 14-44. Historical look at Kathakali dance-drama from its antecedents to present day

performance. Areas of interest are its basis in religious literature and the Hindu cultural idea that music and dance are pathways to salvation. Also appears in *Asian Music*, 18, 2 (1987):14-44.

655. Jones, Clifford R. "A Kerala Village Temple Festival: Ritual and Folk Art Forms as Communicators of Traditional Culture." In *Annals of Oriental Research, Silver Jubilee Volume*, Madras: University of Madras, 1975. 399-420.

656. Jones, Clifford R. and Betty True Jones. *Kathakali: An Introduction to the Dance-Drama of Kerala*. San Francisco: Theatre Arts Books and American Society for Eastern Arts, 1970.

657. Khokar, Mohan. "Dance and Ritual in Manipur." *Sangeet Natak* 10 (1968): 35-47.

658. Kothari, Sunil. "Symbolism in Indian Dance." *The World of Music* 20, 3 (1978): 70-83. On the various symbolisms associated with the dancing Shiva and with Indian dance in general. These include the eight moods (rasa), hand gestures, facial coloring, mask types, and make-up.

659. Kothari, Sunil. "The Kuchipudi Dance-Drama Tradition." In *Dance as Cultural Heritage*, Betty True Jones, ed. Vol. 1. New York: Congress on Research in Dance, 1983. 120-125. On the antiquity and history, both mythological and documented, of this all-male dance form of Andhra Pradesh, its relationship to both temple and court, and its current repertory.

660. Kramrisch, S. *The Presence of Siva*. Princeton: Princeton University, 1981. A thorough and compelling account of Hindu mythology, especially as it relates to Siva. Chap. 12, the Presence of Siva, provides a vivid account of Siva's dance.

661. Lightfoot, Louise. *Dance-rituals of Manipur, India*. Hong Kong: Standard Press, 1959.

662. Lipner, J. "On the Dance in Hinduism." In *Worship and Dance*, Davies, ed. Birmingham: ISWRA, 1975. 83-91.

663. Namboodiri, M.P. Sankaran. "Bhâva as Expressed through the Presentational Techniques of Kathakali." In *Dance as Cultural Heritage*, Betty True Jones, ed. Vol. 1. New York: CORD, 1983. 194-201. Bhâva, one of the eight elemental forms of Rudra (the Vedic god of lightning, often associated with Agni [fire] and Indra), is the personification of 'perpetual becoming' in Vedic literature.

664. Raghavan, V. "Music in Ancient Indian Drama." *Journal of the Music Academy, Madras* 25 (1954): 79-92. An examination of the chapter on music in Bharati's *Natya Sastra* and other texts to show how music and dance developed together in ancient India.

665.   Raghupathy, Sudharani. "Abhinaya and Abhinava Gupta." *Journal of the Music Academy Madras* 57 (1986): 149-61. On Abhinava Gupta's interpretation of the portion on *Abhinaya* (gestures and the feeling states they convey) of the *Natyasastra*.

666.   Rowell, Lewis. "Form in the Ritual Theatre Music of Ancient India." In *Musica Asiatica*, Richard Widdess, ed. Vol. 5. Cambridge: Cambridge University Press, 1988. 140-90.

667.   Singh, Alka. "Manipuri: Dance of the Divine." *India Magazine* 7, 2 (Jan) (1987): 56-65.

668.   *Sangeet Natak*. 97/July-Sept.1990. An issue devoted to the history of temple dance and dancers (devadasi) in Tamil Nadu, Orissa, Karnataka, Andhra Pradesh, Kerala, and Maharashtra. The issue includes essays on the institution of dance in Hindu, Jain, and Buddhist literature and on the socio-religious context of dance.

669.   Thacker, Chaula. *Introduction to Bharat Natyam: An Indian Classical Dance Style*. Southfield, MI: Nadanta, 1989.

670.   Vatsyayan, Kapila. "India: Dance." In *Grove 6*, Vol. 9. 1980. 158-166.

671.   Vatsyayan, Kapila. *Dance Sculpture in Sarangapani Temple*. Madras: Society for Archaeological, Historical, and Epigraphical Research, 1982.

672.   Vatsyayan, Kapila. "Indian Dance and Dance Drama." In *Encyclopedia of Religion*, Mircea Eliade, ed. Vol. 4. 1987. 452-455.

673.   Vatsyayan, Kapila. *Traditions of Indian Folk Dance*. 2nd rev. and enl. ed., New Delhi: Clarion Books associated with Hind Pocket Books, 1987.

INDIA: SHAMANISM

674.   Mahapatra, Sitakant. "Invocation and Ritual Healing in Santal Society." In *Proceedings of the Fifth International Conference on the Study of Shamanism and Alternate Modes of Healing*, Berkeley, CA: Independent Scholars of Asia, 1988. On spirit healers in a major Indian tribe, the Santal. Includes discussion of ritual mantras, invocation songs, and societal reliance on the spirit healers.

675.   Satpathy, Sunil. "Part III of 'Bakens: The Ritual Invocation Songs of the Santals, A Preliminary Statement.'" *Quarterly Journal of the National Centre for the Performing Arts* 9, 1 (1991): 1-18.

676.   Sharma, N.C. "Shamanistic Dance Associated with the Worship of the Snake Goddess Manasa in Assam." *Folklore* 29, 7/July (1988): 145-52.

677.   Sidky, M. H. "Shamans and Mountain Spirits in Hunza." *Asian Folklore Studies* 53, 1 (1994): 67-96. Though nominally Muslim, the Hunza practice nature worship with the *bitan* (shaman) as mediator. Topics covered are the shaman's early life, his functions, his musicians, an oracular seance, a healing, the decline under British rule, and commercialization. In Jammu and Kashmir, India.

INDIA: CHRISTIANITY

678.   Albuquerque, Walter. "Indian Music in Divine Service." In *Musica Indigena*, Josef Kuckertz, ed. Rome: CIMS, 1975. 97-116.

679.   Barboza, Francis Peter. *Christianity in Indian Dance Forms*. Sri Garib Dass Oriental Series, no. 114, Delhi: Sri Satguru Publications, 1990.

680.   Barretto, Lourdino. *Aesthetic Indian Music as a Bridge between Christian and Indian Religious Music*. Ph.D. diss., Pontifical Institute of Sacred Music, 1968.

681.   Dharmaraj, P. S. "Hindu Impact on Christian Fine Arts." In *Influence of Hinduism on Christianity*, G. Robinson, ed. Madurai, India: Tamil Nadu Theological Seminary, 1980. 120-138. On the influence of Hinduism on the architecture, sculpture, art, and dance of Indian Christian churches.

682.   Duncan, Stephen Frederick. *Christian Bhajans: A Study of the Uses of Indigenous Music in the Rites of the Catholic Church on the Subcontinent of India since the Second Vatican Council with Particular Attention to Bhajan and Kirtan*. D.M.A. diss., Memphis State University, 1991. A study of the uses of indigenous music—*bhajan* (devotional songs sung in call and response style) and *kirtan* (group devotional hymns) in the Indian Catholic Church—since Vatican II.

683.   Englund, R. "Christian Dances in India." *Journal of World Association for Christian Communication* 26, 2 (1979).

684.   Popley, H.A. "The Use of Indian Music in Christian Worship." *Indian Journal of Theology* 6 (1957): 80-88.

685.   Rao, Sundara. *Bhakti Theology in the Telugu Hymnal*. Confessing the Faith in India Series, Madras, India: Christian Literature Society, 1983. Devotional theology, the dominant form of religious expression in India, as found in the Christian hymnal in the Telegu language, the language of the state of Andhra Pradesh.

686.   Ross, Israel J. "Ritual and Music in South India: Syrian Christian Liturgical Music in Kerala." *Asian Music* 11, 1 (1979): 80-98. An essay on Syrian Christian music on the southwestern coast of India and its close similarity

to Jewish practice in the same area and in the Middle East. Topics covered are rituals and customs, chant accentuation, mode, motivic analysis, and parallel organum.

687.   Sherinian, Zoe. *The Indigenization of Tamil Christian Music*. Ph.D. diss., in progress.

MODERN SPECULATIONS ON INDIAN MUSIC

688.   Beck, Guy L. *Sonic Theology: Hinduism and Sacred Sound*. Columbia, South Carolina: University of South Carolina Press, 1993. Pt. 1 is on the Vedas, the philosophies of language, and Yoga as the basic sources of a theology of sound in Hinduism; Pt. 2 finds manifestations of sacred cosmic sound in Sakta-Tantra, Saivism, and Vaisnavism.

689.   Bose, Hiren. *Philosophy in Indian Music*. Calcutta: Rupa & Co., 1988. On the religious symbolism and philosophical implications of each of the seven degrees of the Indian musical scale.

690.   Chakravarthy, G.N. *The Concept of Cosmic Harmony in the Rg Veda*. Mysore: University of Mysore, 1966.

691.   Dey, Suresh Chandra. *The Quest for Music Divine*. New Delhi: Ashish Publishing House, 1990. On Indian Hindu metaphysics and music, and the realization of *nada brahman* attainable through music.

692.   During, Jean. "Acoustic Systems and Metaphysical Systems in Oriental Traditions." *The World of Music* 29, 2 (1987): 19-31. An examination of scales and intervals in Arabic and Indian music and their relationship to religious and metaphysical notions of order.

693.   Gottlieb, Robert. "Symbolisms Underlying Improvisatory Practices in Indian Music." *Journal of the Indian Musicological Society* 16, 2 (1985): 23.

694.   Hein, Norvin J. "Caitanya's Ecstasies and the Theology of the Name." In *Hinduism: New Essays in the History of Religions*, Bardwell L. Smith, ed. Leiden: E.J. Brill, 1976.

695.   Killingley, Dermot. "Om: The Sacred Syllable in the Veda." In *A Net Cast Wide: Investigations into Indian Thought in Memory of David Friedman*, Julius J. Lipner, ed. Newcastle-upon-Tyne: Grevatt and Grevatt, 1986.

696.   Mishra, Umesha. "Physical Theory of Sound and its Origin in Indian Thought." In *Allahabad University Studies*, 2. 1926. 239-90. On sound as it is associated with the cakras and on the position of sound according to various philosophical systems.

697.   Mukharji, Justice P. B. "The Metaphysics of Sound." In *Japa Sutram: The Science of Creative Sound*, Swami P. Sarasvati, ed. Madras: Ganesh, 1971.

698.   Musalagaonkar, Vimala. "Music and Sound In Yoga." In *Psychology of Music: Selected Papers*, R.C. Mehta, ed. Bombay and Baroda: Indian Musicological Society, 1980. 44-65.

699.   Naidu, S. Shankar Raju. "Supreme Sound: The Ultimate Reality." *Indian Philosophical Annual* 10 (1974-75): 59-72.

700.   Schramm, Harold. "Nadabrahma: Sound of the Universe." *Music Journal* 23 (1965).

701.   Simms, Robert. "Aspects of Cosmological Symbolism in Hindusthani Musical Forms." *Asian Music* 24, 1 (1992/1993): 67-89. The manner in which Hindusthani musical forms exhibit a formal symbolism of Hindu cosmological doctrine is observed in the concept of *nada*, the Vedas, the raga, rhythm cycles, the correspondence between the first four ratios of the harmonic series with the *mahayuga* ratios, and finally the form of the *dhrupad*.

NEPAL

702.   Ellingson, Ter. "Nasa:Dya:, Newar God of Music." *Selected Reports in Ethnomusicology: Issues in Organology* Vol. 8 (1990): 221-272. A photographic essay on Nasa:Dya, God of Music and Dance, in Newar. Focuses on the many iconographic representations of the 'Formless God,' the rituals, both Hindu and Buddhist, and the instruments, which embody Nasa:Dya or other deities.

703.   Ellingson, Ter. "The Mathematics of Newar Buddhist Music." In *Change and Continuity: Studies in Nepalese Culture of the Kathmandu Valley*, Torino: CESMEO, in press.

704.   Fantin, Mario. *Mani Rimdu, Nepal: The Buddhist Dance Drama of Tengpoche*. R.S. Ahluwalia, transl. Singapore: Toppan Co. ; New Delhi: English Book Store (distr.); New York: W.S. Heinman Imported Books, 1976.

705.   Gellner, David N. *Monk, Householder, and Tantric Priest*. Cambridge: Cambridge University Press, 1992. A close look at how the Tantric Buddhism of the Newar of Nepal works in practice. This detailed ethnography describes the way of life and social organization of the Hindu-Buddhist city of Lalitpur and the role of religion and ritual in the life of its inhabitants.

706.   Hitchcock, John T. and Rex L. Jones, ed. *Spirit Possession in the Nepal Himalayas*. Warminster (England): Aris and Phillips, 1976. Four essays on the subject of spirit possession in Nepal. Though behaviors differ, shamanism is a widely and consistently-used means of seeing the future, diagnosing disease and misfortune, and otherwise bettering the condition of clients.

707.   Jerstad, Luther G. *Mani Rimdu/Sherpa Dance-Drama.* Seattle, WA: University of Washington Press, 1969. A study of a tantric dance-drama (*'chams*) performed at Buddhist monasteries and among the Tibetan Buddhist (Sherpa) peoples of Northeast Nepal.

708.   Kohn, Richard Jay. *Mani Rimdu. Text and Tradition in a Tibetan Ritual.* Ph.D. diss., University of Wisconsin-Madison, 1988. Includes a description and history of the major elements of the festival, including deities, meditative technique and religious dance; a day-by-day descriptive and analytic account of ritual, artistic, and dramatic events; and an annotated translation of the ritual texts.

709.   Mastromattei, Romano. "Shamanism in Nepal: Modalities of Ecstatic Experience." In *Shamanism: Past and Present*, M. Hoppál and O. J. Sadovszky, ed. Budapest, Los Angeles: ISTOR Books, 1989. On the Jhakri shaman of Nepal, including a description of rituals and trance involving chant, drums or brass plate, and a frenzied dance.

710.   Michailovsky, Boyd and Philippe Sagant. "The Shaman and the Ghosts of Unnatural Death: On the Efficacy of a Ritual." *Diogenes: Shamans and Shamanisms: On the Threshold of the Next Millennium*, 158/Summer (1992): 19-37. Special rituals are performed by shamans to appease those who die unnaturally so that they will not return for revenge.

711.   Paul, Robert. "Dumje: Paradox and Resolution in Sherpa Ritual Symbolism." *American Ethnologist* 6, 2/May (1979): 274-304. The masked-dances of the spring Dumje ceremony provide lamas, laymen, and boys an outlet for sexual and aggressive impulses, thereby purging them of repression and guilt and renewing the yearly cycle of agricultural and human fertility.

712.   Poris, Jill. *Shamanistic Music in the Bhuji River Valley of Nepal.* M.A. thesis, University of Wisconsin, 1977.

713.   Schmid, Toni. "Shamanistic Practice in Northern Nepal." In *Studies in Shamanism*, Carl-Martin Edsman, ed. Stockholm: Almqvist and Wiksell, 1967. 82-89. The life and ceremonies of Bön shamans of Northern Nepal. Includes a description of Bön drums and recitation.

714.   Siiger, Halfdan. *The Lepchas: Culture and Religion of a Himalayan People.* Copenhagen: Gyldenal, 1967. Contains translations of songs used in ceremonies in fertility deities.

715.   Tingey, Carol. "An Annotated Bibliography and Discography of Nepalese Musics." *ICTM, UK Chapter* 11 (1985): 14-20. 13 (1987): 35-44.

716.   Tingey, Carol. "Sacred Kettledrums in the Temples of Central Nepal." *Asian Music* 23, 2 (1992): 97-103. A study of *nagarâ bana* (kettle drum

ensemble) of Sivaite and Mother Goddess temple rituals, their construction, divine origin, ritual uses, and sacred qualities.

717.   Wegner, Gert-Matthias. *The Dhimaybaja of Bhaktapur*. Studies in Newar Drumming, I, Wiesbaden, Germany: F. Steiner, 1986. On learning to play the dhimay, large double-headed drums, including the ritual observances involved and the religious ecstasy it is intended to invoke.

SRI LANKA

718.   Ames, M.M. and H.D. Evers. "Buddha and the Dancing Goblins: A Theory of Magic and Religion." *American Anthropologist* 66, February (1964): 75-82. Buddhism and magical healing arts exist side by side in Sri Lanka because they operate in different spheres and thus do not conflict. For a reply, see 67, February (1965): 97-99.

719.   Carter, John Ross. "Music in the Theravada Buddhist Heritage: In Chant, in Song, in Sri Lanka." In *Sacred Sound*, Joyce Irwin, ed. 1983. 127-147. A discussion of early Buddhist attitudes toward music as found in the Pali sources. Two trends are discussed: the prohibiting of monks from listening to music to promote restraint of the senses; and the encouragement of the laity to appreciate and sanction religious music.

720.   "Ceremonial Dances." In *The Veddas*, C.G. Seligman and B.Z. Seligman, ed. Cambridge: The University Press, 1911/repr. 1969. 209-272. A study of the ceremonial dances of the indigenous peoples of Sri Lanka.

721.   Kapferer, Bruce. *A Celebration of Demons: Exorcism and the Aesthetics of Healing in Sri Lanka*. Bloomington: University of Indiana Press, 1983.

722.   Laade, Wolfgang. "The Influence of Buddhism on the Singhalese Music of Sri Lanka." *Asian Music* 25, 1-2 (1993/1994): 51-68. From the arrival of Thêravêdan Buddhism in Sri Lanka in the 3rd century BC, the Singhalese have reinterpreted their myths and adapted their songs to Buddhist content. Hinduism has provided the tangible forms of worship—instruments, dance, and religious pantheon—not found in the more austere orthodox Buddhism.

723.   Obeyesekere, Gananath. *Medusa's Hair: An Essay on Personal Symbols and Religious Experience*. Chicago: 1981. Ecstasy and possession at a Hindu-Buddhist pilgrimage center in Sri Lanka.

724.   Obeyesekere, Ranjini. "The Significance of Performance for its Audience: An Analysis of Three Sri Lankan Rituals." In *By Means of Performance: Intercultural Studies of Theatre and Ritual*, Richard Schechner and Willa Appel, ed. Cambridge: Cambridge University Press, 1990. 118-130.

725. Reed, Susan Anita. *The Transformation of Ritual and Dance in Sri Lanka: Kohombà Kankàriya and the Kandyan Dance*. Ph.D. diss., Brown University, 1991.

726. Seneviratna, Anuradha. "Music Rituals of the Dalada Maligawa." *Sangeeth Natak* (1974). "Rituals and Instruments of the Temple of the Tooth, Kandy" The main Buddhist temple in Kandy, Sri Lanka, is said to have a tooth relic of the Buddha.

727. Seneviratna, Anuradha. "Pancaturya Nada and Hewisi Puja." *Ethnomusicology* 23, 1 (1979): 49-56. A detailed study of the unique offering of sounds performed by drums and other instruments in the daily and weekly services of Buddhist temples. The term *pancaturya nada* (fivefold), the inclusive name for instruments, is derived from the five ways in which instruments are played.

728. Silva Kulatillake, C. de. "Buddhist Chant in Sri Lanka and its Musical Elements." *Jahrbuch fur Musikalische Volks- und Völkerkunde* 10 (1982): 20-32. On the history and evolution of Buddhist chant in Sri Lanka and of the 1500 year history, current context, and choral styles of the didactic Pirit Sajjhayana Buddhist ceremony.

729. Vasantha, Kumara. *Symphony of the Temple Drums: Buddhist Symbolism through Ritual Art*. Kandy, Sri Lanka: Vasantha Kumara, 1993.

730. Zoete, Beryl De. *Dance and Magic Drama in Ceylon*. London: Faber & Faber, 1957. An account in the form of a journal of Kandyan and other Sri Lankan forms of religious, particularly Buddhist, dance and drama.

INDO-ISLAMIC MUSIC; MUSIC OF THE SUFIS

731. Johnston, Sharilee Mehera. *An Aesthetic Model for Qawwali Performance: The Relationship between Music and Sufism*. M.A. thesis, UCLA, 1993.

732. Lawrence, Bruce B. "The Early Chishti Approach to Sama." In *Sacred Sound*, Joyce Irwin, ed. Chico, CA: Scholars Press, 1983. 93-110. On the Indianization of samâ and the stages to the attainment of finding oneself in God through samâ.

733. Malik, M. Saeed. *The Musical Heritage of Pakistan*. Islamabad: Idara Saqafat-e-Pakistan, 1982. Includes comment on the origins of Qawwali and the need it fills for Muslim devotional song.

734. *Music and Qawwali*. Karachi: Peermahomed Ebrahim Trust, 1975.

735. Nasir, Mumtaz. "*Baitak*: Exorcism in Peshawar (Pakistan)." *Asian Folklore Studies* 46, 2 (1987): 159-78.

736.   Nayyar, Adam. *Qawwali*. Islamabad: Lok Virsa Research Centre, 1988. An excellent introduction to the subject of Qawwali in Pakistan.

737.   Pacholczyk, Jozef. "The Status of Sufyana Kalam in Kashmir." In *Maqam: Music of the Islamic World and its Influences*, Robert H. Browning et al., ed. New York: Alternative Museum, 1984. 28-29. A description of the history, function, dance, theory, form and instruments of this genre of Sufi religious music (and the classical music of Kashmir) and an attempt to account for its rapid decline.

738.   Qureshi, Regula Burckhardt. "Indo-Muslim Religious Music, an Overview." *Asian Music* 3, 2 (1972): 15-22. Indo-muslim theorists distinguish between recitation or chant and song. The latter is 'music'; the former, as vocal adornment of a religious text (the Quran), falls outside the realm of worldly pleasure. Two types of religious music are 1) liturgical: *talhin* (cantillation of the Quran in Arabic) and 2) non-liturgical: *nasha'id* (hymns with vernacular text. The latter includes *majlis, qawwali, and milad*.

739.   Qureshi, Regula Burckhardt. *Qawwali, Music of Islamic Mysticism in Pakistan*. New York: Asia Society, 1977.

740.   Qureshi, Regula Burckhardt. "India: Muslim Religious Music." In *Grove* 6, Vol. 9. 1980. 145-147. An introduction to the two broad types of religious music—*talhîn* (liturgical) and *nashâ'id* (non-liturgical, including *majlis, mîlâd*, and *qawwâlî*).

741.   Qureshi, Regula Burckhardt. "Islamic Music in an Indian Environment: The Shi'a Majlis." *Ethnomusicology* 25, 1 (1981): 41-71. A study of the *majlis* (the collection of Islamic Indian hymns and non-liturgical chants). Focus is on contextual background—culture and religion—and particular aspects of the majlis—performers and audience, poetic form, musical form, rhythm, and melody.

742.   Qureshi, Regula Burckhardt. *Qawwali: Sound, Context and Meaning in Indo-Muslim Sufi Music*. Ph.D. diss., University of Alberta, 1981. An analysis of the musical idiom of Qawwali and of its performance context, the shrines of Sufism, with its poetry, ideology, socio-economic setting, and specially trained performers, are integrated through the perspectives of the performer and performance.

743.   Qureshi, Regula Burckhardt. "Qawwâlî: Making the Music Happen in the Sufi Assembly." In *Performing Arts in India: Essays on Music, Dance, and Drama*, Bonnie C. Wade, ed. Lanham, New York: University Press of America, 1983. 118-157. This essay uses *Qawwali*, an Indo-Muslim song genre commemorating dead saints, to demonstrate that music is circumscribed by the social factors that generate it, and that performance is the articulation of the relationship of musical and social factors. A summary of a Qawwali performance in the

abstract is followed by an analysis of a performance. Also in *Asian Music* 18, 2 (Spring-Summer), 1987: 118-57.

744.   Qureshi, Regula Burckhardt. *Sufi Music of India and Pakistan: Sound, Context and Meaning in Qawwali.* Cambridge Studies in Ethnomusicology, Cambridge and New York: Cambridge University Press, 1986. The outstanding work on the performance idiom (*Qawwali*), context (occasion) and process (event) of this "ecstatic culmination of mystical experience".

745.   Qureshi, Regula Burckhardt. *Sufi Music of India and Pakistan.* Cambridge: Cambridge University Press, 1986.

746.   Qureshi, Regula Burckhardt. "Sufi Music and the Historicity of Oral Tradition." In *Ethnomusicology and Modern Music History*, Blum, Bohlman, and Neuman, ed. Chicago: University of Illinois Press, 1991. 103-120. The construction of a history of Sufi music rests almost entirely on information derived from oral tradition and what oral informants consider important concerning such factors as the origins of the poetry and tunes, the authority of the sheikh, ritual, the ownership of specific repertories, and the presence in qawwali of elements of the raga and tala system.

747.   Qureshi, Regula Burckhardt. "'Muslim Devotional': Popular Religious Music and Muslim Identity Under British, Indian and Pakistani Hegemony." *Asian Music* 24, 1 (1992/1993): 111-121. Qawwali is the most popular recorded religious music in South Asia. The author discusses some of the reasons for its popularity, including film and promotion by the record industry.

748.   Qureshi, Regula Burckhardt. "Exploring Time Cross-Culturally: Ideology and Performance of Time in a Sufi Qawwali." *Journal of Musicology* 12, 4 (1994): 491-528. After exploring different concepts of time, Qureshi shows, through the detailed analysis of both the text and music of one song, how *qawwali* offers the listener a duality of time experience: linear, in the sequence of words, pitches, and rhythms, and divine, in the mystic, ecstatic, immediate experience of the Eternal Beloved.

749.   Sadler, Albert William. "Visit to a Chishti Qawwali." *Muslim World* 53, Oct. (1963): 287-292.

750.   Sadler, Albert William. *Mysticism and Devotion in the Music of the Qawwali.* Monographs on Music, Dance, and Theater in Asia, New York: Performing Arts Program of the Asia Society, 1974. A short pamphlet discussing the theological history, spirituality, and ritual of the Qawwali musical tradition.

751.   Sakata, Hiromi Lorraine. "The Sacred and the Profane: *Qawwali* Presented in the Performances of Nusrat Fateh Ali Khan." *The World of Music* 36, 3 (1994): 86-99. An examination of how a spiritual genre retains its integrity in spite of the modifications made in accommodating it to the secular-popular spheres in which it is now often performed.

12

Zoroastrianism and the Parsis of India

752. Boyce, Mary. *A History of Zoroastrianism.* New York and Leiden, Netherlands: E.J. Brill, 1975 (1982)/repr. 1989 (1991).

753. Boyce, Mary. *Zoroastrians: Their Religious Beliefs and Practices.* London: Routledge and Kegan Paul, 1979/repr. 1984. A history of Zoroastrians from the time of Zoroaster to the present. Consult index under rituals, Gathas, Avesta.

754. Boyd, James and Firoze M. Kotwal. "Worship in a Zoroastrian Fire Temple." *The H.B. Wadia Atas Bahram Indo-Iranian Journal* 26, 4 (Dec., 1983): 293-318.

755. Minochehr-Homji, N.D. "Ceremonies and Rituals of the Parsis." In *The Sugar in the Milk: The Parsis of India*, Ram Singh and Nancy Sing, ed. Delhi: Published for Development Education, Madras, by ISPCK, 1986.

756. Modi, J. J. *The Religious Ceremonies and Customs of the Parsees.* Bombay, India: 1937. A thorough description of almost all existing observances.

757. *The Zend-Avesta.* James Darmesteter, transl. Westport, CT: Greenwood Press, 1880-87/repr. 1972. 1880-87 ed., Oxford: Clarendon Press; 1965 repr., Delhi: Motilal Banarsidass.

13

The Ancient Near East

THE ANCIENT NEAR EAST

758.   Farmer, Henry George. "The Music of Ancient Egypt." In *New Oxford History of Music I: Ancient and Oriental Music*, 1957. 255-282.

759.   Farmer, Henry George. "The Music of Ancient Mesopotamia." In *New Oxford History of Music I: Ancient and Oriental Music*, 1957. 228-254.

760.   Galpin, Francis William. *The Music of the Sumerians and Their Immediate Successors, the Babylonians and Assyrians. Described and Illustrated from Original Sources.* 2nd ed., Westport, CT: Greenwood Press, 1955/repr. 1970. Although primarily a study of ancient music instruments, Galpin fills his text with references to mythology and religious symbolism and practice.

761.   Hickman, Hans. "Mesopotamia." In *Grove 6*, Vol. 12. 1980. 196-201.

762.   Kilmer, Anne Draffkorn. *The Cult Song with Music from Ancient Ugarit: Another Interpretation.* Paris (?): E. Leroux (?), 1974. On the songs and music of the Assyro-Babylonian cult of ancient Syria.

763.   Manniche, Lise. *Music and Musicians in Ancient Egypt.* London: British Museum Press, 1991. See especially Chapter 4. 'Music for the gods.'

764.   Polin, Claire C.F. *Music of the Ancient Near East.* New York: Vantage Press, 1954. A study of the compositional ideas and contexts for music of eight ancient Near Eastern cultures.

765.   Sachs, Curt. *The Rise of Music in the Ancient World, East and West.* New York: W.W. Norton & Company, 1943.

766. Sendrey, Alfred. *Music in the Social and Religious Life of Antiquity.* Rutherford: Fairleigh Dickinson University Press, 1974. Also published in Cranbury, NJ: Associated University Presses, Inc. A study of antiquity—Sumeria, Egypt, Babylonia, Assyria, Chaldea, Phoenicia, Greece, Judaea and Rome—with Judaea the central focus of the book.

767. Shanks, H. "World's Oldest Musical Notation Deciphered on Cuneiform Tablet." *Biblical Archaeology Review* 6, 5 (1980): 14-25.

768. Thornton, Debbie Ann. *Music in the Mystery Religions of the Ancient World.* M.A. thesis, Michigan State University, 1988. The similarities revealed by a study of primary and secondary sources and archaeological evidence suggests that there was sharing or borrowing among the cults.

769. Wellesz, Egon, ed. *Ancient and Oriental Music.* New Oxford History of Music, Vol. 1. London/New York: Oxford University Press, 1957.

ANCIENT GREECE

770. Anderson, Warren D. "Plato." In *Grove 6*, Vol. 14. 1980. 853-857. Sec. 1-7 deal with Plato's ideas about the ethical, legal, theoretical, and educational aspects of music; sec. 9-11 describe how later European theorists used these notions—particularly those concerning morality and the relationship of inaudible music to the human soul—to justify their theories.

771. Barker, Andrew. *Greek Musical Writings I. The Musician and His Art.* Barker, Andrew, transl. New York: Cambridge University Press, 1984. Greek poets, historians and essayists on the practical activities of musical performance and composition; Greek philosophers and social critics on the moral, educational and aesthetic dimensions of music.

772. Barker, Andrew. *Greek Musical Writings II. Harmonic and Acoustic Theory.* Barker, Andrew, transl. New York: Cambridge University Press, 1984. This collection of translations of all major Greek theorists is indispensable for an understanding of the two principal traditions: music theory—the theory of actual music—and acoustic theory—through which the order and harmony of the universe can be represented to the human mind.

773. Dodds, E.R. *The Greeks and the Irrational.* Berkeley: University of California Press, 1951. A study of the role of shamanism in Greek culture.

774. Henderson, Isobel. "Ancient Greek Music." In *New Oxford History of Music, I: Ancient and Oriental Music*, London 1957. 336-403.

775. Lawler, Lilian B. *The Dance in Ancient Greece.* Middletown, CT: Wesleyan University Press, 1964/repr. 1978.

776.   Linforth, Ivan M. "Telestic Madness in Plato, Phaedrus 244 CE." In *University of California Publications in Classical Philology*, Vol. 13, no. 6. Berkeley and Los Angeles: University of California Press, 1946. 163-72. Along with prophecy, poetry and love, Socrates considered telestic madness a divine gift. Its function was to restore to sanity, through rites consisting of frenzy and prayerful worship, those beset by mental distress or divine anger.

777.   Linforth, Ivan M. "The Corybantic Rites in Plato." In *University of California Publications in Classical Philology*, Vol. 13, no. 5. Berkeley and Los Angeles: University of California Press, 1946. 121-62. In the Athens of the 5th and 4th centuries BCE, persons consumed with irrational fear could seek release through participation in frenzied dance rites, such as those dedicated to the Corybantic deities. Corybantic dance, accompanied by Phrygian reeds, drum, tambourine and cymbals, brought the participant to a state of transport characterized as god-possessed. Having danced to the point of euphoric exhaustion, the participant would then experience a return to a clear, untroubled state of mind.

778.   Lippmann, Edward A. *Musical Thought in Ancient Greece*. New York, London: Columbia University Press/Da Capo Press, 1964/repr. 1975. Musical thinking as found in conceptions of Harmony (ratios; harmony as sound; harmony as a condition of the cosmos), Theories of Musical Ethics, the Philosophy and Aesthetics of Music, and the Peripatetics.

779.   Lonsdale, Steven. *Dance and Ritual Play in Greek Religion*. Baltimore, MD: Johns Hopkins University Press, 1993. An exploration of the relationship of cultic and festival dance to social and religious institutions in Greece during the archaic and classical periods. Draws on literary texts and archaeological findings.

780.   Meinecke, Bruno. "Music and Medicine in Classical Antiquity." In *Music and Medicine*, D.M. Schullian and M. Schoen, ed. New York: Henry Schuman, 1948. 47-97. A survey of the healing powers of music as found in Greek and Roman mythology and literature.

781.   West, M. L. *Ancient Greek Music*. Oxford: Clarendon Press, 1992. An impressive study of what is known and can be conjectured about this subject.

782.   Winnington-Ingram, R. P. "Ancient Greece." In *Grove 6*, Vol. 1. 1980. 659-672. For Greek subjects in Grove 6, see also Alypius, Aristides, Aristotle, Aristoxenus, Plato, Ptolemy, Pythagoras, Pythagorean Intonation, Ethos.

783.   Winnington-Ingram, R.P. "Aristotle." In *Grove 6*, Vol. 1. 1980. 587-592.

14

Music and Dance in the Bible

MUSIC IN THE OLD AND NEW TESTAMENTS

784.   Hayhoe, G.H. *Music: Its Origin and Use as Recorded in Scripture.* Nepean, Ontario, Canada: Hayhoe, 197?

785.   Jones, Ivor H. "Musical Instruments in the Bible, Pt. 1." *Bible Translator* 37, Jan. (1986): 101-116. On references to shakers, cymbals, jinglets and drums in the Bible.

786.   Jones, Ivor H. "Musical Instruments in the Bible, Pt. 2." *Bible Translator* 38, Jan. (1987): 129-143. Flutes, pipes, shofars, and horns. With tables.

787.   Jones, Ivor H. "Musical Instruments." In *The Anchor Bible Dictionary*, David Noel Freedman, ed. Vol. 4. New York and London: Doubleday, 1992. 934-939.

788.   Kraeling, Carl H. and Lucella Mowry. "Music in the Bible." In *The New Oxford History of Music: Ancient and Oriental Music*, Vol. I. 1957. General overview of religious songs in the Bible and in the early Church, by historical period from the nomadic period to early Christian antiphony and Gnostic hymns.

789.   Larrick, Geary. *Musical References and Song Texts in the Bible*. Studies in the History and Interpretation of Music, Vol. 9, Lewiston, NY/Queenston, Can. /Lampeter, Wales: The Edwin Mellen Press, 1990. Section One provides an alphabetical list of all music terms found in the Bible and the single verses in which the terms are located. Section Two consists of biblical song and canticle texts.

790.   Lovelace, Austin C. "Make a Joyful Noise to the Lord: Biblical Foundations of Church Music." *Point* 2, 1 (1973): 15-27. An examination of specific references to music in the Bible.

791.   Madge, W. *Bible Music and its Development*. London: Chester House Publications, 1977.

792.   Matthews, Victor H. "Music in the Bible." In *The Anchor Bible Dictionary*, David Noel Freedman, ed. Vol. 4. New York and London: Doubleday, 1992. 930-934.

793.   Murphy, Roland E. "The Psalms and Worship." *Ex Auditu* 8 (1992): 23-31.

794.   Ringer, Alexander. "Religious Music in the West." In *Encyclopedia of Religion*, Mircea Eliade, ed. Vol. 10. 1987. 209-216.

795.   Shanks, Hershel, ed. "Ancient Musical Instruments: A Special Section." *Biblical Archaeology Review* 8, 1 (1982): 18-41. Article titles: The Finds that Could Not Be, What did David's Lyre Look Like?, and "Sounding Brass" and Hellenistic Technology: Ancient Acoustical Device Clarifies Paul's Well-known Metaphor.

796.   Shiloah, Ammon. "The *Ud* and Origin of Music." In *Studia Orientalia Memoriae*, D. H. Baneth, Y. Navon, and S. Goitein et al., ed. 1979. 395-407. A study of the biblical figures Jubal and Lamech and the possibility that there is a connection between the *ud* and these "creators" of music.

797.   Strong, James. *The Comprehensive Concordance of the Bible together with Dictionaries of the Hebrew and Greek Words of the Original, with Reference to the English Words*. Iowa Falls, IA: World Bible Publishers, 1890/repr. nd. Useful as an index to all references to music and music instruments in the Bible.

798.   Werner, Eric. "Music; Music Instruments." In *The Interpreters Dictionary of the Bible*, G.A. Buttrick, ed. Vol. 3. 1962. 457-469; 469-476.

799.   Wigoder, Geoffrey. *Illustrated Dictionary & Concordance of the Bible*. New York: Macmillan, 1986. M. Paul Shalom, ed., Old Testament; Benedict T. Viviano, ed., New Testament.

MUSIC IN THE OLD TESTAMENT

800.   Avenary, Hannoch. "Magic, Symbolism and Allegory of the Old-Hebrew Sound-Instruments." *Collectanea historiae musicae* 2 (1956): 21-32. A study of the transition, with the destruction of the 2nd Temple and Jewish state, from the symbolic to the allegoric meaning of music and music instruments.

801.   Bayer, Bathyah. *Material Relics of Music in Ancient Palestine and its Environs: An Archeological Inventory*. Tel-Aviv: Israel Music Institute, 1963. A

survey and inventory of 250 archaeological sites, dating from 3000 BCE to 6th century CE.

802.   Bayer, Bathja. "The Biblical 'Nebel.'" *Yuval* 1 (1968): 89-131. Jerusalem. Based on literary and archaeological evidence, the nebel, mentioned 27 times in the bible, is probably not a harp, but a type of lyre.

803.   Bayer, Bathja. "The Titles of the Psalms: A Renewed Investigation of an Old Problem." *Yuval* 4 (1982): 29-123. The terms were probably added decades after their composition and can support several interpretations according to the historical circumstances in which they were added.   An exclusively musical interpretation is insupportable.

804.   Braun, Joachim. "Iron Age Seals from Ancient Israel Pertinent to Music." *Orbis Musicae* 10 (1990/91): 11-26. Iron Age seals from ancient Israel show the lyre to be the dominant musical instrument both of the cult and in private secular life.

805.   Elkins, Garland. "Difficult Texts from 1 and 2 Kings and 1 and 2 Chronicles." In *Difficult Texts of the Old Testament Explained: The Fifth Annual Fort Worth Lectures*, Wendell Winkler, ed. Hurst, TX: Winkler Publications, 1982. 277-287.

806.   Finesinger, Sol Baruch. "Musical Instruments in the Old Testament." *Hebrew Union College Annual* 3 (1926): 21-75. Vols. 8 and 9, 1931/32, pp. 193-228.   A solid discussion of the shofar and other Biblical instruments.   A full study of the Jewish ritual instruments.

807.   Finesinger, Sol B. "The Shofar." *Hebrew Union College Annual* 8/9 (1931/1932): 193-228. The sound of the shofar invoked either fear or comfort: a review of the Old Testament, Mishna, and Talmud for attitudes concerning the shofar to determine the foundation in Judaic Law for its use.

808.   Flusser, David. "Psalms, Hymns and Prayers." In *Jewish Writings of the Second Temple Period*, Michael Stone, ed. Philadelphia: Fortress Press, 1984. 551-577.

809.   Freedman, David Noel. "But did King David Invent Musical Instruments." *Bible Review* 1, 2, Sum. (1985): 48-51.

810.   Halperin, David. "Music in the Testament of Job." *Yuval* 5 (1986): 356-364. An interpretation of the frequent references to music and music instruments in a Greek pseudoepigrapha from between 100 BCE and 100 ACE.

811.   Herbert, Arthur Sumner. *Worship in Ancient Israel*. Ecumenical Studies in Worship, No. 5, Richmond: John Knox Press, 1959/repr. 1965.

812.   Kleinig, John. *The Lord's Song: The Basis, Function and Significance of Choral Music in Chronicles*. Journal for the Study of the Old Testament. Supplement Series 156, Sheffield, England: JSOT Press, 1993.

813.   Mitchell, Terence C. "The Music of the Old Testament Reconsidered." *Palestine Exploration Quarterly* 124, July-Dec. (1992): 124-143. A scholarly study of the archaeological and Biblical evidence concerning music instruments used in pre-CE Palestine.

814.   Mitchell, Terence C. and R. Joyce. "The Musical Instruments in Nebuchadrezzar's Orchestra." In *Notes on Some Problems in the Book of Daniel*, D.J. Wiseman et al., ed. London: Tyndale Press, 1965. An attempt to unravel the confusion concerning the identity of the instruments named in Daniel.

815.   Mowinckel, S. *The Psalms in Israel's Worship*. Oxford: Oxford University Press, 1962.

816.   Rowley, H.H. *Worship in Ancient Israel: Its Forms and Meaning*. London: SPCK; Philadelphia: Fortress Press, 1967.

817.   Sachs, Curt. "Music in the Bible." In *The Universal Jewish Encyclopedia*, Vol. 8. New York 1939-1948. 46 ff.

818.   Sendrey, Alfred. *Music in Ancient Israel*. New York: Philosophical Library, 1969. A valuable resource on Jewish music up to the 5th and 6th centuries CE. A systematic and exhaustive survey of Biblical and Talmudic references to music, including references to instruments, dance, singing, and women. Includes an extensive bibliography of 19th and early 20th century literature.

819.   Sendrey, Alfred and Mildred Norton. *David's Harp: The Story of Music in Biblical Times*. New York: New American Library, 1964. A popularized version of the topic, from the Patriarchs to 70CE.

820.   Seow, C.L. *Myth, Dance, and the Politics of David's Dance*. Atlanta: HSM, 1989.

821.   Werner, Eric. "The Origin of Psalmody." *HUCA* 25 (1954): 327-345. Repr. in Werner, *Three Ages of Musical Thought*, 19-39. Werner constructs an eleborate historical line in the development of psalmody from its origin in the sacred cries of primitive cults to the established style in 5th and early 6th century C.E. Hebrew, Byzantine, Armenian, Syrian, and Latin contexts.

822.   Werner, Eric. "Musical Aspects of the Dead Sea Scrolls." *MQ* 43, Jan. (1957): 21-37. Repr. in *Three Ages of Musical Thought*, 119-135. This 'first report' mentions musical notation, use of instruments, and evolution of the antiphon.

823.   Wulstan, David. "The Sounding of the Shofar." *Journal of the Galpin Society*, January (1973): 29-46.

DANCE IN THE OLD TESTAMENT

824.   Bayer, Bathja. *Dance in the Bible: The Possibilities and Limitations of the Evidence*. Papers of the International Seminar on the Bible in Dance, Jerusalem: The Israeli Center of the International Theatre Institute, 1979.

825.   Eaton, J. *Dancing in the Old Testament*. Worship and Dance, Davies, ed. Birmingham, Eng.: ISWRA, 1975. 4-15.

826.   Gruber, Mayer I. "Ten Dance-Derived Expressions in the Hebrew Bible." *Biblica* 62 (1981): 328-46. Linguistic, contextual, Talmudic, and cross-cultural approaches to these terms. Also appears in Adams and Apostolos-Cappadona, *Dance as Religious Studies*, 1990.

827.   Lapson, Dvora. "Dance." In *The Universal Jewish Encyclopedia*, Vol. 3. New York: Universal Jewish Encyclopedia Co., 1941. 455-63.

828.   Morgenstern, Julian. "The Etymological History of the Three Hebrew Synonyms for 'To Dance'." *American Oriental Society Journal* 36 (1916): 321-32. HGG, HLL, and KRR, and their cultural significance. These terms and their Assyrian and Arabic equivalents point to early Semitic rites connected with taboo and its removal in both agricultural and shepherd societies.

MUSIC IN THE NEW TESTAMENT

829.   Smith, William Sheppard. *Musical Aspects of the New Testament*. Amsterdam: Uitgeverij W. ten Have N.V., 1962. Chapters cover 1) the Jewish background, 2 and 3) the manner of performance and texts of the earliest Christian worship, 4) secular and illustrative Biblical references, 5) Angelic music, 6) the trumpet, particularly song and the blast of the trumpet, and 7) the New Testament concept of music, ending with the relationship of music to revelation and redemption.

830.   Werner, Eric. "'If I Speak in the Tongues of Men...': St. Paul's Attitude toward Music." *JAMS* 13 (1960): 18-23. Paul's pharisaic background shows itself in his admonitions to early Christians against instrumental music and the singing of women in services and in his advocacy of psalmody and simplicity of chant. Repr. in Werner, *Three Ages of Musical Thought*, 113-118.

15

Judaism

ENCYCLOPEDIAS, BIBLIOGRAPHIES, AND SIDDUR

831.   Heskes, Irene, compiler. *The Resource Book of Jewish Music: A Biblio-graphical and Topical Guide to the Book and Journal Literature and Program Materials.* Music Reference Collection, 3, Westport, CT: Greenwood Press, 1985. An indispensable aid in the study of Jewish music. Fully annotated.

832.   Landman, Isaac, ed. *The Universal Jewish Encyclopedia: An Authori-tative and Popular Presentation of Jews and Judaism since the Earliest Times.* 10 vols. New York: Ktav Publishing House, 1939-48/repr. 1969.   Index edited by Landman, New York: Ktav, 1944/repr. 1969.

833.   Roth, Cecil and Geoffrey Wigoder, ed. *Encyclopedia Judaica.* 2nd, corrected ed., 16 vols. Jerusalem: Macmillan, 1982. 1st ed., 1972.

834.   Scherman, Rabbi Nosson and Rabbi Meir Zlotowitz, ed. *The Complete ArtScroll Siddur: Weekday/Sabbath/Festival. A New Translation and Antholo-gized Commentary.* 2nd ed., Rabbi Nosson Scherman, transl. Brooklyn, NY: Mesorah Publications, Ltd., 1986. The Sabbath and Festival services, in Hebrew and English, with Masoretic accents.

835.   Singer, Isidore, ed. *The Jewish Encyclopedia.* New York: Ktav Publishing House, Inc, 1964. 1st ed., 1907. 12 vols.

836.   Werblowsky, R.J. Zwi and Geoffrey Wigoder, ed. *The Encyclopedia of the Jewish Religion.* "new revised" ed., New York: ADAMA, 1965/updated repr. 1986.

837.   Wigoder, Geoffrey, ed. *The Encyclopedia of Judaism.* New York: Macmillan; London: Collier Macmillan, 1989 (corrected reprint).

HISTORIES, LITURGIES, AND STUDIES

838.   Avenary, Hanoch. *Encounters of East and West in Music: A Collection of Selected Writings*. Tel-Aviv, Israel: Dept. of Musicology, Tel Aviv, 1979. Seventeen previously published articles organized into four categories: music instruments, mode, synagogue and church music, and Jewish folklore.

839.   Avenary, Hanoch. "Music." In *Encyclopedia Judaica*, Cecil Roth, ed. Vol. 12. 1982. 554-678.

840.   Cohen, Selma Jeanne. "Dance." In *Encyclopaedia Judaica*, Vol. 5. Jerusalem: Keter Publishing House, Ltd., 1971. A study of dance throughout Jewish history.

841.   Eisenstein, Judith K. *Heritage of Music: The Music of the Jewish People*. New York: Union of American Hebrew Congregations, 1972. Twenty-eight chapters on a broad range of subjects including liturgical traditions and hymnology.

842.   Elbogen, Isman. *Jewish Liturgy: A Comprehensive History*. Raymond P. Scheindlin, ed. New York: Jewish Theological Seminary of New York, 1993. Orig. 1913.

843.   Gradenwitz, Peter. *The Music of Israel: Its Rise and Growth through 5000 Years*. New York: W.W. Norton, 1949.

844.   Heskes, Irene, ed. *Studies in Jewish Music: Collected Writings of A.W. Binder, with Tributes by Peter Gradewitz, Joseph Yasser, Irene Heskes, and A. Binder*. New York: Bloch Publishing, 1971. A collection of 25 previously published articles on a variety of topics. Biographical introduction by Heskes.

845.   Heskes, Irene. "Miriam's Sisters: Jewish Women and Liturgical Music." *Notes* 48, 4/June (1992): 1193-1202. Biblical authority prevented women from participating in liturgical services for over 2000 years. The field of music gradually opened up to women beginning with the chaos in Europe during the Crusades and especially with Jewish emigration to the US.

846.   Heskes, Irene. *Passport to Jewish Music: Its History, Traditions, and Culture*. Contributions to the Study of Music and Dance, Vol. 33. Westport, CT: Greenwood Press, 1994.

847.   Hofman, S. "Karaites: Musical Tradition." In *Encyclopedia Judaica*, Geoffrey Wigoder, ed. Vol. 10. 1982. col. 783-785.

848.   Idelsohn, Abraham Z. *Jewish Music in its Historical Development*. New York: Schocken, 1956/repr. 1967. The 'classic' study of Jewish music, though now outdated in various areas. Orig. ed., 1929/repr. 1944, New York: Tudor Publishing Co.

849.   Krueger, William Addison. *The Trumpet in Ancient Israel.* M.M. thesis, University of Lowell, 1989. A study of the *shofar* and *hazozerah* against the musical and cultural background of ancient Israel to show why the trumpet is important today and to assist in ethnic understanding.

850.   Kugel, James L. "Is There but One Song." *Biblica* 63, 3 (1982): 329-350. A study of references in midrashic tradition and Origen to Biblical songs that mark ten crucial points in the history of Israel.

851.   Poethig, Eunice Blanchard. *The Victory Song Tradition of the Women of Israel.* Ph.D. diss., Union Theological Seminary, 1986. The Victory Songs ascribed to Miriam, Deborah, and Hannah constitute a distinct musical tradition involving dance, frame drum and song led by women. These songs attest to the importance of women in early Israel and celebrate a revolutionary theology that includes recognition of the role women played in the victory of Yahweh in Israel.

852.   Rothmüller, Aron M. *The Music of the Jews: An Historical Appreciation.* New, revised ed., H.S. Stevens, transl. New York: A.S. Barnes and Co., Inc., 1967. A three-part study of Jewish music: 1) earliest times to the destruction of the 2nd temple; 2) synagogue service and Jewish music from first to 20th century; and 3) new Jewish music of 19th and 20th centuries. 1st ed., 1953/repr. 1960.

853.   Saminsky, Lazare. *Music of the Ghetto and the Bible.* New York: AMS Press, 1934/repr. 1980. A survey of Jewish music, sacred and secular, in Europe and the U.S.

854.   Sendrey, Alfred. *The Music of the Jews in the Diaspora up to 1800: A Contribution to the Social and Cultural History of the Jews.* New York: T. Yoseloff, 1970. A complement to *Music in Ancient Israel* and a scholarly work of formidable scope.

855.   Shiloah, Amnon. *Jewish Musical Traditions.* Detroit: Wayne State University Press, 1992. By the foremost authority on the Arab and Jewish musical traditions, this excellent modern study of Jewish music is the first to consider, in English, oral music of Jewish communities in a sociocultural context.

856.   Shiloah, Amnon. *The Dimension of Music in Islamic and Jewish Culture.* Aldershot, Hampshire, Great Britain; Brookfield, VT: Variorum, 1993. Fifteen essays on the question of how music and culture intersect. The author groups his essays under four thematic headings: the symbolic and metaphorical interpretation of music, the scientific aspect, the transmission of musical knowledge, and the ideological attitude toward music.

857.   Spector, Johanna. "The Role of Ethnomusicology in the Study of Jewish Music." *Musica Judaica* 4 (1981/2): 20-31. Archaeology, physical and cultural

anthropology, linguistics and historical musicology are all necessary for the diachronic and synchronic study of Jewish music. Such a study shows the tenacity of varied oral traditions as well as the strong destructive influence westernization is beginning to exert.

858.   Werner, Eric. "The Jewish Contribution to Music." In *The Jews: Their History, Culture, and Religion*, 3rd ed. Louis Finkelstein, ed. New York: The Jewish Publication Society of America, 1960. 1288-1321. In Biblical times, the contribution includes the psalm form and manner of singing, music as a permanent and indispensable part of solemn worship, the uses of the organ in temple, and melismatic singing (as in Alleluia). Post-biblical contributions include notation, tunes borrowed by the early Christian church, the principle of modality, psalmody, both responsorial and antiphonal, the litany and lesson, the leading or identifying motifs, etc.

859.   Werner, Eric. "Jewish Music." In *Grove 6*, Vol. 9. 1980. 614-634.

860.   Wohlberg, Max. *The Music of the Synagogue*. New York: JMC, 1948. An informative survey of varied styles and forms of synagogue music from Biblical times and the temple era to the development of synagogal liturgy.

861.   Wolberger, Lionel Arie. *Music of Holy Argument: The Ethnomusicology of Talmudic Debate*. Ph.D. diss., Wesleyan University, 1991.

CHANT, MODES, AND TRANSMISSION

862.   Avenary, Hanoch. "The Concept of Mode in European Synagogue Chant." *Yuval* 2 (1971): 11-21. Mode consists not only of modal scale but also of standard motives and their combination. Although synagogue chant may share scales with Roman chant, the range of the melodies and the way motives are combined are not necessarily comparable.

863.   Avenary, Hanoch. "The Earliest Notation of Ashkenazi Bible Chant." *Journal of Jewish Studies* 26 (1975): 132-50. An exploration of the background of Caspar Amman, an Augustinian prior in whose library was found two mss. of Biblical chant from c. 1511, and his relationship with other humanist Hebraists.

864.   Avenary, Hanoch. *The Ashkenazi Tradition of Biblical Chant Between 1500 and 1900: Documentation and Musical Analysis*. Documentation and Studies 2, Tel-Aviv, Israel: Department of Musicology, Tel-Aviv University; Jerusalem: Ministry of Education and Culture, 1978. The construction and comparison of Biblical chant notations from various mid-European traditions.

865.   Avenary, Hanoch. "Second Thoughts about the Configuration of a Synagogue Mode." *Orbis Musicae* 9 (1986/87): 11-16. A hypothesis that the Adoshem-Malach mode is not based on tetrachords as had been previously

maintained, but on the attraction to a central tone of the tones of the upper and lower layers of the melody.

866.   Beckwith, Roger T. "The Courses of the Levites and the Eccentric Psalms Scrolls from Qumran." *Revue de Qumran* 11, 4 (1984): 499-524. An argument that the note on the four liturgical uses for Psalms in 11QPsua explains that the extra texts found in the Eccentric Psalms Scrolls were required by the Levitical singers in order to perform a complete liturgy.

867.   Binder, Abraham Wolf. *Biblical Chant*. New York: Philosophical Library, 1959.

868.   Cohen, Dalia and Daniel Weil. "Progress in Deductive Research on the Original Performance of Tiberian Accents (te'amim)." In *Proceedings of the 9th World Congress of Jewish Studies*, M. Friedman et al., ed. 2. 1986. 265-280.

869.   Cohen, Dalia and Daniel Weil. "The Scale System and Scale of Tiberian Masoretic Cantillations: Were They Pentatonic?—Theoretical Considerations." *Orbis Musicae* 10 (1990/91): 98-117. On the basis of specific criteria, the pentatonic scale is found to be the best candidate for the scale of the Masoretic accents.

870.   Cohen, Francis L. "Cantillation." In *The Jewish Encyclopedia*, Isidore Singer, ed. Vol. 3. New York: Ktav Publishing House, Inc., 1964. 537-549.

871.   Cohon, Baruch J. "The Structure of the Synagogue Prayer-Chant." *JAMS* 3, 1 (1950): 17-32. Prayer chants have a three-part structure consisting of a beginning phrase, an intermediary phrase group, and a concluding phrase. The intermediary group may contain pausal, modulatory, or pre-concluding phrases.

872.   Dotan, A. "Research in Biblical Accentuation: Background and Trends." In *Prolegomenon to Two Treatises on the Accentuation of the Old Testament*, W. Wickes, ed. New York: KTAV Publishing House, 1970. A history of scholarly interest and understanding of the Biblical accentuation system, from the 16th century to the present.

873.   Eisenstein, Judith K. "The Mystical Strain in Jewish Liturgical Music." In *Sacred Sound*, Joyce Irwin, ed. 1983. 35-54.

874.   Flender, Reinhard. *Hebrew Psalmody: A Structural Investigation*. Yuval Monograph Series, Vol. 9. Jerusalem: Magnes Press, The Hebrew University, 1992. A study of the transition of Hebrew psalmody from oral transmission to written. Combines Old Testament scholarship, Judaic studies, and ethnomusicology and includes a good survey and analysis of biblical accents (te'amim).

875.   Frigyesi, Judit and Peter Laki. "Free-form Recitative and Strophic Structure in the Hallel Psalms." *Orbis Musicae* 7 (1979-80): 43-80. An analysis

of the form and musical motives in the Hallel prayer as performed in Hungarian synagogues.

876. Frigyesi, Judit Laki. "Modulation as an Integral Part of the Modal System in Jewish Music." *Musica Judaica* 5 (1982/3): 53-71. Modulation takes three forms: exact transposition of a modal nucleus from one tone level to another; replacement of one modal nucleus by another with the same central tones; and extension of range with a possible change of central tones and melodic emphasis.

877. Gerson-Kiwi, Edith. "The Bards of the Bible." *Studia Musicologica Academiae Scientiarum Hungariae* 7 (1965): 61-70. Budapest. Repr. in the author's *Migrations and Mutations...*, 137-146. The melodies of Hebrew biblical folk literature are compared to chant settings of the same texts by Near Eastern and European Jews, Muslims, Druze, Samaritans and Christian groups.

878. Goldberg, Geoffrey. "Neglected Sources for the Historical Study of Synagogue Music: The Prefaces to Louis Lewandowski's *Kol Rinnah u T'fillah* and *Todah W'simrah*—Annotated Translations." *Musica Judaica* 11, 1 (1989/90): 28-57. An annotated translation of two important prefaces from 19th century Germany.

879. Goldberg, Geoffrey. "Hazzan and Qahal: Responsive Chant in Minhag Ashkenaz." *HUCA* 61 (1991): 203-217.

880. Haik-Vantoura, Suzanne. *The Music of the Bible Revealed: The Deciphering of a Millenary Notation.* Dannis Weber, transl. John Wheeler, ed. Berkeley, CA: BIBAL Press; San Francisco, CA: King David's Harp, 1991. The author claims that her deciphering of the Tiberian-Masoretic notation reveals the true Biblical chant of the 1st and 2nd Temples.

881. Herzog, Avigdor. *The Intonation of the Pentateuch in the Herder of Tunis.* Tel Aviv: Israel Music Institute, 1963. A study of a Biblical chant tradition that developed independently of the synagogue.

882. Herzog, Avigdor. "Masoretic Accents (Musical Rendition)." In *Encyclopedia Judaica*, Geoffrey Wigoder, ed. Vol. 11. 1982. 1098-1112.

883. Hofman, Shlomo. "The Cantillation of the Bible by the Karaites." Proceedings of the Fifth World Congress of Jewish Studies...Jerusalem...1969. Vol. 4. Jerusalem: World Union of Jewish Studies, 1969. 27.

884. Katz, Ruth. "The Reliability of Oral Transmission: The Case of Samaritan Music." *Yuval* 3 (1974): 109-135. The chant of the Samaritans, a distinct Jewish community within Israel, has three styles—syllabic, neumatic, and melismatic—that are characterized by textual and musical troping, a slow controlled vibrato, a three-note scale, and glissandi between notes.

885.   Levine, Joseph A. "Toward Defining the Jewish Prayer Modes with Particular Emphasis on the *Adonay Malakh Mode*." *Musica Judaica* 3 (1980-81): 13-41. Synagogue prayer modes are aggregates of characteristic phrases shared with synagogue Biblical cantillation; they are not comparable to the modes of medieval Christianity.

886.   Levine, Joseph A. "The Biblical Trope System in Ashkenazic Prophetic Reading." *Musica Judaica* 5 (1982/83): 35-52. A study of syllabic, neumatic, and melismatic forms of Biblical reading in various Jewish traditions.

887.   Newhouse, Ruth. *Volume I: The Music of the Passover Seder from Notated Sources (1644-1945). Volume II: Ashkenazi Haggadah—Text Settings from Notated Sources (1644-1945)*. Ph.D. diss., University of Maryland College Park, 1980. A study of over 750 primarily Ashkenazi settings of Haggadah texts reveals 3 or more music settings in a variety of styles for each of approximately 35 Haggadah texts and basic agreement between Ashkenzi and Sephardi traditions regarding the order and content of most Haggadah texts. Three hundred are transcribed.

888.   Nulman, Macy. "The Shirah Melody in the Ashkenazic and Sephardic Traditions." *Journal of Jewish Music and Liturgy* 7 (1984/5): 12-21. On Exodus 15: 1-18. Repr. in M. Nulman, *Concepts of Jewish Music and Prayer*, 137-45. New York: Cantorial Council of America at Yeshiva University, 1985.

889.   Raghavan, V. "The Music of the Hebrews: Resemblances to Samaveda Chant." *Journal of the Music Academy, Madras* 25 (1954): 109-11. A finding that the similarities between the two are overwhelming.

890.   Ravina, Menashe. *Organum and the Samaritans*. Tel Aviv: Israel Music Institute, 1963. A study of the parallel singing of the dissident pre-rabbinic Jewish sect.

891.   Revell, E. J. "Biblical Punctuation and Chant in the Second Temple Period." *Journal for the Study of Judaism in the Persian, Hellenistic and Roman Period* 7, Spring (1976): 181-198.

892.   Revell, E. J. *Biblical Texts with Palestinian Pointing and Their Accents.* Society of Biblical Literature, Masoretic Studies 4, Missoula, Montana: Scholars Press, 1977.

893.   Ringer, Alexander. "Oral Transmission and Literacy: The Biblical Connection." In *IMS12, 1977*, 1981. 423-425. Ringer proposes that oral and written traditions function simultaneously and interactively and that the Masoretic accents of the Hebrew Bible merely determine the traditional limits of liturgical performance, of which "subsequent generations may have to be reminded if proper continuity is to be maintained."

894. Rubin, Emanuel. "Rhythmic and Structural Aspects of the Masoretic Cantillation of the Pentateuch." Proceedings of the Eleventh World Congress of Jewish Studies. Jerusalem, June, 22-29, 1993. Jerusalem: World Union of Jewish Studies, 1994. Division D, Vol. 2: 219-226. A linguistic and musicological re-examination of the underlying rhythmic structure of the *ta'amei hamigra,* based on Medieval sources. Challenges assumptions of Bender and Rosowsky. Concludes with exx. of computer-generated cantillation

895. Schleifer, Eliyahu. "Anticipation in the Ashkenazi Synagogue-Chant." *Orbis Musicae* 9 (1986): 90-102. A description of four ways a liturgical melody is anticipated: 1) Direct anticipation (a change to the mode of the new melody at the end of the previous melody); 2) Complex anticipation systems (a series of musical signals indicating that the singer's function will change); 3) Distant anticipation (the quotation earlier in a service of a melody associated with a later part of the service); and 4) Remote anticipation (the quotation in an earlier service and with a different text of a melody associated with a particular holiday or fast day).

896. Seroussi, Edwin. "Written Evidence and Oral Tradition: The Singing of *Hayom Harat Olam* in Sephardi Synagogues." *Musica Judaica* 11, 1 (1989/90): 1-27. In contrast to how Sephardic liturgical music tradition is commonly perceived, an examination of oral and written sources shows it to have incorporated tunes from the secular sphere and to have undergone periods of renewal.

897. Sharvit, Uri. "The Musical Realization of Biblical Cantillation Symbols (Te'amîm) in the Jewish Yemenite Tradition." *Yuval* 4 (1982): 179-210. Jerusalem: Magnes Press of Hebrew University. The Yemenite Torah reader has three aims: 1) to make the meaning of the verses clear through accurate accentuation of the words and proper demonstration of the syntax of the verses; 2) to distinguish between the different sections of the text as well as the various social contexts of the readings; and 3) to express the social functions of the reading and the status of each event through distinguishing between simple and elaborate renditions of the tune.

898. Spector, Johanna. "The Significance of Samaritan Neumes and Contemporary Practice." In *Studia Musicologica Academiae Scientiarum Hungariae,* Zoltan Kodaly, ed. 7. Budapest 1965. 141-153.

899. Spector, Johanna. "Samaritan Chant." *Journal of the Music Academy, Madras* 38 (1967): 103-112. A discussion of Samaritan history, the Samaritan community in Israel, Samaritan ritual, and the differences between Samaritan and Jewish chant.

900. Spector, Johanna. "Shingli Tunes of the Cochin Jews." *Journal of the Music Academy, Madras* 40 (1969): 80 ff. Reprinted in *Asian Music,* 3, 2:1972:23-28. Historical background of the Jews of Kerala and a description of their synagogue music, both Biblical cantillations and prayer songs.

901.   Spector, Johanna. "Jewish Songs from Cochin, India: With Special Reference to Cantillation and Shingli Tunes." *Proceedings of the Fifth World Congress of Jewish Studies* 4 (1973): 245-65. Jerusalem, World Union of Jewish Studies.

902.   Spector, Johanna. "Yemenite and Babylonian Elements in the Musical Heritage of the Jews of Cochin, India." *Musica Judaica* 7 (1984/5 [1986]): 1-22.

903.   Szabolcsi, A. "A Jewish Musical Document of the Middle Ages: The Most Ancient Noted Biblical Melody." In *Semitic Studies in Memory of Immanuel Löw*, Sandor Scheiber, ed. Budapest: Alexander Kohut Memorial Foundation, 1947. 131 ff.

904.   Topel, Joseph. *Some Aspects of Hebrew Cantillation in Rabbinic and Masoretic Literature*. Cincinnati, OH: HUC-JIR Press, 1962. Scholarly study of Jewish writings that refer to liturgical chant and Biblical musical recitation.

905.   Werner, Eric. *A Voice Still Heard: The Sacred Songs of the Ashkenazic Jews*. University Park, PA: Pennsylvania State University Press, 1976. A study of Ashkenazic cantorial traditions.

906.   Wohlberg, Max. "The Hazzanic Recitative." *Musica Judaica* 10, 1 (1987/88): 40-51. A brief survey with music illustrations and a plea that outdated aspects of text and performance be prudently eliminated.

907.   Yasser, Joseph. "The Cantillation of the Bible: Salomon Rosowsky." *MQ* 44, 3 (1958): 393-401. An essay on the traditional cantillation patterns for chanting the Torah according to Ashkenazic liturgical practice.

908.   Zeitlin, Shneur Zalman and Haim Bar-Dayan. *The Tora and its Cantillation: Book of Shelomo Rosovsky*. Mikra'e Kodesh, Jerusalem: Orient and Occident, 1977.

LITURGY AND MUSIC AFTER 70CE

909.   Adler, Israel. *Musical Life and Traditions of the Portuguese Jewish Community of Amsterdam in the 18th Century*. Jerusalem: Magnes Press, 1974.

910.   Avenary, Hanoch. "The Hasidic Nigun: Ethos and Melos of a Folk Liturgy." *JIFMC* 16 (1964): 60-63. On the background and types of this wordless vocal melody of the popular mysticism of 18th-century Eastern European Jewry.

911.   Avenary, Hanoch. "The Cantorial Fantasia of the 18th and 19th Centuries: A Late Manifestation of the Musical Trope." *Yuval* 1 (1968): 65-85.

A study of improvisational composition in liturgical chant of Ashkenazic synagogues in the western Rhineland.

912.   Bodoff, Lippman. "Music for Jewish Liturgy: Art for Whose Sake?" *Judaism* 36, Winter (1987): 97-103.

913.   Bradshaw, Paul F., ed. *The Making of Jewish and Christian Worship.* Two Liturgical Traditions, Vol. 1. Notre Dame: University of Notre Dame Press, 1991.   Includes articles on Rabbinic Liturgy, Early Jewish Worship, and Worship since the 12th century CE.

914.   Dalven, Rachel and Israel J. Katz. "Three Traditional Judeo-Greek Hymns and Their Tunes." In *The Jews of Ioannina*, Rachel Dalven, ed. Philadelphia: Cadmus Press, 1990. 191-208. Elements of Sephardic, Romaniote and Italian melodies in Jewish-Greek musical traditions.

915.   de Sola, David Aaron. *Sephardi Liturgy.* London: World Sephardi Federation, 1959. English translation of the Hebrew text, based on the Prayer Books of the Late Rev. David Aaron de Sola, with permission of the Spanish & Portuguese congregation of London.

916.   Eisenstein, Judith K. "Medieval Elements in the Liturgical Music of the Jews of Southern France and Northern Spain." *Musica Judaica* 1 (1975/6): 33 ff. A computer study of 6,232 musical motifs suggests that during the 12th and 13th centuries, troubadour melodies served as a two-way conduit between Christian plainchant and the Jewish liturgical chant of Spain and Portugal.

917.   Eisenstein, Judith K. "Tensions in the Music of Jewish Worship." In *Shiv'im: Essays and Studies in Honor of Ira Eisenstein*, Ronald A. Brauner, ed. Philadelphia, PA: Reconstructionist Rabbinical College, 1977. 231-240.

918.   Farmer, Henry George. "Maimonides on Listening to Music." *JRAS* 45 (1933): 867-84. Maimonides' views on the nature and role of music in spiritual expression.

919.   Fenton, Paul. "A Jewish Sufi on the Influence of Music." *Yuval* 4 (1982): 124-130. From the beginnings of Sufism, Jews participated in Sufi ceremonies. The author of this 13th or 14th century document (perhaps David II ben Joshua Maimonides) adduces Biblical support for the use of music in the ecstatic glorification of God.

920.   Fiederer, Adriana. "Continuity and Change: Jewish Italian Liturgical Music in Isreal." In *Proceedings of the Second British-Swedish Conference on Musicology: Ethnomusicology, Cambridge, 5-10 August 1989*, Ann Buckley, Karl-Olof Edström, and Paul Nixon, ed. Göteborgs: Göteborgs Universitet, 1991. 271-83.

921.   Friedland, Eric L. "Jewish Worship since the Period of Its Canonization." In *The Making of Jewish and Christian Worship*, Paul F. Bradshaw and Lawrence A. Hoffman, ed. Two Liturgical Traditions, Vol. 1. Notre Dame, IN: University of Notre Dame Press, 1991. 137-155. Jewish liturgy from the 12th century ACE.

922.   Gerson-Kiwi, Edith. "The Music of Kurdistan Jews: A Synopsis of their Musical Styles." *Yuval* 2 (1971): 59 ff. Also in Werner, *Contributions to a Historical Study of Jewish Music*, 1976: 266-279. The cycle of the liturgical year is in Hebrew and Aramaic, that of the folk year in Arabic and Kurdish. The cantillation shows both the older Babylonian oral style and the later style of Tiberian (Masoretic) notation.

923.   Goldberg, Geoffrey. "Jewish Liturgical Music in the Wake of Nineteenth-Century Reform." In *Sacred Sound and Social Change: Liturgical Music in Jewish and Christian Experience*, Lawrence A. Hoffman and Janet R. Walton, ed. Two Liturgical Traditions, Vol. 3. Notre Dame; London: University of Notre Dame Press, 1992. 59-83.

924.   Goldschmidt, Ernst Daniel et al. "Liturgy." In *Encyclopedia Judaica*, Cecil Roth, ed. 1982. 392-404.

925.   Hirshberg, Jehoash. "Musical Tradition as a Cohesive Force in a Community in Transition: The Case of the Karaites." *Asian Music* 17, 2 (1986): 46-68. Liturgical chant and paraliturgical song play strong roles in maintaining cultural identity among Karaite communities of Egypt.

926.   Hirshberg, Jehoash. "The Role of Music in the Renewed Self-Identity of Karaite Jewish Refugee Communities from Cairo." YTM 21 (1989): 36-56. Refugee status intensified efforts to preserve identity through mytholigization, maintenance of a unique repertory, and individual efforts to expand repertory.

927.   Hoffman, Lawrence A. *Beyond the Text: A Holistic Approach to Liturgy.* Bloomington: Indiana University Press, 1987. A study of prayer must include a knowledge of the significance of prayer to people in their daily lives and of the ritualized patterns through which people make the world uniquely their own.

928.   Hofman, Shlomo. *Music in the Talmud.* Tel Aviv, Israel: Makhon le-musikah Yisreelit, 1974-7, 1989. Talmudic passages on music are cited in the original Aramaic or Hebrew with translation into English, French, and German.

929.   Hofman, Shlomo. "Music Meditation in the Midrashim." In *Proceedings of the Seventh World Congress of Jewish Studies, Held at the Hebrew University of Jerusalem...August 1977*, Vol. 3. Jerusalem: World Union of Jewish Studies, 1980-81.

930. Idelsohn, Abraham Z. "Synagogue Music, Past and Present." *CCAR Yearbook* 33, CC (1923): 344-55. An excellent article, especially for its discussion of the *piyyut*.

931. Idelsohn, Abraham Z. "Songs and Singers in the Synagogue in the 18th Century." *HUCA: Jubilee Volume* 2 (1925): 397-424. Cincinnati: Hebrew Union College. An introduction to the monumental music collection of Eduard Birnbaum, which was installed at Hebrew Union College in 1924.

932. Idelsohn, Abraham Z. "The Ceremonies of Judaism." *The Jewish Layman* 3 (1928-29): 1-9. An outline of the customary liturgical music for all observances of the Jewish calendar.

933. Idelsohn, Abraham Z. "The Kol Nidre Tune." *HUCA* 8-9 (1931/2): 493 ff. Cincinnati: Hebrew Union College. The Kol Nidre text first appears in the 9th century and took its final shape toward the end of the 13th. The literary evidence places the tune between the mid-15th and mid-16th centuries. Internal musical evidence suggests Minnesong influence and Southern Germany as a place of origin.

934. Idelsohn, Abraham Z. *Jewish Liturgy and Its Development.* New York: Schocken Books, 1932/repr. 1967. Both a historical and practical study of the Jewish liturgy.

935. Kanter, Maxine R. "Traditional High Holiday Melodies of the Portuguese Synagogue of Amsterdam." *Journal of Musicological Research* 3, 2 (1981): 223-57. A study of the influence of Spanish Catholic liturgical materials on the liturgical chant of the Sephardic Jews who relocated in the Netherlands in the late 15th century.

936. Kanter, Maxine R. *Traditional Melodies of the Rhymed Metrical Hymns in the Sephardic High Holiday Liturgy: A Comparative Study.* Ph.D. diss., Northwestern University, 1978.

937. Katz, Israel J. "The 'Myth' of the Sephardic Music Legacy from Spain." Proceedings in the Fifth World Congress of Jewish Studies. 4. Jerusalem: World Union of Jewish Studies, 1973. 237-43.

938. Katz, Ruth. "The Singing of Baqqashôt by Aleppo Jews." *Acta Musicologica* 40 (1968): 65-85. Immigrants adapt to 'Westernization' in Israel not by acculturating, but by exaggerated stereotyping of traditional patterns.

939. Kebede, Ashenafi. "Sacred Chant of Ethiopian Monotheistic Churches: Music in Black Jewish and Christian Communities." *Black Perspective in Music* 8, 1 (1980): 21-34.

940. Knapp, Alexander. "Cultural and Denominational Diversity in Jewish Liturgical Music." *ICTM. United Kingdom Chapter Bulletin* 7 (1984): 6-14.

941.   Kollender, Rachael. "The Hierarchy of Fast-Events and its Reflection in the Music of Karaite Synogogue Prayers." *Orbis Musicae* 11 (1993/94): 176-188.

942.   Kollender-Vietchner, Rachel. *The Role of Music in the Karaite Evening and Morning Services of Sabbath in the Community of Ashdod.* M.A. thesis, Bar Ilan University, 1978.

943.   Koskoff, Ellen. *Nigun Composition Among Lubavitcher Hasidim: The Borrowing of Non-Jewish Melodies.* Working Papers in Yiddish and East European Studies, New York: YIVO Institute for Jewish Research, 1978.

944.   Lachmann, Robert. *Jewish Cantillation and Song in the Isle of Djerba.* Jerusalem: Hebrew University, 1940/repr. 1978. Repr. in *Posthumous Works*, 2, E. Gerson-Kiwi, ed. (Jerusalem, 1978). Jewish music on a North African island off the Tunisian shore.

945.   Landman, Leo. *The Cantor—An Historical Perspective: The Study of the Origin, Communal Position and Function of the Hazzan.* New York: CTI of Yeshiva University, 1972. A full, scholarly study of the subject.

946.   Landman, Leo. "Office of the Medieval Hazzan." *Jewish Quarterly Review* 62, Jan. (1972): 156-187; April (1972): 246-276.

947.   Levarie, Siegmund. "Philo on Music." *Journal of Musicology* 9, 1, Winter (1991): 124-130. On the orderly structure of sound, theo-musical observations on the number seven and on various passages in the Bible, and a first-hand account of a festal meeting of the Therapeutae.

948.   Maimonides. "The Responsum of Maimonides [1135-1204] Concerning Music." B. Cohen, transl. *Jewish Music Journal* 2 (1935): 3. English translation of the brief but influential tract on music.

949.   Maimonides, Moses. *Mishneh Torah. Code of Maimonides. Book 8. The Book of the Temple.* Mendell Lewittes, transl. Yale Judaica series, New Haven: Yale University Press, 1957.

950.   Manasseh, Sara. "Who Will Blow the Shofar?: A Case Study of a Thoqe'a." *ICTM. UK Chapter Bulletin* 11 (1985): 21-40.

951.   Manasseh, Sara. "Variation and Stability in Shbahoth: Songs in Praise of the Babylonian Jews." In *Proceedings of the Second British-Swedish Conference on Musicology: Ethnomusicology, Cambridge, 5-10 August 1989*, Ann Buckley, Karl-Olof Edström, and Paul Nixon, ed. Göteborgs: Göteborgs Universitet, 1991. 231-51.

952.   McKinnon, James. "On the Question of Psalmody in the Ancient Synagogue." *Yuval* 6 (1986): 159-192. A re-examination of ancient documents

reveals that the synagogue had no liturgical order before the destruction of the Second Temple in 70CE and that psalm-singing did not become a part of the synagogue service until several centuries later.

953. McKinnon, James W. "The Exclusion of Musical Instruments from the Ancient Synagogue." *Proceedings of the Royal Musical Association* 106 (1979-80): 77-87.

954. Moskovich, Rina Krut. "The Role of Music in the Liturgy of Emigrant Jews from Bombay: The Morning Prayer for the Three Festivals." *Asian Music* 17, 2 (1986): 88-107. Article on the morning prayer songs of the three festivals of Passover, Shavuot, and Sukkot. Focuses on structure and modes and the importance of text, with importance being equated with largeness in music and number of voices.

955. Nulman, Macy. *Concepts of Jewish Music and Prayer.* New York: Cantorial Council of America at Yeshiva University, 1985.

956. Petrovic, A. "Sacred Sephardi Chants in Bosnia." *The World of Music* 24, 3 (1982): 35-51. Traces the historical movement of Sephardi Jews from 15th-century Spain to their near extinction in WWII, and attempts to reconstruct musical services and ceremonies, especially in the early 20th-century reformation period.

957. Reif, Stefan C. "The Early History of Jewish Worship." In *The Making of Jewish and Christian Worship*, Paul F. Bradshaw and Lawrence A. Hoffman, ed. Two Liturgical Traditions, Vol. 1. Notre Dame, IN: University of Notre Dame Press, 1991. 109-136. Jewish liturgy from the fourth century ACE.

958. Rieder, Mary J. "Kol Nidrei: Some Textual and Musical Backgrounds." In *Sacra/Profana: Studies in Honor of Johannes Riedel*, Davidson and Davidson, ed. Minneapolis, MN: Friends of Minnesota Music, 1985. 39-52.

959. Ross, Israel J. "Cross-Cultural Dynamics in Musical Traditions: The Music of the Cochin Jews." *Musica Judaica* 2, 1 (1977-78): 51-72. The cantillation, prayer chants, and semi-religious song and folksong of this 2000-year old settlement, though unique in many ways, all show similarities with Sephardic, Yemenite and Babylonian, Syrian-Christian, and Vedic chant.

960. Sarason, Richard. "The Modern Study of Jewish Liturgy." In *The Study of Ancient Judaism I: Mishnah, Midrash, Siddur*, Jacob Neusner, ed. New York: Ktav, 1981. 107-179. In same volume, also by Sarason, "Recent Developments in the Study of Jewish Liturgy," pp. 180-187.

961. Sarason, Richard. "Religion and Worship: The Case of Judaism." In *Take Judaism, for Example: Studies toward the Comparison of Religions*, Jacob Neusner, ed. Chicago: University of Chicago Press, 1983. 49-65.

962.   Schleifer, Eliyahu. "Jewish Liturgical Music from the Bible to Hasidism." In *Sacred Sound and Social Change*, Lawrence A. Hoffman et al., ed. Two Liturgical Traditions, Vol. 3. Notre Dame, IN: University of Notre Dame Press, 1992. 13-58.

963.   Schleifer, Eliyahu. "Current Trends of Liturgical Music in the Ashkenazi Synagogue." *The World of Music* 37, 1 (1995): 59-72. The current swing toward the use of popular music in all forms of Ashkenazic liturgy is the result such factors as the holocaust, the establishment of the state of Israel, the decline of liturgical art music, new trends in American Jewish music, and Hasidic influence in the preference for religious melodies based on dance tunes and the singing voices of boys.

964.   Seroussi, Edwin. *Schir Hakawod and the Liturgical Music Reforms in the Sephardi Community in Vienna, ca. 1880-1925: A Study of Change in Religious Music*. Ph.D. diss., University of California at Los Angeles, 1988.

965.   Seroussi, Edwin. "Between the Eastern and Western Mediterranean: Sephardic Music after the Expulsion from Spain and Portugal." In *Jews, Christians, and Muslims in the Mediterranean World after 1492*, Alisa Meyuhas Ginio, ed. London, UK; Portland, OR: Cass, 1992. 198-206.

966.   Seroussi, Edwin and Susana Weich-Shahak. "Judeo-Spanish Contrafacts and Musical Adaptations: The Oral Tradition." *Orbis Musicae* 10 (1990/91): 164-194. The practice of adapting Judeo-Spanish folksongs for the singing of Hebrew prayers and *piyyutim* was wide-spread between the 16th and 19th centuries. During the three decades from 1950 to 1980, performers in Israel were interviewed to document this practice.

967.   Sharvit, Uri. *The Role of Music in the Jewish Yemenite Ritual: A Study of Ethnic Persistence*. Ph.D. diss., Columbia University, 1982.

968.   Sharvit, Uri. "Diversity Within Unity: Stylistic Change and Ethnic Continuity in Israeli Religious Music." *Asian Music* 17, 2 (1986): 126-146. Israeli liturgical music is undergoing intentional transformation through the adoption of, abandonment of, or intensifying of certain musical features to change its cultural defining boundaries.

969.   Sharvit, Uri. "Jewish Musical Cualture—Past and Present." *The World of Music* 37, 1 (1995): 3-17. Among Yemenite Jews, singing in parallel fourths and fifths is both a source of aesthetic pleasure and a force for social identity and cohesion.

970.   Shelemay, Kay Kaufman. *The Liturgical Music of the Falasha of Ethiopia*. Ph.D. diss., University of Michigan, 1977.

971.   Shelemay, Kay Kaufman. "A Quarter-century in the Life of a Falasha Prayer." *YIFMC* 10 (1978): 83-108. The changes in the 'beginning' prayer of the

Falasha liturgy between 1947 and 1973 are traced to social and political changes in both Israel and Ethiopia during those years.

972.   Shelemay, Kay Kaufman. "'Historical Ethnomusicology': Reconstructing Falasha Liturgical History." *Ethnomusicology* 24 (1980): 233-258. An attempt to reconstruct a history of Falasha Judaic liturgical tradition from modern oral evidence and comparison with known factors of Jewish and Christian liturgical tradition.

973.   Shelemay, Kay Kaufman. "Seged: A Falasha Pilgrimage Festival." *Musica Judaica* 3, 1 (1980-81): 43-62. A description of a festival that is a syncretism of Judaic, Christian, and indigenous beliefs and practices.

974.   Shelemay, Kay Kaufman. "Zema: A Concept of Sacred Music in Ethiopia." *The World of Music* 24, 3 (1982): 52-63. On Zêmâ, liturgical music of the Jewish Falasha and Christian Ethiopians. Draws parallels and cites divergencies between the two in legends concerning the genesis of the music, the training of the Dabtara as musician, poet and healer, the Zêmâ Bêt schools which emphasize oral tradition, the Christian 'Aqwaqwam Bêt school for dance, and the Qenê Bêt school of poetic composition.

975.   Shelemay, Kay Kaufman. "The Music and Text of the Falasha Sabbath." *Orbis Musicae* 8 (1982/3): 3-22. A description of the Sabbath rituals and music of the Falasha Jews of northwest Ethiopia.

976.   Shelemay, Kay Kaufman. "Jewish Liturgical Forms in the Falasha Liturgy? A Comparative Study." *Yuval* 5 (1986): 372-404. Falasha liturgy is unique in its inclusion of elements that survive in both Jewish and Christian traditions, the absence of universal Jewish elements such as the *shema*, and the attributing of prayers with obvious Jewish content to the Falasha monastic liturgy.

977.   Shelemay, Kay Kaufman. *Music, Ritual, and Falasha History*. Ethiopian Series Monograph No. 17, East Lansing, Michigan: African Studies Center, Michigan State University, 1986/repr. 1990. The author links the liturgical music of Ethiopian Jews to a tradition taught by 14th and 15th century Christian monks. Difficulties with oral transmission of liturgy, socio-cultural change, and the lack of understanding of the text on the part of performers support her thesis.

978.   Shelemay, Kay Kaufman. *A Song of Longing: An Ethiopian Journey*. Urbana, IL: University of Illinois Press, 1991. The author's account of how she came to unravel the mystery of Falasha music and liturgy.

979.   Shiloah, Amnon. "The Attitude Towards Music of Jewish Religious Authorities." In *The Dimension of Music in Islamic and Jewish Culture*, Aldershot, Hampshire, GB; Brookfield, VT: Variorum, 1993. Sec. XII:1-11. From 70 CE, authorities professed a belief that music exercised strong and irresistible effects on the listener's soul, that music was magical, and that it was a

human creation. In cantillation, the text is primary and is thus acceptable so long as the music does not distract from the text. Over the centuries, areas of friction developed over the boundary between liturgical and art music, music used for mystical purposes, the use of instruments, and in general, the boundary between the practical and the ideological.

980.   Sivan, Gabriel A. "Hymns of the Isles." *Judaism: A Quarterly Journal* 155, 39 (1990): 326-337. Jewish religious music in Great Britain.

981.   Solomon, Robbie. "The Music of the Falashas." *Journal of Synagogue Music* 18, 1 (Jul) (1988): 9-10.

982.   Spector, Johanna. "Musical Styles in Near Eastern Jewish Liturgy." *Journal of the Music Academy, Madras* 26 (1955): 122-130. Liturgical music of Samaritan, Yemenite, Kurdish and Persian Jews and the Syrian Christian Church yield a possible common basis for all Jewish cantillation, unique elements and possible early use of harmony among the Yemenite Jews, musical patterns and a reading of the Book of Esther in common, and Near-Eastern elements found in Synagogue and Syrian Church alike.

983.   Spector, Johanna. "Samaritan Chant." *JIFMC* 16 (1964): 66-69. A brief report on the history and current status of Samaritans and Samaritan chant in Israel.

984.   Tasat, Ramón Alberto. *The Cantillation and the Melodies of the Jews of Tangier, Morocco*. Ph.D. diss., University of Texas, Austin, 1993.

985.   Trolin, Clifford. *Movement in Prayer in a Hasidic Mode*. Austin TX: The Sharing Co., 1979. A study of prayer movement from the second century (Rabbi Akiba) to Hasidic prayer in the twentieth century.

986.   Werner, Eric. "The Music of Post-Biblical Judaism." In *New Oxford History of Music I: Ancient and Oriental Music*, 1957. 313-335. Article covers the continuity of the tradition, cantillation of scripture, psalm tones, modal content, influence of poetry, various European traditions, and disintegration due to Hasidism.

987.   Wohlberg, Max. "The Music of the Synagogue as a Source of the Yiddish Folksong." *Musica Judaica* 2 (1977/8): 21-49. Jewish liturgical chant has enriched the songs of homes, workshops, and social gatherings of the young and old, male and female.

16

European Christianity: General References, Histories, Surveys, and Liturgy

BIBLIOGRAPHIES AND SOURCES OF THE MUSIC AND DANCE OF EUROPEAN CHRISTIANITY

988.   Boorman, Stanley et al. "Sources, MS." In *Grove 6*, Vol. 17. 1980. 609-634 (plainchant); 649-702 (polyphony). A listing and discription of the manuscript sources of Western plainchant and polyphony.

989.   Clark, Keith C. *A Selective Bibliography for the Study of Hymns, 1980*. 2nd ed., Springfield, OH: Hymn Society of America, 1980.

990.   Foley, Edward. "Liturgical Music: A Bibliographic Introduction to the Field." *Liturgical Ministry* 3 (1994): 130-143. An indispensible survey of the literature on Jewish and Christian liturgical music. Topics include historical studies (general histories, focused histories), theological studies (on the nature of music/sound, music and the rites, and interplay of music and texts), and pastoral and cultural studies (the culture of worship music; field work and liturgical music).

991.   Gerbrandt, Carl. *Sacred Music Drama: The Producer's Guide*. Princeton, NJ: Prestige, 1993.

992.   Hiley, David. *Western Plainchant*. New York: Oxford University Press, 1993. Includes 65-page bibliography at the front of the book.

993.   Hughes, Andrew. *Medieval Music: The Sixth Liberal Art*. rev. ed., Toronto Medieval Bibliographies 4, Toronto: University of Toronto Press, 1980. A fully annotated bibliography of over 2000 items on all aspects of medieval music.

994.   Jackson, Roland. *Performance Practice: Medieval to Contemporary: A Bibliographic Guide.* New York: Garland, 1988. 1392 entries, fully annotated. See Chap. 2 and 3 in particular for issues related to monody and early polyphony.

995.   Jeffery, Peter. *Re-Envisioning Past Musical Cultures: Ethnomusicology in the Study of Gregorian Chant.* Chicago Studies in Ethnomusicology, Philip V. Bohlman and Bruno Nettl, ed. Chicago and London: The University of Chicago Press, 1992. Contains a 50-page bibliography.

996.   Pfaff, Richard. *Medieval Latin Liturgy: A Select Bibliography.* Toronto Medieval Bibliographies, Vol. 9. Toronto and Buffalo: Toronto University Press, 1982.

997.   Scott, Darwin Floyd. *The Roman Catholic Liturgy and Liturgical Books: A Musical Guide.* UCLA Music Library Bibliography Series, No. 5, Los Angeles: UCLA, 1988.

998.   Szoverffy, Joseph. *A Guide to Byzantine Hymnography: A Classified Bibliography of Texts and Studies.* 2 vols. Brookline, MA: Classical Folia Editions, 1979.

999.   Thompson, Bard. *A Bibliography of Christian Worship.* Metuchen, NJ; London: Amenian Theological Library Association and The Scarecrow Press, 1989. See Part 6: Church Music and Hymnology, pp. 656-740.

1000. Troxell, Kay. *Resources in Sacred Dance: Annotated Bibliography from Christian and Jewish Traditions: Books, Booklets and Pamphlets, Articles and Serial Publications, Media, and Reference Sources.* Peterborough, NH: Sacred Dance Guild, 1991. Rev. of 1986 ed.

1001. Von Ende, Richard C. *Church Music: An International Bibliography.* Metuchen, NJ: Scarecrow Press, 1980. 5445 references to materials in various European languages. A valuable resource.

1002. Wagner, Mary Carol Theresa. *A Practical Annotated Catalog Raisonne: According to the Master Lynn-Peterson Classification, 2nd ed., based on the Ratio Studiorum Prescribed by the Sacred Congregation of Rites for Catholic Education, Standardizing the Cataloging of the Library of Congress in Latin Liturgical Music of the Roman Rite and its Variants, and Including the Holdings of the Catholic University of America.* Typescript,1979. The author reclassifies Catholic liturgical materials and annotates each entry. A monumental and useful undertaking.

1003. Yousif, P. et al. *A Classified Bibliography on the East-Syrian Liturgy.* Rome: Mar Thoma Yogam, 1990. A bibliography in Western languages. See pp. 25-28 for music, hymns, art, and paraliturgical texts.

SOURCE MATERIALS IN TRANSLATION

1004. McKinnon, James. *Music in Early Christian Literature*. James McKinnon, transl. Cambridge Readings in the Literature of Music, Cambridge & New York: Cambridge University Press, 1987. An invaluable collection of 398 passages from the New Testament to the early 5th century, translated into English.

1005. Quasten, J., et al., ed. *Ancient Christian Writers: The Works of the Fathers in Translation*. New York: Newman Press, 1946.

1006. Roberts, Alexander and James Donaldson, ed. *The Ante-Nicene Fathers: Translation of the Writings of the Fathers down to A.D. 325*. 10 vols. Grand Rapids, MI: W.B. Eerdmans, 1885-87/repr. 1956 to 1980. American reprint of the Edinburgh edition, revised and chronologically arranged with brief prefaces and occasional notes by A. Cleveland Coxe.

1007. Strunk, Oliver. *Source Readings in Music History from Classical Antiquity through the Romantic Era*. New York: W. W. Norton, 1950. Eighty-seven selections from Greek and Western sources, through the 19th century.

1008. Weiss, Piero and Richard Taruskin, ed. *Music in the Western World. A History in Documents*. New York: G. Schirmer Books, 1984. One-hundred-fifty-five documents from Greek and Western sources, through 1983.

1009. Wienandt, Elwyn, ed. *Opinions on Church Music: Comments and Reports from Four-and-a-Half Centuries*. Waco, TX: The Markham Press Fund of Baylor University Press, 1974. A valuable compilation of fifty statements by both Catholics and Protestants concerning religious music, from c.1500 to 1972. Drawn from pronouncements of church officials, composers' letters, and published articles and essays.

DICTIONARIES AND ENCYCLOPEDIAS

1010. Cross, Frank L. and Elizabeth A. Livingstone. *The Oxford Dictionary of the Christian Church*. 2nd rev. ed., London: Oxford University Press, 1983.

1011. Davies, J. G., ed. *The New Westminster Dictionary of Liturgy and Worship*. Philadelphia: Westminster Press, 1986.

1012. Kibler, William W. and Grover Zinn, ed. *Medieval France: An Encyclopedia*. Garland Encyclopedias of the Middle Ages, Vol. 2. Hamden, CT: Garland Publishing, 1995. Contains dozens of articles on music and liturgy from the period 987 to 1515.

1013. Laud, Jovian P., Rev. *Dictionary of the Liturgy*. New York: Catholic Book Publishing Co., 1989.

1014. Poultney, David. *Dictionary of Western Church Music.* Chicago: American Library Association, 1991.

HISTORIES

1015. Boorman, Stanley, ed. *Studies in the Performance of Late Medieval Music.* New York/London: Cambridge University Press, 1983. Ten essays cover iconographic evidence concerning performance practice, music instruments and their music, and the purely vocal performance of liturgical polyphony during the 14th and 15th centuries.

1016. Brown, Harold Meyer. *Music in the Renaissance.* Englewood Cliffs: Prentice Hall, 1976.

1017. Brown, Howard Mayer and Stanley Sadie, ed. *Performance Practice: Music before 1600.* The Norton/Grove Handbooks in Music, New York: W.W. Norton, 1990.

1018. Caldwell, John. *Medieval Music.* London: Hutchinson; Bloomington, IN: Indiana University Press, 1978.

1019. Carter, Tim. *Music in the Late Renaissance and Early Baroque Italy.* Longon: Batsford, 1992. A contextual approach to this transitional period.

1020. Cattin, Giulio. *Music of the Middle Ages I.* Steven Botterill, transl. New York, NY: Cambridge University Press, 1985. A study that views medieval monophony as a body of music in its own right, rather than as a preamble to polyphony.

1021. Chanan, Michael. *Musica Practica: The Social Practice of Western Music from Gregorian Chant to Postmodernism.* London; New York: Verso, 1994.

1022. Crocker, Richard and David Hiley, ed. *The Early Middle Ages to 1300.* 2nd ed., The New Oxford History of Music, Vol. 2. Oxford; New York: Oxford University Press, 1990. A completely new history of the Middle Ages in the NOHM series. See individual entries below.

1023. Fassler, Margot and Peter Jeffery. "Christian Liturgical Music from the Bible to the Renaissance." In *Sacred Sound and Social Change: Liturgical Music in Jewish and Christian Experience*, Lawrence A. Hoffman and Janet R. Walton, ed. Two Liturgical Traditions, Vol. 3. Notre Dame, IN: University of Notre Dame, 1992. 84-123. An overview of liturgical and musical developments through the 16th century.

1024. Fenlon, Iain, ed. *Music in Medieval and Early Modern Europe: Patronage, Sources, and Texts.* Cambridge: Cambridge University Press, 1981.

1025. Fenlon, Iain, ed. *The Renaissance: From the 1470s to the End of the Sixteenth Century*. New York: MacMillan, 1989. Fourteen essays on the places, occasions, institutions, and individuals that caused music to be made, and made in the way it was made.

1026. Fleischhauer, Günther. "Ancient Rome." In *Grove 6*, Vol. 1. 1980. 146-153.

1027. Gallo, F. W. *Music of the Middle Ages II*. New York, NY: Cambridge University Press, 1985. A study of the development of polyphony and mensural music in the political, civil and religious context of the period from 1150 to 1450.

1028. Gangwere, Blanche. *Music History from the Late Roman Thru the Gothic Periods, 313-1425: A Documented Chronology*. Westport, CT: Greenwood Press, 1986.

1029. Gangwere, Blanche. *Music History During the Renaissance Period 1425-1520: A Documented Chronology*. Westport, CT: Greenwood, 1991.

1030. Georgiades, Thrysbulos. *Music & Language: The Rise of Western Music Exemplified in Settings of the Mass*. London: Cambridge University Press, 1983.

1031. Gorali, Moshe. *The Old Testament in Music*. Jerusalem: Maron Publishers, 1993. Pt. 2 consists of a list of 5470 settings of Biblical Texts, arranged by composer and by subject. Pt. 3 consists of musical exx. of settings of psalms, liturgical and mystery plays, oratorios, biblical operas, folk songs, vocal and instrumental. Beautifully illustrated. A tremendous work.

1032. Hoppin, Richard H. *Medieval Music*. New York: W.W. Norton, 1978.

1033. Kaldis, Cynthia. *Latin Music through the Ages*. Wauconda, IL: Bolchazy-Carducci Publishers, 1991. Includes English translations of Latin poetry.

1034. Knighton, Tess and David Fallows, ed. *Companion to Medieval and Renaissance Music*. London: Dent and Sons, 1992. Fortynine essays in six sections on 1) the role of taste and temperament in making judgments concerning Medieval and Renaissance music, 2) music and society, 3) form and style (vocal and instrumental genres and techniques of composition), 4) the nature and interpretation of source material, 5) pre-performance decisions, and 6) performance techniques.

1035. Lewis, Anthony and Nigel Fortune. *Opera and Church Music 1630-1750*. The New Oxford History of Music, Vol. 5. New York and London: Oxford University Press, 1975.

1036. McKinnon, James, ed. *Antiquity and the Middle Ages: From Ancient Greece to the 15th Century*. Music and Society, London: Macmillan; Englewood Cliffs, NJ: Prentice Hall, 1990.

1037. Mews, Stuart. "Music and Religion in the First World War." In *The Church and the Arts*, Diana Wood, ed. Oxford, UK; Cambridge, MA: Blackwell Publishers, 1992. 465-475.

1038. Page, Christopher. *Discarding Images: Reflections on Music and Culture in Medieval France*. New York: Oxford University Press; Oxford: Clarendon Press, 1993. A study and rectification of commonly held misconceptions concerning Medieval music and culture. Targets include architecturally-determined musical proportions, incorrect assumptions concerning the audience for double and triple motets, and the attitude that the Middle Ages 'waned.' See reviews and comments in *Early Music*, beginning with Vol. 21, 4 (1993).

1039. Pirrotta, Nino. "Medieval." In *Grove 6*, Vol. 12. 1980. 15-20. A useful introduction to the origin of the term 'medieval' and to the musical context in Latin Europe of the period between 675 and the end of the 14th century.

1040. Pirrotta, Nino. *Music and Culture in Italy from the Middle Ages to the Baroque*. Cambridge, Eng.: Cambridge University Press, 1984. An anthology of writings by the leading authority on Italian music. Many essays place emphasis on the relationship between written and oral traditions of music.

1041. Reese, Gustave. *Music in the Renaissance*. New York: W.W.Norton, 1954. For several decades, the major scholarly work on this period.

1042. Seay, Albert. *Music in the Medieval World*. 2nd ed., Englewood Cliffs, NJ: Prentice-Hall, Inc., 1975.

1043. Stevens, J. *Words and Music in the Middle Ages: Song, Narrative, Dance and Drama, 1050-1350*. London/New York: Cambridge University Press, 1986. Part 1: "Number in Music and Verse" covers conductus, sequence, lai and planctus. Part 2: "Relations of Speech, Action, Emotion, and Meaning" includes speech and melody in Gregorian Chant and Liturgical Drama. Part 3: "Melody, Rhythm and Meter" includes sections on theorists and paleography.

1044. Strohm, Reinhard. *The Rise of European Music, 1380-1500*. New York, NY: Cambridge University Press, 1993. The most comprehensive study of the music of this period by a single author since Reese's surveys. Alternates between closely detailed description of specific exemplary works and panoramic views of the social, political, and cultural contexts out of which they emerged.

1045. Wienandt, Elwyn A. *Choral Music of the Church*. Music Reprint Series, New York: Da Capo, 1965/repr. 1980. A historical survey of the choral music for the Roman Catholic, Anglican, and Lutheran liturgies from its beginnings to the early 1960's.

1046. Wilson, David Fenwick. *Music of the Middle Ages: Style and Structure.* New York: Schirmer, 1990. A study of Medieval music as viewed through the theoretical thought of the age, with music illustrations and study assignments in analysis and composition at the end of many of the seventeen chapters.

1047. Wilson-Dickson, Andrew. *The Story of Christian Music: From Gregorian Chant to Black Gospel: An Authoritative Illustrated Guide to all the Major Traditions for Music for Worship.* Oxford, Eng./Batavia, IL: Lion Publications, 1992. A generously illustrated but textually brief and sometimes dated history of Christian music from its origins and survey of worship of Christian congregations throughout the world today.

PHILOSOPHIES AND THEOLOGIES OF CHURCH MUSIC

1048. Berglund, Robert. *A Philosophy of Church Music.* 2nd ed., St. Paul, MN: Bethel Publications, 1985.

1049. Best, Harold M. *Music Through the Eyes of Faith.* San Francisco, CA: Harper, San Francisco, 1993. An argument for musical pluralism in a pluralistic world.

1050. Davis, Henry Grady. "Theology in Relation to Arrangements for Music in the Church." *Response* 3, Pentecost (1961): 3-12. Davis points up the failures of church architecture to facilitate Christian worship through music. The author provides theological as well as musical considerations for new designs.

1051. Eaton, John H. "Music's Place in Worship: A Contribution from the Psalms." In *Prophets, Worship and Theodicy: Studies in Prophetism, Biblical Theology and Structural and Rhetorical Analysis and on the Place of Music in Worship*, J. Barton R. Carroll, et al., ed. Leiden, Netherlands: E. J. Brill, 1984. 85-107.

1052. Epstein, Heidi. *The Nature of the Relationship between Music and Theology According to Oskar Sohngen and Oliver Messiaen.* M.A., McGill University, 1990. Protestant theologian Oskar Söhngen's three categories of relationship between music and theology—music as science, as worship, and as creatura—all find implicit use in the works of Oliver Messiaen.

1053. Gardner, James Earl. *An Examination of Selected Aspects of Marxist and Christian Musical Aesthetics.* DMA dissertation, Southwestern Baptist Theological Seminary, 1982. An examination of how non-musical content is expressed through musical style. Why music exists and how it functions according to Orthodox Marxism, Critical Marxism, Radical Christianity, Popular Christianity, and Intellectual Christianity. How aesthetics is affected when made subservient to idiology.

1054. Harnoncourt, Philipp. "If They Don't Sing It, They Don't Believe It: Singing in the Worship Service: Expression of Faith or Unreasonable Liturgical Demand?" In *The Hymnology Annual*, V. Wicker, ed. 1. 1991. 4-35.

1055. Hazelton, Roger. *A Theological Approach to Art*. Nashville: Abingdon Press, 1967. The religious use of the arts is examined from the standpoints of art as disclosure, as embodiment, as vocation, and as celebration.

1056. Johansson, Calvin M. *Music and Ministry: A Biblical Counterpoint*. Peabody MA: Hendrickson Publishers, 1984. Because music is abstract and ephemeral, it can explore the mystery of God's transcendence and engender the awe experienced in contemplating the Holy in a way that words alone cannot. It does this through such characteristics as continuity, variety and unity, hierarchy, the 'self-worth' of every detail, order and freedom, climax, balance, symmetry, economy—all of which 'participate in the universal principles found in all of existence' and give to great music its 'rightness' or internal truth.

1057. Johansson, Calvin M. *Disciplining Music Ministry: Twenty-first Century Directions*. Peabody, MA: Hendrickson Publishers, 1992.

1058. Johnson, Lawrence J. *The Mystery of Faith: The Ministers of Music*. Washington D.C.: Pastoral Press, 1983.

1059. Joncas, J. Michael. "Semiotics and the Analysis of Liturgical Music." *Liturgical Ministry* 3, Fall (1994): 144-154. A presentation of the basic concepts of semiotics—the science of *how* signs acquire meaning—in general, of how these concepts have been applied to the analysis of music, and of how they may be applied to the critiquing of liturgical music.

1060. Leaver, Robin A. *The Theological Character of Music in Worship*. Church Music Pamphlet Series, St. Louis, MO: Concordia Publishing House, 1985/repr. 1989. Originally published as Chapter 3 of Routley: *Duty and Delight,* pp. 47-64. An examination of music in worship based on criteria by Erik Bentley and Paul Waitman Hoon and with reference to the theological categories of liturgy, doctrine, and proclamation.

1061. Leaver, Robin A., James H. Litton, and Carlton R. Young, ed. *Duty and Delight: Routley Remembered: A Memorial Tribute to Erik Routley (1917-1982), Ministry, Church Music, Hymnody*. Carol Stream, IL: Hope Publishing Co; Norwich, Norfolk: Canterbury Press, Norwich, 1985.

1062. Lee Joong-Tai. *The Position and Meaning of Music in Worship*. D.Min. diss., Fuller Theological Seminary, School of Theology, 1984.

1063. Lovelace, Austin C. and William C. Rice. *Music and Worship in the Church*. Rev. and enl. ed., Nashville, KY: Abingdon Press, 1976.

1064. Martin, David A. "Music and Religion: Ambivalence Towards "the Aesthetic"." *Religion* 14, July (1984): 269-292. A study of the tension between the Christian religion and "the aesthetic" according to four basic and often incompatible attitudes: 1) as the sonic aspect of prayer, music must be subordinate to prayer, 2) music must be "worthy" of worship, 3) any kind of music will do as long as it gets the evangelical message across, and 4) music itself is God's revelation to man. The various devices and methods composers have used to evoke "the holy" are also analysed.

1065. Mitchell, Robert H. *Ministry and Music*. Westminster Press: 1978. See especially Chap. 5: Music and Worship, and Chap. 8: Age of Rock or Rock of Ages.

1066. Moger, Peter. *Music and Worship: Principle to Practice*. Bramcote, Nottingham: Grove Press, 1994. A brief but valuable account of attitudes toward music from the Bible to the present, issues concerning music and theology, and music for worship.

1067. Nelson, Edward W. *Music and Worship*. El Paso, TX: Casa Bautista de Publicaciones, 1985.

1068. Oldham, Larry Eugene. *Biblical Foundations for Ministry Through Music*. DMA, Southwestern Baptist Theological Seminary, 1983. A finding that music in the life of the church is validated, not by its artistic value, as has been the practice since the Renaissance, but by its functioning to glorify God and edify the corporate worshippers.

1069. Poole, Thomas Daryl. *Towards an Integration of Music and Theology: Suggestions for the Construction of a Theological Definition of Music*. D.M.A., Southern Baptist Theological Seminary, 1988. An examination of music treatises from the ancient Greeks through 1950 according to methods by Tillich and Gilkey yield four definitions of music: the Pythagorean Model, the Divine Art Model, the Prophetic-Priestly Model, and the Ultimate Realities Model. Only the last is judged to satisfy the theological criterion—music's expression of and participation in Ultimate Concern—and is suggested as a way of defining music theologically.

1070. Pottie, Charles S. *A More Profound Alleluia! Gelineau and Routley on Music in Christian Worship*. Washington, DC: Pastoral Press, 1984. For Gelineau, the value of music is its capacity to deepen the mystery of liturgical actions for the liturgical assembly. For Routley, music heightens God's word as given in Scripture. For both, music has the symbolic power to communicate "God's love in Christ to the worshipping community."

1071. Riedel, Scott. "Technology, Music, and Today's Liturgy." *Liturgical Ministry* 3, Fall (1994): 160-163.

1072. Routley, Erik. *The Church and Music: An Enquiry into the History, the Nature, and the Scope of Christian Judgment on Music*. Rev. ed., London: Gerald Duckworth and Co., Ltd., 1967/repr. 1978. A survey of Christian views toward music in nine historical periods, beginning with the pre-Christian background and ending with the first half of the 20th century.

1073. Routley, Erik. *Church Music and the Christian Faith*. Carol Stream IL: Agape, 1978. A study of the judgments and disputes about the role of music in Christian churches during the last three centuries. Routley provides Biblical background for such judgments with particular emphasis on the role and music of J.S. Bach, and concludes with a chapter on methods of criticism and on Good and Bad Music.

1074. Routley, Erik. *The Divine Formula: A Book for Worshipers, Preachers, and Musicians, and All Who Celebrate the Mysteries*. Princeton, NJ: Prestige Publications, 1986. The formula consists of The Story of Salvation, The Pattern of Scripture, The Law of God, Revelation, and The Moral Imperatives.

1075. Schueller, Herbert. *The Idea of Music: An Introduction to Musical Aesthetics in Antiquity and the Middle Ages*. Kalamazoo, MI: Medieval Institute Publications, Western Michigan University, 1988.

1076. Seel, Thomas Allen. *A Theology of Music for Worship Derived from the Book of Revelation*. Studies in Liturgical Musicology, Vol. 3. Metuchen, NJ: Scarecrow Press, 1995. A dramatic approach to the Book of Revelation shows its eschatology to have been expressed in terms of the best music traditions of the past. Forms of music, performing groups, and performance practice within the Book are traced historically through the early pagan, Jewish, Greek, Roman, and early church periods. From this historical perspective, ten guideposts—a theology of music—are developed, which are historically, biblically and eschatologically supported and made relevant to the contemporary church musician. A revision of DMA diss., Southern Baptist Theological Seminary.

1077. Skeris, Robert A. *Chroma Theou: On the Origins and Theological Interpretation of the Musical Imagery used by the Ecclesiastical Writers of the First Three Centuries, with Special Reference to the Image of Orpheus*. Musicae Sacrae Melethmata, 1, Alotting: A. Coppenrath, 1976.

1078. Söhngen, Oskar. "Music and Theology: A Systematic Approach." In *Sacred Sound*, Joyce Irwin, ed. Chico: Scholars Press, 1983. 1-19. Christian music has a theological content from three standpoints: the mathematical (the correlation between the motion of the heavenly bodies and the simple ratios found in musical intervals), the mediational (music as worship, music intimately linked to liturgical action), and the revelatory (Luther's concept of music as the sounding image of God's creation).

1079. Steckel, Clyde J. "How Can Music Have Theological Significance?" *Black Sacred Music* 8, Spring (1994): 13-35. Music can be theologically significant in three ways: through the expression of feelings and emotions associated with religious texts and contexts, through its capacity to present alternative domains and new visions of life-experience, and through its power to transform the lives of participants.

1080. Tucci, Douglass S. "High Mass as Sacred Dance." *Theology Today* 34, Ap. (1977): 58-72. Tucci closely examines Roman Catholic and Anglican liturgy as art with attention to how that art form reflects, informs and interprets church architecture.

1081. Wilkey, Jay W. "Prolegomena to a Theology of Music." *Review and Expositor* 69 (1972): 507-517.

1082. Wilkey, Jay W. "Music as Religious Expression in Contemporary Society." *Review and Expositor* 69, Spring (1972): 199-216.

PSALMODY AND HYMNODY

1083. Anderson, Warren et al. "Hymn." In *Grove 6*, Vol. 8. 1980. 836-851. An excellent overview of the hymn in both Catholic and Protestant Christianity.

1084. Dunstan, Alan. *The Use of Hymns*. Bury St. Edmunds: Kevin Mayhew, 1990.

1085. Dunstan, Alan. "Hymnody in Christian Worship." In *The Study of Liturgy*, 2nd, rev. ed. Jones, Wainwright, Yarnold, and Bradshaw, ed. New York: Oxford University Press, 1992. 507-519.

1086. English, Joan Pritcher. *Criteria for the Reform and Renewal of Contemporary Musical Forms in Christian Worship*. Ph.D. dissertation, Emory University, 1985. On the devotional use of hymns in churches.

1087. Julian, John, ed. *A Dictionary of Hymnology: Setting Forth the Origin and History of Christian Hymns of All Ages and Nations, with...Historical Articles on National and Denominational Hymnody, Breviaries, Missals, Primers, Psalters, Sequences, etc*. Rev. ed., 2 vols. Grand Rapids, MI: Kregel Publications, 1907/repr. 1985. 1st. ed., 1892; rev. ed. with new suppl.,1907. Still the most exhaustive study of this subject.

1088. Lovelace, Austin C. *The Anatomy of Hymnody*. Nashville, TN: Abingdon Press, 1965. A study of hymnic prosody and rhyme and how different meters have been set to music.

1089. Manwaring, Randle. *A Study of Hymn-Writing and Hymn-Singing in the Christian Church*. Texts and Studies in Religion, 50, Lewiston, NY: The Edwin Mellen Press, 1990. Traces the history of hymn-writing and singing, with special emphasis on the development of English hymnody.

1090. Robertson, Charles, ed. *Singing the Faith: Essays by Members of the Joint Liturgical Group on the Use of Hymns in Liturgy*. Norwich, Eng.: Canterbury Press, 1990. Seventeen articles on the use of hymns in various Christian denominations.

1091. Routley, Erik. *A Panorama of Christian Hymnody*. Collegeville, MN: Liturgical Press, 1979. A collection of hymn texts from 28 sources, with commentary on each group.

1092. Routley, Erik. *Christian Hymns, an Introduction to their Story*. Princeton, NJ: Prestige Publications, 1980. 6 cassettes in book format. From beginnings to 1900.

1093. Routley, Erik. *The Music of Christian Hymns*. Chicago: G.I.A. Publications, 1981. A study of 605 hymn tunes, divided into 27 groups, with commentary on each group. Tunes span almost 2000 years, from plainchant to the present. Contains an extensive list of hymnals and a lengthy bibliography.

1094. Routley, Erik. *Christian Hymns Observed: When in our Music God is Glorified*. Princeton, NJ: Prestige Publications, 1982.

1095. Werner, Eric et al. "Psalm." In *Grove 6*, Vol. 15. 1980. 320-335. An excellent overview of musical settings of the Psalms from Biblical times to the present.

1096. Wicker, Vernon, ed. *The Hymnology Annual: An International Forum on the Hymn and Worship*. Vol. 1. Berrien Springs, MI: Vande Vere Publishing, 1991. A collection of 19 articles from various denominations, disciplines, and cultures.

1097. Wicker, Vernon, ed. *The Hymnology Annual: An International Forum on the Hymn and Worship*. Vol. 2. Berrien springs, MI: Vande Vere Publishers, 1992. A collection of 17 articles from various denominations, disciplines, and cultures.

EARLY LITURGY: DOCUMENTS IN TRANSLATION

1098. Brightman, F.E. *Liturgies Eastern and Western, being the Texts, Original or Translated of the Principal Liturgies of the Church*. Oxford, England: Oxford University Press, 1896/repr. 1967.

1099. Deiss, Lucien, ed. *Springtime of the Liturgy*. Matthew J. O'Connell, transl. Collegeville, MN: Liturgical Press, 1979. Translated from the French. Liturgical texts of the first four centuries.

1100. Hamman, Adelbert, ed. *The Mass: Ancient Liturgies & Patristic Texts.* Alba patristic library, Thomas Halton, ed. Staten Island, NY: Alba House, 1967. Translation of *La Messe; liturgies anciennes et textes patristiques.*

1101. Thompson, Bard, ed. *Liturgies of the Western Church.* Philadelphia PA: Fortress Press, 1980. Translations of liturgies from Justin Martyr (ca. 155 AD) to John Wesley (1784).

1102. Whitaker, E.C. *Documents of the Baptismal Liturgy.* 2nd ed., London, England: The Society for Promoting Christian Knowledge, 1970.

1103. White, James F. *Documents of Christian Worship. Descriptive and Interpretive Sources.* Louisville: Westminster/John Knox Press, 1992.

LITURGY, EAST AND WEST

1104. Adam, Adolf. *Foundations of Liturgy: An Introduction to Its History and Practice.* Matthew J. O'Connell, transl. Collegeville, MN: The Liturgical Press, 1992. Orig. German, 1985. A study of the history and functions of the liturgy and of specific sacraments.

1105. Baldovin, John F. *The Urban Character of Christian Worship: The Origins, Development and Meaning of Stational Liturgy.* Orientalia Chyristiana Analecta, 228. Rome: Ponteficium Institutum Studiorum Orientalium, 1987. A comparison of Sunday worship on different feast days, conducted by official church hierarchy at various churches in the cities of Rome, Jerusalem, and Constantinople through late antiquity.

1106. Baldovin, John F. "Christian Worship to the Eve of the Reformation." In *The Making of Jewish and Christian Worship*, Paul F. Bradshaw and Lawrence A. Hoffman, ed. Two Liturgical Traditions, Vol. 1. Notre Dame, IN: University of Notre Dame Press, 1991. 156-183.

1107. Baumstark, Anton. *Comparative Liturgy.* F.L. Cross, ed. London: A.R. Mowbray, 1958. An examination of all Christian rites of Europe, Southwest Asia, Northwest Africa, the Near East and India—18 liturgies in all that originated before the 16th century—in order to determine fundamental rules about the collective structure of ritual.

1108. Bradshaw, Paul F. "Ten Principles for Interpreting Early Christian Liturgical Evidence." In *The Making of Jewish and Christian Worship*, Paul F. Bradshaw and Lawrence A. Hoffman, ed. Two Liturgical Traditions, Vol. 1. Notre Dame, IN: University of Notre Dame Press, 1991. 3-21. Guidelines from one of the leaders in the modern re-examination of early Christian liturgy.

1109. Harper, John. *The Forms and Orders of Western Liturgy from the Tenth to the Eighteenth Century. A Historical Introduction and Guide for Students and Musicians*. London/New York: Oxford University Press, 1991. A mass of material brought together into a single volume. A good starting point for a study of later Christian liturgy, though biased toward musical and liturgical practice in England.

1110. Jones, Cheslyn, Geoffrey Wainwright, Edward Yarnold SJ, and Paul Bradshaw, ed. *The Study of Liturgy*. rev. ed., New York: Oxford University Press, 1992. A highly regarded resource for the study of Christian liturgy. Essays written by Anglican, Roman Catholic, Methodist, Reformed and Orthodox scholars. Includes information on contemporary revisions of the liturgy in various Christian denominations. First ed. publ. in New York: OUP, 1978.

1111. Kilmartin, Edward. *Christian Liturgy: Theology and Practice, Vol. 1: Systematic Theology of Liturgy*. Kansas City, MO: Sheed and Ward, 1988.

1112. King, A. A. *Liturgies of the Primatial Sees*. Milwaukee, WI: 1957. Includes Ambrosian, Gallican and Mozarabic rites.

1113. King, A. A. *Liturgies of the Past*. London, New York: Longmans Green; Milwaukee, WI: Bruce Publishing Co., 1958. Includes Beneventan, Ambrosian, Celtic, and English Medieval liturgies.

1114. Stringer, Martin D. "Liturgy and Anthropology: The History of a Relationship." *Worship* 63 (1989): 503-21. After observing that neither anthropology nor sociology have studied Christian worship as such, Stringer reviews what major studies of liturgy there are (Baumstock, Dix, Taft, Kavanagh), then discusses questions concerning liturgy to which anthropology and other disciplines might provide answers: what happens in worship, what meanings might it have, how can the non-verbal, experiential aspects of worship be analyzed?

1115. Taft, Robert. *Beyond East and West: Problems in Liturgical Understanding*. NPM Studies in Church Music and Liturgy, Washington, DC: Pastoral Press, 1984.

1116. Taft, Robert. *The Liturgy of the Hours in East and West: The Origins of the Divine Office and Its Meaning for Today*. Collegeville, MN: Liturgical Press, 1986. A study of the Daily Hours in the Armenian, Assyro-Chandean, West-Syrian and Maronite, Coptic, Ethiopian, Byzantine, Latin, and early Protestant liturgies. Extensive bibliographies on each.

1117. Van Olst, Ernst H. *The Bible and Liturgy*. Grand Rapids, MI: Eerdmans, 1991.

1118. Wegman, Herman. *Christian Worship in East and West: A Study Guide to Liturgical History*. Gordon W. Lathrop, transl. New York: Pueblo Press, 1985. German original, 1976.

EARLY LITURGY: STUDIES

1119. Baldovin, John F. *Liturgy in Ancient Jerusalem*. Bramcote, Nottingham: Grove Books Ltd., 1989. An examination of the Christian liturgy in Jerusalem from 312 (the conversion of Constantine) to 638 (the Islamic conquest).

1120. Bastiaensen, Antoon A.R. "Psalmi, Hymni, and Cantica in Early Jewish-Christian Tradition." In *Studia Patristica*, E. Livingston, ed. Vol. 21. 1989. 15-26. A study of the Greek terms "psalmos," "ode," and "hymnos" in early Christian literature.

1121. Bradshaw, Paul F. *Daily Prayer in the Early Church: A Study of the Origins and Early Development of the Divine Office*. New York: Oxford University Press, 1982. A detailed study of the early texts reveals the Offices to be monastic in origin and their time and content to vary according to time and place.

1122. Bradshaw, Paul F. *Ordination Rites of the Ancient Churches of East and West*. New York: Pueblo, 1990. On the ordination rites of Bishop, Presbyter, Deacon, Deaconess and minor orders throughout the ancient Christian world. Pt. 1: Commentary; Pts 2 & 3: the Texts. A re-evaluation of the earliest documents with their emphasis on teaching and the ministering of discipline.

1123. Bradshaw, Paul F. *The Search for the Origins of Christian Worship: Sources and Methods for the Study of Early Liturgy*. New York: Oxford University Press, 1992. An eminent scholar describes the history, sources, principles, problems and pitfalls of a subject that is now seen to be far more complex than previously thought. A necessary starting place for a study of Christian liturgy from its complex and varied beginnings in the first century through the fourth century.

1124. Cabaniss, Allen. *Pattern in Early Christian Worship*. Macon, GA: Mercer University Press, 1989.

1125. Cullman, Oscar. *Early Christian Worship*. A. Stewart Todd and James B. Torrance, transl. Philadelphia, PA: The Westminster Press, 1978.

1126. Ferguson, Everett. "The Active and Contemplative Lives: The Patristic Interpretation of Some Musical Terms." In *Studia Patristica*, E. Livingstone, ed. Vol. 16. 1985. 15-23. A study of the interpretations of music terms in the Psalms by the 4th century Greek philosopher Didymus, the Blind, of Alexandria.

1127. Jasper, R.C.D. and G.J. Cuming. *Prayers of the Eucharist: Early and Reformed*. 3rd ed., New York, NY: Pueblo, 1987.

1128. Jeffery, Peter. "The Introduction of Psalmody into the Roman Mass by Pope Celestine I (422-432): Reinterpreting a Passage in the *Liber Pontificalis*." *Archiv für Liturgiewissenschaft* 26 (1984): 147-65.

1129. Martin, Ralph P. *Carmen Christi: Philippians ii 5-11 in Recent Interpretation and in the Setting of Early Christian Worship.* Rev. ed., Grand Rapids, MI: Eerdmans, 1983. 1st ed., 1967.

1130. McKinnon, James. "The Fourth-Century Origin of the Gradual." *Early Music History* Vol. 7 (1987): 91-106. The unprecedented wave of enthusiasm for psalmody that swept from east to west during the second half of the fourth century argues in favor of a fourth-century origin for this psalm-based form.

1131. Mowry, L. "Revelation 4-5 and Early Christian Liturgical Usage." *Journal of Biblical Literature* 71 (1952): 75-84.

1132. Spinks, Byron D. *The Sanctus in the Eucharistic Prayer.* Cambridge and New York: Cambridge University Press, 1991. A speculation that the inclusion of the Sanctus in the Eucharistic Prayer took place at different locations and times, and a history of its use since the 4th century.

1133. Talley, Talley J. *The Origins of the Liturgical Year.* New York: Pueblo Publishing Co., 1986. An new appraisal, based on a study of ancient documents, of the varied early liturgies of Easter, Christmas, and Lent, and how they evolved.

JUDAISM AND CHRISTIAN ANTIQUITY

1134. Avenary, Hanoch. "Formal Structure of Psalms and Canticles in Early Jewish and Christian Chant." *Musica Disciplina* 7 (1953): 1 ff. Comparison of early Christian psalmody with psalmody as described in the Thalmud leaves the answers to most questions about the relationship between the two largely conjectural.

1135. Avenary, Hanoch. *Studies in the Hebrew, Syrian and Greek Liturgical Recitative.* Tel Aviv: Israel Music Institute, 1963. A study of the stages of the development, notation, musical styles and interrelationship of these branches of religious chant.

1136. Avenary, Hanoch. "Reflections on the Origins of the Alleluia-Jubilus." *Orbis Musicae. Tel-Aviv University,* 6 (1978): 34-42. The Jubilus of the Alleluia has no Jewish equivalent; it is a formalization of early Christian visionary glossolalia.

1137. Avenary, Hanoch. "Contacts between Church and Synagogue Music." In *Proceedings of the World Congress on Jewish Music, Jerusalem, 1978,* J. Cohen, ed. Tel Aviv: The Institute for the Translation of Hebrew Literature, 1982. 89-106.

1138. Bockmåhl, Markus. "The Trumpet Shall Sound: Shofar Symbolism and its Reception in Early Christianity." In *Templum Amicitiae,* W. Horbury, ed.

1991. 199-225. After surveying the liturgical and symbolic role of the shofar in ancient Judaism, the author attempts to account for the lack of liturgical function for the shofar in early Christianity through a study of Patristic apologetic and philosophical writings.

1139. Buchanan, George. "Worship, Feasts, and Ceremonies in the Early Jewish-Christian Church." *NTS* 26 (1980): 279-297.

1140. Cohen, Judith, ed. *Proceedings of the World Congress on Jewish Music Jerusalem 1978*. Tel Aviv, Israel: Institute for Translation of Hebrew Literature, 1982. Summaries and abstracts of several dozen papers including many on Jewish and Christian chant.

1141. Di Sante, Carmine. *Jewish Prayer: The Origins of Christian Liturgy*. Matthew J. O'Connell, transl. New York: Paulist Press, 1991.

1142. Fellerer, K.G. "Jewish Elements in Pre-Gregorian Chants." In *Proceedings of the World Congress on Jewish Music, Jerusalem 1978*, J. Cohen, ed. Tel Aviv: The Institute for the Translation of Hebrew Literature, 1982. 115-118.

1143. Fisher, Eugene J. *The Jewish Roots of Christian Liturgy*. New York: Paulist Press, 1990.

1144. Flusser, D. "Jewish Roots of the Liturgical Trishagion." In *Immanuel*, 3. 1973-4. 37 ff.

1145. Foley, Edward. "The Cantor in Historical Perspective." *Worship* 56 (1982): 194-213. In both the Judaism and the Christianity of the first century CE, group prayer was lead by a member of the congregation chosen more for his leadership than his musical abilities. Only as the religious traditions began to distinguish between the spoken and the sung, with the latter taking on ever-increasing complexity, were singing duties assigned to the professional singer— the hazzan and the cantor. By the late 4th century, the singing had taken precedence over what was being sung, a situation commented on with alarm by Augustine. The author urges a return to the tradition of the prayer leader.

1146. Gerson-Kiwi, Edith. *Migrations and Mutations of the Music in East and West: Selected Writings*. Tel Aviv: Tel Aviv University, 1980. See Part B: Sacred Chant in Cult and Religion (on the relationship of early Jewish and Christian Chant).

1147. Gerson-Kiwi, Edith, Chairman. "Mediterranean Studies: Chant Traditions and Liturgy." In *IMS12, 1977*, 1981. 402-435.

1148. Pressacco, Gilberto. "Musical Traces of Markan Traditions in the Mediterranean Area." *Orbis Musicae* 11 (1993/94): 7-72. A search through historical documents from the Old Testament and Philo to the 16th century for references to Markan communities around the Mediterranean that had dance as a common cultural feature and that persisted until the 17th century.

1149. Smith, J. A. "The Ancient Synagogue, the Early Church and Singing." *Music and Letters* 65 (1984): 1-16. Contrary to received opinion, current research indicates that psalm-singing was not part of the synagogue service during the first century and that the Jewish private religious assembly was the source of such singing for the early Christians.

1150. Smith, J. A. "First-Century Christian Singing and its Relationship to Contemporary Jewish Religious Song." *Music and Letters* 75, 1 (1994): 1-15. Due to the ambiguities in both Biblical and extra-Biblical literature and to questions about the sources of this literature, what Christians sang during the first century cannot be verified. All that can be said with certainty is that by some early date Christians sang Jewish hymns.

1151. Vecchi, Giuseppe. "Music, Liturgy, Hebrew Psalmody, and the Bolognese Historians." In *IMS12, 1977*, 1981. 428-430. A comment on the contributions that scholars Ercole Bottrigari and Padre Martini made to the study of Hebrew liturgical psalmody.

1152. Werner, Eric. *The Sacred Bridge. The Interdependence of Liturgy and Music in Synagogue and Church during the First Millennium [I]*. New York: Da Capo, 1959/repr. 1979. Eighteen essays on Jewish and Christian music and liturgy and their interdependence up to the 10th century.

1153. Werner, Eric. *Three Ages of Musical Thought*. New York: Da Capo, 1981. Essays on Judaica, the Renaissance, and Mendelssohn. 'Judaica' includes 11 essays on Jewish and early Christian music and Greek and Arab philosophies of music.

1154. Werner, Eric. "The Hebrew Background of the Te Deum." *Eretz-Isra'el* Vol. 16 (H. Orlinsky volume) (1982). The Te Deum is a prototype of early non-metrical hymns (or 'spiritual songs' as in Eph. 5:19). It consists of distinct elements from biblical and post-biblical Jewish texts, early Christology, and a militancy reflective of Roman imperialism. Werner takes each segment and shows its origin. The tune also shows strong resemblance to a melody/mode common during the first four centuries CE—a time prior to Ambrose and Augustine and the divorce of Christianity from its Jewish origins.

1155. Werner, Eric. *The Sacred Bridge. The Interdependence of Liturgy and Music in Synagogue and Church during the First Millennium [II]*. Vol. II. New York: KTAV Publishing House, Inc., 1984. Dated material of often questionable scholarship. The reviews highlight the changes that have taken place in early Christian scholarship in the last few decades. See Peter Jeffery in *Jewish Quarterly Review* 77: 283-98; Paul F. Bradshaw in *Second Century—A Journal of Early Christian Studies*. Vol. 6, No. 4: 249-252; Theodore Karp, Melos Velimirovic, and Richard Sarason in *Musica Judaica* 8, 1 (1985-86): 887-94.

1156. Werner, Eric. "Music and Religion in Greece, Rome and Byzantium." In *Encyclopedia of Religion*, Mircea Eliade, ed. Vol. 10. 1987. 204-209.

1157. Wilkinson, John. "Jewish Influences on the Early Christian Rite of Jerusalem." *Muséon* 92 (1979): 347-359.

MUSIC OF CHRISTIAN ANTIQUITY

1158. Fenwick, John R. K. *The Anaphoras of St. Basil and Saint James: An Investigation into their Common Origin*. Orientalia Christiana Analecta, 240. Rome: Pontificum Institutum Orientale, 1992. A study of the Lord's Supper in the Rite of Jerusalem.

1159. Ferguson, Everett. "Psalm-Singing at the Eucharist: A Liturgical Controversy in the Fourth Century." *Austin Seminary Bulletin* 98 (1983): 52-77.

1160. Foley, Edward. *Foundations of Christian Music: The Music of Pre-Constantinian Christianity*. Bramcote: Grove, 1992. A five-part overview of Christian music during the first three centuries CE.

1161. Hannick, Christian. "Christian Church, Music of the Early." In *Grove 6*, Vol. 4. 1980. 363-71.

1162. Hollemann, A.W. "The Oxyrhynchus Papyrus 1786 and the Relationship between Ancient Greek and Early Christian Music." *Vigiliae Christianae* 26, 1/March (1972): 1-17. The papyrus deliberately demonstrates the inadequacy of Greek notation, which is designed to record metric quantity, in notating the more fluid melodies of early Christian hymnody.

1163. Jeffery, Peter. "Lost Melodies of the Rite of Jerusalem, and Partial Survivals in the Byzantine and Latin Chant Repertoires." *The Seventeenth International Byzantine Congress 1986: Abstracts of Short Papers* (1986): 154-55. Washington, DC: US National Committee for Byzantine Studies

1164. Jeffery, Peter. "The Formation of the Earliest Christian Chant Traditions: Four Processes That Shaped the Texts." *PRISM: Yale Institute of Sacred Music, Worship and the Arts* 14, December (1990): 10-13. The processes are the selection of the source text, text modification, the emergence of chant collections, and the work of reformers and standardizers.

1165. Jeffery, Peter. "The Lost Chant Tradition of Early Christian Jerusalem: Some Possible Melodic Survivals in the Byzantine and Latin Chant Repertories." In *Studies in Medieval and Early Modern Music*, Iain Fenlon, ed. Vol. 11. Cambridgeshire; New York: Cambridge University Press, 1992. 151-190.

1166. Jeffrey, Peter. "The Earliest Christian Chant Repertory Recovered: The Georgian Witnesses to Jerusalem Chant." *JAMS* 47, 1 (1994): 1-38. Newly available sources of the Georgian liturgy document the Jerusalem rite as using the Greek language from the 4th to the 12th century, the first repertory committed to writing and the first to document the eight-mode system. These sources offer many avenues to showing how the Jerusalem repertory influenced Gregorian, Latin, Syriac, and Armenian rites.

1167. Levy, Kenneth. "Mediterranean Musical Liturgies: The Quest for Origins." In *IMS12, 1977*, 1981. 413-414. A plea that the origins of and relationships between the six complete musical liturgies preserved from the Middle Ages—the Gregorian-Roman, Roman, Milanese, Mozarabic, Byzantine-Greek and the later Slavonic—and the written fragmentary remains of other early repertories—the Beneventan of South Italy, a tradition of North Italy, the Celtic and Gallican of Northern Europe, and the Armenian, Georgian and Ethiopic of the East—be studied more fully.

1168. McKinnon, James. "Christian Antiquity." In *Antiquity and the Middle Ages From Ancient Greece to the 15th Century*, James McKinnon, ed. Music and Society, Englewood Cliffs, NJ: Prentice Hall, 1990. 68-87.

1169. McKinnon, James. "Desert Monasticism and the Later Fourth-Century Psalmodic Movement." *Music and Letters* 75, 4 (1994): 505-521. A study of the development of psalmody from the continuous form sung in desert and Eastern monastic Offices to relatively austere melodies, to the the more elaborate modal hymns sung in a Western center such as 4th-century Milan.

1170. Quasten, Johannes. "The Liturgical Singing of Women in Christian Antiquity." *The Catholic Historical Review* 27 (1941): 149 ff.

1171. Quasten, Johannes. *Music and Worship in Pagan and Christian Antiquity.* 2nd ed., Boniface Ramsey, O.P., transl. NPM Studies in Church Music and Liturgy, Washington, DC: National Association of Pastoral Musicians, 1973/ repr. 1983. Orig. ed. publ. in German, 1929; 2nd ed. 1973. An important study, from mostly Greek sources, of early Christian worship in the context of Greek and Roman practices.

17

The Church of Rome

DICTIONARIES AND ENCYCLOPEDIAS

1172. Carroll, Joseph Robert. *Compendium of Liturgical Music Terms*. Toledo, OH: Gregorian Institute of America, 1964.

1173. Fink, Peter, ed. *The New Dictionary of Sacramental Worship*. Collegeville, MN: Liturgical Press, 1990. On Roman Catholic liturgy, compiled in the spirit of the reforms of Vatican II.

1174. McDonald, William J. et al., ed. *The New Catholic Encyclopedia*. 18 vols. New York: McGraw Hill Book Company, 1967-1989. Includes three supplements, from 1967 to 1989. See entries under Sacramentaries; Requiem Mass, Liturgy of; Liturgy (Latin Rite); Requiem Mass, Music of; Music. See also the names of the various rites.

LITURGY

1175. "[Liturgical Books]." In *Grove 6*, 1980. See "Antiphoner," "Breviary," "Missal," "Psalter," "Kyriale," and "Tonary."

1176. "[Liturgy of the Roman Rite]." In *Grove 6*, 1980. See "Liturgy and liturgical books", "Divine Office," "Little Hours," "Liturgy of the Hours," and "Ordo cantus missae.".

1177. Baltzer, Rebecca A. "The Geography of the Liturgy at Notre-Dame of Paris." In *Plainsong in the Age of Polyphony*, Thomas Forrest Kelly, ed. Cambridge Studies in Performance Practice, Cambridge, England; New York: Cambridge University Press, 1992.

1178. Crocker, Richard. "Liturgical Materials of Roman Chant." In *NOHM II*, 1990. 111-145.

1179. Dyer, Joseph. "Psalmody and the Roman Mass." *Studies in Music from the University of Western Ontario* Vol. 10 (1987): 1-24.

1180. Jeffery, Peter. *Chant, Liturgy, and Culture*. NPM Studies in Church Music and Liturgy, Washington, DC: Pastoral Press, 1992.

1181. Jungmann, Joseph A. *The Mass of the Roman Rite: Its Origins and Development*. 2 vols. Francis A. Brunner, transl. Westminster, MD: Christian Classics, 1951/repr. 1955, 1986. For many years, an unsurpassed classic.

1182. King, Archdale Arthur. *The Liturgy of the Roman Church*. London: Longmans, Green and Co.; Milwaukee, WI: Bruce Publishing Co., 1957.

1183. Sandon, Nick, ed. *The Octave of the Nativity: Essays and Notes on Ten Liturgical Reconstructions for Christmas*. London: British Broadcasting Corporation, 1984. A reconstruction of the eucharistic celebration as it might have been conducted at ten different churches between 902 and 1656.

1184. Vogel, Cyrille. *Medieval Liturgy: An Introduction to the Sources*. Rev. ed., William G. Storey and Niels Krogh Rasmussen, transl. National Association of Pastoral Musicians Studies in Church Music and Liturgy, Washington, DC: Pastoral Press, 1986. 2nd French edition, 1981. An introduction to the basic documents of the Latin liturgy by a leading liturgical scholar.

MUSIC: HISTORIES AND STUDIES

1185. Fellerer, Karl Gustav. *The History of Catholic Music*. Francis A. Brunner, transl. Westport, CT: Greenwood Press, 1961/repr. 1979.

1186. Jungmann, Josef A. *The Mass: An Historical, Theological, and Pastoral Survey*. Collegeville, MN: Liturgical Press, 1976.

1187. McKenna, Edward. "Music, Styles of Liturgical." In *The New Dictionary of Sacramental Worship*, Fink, ed. 1990. 870-881.

1188. Miller, Ronald Sherman. *The Repertory of Ms MR8: A Medieval Pauline Antiphoner Plus a Portfolio of Compositions*. Ph.D. dissertation, UC, Santa Barbara, 1992. A study of the only surviving complete, one-volume Antiphoner of the Pauline order in Hungary. The order was founded in 1215. The ms. dates from the late 15th century.

1189. Nemmers, Erwin E. *Twenty Centuries of Catholic Church Music*. Westport, CT: Greenwood, 1949/repr. 1978. 1949 ed. Milwaukee: Bruce.

1190. Pruett, James W. "Requiem mass." In *Grove 6*, Vol. 15. 1980. 751-755.

1191. Sanders, Ernest H., et al. "Motet." In *Grove 6*, Vol. 12. 1980. 617-47. An excellent concise history of the motet of the Middle Ages, Renaissance, Baroque, and after 1750.

1192. Sparksman, Brian Joseph. *The Minister of Music in the Western Church: A Canonical-historical Study.* J.C.D. thesis, Catholic University of America, 1980/1985.

1193. Weakland, Rembert G., O.S.B., et al. "Music." In *New Catholic Encyclopedia*, William McDonald, ed. Vol. 10. New York 1967. 88-139.

PHILOSOPHIES AND THEOLOGIES OF MUSIC

1194. "[Western Catholic Church Theologians]." In *Grove 6*, 1980. See "Ambrose," "Augustine of Hippo," and "Isidore of Seville."

1195. Augustine, St. *On Music: De Musica.* R. C. Taliaferro, transl. The Fathers of the Church, Vol. 2. New York: Cima Publishing Company, 1947. 153-379.

1196. Caldwell, John. "The 'De Institutione Arithmetica' and the 'De Institutione Musica.'" In *Boethius. His Life, Thought and Influence*, Oxford: Basil Blackwell, 1981. 135-154. A study of what Boethius owed to past writers, especially Nicomachus and Ptolemy, as well as of what was distinctively Boethian: a personal conviction that music has the power to elevate or corrupt. Chap. 2 of 'Musica' contains the famous three-fold division of music into *musica mundana, musica humana,* and *musica instrumentalis*, the latter two referring not to vocal and instrumental music, but to music of the soul and of the body.

1197. Cole, Basil. "Music and Spirituality." *The Homiletic and Pastoral Review* 95, 8 (1995). A theology of music according to Thomas Acquinas: God participates in the world through the beautiful. Music can raise one's thoughts to the worship of God through the three properties of beauty: clarity, order and proportion, and splendor of form. Beauty—and the beautiful in music—also promote unity, contemplation, and devotion.

1198. Forman, Robert J. "Augustine's Music: 'Keys' to the Logos." In *Augustine on Music: An Interdisciplinary Collection of Essays*, Richard La Croix, ed. Studies in the History and Interpretation of Music, Lewiston, NY: E. Mellen Press, 1988. 17-27.

1199. LaCroix, Richard, ed. *Augustine on Music: An Interdisciplinary Collection of Essays.* Studies in the History and Interpretation of Music, Lewiston, NY: E. Mellen Press, 1988.

1200. Portnoy, Julius. *The Philosopher and Music: A Historical Outline.* New York: Da Capo Press, 1955/repr. 1980. Beginning with its origins in Greek concepts, Portnoy examines what music was to Medieval man.

1201. Slocum, Kay Brainerd. *'Speculum Musicae': Jacques de Liege and the Medieval Vision of God.* Ph.D. dissertation, Kent State University, 1987. *Speculum Musicae* is a university-schooled, philosophical argument for the retention of traditional, modal rhythms, based as they are on the sacred and symbolic number three.

1202. Walhout, Donald. "Augustine on the Transcendent in Music." *Philosophy and Theology* 3, Spring (1989): 283-292. Basing his argument on Augustine's *De Musica*, the author focuses on the aspect of music that can bring the listener to a point of union with transcendent reality.

18

Western European Plainchant

EASTERN AND WESTERN PLAINCHANT

1203. Dubowshik, Rosemary. *A Chant for Feasts of the Holy Cross in Jerusalem, Byzantium, and Medieval Europe.* Ph.D. diss., Princeton University, 1993. A tracing of the Latin antiphon "Crucem tuam adoramus domine" from its Greek origins through Georgian, Armenian, Syrian, Coptic, Ethiopian versions, and five distinct Latin recensions.

1204. Levy, Kenneth. "Plainchant: Chant in East and West." In *Grove 6*, Vol. 15. 1980. 800-805. See for extensive bibliography.

WESTERN PLAINCHANT: GENERAL REFERENCES

1205. Emerson, John A. "Plainchant: Western Plainchant." In *Grove 6*, Vol. 15. 1980. 805-832. See for extensive bibliography.

1206. Hiley, David. "Plainchant Transfigured: Innovation and Reformation through the Ages." In *Antiquity and the Middle Ages*, Englewood Cliffs, NJ: Prentice Hall, 1990. 120-142.

1207. Hiley, David. "Chant." In *Performance Practice: Music before 1600*, Howard Mayer Brown and Stanley Sadie, ed. The Norton/Grove Handbooks in Music, New York: W.W. Norton, 1990. 37-54.

1208. Hiley, David. *Western Plainchant: A Handbook.* Oxford: Clarendon Press; New York: Oxford University Press, 1993. An indispensible, up-to-date study of every aspect of the subject. Includes a 65-page bibliography.

1209. Hughes, Andrew. *Medieval Manuscripts for Mass and Office: A Guide to Their Organization and Terminology*. Toronto & Buffalo: University of Toronto Press, 1982. An ordered presentation of a vast amount of material, annotated fully and in great detail.

1210. Nowacki, Edward. "The Syntactical Analysis of Plainchant." In *IMS12, 1977*, 1981. 191-201. Nowacki demonstrates an analytical technique by which chants are classified not by melodic stereotypes or centonate content, but by the underlying syntactical structure of the melody. This method is best able to show the relationship between chants the other methods call unique, free or variant.

1211. Paxton, Frederick S. *Christianizing Death: The Creation of a Ritual Process in Early Medieval Europe*. Ithaca, NY: Cornell University Press, 1990.

1212. Werf, Hendrik van der. *The Emergence of Gregorian Chant: A Comparative Study of Ambrosian, Roman, and Gregorian Chant*. Rochester, NY: H. van der Werf, 1983. Neither Gregorian Chant nor Roman Chant developed from the other; both derived from parent melodies that were not preserved. Although the texts for the Proper and Ordinary were codified during the reign of Charlemagne, the transition from re-improvised melody to fixed melody lasted several centuries thereafter.

GREGORIAN CHANT

1213. [Latin Rites-Gregorian: Music and Liturgy]. In *Grove 6*, 1980. For the music of the Roman rite, see "Gregorian Chant." See also "Rome."

1214. [Later Medieval Music and Techniques]. In *Grove 6*, 1980. See "Processional," "Prosa," "Prosula," "Sequence," "Tract," "Trope," "Lauda Spirituale," "Centonization," "Inflection," and "Responsory."

1215. [Mass Items]. In *Grove 6*, 1980. For an account of the music for individual items in the mass and daily offices, see "Ordinary chants," "Proper chants," "Proper of the time," "Proper of the Saints," as well as "Alleluia," "Agnus Dei," "Benedicamus Domino," "Benedicite," "Benedictus," "Communion," "Credo," "Doxology," "Epistle," "Gloria," "Gospel," "Introit," "Invitatory," "Kyrie Eleison," "Lord's Prayer," and "Offertory." See also "Litany."

1216. [Psalmody; Hymnody]. In *Grove 6*, 1980. For psalmody, see "Psalm," "Antiphonal Psalmody," "Direct Psalmody," "Responsorial Psalmody," and "Antiphon." See also "Hymn."

1217. Atkinson, Charles. "The Earliest Agnus Dei Melody and its Tropes." *JAMS* 30 (1977): 1-19. Through examination of various early collections of Agnus Dei chants, Atkinson argues that the Agnus Dei was performed long before it was written down and that the embellishing verses may be considered trope, as they are frequently designated *tropi* in manuscripts.

1218. Atkinson, charles. "'O amnos tu theu: The Greek Agnus Dei in the Roman Liturgy from the Eighth to the Eleventh Century." *Kirchenmus-ikalisches Jahrbuch* 65 (1981): 7-30.

1219. Binford-Walsh, Hilde Marga. *The Melodic Grammar of Aquitanian Tropes*. Ph.D. diss., Stanford University, 1992. A description of the melodic style of Aquitanian tropes through the application of musico-textual, probabilistic, and statistical analysis to melodies written in neumatic notation.

1220. Bjork, David. "Early Settings of the Kyrie Eleison and the Problem of Genre Definition." *JPMMS* 3 (1980): 40-48. A study of Kyrie settings, composed from the 9th through 11th centuries in Frankish, German, North Italian, Beneventan, and Old Roman regions, shows that Kyrie settings were extremely varied in length and melodic content.

1221. Bjork, David. "The Kyrie Trope." *JAMS* 33 (1980): 1-41. The delineation between Kyries and Kyrie tropes is found mainly in the musical independence of the tropes. Several Kyries from various sources are examined.

1222. Blachly, Alexander. "Some Observations on the "Germanic" Plainchant Tradition." *Current Musicology*. 45-47 (1990): 85-118. Germany retained neumatic notation after the adoption of staff notation in the rest of Europe. Dating from the 9th century, German chant style was a major branch of Gregorian tradition; its relationship to other contempory styles has yet to be determined.

1223. Boyce, James. *Cantica Carmelitana: The Chants of the Carmelite Office*. Ph.D. diss., New York University, 1985.

1224. Boyce, James. "The Medieval Carmelite Office Tradition." *Acta Musicologica* 62, 2-3 (1990): 119-151. A description of the detailed organization of early 14th through early 15th Carmelite feasts, varied sources of feasts, ways of combining liturgy and theology, and methods of preserving and utilizing treasured chant melodies. Includes lists of feasts, extant mss. and transcriptions.

1225. Brooks-Leonard, John Kenneth. *Easter Vespers in Early Medieval Rome: A Critical Edition and Study*. Ph.D. diss., University of Notre Dame, 1988. A historical, liturgical analysis of the Easter Vespers and a reconstruction of the rubrics, texts, and music of the service based on the oldest extant sources and arranged in the order of service.

1226. Cardine, Eugéne. *An Overview of Gregorian Chant: XVI of Etudes Gregoriennes*. From Solesmes about the Chant, Orleans, MA: Paraclete Press, 1992.

1227. Chen, Matthew Y. "Toward a Grammar of Singing: Tune-Text Association in Gregorian Chant." *Music Perception* 1 (1983): 84-122.

1228. Crocker, Richard. "The Troping Hypothesis." *MQ* 52 (1966): 183-203. Crocker posits that tropes, both melody and text, are new compositions and are found only in the Introit, Offertory, Communion, Gloria, and Sanctus. The Kyrie and Agnus Dei present a problem in that the 'official' 9th-10th century text cannot be determined from the trope. Alleluia sequentiae are also distinguished from tropes.

1229. Crocker, Richard. *The Early Medieval Sequence.* Berkeley: University of California Press, 1977. A thorough study, with transcriptions, of the 33 sequences of *Liber Hymnorum* by the 9th-century monk of St. Gall, Notker Balbulus.

1230. Crocker, Richard. "Matins Antiphons at St. Denis." *JAMS* 39, 3 (1986): 441-490. When the repertories are compared, the Matins Antiphons at St. Denis shows little influence of Gregorian or Old Roman chant.

1231. Crocker, Richard. "Medieval Chant." In *NOHM II*, 1990. 225-309.

1232. Crocker, Richard. "Chants of Roman Office." In *NOHM II*, 1990. 146-173.

1233. Crocker, Richard. "Chants of Roman Mass." In *NOHM II*, 1990. 174-222.

1234. Dobszay, László. "Plainchant in Medieval Hungary." *JPMMS* 13 (1990): 49-82. The process of selecting, completing, and distributing Latin chant in Hungary was begun in the 11th century. Dobszay studies the repertory and liturgy, notation and mss., and circumstances for Latin chant in Hungary. With biblio., transcriptions, and photos from chant mss.

1235. Dyer, Joseph. "The Offertory Chant of the Roman Liturgy and its Musical Form." *Studi Musicali* 11 (1982): 3-30.

1236. Dyer, Joseph. "Monastic Psalmody of the Middle Ages." *Revue Bénédictine* 99 (1989): 41-74.

1237. Dyer, Joseph. "The Singing of Psalms in the Early-Medieval Office." *Speculum* 64, July (1989): 535-578.

1238. Evans, P. *The Early Trope Repertory of Saint Martial de Limoges.* Princeton, NJ: Princeton University Press, 1970. Medieval mss. use the term 'tropus' to denote only 1) additions to the antiphonal chants of the Proper of the Mass and 2) additions to the chants of the Ordinary. This study and transcription of the earliest fully transcribable St. Martial troper, Paris 1121, from the early 11th century, covers the meaning and historical position of the tropes, the tropers themselves, trope texts, and musical structure.

1239. Falconer, Keith Andrew. *Some Early Tropes to the Gloria.* Ph.D. diss., Princeton University, 1989. Tropes to the Gloria are unusually long, spread widely among the sources, and widely divergent. Some date as early as the 9th century and are closest to Gallican chant in style.

1240. Fassler, Margot. "The Office of the Cantor in Early Western Monastic Rules and Customaries: A Preliminary Investigation." *Early Music History* Vol. 5 (1985): 29-52. Fassler traces the ascent of the cantor, through the 6th to the 11th centuries, to director of all aspects of music-making, and his eventual decline, by the end of the 11th century, when the offices of cantor and librarian became fused into a single office embracing the duties of both.

1241. Fassler, Margot. "The Role of the Parisian Sequence in the Evolution of Notre-Dame." *Speculum* 62, Apr. (1987): 345-374.

1242. Fassler, Margot. *Gothic Song: Victorine Sequences and Augustinian Reform in Twelfth-Century Paris.* New York, NY: Cambridge Univerisity Press, 1993. A richly documented survey of late 12th-century sequence, a devotional form championed at the Abbey of St. Victor in Paris.

1243. Flynn, William. *Paris, Bibliotheque de L'Arsenal, MS 1169: The Hermeneutics of Eleventh-century Burgundian Tropes and their Implications for Liturgical Theology.* Ph.D. diss., Duke University, 1992. Tropes served important pedagogical goals by teaching grammar and rhetoric, scriptural exegesis, and musical styles and verse forms. They supported widely held hermeneutic norms, evoked specific affective responses to the liturgical celebration, and supported a liturgical way of 'reading' texts.

1244. Gebr, Adela. *The Role of the Franciscans in the Development of Early Sacred and Secular Monophony.* Ph.D. diss., USC, 1983. The Franciscans enriched 13th-century liturgical monophony with a vast repertory of Hymns and Sequences, as well as with over 770 rhymed offices and a large repertory of laude. Their constant traveling stimulated the exchange, development and propagation of new ideas concerning many genres and their widespread dissemination.

1245. Gradenwitz, Peter. "Mediterranean Liturgy in Western Art Music." In *IMS12, 1977,* 1981. 405-407.

1246. Gümpel, Karl-Werner. "Cantus Eugenianus-Cantus Melodicus." In *IMS12, 1977,* 1981. 407-413. A description of a chant tradition—a version of Gregorian Chant embellished by certain melodic and rhythmic ornamentations— at the Cathedral of Toledo, Spain, from 1448 to 1851.

1247. Haller, Robert B. *Early Dominican Mass Chants: A Witness to Thirteenth Century Chant Style.* Ph.D. diss., Catholic University of America, 1986. The first study of the earliest known sources of Dominican chant, as it existed prior to the reform of Humbert of Romans in 1256.

1248. Halmo, Joan. *Medieval Office Antiphons for the Paschal Triduum-Easter.* Ph.D. diss., The Catholic University of America, 1993. A study of 142 antiphons in 12 mss. from late 10th to late 13th centuries, with 30 examined closely as to modal and melodic characteristics, variant readings, text sources of psalms in relation to anthphons, and liturgical and spiritual context.

1249. Herbert, R. "Singer, Text, and Song." *Parabola* 14, 4 (1989): 17-23. On the relationship of singer, text, and song in Gregorian chant.

1250. Hiley, David. "Rouen, Bibliotheque-Municipale, MS-249 (A.280) and the Early Paris Repertory of Ordinary of Mass Chants and Sequences." *Music and Letters* 70, 4 (1989): 467-482.

1251. Hughes, Andrew. "Modal Order and Disorder in the Rhymed Office." *Musica Disciplina* 37 (1983): 29-52. An attempt to discern order in the texts and chants for thousands of Proper offices, compiled or composed between the 10th and 16th centuries. Promising approaches involve grouping chants by mode and determining how various orderings and shufflings of chant are distributed in all the mss. of a single office.

1252. Jacobsson, Ritva, ed. *Pax et Sapientia: Studies in Text and Music of Liturgical Tropes and Sequences in Memory of Gordon Anderson.* Stockholm, Sweden: Almqvist & Wiksell International, 1986.

1253. Johnsen, P. "Integrative Devices in Gregorian Chant." *American Journal of Semiotics* 8, 3 (1991): 83-105.

1254. Johnstone, John Gearey. *The Offertory Trope: Origins, Transmission, and Function.* Ph.D. diss., The Ohio State University, 1984. This study shows that Offertory tropes, which were wide spread during the 9th and 10th centuries, paralleled their base chants in syntax and structure. Many paraphrase the texts of the chants they introduce, thereby queuing their performance.

1255. Kelly, Thomas Forrest. "Introducing the Gloria in Excelsis." *JAMS* 37 (1984): 479-506. Tropes introducing the Gloria developed along a restricted line when limited to those occasions when only a bishop could intone the Gloria and when used only at Easter. When these restrictions relaxed, introductory trope composition moved to a festival rather than a ceremonial focus and was widely cultivated until the tradition of troping died out.

1256. Lee, Katharine W. *Chant: The Origins, Form, Practice, and Healing Power of Gregorian Chant.* New York: Bell Tower, 1994.

1257. McKinnon, James. "The Patristic Jubilus and the Alleluia of the Mass." In *IMS Study Group 'Cantus Planus...Hungary...1988*, Budapest: Hungarian Academy of Sciences Institute for Musicology, 1990. 61-70.

1258. McKinnon, James. "The Emergence of Gregorian Chant in the Carolingian Era." In *Antiquity and the Middle Ages from Ancient Greece to the Fifteenth Century*, James McKinnon, ed. Englewood, NJ: Prentice Hall, 1990. 88-119.

1259. McKinnon, James. "The Eighth-century Frankish-Roman Communion Cycle." *JAMS* 45, 2 (1992): 179-228. McKinnon shows that the Communion texts for the entire temporale reveal thematic and symmetrical patterns, which are the result of revision and composition that began in the Roman schola cantorum of the later 7th century and concluded with the participation of the Franks. He also shows that the 10 Communion chants being studied had melodies that pre-existed as antiphons and that three of them were Frankish additions to the liturgy.

1260. Metzinger, Joseph Paul. *The Liturgical Function of the Entrance Song: An Examination of the Introits and Introit Tropes of the Manuscript Piacenza, Archivio Capitolare, 65*. D.M.A., The Catholic University of America, 1993. A study of the function, text, and music of early Introits and Introit tropes, and a comparison of the 11th-century trope melodies and texts with those of the much earlier Introits.

1261. Nowacki, Edward. "The Gregorian Office Antiphons and the Comparative Method." *Journal of Musicology* 4 (1985): 243-75. The author begins by repeating the commonly held assumption that, based on simple comparison, only 60% of Old Roman and Frankish office antiphon texts share the same melody. To refine the tools of comparison, the author lays out four stages in the chronological development of the Divine Office and proposes a breach in the tradition of melody/text association to account for the non-correspondence during the years that predate the adoption of Gregorian chant by the Franks. He then argues that Old Roman mss. do not transmit fixed works, but provide information concerning desired melodic assignment and examples illustrating how melodies of a specified type go. Even texts with the same melodic assignment should not be considered variants of the same work, but only variants of the same melody type, and thus equal to all other versions of that type.

1262. Olexy, Ronald Thomas. *The Responsories in the 11th-century Aquitanian Antiphonal: Toledo, Bibl. Cap. 44.2**. Ph.D. diss., The Catholic University of America, 1980. Digital technology is used to sort and order the 941 responsories of this antiphonal.

1263. Pieper, Brenda K. *A Study of Marian Worship: The Influence of Marian Devotion upon Music in the Middle Ages and Renaissance*. M.M. thesis, Baylor University, 1990.

1264. Reier, Ellen Jane. *The Introit Trope Repertory at Nevers: Mss Paris B.N. Lat. 9449 and Paris B.N. N.A. Lat. 1235*. Ph.D. diss., U.C., Berkeley, 1981. Introit tropes from two non-Aquitanian mss., though dating from the mid-11th century and the 12th century, descend from what is probably the earliest tradition of Proper trope composition. When compared to Aquitanian melodies for the same trope text, the Nevers melodies show stronger modal and structural differences with respect to Gregorian style.

1265. Ridder, R. Todd. *Musical and Theological Patterns Involved in the Transmission of Mass Chants for the Five Oldest Marian Feasts: An Examination of Proper Chants and Tropes in a Select Group of Medieval Manuscripts*. Ph.D. diss., The Catholic University of America, 1993. A study of Marian mass propers and tropes in 49 sources from the 9th to 14th centuries reveals important currents in liturgico-musical development and changes in the medieval church's reflection on the meaning of Mary.

1266. Roederer, Charlotte. *Eleventh-century* Aquitanian *Chant: Studies Relating to a Local Repertory Processional Antiphons*. Ph.D. diss., Yale University, 1971.

1267. Schneider, Marius. "On Gregorian Chant and the Human Voice." *The World of Music* 24, 3 (1982): 3-22. An exploration of psalmody and mass chants, their steadfast yet restrained construction and performance, a brief look at modes, and a search for transcendence through the voice, whether speaking or chanting, as an instrument of power, sacrifice and praise.

1268. Sevestre, Nicole. "The Aquitanian Tropes of the Easter Introit: A Musical Analysis." *Journal of Plainsong and Medieval Music* 3 (1980): 26-40. This repertory is unoriginal, restricted, and formulaic, a reworking of traditional material, lacking in conviction and organization. It also does not correspond to pure Gregorian formulas.

1269. Sherr, Richard. "The Performance of Chant in the Renaissance and its Interactions with Polyphony." In *Plainsong in the Age of Polyphony*, Thomas Forrest Kelly, ed. Cambridge Studies in Performance Practice, Cambridge, England; New York: Cambridge University Press, 1992. 178-208.

1270. Smith, F. J. "Some Aspects of Mediaeval Music Theory and Praxis: The Ordo Minorum and its Place in Cultural History." In *Franciscan Studies*, S. F. Brown, ed. Vol. 32. 1972. 187-202. Smith documents the significant role of Franciscan friars in the history, theory and composition of Medieval sacred music.

1271. Stapert, Calvin. "Gregorian Chant and the Power of Emptiness." In *Faith Seeking Understanding: Learning and the Catholic Tradition: Selected Papers...*, George C. Berthold, ed. Manchester, NH: Saint Anselm College Press, 1991. 107-115. Stapert reflects on the role of Gregorian Chant in furthering Christian growth as it relates to the paradox of riches arising from 'emptiness.'

1272. Steiner, Ruth. "The Music for a Cluny Office of Saint Benedict." In *Monasticism and the Arts*, Timothy Verdon et al., ed. Syracuse, NY: Syracuse University Press, 1984. 81-113. A reflection on the role of musical texts and compositions, especially the chanting of the Hours, in shaping monastic imagination in 11th-century Europe.

1273. Van Deusen, Nancy. *Music at Nevers Cathedral: Principal Sources of Mediaeval Chant*. Institute of Mediaeval Music, Vol. 30. Henryville, Quebec: Institute of Mediaeval Music, 1980.

1274. Waddell, Chrysogonus, OCSO. "The Vidi Aquam and the Easter Morning Procession: Pages from the Prayerbook of a Fifteenth-Century Cistercian Nun." *Liturgy O.C.S.O.* 21, 3 (1987): 3-56.

CHANT RHYTHM AND PERFORMANCE

1275. Belan, William Lee. *The Conducting of Gregorian Chant: A Study of Chironomy as Applied to the Semiology of Neumatic Notation, With Performance Editions of Five Selected Examples of Gregorian Chant*. D.M.A. Thesis, University of Oklahoma, 1984. This study provides guidelines for the interpretation of chant notation and shows how to conduct chant according to Solesmes practice.

1276. Brunner, Lance W. "The Performance of Plainchant." *Early Music* Vol. 10 (1982): 317-328. Recent re-examinations of original chant notation indicate fresh departures from the Solesmes method. One is Cardine's suggestion of slight agogic lengthenings. Another is the performances of Schola Antiqua.

1277. Cardine, Eugene. *Is Gregorian Chant Measured Music?* Solesmes: Abbaye Saint-Pierre, 1964.

1278. Cardine, Eugene. *Gregorian Semiology*. Robert M. Fowels, transl. Solesmes: Abbaye Saint-Pierre de Solesmes, 1982. French orig., 1970. Extensive, detailed discussion of new ways of considering chant rhythm. One possibility: Chant neumes have two meanings: melodic and expressive. Three different forms of the same neume may indicate three different beamings of the same notes and, hence, three different phrasings.

1279. Carroll, Joseph Robert. *A Guide to Gelineau Psalmody: Musical Settings, Preparing the Choir, the Use of the Psalms, Analyses of Variations of the Psalms, Conducting Psalm Festivals*. Toledo, OH: Gregorian Institute of America, 1965.

1280. Fassler, Margot. "Accent, Meter, and Rhythm in Medieval Treatises 'De Rithmis.'" *Journal of Musicology* 5 (1987): 164-190.

1281. Huglo, Michael. "Notated Performance Practices in Parisian Chant Manuscripts of the Thirteenth Century." In *Plainsong in the Age of Polyphony*, Thomas Forrest Kelly, ed. Cambridge Studies in Performance Practice, Cambridge, England; New York: Cambridge University Press, 1992. 32-44.

1282. Jeffery, Peter. "The New Chantbooks from Solesmes." *Notes* 47, 4/June (1991): 1039-1063. On the 1983 edition of the *Liber Hymnarius* and its explanations of neumes, reading the neumes, rhythmic values, and repercussion and elision of vowels.

1283. Murray, Gregory. *Plainsong Rhythm, the Editorial Methods of Solesmes.* Exeter: Catholic Records Press, 1956.

1284. Page, Christopher. *Summa Musice: A Thirteenth Century Manual for Singers.* Musical Texts and Monographs, Cambridge: Cambridge University Press, 1991. An edition and translation of a guide to plainchant performance, with commentary on its usage (schoolrooms), place and time of origin (Bavaria, c. 1200), and authors (two).

MODES AND MODAL THEORY

1285. Allaire, C.G. "The Theory of Hexachords, Solmization and the Modal System." *Musicae Sacrae Disciplina* 24 (1972).

1286. Atkinson, Charles M. "'Harmonia' and the 'Modi' quos abusive tonos dicimus'." *Atti del XIV Congresso della Società internazionale di musicologia* Vol. 3 (1987): 485-500. A demonstration of the influence of Boethius' terminology on the anonymous author of the late 9th-century treatise *Musica Enchiriadis*. The latter's preference for the term 'modus' over 'tonus' to describe the transposing of scales set the stage for a truly Medieval theory of melodic modes.

1287. Bailey, Terence. *The Intonation Formulas of Western Chant*. Pontifical Institute of Mediaeval Studies, No. 28, Toronto, Canada: Pontifical Institute of Mediaeval Studies, 1974. A history and edition of intonation formulas—short melodies that represent the 8 modes of Gregorian Chant—from neumed sources of the 11th century and earlier.

1288. Bailey, Terence. "Accented and Cursive Cadences in Gregorian Psalmody." *JAMS* 29 (1976): 463-71. By the 10th century, the time of the earliest chantbooks and named tonaries, accentual median and terminal cadences existed alongside the earlier practice of cursive cadences. By making all cadences accentual, the Solesmes editors have created consistency where historically none existed.

1289. Boethius, Anicius Manlius Severinus. *Fundamentals of Music [De institutione musica]*. Calvin M. Bower, transl. Music Theory Translation Series, New Haven, CT: Yale University Press, 1989.

1290. Chadwick, Henry. *Boethius: The Consolations of Music, Logic, Theology, and Philosophy*. Oxford, England: Oxford University Press, 1981. An analysis of Boethius' s *Consolations* (524-525). Chadwick shows Boethius's concern with music (see pp. 78-101) to be almost entirely theoretical and rooted in Pythagorean mathematical philosophy, especially that of Nicomachus.

1291. Dyer, Joseph. "On the Monastic Origins of Western Music Theory." In *IMS Study Group 'Cantus Planus'...Hungary...1988*, Laszlo Dobszay et al., ed. Budapest: Hungarian Academy of Sciences Institute for Musicology, 1990. 199-225.

1292. Gushee, Lawrence A. "Questions of Genre in Medieval Treatises on Music." In *Gattungen der Musik in Einzeldarstellungen: Gedenkschrift für Leo Schrade...*, Higini Angles et al., ed. Bern and Munich: Francke, 1973. 365-433.

1293. Hansen, Finn Egeland. *The Grammar of Gregorian Tonality: An Investigation Based on the Repertory in Codex H 159, Montpellier*. Shirley Larsen, transl. Copenhagen: Dan Fog, 1979. A study of tonality on the basis of tensity between primary and secondary tones as aspects of the modal 'coding' of chants. Categorizes according to an elaborate system the whole repertory of Montpellier.

1294. Huglo, Michel. "The Study of Ancient Sources of Music Theory in the Medieval Universities." In *Music Theory and its Sources: Antiquity and the Middle Ages*, André Barbera, ed. Notre Dame, IN: University of Notre Dame Press, 1990. 150-172.

1295. Merkley, Paul. *Modal Assignment in Northern Tonaries*. Ottawa, Canada: Institute of Mediaeval Music, 1992.

1296. Palisca, Claude, ed. *Hucbald, Guido and John on Music*. Warren Babb, transl. New Haven, CT: Yale University Press, 1980. Three medieval treatises: *De Harmonica Institutione*, by Hucbald of Saint Amand; *Micrologus*, by Guido d'Arezzo; and *De Musica* by Johannes Afflighemensis.

1297. Pesce, Dolores. *The Concept of the Affinities in Theoretical Writings on Music from c.900 to c.1550*. Ph.D. diss., University of Maryland College Park, 1982. A three-fold study of the task of reconciling an inherited chant repertory with an *a posteriori* modal classification scheme, the functional interpretation of an existing tonal system, the gamut, and a way to deal with both tasks, namely, *affinitas*. A study of affinities, *affinales*, and the hexachord system.

1298. Pesce, Dolores. *The Affinities and Medieval Transposition*. Bloomington, IN: Indiana University Press, 1987.

1299. Planer, John Harris. *The Ecclesiastical Modes in the Late Eighth Century*. Ph.D. diss., 1970.

1300. Powers, Harold. "Mode." In *Grove 6*, 1980.

1301. Wingell, R. "Hucbald of St. Amand and Carolingian Music Theory." In *Festival Essays for Pauline Alderman*, Provo, UT 1976. 19 ff.

1302. Wulstan, David. "The Origin of the Modes." *Studies in Eastern Chant* Vol. 2 (1971): 4-20. Modes seem to have originated as or to be associated with 1) separate classes of spells as well as 8-day liturgies in ancient Babylon and Judaism, 2) Greek instrument tunings that became associated with the magical number 8, 3) melodic formulae for cantillation of psalms, 4) identification of modes with final note of chant, 5) identification of modes with scales.

ORAL AND LITERATE TRANSMISSION; NOTATION

1303. [Notational systems]. In *Grove 6*, 1980. For articles related to notation, see "Chieronomy," "Melisma," "Neuma," "Notation," "Ekphonetic Notation," "Neumatic Notations," "Pitch Notation," and "Solmization."

1304. Engberg, Sysse Gudrun. "Ekphonetic Chant—The Oral Tradition and the Manuscripts." In *Symposion für Musikologie: Byzantinische Musik 1453-1832 als Quelle musikalischer Praxis und Theorie vor 1453*, Jørgen Raasted, ed. 16. Internationaler Byzantinistenkongress, Wien, 4.-9. Oktober 1981: Akten 2/7. Jahrbuch der österreichischen Byzantinistik 32/7, Vienna: Verlag der öster-reichischen Akademie der Wissenschaften, 1982. 41-48. Mss show chant to have acquired fixed melodic form well before the appearance of the earliest surviving mss, rather than at the time of notation as argued by Treitler and Hucke.

1305. Haar, James. "Monophony and the Unwritten Tradition." In *Performance Practice: Music before 1600*, Howard Mayer Brown and Stanley Sadie, ed. New York: W.W. Norton, 1990. 185-200.

1306. Hucke, Helmut. "Toward a New Historical View of Gregorian Chant." *JAMS* 33, 3 (Fall) (1980): 437-467. An updating of the general overviews of chant by Apel, Wagner, and the school of Solesmes. Argues for comparative analysis of the various chant traditions and for the study of the relationship between oral and written transmission.

1307. Hughes, David G. "Evidence for the Traditional View of the Transmission of Gregorian Chant." *JAMS* 40 (1987): 377-404. With respect to the Proper chants of the Mass, Gregorian Chant was fully fixed as to pitch before it was disseminated throughout and beyond the Carolingian Empire and well before the earliest surviving mss. Minor variants were mishearings rather than misreadings—suggesting that chants were written from dictation rather than by copying another manuscript. Microtones were once used, and substantive variants were regional. See JAMS. 41, 3 (1988) and 42, 2 (1989) for exchange between Hughes, Treitler, and Werf.

1308. Jeffery, Peter. *Re-Envisioning Past Musical Cultures: Ethnomusicology in the Study of Gregorian Chant*. JAMS, Philip V. Bohlman and Bruno Nettl, ed. Chicago and London: The University of Chicago Press, 1992. A controversial study of Gregorian Chant, the New Historical View, and the problem of the relationship between oral and written traditions. Argues for studying oral transmission in present-day cultures as a way to understand chant transmission. Contains a 50-page bibliography. See reviews by Leo Treitler in *JAMS*, 47, 1 (1994): 137-171 and Nowacki in *Notes*, 50, 3 (1994): 913-917.

1309. Jeffery, Peter. "Rome and Jerusalem: From Oral Tradition to Written Repertory in Two Ancient Liturgical Centers." In *From Rome to the Passing of the Gothic: Festschrift for David G. Hughes*, Graeme Boone, ed. Cambridge, MS: Harvard University Music Department, forthcoming.

1310. Jonsson, Rittva and Leo Treitler. "Medieval Music and Language: A Reconsideration of the Relationship." In *Studies in the History of Music I: Music and Language*, New York 1983. 1-23.

1311. Kleeman, Janice. "The Parameters of Musical Transmission." *The Journal of Musicology* 4 (1985-6): 1-22.

1312. Levy, Kenneth. "Charlemagne's Archetype of Gregorian Chant." *JAMS* 40 (1987): 1-30. A proposal for late 8th-century France as the date and place of the first use of neumatic notation, to effect a changeover from Gallican to Gregorian repertories. See Communications in JAMS 41, March (1988): 566-578, for arguments by Treitler for a later date, c. 900 CE.

1313. Levy, Kenneth. "On the Origin of Neumes." *Early Music History* Vol. 7 (1987): 59-90. Levy proposes a three stage development of early neumes: 1) both graphic (pitch centered) and gestural; 2) a nuance-poor 'Charlemagne's archetype,' c. 800 and now lost, based on gestural neumes; 3) neume species, c. 900.

1314. Levy, Kenneth. "The Two Carolingian Archetypes of Gregorian Chant." *Atti del XIV Congresso della Società internazionale di Musicologia* Vol. 3 (1987): 501-504. An argument for at least a century's development of neume notation before the appearance of the first mss, c. 900.

1315. Levy, Kenneth. "On Gregorian Orality." *JAMS* 43, 2 (1990): 185-227. An assertion that Gregorian Chant was stabilized at a certain point in its oral transmission, but that the unstable phases account for divergences in sources at the time of written transmission. See Communications in *JAMS* 44, (1991): 185-227, for exchanges between Levy, Werf, and Treitler.

1316. McGee, William and Paul Merkley. "The Optical Scanning of Medieval Music." *Computers and the Humanities* 25, 1 (Feb., 1991): 47-53. When Medieval music is scanned, the recognition of pitches is accomplished through the location and elimination of staff lines and a process of pattern recognition—

in effect, through the converting of square notation into the earlier cheironomic neumes.

1317. Nettheim, Nigel. "On the Accuracy of Musical Data, with Examples from Gregorian Chant and German Folksong." *Computers and the Humanities* 27, 2 (April, 1993): 111-120. Now that large data-bases of melodies are becoming available, one method for controlling the quality or accuracy of musical data is the investigation of unusual melodic progressions.

1318. Pirrotta, Nino. "New Glimpses of an Unwritten Tradition." In *Words and Music: The Scholar's View: A Medley of Problems and Solutions Compiled in Honor of A. Tillman Merritt*, Laurence Berman, ed. Cambridge, MA: Harvard University Department of Music, 1972. 271-291. Repr. with an appendix in Pirrotta, *Music and Culture in Italy from the Middle Ages to the Baroque*. Cambridge, MA: Harvard University Press. 1984: 51-71, 377-80.

1319. Planchart, Alejandro. "The Transmission of Medieval Chant." In *Music in Medieval and Early Modern Europe: Patronage, Sources and Texts*, Iain Fenlon, ed. Cambridge: Cambridge University Press, 1981. 347-63.

1320. Planchart, Alejandro. "On the Nature of Transmission and Change in Trope Repertories." *JAMS* 41 (1988): 215-49. Tropes were transmitted by both oral and written means, though written transmission was dominant. Yet, since tropes did not have the immutable status Gregorian Chant had, local taste permitted alteration of the tropes.

1321. Pompilio, Angel. "Atti del XIV Congresso della Società Internazionale di Musicologia." Torino, IT: EDT, 1987. 485-571. Contains seven papers on the theory and transmission of Medieval plainchant

1322. Rastall, R. *The Notation of Western Music: An Introduction*. London: Dent; New York: St. Martin's Press, 1983. Provides a clear guide to medieval notation.

1323. Robertson, Anne Walters. "Benedicamus Domino: The Unwritten Tradition." *JAMS* 41, 1 (1988): 1-62. A study of the prestige and pervasiveness of the Benedicamus and of how the ease of applying improvisitory practices to the Benedicamus encouraged a multiplicity of settings. Both factors lead to the chant's being interconnected with other forms such as responsory tropes, polyphonic responsories, alleluias, and motets.

1324. Treitler, Leo. "Homer and Gregory: the Transmission of Epic Poetry and Plainchant." *MQ* 60 (1974): 333-72. Treitler proposes a model of how oral tradition worked in Gregorian Chant, its parallel to the Homeric tradition, and how it stayed within the boundaries of the oral learning 'tradition' and the realistic limitations of cognitive processes.

1325. Treitler, Leo. "Centone Chant: Übles Flickwerk or E pluribus unus?" *JAMS* 28 (1975): 1-23. To maintain that chants are either a hodge-podge of melodic motives or the result of a uniform act of creation is to obscure the generative procedures of oral composition and the processes of redaction and rationalization associated with writing chants down.

1326. Treitler, Leo. "Oral, Written, and Literate Process in the Transmission of Medieval Music." *Speculum* 56 (1981): 471-91.

1327. Treitler, Leo. "The Early History of Music Writing in the West." *JAMS* 35 (1982): 237-79. Symbolic vs iconic notation: a study of the ways early music notation functioned.

1328. Treitler, Leo. "Reading and Singing: On the Genesis of Occidental Music-Writing." *Early Music History* Vol. 4 (1984): 135-208.

1329. Treitler, Leo. "Orality and Literacy in the Music of the Middle Ages." *Parergon: Bulletin of the Australian and New Zealand Association for Medieval and Renaissance Studies* Vol. (new series) 2 (1984): 143-74.

1330. Treitler, Leo. "Reading and Singing: On the Genesis of Occidental Music-Writing." *Early Music History* Vol. 4 (1984): 135-208. A proposition that neumatic notation developed first in the Carolingian Empire in the late 8th century, spread next to Britain, and then, in the 11th century, to South Italy.

1331. Treitler, Leo. "From Ritual through Language to Music." *Schweizer Jahrbuch für Musikwissenschaft*, New Series 2 (1984): 109-23.

1332. Treitler, Leo. "Oral and Literate Style in the Regional Transmission of Tropes." *Studia Musicologica Academiae Scientiarum Hungaricae* Vol. 27 (1985): 171-83.

1333. Treitler, Leo. "Orality and Literacy in the Music of the European Middle Ages." In *The Oral and the Literate in Music*, Tokumaru and Yamaguti, ed. Tokyo: Academia Music, 1986. 38-56. Between the 9th and 13th centuries, literate transmission of chant ran parallel to strong oral traditions, but made possible the development of certain stylistic tendencies in composition. Includes a description of the oral features of a notated Roman chant.

1334. Treitler, Leo. "Paleography and Semiotics." In *Musicologie Médiéval...*, Michel Huglo, ed. Paris and Geneva: H. Champion, 1987. 17-27.

1335. Treitler, Leo. "The History of Gregorian Chant before the Age of Music Writing." *JAMS* 44, 3 (1991): 513-517.

1336. Treitler, Leo. "The 'Unwritten' and 'Written Transmission' of Medieval Chant and the Start-up of Musical Notation." *Journal of Musicology* 10, 2

(1992): 131-191. A study of systems of Medieval notation, their piecemeal development, and their relationship to unwritten vocal chant traditions.

1337. Uduvich, Joann. *Modality, Office Antiphons, and Psalmody: The Musical Authority of the Twelfth-Century Antiphonal from St. Denis*. Ph.D. diss., The University of North Carolina at Chapel Hill, 1985. An evaluation of the antiphonal's musical text shows the consistent placement of ending formulas (*differentiae*) for the psalm recitations in the outside margins to have been part of the original design and to be an intelligent attempt to grapple with certain problems encountered in the writing-down of the entire office repertory in the 'new' pitch-accurate notational system.

NON-GREGORIAN LATIN CHANT TRADITIONS

General Reference

1338. Levy, Kenneth. "Latin Chant Outside the Roman Tradition." In *NOHM II*, 1990. 69-110.

Ambrosian Chant

1339. Bailey, Terence. "Ambrosian Psalmody: An Introduction." In *Studies in Music from the University of Western Ontario* 2, 1977. 65-78.

1340. Bailey, Terence. "Ambrosian Psalmody: The Formulae." *Studies in Music from the University of Western Ontario* Vol. 3 (1978): 72-96.

1341. Bailey, Terence. "Ambrosian Choral Psalmody: The Formulae." In *Studies in Music from the University of Western Ontario 3*, 1978. 72-96.

1342. Bailey, Terence. "Ambrosian Chant in Southern Italy." *JPMMS* 6 (1983): 1-7. Employing both musical and historical evidence, Bailey shows that composers of Beneventan chant adopted and adapted items of Ambrosian chant. This was probably done to resist Roman-Gregorian encroachment by showing affiliation with the only rival to Gregorian domination in the matter of ecclesiastical chant.

1343. Bailey, Terence. *The Ambrosian Alleluias*. Egham, Surrey: Plainsong & Mediaeval Music Society, 1983. The alleluia is one of the most ancient of ecclesiastical genres and has the most elaborate and complex development. This study presents a history and edition of the genre in the Milanese rite.

1344. Bailey, Terence. "Milanese Melodic Tropes." *JPMMS* 11 (1988): 1-12.

1345. Bailey, Terence. *The Melodic Tradition of the Ambrosian Office-Antiphon*. Ottawa, Canada: Institute of Mediaeval Music, 1989 (1990).

1346. Bailey, Terence. *Antiphon and Psalm in the Ambrosian Office*. Ottawa, Canada: Institute of Mediaeval Music, 1994. A study of the liturgies of Milan's two cathedrals, antiphons and the practice of antiphony, the sequential reading of the psalms in early Christian liturgy and in Milan, and fixed assignments of psalms in Matins and Vespers.

1347. Baroffio, Giacomo Bonifazio. "Ambrosian [Milanese] Rite, Music of the." In *Grove 6*, Vol. 1. 1980. 314-320.

1348. Halperin, D. *Contributions to a Morphology of Ambrosian Chant*. Ph.D. diss., Tel-Aviv University, 1986.

1349. Jesson, Roy Hart. *Ambrosian Chant, the Music of the Mass*. Ph.D. diss., Indiana University, 1955.

1350. Weakland, Rembert G. "The Performance of Ambrosian Chant in the Twelfth Century." In *Aspects of Medieval and Renaissance Music: A Birthday Offering to Gustave Reese*, Jan La Rue, ed. New York: Pendragon Press, 1966/repr. 1978. 856-866. Explores information not given directly by the music but in other mss. concerning such matters as the hierarchy of personnel involved in the performance the Milanese liturgy, the number of singers, which chants are solo and which are choral, and who is assigned to sing each chant.

Beneventan Chant

1351. Kelly, Thomas Forrest. "Palimpsest Evidence of an Old-Beneventan Gradual." *Kirchenmusikalisches Jahrbuch* 67 (1983): 5-23.

1352. Kelly, Thomas Forrest. "Montecassino and the Old Beneventan Chant." *Early Music History* Vol. 5 (1985): 53-83. Of the entire Beneventan repertory, only two 11th-century chant mss. survived papal suppression.

1353. Kelly, Thomas Forest. "Beneventan and Milanese Chant." *Journal of the RMA* 112 (1987): 173-195.

1354. Kelly, Thomas Forest. *The Beneventan Chant*. Cambridge Studies in Music, Cambridge and New York: Cambridge University Press, 1989. A thorough study of one of the oldest surviving bodies of Western music, the Latin church music of the duchy of Benevento in southern Italy before the spread of Gregorian chant. Topics include political and ecclesiastical context, sources, style, liturgy, history, and relationship to other repertories. Rev. by James McKinnon in *Early Music History* Vol. 4, 1992: 314-323.

1355. Kelly, Thomas Forrest. "Beneventan Liturgy and Music in Tuscany." *Ricerche di Storia Dell Arte* Vol. 49 (1993): 51-54.

1356. Schlager, Karlheinz. "Beneventan Rite, Music of the." In *Grove 6*, Vol. 2. 1980. 482-484.

Gallican Chant

1357. Babcock, R.G. "The Luxeuil Prophets and the Gallican Liturgy." *Scriptorium* 47, 1 (1993): 52-55. Luxeuil-Lectionary, Paris, BN-Lat-9427.

1358. Gough, Austin. "The Roman Liturgy, Gregorian Plainchant, and the Gallican Church." *Journal of Religious History* 11 (1981): 536-557.

1359. Hiley, David. "Neo-Gallican Chant." In *Grove 6*, Vol. 13. 1980. 105-107.

1360. Huglo, Michel. "Gallican Rite, Music of the." In *Grove 6*, Vol. 5. 1980. 113-124.

1361. Levy, Kenneth. "Toledo, Rome and the Legacy of Gaul." In *Early Music History: Studies in Medieval and Early Modern Music*, Iain Fenlon, ed. Vol. 4. Cambridge: Cambridge University Press, 1984. 49-100. Comparison of surviving Gallican Chant mss. with Mozarabic and Gregorian sources allows two to three dozen Gregorian non-psalmic Offertories to be reclaimed by the Gallican rite.

Mozarabic Chant

1362. Brockett, Clyde W. *Antiphons, Responsories and other Chants from the Mozarabic Rite*. Wissenschaftliche Abhandlungen-Musicological Studies, Brooklyn, NY: Institute of Mediaeval Music, 1968. Ph.D. diss.. Columbia University, 1965. A study in two parts: 1) History: liturgical books, historical concepts, and notation; and 2) Structure and Usage: the antiphons, responsories, and other chants, and a perspective. Although the notation is unreadable, what can be adduced is that Mozarabic chant, from its wellspring in the 7th century, has little in common with other bodies of chant.

1363. Gonzálvez, Ramon. "The Persistence of the Mozarabic Liturgy in Toledo after A.D. 1080." In *Santiago, Saint-Denis, and Saint Peter: The Reception of the Roman Liturgy in Léon-Castile in 1080*, Bernard F. Reilly, ed. New York: Fordham University Press, 1985. 157-185. Beginning with Gregory VII (1080), forces in Rome and within Spain attempted to Romanize the Spanish liturgy. The Mozarab minority, however, held on to its liturgy until the late 13th and 14th centuries, when social and economic factors reduced the minority to marginality. Although preserved in notation, the liturgy ceased to be viable by the end of the 15th century.

1364. Imbasciani, Vito D. *Cisneros and the Restoration of the Mozarabic Rite*. Ph.D. diss., Cornell University, 1979.

1365. Randel, Don M. *The Responsorial Psalm Tones for the Mozarabic Office.* Princeton, NJ: Princeton University Press, 1969. Topics are the Lion and Rioja traditions and their sources, northern fragments, Toledo sources, and the origin and relationship of the traditions.

1366. Randel, Don M. "Responsorial Psalmody in the Mozarabic Rite." *Etudes grégoriennes* 10 (1969): 87-116.

1367. Randel, Don M. "Mozarabic Rite, Music of the." In *Grove 6*, Vol. 12. 1980. 667-675.

1368. Randel, Don M. "Antiphonal Psalmody in the Mozarabic Rite." In *IMS12, 1977,* 1981. 414-422. An exploration of modal systems and formulaic phrases in Mozarabic chant and a comparison of these systems with the systems in Gregorian chant.

Old Roman Chant

1369. Connolly, Thomas. "Introits and Archetypes: Some Archaisms of the Old Roman Chant." *JAMS* 25 (1972): 157-74. Gregorian Introits differ from the Old Roman in the relaxation of three prominent formulaic patterns; 1) type melodies in psalmodic recitation, 2) repeated psalm tone structures within the antiphon, and 3) final cadence types.

1370. Connolly, Thomas. "Musical Observance of Time in Early Roman Chant." In *Studies in Musicology in Honor of Otto E. Albrecht,* John Walter Hill, ed. Kassel: Barenreiter; Clifton, NJ: European American Music Distributors Corp., 1980. 3-18.

1371. Cutter, Paul F. "The Question of the 'Old-Roman' Chant: A Reappraisal." *Acta Musicologica* 39 (1967): 2 ff. If the notated Gregorian chant of 9th-century France was the oral chant of contemporary Rome, then the 11th-century Roman mss. represent two centuries of further development of Old Roman chant.

1372. Cutter, Paul F. "The Old Roman Tradition: Oral or Written?" *JAMS* 20 (1967): 167-181. The 11th-century mss. of Old Roman chant are an attempt to preserve a body of oral chant that is later in its development and is hence more florid in character than is the less florid Gregorian chant found in earlier mss. from France.

1373. Cutter, Paul F. "Oral Transmission of the Old-Roman Responsories?" *MQ* 62 (1976): 182-194. Furthers a study by Treitler on oral transmission of chant. Juxtaposition of the Gregorian responsory repertory with the Old Roman responsory repertory points to the economy of musical phrases in an oral tradition.

1374. Dyer, Joseph. *The Offertories of Old-Roman Chant: A Musico-Liturgical Investigation*. Ph.D. diss., Boston University, 1971.

1375. Dyer, Joseph. "Latin Psalters, Old Roman and Gregorian Chants." *Kirchenmusikalisches Jahrbuch* 68 (1984): 11-30.

1376. Hucke, Helmut. "Gregorian and Old Roman Chant." In *Grove 6*, Vol. 7. 1980. 693-7.

1377. Murphy, Joseph. *The Communions of the Old Roman Chant*. Ph.D. diss., University of Pennsylvania, 1977.

1378. Nowacki, Edward. *Studies on the Office Antiphons of the Old Roman Manuscripts*. Ph.D. diss., Brandeis University, 1980. This study of over 1200 pieces from two mss., dating from 1071 to the mid-thirteenth century, shows that taxonomic classification yields only superficial similarities, whereas a hierarchically layered system of classification reveals underlying structural similarities that form the basis for potentially unlimited numbers of different derivatives.

1379. Nowacki, Edward. "Text Declamation as a Determinant of Melodic Form in the Old Roman Eighth-Mode Tracts." *Early Music History* Vol. 6 (1986): 193-226. An analysis of Old Roman melodies in relation to the poetic and syntactic structures of the texts reveals that the these structures determine to a remarkable degree the chant's melodic shape, that melody is uniform in identical textual conditions, and that the Old Roman composers achieved a setting in which the text was easily understood and vivid to the imagination. Includes tables showing the relationship of text declamation to melodic shape.

1380. Van Deusen, Nancy M. *An Historical and Stylistic Comparison of the Graduals of Gregorian and Old Roman Chant*. Ph.D. diss., Indiana University, 1972.

Other Chant Traditions

1381. Fleischmann, Aloys. "Celtic Rite, Music of the." In *Grove 6*, 1980. 52-54.

1382. Hiley, David. "The Chant of Norman Sicily: Interaction between the Norman and Italian Traditions." *Studies in Music History* Vol. 30, 1-4 (1988): 379-391.

1383. Jordan, Peter Gray. *The Liturgical Music of Medieval Brittany: Study of the Manuscript Sources and Musical Variants*. Ph.D. diss., Harvard University, 1978. On the liturgical music of the Celtic church.

1384. Levy, Kenneth. "Ravenna Rite, Music of the." In *Grove 6*, Vol. 15. 1980. 621-622.

19

Western European Polyphony

MUSIC IN INDIVIDUAL PLACES, COURTS, AND INSTITUTIONS

1385. Brobeck, John T. "Musical Patronage at the Royal Chapel, France, under Francis I." *JAMS* 48, 2 (1995): 187-239.

1386. Borders, James Matthew. *The Cathedral of Verona as a Musical Center in the Middle Ages: Its History, Manuscripts, and Liturgical Practice*. Ph.D. diss., University of Chicago, 1983. An examination of the organization and musical activities of the cathedral chapter and the development of the liturgy and sacred music in one of the premier religious establishments of medieval Italy (9th through 14th centuries).

1387. Curtis, Liane Renee. *Music Manuscripts and Their Production in Fifteenth-Century Cambrai*. Ph.D. diss., The University of North Carolina at Chapel Hill, 1991. Rare northern ms. sources of chant and polyphony document the high priority of chant in the musical life of the cathedral, the use of choirboys in polyphony earlier than 1417, and the role of the cathedral scribe.

1388. Dean, Jeffrey J. *The Scribes of the Sistine Chapel, 1501-1527*. Ph.D. diss., 1984. An analysis of the work of Johannes Orceau, Claudius Gellandi, Claudius Bouchet, and other music scribes.

1389. Fenlon, Iain. *Music and Patronage in Sixteenth-Century Mantua*. Cambridge/New York: Cambridge University Press, 1982. Vol. 1. Text. Vol. 2. Anthology.

1390. Fenlon, Iain. "Patronage, Music, and Liturgy in Renaissance Mantua." In *Plainsong in the Age of Polyphony*, Thomas Forrest Kelly, ed. Cambridge Studies in Performance Practice, Cambridge, England; New York: Cambridge University Press, 1992. 209-235. A study of the liturgy, chapel traditions, and

politics in Mantua under the Gonzagas; the unique, restrained plainsong repertory for mass at the ducal basilica of Santa Barbara; and the polyphonic masses
that were composed to these chants by Wert, Palestrina and others to bring
prestige to the basilica.

1391. Forney, Kristine K. "Music, Ritual and Patronage at the Church of Our
Lady, Antwerp." *Early Music History* Vol. 7 (1987): 1-57. On the decisive role
of the lay devotional congregation in promoting the use of polyphony in 14th-
and 15th-century Antwerp and in supporting a strong musical establishment.

1392. Haggh, Barbara Helen. *Music, Liturgy, and Ceremony in Brussels, 1350-
1500*. Ph.D. diss., University of Illinois at Urbana-Champaign, 1988. Systems
of endowment and incorporation allowed wealthy parishioners to shape sacred
ceremony and permitted the introduction and maintenance of polyphony and
organ music.

1393. Johnson, Glenn Pierr. *Aspects of Late Medieval Music at the Cathedral of
Amiens*. Ph.D. diss., Yale University, 1991. Amiens flourished during the
thirteenth through mid-fourteenth centuries, becoming a center for both polyphony and secular monophony. This work documents the ways cathedral clerics
insured that the liturgy at Amiens was sufficiently solemn.

1394. Kendrick, Robert L. *Genres, Generations and Gender: Nuns' Music in
Early Modern Milan, c. 1550-1706*. Ph.D. diss., New York University, 1993.
Conditioned by order-specific liturgy and piety, contemporary devotional trends,
and ideas of gender-specific spirituality, Milanese nuns had ample scope for
singing, instrument playing, and the composition of polyphonic devotional
music in a variety of styles.

1395. Lockwood, Lewis. *Music in Renaissance Ferrara 1400-1505. The
Creation of a Musical Center in the Fifteenth Century*. Cambridge, MA:
Harvard University Press, 1984. The Este court in Ferrara was home to such
composers as Dufay (in the 1430s), Josquin (1503-04), and Obrecht (1504-05).
Archival materials are used to construct a detailed picture of the rich intellectual
and musical life in Ferrara during the 15th century.

1396. Monson, Craig A. "Disembodied Voices: Music in the Nunneries of
Bologna in the Midst of the Counter-Reformation." In *The Crannied Wall:
Women, Religion, and the Arts in Early Modern Europe*, Craig A. Monson, ed.
Ann Arbor, MI: University of Michigan Press, 1992. 191-210. In spite of the
almost complete walling-off of nuns from the outside world, they managed to
employ diverse genres of musical performance—monody, cori spezzati, and
concertato—and maintain a rich if rarified musical life.

1397. Robertson, Anne Walters. *The Service-Books of the Royal Abbey of Saint-
Denis: Images of Ritual and Music in the Middle Ages*. Oxford Monographs on
Music, New York: Oxford University Press, 1991. A reconstruction of the
liturgical and musical history of St. Denis, from its founding in the 5th century

through the height of its glory in the 12th and up to the 15th. A masterly study of service books and other original sources.

1398. Saunders, Suparmi Elizabeth. *The Dating of the Trent Codices from Their Watermarks: With a Study of the Local Liturgy of Trent in the Fifteenth Century.* Outstanding Dissertations in Music from British Universities, New York: Garland Publications, 1989.

1399. Sherr, Richard. "Music and the Renaissance Papacy: The Papal Choir and the Fondo Cappella Sistina." In *Rome Reborn: The Vatican Library and Renaissance Culture*, Anthony Grafton, ed. Washington D.C.: Library of Congress; New Haven, CT: Yale University Press, 1993. The author uses reproductions of engravings, paintings, miniatures, early printed editions, and mss. contained in the Vatican library to document the life of the members of the Papal Choir and its repertory. A lavishly illustrated book; a visual treasure.

1400. Starr, Pamela F. *Music and Music Patronage at the Papal Court, 1447-1464.* Ph.D. diss., Yale University, 1987. On the music and musicians of the Papal Court and the salaries and pensions paid to the musicians.

1401. Starr, Pamela F. "Rome as the Centre of the Universe: Papal Grace and Musical Patronage." In *Studies in Medieval and Early Modern Music*, Iain Fenlon, ed. Vol. 11. Cambridgeshire; New York: Cambridge University Press, 1992. 223-263.

1402. Strohm, Reinhard. *Music in Late Medieval Bruges.* rev. ed., Oxford: Clarendon Press, 1990. First publ., 1985. At the end of the Middle Ages, Bruges was the artistic and commercial center of Flanders, an urban community with a coherent artistic policy and practice. This lasted until c1477, with the fall of Charles the Bold and the simultaneous arrival and competition of the Renaissance and the Reformation. Strohm documents the people of Bruges, their institutions—the churches, convents, confraternities, the city and court—and the musical repertory these engendered.

1403. Tomasello, Andrew. *Music and Ritual at Papal Avignon, 1309-1403.* Studies in Musicology, Charlotte NC: UMI Research Press, 1983. A study of the roles played by the French papal chapel college singers and papal servers and chaplains, and of their influence into the 15th and 16th centuries.

1404. Tomasello, Andrew. "Ritual, Tradition, and Polyphony at the Court of Rome." *Journal of Musicology* 4, 4 (1985-86): 447-471.

1405. Walters, Anne Elizabeth. *Music and Liturgy at the Abbey of Saint-Denis, 567-1567.* Ph.D. diss., Yale University, 1984. A study of 43 chant mss. reveal 1000 years of the abbey's musical and liturgical life, including remnants of the ancient Gallican tradition, chants of the Greek mass, many hitherto undiscovered melodies, and sequences contrafacted at the abbey.

1406. Wright, Craig. *Music at the Court of Burgundy 1363-1419: A Documentary History*. Musicological Studies, Vol. 28. Henryville, PA: Institute of Mediaeval Music, 1979. Chronicles and account books form the basis for this study of both the secular and sacred music of the Burgundy court.

1407. Wright, Craig. *Music and Ceremony at Notre Dame of Paris, 500-1500*. Cambridge Studies in Music, Cambridge, New York: Cambridge University Press, 1989. Nine essays on all aspects of the musical life of the Parisian cathedral of Notre Dame, including early Parisian chant, liturgy and ceremony, choral and organ repertories through the Late Middle Ages, administration, and relationship of cathedral to court. For a lengthy review, see Thomas B. Payne in *Journal of Musicological Research*, 12, Supplement (1992): S3-S18.

ORGANUM

1408. [Early Medieval Polyphony]. In *Grove 6*, 1980. For early polyphony, see "Organum and Discant," "Conductus," "Motet," "Rhythmic Modes," "St. Martial," and "Notre Dame."

1409. Bonderup, Jens. *The Saint Martial Polyphony: Texture and Tonality: A Contribution to Research in the Development of Polyphonic Style in the Middle Ages*. Copenhagen: Dan Fog Musikforlag, 1982.

1410. Crocker, Richard. "Rhythm in Early Polyphony." *Current Musicology*, 45-47 (1990): 147-178. Although 12th-century polyphony permits no consistent system of rhythm and was perhaps the result of various experiments at combining the upper voice with the lower, an isosyllabic hypothesis—which states that the syllable is the primary rhythmic unit and that syllables are approximately equal in length—offers the best starting point for aligning the two voices. Also suggested are the placing of consonances at the *end* of a syllable (rather than at the beginning) and the existence of three note values in Leonin: the short, the long, and the ternery long.

1411. Fuller, Sarah Ann. *Aquitanian Polyphony of the Eleventh and Twelfth-Centuries*. Ph.D. diss., UCB, 1969. The repertory of the "Saint Martial School" is in Aquitanian notation and contains seven distinct sources of para-liturgical polyphony. A masterly study of the literary background and ritual function, sources, notations, proses, poetic structure and music form, and contrapuntal structure of the Aquitanian repertory. A case is made for unmeasured rhythm and for the direct connection of Aquitanian *versus* to the polyphony of Parisian conductus.

1412. Fuller, Sarah Ann. "Discant and the Theory of Fifthing." *Acta Musicology* 50 (1978): 241-75. Thirteenth and early 14th-century treatises indicate that singing with frequent parallel fifths was a special kind of 2-part singing, separate from, and equal and contemporaneous to, that of organum and discant.

1413. Fuller, Sarah Ann. "The Myth of 'Saint Martial' Polyphony: A Study of the Sources." *Musica Disciplina* 33 (1979): 5-26.

1414. Fuller, Sarah Ann. "Theoretical Foundations of Early Organum Theory." *Acta Musicologica* 53 (1981): 52-84. John of Garland was the first to make metric organization, rather than consonance, the primary factor in the organization of vertical sonorities. His clear differentiation between consonance and dissonance, and the coordination of consonance with and its subordination to metrically strong beats have lasted as organizing principles until the beginning of the 20th century.

1415. Fuller, Sarah Ann. "Early Polyphony." In *NOHM II*, 1990. 485-556.

1416. Gillingham, Bryan. *Modal Rhythm*. Ottawa, Canada: Institute of Medieval Music, 1986. A study of the development of lyric poetry and the modal system. After a detailed explanation of the latter, the author examines the rhythm of conductus and organum, trope, sequence and versus, and secular song—all of which set metrical poetry.

1417. Gushee, Marion S. "The Polyphonic Music of the Medieval Monastery, Cathedral and University." In *Antiquity and the Middle Ages*, James McKinnon, ed. Englewood Cliffs, NJ: Prentice Hall, 1990. 143-169.

1418. Karp, Theodore. *The Polyphony of Saint Martial and Santiago de Compostela*. Berkeley: University of California Press, 1992. An analytical and statistical rather than contextual or liturgical study.

1419. Knapp, Janet. "Polyphony at Notre Dame of Paris." In *NOHM II*, 2nd ed. 1990. 557-635.

1420. Tischler, Hans. "Four Styles of Notre Dame Organa." *Orbis Musicae* 8 (1982-83): 44-53. Four styles of Notre Dame organum—organum purum, copula, discant, and pseudo discant—are based on examples found in Johannes de Garlandia's *De Mensurabili Musica*.

1421. Tischler, Hans. "The Evolution of the Magnus Liber Organi." *MQ* 70, 2 (1984): 163-174. By comparing the chants of F, W1 and W2 on the basis of specific musical criteria, Tischler arrives as a three-stage model for the evolution of the chants.

1422. Treitler, Leo. "Musical Syntax in the Middle Ages: Background to an Aesthetic Problem." *Perspectives in New Music* 4 (1965): 75-85. Music created of the ordered rhythmic movement toward tonal goals and the building of musical structures of complementary phrases had its beginning in the Middle Ages. This model lasted until the beginning of the 20th century.

1423. Wallace, Robin. "The Role of Style in the Notre-Dame Period: A Preliminary Study." *The Journal of Musicological Research* 12, 4 (1993): 253-273.

1424. Werf, Hendrik van der. *Integrated Directory of Organa, Clausulae, and Motets of the Thirteenth Century.* Rochester, NY: H. van der Werf, 1989.

1425. Werf, Hendrik van der. *The Oldest Extant Part Music and the Origin of Western Polyphony.* 2 vols. Rochester, NY: H. van der Werf, 1993. A study of the Aquitanian and Calixtine repertories. Deals with the polyphonic structure, status of the mss., oral element in the transmission of the music, verbal texts, rhythmic interpretation, and chromatic alteration, and the perplexing question of their liturgical function.

1426. Wright, Craig. "Leoninus, Poet and Musician." *JAMS* 39 (1986): 1-35. Wright reconstructs the life of Leoninus through church documents, Leonin's poetry and music, and what is commonly known about composers of polyphonic church music in this period.

1427. Yudkin, Jeremy. "The Copula According to Johannes de Garlandia." *Musica Disciplina* 34, 1 (1980): 67-84. According to Garlandia, St. Emmeram, and Anon. IV, the *copula* is a distinct form of polyphony, characterized by sectionalization and melodic sequence over a held tenor-tone. The theorists differ as to the number of voices involved (2 or 3) and the way the tenor was performed: as a sustained tone (Garlandia) or as subject to modal rhythm.

1428. Yudkin, Jeremy. "The Rhythm of Organum Purum." *Journal of Musicology* 2, 4 (1983): 355-76. After reviewing the writings of 25 scholars on the interpretation of rhythm in the duplum of organum duplum, Yudkin cites evidence in treatises of Johannes de Garlandia, Anonymous of St. Emmeram, and Anonymous IV that *organum purum* was not to be performed with modal rhythm, but that the length of the longs and shorts was to be determined by context.

1429. Yudkin, Jeremy. "The Anonymous of St. Emmeram and Anon. IV on the Copula." *MQ* 70, 1 (1984): 1-22. See also the author's translation of the *Anonymous of St. Emmeram.*

MASS AND MOTET TO 1400; CONDUCTUS

1430. Anderson, Gordon. "The Rhythm of the Monophonic Conductus in the Florence Manuscript as Indicated in Parallel Sources in Mensural Notation." *JAMS* 31 (1978): 480-89. Parallel mensural versions of conductus provide the clue to the convincing transcription of monophonic conductus: through the use of broadly interpreted iambic rhythms.

1431. Corrigan, Vincent J. *The Style of the Notre Dame Conductus.* 2 vols. Ph.D. diss., Indiana University, 1980. A study of the pitch, rhythm and form of the 3 and 4-part conductus and the problems involved in their transcription.

1432. Crocker, Richard. "French Polyphony of the 13th Century." In *NOHM II*, 1990. 636-678.

1433. Everist, Mark. *French Motets in the Thirteenth Century: Music, Poetry, and Genre.* Cambridge/New York: Cambridge University Press, 1994. A study of ms. sources, word-note relationships, musical and textual references in one motet to other works, and poetic and musical patterns in specific works. Major emphasis is placed on the word-music relationship within and between works, especially as it appears in the refrains.

1434. Falck, Robert. *The Notre Dame Conductus: A Study of the Repertory.* Musicological Studies, Vol. 33. Henryville, PA: Institute of Medieval Music, 1981.

1435. Fischer, K. von. "The Sacred Polyphony of the Italian Trecento." *PRMA* 100 (1973/4): 143-157. A survey of a repertory that is larger and has greater stylistic complexity than previously thought.

1436. Gillingham, Bryan. "A New Etiology and Etymology for the Conductus." *MQ* 75, 1 (1991): 59-73. Conductus was not originally conceived as music for processions; textual, etymological and musical evidence indicates that it began as a hybrid of the 12th-century hymn and sequence—a strophic form based on sequence poetry. The simplicity of this form made polyphonic setting a relatively simple matter.

1437. Kidwell, Susan Allison. *The Integration of Music and Text in the Early Latin Motet.* 2 vols. Ph.D. diss., University of Texas at Austin, 1993. Forty-five early Latin motets are studied as to properties of source clausulae, text underlay, text properties such as syntactic and symantic divisions, poetic assonance, and tenor quotation, in order to show how the articulation of musico-poetic structure, and the rhetorical interaction of music and text enhance the liturgical message of each motet.

1438. Leech-Wilkinson, Daniel. "Ars Antiqua—Ars Nova—Ars Subtilior." In *Antiquity and the Middle Ages*, James McKinnon, ed. Englewood Cliffs, NJ: Prentice Hall, 1990. 218-240. A study of the transition from 13th to 14th-century styles.

1439. Leech-Wilkinson, Daniel. *Machaut's Mass: An Introduction.* London: Oxford University Press, 1990. Detailed analysis shows Machaut to have conceived the 4-part texture as a whole rather than one line at a time. Includes performance guide and discussion of Machaut's life and possible liturgical functions of the Mass.

1440. Pesce, Dolores. "A Revised View of the Thirteenth-Century Latin Double Motet." *JAMS* 40, 3 (1987): 405-442. Rather than being a 'peripheral' phenomenon, the Continental Latin double (or bitextual) motet contains features also found in motets linked to the Notre Dame tradition. Although these motets have both French and non-French features, musical and ms. evidence supports their position in the center of French motet composition.

1441. Robertson, Anne Walters. "The Mass of Guillaume de Machaut in the Cathedral of Reims." In *Plainsong in the Age of Polyphony*, Thomas Forrest Kelly, ed. Cambridge/New York: Cambridge University Press, 1992. 100-139. Archival material, service books, and church architecture shed light on the liturgical, musical and spatial context in which Machaut worked and in which he composed the mass.

1442. Sanders, Ernest. "Conductus and Modal Rhythm." *JAMS* 38 (1985): 439-469. The origin of musical rhythm, especially in music before c. 1210, was in no way influenced by poetic (modal) rhythm; composers were often oblivious to accentual and rhythmic patterns in music.

1443. Smith, Norman E. "The Earliest Motets: Music and Words." *JRMA* 14, 2 (1989): 141-163. After surveying early scholarly opinion concerning which came first, early French and Latin motets or related discant clausulae, the author compares the notation of Latin motets to that of clausulae and determines that 1) most of the motets were based on clausulae and 2) the earliest motet writers were scrupulous in their reproductions of the clausulae models in all of their musical detail.

1444. Wathey, Andrew. "The Motets of Philippe de Vitry and the Fourteenth-century Renaissance." *Early Music History* Vol. 12 (1993): 119-151.

POLYPHONY, 1400-1600

1445. Berger, Anna Maria Besse. *Mensuration and Proportion Signs: Origin and Evolution*. Oxford: Clarendon Press, 1993. A detailed study of the signs that signify the mensural system.

1446. Bloxam, Mary Jennifer. *A Survey of Late Medieval Service Books from the Low Countries: Implications for Sacred Polyphony, 1460-1520*. Ph.D. diss., Yale University, 1987.

1447. Bloxam, M. Jennifer. "Sacred Polyphony and Local Traditions of Liturgy and Plainsong: Reflections on Music by Jacob Obrecht." In *Plainsong in the Age of Polyphony*, Thomas Forrest Kelly, ed. Cambridge Studies in Performance Practice, Cambridge, England; New York: Cambridge University Press, 1992. 140-177. For centuries prior to the Tridentine reforms, the structure of the liturgical year and the plainsong repertory varied from city to city. Bloxam uses two masses and a motet by Obrecht to demonstrate the local usages and sources of chant employed in the four northern cities where Obrecht worked.

1448. Brothers, Thomas. "Vestiges of the Isorhythmic Tradition in Mass and Motet, ca. 1450-1475." *JAMS* 44, 1/Spring (1991): 1-56. A study of 'modus disposition' and 'number disposition' as vestiges of isorhythmic construction, and an investigation of a chain of influence from Du Fay through Busnoy to Josquin based on isorhythmic tradition.

1449. Busse-Berger, Anna Maria. "Musical Proportions and Arithmetic in the Late Middle Ages and Renaissance." *Musica Disciplina* 44 (1990): 89-118. Late Medieval and Renaissance theorists and composers derived their system of mensural proportion, not from Euclid and Boethius, but from texts in commercial arithmetic, and particularly from the Rule of Three, a formula that came from 7th-century India, through Arabic writings, to Italy and the writings of Leonardo Fibonacci at the beginning of the 13th century.

1450. Caldwell, John. "Plainsong and Polyphony 1250-1550." In *Plainsong in the Age of Polyphony*, Thomas Forrest Kelly, ed. Cambridge Studies in Performance Practice, Cambridge, England; New York: Cambridge University Press, 1992. 6-31. Through the 13th century, plainsong was probably performed in equal note values. In the succeeding centuries, when polyphony and plainsong were performed in alternation, accommodations of plainsong to polyphony had to be reached with respect to pitch, mode, and rhythm.

1451. Cavanaugh, Philip. "Early Sixteenth Century Cycles of Polyphonic Mass Propers: An Evolutionary Process or the Result of Liturgical Reforms." *Acta Musicologica* 48 (1976): 151-165.

1452. Dixon, Graham. "Palestrina Quatercentenary." *Early Music* (1994): complete issue. Seven articles on different aspects of Palestrina's music.

1453. Fallows, David. "Specific Information on the Ensembles for Composed Polyphony, 1400-1474." In *Studies in the Performance of Late Medieval Music*, Stanley Boorman, ed. London: Cambridge University Press, 1983. 109-160. Instruments were not used in the performance of composed polyphony during this period. Records from the Court of Burgundy, as well as Dufay's will, provide information concerning the use of boy sopranos and male falsettists and in general more singers on the upper voice than on the lower two or three voices. Bottom lines without text were most likely vocalized by a single singer.

1454. Funkhouser, Sara Ann. *Heinrich Isaac and Number Symbolism: An Exegesis of Commemorative Motets Dedicated to Lorenzo de' Medici and Maximilian I*. D.M.A., University of Missouri, Kansas City, 1981. A demonstration that Isaac used golden mean, Fibonacci, and Pythagorian proportional systems, and gematria, qabalistic and other types of number symbolism consciously and consistently in all levels of form in the works under study.

1455. Goldberg, Clemens. "Text, Music, and Liturgy in Johannes Ockeghem's Masses." *Musica Disciplina* 44 (1990): 185-232. In Ockeghem's musically expressive and rhetorically symbolic settings of the 'qui tollis peccata mundi' sections of his Mass Glorias, the author finds evidence that late 15th-century composers (and artists in general) sought 'grace' in a personal relation to God at a time when grace was found to be missing from a Church considered corrupt.

1456. Judd, Cristle Collins. "Modal Types and Ut, Re, Mi Tonalities: Tonal Coherence in Sacred Vocal Polyphony from about 1500." *JAMS* 45, 3 (1992): 428-467. A study of modal structures or melodic-contrapuntal paradigms of tonal coherence in Josquin's motets based on concepts by Pietro Aron and Glarean.

1457. Kugle, Karl. *The Manuscript Ivrea, Biblioteca Capitolare 115: Studies in the Transmission and Composition of Ars Nova Polyphony.* Ph.D. diss., New York University, 1993.

1458. Leech-Wilkinson, Daniel. *Compositional Techniques in the Four-Part Isorhythmic Motets of Philippe de Vitry and his Contemporaries.* Outstanding Dissertations in Music from British Universities, New York/London: Garland Publishing, 1989. See JAMS 46, 2 (1993): 295-305.

1459. Nugent, G. "Anti-Protestant Music for Sixteenth-Century Ferrara." *JAMS* 43, 2 (1990): 228-291. A study of three pieces, including a Te Deum with a text cursing Martin Luther, that exemplify anti-Protestant religious and political propaganda invested in music through the order of political leaders.

1460. Reynolds, Christopher A. "The Counterpoint of Allusion in Fifteenth-century Masses." *JAMS* 45, 2/Summer (1992): 228-260. A study of the likelihood that the melodic references to chansons that were embedded in the contrapuntal voices of 15th-century masses functioned to interpret or amplify the meaning of the (unsung) text of the chanson melody serving as the tenor.

1461. Ward, Tom R. "The Polyphonic Office Hymn and the Liturgy of 15th-Century Italy." *Musica Disciplina* 26 (1980): 161-188. Large numbers of polyphonic hymns exist in ms. collections of 15th and early 16th-century Italy. They were performed in cycles the contents of which were determined by three factors: the occasions on which polyphony was performed as determined by its liturgical rank, the text assignment for these occasions as determined by local tradition, and the chant melody traditionally associated with each text. The appropriate chant melody was usually incorporated into the polyphonic setting.

1462. Woodruff, Lawrence Theodore. *The Missae de Beata Virgine c. 1500-1520: A Study of Transformation from Monophonic to Polyphonic Modality.* Ph.D. diss., North Texas State University, 1986.

1463. Wright, Craig. "Dufay's Nuper Rosarum Flores: King Solomon's Temple, and the Veneration of the Virgin." *JAMS* 47, 3 (1994): 395-441. The durational ratios in Dufay's motet are based, not on the structural proportions of the cathedral of Florence, but on the dimensions of the Temple of Solomon as given in I Kings 6:1-20 and the numerical symbolism associated with the Virgin Mary.

POLYPHONY, 1600-1800

1464. Brough, Delma. *Polish Seventeenth-Century Church Music: With Reference to the Influence of Historical, Political, and Social Conditions*. New York: Garland Publishers, 1989. A study of several cathedral cities, the Jesuits, the Piarits, and the Collegiate church at Lowicz, and their influence on different types of religious choral music.

1465. Carver, Anthony F. *Cori Spezzati*. Vol. 2. New York, NY: Cambridge University Press, 1988. Vol. 1, *The Development of Sacred Polychoral Music to the Time of Schutz*, traces the development of polychoral church music from its beginnings in the early 1500s to the works of Gabrieli and Schütz and treats in depth the music of such major composers as the Gabrielis, Lasso, Palestrina, and Victoria, as well as some important German composers. Vol. 2, *An Anthology of Sacred Polychoral Music*, consists of seventeen complete compositions.

1466. Eby, Jack. "Music at the Church of the SS Innocents, Paris, in the Late 18th Century." *JRMA* 117, 2 (1992): 247-269. For the four wealthiest churches of Paris—Notre Dame, Sainte-Chapelle, St. Germain l'Auxerrais, and SS Innocents—the most important musical genre of the period was the century old *grand motet*, a multi-movement work for soloists, chorus and orchestra. This study documents the occasions, budgets, and *maitres* associated with music at SS Innocents until its destruction for urban renewal in the late 1780s.

1467. Gianturco, Carolyn. "'Cantate Spirituali e Morali' with a Description of the Papal Sacred Cantata Tradition for Christmas 1676-1740." *Music & Letters* 73, 1/Feb. (1992): 1-30. Sacred cantatas, with Christ as the central figure, were performed after the First Vespers of Christmas with the Pope in attendance. Moral cantatas, which seem to be closely related to oratorios, were probably performed on both private and public occasions.

1468. Kirwan-Mott, Anne. *The Small-Scale Sacred Concertato in the Early Seventeenth Century*. 2 vols. Ann Arbor, MI: UMI Research Press, 1981. Vol. 1, Commentary; Vol. 2, transcription of works in Latin and German.

1469. Nelson, Bernadette. "*Alternatim* Practice in Seventeenth-Century Spain: The Integration of Organ Versets and Plainchant in Psalms and Canticles." *Early Music* Vol. 22, 2 (1994): 239-260. On the successful integration of organ music with the performance of psalms and canticles. Topics include the role of the organ, melodic formulae and pitch of psalm tones, *alternatim* practice and transposition, and psalm-tone transposition at the organ. Also discusses the retention of modal integrity with the approach of tonality and equal temperament.

1470. Noske, Frits. *Music Bridging Divided Religions: The Motet in the Seventeenth-Century Dutch Republic.* Wilhelmshaven, Ger.:F. Noetzel, Heinrichshofen-Books; New York: C.F. Peters, 1989. Throughout 17th-century Holland, Catholics and Protestants united to sing settings of sacred texts in the non-liturgical context of the collegium museum. Vol. 1, History; Vol. 2. Transcription.

1471. Potter, Susan R. *The Petit Motet in Parisian Printed Sources from 1647-1689.* 2 vols. Ph.D. diss., Rutgers University, New Jersey, 1993. An examination of over 270 motets composed by six composers during the reign of Loius XIV. Focuses on the relationship between the music, which embodies the ideals of logic and clarity, and the Latin texts, most of which are Biblical or liturgical, and how these elements expressed personal religious sentiment or were used for intimate devotions.

1472. Roche, Jerome. *North Italian Church Music in the Age of Monteverdi.* Oxford: Clarendon Press, 1984.

NON-LITURGICAL RELIGIOUS MONODY AND POLYPHONY TO 1700

1473. Barr, Cyrilla. *The Monophonic Lauda and the Lay Religious Confraternities of Tuscany and Umbria in the Late Middle Ages.* Kalamazoo, MI: Medieval Institute Publications, Western Michigan University, 1988. An examination of the turbulent social conditions of the late 13th century, with its flagellant fraternaties, and the devotional popular hymnody found in Cortona 91, one of only two of the two hundred laude mss. that contain music.

1474. Boenig, Robert. "Music and Mysticism in Hildegard von Bingen's *O Ignis Spiritus Paracliti.*" *Studia Mystica* Vol. 9, No. 3, Fall (1986): 60-72.

1475. Brown, Howard Mayer. "The Mirror of Man's Salvation: Music in Devotional Life about 1500." *Renaissance Quarterly* 43, Wint. (1990): 744-773. On devotional motets published in four service book anthologies by Petrucci.

1476. Epstein, Marcy J. *'Prions en Chantant': An Edition with Commentary of the Old French Devotional Songs in the Manuscripts Paris, Bibliotheque Nationale Fr. 24406 and Bibliotheque Nationale N. A. Fr. 1050.* Ph.D. diss., University of Toronto, 1981. A study and transcription of 61 trouvere devotional songs from the 13th century shows them to be more expressive and less didactic than most other devotional lyric traditions.

1477. Grier, James Norman. "Scribal Practices in the Aquitanian Versaria of the Twelfth Century: Towards a Typology of Error and Variant." *JAMS* 45, 3 (1992): 373-427. For versaria that exist in two or more versions, the author distinguishes between five types of errors and five types of variants and attempts to account for these phenomena in circumstances in the transmission and practice of the music.

1478. Grier, James Norman. *Transmission in the Aquitanian Versaria of the Eleventh and Twelfth Centuries.* Ph.D. diss., University of Toronto, 1985. A study of one of the earliest extensive, surviving collections of monophonic and polyphonic non-liturgical sacred music. This study establishes the history of each piece as it passed from ms. to ms., singer to singer, in a context which permitted and even encouraged singers to insert variants intentionally.

1479. Holsinger, Bruce Wood. "The Flesh of the Voice: Embodiment and the Homoerotics of Devotion in the Music of Hildegard of Bingen." *Signs* 19, 1 (1993): 92-125. A study of how Hildegard of Bingen links religious devotion to sexual aspects of the female body and exhibits in her music rather than through her texts the subversiveness of women to patriarchal authority and tradition.

1480. Huseby, Gerardo Victor. *The 'Cantigas de Santa Maria' and the Medieval Theory of Mode.* Ph.D. diss., Stanford University, 1983. This study of 415 cantigas shows their melodic features to be closely related to the theoretical formulation of the system of eight modes found in treatises from the 11th through the early 14th centuries.

1481. Jeffery, Peter. "Popular Culture on the Periphery of the Medieval Liturgy." *Worship* 55 (1981): 419-27. A study of Medieval musical genres that enabled lay persons to participate in worship, especially in the areas of preaching, pilgrimages, and the houses of women's religious orders.

1482. Jeskalian, Barbara J. "Hildegard of Bingen: Her Times and Music." *Anima* 10, Fall (1983): 7-13. A discussion of the music and times of the 12th-century German composer, poet, dramatist, painter, herbalist, and mystic.

1483. Joldersma, Hermina. "Appropriating Secular Song for Mystical Devotion in the Late Middle Ages: The Tannhäuser Ballad in Brussels MS II, 2631." *Mystics Quarterly* 18, Mar. (1992): 16-28. An examination of the route by which a secular song of the Netherlandic late-Medieval period came to be transformed into a vernacular religious song used by the Franciscan Tertiary. The author argues for the strong influence of the mystics.

1484. Knapp, Janet. "Musical Declamation and Poetic Rhythm in an Early Layer of Notre Dame Conductus." *JAMS* 32 (1979): 383-407. In the early Notre Dame conductus, a trochaic poetic pattern did not assume first mode rhythm: sources show many instances of fifth mode equal measured style.

1485. Kreitner, Kenneth. "Minstrels in Spanish Churches, 1400-1600." *Early Music* 20, Nov. (1992): 532-546. A study of the distinctive Spanish practice of employing minstrels, with the instruments that they used, for limited functions in church services.

1486. Macey, Patrick. "The Lauda and the Cult of Savonarola." *Renaissance Quarterly* 45, 3/Autumn (1992): 439-483. After the death of Savonarola in 1498, *laude*, a type of devotional hymn, were used by his followers to keep alive his anti-status-quo religious and political beliefs.

1487. Noske, Frits. *Saints and Sinners: The Latin Musical Dialogue in the Seventeenth Century.* Oxford: Clarendon Press; New York: Oxford University Press, 1993. A history and survey, with transcriptions, of the 17th century Biblical and non-Biblical Latin dialogue set to music. Largely Italian and Catholic, the dialogues were included in the liturgy for educational and instructional purposes.

1488. Pfau, Marianne Richert. *Hildegard von Bingen's 'Symphonia Armonie Celestium Revelationum': An Analysis of Musical Process, Modality, and Text-Music Relations.* Ph.D. diss., SUNY at Stony Brook, 1990. Known collectively as Symphonia, the sacred compositions of the 12th-century abbess are seen as evolving processes that involve the interrelationship of melody and language (Chap. 2). Later chapters treat Hildegard's indiosyncratic tone system, analyze text-music relations in songs, and discuss a rhetoric based on phonetic, syntactic and semantic interrelations between language and music.

1489. Stevens, John. "Medieval Song." In *NOHM II*, new ed. Richard Crocker, ed. Oxford, New York: Oxford University Press, 1990. 357-451.

MUSICAL INSTRUMENTS IN RELIGIOUS MUSIC TO c.1700

1490. Bonta, S. "The Use of Instruments in Sacred Music in Italy 1560-1700." *Early Music* 18, 4/Nov. (1990): 519-532.

1491. Bush, Douglas Earl. *The Liturgical Use of the Organ in German Regions Prior to the Protestant Reformation: Contracts, Consuetudinaries, and Musical Repertories.* Ph.D. diss., University of Texas at Austin, 1982. A study of contracts, liturgical books, and various collections of music, particularly those relating to Arnolt Schlick (early 16th century) concerning organ music.

1492. Cox, Vivia Jean. *An Investigation of the Origin of Bells in the Western Christian Church Based upon a Study of Musical Instruments Used within Worship Services at Major Religious Shrines of Europe and the Middle East (500B.C.E.-800 C.E.): The Parthenon, the Jewish Temple, Hagia Sophia, and St. Peter's.* Ph.D. diss., Florida State University, 1990. The practice of ringing bells at St. Peters, which already existed in the middle of the eighth century, has no precedents in Greek, Jewish, or Eastern Orthodox tradition. This practice appears to have been derived from other, as yet unknown, sources. Possibilites include religious shrines in Egypt, Syria, and northern India. There may be a link between bell ringing in ancient Buddhism and Hellenistic culture of the Middle East.

1493. Korrick, Leslie. "Instrumental Music in the Early 16th-century Mass: New Evidence." *Early Music* 18, 3 (1990): 359-369.

1494. McKinnon, James. *The Church Fathers and Musical Instruments.* Ph.D. diss., Colombia University, 1965.

1495. McKinnon, James. "The Meaning of the Patristic Polemic against Musical Instruments." *Current Musicology* 1 (1965): 69-82. The vehement and uniform antipathy to instruments in liturgy during the patristic period was based on a moral aversion to instruments, associated as they were with entertainment and pagan cults, and on a liturgy in which instruments would have been irrelevant and inappropriate.

1496. McKinnon, James. "Musical Instruments in Medieval Psalm Commentaries and Psalters." *JAMS* 21 (1968): 3-20. Music instruments other than the organ were not employed in the medieval liturgy; literary references are allegorical and iconographic. Documents never show monks playing instruments.

1497. McKinnon, James. "The Tenth Century Organ at Winchester." *The Organ Yearbook* 5 (1974): 4-19.

1498. McKinnon, James. "Representations of the Mass in Medieval and Renaissance Art." *JAMS* 31, 1 (1978): 21-52. Pictorial evidence supports the view that *a cappella* ecclesiastical performance of liturgical music was the norm during the 15th century, although there were scattered exceptions. Employment of instruments increased during the 16th century, with Spain taking the lead, followed by Italy and England. France does not adopt the practice until after the close of the century.

1499. McKinnon, James. "Fifteenth-Century Northern Book Painting and the A Cappella Question: An Essay in Iconographic Method." In *Studies in the Performance of Late Medieval Music*, Stanley Boorman, ed. London: Cambridge University Press, 1983. 1-18. Of the hundreds of 15th-century Flemish and French artworks that depict liturgical events, many include singers, but none includes instruments other than the organ. On the basis of five criteria, McKinnon concludes that during this period, liturgical music was performed without the participation of instruments.

1500. Page, Christopher. "Instruments and Instrumental Music before 1300." In *NOHM II*, Richard Crocker, ed. Oxford, New York: Oxford University Press, 1990. 451-484.

1501. Schaefer, Edward E. *The Relationship between the Liturgy of the Roman Rite and the Italian Organ Literature of the Sixteenth and Seventeenth Centuries.* DMA diss., Catholic University of America, 1985. Combining the musical taste of the time with current liturgical norms, the history of organ music paralleled the history of the liturgy.

1502. Schroeder-Sheker, Therese. "The Use of Plucked-Stringed Instruments in Medieval Christian Mysticism." *Mystics Quarterly* 15, Spr. (1989): 133-139. On the mystical use of instruments by Mechtild of Hacheborn (13th century).

1503. Van Deusen, Nancy. "Medieval Organologies: Augustine vs Cassiodor on the Subject of Musical Instruments." In *Augustine on Music: An Interdisciplinary Collection of Essays*, Richard R. La Croix, ed. Lewiston, NY: E. Mellen Press, 1988. 53-96. Van Deusen contrasts Augustine's practical, pastoral and influential commentary on the place of musical instruments with Cassiodor's more academic, philosophical and nuanced approach.

1504. Williams, Peter F. "How Did the Organ Become a Church Instrument: Questions Towards an Understanding of Benedictine and Carolingian Cultures." In *Visitatio Organorum*, A. Dunning, ed. Vol. 2. 1980. 603-618.

1505. Williams, Peter F. *The Organ in Western Culture, 750-1250*. Cambridge Studies in Medieval and Renaissance Music, New York: Cambridge University Press, 1993. A thorough examination of all sources concerning the nature, uses, and methods of performance of the organ at different times and places during the Middle Ages. Special attention is paid to European monasticism around 1000 AD, and particularly to the resourcefulness of the Benedictine reformers.

1506. Williams, Peter F. *The King of Instruments: How Churches Came to Have Organs*. London: SPCK, 1993.

20

Liturgical Reforms of the 19th and 20th Centuries. Vatican II (1962–1965)

VATICAN DOCUMENTS

1507. Abbot, Walter M., ed. *The Documents of Vatican II with Notes and Comments by Catholic, Protestant and Orthodox Authorities.* Piscataway, NJ: New Century Publishers, 1974.

1508. Catholic Church. National Conference of Catholic Bishops. Bishops' Committee on the Liturgy. *Liturgical Music Today: A Statement of the Bishops' Committee on the Liturgy on the Occasion of the Tenth Anniversary of Music in Catholic Worship.* Washington, DC: Bishops' Committee on the Liturgy, National Conference of Catholic Bishops, 1982.

1509. "Constitution on the Sacred Liturgy of the Second Vatican Council." In *Documents of Vatican II*, Austin P. Flannery, ed. Grand Rapids, MI: Eerdman's, 1984. 1-282.

1510. Hayburn, Robert F. *Papal Legislation on Sacred Music, 95 A.D. to 1977 A.D.* Collegeville, MN: Liturgical Press, 1979. A study of papal legislation with translation of generous portions of the original texts.

1511. Huck, Gabe, ed. *The Liturgy Documents: A Parish Resourch.* Chicago, IL: Liturgy Training Publications, 1991. This collection includes "Constitution on the Sacred Liturgy," "Music in Catholic Worship," and "Liturgical Music Today".

1512. O'Brien, Thomas C., ed. *Documents on the Liturgy, 1963-1979: Conciliar, Papal, and Curial Texts/International Commission on English in the Liturgy.* Thomas O'Brien, transl. Collegeville, MN: The Liturgical Press, 1982.

1513. Pius XII, Pope. *Musicae Sacrae Disciplina*. Washington, DC: National Catholic Welfare Conference, 1956. Encyclical Letter. Repr. in *Sacred Music*, 118, 4 (1991): 7-17.

1514. Seasoltz, Kevin. *The New Liturgy: A Documentation. 1903-1965*. New York: Herder and Herder, 1966.

1515. Society of St. Gregory of America. Music Committee. *The White List of the Society of St. Gregory of America: With a Selection of Papal Documents and other Information Pertaining to Catholic Church Music*. Glen Rock, NJ: The Society, 1947/repr. 1958. Reissued in 1958 with supplement. Separate supplements to the 4th ed. issued in 1951 and 1953.

1516. Vatican Council [2nd: 1962-1965]. *Constitution of the Sacred Liturgy*. Collegeville, MN: Liturgical Press, 1963. In Latin and English.

STUDIES

1517. Adam, Adolf. *The Liturgical Year: Its History and its Meaning after the Reform of the Liturgy*. New York: Pueblo Publishing Company, 1981. Original German, 1979.

1518. Barnes, Andrew E. "Religious Reform and the War against Ritual." *Journal of Ritual Studies* 4 (1990): 127-33.

1519. *Baptism, Eucharist and Ministry*. Geneva: World Council of Churches, 1982. Ecumenical views on sacraments and Christian union, with emphasis on such topics as baptism and the Lord's Supper.

1520. *Baptism, Eucharist and Ministry 1982-1990: Report on the Process and Responses*. Geneva: World Council of Churches, 1990. Ecumenical views on Christian liturgy, compiled by the Commission on Faith and Order of the World Council of Churches.

1521. Bergeron, Katherine Ann. *Representation, Reproduction, and the Revival of Gregorian Chant at Solesmes*. Ph.D. diss., Cornell University, 1989. An examination of the graphological aspects of the revival of Gregorian Chant and the attempts to define and regulate Gregorian rhythm for all time.

1522. Browne, Deirdre. "The Contemporary Composer and Liturgical Reform." *Worship* 61, Jan. (1987): 16-25. Browne develops four themes: the composer as artist, the relationship between composer and church, possible responses to the demand for new liturgical music, and solutions to current difficulties.

1523. Bugnini, Annibale. *The Reform of the Liturgy 1948-1975*. Matthew J. O'Connell, transl. Collegeville, MN: The Liturgical Press, 1990. Italian original, 1983.

1524. Carroll, Catherine A. *A History of the Pius X School of Liturgical Music: 1916-1969*. St. Louis, MO: Society of the Sacred Heart, 1989. The story of the rise and demise of the Pius X School of Liturgical Music in Manhattanville, N.Y, and of its faculty who championed the use of Latin chant.

1525. *The Crisis of Liturgical Reform*. Concilium: Theology in the Age of Renewal, Vol. 42, New York: Paulist Press, 1969.

1526. Day, Thomas. "Twentieth-century Church Music: An Elusive Modernity." *Communio: International Catholic Review* Vol. 6 (1979): 236-256.

1527. Day, Thomas. *Why Catholics Can't Sing: The Culture of Catholicism and the Triumph of Bad Taste*. New York: Crossroad, 1990. An attack on the factors that have led to a decline in quality of Catholic singing: Vatican II, a pervasive 1960's mentality, folksy jargon, feel-good lyrics, the use of speaker systems, a focus on one singer-the cantor, etc. See whole issue of *Pastoral Music* 15, 6, 1991, for a rebuttal: "Why Catholics Can Sing."

1528. DeSanctis, Michael Edward. *Some Artistic Aspects of Catholic Liturgical Reform: A Comparative Study of the Influence of Vatican Council II on Music and Architecture for the Liturgy*. Ph.D. diss., Ohio University, 1985. This study of the Liturgical Movement, major articles of liturgical law, and four contemporary settings of the Ordinary of the Mass, proposes that the simplification and regionalization evident in the Mass settings indicates that sanctity as an intrinsic quality and elaborate artistic magnification are less important than accommodation to active participation of the liturgical assembly.

1529. Dimock, G. "Baroque Liturgy on Trial." *Sacred Music* 116, 2/Summer (1989): 19-24. A defense of Baroque arts against the charge of being too theatrical to be sacred. Modern church music, in its quest for the immediately appealing, has settled for the banal and could benefit from the transcendence of the Baroque.

1530. Dinges, William D. "Ritual Conflict as Social Conflict: Liturgical Reform in the Roman Catholic Church." *Sociological Analysis* 48, 2 (1987-8): 138-58.

1531. Dix, Gregory. *The Shape of the Liturgy*. 2nd, rev. ed., New York: Seabury, 1982. The classic of liturgical theory. Stresses the impact of social context on the development of liturgy. With additional notes by P.V. Marshall.

1532. Doran, Carol and Thomas Troeger. "Recognizing an Ancient Unity: Music and Liturgy as Complementary Disciplines." *Worship* 60 (1986): 386-398.

1533. Draeger, Hans-Heinz. "The Order of the Arts in the Catholic Service." In *Paul A. Pisk. Essays in his Honor*, John Glowacki, ed. Austin, TX: University of Texas, 1966. Draeger employs the terms *mimesis* (imitation of nature) and *poiesis* (the uniquely human creative capacity) to explain why music occupies the highest place of the arts in the Catholic liturgy: music alone attains to the transcendency of the liturgy, with chant, sacred polyphony, and popular hymns being the order of approved forms of music.

1534. Foley, Edward. *Music in Ritual: A Pre-Theological Investigation.* American Essays In Liturgy, Washington, DC: The Pastoral Press, 1984. An investigation of music in ritual and a designation of music as power, communication, language, and symbol. Concludes that music fills a void in worship with its symbolic import and is an integral part of ritual.

1535. Foley, Edward. "Liturgical Musicology Redux." *Worship* 64 (1990): 264-8. While agreeing with Mannion (see entries in this section) that things are not as good as they could be, Foley points to the scholars' work and participation in liturgical music that is taking place today, thereby disputing the main contentions of Mannion (and Peter Jeffery) to the contrary.

1536. Foley, Edward. "Music, Liturgical." In *The New Dictionary of Sacramental Worship*, S.J. Peter E. Fink, ed. Collegeville, MN: Liturgical Press, 1990. 854-870.

1537. Foley, Edward. "Music in Catholic Worship," and "Liturgical Music Today." In *The Liturgy Documents. A Parish Resource*, Gabe Huck, ed. Chicago: Liturgy Training Program, Archdiocese of Chicago, 1991. 269-291, 292-312.

1538. Foley, Edward. "Toward a Sound Theology." *Studia Liturgica* 23, 2 (1993): 121-139. Foley answers the question "is music integral to worship?" by pointing to the properties of music and of sound itself that also describe our experience of God as understood in the Judeo-Christian tradition: Sound provides the experience of impermanence, the intangible, activity, engagement, and the personal. These correlate to our understanding of God as historical, elusive presence, dynamic, relational, and personal.

1539. Foley, Edward, Sue Seid-Martin, Fred R. Anderson, and Virgil C. Funk. "Tradition and Enculturation in the Music of the Liturgy: A Symposium." *Proceedings of the Annual Meeting of the North American Academy of Liturgy, Nashville, Tennessee, 2-5 January 1989* (1989): 40-60. Valparaiso, IN: North American Academy of Liturgy

1540. Franklin, R.W. "Guéranger and Pastoral Liturgy: A Nineteenth Century Context." *Worship* 50, 2 (1976): 146-162.

1541. Franklin, R.W. "The Nineteenth Century Liturgical Movement." *Worship* 52, 1 (1978): 12-39.

1542. Funk, Virgil C., ed. *Music in Catholic Worship/the Bishops' Committee on the Liturgy. The NPM Commentary: A Collection of Articles First Published in Pastoral Music Magazine.* 2nd, rev. ed., Washington, DC: The Pastoral Press,

1983. The 1972 guidelines for liturgical renewal, with commentaries on the quidelines published between 1976 and 1980 in *Pastoral Music Magazine*.

1543. Funk, Virgil C. and Gabe Huck, ed. *Pastoral Music in Practice: A Collection of Articles First Published in Pastoral Music Magazine*. Washington, DC: The Pastoral Press, 1981. Includes articles by Weakland and Gelineau.

1544. Gamber, Klaus. *The Reform of the Roman Liturgy: Its Problems and Background*. San Juan Capistrano: Una Voce Press; Harrison, NY: Foundation for Catholic Reform, 1993.

1545. Gelineau, Joseph. *Psalmody in the Vernacular, the Theory and Application of the Gelineau Method of Psalmody*. Toledo, OH: Gregorian Institute of America, 1965.

1546. Gelineau, Joseph. *The Liturgy Today and Tomorrow*. New York: Paulist Press, 1978. On the difficulties of maintaining the laity's interest in the liturgy and steps that can be taken to make the liturgy both available and evocative.

1547. Gelineau, Joseph. *Learning to Celebrate: The Mass and Its Music. 16 Suggested Approaches*. Mary Anselm Grover, SNJM, transl. Washington, DC: Pastoral Press, 1985.

1548. Gelineau, Joseph. "The Path of Music." In *Music and the Experience of God*, 1989. 135-147. On the element of music in the Christian liturgy as it relates to the voice, the word, the hymn, and 'the song of the bride'.

1549. Gelineau, Joseph. "Music and Singing in the Liturgy." In *The Study of Liturgy*, 2nd, rev. ed. Wainwright, Jones, Yarnold, and Bradshaw, eds. New York: Oxford University Press, 1992. 493-507.

1550. Halmo, Joan and Todd Ridder. "Liturgical Musicology." *Worship* 64 (1990): 460-2. On academic institutions that offer programs in liturgical music.

1551. Hanshell, D. "The Shape of Things to Come in Liturgy." *Sacred Music* 119, 4 (1992): 15-18.

1552. Herring, William. *The Role of Music in the New Roman Liturgy*. Oak Park IL: American Catholic Press, 1971.

1553. Hucke, Helmut. "Church Music." In *The Church and the Liturgy*, Johannes Wagner, ed. Concilium: Theology in the Age of Renewal, Liturgy Vol. 2, Glen Rock, NJ: Paulist Press, 1964. 111-134. An examination of the far-reaching implications of Vatican II for Catholic music, and specifically of the call for the close linking of music to the liturgy, the direct involvement of the congregation, and the use of a great range of musical styles.

1554. Hucke, Helmut. "The Roman Instruction on Music in the Liturgy." *Concilium* Vol. 32 (1968): 119-138. A description of the instructions issued in *Musicam Sacram* of 1967 compared to those of *De Musica Sacra et Sacra Liturgia* of 1958. The removal of the term "sacred music" from the later tract indicates the view that music is to be an integral outgrowth of the liturgical action, not a mere embellishment to it. No restrictions are made with respect to style, and local churches have greater autonomy in choice of music and musical forces.

1555. Hucke, Helmut. "Jazz and Folk Music in the Liturgy." In *The Crisis of Liturgical Reform*, Concilium: Theology in the Age of Renewal, Vol. 42, New York and Glen Rock, NJ: Paulist Press, 1969. 138-72. A description of new forms of church music, a survey of usages of folk and popular music in various locations in the Catholic world, and an argument that any music used in liturgy should be so used for its appropriateness, not its popular appeal.

1556. Hucke, Helmut. "Towards a New Kind of Church Music." In *Liturgy in Transition*, Hermann Schmidt, ed. Concilium: Theology in the Age of Renewal, Vol. 62, New York: Herder & Herder, 1971. 87-97. A call for abandoning traditional categories and the attempt to preserve particular repertories and instead for developing a music that is appropriate both to the liturgy and to each worshipping community.

1557. Hucke, Helmut, Réné Reboud, Erhard Quack, and Stephen Mbunga. "New Church Music in the Vernacular." In *The Church Worships*, Johannes Wagner and Heinrich Rennings, ed. Concilium: Theology in the Age of Renewal Vol. 12, New York and Glen Rock, NJ: Paulist Press, 1966. 93-130. Brief articles on church music in France, Germany, Tanzania, Indonesia, and Australia.

1558. Huijbers, Bernard. "Liturgical Music after the Second Vatican Council." In *Symbol and Art in Worship*, Luis Maldonado and David Power, ed. Concilium: Religion in the Eighties 132 (1980, no. 2), New York: Seabury Press, 1980. 101-111. An investigation of sacred music from three standpoints: 1) the interaction between music and other elements of the liturgy; 2) the dual roles of the congregation as celebrants and as performers; and 3) the interaction between musical elements and the contents of the liturgy.

1559. Jeffery, Peter. "Chant East and West: Toward a Renewal of the Tradition." In *Music and the Experience of God*, Collins, Power, and Burnim, ed. Concilium: Religion in the Eighties, Edinburgh: T. and T. Clark, 1989. 20-29. An appeal for the application of information from both historical and anthropological disciplines to heal the rift between "sacred music" and "pastoral music" advocates.

1560. John Paul II. "Music: An Essential Part of Liturgy." *Sacred Music* 116, 2/Summer (1989): 29.

1561. Kilmartin, E.J. *Christian Liturgy: Theology and Practice.* I. Systematic Theology of the Liturgy, Kansas City: Sheed & Ward, 1988. On Roman Catholic ligurgy.

1562. Kock, Gerard. "Between the Altar and the Choir-loft: Church music— Liturgy or Art." In *Music and the Experience of God*, 1989. 11-19. On the Second Vatican Council and Consociatio Internationalis Musicae Sacrae (CIMS).

1563. Lang, Paul Henry. "The *Patrimonium Musicae Sacrae* and the Task of Sacred Music Today." *Sacred Music* 93 (1966-67): 119-31. A plea to reintroduce high artistic standards and the findings of modern scholarship into liturgical music, as well as a recognition of the increased involvement of the congregation.

1564. Lanners, Norita. *Chant: From Gueranger to Gelineau.* American Essays in Liturgy 2, Washington, DC: The Pastoral Press, 1984. A description of liturgical reform from 1833, the founding of the Benedictine Abbey of Solesmes by Guéranger, to the 1980's, with emphasis on the reforms by Joseph Gelineau.

1565. Licon, Peggy Ann. *Twentieth-century Liturgical Reform in the Catholic Church and a Sample of Current Choral Literature.* D.M.A., Arizona State University, 1989. The current trend to exclude the parish or cathedral choir is the result of a gross misinterpretation of Vatican II directives concerning participation of the congregation and the use of vernacular.

1566. MacCarthy, P.T. "Listening and Liturgy." *Sacred Music* 120, 3/Fall (1993): 34-38.

1567. Mannion, M. Francis. "Liturgy and the Present Crisis of Culture." *Worship* 62 (1988): 98-123. The modern liturgy has had limited success in generating social transformation; modern culture, however, has damaged considerably the perception and practice of the liturgy. Topics include the subjectification of reality, the intimization of society, and the politicization of culture.

1568. Mannion, M. Francis. "The Need for an Adequate Liturgical Musicology." *Worship* 64 (1990): 78-81. A response in agreement with Peter Jeffery that until the liturgical renewal movement enlists the aid of serious scholarship in the area of music, the Catholic church will be hopelessly polarized between proponents of traditional classical music and those of the latest in pop church music fads. Unfortunately, very few universities offer degree programs in liturgical music.

1569. Morris, Brian. *Ritual Murder: Essays on Liturgical Reform.* Manchester: Carcanet New Press, 1980.

1570. Murray, Gregory. *Music and the Mass: A Personal History*. Essex, Eng.: Kevin Mayhew, 1977.

1571. Nash, A. "The Liturgy Vacuum: A Personal Viewpoint." *Sacred Music* 119, 2 (1992): 11-17. In the past, plainsong and polyphony *were* the liturgy. With the recent reforms, non-sacramental hymns, often from Protestant and popular or folk sources, have replaced the traditional chant texts. The liturgy has been replaced by hymn-singing. Let the liturgical music of the Latin rite return to be the soil for new vernacular chant and music.

1572. Nocent, Ardien. "Word and Music in the Liturgy." In *Music and the Experience of God*, Collins, Power, and Burnim, ed. 1989. 127-134. Nocent asserts that the ideal of worshipful expression is in music, but in a music that resembles the forms of the Old and New Testaments: little or no instrumentation and with an emphasis on the text as proclamation, not mere statement.

1573. Overath, Johannes, ed. *Sacred Music and Liturgy Reform after Vatican II: Proceedings of the Fifth International Church Music Congress, Chicago-Milwaukee, August 21-28, 1966*. Rome: Consociatio Internationalis Musicae Sacrae, 1969.

1574. Overath, Johannes. *Crux et Cithera: Selected Essays on Liturgy and Sacred Music*. Robert A. Skeris, transl. Altotting: Verlag Alfred Coppenrath, 1983.

1575. Pierce, Joanne M. "Early Medieval Liturgy: Some Implications for Contemporary Practice." *Worship* 65, 6 (Nov., 1991): 509-522. The adaptation of the Roman Liturgy, with its terse, sparce phrasing, in France and Germany from the late 8th- through the late 11th-centuries suggests that creative solutions may once again solve the problems of a liturgy in transition.

1576. Pitre, Richard. *Preliminary Consideration for a Theological Anthropology of Music*. M.Th. thesis, Jesuit School of Theology at Berkeley, California, 1988. In line with the dictates of Vatican II, Pitre enlists Zuckerkandl (the phenomenology of music), Maurice Merleau-Ponty (the phenomenology of the body) and Schenker (tone-directed motion) in order to move from an idiologically-based use of music in ritual to one that explores music's ability to creatively control time and engender inter-subjective unity.

1577. Pol-Topis, Margaret, Kevin Donovan et al., ed. *Growing in Church Music: Proceedings of a Meeting on "Why Church Music"*. Washington, DC: Universa Laus, 1979. Articles by Hucke, East, Costa, Huijbers and Gelineau on Catholic music since Vatican II.

1578. Quinn, Frank C. *Music in Catholic Worship: The Effect of Ritual on Music and Music on Ritual*. Proceedings of the Annual Meeting of the North American Academy of Liturgy, Nashville, Tennessee, 2-5 January 1989, 161-76, Valparaiso, Indiana: North American Academy of Liturgy, 1989.

1579. Schmemann, Alexander. *Introduction to Liturgical Theology.* Asheleigh E. Moorhouse, transl. 3rd ed. Crestwood, NY: St. Vladimir's Seminary Press, 1986.

1580. Schmitt, Francis P. *Church Music Transgressed: Reflections on "Reform."* New York: Seabury Press, 1977. Everyone knows today's church music is agonizingly crude and banal, yet no one will state the obvious. An eloquent and delightfully written defense by a Capuchin friar from 1529 of art—or skillfully written—music as functional in the highest sense.

1581. Schneider, Marius. "On Gregorian Chant and the Human Voice." *The World of Music* 24, 3 (1982): 3-21. Schneider proposes that Gregorian chant, as sound befitting words addressed to God, holds a special function not only in the musical traditions that have survived until today, but also on a subconscious level through the inherent qualities of the chant.

1582. Scott, Darwin Floyd, compiler and annotater. *The Roman Catholic Liturgy and Liturgical Books: A Musical Guide.* 3rd ed., UCLA Music Library Bibliography Series, no. 5, Los Angeles, CA: UCLA, 1988.

1583. Seasoltz, R. Kevin. *New Liturgy, New Laws.* Collegeville, MN: Liturgical Press, 1980. An overview of the changes in the sacraments, liturgical books, liturgy, and other issues brought about by Vatican II. Includes an extensive bibliography of official documents pertaining to liturgical renewal.

1584. Simmons, Robert M. "Syncretism in Sacred Music: Corridor to Intentional Inclusiveness." *Journal of Theology* 96 (1992): 60-76. Advocates and provides the criteria for the blending of compatible musical elements of African-American and Euro-American sacred music as a way of consciously promoting inclusivity in church membership.

1585. Sinclair, Jane. *Keeping in Tune with Heaven: A Response to the Report of the Archbishops' Commission on Church Music.* Grove Worship Series, No. 122, Bramcote, Notts: Grove Books, 1992.

1586. Skeris, Robert A., ed. *Cum Angeles Canere: Essays on Sacred Music and Pastoral Liturgy in Honour of Richard J. Schuler, 1920-1990.* Saint Paul, MN: Catholic Church Music Associates, 1990.

1587. Skeris, Robert A. *Divini Cultus Studium: Studies in the Theology of Worship and of its Music.* Altotting: Verlag Alfred Coppenrath, 1990.

1588. Skeris, Robert A. "Liturgical Music and the Restoration of the Sacred." *Sacred Music* 118, 2 (1991): 7-14. and 119, 3 (1992): 7-22.

1589. Starkhouse, Max. "Ethical Vision and Musical Imagination." *Theological Education* 31, 1 (1994): 149-164.

1590. Stefani, Gino. "Does the Liturgy Still Need Music?" In *The Crisis of Liturgical Reform*, Concilium: Theology in the Age of Renewal 42, 1969. 71-86. In contrast to arguments for the use of words, arguments that are basically theological, the traditional arguments for the use of music in liturgy are more anthropological and sociological. The modern approach should encourage an openness to the use of music of various types when appropriate to text and occasion.

1591. Turner, Victor. "Ritual, Tribal and Catholic." *Worship* 50 (1976): 504-26. A comparison of Pre-Conciliar and Ndembu (Zambian) rituals. By catering to fashion and fads in its liturgy, Roman Catholicism is in danger of loosing the sense of presence, rich symbolism, community, and unity of performer with the performed that characterizes deep ritual.

1592. Universa Laus. "The Music of Christian Ritual: Universa Laus Guidelines 1980." *Universa Laus, An International Study Group for Liturgical Music: Bulletin 30* (1980): 4-15.

1593. Universa Laus. "Music in Christian Celebration: A Document Prepared by Universa Laus." *Music and Liturgy* 6, 3 & 4 (1980): 151-161. A set of 10 principles or frames of reference formulated by a group of liturgical musicians to deal with Vatican II, the encounter of worship and culture, and the results of the new cross-fertilization of academic disciplines.

1594. Weakland, Rembert. "Music as Art in Liturgy." *Worship* 41 (1967): 5-15. An article on the direction of music in the Catholic church after Vatican II—that music must serve the liturgy—and his assessment that, because music has always taken precedence over the liturgy, there was no liturgical golden age and that the Romantic period mistakenly considered the Medieval period as the height of the Christian aesthetic.

1595. Winter, Miriam T. *Why Sing? Toward a Theology of Catholic Church Music*. Washington, DC: Pastoral Press, 1984.

21

Orthodox and Other Non-Latin Christian Rites: Liturgy and Music

ORTHODOX LITURGIES AND MUSIC

General Reference

1596. [Non-Latin Rites: Music and Liturgy]. In *Grove 6*, 1980. For music of the Non-Latin rites, see "Armenian Rite," "Byzantine Rite," "Coptic Rite," "Ethiopian Rite," and "Georgian Rite," as well as "Russian and Slavonic Church music," and "Syrian Church music." See also "Severus of Antioch."

Liturgies of the Orthodox Rites

1597. Bria, Ion. "Dynamics of Liturgy in Mission." *International Review of Mission* 82 (1993): 317-325. Liturgy is central to Orthodox Christianity. Ways are discussed to strengthen liturgy and to establish liturgical training and church music schools.

1598. Catholic Church, The. *The Byzantine Liturgy. A New English Translation of the Liturgies of St. John Chrysostom and St. Basil the Great.* 2nd ed., New York: Fordham University, Russian Center, 1958.

1599. Kucharek, Casimir. *The Byzantine-Slav Liturgy of St. John Chrysostom, Its Origin & Evolution.* Allendale, NJ: Alleluia Press, 1971.

1600. Levy, Kenneth. "Liturgy and Liturgical Books: Greek Rite." In *Grove 6*, Vol. 11. 1980. 86-88.

1601. Levy, Kenneth. "Divine Liturgy." In *Grove 6*, Vol. 5. 1980. 507-508.

1602. Mancuso, Laurence, ed. *The Divine Liturgy*. New Canaan, CT: Byzantine Franciscans, 1965. Liturgy of Saint John Chrysostom.

1603. Mathews, Thomas. *The Early Churches of Constantinople: Architecture and Liturgy*. University Park and London: Pennsylvania State University Press, 1980. Consult index for references to music.

1604. Orthodox Eastern Church. *The Orthodox Liturgy, Being the Divine Liturgy of S. John Chrysostom and S. Basil the Great, according to the Use of the Church of Russia*. London: Society for the Promoting Christian Knowledge for the Fellowship of Ss. Alban and Sergius, 1939. The short and long forms of the basic liturgy of the Byzantine and other non-Latin rites.

1605. Orthodox Eastern Church. *The Orthodox Liturgy: Being the Divine Liturgies of S. John Chrysostom and S. Basil the Great and the Divine Office of the Presanctified Gifts: Together with the Ordering of the Holy and Divine Liturgy, the Office of Preparation for the Holy Communion, the Prayers of Thanksgiving after the Holy Communion*. London/New York: Oxford, 1982.

1606. Schulz, Hans-Joachim. *The Byzantine Liturgy: Symbolic Structure and Faith Expression*. Matthew J. O'Connell, transl. New York: Pueblo, 1986. German original publ. 1980.

1607. Solovii, Meletius Michael. *The Byzantine Divine Liturgy: History and Commentary*. Demetrius Emil Wysochansky, transl. Washington: Catholic University of America Press, 1970. A comprehensive study of the Byzantine Divine Liturgy. Part 1 covers the historical development; Part 2 describes the three components of the Divine Liturgy: The Proskomide (Offering), the Liturgy of the Cathechumens, and the Liturgy of the Faithful.

1608. Taft, Robert. "How Liturgies Grow: The Evolution of the Byzantine Divine Liturgy." *Orientalia Christiana Periodica* 43 (1977): 335-378.

1609. Taft, Robert. "The Liturgy of the Great Church." *Dumbarton Oaks Papers* 34-35 (1980-81): 45-75.

1610. Taft, Robert. *The Byzantine Rite: A Short History*. Collegeville, MN: Liturgical Press, 1992.

1611. Vasileios of Stravronikita. *Hymn of Entry: Liturgy and Life in the Orthodox Church*. Crestwood, NY: St Vladimir's Seminary Press, 1984.

1612. Wybrew, Hugh. *The Orthodox Liturgy: The Development of the Eucharistic Liturgy in the Byzantine Rite*. London: SPCK, 1989; Crestwood, NY: St. Vladimir's Seminary Press, 1990.

Byzantine Church Music

1613. [Byzantine Musical Forms and Modes]. In *Grove 6*, 1980.   See "Alleluia," "Kanon," "Kontakion," "Oktoechos," "Echos," "Enechema," "Troparion," and "Hiermologion."

1614. Biezen, Jan van. "The Middle-Byzantine Kontakion-Notation of Codex Ashburnhamensis and the Akathestos Hymn." *Orbis Musicae* 1, 2 (1972): 147-174. The most famous of all Greek hymns newly transcribed according to the author's assumptions concerning binary rhythms in 12th century Byzantine notation.

1615. Cavarnos, Constantine. *Byzantine Sacred Music: The Traditional Music of the Orthodox Church, its Nature, Purpose, and Execution*. Belmont, MA: Institute for Byzantine and Modern Greek Studies, 1974.

1616. Chrysaphes, Manuel. *The Treatise of Manuel Chrysaphes, the Lampadarios [1440-1463]: On the Theory of the Art of Chanting and on Certain Erroneous Views that Some Hold about it*. Monumenta Musicae Byzantinae, Vienna: Verlag der Osterreichischen Akademie der Wissenschaften, 1985.

1617. Conomos, Dmitri E. *Byzantine Trisagia and Cheroubika of the 14th and 15th Centuries: A Study of Late Byzantine Liturgical Chant*. Thessaloniki: Patriarchal Institute for Patristic Studies, 1974. A thorough, scholarly study of the musical style of late Byzantine chant.

1618. Conomos, Dmitri E. "Change in Early Christian and Byzantine Liturgical Chant." *Studies in Music from the University of Western Ontario* 5 (1980): 49-63.

1619. Conomos, Dimitri E. "Experimental Polyphony, 'According to the... Latins,' late Byzantine Psalmody." *Early Music History* Vol. 2 (1982): 1-16.

1620. Conomos, Dmitri E. "The Trisagion Hymn." *Orthodox Church Music* I (1983).

1621. Conomos, Dmitri E. *Byzantine Hymnography and Byzantine Chant*. Brookline, MA: Hellenic College Press, 1984.

1622. Conomos, Dmitri E. *The Late Byzantine and Slavonic Communion Cycle: Liturgy and Music*. Dumbarton Oaks Studies, Vol. 21. Washington, DC: Dumbarton Oaks Research Library and Collection, 1985.

1623. Conomos, Dimitri E. "The Monastery of Putna and the Musical Tradition of Moldavia in the 16th century." In *Music in Medieval Moldavia, 16th Century*, Anne Elizabeth Pennington, ed. Bucharest: Musical Publishing House, 1985. 222-266. A comparison of nine 16th-century anthologies containing chant in

Greek, Serbian and Romanian reveal Putna to have been an international center of Eastern chant.

1624. Engberg, G. "Greek Ekphonetic Neumes and Masoretic Accents." *Studies in Eastern Chant* Vol. 1 (1966): 37-49. A comparison of specific Greek text settings in Sinaiticus 8 with the same texts set with Masoretic notation reveal a surprising correspondence, but there is not yet enough data to show that ekphonetic notation originated in Masoretic accents.

1625. Gertsman, Evgenij V. "Modern Perception of Ancient Greek and Byzantine Music." *Orbis Musicae* 10, 1 (1990/1): 39-49. The further removed we are in time from another epoch, the less we have in common with it. It is necessary, therefore, in order to understand an ancient music, to set aside our own practices and to approach it in terms of its own musical methods.

1626. Habbi, Antun. *Short Course in Byzantine Ecclesiastical Music*. Newton, MS: Greek Melkite Catholic Diocese of Newton in the United States, 1988.

1627. Hannick, Christian, ed. *Fundamental Problems of Early Slavic Music and Poetry*. Studies on the Fragmenta Chiliandarica Palaeo-Slavica 2. Monumenta Musicae Byzantinae, Subsidia 6, Copenhagen: Munksgaard, 1978. Articles by Hannick, Mares, Bugge, Radojicic, Velimirovic, Levy, and Gove.

1628. Hannick, Christian and V.D. van Aalst, ed. *Rhythm in Byzantine Chant*. Hernen, Netherlands: A.A. Bredius Foundation, 1991. A collection of articles in English, German, and French.

1629. Harris, Simon. "The Byzantine Responds for the Two Sundays before Christmas." *Music and Letters* 74, 1 (Feb., 1993): 1-15. The Psaltika and Asmatika, two collections of 13th century chants that share features characteristic of much earlier chant traditions, are said to possess a grandeur that has no equal in Western chant traditions. Includes discussion of the relationship of the chants in the collections.

1630. Karavites, Peter. "Gregory Nazianzinos and Byzantine Hymnography." *Journal of Hellenic Studies* 113 (1993): 81-98. Speeches of the 4th century orator Gregory Nazianzinos became, from the 6th century to the 11th, the source of hymns that are still sung in the Orthodox Church today.

1631. Kazhdan, Alexander P., ed. *The Oxford Dictionary of Byzantium*. 3 vols. New York: Oxford University Press, 1991. Covers the 1100-year history of Byzantium. See for entries on liturgy, music, and music instruments.

1632. Levy, Kenneth. "The Byzantine Sanctus and its Modal Tradition in East and West." *Annales Musicologiques* 6 (1958-63): 7-67.

1633. Levy, Kenneth. "The Earliest Slavic Melismatic Chants." In *Fundamental Problems of Early Slavic Music and Poetry*, Christian Hannick, ed. Studies on the Fragmenta Chiliandarica Palaeo-Slavica 2. Monumenta Musicae Byzantinae, Subsidia 6, Copenhagen: Munksgaard, 1978. 197-210.

1634. Levy, Kenneth. "Byzantine Rite, Music of the." In *Grove 6*, Vol. 3. 1980. 553-566.

1635. Levy, Kenneth. "The Slavic Reception of Byzantine Chant." In *Christianity and the Arts in Russia*, William Craft Brumfield and Milos Velimirovic, ed. Cambridge, England; New York: Cambridge University Press, 1991. Levy theorizes that the Slavs received Byzantine hymnody with memory-aid neumes and that later musical traditions continued the practice of notation.

1636. Lungu, N., G. Costea, and I. Croitoru. *A Guide to the Music of the Eastern Orthodox Church*. Nicholas K. Apostola, transl. Nicholas K. Apostola, ed. Brookline, MA: Holy Cross Orthodox Press, 1984.

1637. Metsakis, K. "The Hymnography of the Greek Church in the Early Christian Centuries." *Jahrbuch der österreichischen Byzantinistik* 20 (1971): 31 ff.

1638. Moran, Neil K. *The Ordinary Chants of the Byzantine Mass*. 2 vols. Hamburger Beitrage zur Musikwissenschaft, Bd. 12, Hamburg: Verlag der Musikalienhandlung K.D. Wagner, 1975. Vol. 1 discusses the history, sources, liturgics, and chants of the Byzantine mass. Vol. 2: Critical Edition.

1639. Raasted, Jørgen. "Byzantine Chant in Popular Tradition." *Université de Copenhague, Cahiers de l'Institut du Moyen-âge grec et latin* Vol. 31 (1979): 39-49, 78-81.

1640. Raasted, Jørgen. "Troping Techniques in Byzantine Chant." In *Research on Tropes: Proceedings of a Symposium Organized by the Royal Academy of Literature, History and Antiquities and the Corpus Troporum, Stockholm, June 1-3, 1981*, Iversen, ed. Kungl. Vitterhets Historie och Antikvitets Akademien, Konferenser 8, Stockholm: Almqvist & Wiksell, 1983.

1641. Raasted, Jørgen. *The Hagiopolites: A Byzantine Treatise on Music Theory*. Copenhagen: Université de Copenhague, 1983.

1642. Deleted.

1643. Revell, E. J. "Hebrew Accents and Greek Ekphonetic Neumes." *Studies in Eastern Chant* Vol. 4 (1979): 140-70. Crestwood, NY: St. Vladimir's Seminary Press. Argues that the basic function of accent signs was musical and that their function as punctuation markers was secondary. A comparison of Hebrew, Greek and Syriac Biblical accentuation and the accentuation of Rabbinic texts shows Hebrew accents to be distinctively different from the rest. Greek accents may have derived from Mishnaic and other Rabbinic texts, but a direct connection between the Greek and Masoretic systems is not supportable.

1644. Schidlovsky, Nicolas. *The Notated Lenten Prosomoia in the Byzantine and Slavic Traditions*. Ph.D. diss., Princeton University, 1983. Based on previously unavailable Slavic notated sources, this analysis of early Byzantine and Slavic notation indicates a divergence, from a common origin, dating back at least to the 11th century, and offers a rare glimpse into the relationship between words and music in an orally-based traditon.

1645. Strunk, Oliver. *Essays on Music in the Byzantine World*. New York: 1977. Republication of 22 articles on Byzantine chant, 1942-1973. Topics include the Byzantine modal system, notation of Byzantine chant, various categories of chant, melody construction, recent research, and the influence of Eastern chant on that of the West.

1646. Touliatos-Banker, Diane. *The Byzantine Amomos Chant of the Fourteenth and Fifteenth Centuries*. Thessaloniki: Patriarchikon Hidryma Paterikon Meleton (Patriarchal Institute of Patristic Studies), 1979/repr. 1985. A history of the incorporation of Psalm118 [or Ps. 119 in Jewish and English Bibles] into the Byzantine liturgy (the chanted services of the Sunday morning office and funeral services) and a study of some of its many music settings. 73 of the 176 verses are found to have been set to melody and a number are attributed to specific composers.

1647. Touliatos-Banker, Diane. "Solmisation in the Ancient Greek and Byzantine Traditions." In *Proceedings of the 7th International Congress of Musicology 'Musica Antiqua Europae Orientalis'*, Bydgoszcz, Poland 1985. 553-73.

1648. Trypanis, C. "On the Musical Rendering of the Early Byzantine Kontakia." *Studies in Eastern Chant* Vol. 1 (1966): 104 ff. Oxford. The stanzas of a 13th century *kontakion*, with their highly melismatic lines, were performed with great freedom and variety. In a 6th and 7th *kontakion*, with its more syllabic setting, the music was the same for each stanza.

1649. Velimirovic, Milos. "The Byzantine Heirmos and Heirmologion." In *Gattungen der Musik in Einzeldarstellungen: Gedenkschrift Leo Schrade*, Wulf Arlt, Ernst Lichtenhahn, Hans Oesch, and Max Hass, ed. Vol. 1. Bern and Munich: Francke, 1973. 192-244.

1650. Velimirovic, Melos. "Egon Wellesz and the Study of Byzantine Chant." *MQ* 62 (1976): 265-277. An appreciation of the immense contribution Wellesz made to the study of Byzantine Chant.

1651. Velimirovic, Milos. "Attainments and Tasks in the Study of Contacts between Byzantium and the Slavs of the Eastern Mediterranean." In *IMS12, 1977*, 1981. 430-433. Paper on the Byzantine links to Slavic chant, the liturgical books imported from Byzantium, and the problem of later mss.

1652. Velimirovic, Milos. "Byzantine Chant." In *NOHM II*, Richard Crocker, ed. 1990. 26-68.

1653. Wellesz, Egon. *A History of Byzantine Music and Hymnography*. 3rd ed., London: Oxford University Press, 1963. 1st ed., 1949; 2nd ed., 1961/repr. 1971.

1654. Wellesz, Egon. "Byzantine Music and Liturgy." In *The Cambridge Medieval History*, Vol. IV, Part 2.: Cambridge University Press, 1967. 134-160.

Russian Church Music

1655. Ambrose, Brother [1849-1909]. *A Short Introduction to Znamenny Chant and its Notation*. S.l.: Old Ritualist Society, 1980. On the history and notation of Russian monophonic chant.

1656. Beliaev, Viktor. "Early Russian Polyphony." In *Studia Memoriae Belae Bartok Sacra*, 3rd ed. London: Boosey and Hawkes, 1959. 311-330. A transcription of 2 and 3-voice *strochny* singing (liturgical melody with simultaneous ornamentation) from the 11th to 16th centuries and *znamenny* chant in 3-voice parallel style. Beliaev discusses the problems the notation has caused his predecessors.

1657. Brill, Nicholas. *History of Russian Church Music, 988-1917*. 2nd ed., Bloomington, ILL: Brill, 1982. Consists of an overview of the history of Russian church music (Ch. 1-5), the Divine Liturgy (Ch. 6), music for the imperial chapel and other choirs (Ch. 7-10), and important composers from Tchaikovsky to the present. Includes music in America.

1658. Dolskaya-Ackerly, Olga. "The Sacred Kant in 17th-century Russian Music." *Hymn* 39, Jan. (1988): 10-17. The author provides an overview of developments in Russian polyphony with attention to the impact of Western styles of composition and the transitional role of the Kant.

1659. Gardner, Johann von. *Russian Church Singing*. Vladimir Morosan, transl. Crestwood, NY: St. Vladimir's Seminary Press, 1980. A translation of *System und Wesen des russischen Kirchengesanges*. Vol. 1: Orthodox Worship and Hymnography.

1660. Gusejnova, Zivar. *Russian Znamenny Chant in the First Half of the XVIIth Century*. Cantus Planus 2: Papers Read at the Fourth Meeting, Pecs, Hungary, 3-9 September 1990, Budapest: Institute for Musicology, Hungarian Academy of Sciences, forthcoming.

1661. McCredie, A. "Some Aspects of Current Research into Russian Liturgical Chant." *MMA* 6 (1972): 55-152.

1662. Morosan, Valdimir. *Choral Performance in Pre-Revolutionary Russia.* Russian Music Studies, No. 17, Ann Arbor, MI: UMI Research Press, 1985. Originally an A.Mus.D. thesis: University of Illinois at Urbana-Champaign, 1984.

1663. Morosan, Vladimir. "Liturgical Singing or Sacred Music?: Understanding the Aesthetic of the New Russian Choral School." In *Christianity and the Arts in Russia*, William Craft Brumfield and Milos Velimirovic, ed. Cambridge, England; New York: Cambridge University Press, 1991. The author attempts to bring clarity and precision to the use of teminology for the musical traditions of the Russian church with particular attention to developments of the late 19th and early 20th centuries.

1664. Roccasalvo, Joan L. *The Plainchant Tradition of Southwestern Rus'.* East European Monographs 202, Boulder, CO: East European Monographs, 1986. Also publ. by Columbia University Press, New York. Originally a dissertation: *The Plainchant Tradition of Southwestern Rus': Kiev-Lviv-Subcarpathian Rus'.* This first English-language study of Carpathian-Ruthenian plainchant demonstrates its dependence on the melodic formulae of the southwestern branch of Znamenny chant, the chant of ancient Rus'.

1665. Roccasalvo, Joan L. "The Znamenny Chant." *MQ* 74, 2 (1990): 217-241. Liturgical chant traditions of the Russian people of Kiev.

1666. Roccasalvo, Joan L. "The Role of Religion in the Development of the Znamenny-Rusin Chant." *Diakonia* 26, 1 (1993): 41-66. The response of Hungarian orthodoxy to the Protestant Reformation and Jesuit missionaries in the 16th century was the establishment of brotherhoods to promote Orthodox chant through liturgical books and education.

1667. Swan, Alfred. "The Znamenny Chant of the Russian Church." *MQ* 26 (1940): 232-243, 365-380, 529-545. Part I. Historical back-ground and enumeration of the sections in the 5 song books to be used in analysis. Part II. Analysis of the monophonic chant. Part III. Discussion of notation in medieval chant, of mss. from 988-1240 C.E., and an inquiry into the composers of the chant.

1668. Swan, Alfred. "Russian Church Music." In *Grove 5*, 1954.

1669. Velimirovic, Milos. "Russian and Slavonic Church Music." In *Grove 6*, Vol. 16. 1980. 337-46.

1670. Vladyshevskaia, Tatiana. "On the Links between Music and Icon Painting in Medieval Rus." In *Christianity and the Arts in Russia*, William Craft Brumfield and Milos Velimirovic, ed. Cambridge, England; New York: Cambridge University Press, 1991. 14-29. A study of the parallel and complementary themes of Russian music, iconography and literature.

Serbian and Slavonic Church Music

1671. Doliner, Gorana. "Traditional Church Singing in Kraljevica (Croatia): The Work of Lujza Kozinovic." *The World of Music* 33, 2 (1991): 50-64. Although women were banned from creating church rituals in earlier centuries, the work of sister Lujza Kozinovic in preaching and composing music casts doubt on whether this rule was always adhered to.

1672. Conomos, Dimitri. "The Byzantine Legacy in Slavonic Chant." In *The Legacy of St. Vladimir: Byzantium, Russia, America*, J. Breck, J. Meyenforff, and E. Silk, ed. Crestwood, NY: St. Vladimir's Seminary Press, 1990. Conomos establishes both the strong Byzantine influence on Slavonic sacred music and the indigenous Slavonic roots that shaped the tradition.

1673. Petrovic', D. "Church Elements in Serbian Ritual Songs." In *Beitraege zur Musikkultur des Balkans, 1: Walter Wünsch zum 65. Geburtstag*, R. Flotzinger, ed. Graz 1975. 109.

Ukrainian Church Music

1674. Antonowycz, Myroslaw. *The Chants from the Ukrainian Heirmologia.* Bilthoven: A.B. Creyghton, 1974.

1675. Kononenko, Natalie O. "The Influence of the Orthodox Church on Ukrainian *Dumy*." *Slavic Review* 50, 3 (1991): 566-75. Oral epic songs of military subject matter give a religious and moral rather than a military explanation of events.

1676. Taft, Robert. "The Structural Analysis of Liturgical Units: An Essay on Methodology." *Worship* 52, July (1978): 314-329.

MUSIC AND LITURGY OF THE NON-CHALCEDONIAN ORTHODOX RITES

General References

1677. Day, Peter D. *Eastern Christian Liturgies: The Armenian, Coptic, Ethiopian, and Syrian Rites; Eucharistic Rites with Introductory Notes and Rubrical Instructions.* Shannon: Irish University Press, 1972.

1678. Velimirovic, Milos. "Christian Chant in Syria, Armenia, Egypt and Ethiopia." In *NOHM II*, Richard Crocker, ed. 1990. 3-25.

Armenian Church Music

1679. Hannick, Christian. "Armenian Rite, Music of the." In *Grove 6*, Vol. 1. 1980. 596-99.

1680. Henrotte, Gayle A. "Armenian Liturgical Music: An Encounter in Jerusalem." *Miscellanea Musicologica: Adelaide Studies in Musicology* 11 (1980): 215-25.

1681. Sarafian, Krikor A. *The Armenian Apostolic Church: Her Ceremonies, Sacraments, Main Feasts and Prominent Saints.* Fresno, CA: 1959. Textbook for Sunday schools of the California Diocese of the Armenian churches.

1682. Winkler, Garbriele. "The Armenian Night Office I: The Historical Background of the Introductory Part of *Gisheratyn Zham.*" *Journal of the Society for Armenian Studies* 1 (1984): 93-113. Part II: The Unit of Psalmody, Canticles, and Hymns. *Revue des Études Arméniennes.* 17 (1983): 471-551.

Coptic Church Music

1683. Bennett, John Paul. *Music in the Coptic Church of Egypt and Ethiopia.* MA MusEd, Washington, 1945. A history of the Coptic Church and liturgy, with a description of the music system, instruments, notation, modes and a comparison with Gregorian Chant.

1684. Borsai, Ilona. "Coptic Rite, Music of the." In *Grove 6*, Vol. 4. 1980. 730-4.

1685. Butler, A.J. *Ancient Coptic Churches of Egypt.* 2 vols. London: Oxford University Press, 1884. An account of the practices in Egyptian Coptic churches of over a century ago.

1686. Erian, Nabila Meleka. *Coptic Music—an Egyptian Tradition.* Ph.D. diss., University of Maryland, Baltimore County, 1986. The religious music of Egyptian Christians is examined from the standpoints of 1) historical origins, distribution, important figures, transmission, and liturgy, and 2) musical features: text-music relationships, performing styles, tones, forms, structure, and genres as well as relationship to other Egyptian chant traditions.

1687. Gillespie, John. "The Egyptian Copts and Their Music." *Church Music* 1 (1971): 18-28. On the first-century origins, language, and liturgy of the Copts, mss. and modern edd., and pre-Christian Egyptian, Hebrew, Greco-Byzantine and Arabic influences. Describes history and general characteristics of Coptic chant.

1688. Gillespie, John. "Coptic Chant: A Survey of Past Research and a Projection for the Future." In *The Future of Coptic Studies*, R. McL. Wilson, ed. Coptic Studies 1, Leiden: E.J. Brill, 1978.

1689. Kebede, Ashenafi and K. Suttner. *Ethiopia: The Music of the Coptic Church.* Berlin, Germany: 1969.

1690. Khs-Burmeister, O.H.E. *The Egyptian or Coptic Church: A Detailed Description of her Liturgical Services and the Rites and Ceremonies Observed in the Administration of her Sacraments.* Publications de la Societe d'archeologie copte, Cairo: np, 1967.

1691. Khs-Burmeister, O.H.E., transl. *Ordination Rites of the Coptic Church.* Cairo: Société d'archeologie Copte, 1985.

1692. Robertson, Marian. "The Reliability of the Oral Tradition in Preserving Coptic Music, Part II: Comparison of Three Musical Transcriptions of an Extract from the Liturgy of St. Basil." *Bulletin de la Société d'Archéologie Copte* 26 (1984): 83-93.

1693. Robertson, Marian. "The Reliability of the Oral Tradition in Preserving Coptic Music: A Comparison of Two Recordings of the Hymn 'Tenouosht....'" *Bulletin de la Société d'Archéologie Copte* 27 (1985): 73-85.

1694. Robertson, Marian. "Vocal Music in the Early Coptic Church." *Coptologia* 6 (1985): 23-27.

1695. Taft, Robert. "Praise in the Desert: The Coptic Monastic Office Yesterday and Today." *Worship* 56 (1982): 513-36.

Ethiopian Church Music

1696. Hammerschmidt, E. *Studies in the Ethiopic Anaphoras.* 2nd rev. ed., Stuttgart: 1987. A study of Ethiopian Christian liturgy.

1697. Hannick, Christian. "Ethiopian Rite, Music of the." In *Grove 6*, Vol. 6. 1980. 272-5.

1698. Kebede, Ashenafi. *The Music of Ethiopia: Its Development and Cultural Setting.* Ph.D. diss., Wesleyan University, 1971. A history of sources of Ethiopian music, its songs types and texts, music instruments, the Azmaris, music of contemporary Ethiopia, and music transcription. Early chapters explore Arab, Jewish (1st millenium BCE) and Christian (4th century CE) cultures in Ethiopia and the religious chant of the latter two.

1699. Kebede, Ashenafi. "Sacred Chant of Ethiopian Monotheistic Churches: Music in Black Jewish and Christian Communities." *Black Perspective in Music* 8, 1 (1980): 21-34.

1700. Lepisa, Tito. "The Three Modes and the Signs of the Songs in the Ethiopian Liturgy." Proceedings of the Third International Conference of Ethiopian Studies. II. Addas Ababa: 1970. 162-187. A study of notational signs found within mss. of Ethiopian chant

1701. Powne, Michael. *Ethiopian Music: A Survey of Ecclesiastical and Secular Ethiopian Music and Instruments.* Westport, CT: Greenwood Press, 1966/repr. 1980. Chap. 4, Ecclesiastical Music (84-119) discusses the history, notation, "modes," legends, and music training in the Ethiopian Church and the lack of documents to make possible a thorough study.

1702. Shelemay, Kay Kaufman. "The Musician and Transmission of Religious Tradition: The Multiple roles of the Ethiopian däbtära." *Journal of Religion in Africa* 22, 3 (1992): 242-260. A study of the multi-faceted education of a group of musicians whose activities are at the center of Ethiopian Christian musical practice and of the careers available to them—traditionally that of mendicant, merchant or healer—in rapidly changing social conditions.

1703. Shelemay, Kay Kaufman, Peter Jeffery, and Ingrid Monson. "Oral and Written Transmission in Ethiopian Christian Chant." In *Studies in Medieval and Early Modern Music*, Iain Fenlon, ed. Vol. 12. Cambridgeshire; New York: Cambridge University Press, 1993. 55-118. Although founded in the 4th century, the Ethiopian Christian church began to notate its liturgical music only in the 16th century. A study of the relationship between oral and written transmission in contemporary Ethiopian chant may thus reveal valuable information concerning the same relationship with respect to Latin chant some thousand years ago. The authors approach Ethiopian chant from three standpoints. Shelemay addresses the methods and problems involved in using modern sources to achieve historical reconstruction. Jeffery examines the manuscript evidence from the 13th century to the present. And Monson explores evidence from the modern oral tradition. The conclusion summarizes the historical factors that lead to the use of notation to preserve liturgical chant, but asserts that while such factors have influenced chant transmission, they were never intended to replace oral transmission.

Syrian Church Music

1704. Cody, Aelred. "The Early History of the Octoechos in Syria." In *East of Byzantium: Syria and Armenia in the Formative Period*, Nina Garsoïan et al., ed. Washington, DC: Dumbarton Oaks Center for Byzantine Studies, 1982. 89-113.

1705. Husmann, Heinrich. "The Practice of Organum in the Liturgical Singing of the Syrian Churches of the Near and Middle East." In *Aspects of Medieval and Renaissance Music: A Birthday Offering for Gustave Reese*, Jan LaRue, ed. New York: Pendragon, 1966/repr. 1978. 435-39. Husmann proposes that organum at the fourth is of Syrian origin and develops a theory of the development of organum from his encounters within various churches.

1706. Husmann, Heinrich. "Syrian Church Music." In *Grove 6*, Vol. 18. 1980. 472-81.

UNIATE CHURCH/EASTERN CATHOLIC: MARONITES

1707. Hage, Louis. *Maronite Music*. Carreras Arab Lectures 7, London: Longman for the University of Essex, 1978.

1708. Macomber, William F., S. J. "A Theory on the Origins of the Syrian, Maronite and Chaldean Rites." *Orientalia Christiana Periodica* 39 (1973): 235-42.

OTHER NON-LATIN CHURCH MUSIC OF THE NEAR EAST

1709. Cohen, Dalia. "The Meaning of the Modal Framework in the Singing of Religious Hymns by Christian Arabs in Israel." *Yuval* 2 (1971): 23-57. Modal elements in these hymns consist of central tones and the intervals between them, 3-5 tone subdivisions of these intervals, a collection of characteristic musical motifs and their order of appearance, and tonal skeletons, with stable and unstable tones.

1710. Cohen, Dalia. "Theory and Practice in Liturgical Music of Christian Arabs in Israel." In *Studies in Eastern Chant*, Vol. 3. London: Oxford University Press, 1973. 1-50. On the performance of liturgical chant and the concepts of the performers about the chant. Although the existence of a framework was evident in the performances, little correspondance was found between theory and practice with respect to intonation system, internal organization of scales, or the relationships of the seconds.

1711. Foley, Rolla. *Song of the Arab, the Religious Ceremonies, Shrines, and Folk Music of the Holy Land Christian Arab*. New York: Macmillan, 1953.

1712. Hannick, Christian. "Georgian Rite, Music of the." In *Grove 6*, Vol. 7. 1980. 241-243.

1713. Isiah, Yousef Aziz. *The Folk Hymns of the Evangelical Churches in Egypt: An Analytical Study*. M.A. thesis, University of Maryland, Baltimore County, 1985.

22

Religious Music in Great Britain

HISTORIES AND SURVEYS

1714. Baldwin, David. *The Chapel Royal: Ancient and Modern.* London: Duckworth, 1990. A history of Chapel Royal from the time of ancient Rome to the present day.

1715. Caldwell, John. *The Oxford History of English Music. Vol.1: From the Beginnings to c. 1715.* The Oxford History of English Music, New York: Oxford University Press, 1992. A chronological study, based on the most recent research, with musical analysis, historical context, and critical assessment.

1716. Flanagan, David Timothy. *Polyphonic Settings of the Lamentations of Jeremiah by Sixteenth-Century English Composers.* Ph.D. diss., Cornell University, 1990. 2 vols.

1717. Harper, John. *A History of Music in the English Church from Bede to the Present Day.* Forthcoming.

1718. Le Huray, Peter and John Morehen. *English Choral Practice c.1400-c.1650: A Memorial Volume to Peter le Huray.* Cambridge Studies in Performance Practice, Vol. 5. Cambridge; New York: Cambridge University Press, 1995.

1719. Moroney, Michael Davitt. *Under Fower Sovereygnes: Thomas Tallis and the Transformation of English Polyphony.* Ph.D. diss., UC, Berkeley, 1980. Thomas Tallis, more than any other composer, embodied the changes that took place during the reigns of Henry VIII, Edward, Mary, and Elizabeth: A study of the transformations in Tallis' music along with the compositions of one major composer in each reign: Taverner, Tye, Sheppard and Byrd.

1720. Parry, W.H. *Thirteen Centuries of English Church Music*. New York: Gordon Press, 1977. 2nd, enl. ed., 1946.

1721. Price, David C. *Patrons and Musicians of the English Renaissance*. Cambridge/New York: Cambridge University Press, 1981. See Chap. 2. 'The Reformation Crisis' and Chap. 4. 'Private Music and Religious Faith.' Both document the flight of musicians in both Catholic and Protestant institutions to private service, for both secular and religious music making.

1722. Routh, Francis. *Early English Organ Music from the Middle Ages to 1837*. New York: Barnes & Noble Books; London: Barrie and Jenkins, 1973. With the publication of Musica Britannica in the 1950s, the door to England's musical past opened. This book documents the history of English organs, organ music, and composers thereof.

1723. Sheldon, Robin, ed. *In Spirit and In Truth: Exploring Directions in Music in Worship Today*. London: Hodder & Stoughton, 1989. Ten essays on current trends in church music, Roman Catholic and Protestant, in England.

1724. Spink, Ian, ed. *The Blackwell History of Music in Britain*. Oxford: Blackwell, 1988-1995. A semi-specialized series for students, teachers, and dedicated music lovers. In 5 volumes.

ROMAN CATHOLIC MUSIC IN GREAT BRITAIN

1725. Allenson, Stephen. "The Inverness Fragments: Music from a Pre-Reformation Scottish Parish Church and School." *Music and Letters* 70, 1/Feb. (1989): 1-45. A study of the Inverness Fragments in an attempt to glean background information about the repertory and musical style employed in ordinary parishes.

1726. Bailey, Terence W. *The Processions of Sarum and the Western Church*. Pontifical Institute of Medieval Studies: Studies and Texts, 21, Toronto: 1971. The most comprehensive study of processions in secular liturgy.

1727. Bakerman, William Edward. *The Use of Sarum: A Study of the Mass Liturgy and the Chants of the Ordinary*. M.A. thesis, University of Orgeon, 1978.

1728. Benham, Hugh. *Latin Church Music in England, Fourteen Sixty to Fifteen Seventy-Five*. Music Reprint Series, New York: Da Capo Press, 1977/repr. 1980.

1729. Berry, Mary. "Sarum Rite, Music of the." In *Grove 6*, Vol. 16. 1980.

1730. Bokerman, William Edward. *The Use of Sarum: A Study of the Mass Liturgy and the Chants of the Ordinary*. M.A. thesis, University of Oregon,

1978. The modifications of the Roman mass for use at the Cathedral of Salisbury between the 13th and 16th centuries.

1731. Bowers, Roger. "The Musicians of the Lady Chapel of Winchester Cathedral Priory, 1402-1539." *Journal of Ecclesiastical History* 45, 2 (1994): 210-227. By the end of the Middle Ages, 40 or 50 groups of professional musicians were maintained in British monasteries for daily corporate worship of the Virgin Mary. Using the documents that have survived, Bowers documents the institution of such a choir at Winchester Cathedral in the early 13th century, its history, duties and repertory, and its complete extinction, along with that of all other such choirs, by the middle of the 16th century—a casualty of the Reformation.

1732. Brannon, Patrick V. "The Search for the Celtic Rite." In *Music and the Church*, Gerard Gillen and Harry White, ed. Vol. 2. Dublin: Irish Academic Press, 1993. 13-40. No examples of notation in any Irish liturgical mss. survive prior to 1000. A comparison of the incipits of Irish Sarum, English Sarum, and early Gregorian melodies yields both commonalities and dissimilarities with respect to both music and liturgy. Texts and chants for Irish saints, as added to the English Sarum Office mss. used in Ireland, reveal a variety of souces for the melodies, including England, the continent, and, possibly, Celtic chants native to Ireland.

1733. Brannon, Patrick V. *A Contextual Study of the Four Notated Sarum Divine Office Manuscripts from Anglo-Norman Ireland*. Ph.D. diss., Washington University, 1990. On the role of Sarum manuscripts in the Office liturgy of the 15th century Celtic Church.

1734. Cain, Elizabeth Ann. *English Chant Tradition in the Late Middle Ages: The Introits and Graduals of the Temporale in the Sarum Gradual*. Ph.D. diss., Harvard University, 1982. Until this study, two 15th and 16th century chant traditions have been assumed: Northern and Latin. This study shows that Sarum chant practice often stands with that of York, Hereford and Rouen against Paris, and with Paris against the 'standard' reading, suggesting a third, Northern French-Normal-English group, within which there is a unified Anglo-Norman group.

1735. Chadd, D. F. L. "Liturgy and Liturgical Music: The Limits of Uniformity." In *Cistercian Art and Architecture in the British Isles*, C. Norton and C. Park, ed. Cambridge, Eng., New York, NY: Cambridge University Press, 1986. 299-314. An attempt to document the musical and liturgical deviations that developed despite the order's ideal of uniformity between houses.

1736. Crocker, Richard. "Polyphony in England in the 13th Century." In *NOHM II*, 1990. 679-720.

1737. Droste, Diane Lynne. *The Musical Notation and Transmission of the Music for the Sarum Use, 1225-1500*. Ottawa: National Library of Canada,

1984. This study of later square notation shows that variants exist due to personal habit of the scribe, datable developments in the notation, and learned local or regional variations. Variants due to copying error and later used as an exemplar ceased c.1385, suggesting a break in the tradition.

1738. Eden, Bradford Lee. *The Thirteenth-Century Sequence Repertory of the Sarum Use*. Ph.D. diss., University of Kansas, 1991.

1739. Floyd, Malcolm. "Processional Chants in English Monastic Sources." *JPMMS* 13 (1990): 1-48.

1740. Fugler, Stephen Paul. *Pre-Compositional Mathematical Planning in Mass Settings by Nicholas Ludford and Robert Fayrfax*. Ph.D. diss., University of Exeter, 1990. Against surveys of music as a mathematical art, including the highly complex topic of number symbolism, and the work of five scholars on mathematical structures in early music, the author demonstrates the precompositional mathematical planning in works by Ludford and Fayrfax, and shows how one work was "derived from a single 'perfect' number in the most rigorous manner".

1741. Galles, P.L.C.M. "Church Music in Private Chapels." *Sacred Music* 116, 4 (1989): 11-15. Prohibited by the Council of Trent (1563) and reinstated by the Code of Canon Law (1983), royal chapels, at first modest in size (in the 12th century), grew to large proportions by the beginning of the 15th century. Henry VIII's chapel had 18 to 21 chaplains; chapels of the nobility often had from 4 to 16 male singers.

1742. Gillen, Gerard and Harry White, ed. *Music and the Church*. Irish Musical Studies, Vol. 2. Dublin: Irish Academic Press, 1993.

1743. Grindle, W.H. *Irish Cathedral Music: A History of Music at the Cathedrals of the Church of Ireland*. Belfast: Institute of Irish Studies, Queen's University of Belfast, 1989.

1744. Harrison, Frank L. *Music in Medieval Britain*. 4th ed., Buren, Netherlands: F. Knut, 1958/repr. 1980. A major study of religious music in Great Britain from the Norman invasion in the 11th century into the 16th century.

1745. Haworth, Kenneth William. *The Use of Sarum: The Worship and Organisation of Salisbury Cathedral in the Middle Ages*. Salisbury: Friends of Salisbury Cathedral, 1973.

1746. Hiley, David. "The Norman Chant Traditions: Normandy, Britain, Sicily." *Proceedings of the Royal Musical Association* 107 (1980-1): 1-33.

1747. Hiley, David. "Ordinary of Mass Chants in English, North French and Sicilian Manuscripts." *JPMMS* 9 (1986): 1-128.

1748. Hiley, David. "Thurstan of Caen and Plainchant at Glastonbury: Musicological Reflections on the Norman Conquest." In *Proceedings of the British Academy*, 72. London: British Academy, 1987. 57-90.

1749. Hofman, May and John Morehen compilers. *Latin Music in British Sources, c1485-c1610*. Early English Church Music, London: Published for the British Academy: Stainer and Bell, 1987.

1750. Jenkins, Glynn Edwin. *Latin Polyphony in Scotland, 1500-1560: (with Studies in Analytical Techniques)*. Ph.D. diss., University of Exeter, 1988. Vol. 1 is a study of the Dunkeld Partbooks and a possible scribe. Vol. 2 contains selections of music of eight French and English composers represented in the partbooks.

1751. Kirkman, Andrew. "The Transmission of English Mass Cycles in the Mid to Late-Fifteenth Century: A Case Study in Context." *Music and Letters* 75, 2 (1994): 180-199. Although the cyclic cantus firmus mass was invented in 15th-century England, the destruction of mss. has made it nearly impossible to trace the details of its transmission to the Continent. The author highlights the difficulties by attempting to account for the variants in four versions of the same mid-century English mass.

1752. Lefferts, Peter. *The Motet in England in the Fourteenth Century*. Ann Arbor, MI: UNI Research Press, 1986. A study of a repertory of 14th-century polyphony, equal in importance to repertories of contemporary France and Italy, as to typology of motet structures, notations, and texts. In many ways a repertory that developed in relative isolation from those on the continent, it reveals a number of distinct archetypes for motet construction, several lines of notational development, and interests in musical variation and motivic work, in exploiting the designs of unusual tenors, and in numerical proportion.

1753. Lefferts, Peter. "Medieval England, 950-1450." In *Antiquity and the Middle Ages*, James McKinnon, ed. Englewood Cliffs, NJ: Prentice Hall, 1990. 170-196.

1754. Lefferts, Peter and Margaret Bent. "New Sources of English Thirteenth and Fourteenth Century Polyphony." *Early Music History* Vol. 2 (1982): 273-362.

1755. Lefferts, Peter. "Cantilena and Antiphon: Music for Marian Services in Late Medieval England." *Current Musicology* Jan.-Dec., 45-47 (1990): 247-282. A study of the Lady mass in the use of Salisbury and of Marian sequences, offertories, antiphons, and the Cantilena repertory in 14th and early 15th century England.

1756. Losseff, Nicky. *The Best Concords: Polyphonic Music in Thirteenth-Century Britain*. Outstanding Dissertation in Music from British Universities, New York: Garland Publishing, 1994. A study of the relationship of English and

'Notre-Dame' polyphony in the 13th century, with special attention to the wide variety of styles embraced by the term 'conductus'.

1757. Planchart, A. *The Repertory of Tropes at Winchester*. 2 vols. Princeton, NJ: Princeton University Press, 1977. Vol. 1. A study of the repertory and liturgy of the Proper and Ordinary tropes of the Winchester and Canterbury Tropers. Vol. 2. An inventory of the mss.

1758. Rankin, Susan and David Hiley, ed. *Music in the Medieval English Liturgy: Plainsong and Medieval Music Society Centennial Essays*. London/ New York: Oxford University Press; Oxford: Clarenden Press, 1993. Twelve essays in three groups: 1) Liturgy and liturgical music in the 11th century (with three essays on the Winchester Troper); 2) Liturgical uses and genres in Medieval England (alleluias, antiphons, rhymed offices and the relationship between liturgy and vernacular music); and 3) Liturgical polyphony in later Medieval England.

1759. Sanders, Ernest. "Worcester Polyphony." In *Grove 6*, Vol. 20. 1980. 524-28.

1760. Smith, William Liddell. *The Burial Agenda and Associated Music in Pre-Reformation England: Cambridge University Library Manuscript FF.6.21*. Ph.D. diss., University of Minnesota, 1985. A study of Christian burial practice from 980 to c. 1400.

1761. Summers, William John. "The Establishment and Transmission of Polyphonic Repertories in England, 1320-1399." *Atti del XIV Congresso della Società internazionale di Musicologia* 3 (1987): 659-672. A finding "that a significant number of institutions were populated by persons capable of composing, notating and singing" a large repertory of polyphonic music. Includes a table of 85 14th-century ms. sources.

1762. Woods, Isobel. "'Our awin Scottis use': Chant Usage in Medieval Scotland." *Journal of the Royal Musical Association* 112 (1987): 21-37.

PROTESTANT MUSIC IN GREAT BRITAIN

1763. Bishop, Selma L. *Isaac Watt's Hymns and Spiritual Songs (1707) A Publishing History and a Bibliography*. Ann Arbor MI: Pierian Press, 1974.

1764. Blizzard, Judith. *Borrowings in English Church Music 1550-1950*. London: Stainer and Bell, 1990. In three sections: music borrowed from sacred sources, from secular sources, and borrowings of musical style. On the sources of responds, services, and anthems, etc., their composers, and the export of British church music to the U.S.

1765. Chappell, Paul. *Music and Worship in the Anglican Church, 1597-1967.* London: Faith Press, 1968. Topics: Beginnings, Reformation, Golden Age and Puritanism, Restoration, Age of Oratorio, Victorian Age, and Liturgical Reform and Experiment. Emphasis is on the architectural setting of public worship.

1766. Church of England. Archbishops' Commission on Church Music. *In Tune with Heaven: The Report of the Archbishops' Commission on Church Music.* London: Church House Publishing and Hodder & Stoughton, 1992.

1767. Cuming, Geoffrey J. *A History of Anglican Liturgy.* 2nd ed., London: 1982.

1768. Davie, Donald. *The Eighteenth-Century Hymn in England.* Cambridge Studies in 18th-century English Literature & Thought, Vol. 19. Cambridge, Eng.: Cambridge University Press, 1993.

1769. East, John Michael. "The Challenge of Vatican II to the English Tradition." In *Growing in Church Music: Proceedings of a Meeting on "Why Church Music?",* Margaret Pol-Topis and Kevin Donovan et al., eds. Washington, DC: Universa Laus, 1979. 1-15. East reflects on the needs both to raise standards and to expand horizons in attempting to bring the English sacred music tradition in line with Vatican II reforms.

1770. Fellowes, Edmond H. *English Cathedral Music from Edward VI to Edward VII.* rev. 5th ed., London: Methuen, 1974. 5th ed., revised by J.A. Westrup, 1969. A study of the service and the anthem from the introduction of the Prayer Book (1549) to the mid-19th century.

1771. Gallaway, Craig. "Patterns of Worship in Early Methodist Hymnody and the Task of Hymnal Revision." *Quarterly Review* 7, Fall (1987): 14-29.

1772. Galles, DLCM. "Anglican-Use Sacred Music." *Sacred Music* 116, 1 (1989): 11-15. In the 1980s, the Roman Catholic church approved 'The Book of Divine Worship," an Anglican liturgy for Anglican converts to Roman Catholicism. Steps need to be taken to insure that the rich heritage of Anglican music and that of Eastern Rite Catholics are fostered and cultivated.

1773. Ingles, Faith Petra. *The Role of Wesleyan Hymnody in the Development of Congregational Song.* D.M.A., Combs College of Music, 1986. A study of the relationship between Wesleyan hymnody and the development of congregational song. The Wesleys' hymnody, combining objective theology, scriptural reference, and subjective response, is the very song and soul of the Reformation. Though widely influential, the hymnody remains misunderstood and much remains unknown and unsung.

1774. Inglis, James. *The Scottish Churches and the Organ in the Nineteenth Century.* Ph.D. diss., University of Glasgow, 1987. From 1807, the first use of a musical instrument in public worship by any Presbyterian congregation in

Scotland, through the 19th century, a controversy existed re. the use of organs. This study documents the adoption of instrumental music in each of the major Scottish denominations.

1775. Le Huray, Peter. *Music and the Reformation in England 1548-1660.* London: Cambridge University Press, 1967/repr. 1978.

1776. Miller, Terry E. "Oral Tradition Psalmody Surviving in England and Scotland." *The Hymn* 35, 1 (1984): 15-22.

1777. Morehen, J. *The Sources of English Cathedral Music, c. 1600-1640.* Ph.D. diss., University of Cambridge, 1969.

1778. Nicholson, David, ed. *Liturgical Music in Anglican Benedictine Monasticism.* St. Benedict, OR: Mount Angel Abbey, 1990.

1779. Obelkevich, Jim. "Music and Religion in the Nineteenth Century." In *Disciplines of Faith: Studies in Religion, Politics, and Patriarchy,* Jim Obelkevich, Lyndal Roper, and Raphael Samuel, ed. London, UK; New York, NY: Routledge & Kegan Paul, 1987. 550-565. A brief but interesting view of trends in religious music from Victorian England to the present. Organs, choirs, and hymns were the main elements in the urban religious music of Victorian England. The tunes themselves were sentimental and the setting richly self-absorbed. Whereas in 19th-century Germany, secular music became the new religion, religious music, especially oratorios, filled the same role in England.

1780. Padfield, Marsha Lou. *The Interaction of Belief and Movement: An Examination of the Type and Function of Movement in the Anglican Church.* Ph.D. diss., The Union Institute, 1991.

1781. Patrick, Millar. *Four Centuries of Scottish Psalmody.* London: Oxford University Press, 1949.

1782. Payne, Ian. *The Provision and Practice of Sacred Music at Cambridge Colleges and Selected Cathedrals, c. 1547-c1646: A Comparative Study of the Archival Evidence.* Outstanding diss. in music from British Universities, New York: Garland Publishers, 1993.

1783. Phillips, Peter. *English Sacred Music, 1549-1649.* Oxford: Gimmell, 1991.

1784. Quantrille, Wilma Jean. *The Triune God in the Hymns of Charles Wesley.* Ph.D. diss., Drew University, 1989. As declared in Wesley's hymn texts, the Trinity is the central doctrine of the Christian faith, the interpreting principle of the history of salvation. Though Wesley's concerns were evangelical and doxological, he was careful to affirm correct doctrine in his hymns.

1785. Rainbow, Bernarr. *English Psalmody Prefaces: Popular Methods of Teaching, 1562-1835*. Kilkenny, Ireland: Leslie Hewitt for Boethius Press, 1982.

1786. Routley, Erik. *English Hymns and their Tunes: A Survey*. Guildford: Hymn Society of Great Britain and Ireland, 1981.

1787. Shaw, Watkins. *The Succession of Organists of the Chapel Royal and the Cathedrals of England and Wales from c.1538*. New York: Oxford University Press, 1991. English cathedral life from the 16th century to the present from the viewpoint of those in the most enduring of England's musical professions.

1788. Spink, Ian. *Restoration Cathedral Music: 1660-1714*. Oxford Studies in British Church Music, Oxford, UK: Clarendon Press; New York: Oxford University Press, 1995.

1789. Stevens, Denis. *Tudor Church Music*. New York: Da Capo, 1955/repr. 1973.

1790. Temperley, Nicolas. "John Playford and the Metrical Psalms." *JAMS* 25 (1972): 331-78. Playford's book of psalm tunes sought to give English psalmody uniformity and dignity. Provides a history of psalmody before Playford and a thorough look at Playford's books on music.

1791. Temperley, Nicolas. "Psalmody: England." In *Grove 6*, Vol. 15. 1980. 337-345.

1792. Temperley, Nicholas. *The Music of the English Parish Church*. 2 vols. Cambridge Studies in Music, London: Cambridge University Press, 1980. Vol. 1: text; Vol. 2: anthology.

1793. Treacy, Susan. *English Devotional Song of the Seventeenth Century in Printed Collections from 1638-1693: A Study of Music and Culture*. Ph.D. diss., North Texas State University, 1986.

1794. Warren, James I. *O for a Thousand Tongues: The History, Nature, and Influence of Music in the Methodist Tradition*. Grand Rapids, MI: F. Asbury Press, 1988.

1795. Wienandt, Elwyn A. and Robert H. Young. *The Anthem in England and America*. New York: Free Press, 1970.

1796. Wilson, Ruth Mack. *Anglican Chant and Chanting in England and America, 1660-1811*. Ph.D. diss., University of Illinois at Urbana-Champaign, 1988. This study traces the various changes and implementations made by cathedrals, collegiate chapels and churches, and parish churches after the Latin Offices and Mass were consolidated and translated into English.

23

Protestant Music on the European Continent

MUSIC AND PROTESTANT THEOLOGY

1797. Bailey, Adrienne Thompson. "Music in the Liturgies of the Reformers: Martin Luther and John Calvin." *Reformed Liturgy and Music* 21, Spr. (1987): 74-79.

1798. Buszin, Walter E. "Luther's Quotes on Music." *Journal of Church Music* 13 (1971): 2-7.

1799. Dunning, Albert. "Calvin, Jean." In *Grove 6*, Vol. 3. 1980. 630-632.

1800. Garside, Charles W. "Calvin's Preface to the Psalter: A Re-Appraisal." *MQ* 37 (1951): 566-577. Calvin's notions on music are re-examined on the basis of his Preface to the Genevan Psalter. They are 1) the melody must have weight and majesty, 2) only the psalms are an appropriate text, 3) music is inextricably linked with prayer and forms an integral part of the church service.

1801. Garside, Charles W. *The Origins of Calvin's Theology of Music, 1536-1543*. Philadelphia, PA: American Philosophical Society, 1979.

1802. Hommes, N.J. "Let Women be Silent in Church: A Message Concerning the Worship Service and the Decorum to be Observed by Women." *Calvin Theological Journal* 4 (1969): 5.

1803. Horne, Brian L. "A Civitas of Sound: On Luther and Music." *Theology* 88, Jan. (1985): 21-28. Music occupied a central position in Luther's thinking because, as the most abstract of the arts, it represented the order of God's creation.

1804. Leaver, Robin A. "Zwingli, Ulrich." In *Grove 6*, Vol. 20. 1980. 725-726.

1805. Leaver, Robin A. "Then the Whole Congregation Sings: The Sung Word in Reformation Worship." *Drew Gateway* 60, Fall (1990): 55-73. An argument for liturgical musicology and the necessity of considering music as an essential part of liturgy. Examples include the medieval mass and Calvin's Geneva liturgy, with detailed consideration given Luther's German Mass.

1806. Leaver, Robin A. and Ann Bond. "Luther, Martin." In *Grove 6*, Vol. 11. 1980. 365-371.

1807. Pietsch, Helen. "On Luther's Understanding of Music." *Lutheran Theological Journal* 26, Dec. (1992): 160-168.

1808. White, Susan J. "Christian Worship since the Reformation." In *The Making of Jewish and Christian Worship*, Paul F. Bradshaw and Lawrence A. Hoffman, ed. Two Liturgical Traditions, Vol. 1. Notre Dame, IN: University of Notre Dame Press, 1991. 184-206.

HISTORIES AND SURVEYS

1809. Blume, Friedrich, et al. *Protestant Church Music*. New York: W.W. Norton, 1974.

1810. Davidson, James Robert. *A Dictionary of Protestant Church Music*. Metuchen, NJ: Scarecrow Press, 1975.

1811. Etherington, Charles L. *Protestant Worship Music: Its History and Practice*. Westport CT: Greenwood Press, 1962/repr. 1978.

1812. Gérold, T. "Protestant Music on the Continent." In *New Oxford History of Music*, Vol. 4. London, England: Oxford University Press, 1968. 419-64.

1813. Leaver, Robin A. "Christian Liturgical Music in the Wake of the Protestant Reformation." In *The Sacred Sound and Social Change: Liturgical Music in Jewish and Christian Experience*, Lawrence A. Hoffman and Janet Roland Walton, ed. Two Liturgical Traditions, Vol. 3. Notre Dame: University of Notre Dame Press, 1992. 124-145. On Lutheran and Anglican musical responses to the Reformation.

1814. Riedel, Johannes, ed. *Cantors at the Crossroads: Essays on Church Music in Honor of Walter E. Buszin*. St. Louis, MO: Concordia Publishing House, 1967. 20 essays on traditional and 20th-century Protestant church music.

1815. Seeley, G.S. *German Protestant Choral Music since 1925*. Ph.D. diss., University of Southern California, 1969.

1816. Steinitz, P. "German Church Music." In *New Oxford History of Music*, Vol. 5. London: Oxford University Press, 1975. 557-776.

1817. Temperley, Nicolas. "Hymn: Protestant." In *Grove 6*, Vol. 8. 1980. 846-851.

1818. Youens, Susan Lee. *Music and Religion in the French Reformation and Counter-Reformation*. Ph.D. diss., University of Santa Barbara, 1975.

LUTHERAN MUSIC AND THEOLOGY

1819. Barker, J.W. "Sociological Influences upon the Emergence of Lutheran Music." *MMA* 4 (1969): 157-98.

1820. Bond, Ann. "Plainsong in the Lutheran Church." *Musical Times* 114 (1973): 582-587, 993-997, 1114-1118. Although a radical in doctrine, Luther loved the Medieval liturgy and recommended high mass with plainsong in Latin whenever possible. Pt. 1. Plainsong survived in the Lutheran liturgy in three sung forms: Latin plainsong, metrical paraphrases in German, and in harmonized versions. The first two were sung in alternation by a choir, a practice that lasted into the 18th century. In harmonized versions, such as by Schein in the early 17th century, melismas were mercilessly pruned so that the text could fit a regular harmonic structure. Plainsong also survived in organ music. Part II covers plainsong hymns and sequences for organ from 1600-1750. Part III covers canticles and songs and the ordinary of the mass for the same period.

1821. Brouwer, Frans. "Church Music in Iceland During the Nineteenth Century." In *Ars et Musica in Liturgia...* Frans Brouwer and Robin Leaver, eds. Metuchen, NJ: Scarecrow Press, 1994. 13-31. The only music heard during regular services of the Lutheran Church was the congregational song, usually unaccompanied, and the chant sung by the minister. This centuries-old conservatism is attributed to the need to preserve national identity under domination by the Danes, Iceland's low economic status, and cultural isolation. Toward the end of the nineteenth century, four-part chorale harmonizations to be sung by a choir were introduced and have become popular.

1822. Buszin, Walter E. "Music of the Lutheran Church." In *The Encyclopedia of the Lutheran Church*, Vol. 3. Minneapolis, MN 1965. 62 ff.

1823. Buszin, Walter E. "Criteria of Church Music in the 17th and 18th Centuries." In *Festschrift Theodore Hoelty-Nickel: A Collection of Essays on Church Music*, Newman W. Powell, ed. Valparaiso, IN: Valparaiso University, 1967. 13 ff. For Bach and Schütz, the text inspired the music and was set so as to be understood. After about 1720, Lutheran theology, liturgy, and church music suffered at the hands of rationalism and secularism and have yet to recover.

1824. Finney, Chanson. *The Development of the Lutheran Kantorei in the Early Sixteenth Century*. Thesis, University of Louisville, 1970.

1825. Geier, Martin. *Music in the Service of the Church: The Funeral Sermon for Heinrich Schutz*. Robin A. Leaver, transl. St. Louis, MO: Concordia Publishing House, 1984.

1826. Gould, Ronald Lee. *The Latin Lutheran Mass at Wittenberg, 1523-1545; A Survey of the Early Reformation Mass and the Lutheran Theology of Music, as Evidenced in the Liturgical Writing of Martin Luther, the Relevant Kirchen-ordnungen, and the Georg Rhau Muskidrucke for the Hauptgottesdienst*. Ph.D. diss., Union Theological Seminary, 1970.

1827. Hill, David Stuart. *The Persistance of Memory: Mode, Trope, and Difference in the Passion Chorale*. Ph.D. diss., State University of New York at Stony Brook, 1994. Continuity in chorale composition from Hassler to Bach.

1828. Irwin, Joyce. "Shifting Alliances: The Struggle for a Lutheran Theology of Music." In *Sacred Sound*, Joyce Irwin, ed. 1983. 55-69. By the end of the 17th century, several emphases concerning music had hardened into irreconcilable positions: the importance of the text, the sincerity and devotion of the worshipper, the importance of congregational participation, and the inherent sacredness of music itself. Advocates of all positions found support in the writings of Luther.

1829. Irwin, Joyce *Neither Voice Nor Heart Alone: German Lutheran Theology of Music in the Age of the Baroque*. American University Studies. Series 7, Theology and Religion, Vol. 132, New York: P. Lang, 1993. Pt. 1, 'The Formulation of the Lutheran Orthodox Theology of Music,' deals with such polarities as freedom and obligation, psychology and spirituality, and the sacred and secular. Pt. 2, 'Synthesis and Antithesis,' surveys the theologies of various pre-Pietists. Pt. 3. 'From Pietism to the Enlightenment,' looks at worship as edification, the regeneration of musicians, music and adiaphora, and the cantata debate. Concludes with 'Finale: J.S. Bach—a Musician, not a Theologian.'

1830. Jones, Robert Kent. *The Confessional Theology of Heinrich Schütz: A Musical, Theological, and Liturgical Analysis of His 'Musikalische Exequien'*. Ph.D. diss, Claremont Graduate School, 1994.

1831. Leaver, Robin A. *The Liturgy and Music: A Study of the Use of the Hymn in Two Liturgical Traditions*. Bramcote, Hants.: Grove Books, 1976. On the use of hymns in the Church of England and the Lutheran Church.

1832. Leaver, Robin A. "Theological Dimensions of Mission Hymnody: The Counterpoint of Cult and Culture." *Worship* 62 (1988): 316-331.

1833. Leaver, Robin A. "The Lutheran Reformation." In *The Renaissance from the 1470s to the End of the Sixteenth Century*, New York: MacMillan, 1989. 263-285. On Luther and Lutheran music in Wittenberg, Leipzig, and Augsburg.

1834. Marshall, Robert L. "Chorale." In *Grove 6*, Vol. 4. 1980. 312-321. See also for all other forms based on the chorale.

1835. Marshall, Robert L. "Chorale settings." In *Grove 6*, Vol. 4. 1980. 323-338.

1836. Mihok, Shirley Mae. *Music in the Divine Liturgy of Slovak Lutheran Worship*. D.A. thesis, Ball State University, 1982. A study of three 20th-century liturgical settings, composed between 1922 and 1965, reveals the influence of Slav, Latin, Czech, and German sources.

1837. Ottermann, Reino E. "The Role of Music in Devotional Life." *Scriptura* 3 (1981): 19-29. On the role of music in devotional life within the Lutheran church and on music as "a foretaste of eternal life".

1838. Robinson-Hammerstein, Helga. "The Lutheran Reformation and its Music." In *Transmission of Ideas in the Lutheran Church*, Helga Robinson-Hammerstein, ed. 1989. 141-171.

1839. Rupprecht, Oliver C. "The Modern Struggle for Standards in Religious Music: A Theological-musical Appraisal Viewing the Work of Luther, Bach, and Mendelssohn." *Concordia Journal* 9, July (1983): 124-139. A questioning of the relationship between the features of music and their theological implications and uses, and a plea for the continued application of the spiritual values found in traditional music.

1840. Schalk, Carl. *Music in Lutheran Worship*. St. Louis MO: Concordia Publishing House, 1983.

1841. Söhngen, Oskar. "Fundamental Considerations for a Theology of Music." *The Musical Heritage of the Church* 4 (1954): 1-19. Of the pronouncements on music by the three Protestant reformers, only on Luther's can a theology of music be based: only Luther considered music, like the Word, to be a gift of God.

1842. Suojanen, Paivikki. *Finnish Folk Hymn Singing: Study in Music Anthropology*. Tampere, Finland: University of Tampere Institute for Folk Tradition, 1984. A study of folk hymn singing among members of a revivalist Beseecherite Lutheran sect in southwestern Finland. Chapters deal with hymn singing, places and occasions for hymn singing, what is sung, and the meaning of hymn.

1843. Walker, Paul, ed. *Church, Stage, and Studio: Music and Its Contexts in Seventeenth-Century Germany*. Ann Arbor, MI: UMI Research Press, 1990. Includes essays on Buxtehude in the context of 17th century music, 17th century German organ music, the sacred organ works of Samuel Scheidt, Buxtehude's expressive chorale preludes, and Schütz's *Musikalische Exequien*.

1844. Webber, Geoffrey. *North German Church Music in the Age of Buxtehude.* Oxford Monographs on Music, New York: Clarendon Press, 1995. A study of the church music of Buxtehude's contemporaries and of the influence of contemporary Italian church music. Also considers the music's religious and social context and performance practice.

1845. Westendorf, Craig Jon. *The Textual and Musical Repertoire of the Spruchmotette.* D.M.A., University of Illinois at Urbana-Champaign, 1987. A history of late Renaissance and early Baroque motets based strictly on the German translation of the Bible; a survey of the theology of Scripture and concomitant tenets of devotional, pastoral theology in the late 16th and early 17th centuries; a catalogue of over 1500 Spruchmotetten and their concordances; and a description of strictly musical aspects.

1846. Windh, J.E. *Early Lutheran Masses.* Ph.D. diss., Univ. of Illinois, 1971.

1847. Youens, Laura Seale. *Music for the Lutheran Mass in Leipzig. Universitatsbibliothek, MS Thomaskirche 49/50.* Ph.D. diss., Indiana University, 1978.

THEOLOGICAL ASPECTS OF THE MUSIC OF J. S. BACH

1848. Ellis, John Robert. *Treatment of the Trumpet in the Bible and its Relationship to the Sacred Solo Arias with Obbligato Trumpet by Johann Sebastian Bach.* DMA diss., Arizona State University, 1984. A comparison of Bach's use of the trumpet to its occurences in Jewish tradition to c. 70AD shows Bach's employment of the trumpet reflected Biblical usage.

1849. Froehlich, Karlfried. "Luther's Hymns and Johann Sebastian Bach." *Lutheran Theological Seminary Bulletin* 66, 1, Wint. (1986): 3-29.

1850. Holborn, Hans Ludwig. *Bach and Pietism: The Relationship of the Church Music of Johann Sebastian Bach to Eighteenth Century Lutheran Orthodoxy and Pietism with Special Reference to the Saint Matthew Passion.* D. Min. Thesis, Claremont School of Theology, 1976.

1851. Krapf, Gerhard. "Bach's Use of the Chorale as an Agent of Exegesis." *Religious Studies and Theology* 6, 1-2/Jan.-May (1986): 20-26.

1852. Maxwell, David R. "Theological Symbolism in the Organ Works of J. S. Bach." *Concordia Journal* 19, Apr. (1993): 148-162.

1853. Minear, Paul S. "Bach and Today's Theologians." *Theology Today* 42, July (1985): 201-210. Bach's vocation is seen as that of "a liturgical, narrative, exegetical, Christocentric theologian." He is viewed as both a pre-modern and a post-liberal thinker.

1854. Olson, Howard S. "Johann Sebastian Bach: God's Musical Ambassador." *Africa Theological Journal* 14, 1 (1985): 19-34.

1855. Saler, June Lee. *The Theological Influence of the Pietist Movement on the Texts of Bach's Sacred Cantatas.* M.A. thesis, California State University, 1982. Saler documents Pietist influence with attention to the concept of *unio mystica* as found in cantata texts.

1856. Simon, Carl Geoffrey. *Musical Iconography in the Sacred Cantatas of Johann Sebastian Bach.* D.M.A., Peabody Institute of the Johns Hopkins University, 1980. A study of 96 of Bach's sacred cantatas composed from 1707 through 1749 reveals four types of musical icons: the single word/phrase icon; the symbolic figuration icon; the conceptual icon; and the icon of literary allusion. Bach's extensive use of such icons indicates Bach's primary purpose to be theological. Bach, both consummate musician and well-versed Lutheran, placed music at the service of the Word of God.

1857. Smith, Timothy A. "Bach and the Cross." *Christian Scholar's Review* 22, 3 (1993): 267-290. Symbolism in the notation of Bach's music.

1858. Stapert, Calvin. "Bach as Theologian: A Review Article." *Reformed Journal* 37, May (1987): 19-27.

1859. Stiller, Gunther. *Johann Sebastian Bach and Liturgical Life in Leipzig.* Herbert J.A. Bouman, Daniel F. Poellot, Hilton C. Oswald, transl. Robin A. Leaver, ed. St. Louis, MO: Concordia Publishing House, 1984.

1860. Westermeyer, Paul. "Grace and the Music of Bach." *Christian Century* 102, Mar. (1985): 291-294. A finding that the source of grace in Bach's music is the grace that is the source of the music itself.

1861. Young, W. Murray. *The Sacred Dramas of J.S. Bach: A Reference and Textual Interpretation.* Jefferson, NC; London: McFarland, 1994.

OTHER EUROPEAN RELIGIOUS MUSIC

1862. Abel, Timothy D. *Handel's Messiah as Proclamation: A Study in Building a Theology for Sacred Music Performances.* D. Min. diss., Southern Methodist University, 1990.

1863. Barrett, Aubrey Wayne, Jr. *A Study of the Choral Music Tradition in Hungarian Baptist Churches: Its History, Leadership, Literature, Personnel, and Practice, Including an Anthology of Representative Choral Works.* D.M.A., The University of Iowa, 1992. A study of Hungarian Baptist church music from 1873 to the present, primary leaders, publications and choral anthologies, socio-political contexts, and choirs.

1864. Greene, David B. "Handel's Messiah: Music, Theology, and Ritual." *Soundings* 75, Spr. (1992): 43-59.

1865. Johanson, John H. "Moravian Hymnody." *The Hymn*. 30, 3 (1979): 167-177. On the hymnody of the ancient Unitas Fratrum, the original church founded in Bohemia in the mid-15th century. 30, 4 (1979): 230-239. On the hymnody of the Renewed Moravian Church, founded in Saxony in 1727.

1866. Knudsen, T. "Ornamental Hymn/Psalm Singing in Denmark, the Faroe Islands, and the Hebrides." *DFS Information* 68, 2 (1968).

1867. Lange, Barbara Rose. *Holy Brotherhood: The Negotiation of Musical Style in a Gypsy and Magyar Pentecostal Church*. Ph.D. diss., University of Washington, 1993.

1868. Leaver, Robin A. *Goostly Psalmes and Spirituall Songes: English and Dutch Metrical Psalms from Coverdale to Utenhove, 1535-1566*. Oxford Studies in British Church Music, New York: Oxford University Press, 1991.

1869. Letkemann, Peter. *The Hymnody and Choral Music of Mennonites in Russia, 1789-1915*. Ph.D. diss., University of Toronto, 1986. A history of Mennonite music, beginning with unison congregational singing as the only form of music to four-part harmony, choral societies and instrumental music in every village by the Russian Revolution.

1870. Lieseberg, Ursula. "The Martyr Songs of the Hutterite Brethren." *Mennonite Quarterly Review* 67 (1993): 323-336. The Anabaptists were a peaceful religious group whose members suffered bloody executions during the 16th century. This essay lists and describes the martyr songs that reflect this history.

1871. Nilsson, Ann-Marie. *On Liturgical Hymn Melodies in Sweden during the Middle Ages: Summary and Comments on Four Articles and a Research Project*. Goteborg: Musikvetenskapliga Institutionen, 1991. On the sources of Swedish hymnody (England among them) and the problem of variants.

1872. Sommerville, C. John. "The Religious Music of the 20th and 21st Centuries." *Religion* 14, July (1984): 245-267. The religious compositions of Britten, Webern, Vaughan Williams, Stravinsky, Schönberg, Poulenc, and Messiaen are used to argue that a high level of religious music composition will continue well into the future.

1873. Stanley, Glenn. *The Oratorio in Prussia and Protestant Germany: 1812-1848*. Ph.D. diss., Columbia University, 1988. A study focussing on the context in which Spohr, Loewe, Mendelssohn and others composed the oratorio.

1874. Wells, Melvin A., Jr. *Settings of the Passion Story in the Nineteenth Century*. D.M.A., Southwestern Baptist Theological Seminary, 1990.

24

Liturgical Dance and Drama

DANCE AND DRAMA IN PRE-20TH-CENTURY CHRISTIANITY

1875. Brockett, Clyde, Jr. "A Previously Unknown 'Ordo Prophetarum' in a Manuscript Fragment in Zagreb." *Comparative Drama* 27, 1 (1993): 114-127. A unique version of the medieval music-drama 'Ordo Prophetarum, written in a notation that dates from the late 12th or early 13th century, proves that the composition of medieval music-dramas developed along more than one tradition.

1876. Brooks, Lynn Matluck. "The Catholic Church and Dance in the Middle Ages." In *Focus on Dance X: Religion and Dance*, Dennis J. Fallon and Mary Jane Wolbers, ed. Reston, VA: American Alliance for Health, Physical Education, Recreation and Dance, 1982.

1877. Brooks, Lynn Matluck. *The Dances of the Processions of Seville in Spain's Golden Age*. Kassel, Germany: Edition Reichenberger, 1988. A study of the religious dances of 16th and 17th century Seville and the social and cultural context in which they developed. Originally appeared as Ed.D. Thesis, Temple University, 1985.

1878. Carroll, William. *The Bible in Drama and Dance at the Jesuit Colleges of the 16th to 18th Centuries*. Papers of the International Seminar on the Bible in Dance, Jerusalem: The Israeli Center of the International Theatre Institute, 1979.

1879. Chirovsky, A. "Revelation and Liturgy: The Epiphanic Function of the Human Body in Byzantine Worship." *Diakonia* 13, 2 (1978): 111-119.

1880. Collins, Fletcher, Jr. *Production of Medieval Church Music-Drama*. Charlottesville, VA: University Press of Virginia, 1972.

1881. Daniels, Marilyn. *The Dances in Christianity: A History of Religious Dance through the Ages.* Ramsey, NJ: Paulist Press, 1981. A readable historical overview of Christian dance through the centuries with particular attention paid to the Early Church, Medieval and late-Medieval periods, and the Renaissance and Post-Renaissance periods. Current dancers producing church-based work are profiled in the final chapter.

1882. Davidson, Audrey Ekdahl, ed. *Holy Week and Easter Ceremonies and Dramas from Medieval Sweden.* Early Drama, Art, and Music Monograph Series, No. 13, Kalamazoo, MI: Medieval Institute, 1990.

1883. Davies, J.G., ed. *Worship and Dance.* Birmingham, Eng.: University of Birmingham Institute for the Study of Worship and Religious Architecture (ISWRA), 1975. A collection of essays concerned with the past, present and future of Christian dance. Among the topics presented are dance in church buildings, a theology of dance, eroticism in Christian dance, and Pentecostal dance traditions.

1884. Davies, J. G. *Liturgical Dance: An Historical, Theological and Practical Handbook.* London: SCM Press Ltd, 1984. A collection of ten stimulating and broad-ranging essays on the relationship of worship and dance. Topics include dance in the Bible, in church, and in church buildings, a theology of dance, and specific types of religious dance. Includes an extensive bibliography.

1885. De Sola, Carla. "Dance, Liturgical." In *The New Dictionary of Sacramental Worship*, Fink, ed. 1990. 314-319.

1886. Deiss, Lucien. *Dance for the Lord.* Schiller Park, IL: World Library Publications, 1975. The author supports the use of liturgical dance with references to the Old and New Testaments, early church councils and modern writing. Includes illustrated choreography for eleven liturgical dances to music by the author.

1887. Dewey, Arthur J. "The Hymn in the Acts of John: Dance as Hermeneutic." *Semeia* 38, Apocryphal Acts of Apostles issue (1986): 67-80. The hymn and the round dance to which it was performed combine to lead to a state of ecstasy. (This contention is qualified by Jean-Daniel Kaestli, pp. 81-88).

1888. Enders, J. "Visions with Voices: The Rhetoric of Memory and Music in Liturgical Drama." *Comparative Drama* 24, 1 (1990): 34-54.

1889. Fallon, Dennis J. and Mary Jane Wolbers, ed. *Focus on Dance X: Religion and Dance.* Focus on Dance, Vol. 10. Reston, VA: American Alliance for Health, Physical Education, Recreation, and Dance, 1982. A collection of 22 essays by both professional dancers and others on the relationship between dance and religion from Christian, Jewish, Native American, ancient, and 'primitive' perspectives. Articles are divided into four catagories: 1) History of

Dance and Religion, 2) Dance and Organized Religion, 3) Spiritual Expression and Prayer, 4) Dance in Places of Worship.

1890. Fassler, Margot. "The Feast of Fools and Danielis Ludus: Popular Tradition in a Medieval Cathedral Play." In *Plainsong in the Age of Polyphony*, Thomas Forrest Kelly, ed. Cambridge: Cambridge University Press, 1992. 65-99. Fassler demonstrates that the Play of Daniel was part of the Feast of Fools celebration, which took place once a year on the octave of Christmas. As such, it is jocular and tension-releasing in character, allowing as it did the community of minor clergy at Beauvais Cathedral to assume the roles of the church hierarchy for one day. In the play, the Babylonians were comic characters, buffoons, whose boisterous behavior in a cathedral was part of the irreverence of this occasion. The play should thus be played for its comedic values—an example of Medieval entertainment for the general public.

1891. Flanigan, C. Clifford. "The Roman Rite and the Origins of the Liturgical Drama." *University of Toronto Quarterly* 43 (1974): 263-84.

1892. Gagne, Ronald, Thomas A. Kane, and Robert VerEecke. *Introducing Dance in Christian Worship*. Washington, DC: The Pastoral Press, 1984. The authors reflect on the past, present and future of Judeo-Christian cultic movement and liturgical dance from a Catholic theological perspective. Includes an annotated bibliography and a detailed chronology of liturgical dance (300-1800 CE). With an introduction by Carla DeSola.

1893. Hardison, O.B., Jr. "European Religious Drama." In *Encyclopedia of Religion*, Mircea Eliade, ed. Vol. 4. 1987. 470-474.

1894. Hollenweger, W.J. "Danced Documentaries: The Theological and Political Significance of Pentecostal Dancing." In *Worship and Dance*, Davies, ed. Birmingham: ISWRA, 1975. 76-82.

1895. Kazarow, Patricia A. "Text and Context in Hildegard of Bingen's *Ordo Virtututm*." In *Maps of Flesh and Light: The Religious Experience of Medieval Women Mystics*, Ulrike Wiethaus, ed. Syracuse, NY: Syracuse University Press, 1993. 127-151. A study of *Ordo Virtutum*, the first extant liturgical morality play, in its musical, theological, and drama-historical contexts. A description of the play's staging, music and text, the dramatic milieu of its day, and the relationship between Hildegard's music and theology. This relationship is discussed on four levels of meaning: the literal, the moral, the allegorical, and the anagogical.

1896. Marks, Joseph E., III, ed. *The Mathers on Dancing, An Arrow Against Profane and Promiscuous Dancing, A Bibliography of Anti-Dance Books 1865-1963*. Brooklyn, N.Y.: Dance Horizons, 1975. The sermons and writings of Increase and Cotton Mather on dance and worship. Some examples of acceptable dance are included.

1897. Maynard, Susan Watkins. *Dance in the Arts of the Middle Ages*. Ph.D. diss., Florida State University, 1992. Dance as the subject of works of art and the symbol of human values is examined for what these sources reveal about the attitudes, emotions, and beliefs connected with dance through the early sixteenth century.

1898. McGee, T. J. "The Liturgical Placement of the *Quem Quaeritis* Dialogue." *JAMS* 29 (1976): 1-29. Rather than beginning as a trope, this dialogue probably formed part of a ceremony that was separate from the Easter Mass.

1899. Miller, James L. *Measures of Wisdom: The Cosmic Dance in Classical and Christian Antiquity*. Toronto: University of Toronto Press, 1986. A presentation of the shifting philosophical interpretations of dance in the first six centuries of Christian thought. Nine distinct if overlapping phases are discussed: 1) Old Platonic, 2) Judeo-Hellenistic, 3) Gnostic, 4) Early Neo-Platonic, 5) Middle Platonic, 6) Heliotropic/Cosmopoetic, 7) Greek Patristic, 8) Late Neo-Platonic, and 9) the Angelic Phase.

1900. Norton, Michael L. "'Sermo in Cantilena': Structure as Symbol in 'Imago Sancti Nicolai'." *Comparative Drama* 27, 1 (1993): 83-99. The symbolic numbers three and five and rhetorical symbols of loss and restoration are imbedded in the music, text, and dramatic form of the 12th century St. Nicholas drama to convey structural symbols of Christianity.

1901. Pagels, Elaine H. "To the Universe Belongs the Dancer." *Parabola: The Magazine of Myth and Tradition* 4, 2 (1979): 6-9. An account of a dance by Jesus and his followers in the *Acts of John*, an extra-Biblical early Christian text.

1902. Rankin, Susan. "Musical and Ritual Aspects of *Quem queritis*." In *Liturgische Tropen*, Gabriel Silagi, ed. Munich 1985. 181-192.

1903. Rankin, Susan. *The Music of the Medieval Liturgical Drama in France and England*. Outstanding Dissertations in Music from British Universities, New York and London: Garland, 1989. Orig., Ph.D. diss., Un. of Cambridge, 1982.

1904. Rankin, Susan. "Liturgical Drama." In *NOHM II*, Richard Crocker, ed. 1990. 310-356.

1905. Rankin, Susan. "The Divine Truth of Scripture: Chant in the Roman de Fauvel." *JAMS* 47, 2 (1994): 203-243. An allegory of the vice-ridden French royal court, the Roman de Fauvel contains 169 musical pieces, monophonic and polyphonic, French and Latin. This study examines the origin of the chant-based pieces and the reasons for their inclusion.

1906. Rock, Judith and Norman Mealy. *Performer as Priest and Prophet: Restoring the Intuitive in Worship through Music and Dance*. New York: Harper and Row, 1988. A five-part dialogue between a dancer (Rock) and a musician

(Mealy) on the healing possibilities of the performing arts within Christian Church Communities.

1907. Schneider, Paul G. *The Mystery of the Acts of John: An Interpretation of the Hymn and the Dance in Light of the Acts' Theology*. Distinguished Diss. Series, Vol. 10. San Francisco: Mellen Research University Press, 1991. The Acts of John contains a sacrament made up of an introductory hymn, the main hymn, and a dance during which the participants become identical with the Lord, the salvific gnosis is received, and the Pleroma is visible before them. The sacrament concludes with mystagogical instructions concerning what they have have experienced.

1908. Sevestre, Nicole. "The Aquitanian Tropes of the Easter Introit." *JPMMS* 3 (1980): 26-39.

1909. Smoldon, William L. *The Music of the Medieval Church Dramas*. Cynthia Bourgeault, ed. London: Oxford University Press, 1980.

1910. Stevens, John. "Medieval Drama, II. Liturgical Drama." In *Grove 6*, Vol. 12. 1980.

1911. Trachte, Sharon Reed. *Doctrine and Aesthetics in French Christmas Liturgical Drama*. Ph.D. diss., SUNY at Binghamton, 1987. This study challenges received opinion that the earliest dramatic representations did not constitute drama because they were didactic. In fact, in 11th-century versions of the Officium Stellae drama, the psychological and dramatic co-existed with the didactic and were reciprocal in their relationship.

1912. Wallace, Robin. "The Role of Music in Liturgical Drama: A Revaluation." *Music and Letters* 45 (1984): 219-28.

1913. Wright, Stephen K. "The 'Ingressus Pilatus' Chant in Medieval German Drama." *Comparative Drama* 28, 3 (1994): 348-366.

DANCE AS MODERN LITURGY

1914. Adams, Doug, ed. *Papers Presented at the International Seminar on the Bible in Dance, Jerusalem, Aug. 5-9, 1979*. Nineteen papers on the Bible in dance. Typescript at Graduate Theological Union Library, Berkeley, CA.

1915. Adams, Doug. *Congregational Dancing in Christian Worship*. Richmond, CA: The Sharing Company, 1984. Congregational dance in Biblical, historical and theological perspectives, with suggestions for congregational dance in relation to community, repentence, rejoicing and rededication.

1916. Adams, Doug. *Changing Biblical Imagery and Artistic Identity in Twentieth Century Liturgical Dance*. Richmond, CA: The Sharing Press, 1985.

A study of liturgical dance and other dance rituals from the 1920s through the 1970s. Includes suggestions for those texts and themes that provide most effective engagement of a congregation.

1917. Adams, Doug and Diane Apostolos-Cappadona, ed. *Dance as Religious Studies.* New York: Crossroad, 1990. Fifteen essays on traditional and modern religious dance, especially in relation to and inspired by the Bible.

1918. Adams, Douglas and Judith Rock. "Biblical Criteria in Modern Dance: Modern Dance as Prophetic Form." In *Dance as Religious Studies,* Doug Adams and Diane Apostolos-Cappadona, ed. Richmond, CA: The Sharing Co., 1982. 80-91. Rather than focusing on Biblical subject matter, this paper focuses on how Biblical faith and values may be reflected in the esthetics of modern dance technique and choreography: an application to dance of Paul Tillich's four categories of relationship between religion and visual art.

1919. Adams, Doug et al., ed. *The Bible in Dance.* Switzerland; U.S.: Harwood Academic Publishers, 1992. Ten articles by such authors as Doug Adams, Judith Rock, and Giora Manor on various aspects of biblical dance.

1920. Allan, John. "Music, Movement and Silence in Worship." *Christian Brethren Review* 39 (1988): 63-78.

1921. Barton, Anne. *Shall We Dance.* Grove Worship Series, No. 119, Bramcote, Nottingham: Grove Books, 1991. On the religious aspects of modern Christian dance.

1922. Blogg, Martin. *Dance and the Christian Faith: Dance, a Form of Knowing.* London: Hodder and Stoughton/David and Charles, 1987. A scholarly discussion of religious dance as it appears in the disciplines of sculpture, education, and art.

1923. Challingsworth, Nell. *Liturgical Dance Movement: A Practical Guide.* London: Mowbray, 1982. With a Foreword by the Bishop of Croydon.

1924. Combs, Jo Anne. *Christian Sacred Dance: An Ethnography of Performance and Symbolic Interactionism.* Ph.D. diss., UCLA, 1992. The perceptions, assessments, opinions, values and meanings that dancers hold of dance in religious settings.

1925. De Sola, Carla. *The Spirit Moves: A Handbook of Dance and Prayer.* Austin, TX: The Sharing Co., 1977/repr. 1986. After a brief reflection on the natural and beneficial relationship between dance and prayer, the author devotes the rest of the book to descriptions of and guides to movement meditation, circle dance, biblically-based dance and ritualistic dance. 1977 ed., Washington, DC: Liturgical Conference.

1926. Deiss, Lucien and Gloria Weyman. *Liturgical Dance*. Phoenix, AZ: North American Liturgy Resources, 1984. A study of the relationship of Christian dance to human nature, sacramental theology and the theology of worship. Includes suggestions for a vocabulary of movements to be used in services.

1927. Deitering, Carolyn. "Movement Prayer, A Learning Experience - A Worship Experience." *NICM Journal* 7, Fall (1982): 24-30.

1928. Deitering, Carolyn. *The Liturgy as Dance and the Liturgical Dancer*. New York: Crossroad Publishing Co., 1984. In a personal yet practical style, Deitering lays out her vision of a Catholic theology of liturgical dance based on the Catholic mass, teaching, and canon law.

1929. Engle, Mark C. "Movement in the Eucharist." *Saint Luke's Journal of Theology* 26, Dec. (1982): 11-22. A presentation of the theory and practice of dance and the liturgy, geared to the experimental reader.

1930. Fisher, Constance. *Dancing the Old Testament: Christian Celebrations of Israelite Heritage for Worship and Education*. Austin: The Sharing Co., 1980. Chapters deal with roots, life cycle, prophetic and victory dances, and weekly and yearly celebration.

1931. Fisher, Constance. *Music and Dance: In the Worship Program of the Church*. Austin TX: The Sharing Co., 1981.

1932. Fisher, Constance and Doug Adams. *Dancing with Early Christians*. Richmond, CA: The Sharing Co., 1983. After introductory chapters on the development of Christian belief and liturgy during the first three centuries, the author provides the dialog and choreography for four groups of dances and ritual celebration expressive of central Christian beliefs. Chapters are entitled 1) Lord of the Dance, 2) The Living Sacrifice, 3) Dancing with Angels, and 4) The Celebration of Faith.

1933. Hoare, Timothy Douglas. *On the Aesthetic and the Religious Dimensions of the Classical Theatre of Thailand: Performance as a Theological Agenda for Christian Ritual Praxis*. Ph.D. diss., Graduate Theological Union, 1992.

1934. Hume, Janelle Beckwith. *Dancing for God: A Clarification of the Distinguishing Characteristics of Christian Dance Worship*. M.A. thesis, University of Oregon, 1982.

1935. Jasper, R.C. P. *Worship and Dance Today: A Survey*. Worship and Dance, Davies, ed. Birmingham, Eng.: ISWRA, 1975. 22-28.

1936. Krosnicki, Thomas A. "Dance Within the Liturgical Act." *Worship* 61 (1987): 349-357.

1937. MacLeod, Marian B. *Dancing Through Pentecost: Dance Language for Worship from Pentecost to Thanksgiving.* Austin, TX: The Sharing Co., 1981.

1938. Manor, Giora. *The Gospel According to Dance: Choreography and the Bible from Ballet to Modern.* New York: St. Martin's Press, 1980. An illustrated study of 20th-century settings by noted choreographers of Bible stories.

1939. Mead, Patriceann J. *Experiencing the Ineffable: Traditional and Ritual Dances from West Africa and Brazil as Inspiration for Modern Dance.* M.A. thesis, S.U.N.Y College at Brockport, 1993.

1940. Mealy, Cynthia Linell. *Historical Foundations for Dancing the Eucharist: An Essay Developing Liturgical Guidelines for the Incorporation of Dance in the Episcopal Eucharistic Rite II, on the Basis of a History and Commentary of the Rite.* 1983. Drawing inspiration from Medieval and Anglican architecture, music and ceremonial expression as well as the religious traditions of the Episcopal Church, the author develops guidelines for the role of dance within the ongoing liturgical reform movement.

1941. Mealy, Norman and Rock Judith, ed. *Music, Dance, and Religion: The Performing Arts in Worship.* Englewood Cliffs, NJ: Prentice-Hall, 1985.

1942. Mealy, Norman and Judith Rock, ed. *Performer as Priest and Prophet: Restoring the Intuitive in Worship through Music and Dance.* San Francisco: Harper & Row, 1988.

1943. Pruett, Diane Milhan. "Duncan's Perception of Dance in Religion." In *Focus on Dance X: Religion and Dance*, 1982.

1944. Reed, Carlynn. *And We Have Danced: A History of the Sacred Dance Guild and Sacred Dance: 1958-1978.* Austin: The Sharing Co., 1978. Formed at a time when dance at the altar was being tentatively explored, the SDG has been an active force in encouraging liturgical dance.

1945. Rock, Judith. *Theology in the Shape of Dance: Using Dance in Worship and Theological Process.* Austin, TX: The Sharing Co., 1977. Rock asks and answers four primary questions concerning Christian dance: 1) what makes an effective religious dance? 2) how does that dance function in Christian theology and worship? 3) how does one establish critical standards for Christian dance? and 4) what are the responsibilities of the Christian dancer?

1946. Rudolph, Amelia. *Walk and Talk, Text and Contacts: An Exploration of Dance and Religious Studies.* M.A. thesis, Graduate Theological Union, 1990.

1947. Sequeira, A. Ronald. "Liturgy and Dance: On the Need for an Adequate Terminology." *Studia Liturgica* 17 (1987): 157-165.

1948. Shields, Katina. *Dance as Worship: A Case Study of Congregational Response*. M.A. thesis, UCLA, 1985.

1949. Siegel, Marcia B. *The Shapes of Change: Images of American Dance*. Berkeley, Ca: University of California Press, 1979/repr. 1985. Includes discussion of Negro Spirituals, Shakers and some of Graham's works.

1950. Sigler, Anne. *To Be a Dancing Body: Visions in Sacred Dance*. MA, Pacific School of Religion, 1989. A transcript of a 3-part video presentation. Parts 1 and 3 are concerned with the use of dance within contemporary Christian communities. Part 2 explores religious judgements about the body and the impact of such judgements on the role of dance.

1951. Tarter-Strobel, Craig. *The Use of Dance as a Hermeneutical Tool for Interpreting the Theology of John Calvin*. M.A. thesis, Pacific School of Religion, 1986. Strobel presents the thesis that dance, due to its capacity to establish immediacy and facilitate participatory thinking, is an especially useful tool for hermeneutical work. The author uses his own dance-based hermeneutical exploration of the *Institutes* of John Calvin as an illustration of this approach.

1952. Taussig, Hal. *Dancing the New Testament: A Guide to Texts*. Richmond, CA: The Sharing Co., 1977. Suggestions for style and location for choreography based on seven categories of New Testament passages that relate directly to dance: hymns and hymn fragments, initiation rites, enthronement ceremonies, eucharist-related, dramatic narrative, and resurrection proclamations.

1953. Taussig, Hal. *The Lady of the Dance: A Movement Approach to Biblical Figures of Wisdom in Worship*. Richmond, CA: The Sharing Co., 1981. Suggestions on how to dance some 100 Old and New Testament texts that involve figures of wisdom.

1954. Taussig, Hal. *New Categories for Dancing the Old Testament*. Richmond, CA: The Sharing Co., 1981. An approach to Biblical dance based on category of texts: songs, psalms, oracles, prophetic liturgies, temple/synagogue liturgies, monarchial ceremony, sacrifices, covenant ceremonies, agricultural feasts, passover texts, poetry, Exodus related texts, J narratives, and passages related to wisdom.

1955. Van Tine, Mary Patricia. *Human Energy Fields and Movement in Ritual Dance*. M.S. thesis, UCLA, 1977. The application of the psychology of movement to modern ritual dance.

1956. Wise, Joseph. *The Body at Liturgy*. Phoenix, AZ: North American Liturgy Resources, 1972.

1957. Youngerman, Suzanne. "Theatrical and Liturgical Dance." In *Encyclopedia of Religion*, Mircea Eliade, ed. Vol. 4. 1987. 221-236.

25

Islam

GENERAL REFERENCES

1958. al-Faruqi, Lois Ibsen. "The Shari'ah on Music and Musicians." In *Islamic Thought and Culture*, Herndon, VA: International Institute of Islamic Thought, 1982. 27-52.

1959. al-Faruqi, Lois Ibsen. "Music, Musicians and Muslim Law." *Asian Music* 17, 1 (1985): 3-36. Genres of music are ranked according to the degree to which they are sanctioned or un-sanctioned, from Qur'anic chant at one extreme to sensuous music at the other. Careful attention is given to the sources, associations between musical and non-musical activities, and terminology with respect to music, musicians, and Muslim law.

1960. al-Faruqi, Lois Ibsen. "Islamization through the Sound Arts." *American Journal of Islamic Social Sciences* 3, Dec. (1986): 171-180. Al Faruqi proposes the term "handasah al saut" to describe Islamic sound art that arises out of and expresses the message of the culture of Islamic people. She traces the religio-historic attitudes toward the sound arts and makes a case for their current importance.

1961. al-Faruqi, Lois Ibsen. "The Mawlid." *The World of Music* 28, 3 (1986): 79-89. Music that is used to celebrate the birth and other events in the life of the prophet Muhammad.

1962. Browning, Robert H. et al., ed. *Maqâm: Music of the Islamic World and its Influences*. New York, NY: Alternative Museum, 1984.

1963. Denny, Walter. "Music and Musicians in Islamic Art." *Asian Music* 17, 1 (1985): 37-68. Includes a discussion of the *adhan* (call to prayer) and religious as well as the cosmological symbolism of music instruments, as represented in Islamic art.

1964. Farmer, Henry George. "The Music of Islam." In *The New Oxford History of Music I: Ancient and Oriental Music*, 3rd ed. 1957. 421-478.

1965. Gibb, H. A. R. et al., ed. *The Encyclopedia of Islam, New Edition Prepared by a Number of Leading Orientalists*. Leiden: Brill; London: Luzac, 1965/repr. 1986. Index compiled by Larry Feldman, publ. in Amherst, MA, by University of Massachusetts Press, 1975.

1966. Houtsma, M.T., T.W. Arnold, R. Basset, and R. Hartmann, ed. *The Encyclopaedia of Islam: A Dictionary of the Geography, Ethnography and Biography of the Muhammadan Peoples...* Leyden, Netherlands: E.J. Brill, 1954/repr. 1960. 4 vols. with supplement. 1st ed., 1913-1938.

1967. Nasr, Sayyed Hossein. "Music." In *Islamic Art and Spirituality*, Albany, NY: State University of New York Press, 1987. 149-74. Two chapters, entitled "Islam and Music: The View of Ruzbahan Baqli, the Patron Saint of Shiraz," and "The Influence of Sufism on Traditional Persian Music," are both geared toward the believer and are presented in a meditational style.

1968. Neubauer, Eckhard. "Islamic Religious Music." In *Grove 6*, Vol. 9. 1980. 342-349.

1969. Sawa, George Dimitri. "Music, Islamic Attitudes Toward." In *Dictionary of the Middle Ages*, Vol. 8. 1987. 550-61.

1970. Shiloah, Amnon. "Music and Religion in the Middle East." In *Encyclopedia of Religion*, Mircea Eliade, ed. Vol. 10. 1987. 182-185.

1971. Shiloah, Amnon. *The Dimension of Music in Islamic and Jewish Culture*. Aldershot, Hampshire, Great Britain; Brookfield, VT: Variorum, 1993. Fifteen essays on the question of how music and culture intersect. The author groups his essays under four thematic headings: the symbolic and metaphorical interpretation of music, the scientific aspect, the transmission of musical knowledge, and the ideological attitude toward music.

1972. Shiloah, Amnon. *Music in the World of Islam: A Socio-Cultural Study*. Detroit, MI: Wayne State University Press, 1995. See Ch. 4, 'Islam and Music,' and Ch. 5, 'The Science of Music.'

QUR'ANIC CHANT

1973. al-Faruqi, Lois Ibsen. "Accentuation in Qur'anic Chant: A Study in Musical Tawazun." *YIFMC* 10 (1978): 53-68. Al-Faruqi analyses five primary forms of accentuation Qur'anic chant: pitch, intensity, duration, ornamention, and vocal timbre. Includes examples of compositions.

1974. al-Faruqi, Lois Ibsen. "The Cantillation of the Qur'an." *Asian Music* 19, 1 (Fall-Winter) (1987): 2-25. An exhaustive study, in four sections: the oral tradition, characteristics of the text, characteristics of cantillation, and the chanter or *qâri*.

1975. Cagatay, N. "The Tradition of Mavlid Recitations in Islam, particularly in Turkey." *Studia Islamica* 28 (1968): 127 ff.

1976. Denny, Frederick M. "Qur'an Recitation: A Tradition of Oral Performance and Transmission." *Oral Tradition* 4, 1-2 (Jan-May) (1989): 5-26.

1977. Kusic, Dane. "Topical Peculiarity of Terminology in the Reading of the Kur'an in Turkey." *Turkish Music Quarterly* 4, 1 (1991): 1-8.

1978. McClain, Ernest G. *Meditations through the Quran*. York Beach: Nicolas-Hays, 1981.

1979. Nelson, Kristina. "Reciter and Listener: Some Factors Shaping the Mujawwad Style of Qur'ânic Reciting." *Ethnomusicology* 26 (1982): 41-47. In Egyptian style, reciters, in order to avoid fixing the melody and to create a more effective recitation, are guided by the verbal responses of the listeners.

1980. Nelson, Kristina. *The Art of Reciting the Qur'ân*. Modern Middle East Series 11, Austin: University of Texas Press, 1985. Written sources from Egypt have set the standards for Qur'an recitation throughout the Muslim world.

1981. Pacholczyk, Jozef Marcin. "Vibrato as a Function of Modal Practice in the Qur'an Chant of Shaikh 'Abdu'l-Basit 'Abdu's Samad." *Selected Reports in Ethnomusicology* 2, 1 (1974): 33-41. A description of the use of vibrato on different tones in different modes of Qur'anic chant as practiced by Shaikh 'Abdu'l-Bâsit 'Abdu's Samad.

1982. Quasem, Muhammad Abul. *The Recitation and Interpretation of the Qur'an: al-Ghazzali's Theory*. Muhammad Abul Quasem, transl. Boston: Kegan Paul International, 1979/repr. 1982. *Ihya' 'ulum al-din*. Book 8. English.

1983. Wegner, Ulrich. "Transmitting the Divine Revelation: Some Aspects of Textualism and Textual Variability in Qur'anic Recitation." *The World of Music* 28, 3 (1986): 57-78. On the transmission of the Qur'an from its oral beginnings to the careful transition to a written tradition. Problems of the written tradition, such as vowel length and consistent emphasis on text are discussed. Regional chant is compared to a sung folk poetry of the same locale.

REGIONAL RELIGIOUS MUSIC

1984. al-Faruqi, Lois Ibsen. "The Status of Music in Muslim Nations: Evidence from the Arab World." *Asian Music* 12, 1 (1981): 56-84. First part of article defines "religious music" as understood in Islam and explores various criteria for what may be included in this category.

1985. Blum, Stephen. "Iran." In *Grove 6*, Vol. 9. 1980. 292-309. See especially §II, 2: Religious recitation.

1986. Crapanzano, Vincent. *The Hamadsha: An Essay in Moroccan Ethnopsychiatry*. Berkeley, CA: University of California Press, 1973. Possession trance and self-mutilation in a Moroccan Islamic religious brotherhood.

1987. Jones, Lura Jafran. *The 'Isawiya of Tunisia and Their Music*. Ph.D. diss., University of Washington, 1978.

1988. Kerbage, Toufic. "Musical Ecstasy and Functional Harmony in Arabic Music." *Al Ma'thurat Al Sha'biyyah* 1, 3 (1986): 29-39, 90-103.

1989. Mahdi, Salah El. "North Africa." In *Grove 6*, Vol. 13. 1980. 287-292. See especially §5: Religious Music, and §6: Music for events in the life cycle.

1990. Markoff, Irene. "The Role of Expressive Culture in the Demystification of a Secret Sect of Islam: The Case of the Alevis of Turkey." *The World of Music* 28, 3 (1986): 42-56. Music and dance in a Muslim Sufi sect that retains elements of its nomadic past.

1991. Pennanen, Risto Pekka. "The God-Praising Drums of Sarajevo." *Asian Music* 25, 1-2 (1993/1994): 1-7. A brief study of Islamic ritual drums and metallic percussion in Islamic brotherhoods of Sarajevo.

1992. Pennanen, Risto Pekka. "All-Comprehending, United and Divine. The Myth of *ilahiiya* Hymns in Sarajevo." *The World of Music* 36, 2 (1994): 49-67.

1993. Racy, Ali Jihad. "Druze music." In *Grove 6*, Vol. 5. 1980. 652-656.

1994. Reckord, Thomas Martin. *Chant in Popular Iranian Shi'ism*. Ph.D. diss., University of California, Los Angeles, 1987. A study of the three principal genres of unmetered religious chant of mourning—*madh, musibat*, and *rawayat*—as to context, terminology, rhythm and mode.

1995. Reinhard, Kurt. "Turkey." In *Grove 6*, Vol. 19. 1980. 268-78. See especially §4, i: Religious music.

1996. Sakata, Hiromi Lorraine. "The Complementary Opposition of Music and Religion in Afghanistan." *The World of Music* 28, 3 (1986): 33-41. An elucidation of the music/non-music dichotomy in Islamic Afghanistan. Performance with religious intent is not considered music. Prohibition is caused by improper usage.

1997. Schuyler, P. D. "Music and Meaning among the Gnawa Religious Brotherhood of Morocco." *The World of Music* 23, 1 (1981): 3-13. The Gnawa Religious Botherhood believe that their music communicates on a level beyond the textual overlay and that people as well as spirits listen to and obey the ritual music's instructions.

1998. Schuyler, R.H. "The Rwais and the Zawia Professional Musicians and the Rural Religious Elite in Southwestern Morocco." *Asian Music* 17 (1985): 114-131. Though often reproached, Muslim musicians are able to play *ahwash*, communal dance music that still resembles pre-Islamic ritual music, by incorporating Muslim religious elements into their performance.

1999. Slobin, M. *Music in the Culture of Northern Afghanistan*. Tucson AZ: University of Arizona Press, 1976. Slobin's aim is to detect patterns of inter-ethnic and religious contact through an examination of the musical styles of the region. Religious, specifically Islamic, music is treated within this context.

2000. Stone, Ruth M. "Sound and Rhythm in Corporate Ritual in Arabia." In *Music and the Experience of God*, Collins, Power, and Burnim, ed. 1989. 73-81. An article on the Muslim call to prayer, prayer chants and the music of the month of Ramadan, the month of daytime fasting and prayerful, musical evenings.

MUSIC AND DANCE OF THE SUFIS

2001. al-Faruqi, Lois Ibsen. "Al Ghazali on Samâ." In *Essays in Islamic and Comparative Studies*, Herndon, VA: International Institute of Islamic Thought, 1982. 43-50.

2002. al-Hujwiri, 'Ali ibn Uthman. *The Kashf al-Mahjub (The Unveiling of the Veiled), the Oldest Persian Treatise on Sufism by al-Hujwiri*. R. A. Nicholson, transl. Gibb Memorial Series, 17, Lahore: Islamic Book Foundation, 1911/repr.1970. A mystical treatise on the principles and elements of Sufism. Chapter 25 discusses the place and purpose of dancing, poetry and chanting.

2003. Algar, Hamid. "Some Notes on the Naqshbandi *Tariqat* in Bosnia." *Studies in Comparative Religion* 9 (1975): 69-97. A history of this order. Includes a vivid description of a *dhikr* ceremony in a village near Sarajevo.

2004. Baily, John. "Qawwali in Bradford: Traditional Music in a Muslim Community." In *Black Music in Britain: Essays on the Afro-Asian Contribution to Popular Music*, Paul Oliver, ed. Buckingham: Open University Press, 1990. 153-65.

2005. Birge, John Kingsley. *The Bektashi Order of Dervishes*. New York: AMS Press, 1937/repr. 1982. A thorough study of this Turkish order. Movement, music and chant, although mentioned throughout the text, are covered most fully in Chapter 4 of Part 1, entitled Rites and Practices.

2006. Crow, Douglas Karim. "Samâ: The Art of Listening in Islam." In *Maqam: Music of the Islamic World and Its Influences*, Robert H. Browning et al., ed. New York, NY: Alternative Museum, 1984. On samâ (spiritual audition) as a basic technique in Sufism. Focuses on the primacy of the sense of hearing, theoretical discourse, and the state of the auditor in a samâ ceremony.

2007. During, Jean. "Revelation and Spiritual Audition in Islam." *The World of Music* 24, 3 (1982): 68-81. Provides a spiritual and metaphysical background for an examination of a variety of forms of the chanting of the Koran, particularly *samá* and *dhikr*. Concludes with a description of different kinds of samâ (audition).

2008. Elias, Jamal J. "A Kubrawi Treatise on Mystical Visions: The risala-yi nuriyya of Ala' Ad-Sawla As-Simnani." *Muslim World* 83 (1993): 68-80. A translation of a 13th-century treatise, one of the very few treatises to describe first hand the lights a mystic experiences while practicing *dhikr*.

2009. Farmer, Henry George, transl. *Music: The Priceless Jewel*. Collection of Oriental Writers on Music, Bearsden, Scotland: Farmer, 1942. From the 'Kitab al'iqd al-farid' of Ibn 'Abd Rabbihi (d. 940).

2010. Friedlander, Ira, ed. *The Whirling Dervishes: Being an Account of the Sufi Order, Known as the Mevlevis and Its Founder, the Poet and Mystic, Mevlana Jalau'ddin Rumi*. New York: Collier Books, 1975. A description of the founder of the Islamic religious order known as Sufism and the whirling dance practiced by its adherents.

2011. Frishkopf, Michael. *Music, Emotion and Meaning in the Sufi Dhikr of Egypt*. Ph.D. diss., in progress.

2012. Hurwitt, Jannika. "With the Whirling Dervishes in Konya." *Gnosis*, 11, Spring (1989): 28-32. A description of the whirling dance and a history of its foundation and its founder, the Sufi saint and poet Jelaluddin Rumi.

2013. Hussaini, S.S. Khusro. *Sayyid Muhammad al-Husayni-i Gisudaraz (721/1321-825/1422) on Sufism*. M.A. thesis, McGill University, 1976. Chapter III: Audition of Music (Sama'): 140-219.

2014. Ibn abî l-Dunya and Majd al-Din (Ahmad) al-Ghazzali. *Tracts on Listening to Music. Being Dhamm al-malahi by Ibn abî l-Dunya and Bawariq al-ilma by Majd al-Din al-Tûsi al-Ghazzalî*. Oriental Translation Fund, New Series 34, James Robson, ed. London: Royal Asiatic Society, 1938. London. Al-

Ghazzalî's tract is an important early 12th century statement on Sufi music and dance.

2015. Kennedy, J.G. and Hussein Fakim. "Nubian Dhikr Rituals and Cultural Change." *Muslim World* 64 (1974): 205-219. A descriptive study of two *dhikr* ceremonies in Egyptian Nubia.

2016. Khan, Hazrat Inayat. *The Sufi Message of Hazrat Inayat Khan. Vol. II: The Mysticism of Sound; Music, etc.* London: Barrie and Jenkins, 1960/repr. 1969, 1970. Includes "The Mysticism of Sound" (1923) and "Music" (1921). Has appeared in several editions.

2017. Lewis, Samuel L. *Spiritual Dance and Walk: An Introduction from the Work of Murshid Samuel L. Lewis (Sufi Ahmed Murad Chisti).* 2nd ed., San Francisco: Sufi Islamia/Prophecy Publications, 1978/repr. 1983. Arranged in a two-part format, this book is meant to serve as an introduction to the Dances of Universal Peace and the writings of the dance movement's founder, Samuel Lewis. Part One contains essays by Lewis and his disciples on the history, philosophy and spirituality of the Sufi-based dances. Part Two contains instructions for over 40 of the dances.

2018. Maier, John. "Silence and Ecstasy: Watching the Sufis Dance." *Journal of Ritual Studies* 4, 1 (1990): 41-64.

2019. Michon, Jean Louis. "The Spiritual Practices of Sufism." In *Islamic Spirituality: Foundations*, Katherine O'Brien, ed. New York, NY: The Crossroad Publishing Company, 1987. 265-293. Later sections pertain to spiritual meetings and sung and recited texts used during the meetings, such as the *dhikr*, the *wird*, hymns, and sacred dances.

2020. Michon, Jean Louis. "Sacred Music and Dance in Islam." In *Islamic Spirituality: Manifestations*, Seyyed Hossein Nasr, ed. New York, NY: The Crossroad Publishing Company, 1991. 469-504. A discussion of the ambivalent place of music in Islam (music as both physical and corporeal; music as mathematical), the spiritual concert and its elements (instruments, modes, rhythm, and the human voice), Quranic psalmody, Call to Prayer, Praises upon the Prophet, ecstatic dance, Qawwali, religious music of the Kurds and of Shi'ite Iran.

2021. Nakamura Kojiro, tr. *Ghazali on Prayer*. Tokyo, Japan: University of Tokyo Press, 1973. One book from the *Iyha...* entitled "Book of Invocations and Supplications." In the Introduction, the translator provides an analysis of the mystical concepts of *dhikr* (recalling the names of God) and *du'â* (supplication).

2022. Osman, Ahmed Ibrahim. *In Praise of the Prophet: The Performance and Thematic Composition of the Sudanese Religious Oral Poetry.* Ph.D. diss., Indiana University, 1990. Influenced by Sufism, *madih nabawi* (poetry in praise of the Prophet Muhammad) is performed only by expert performers during community ceremonial and ritual events. Composed and rehearsed in seclusion, a performance of *madih nabawi* consist of lyrics, dance, music (drum accompaniment), and kinesics.

2023. Poche, Christian. "Zikr and Musicology." *The World of Music* 20, 1 (1978): 59-71. Begins with a description of various traditions of Zikr and a consideration of the *munshed*, the singer of hymns, in particular. Concludes with a detailed description of a ceremony in Syria.

2024. Schimmel, Annemarie. *Mystical Dimensions of Islam.* Chapel Hill: University of North Carolina Press, 1975.

2025. Shiloah, Amnon. "The Role and Nature of Music in the Practice of the *Sama.*'" In *IMS12*, Daniel Heartz and Bonnie Wade, ed. Kassel: Baerenreiter, 1981. 425-428.

2026. Uzel, Nezih. "Music of the Mevlevi Dervishes." In *The Whirling Dervishes*, Ira Friedlander, ed. New York: Collier Books, 1975. 127-141.

2027. Waugh, Earl H. *The Munshidin of Egypt: Their World and their Song.* Studies in Comparative Religion, Columbia, SC: University of South Carolina Press, 1989. A study of the Sufis of Egypt and their music. Waugh attempts to understand and explain, through observation, interview, and recording sessions, the meaning behind the functions of the *munshid* singers as they understand themselves. Before presenting a detailed survey of the musical repertory and traditions, the author first places the mystic singers in cultural, religious, and psychological contexts.

2028. Waugh, Earle H. "Ritual Leadership in the Dhikr: The Role of the Munshidin in Egypt." *Journal of Ritual Studies* 5, Wint. (1991): 93-108. There is more to *dhikr* than going into trance: encounter, therapy, worship, affirmation, penance, confession, self-assessment and identity, kinship, and the re-enactment of a covenant with God—all are part of *dhik*r, and it is the role of the *munshi*d to see that these take place in an orderly, even highly structured, way.

2029. Yarmolinsky, Benjamin. *The Music of the Jillala: A Repertoire of Spirits.* Ph.D. diss., City University of New York, 1992. A study of Sufi music in Morocco.

26

Music, Mathematics, and Mysticism

THE SCHOOL OF PYTHAGORAS AND THE HARMONY OF THE SPHERES: ORIGINAL WORKS IN TRANSLATION

2030. Aristides Quintilianus. *On Music, in Three Books*. New Haven: Yale University Press, 1983. Translated, with an Introduction, Commentary and Annotations, by Thomas J. Mathiesen. One of the principal sources of Pythagorean thought. Vol. 1: The Theory of Music; Vol. 2: Ethics and Education; Vol. 3: Arithmetic (Pythagorean mathematics).

2031. Barker, Andrew. *Greek Musical Writings II. Harmonic and Acoustic Theory*. Barker, Andrew, transl. New York: Cambridge University Press, 1984. This collection of translations of all major Greek theorists is indispensable for an understanding of the two principal traditions: music theory—the theory of actual music—and acoustic theory—through which the order and harmony of the universe can be represented to the human mind.

2032. Godwin, Joscelyn, ed. *The Harmony of the Spheres. A Sourcebook of the Pythagorean Tradition in Music*. Rochester: Inner Traditions International, 1993. A comprehensive collection of speculative thinkings concerning the relationship between numbers, music, the cosmos, and man, by 52 authors from Plato through the 19th century. Includes many original translations by the editor.

2033. Levin, Flora R., trans. *The Manual of Harmonics of Nichomacus the Pythagorean*. Grand Rapids, MI: Phanes Press, 1994. The first complete translation into English of this important work of the Pythagorean school from the 2nd century C.E. Each chapter is followed by an extended commentary by the translator.

THE SCHOOL OF PYTHAGORAS: STUDIES

2034. Anderson, Warren. "Ethos." In *Grove 6*, Vol. 6. 1980. 282-287. A discussion of the capacity of music to convey ethical attitudes.

2035. Barbara, C. André. *The Persistence of Pythagorean Mathematics in Ancient Musical Thought*. Ph.D. diss., University of North Carolina, 1980.

2036. Fideler, David. "Orpheus and the Mysteries of Harmony. Is the Universe Governed by the Same Laws that Rule the Harmonies of Music?" *Gnosis* 27, Spring (1993): 21-27.

2037. Haar, James. "Pythagorean Harmony of the Universe." In *The Dictionary of the History of Ideas*, Philip Wiener, ed. 1973. 38-42. On the Pythagorean theory of 'music of the spheres,' its possible origins in either Chaldean or Jewish thought, its elaboration by other Greek philosophers, and its persistence through the Middle Ages to the 20th century.

2038. Haar, James. "Music of the Spheres." In *Grove 6*, Vol. 12. 1980. 835-36.

2039. Iamblichus. *The Theology of Arithmetic: on the Mystical, Mathematical and Cosmological Symbolism of the First Ten Numbers*. Grand Rapids, MI: Phanes Press, 1988.

2040. Levin, Flora R. *The Harmonics of Nicomachus and the Pythagorean Tradition*. University Park, PA: American Philological Association, 1975. Levin begins this scholarly study of Nicomachus's *Harmonikon Enchiridion* with the misquotation of Plato that it contains. She examines the work in light of its goals and historical context and in reference to contemporary thinkers.

2041. Macaulay, Anne. "APOLLO: The Pythagorean Definition of God." In *Homage to Pythagoras*, Lindisfarne Letter no. 14, West Stockbridge, MA 1982. 85-109.

2042. McClain, Ernest G. *The Pythagorean Plato: Prelude to the Song Itself*. Stony Brook: Nicolas-Hays, 1978. An argument for the musical interpretation of numbers in Greek mythology.

2043. Schimmel, Annemarie. "Numbers: An Overview." In *Encyclopedia of Religion*, Mircea Eliade, ed. Vol. 11. 1987. 13-19. A general overview of the religious valorization and symbolism of numbers.

2044. Thesleff, Holger. "Pythagoreanism." In *Encyclopaedia Britannica*, Vol. 25. 1993. 578-581.

2045. Wellesz, Egon. "Music in the Treatises of Greek Gnostics and Alchemists." *Ambix* 4 (1951): 145-158.

ARABIC WRITINGS AND STUDIES

2046. Madian, Azza Abd al-Hamid. *Language-music Relationships in Al-Farabi's Grand Book of Music*. Ph.D. thesis, Cornell University, 1992.

2047. Nasr, Seyyed Hossein. *An Introduction to Islamic Cosmological Doctrines*. Boulder, CO: Shambhala, 1978. A study of the cosmological formulations of Ikhwan al-Safa, al Biruni and Ibn Sina.

2048. Shiloah, Amnon (translator). *The Epistle on Music of the Ikhwan al-Safa*. Tel-Aviv: Tel-Aviv University, 1978. With an introduction by the translator.

JEWISH WRITINGS AND STUDIES

2049. Halevi, Z'ev ben Shimon. *Kabbalah: Tradition of Hidden Knowledge*. London: Thames & Hudson, 1979.

2050. Idel, Moshe. "Music and Prophetic Kabbalah." *Yuval* 4 (1982): 150-69. According to Abulafia and his school, note-combining and letter-combining are similar and lead to the raising up of the soul. Music used in combination with the pronouncing of Names is the path to arrive at prophecy. Idel also includes the differing views of contemporaries concerning the value of music.

2051. Idel, Moshe. "Mystical Techniques." In *Kabbalah. New Perspectives*, New Haven, CT: Yale University Press, 1988. 74-111. Idel describes four techniques: weeping, the ascent of the soul, combining the letters of the Divine Name, and visualizing of colors and Kabbalistic prayer. All involve vocalization in the form of hymns, letters, or repetitions of the Divine Name.

2052. Idel, Moshe. *The Mystical Experience in Abraham Abulafia*. Jonathan Chipman, transl. Albany: State University of New York Press, 1988. Abulafia's mystical experience, which took place in 1280, consisted of the union of the highest part of his being, the human intellect, with the divine intellect. This was achieved through his concentrating on the letters of the divine name, transposed and re-combined, and set to various tunes. Abulafia's form of Kabbalah, the prophetic or ecstatic form achieved in solitude, differed from the dominant, theosophical form, conducted communally. Transl. from the Hebrew.

2053. Idel, Moshe. "Abraham Abulafia and Unio Mystica." In *Studies in Ecstatic Kabbalah*, Albany: State University of New York Press, 1988. 1-32.

2054. Shiloah, Amnon. *Music Subjects in the Zohar: Texts and Indices*. Yuval Monograph Series, Vol. 5. Jerusalem: Hebrew University, Magnes Press, 1977.

2055. Shiloah, Amnon. "The Chapter on Music in Ibn Falaquera's 'Book of the Seeker.'" *Proceedings of the Fourth World Congress of Jewish Studies* 2

(1978): 373-77. Full name: Shemtov ben Joseph Falaquera, 13th century Spanish or south French philosopher who aimed at reconciling Judaism with philosophy.

2056. Shiloah, Amnon. "The Symbolism of Music in the Kabbalistic Tradition." *The World of Music* 22 (1978): 56-69. Examines the symbolism and manifestations of music and meditation, man working though music to influence the destiny of the universe, and music of the cosmos and angels.

2057. Sperling, Harry and Maurice Simon trans. *Zohar*. 2nd ed., 5 vols. New York: Soncino Press, 1949, 1984. The classic text in Jewish mysticism, published in Spain between 1285 and 1300. Orig. English ed., 1931-34.

2058. Tishby, Isaiah, ed. *The Wisdom of the Zohar*. 3 vols. The Litman Library of Jewish Civilization, London: Oxford University Press, 1986, 1989, 1991.

2059. Werner, Eric and Isaiah Sonne. "The Philosophy and Theory of Music in Judaeo-Arabic Literature." *HUCA* 16 (1941): 251-319, the essay, 17 (1942-43): 511-573, the translations. Repr. in Werner's *Three Ages of Musical Thought*, pp. 137-206. A valuable survey of the cosmological, ethical and theological thought of such Medieval Jewish authors as Moses Maimonides, Moses Abulafia, Falaquera Isaac ben Abraham ibn Latif, Honein-Alhurizi, Saadia Gaon, etc.

2060. Wolfson, Elliot. "Biblical Accentuation in a Mystical Key: Kabbalistic Interpretations of the *Te'amim*." *Journal of Jewish Music and Liturgy* 12 (1989-90): 1-13. On the different levels and types of meaning of the letters, vowels, and accents of the Hebrew alphabet.

CHRISTIANITY AND HUMANISM: ORIGINAL WORKS IN TRANSLATION

2061. Clement of Alexander. "Exhortation to the Greeks 1." The Ante-Nicene Fathers, Vol. 2. Grand Rapids, MI: W.B. Eerdmans Publishing Co., 1965-70.

2062. Clement of Alexander [150-c215]. *Stromata, Chap. 5: On the Mystical Meanings in the Proportions of Numbers, Geometrical Ratios, and Music*. Loeb Classical Library, Cambridge: Harvard University Press, 1960.

2063. Dionysius Areopagita, Pseudo-. *The Divine Names and Mystical Theology*. Milwaukee: Marquette Press, 1980.

2064. Dionysius the Areopagite. *The Mystical Theology and The Celestial Hierarchies*. Editors of the Shrine of Wisdom, transl. Surrey: Shrine of Wisdom, 1965. Also known as Pseudo-Dionysius, to distinguish this 6th century Syrian monk from the first century biblical figure. Pseudo-Dionysius was an important influence in the Neo-Platonic trend in Medieval Christian doctrine.

CHRISTIAN AND HUMANISTIC STUDIES

2065. Amman, Peter J. "The Musical Theory and Philosophy of Robert Fludd." *Journal of the Warburg and Courtauld Institutes* 30 (1967): 198-277.

2066. Barton, Todd. *Robert Fludd's Temple of Music: A Description and Commentary.* MA thesis, University of Oregon, 1978.

2067. Bukofzer, Manfred. "Speculative Thinking in Medieval Music." *Speculum* 17 (1942): 165-180. Things unrelated in sound and effect may yet be related by the power of the mind through proportion and number: illustrations of how practical music can demonstrate speculative ideas.

2068. Chamberlain, D.S. "Wolboro of Cologne (d. 1167): A Zenith of Music Imagery." *Mediaeval Studies* 33 (1971): 114-126. On music as metaphor for religious and moral activity and on how music imagery can signify all kinds of moral and religious qualities.

2069. d'Olivet, Antoine Fabre (1767-1825). *Music explained as Science and Art: and Considered in its Analogical Relations to Religious Mysteries, Ancient Mythology, and the History of the World.* Joscelyn Godwin, transl. Rochester, VT/New York: Inner Traditions/Harper and Row, 1987.

2070. Fideler, David. *Jesus Christ, Sun of God: Ancient Cosmology and Early Christian Symbolism.* Wheaton, IL: Quest Books (Theosophical Publishing House), 1993.

2071. Finney, Gretchen Ludke. "Harmony or Rapture in Music." In *The Dictionary of the History of Ideas*, Philip Wiener, ed. 1973. 388-395. On the origin of three speculative approaches to music current during the Renaissance: music as a mathematical key to universal order, music as an image of the soul's harmony and as a bridge between the soul and heaven, and music as a vehicle of World Spirit.

2072. Gautier, Daniel. "Maps of the Eternal." *Gnosis* #27, Spring (1993): 28-35. A demonstration of how number and proportion were applied to the construction of Gothic Cathedrals.

2073. Godwin, Joscelyn. "The Golden Chain of Orpheus: A Survey of Musical Esotericism in the West." *Temenos* (1984): 4: 7-25 and 5: 211-239.

2074. Haar, James. *Musica Mundana: Variations on a Pythagorean Theme.* Ph.D. diss., Harvard University, 1960.

2075. Hollander, John. *The Untuning of the Sky.* Princeton, NJ: Princeton University Press, 1961. A study of English poetry between 1500 and 1700 that contains much information about the philosophical and mathematical aspects of Medieval music.

2076. Irwin, Joyce L. "Celestial Harmony in Baroque Lutheran Writings." *Lutheran Quarterly n.s.* 3, Aut. (1989): 281-297. On the writings of Johann Matthaeus Meyfart (1590-1642).

2077. McKinnon, James W. "Jubel or Pythagoras: Who is the Creator of Music?" *MQ* 64, 1 (1978): 1-28. A study of two opposing attitudes towards music and music instruments and their influence up to the 18th century.

2078. Pallis, Marco. "The Metaphysics of Musical Polyphony." *Studies in Comparative Religion* 10, 2, Spring (1976): 105-108. Analyzes polyphony in terms of unity, multiplicity, change, stasis, and as a reflection of divine presence.

2079. Scillia, Charles E. "Meaning and the Cluny Capitals: Music as Metaphor." *Gesta* 27, 1-2 (1988): 133-148.

2080. Stephenson, Bruce. *The Music of the Heavens. Kepler's Harmonic Astronomy.* Princeton, NJ: Princeton University Press, 1994. After a survey of theories, from Plato to Boethius, associating music with the cyclic motion of the planets, the author highlights Ptolemy's *Harmonics*, then concludes with a penetrating study of Kepler's *Harmonice Mundi* (1619).

2081. Tomlinson, Gary. *Music in Renaissance Magic: Toward a Historiography of Others.* Chicago/London: University of Chicago Press, 1993. A comprehensive archaeological study of speculative thought during the Renaissance on the role of music in the occult sciences—astrology, demonology, theurgy, numerology, cabbala, and witchcraft. Includes discussion of the relationship of music to the motion of heavenly bodies, 'modes and planetary song,' shamanism, ancient dionysiac rites etc.

2082. Walker, Daniel Pickering. *Studies in Musical Science in the Late Renaissance.* London: Warburg Institute, University of London, 1978. Includes chapters on the Harmony of the Spheres and Kepler's Celestial Music, as well as on 16th and 17th-century theory and views on intonation.

2083. Werner, Eric. "The Last Pythagorean Musician: Johannes Kepler." In *Aspects of Medieval and Renaissance Music: A Birthday Offering to Gustave Reese*, Jan LaRue, ed. New York: W.W. Norton & Co., 1966. 867-882. An introduction to and discussion of Kepler's theory on the music of the spheres, how he modified Greek theory, Zarlino's concept of the 3rd, and other notions of music and astronomy to come to his own conclusions. Also in Eric Werner. *Three Ages of Musical Thought.* New York: Da Capo Press, 1981: 293-308.

SPECULATIVE MODERN THOUGHT

2084. Collin, Rodney. *The Theory of Celestial Influence: Man, the Universe, and Cosmic Mystery.* Dulverton, Eng.: Watkins, 1954/rep. 1958, 1980.

236   Music, Mathematics, and Mysticism

2085. Godwin, Joscelyn. "The Revival of Speculative Music." *MQ* 68 (1982): 373-389. An exploration of the 'historical' and 'actual' paths of speculative music in the late 20th century, 'historical' being the unalterable physical properties, and 'actual' being the conditioned societal responses—mythologies, styles, etc.

2086. Godwin, Joscelyn. *Harmonies of Heaven and Earth. The Spiritual Dimension of Music from Antiquity to the Avant-Garde.* Rochester: Inner Traditions International, 1987.

2087. Godwin, Joscelyn, ed. *Cosmic Music. Three Musical Keys to the Interpretation of Reality.* Rochester: Inner Traditions International, 1989. Essays by Marius Schneider, Rudolf Haase, and Hans Erhard Lauer, with extracts from Kepler in an appendix.

2088. Godwin, Joscelyn. *The Mystery of the Seven Vowels/In Theory and Practice.* Grand Rapids: Phanes Press, 1992. An exploration of the relationship between the seven vowels, harmonics, and the laws of number held to govern the universe.

2089. Godwin, Joscelyn. *Music and the Occult. French Musical Philosophies 1750-1950.* Rochester, NY: University of Rochester Press, 1995. On the theories of d'Olivet, Fourier, Wronski, and other French Pythagoreans.

2090. Haase, Rudolf. "Harmonics and Sacred Tradition." In *Cosmic Music*, Joscelyn Godwin, ed. Rochester, Vermont: Inner Traditions, 1989. 91-110.

2091. Hamel, Peter Michael. *Through Music to the Self. How to Appreciate and Experience Music Anew.* Boulder: Shambhala, 1979.

2092. Hammil, Carrie Esther. *The Celestial Journey and the Harmony of the Spheres in English Literature, 1300-1700.* Fort Worth, TX: Texas Christian University Press, 1980.

2093. Hayes, Michael. *The Infinite Harmony: Musical Structures in Science and Theology.* London: Weidenfeld and Nicolson, 1994.

2094. Hodson, Geoffrey. *Music Forms: Superphysical Effects of Music Clairvoyantly Observed.* Adyar, India: Theosophical Publishing House, 1979. Visual representations of eight pieces of classical music 'clairvoyantly observed'.

2095. Kavanaugh, James Vincent. *Music and American Transcendentalism: A Study of Transcendental Pythagoreanism in the Works of Henry David Thoreau, Nathaniel Hawthorne and Charles Ives.* Ph.D. diss., Yale University, 1978.

2096. Kayser, Hans. *Akróasis: The Theory of World Harmonics.* Robert Lilienfeld, transl. Boston: Plowshare Press, 1970.

2097. Lewis, Robert C. *The Sacred Word and its Creative Overtones: Relating Religion and Science through Music.* 2nd ed., Oceanside, CA: Rosicrucian Fellowship, 1990. With the first five verses of the Gospel of John as his starting point, the author sees the different forms of life as the result of vibratory processes controlled by numerical relationships similar to those of the harmonic series. Explores the properties of various intervals and other aspects of music.

2098. McClain, Ernest G. *The Myth of Invariance. The Origin of the Gods, Mathematics and Music from the Rg Veda to Plato.* York Beach: Nicolas-Hays, Inc, 1984 (1976). McClain draws on Egyptian, Babylonian, Hindu, Hebraic, Greek and Christian sources to show "how correspondences between numerical *quantity* and tonal *quality* became a science governing temples and calendars in diverse cultures while carrying a common spiritual tradition across the barriers of time, space, and language".

2099. McMullin, Michael. "The Zodiac and the Twelve Tones of the Musical Scale." *The Astrological Journal* (Spring, 1984).

2100. Meyer-Baer, Kathi. *Music of the Spheres and the Dance of Death. Studies in Musical Iconology.* Princeton: Princeton University Press; New York: Da Capo Press, 1970/repr. 1984.

2101. Mitchell, John. *The Dimensions of Paradise: The Proportions and Sacred Numbers of Ancient Cosmology.* London: Thames & Hudson, 1981.

2102. Murchie, Guy. *Music of the Spheres: The Material Universe, from Atom to Quasar, Simply Explained.* New York: Dover, 1967. See Chapter 11, pp. 359-413: 'Of Waves and Music.' See also the index for many references to music.

2103. Roustit, Albert. *Prophecy in Music: Prophetic Parallels in Music History.* John A. Green, transl. Paris: "D.K. Paris Ve," 1975. With a Preface by Olivier Messiaen.

2104. Rudhyar, Dane. *The Magic of Tone and the Art of Music.* Boulder: Shambhala, 1982.

2105. Scott, Cyril. *Music, its Secret Influence Throughout the Ages.* rev. ed., New York: Weiser, 1959/repr. 1969.

2106. Steiner, Rudolf. *Eurhythmy as Visible Music.* V. and J. Compton-Burnett, transl. London: Rudolf Steiner Press, 1977.

2107. Deleted

27

Sub-Saharan Africa

GENERAL REFERENCES AND BIBLIOGRAPHIES

2108. Adamczyk, Alice J. *Black Dance: An Annotated Bibliography*. Garland Reference Library of the Humanities, Vol. 558, New York: Garland Press, 1989.

2109. Bascom, William R. and Melville J. Herskovits, ed. *Continuity and Change in African Cultures*. Chicago: The University of Chicago Press, 1959. For relevant material, consult index under dance, drums, music, and possession.

2110. Beattie, John and John Middleton, ed. *Spirit Mediumship and Society in Africa*. New York: Africana Publishing Corporation, 1969. Also publ. as *Spirit Mediumship in Bunyoro*, by Routledge and Kegan Paul, London. Thirteen essays on spirit mediumship and possession in as many cultures of Sub-Saharan Africa. See Introduction for description of basic types of dissociation, functions, powers, practices, practitioners, and cultural contexts.

2111. Blakely, Thomas D., W.E.A. Beek, and Dennis L. Thomson, ed. *Religion in Africa: Experience and Expression*. London: J. Currey; Portsmouth, NH: Heinemann, 1994. Twenty essays, including one on the African origins of Candomblé, by Mikelle Smith Omari, and another on the reality of the "Drums of Affliction," by John M. Janzen.

2112. De Lerma, Dominique-René. *Bibliography of Black Music*. 4 vols. Westport, CT: Greenwood Press, 1981-84. 1: Reference Materials (1981); 2: Afro-American Idioms (1981); 3: Geographical Studies (1982); 4: Theory, Education and Related Studies (1984). An exhaustive though unannotated bibliography of materials on Africa and the Western hemisphere. See especially vol. 4, 111-137: Dance, and 192-208: Theology and Liturgy.

2113. Emezi, Herbert O. "A Bibliography of African Music and Dance—the Nigerian Experience, 1930-1980." *Current Bibliography on African Affairs* 18, 2 (1985-86): 117-47.

2114. Gray, John. *African Music: A Bibliographic Guide to the Traditional, Popular, Art, and Liturgical Musics of Sub-Saharan Africa*. African Special Bibliographic Series, no. 14, New York: Greenwood Press, 1991. See index for church music, dance, and trance. Partially annotated. 5802 entries, including discographies. Includes references in English, French, German, Italian and Russian.

2115. Lems-Dworkin, Carol. *African Music: A Pan-African Annotated Bibliography*. London & New York: Hans Zell, 1991. 1703 items. See index under church music, religious music, possession, and entries under specific countries.

AFRICAN MUSIC, DANCE, AND DRAMA

2116. Adegbite, Ademola. "The Concept of Sound in Traditional African Religious Music." *Journal of Black Studies* 22, 1 (Sep) (1991): 45-54. According to traditional African belief, sound itself acts as a metaphysical agent capable of evoking psychic forces of tremendous potency. Sound in the form of music, on the other hand, acts as a bridge or channel between the spiritual and material planes of existence.

2117. Anyanwu, K. Chukwulozie. "Sound as Ultimate Reality and Meaning: The Mode of Knowing Reality in African Thought." *Ultimate Reality and Meaning* 10, Mar. (1987): 29-38.

2118. Biebuyck, Daniel P. "African Religious Drama." In *Encyclopedia of Religion*, Mircea Eliade, ed. Vol. 4. 1987. 462-465.

2119. Brandel, Rose. "The Music of African Circumcision Rituals." *JAMS* 7 (1954): 52 ff. Music for circumcision is magical, frozen in form, reduced in melodic intervals, and therefore a source for all other musical life. Circumcision is viewed as "food for the Gods."

2120. Diallo, Yaya and Mitchell Hall. *The Healing Drum: African Wisdom Teachings*. Rochester, VT: Destiny Books, 1989. Also published as *The Healing Drum: African Ritual Healing with Music*.

2121. Drewal, Margaret Thompson. "Ritual Performance in Africa Today." *The Dance Review* 32, 2 (Summer) (1988): 25-30. An introduction to an issue of *The Dance Review* devoted to nine kinds or aspects of ritual performance in Africa.

2122. Euba, Akin. *Essays on Music in Africa*. 2 vols. Bayreuth, Germany: IWALEWA-Haus, Universität Bayreuth, 1988.

2123. Fiagbedzi, Nissio. *Religious Music Traditions in Africa: A Critical Evaluation of Contemporary Problems and Challenges: An Inter-Faculty Lecture Delivered on Thursday, 17 August, 1978.* Accra, Ghana: Ghana Universities Press, 1979. An informative presentation of music in Christian, Islamic and indigenous religions, with useful definitions and examples of the conflict between dogma and practice.

2124. Grund-Khaznader, Francoise. "Masked Dances and Ritual in Tanzania, Mozambique and Zambia." *The Drama Review* 25, Winter (1981): 25-38. An investigation of the Makishi, Nyau, and Midimu ritual dances.

2125. Harrison, Daphne D. "Aesthetic and Social Aspects of Music in African Ritual Settings." In *More Than Drumming...*, Irene V. Jackson, ed. Westport, CT: Greenwood Press, 1985. 49-65. Includes a description of the aesthetic aspects—the drama, music and dance—of rituals that involve possession trance.

2126. Hartigan, Royal. *The Drum: Concepts of Time and No Time from African, Latin American, and African-American Origins.* MA thesis, Wesleyan University, 1983.

2127. Huet, Michel. *The Dance, Art and Ritual of Africa.* New York: Pantheon, 1978. A collection of 256 vivid, 9 1/2 by 11 1/2, black and white and color illustrations from Guinea Coast, Western Sudan, and Equatorial Africa.

2128. Jackson, Irene V., ed. *More Than Drumming: Essays on African and Afro-Latin Music and Musicians.* Contributions in Afro-American and African Studies, Vol. 80. Westport, CT: Greenwood Press, 1985. A collection of essays that deals with Sub-Saharan African and Afro-Latin issues and materials.

2129. Kebede, Ashenafi. *Roots of Black Music: The Vocal, Instrumental and Dance Heritage of Africa and Black America.* Englewood Cliffs, NJ: Prentice-Hall, 1982.

2130. Merriam, Alan P. "Music Bridge to the Supernatural." *Tomorrow's Magazine* 5, 4 (1957): 61-67.

2131. Niangoran-Bouah, Georges. "The Talking Drum: A Traditional Instrument of Liturgy and of Mediation with the Sacred." In *African Traditional Religions in Contemporary Societies*, J. Olupona, ed. 1991. 81-92. The drum is to Africans what the Bible and Quran are to Christians and Muslims: it is sacred, it is the repository of history, of values, and of the divine word, and it is the preferred mediator between humans and the sacred.

2132. Nketia, J.H. Kwabena. *African Gods and Music.* Legon, Ghana: Institute of African Studies, University of Ghana, 1965. See also *Universitas*, Vol. 4, #4, 3-7.

2133. Nketia, J. H. Kwabena. *The Music of Africa*. New York: W. W. Norton, 1974.

2134. Nketia, J.H. Kwabena. "Music and Religion in Sub-Saharan Africa." In *The Encyclopedia of Religion*, Mircea Eliade, ed. Vol. 10. 1987. 172-176.

2135. Nketia, J.H. Kwabena. "Musical Interaction in Ritual Events." In *Music and the Experience of God*, Collins, Power, and Burnim, ed. Concilium Vol. 202. 1989. 111-124. A discussion of the modes of interaction between music and ritual in Ghana: music sustains ritual occasions, provides context, serves as a form of worship, and instigates desired behavioral patterns.

2136. Roberts, John S. *Black Music of Two Worlds*. New York: Praeger, 1972.

2137. Ukpokodu, I. Peter. "Plays, Possession, and Rock-and-Roll: Political Theatre in Africa." *The Drama Review* 36, 4/Winter (1992): 28-53.

2138. Walker, Sheila S. *Ceremonial Spirit Possession in Africa and Afro-America. Forms, Meanings, and Functional Significance for Individuals and Social Groups*. Leiden: E.J. Brill, 1972. A study of spirit possession phenomena from the standpoints of neurophysiology, hypnosis, the socialization process, cult determinism, mental illness and therapy, the effects of social disorganization, and their implications on concepts of normality and abnormality. Music (the 'sacred rhythms of drums') is only one of several ways in which trance can be induced, the others including drugs, sensory deprivation, hypnosis, and stress.

WEST AFRICA AND WEST CENTRAL AFRICA

2139. Bascom, William. *Ifa Divination: Communication between Gods and Men in West Africa*. Bloomington, IN: Indiana University Press, 1969. A study of sacred texts of the Ifa.

2140. Erlmann, V. "Trance and Music in the Hausa *Boorii* Spirit Possession Cult in Niger." *Ethnomusicology* 26 (1982): 49. Like humans, spirits are susceptible to praise songs. Musician specialists must thus provide such songs for each of more than 400 spirits, to induce them to participate in trance ritual. The author investigates musical, cultural, physiological, and psychological aspects of this group's rituals.

2141. Gorer, Geoffrey. "The Function of Different Dance Forms in Primitive African Communities." In *The Function of Dance in Human Society*, 2nd ed. Franz. Boas, ed. New York: Dance Horizons, 1972. Includes a description of several religious dances, including a Wolof trance dance designed to reveal the identity of a sorcerer.

2142. Griaule, Marcel. *Conversations with Ogotemmêli: An Introduction to Dogon Religious Ideas*. London: Oxford University Press, 1965/repr. 1970.

Mali. The rich tapestry of Dogon religion, explained in 33 conversations. See Day 28, on dancing and the rituals of which it is a part.

2143. Monts, Lester P. "Vai Women's Roles in Music, Masking, and Ritual Performance." In *African Musicology: Current Trends, Volume I: A Festschrift Presented to J.H. Kwabena Nketia*, Jacqueline Djedje and William G. Carter, ed. Los Angeles: University of California Crossroads Press, 1989. 219-35. Women play a more active role in traditional ritual occasions than do men in this Muslim society. They play the central role in masked dance ceremonies propitiating unseen spirit powers whose life-giving forces control one's daily existence.

2144. Nevadomsky, Joseph, with Norma Rosen. "The Initiation of a Priestess: Performance and Imagery in Olokun Ritual." *TDR: The Drama Review* 32, 2 (Summer) (1988): 186-207. Benin. A detailed account of a fertility ritual by initiate Norma Rosen.

2145. Shaw, R. Daniel. *Kandila: Samo Ceremonialism and Interpersonal Relationships*. Ph.D. diss., 1991. Western Sudan.

2146. Somé, Malidoma Patrice. *Of Water and the Spirit: Ritual, Magic, and Initiation in the Life of an African Shaman*. New York: Jeremy P. Tarcher/ Putnam, 1994. The author's account of his childhood in Upper Volta (Burkina Faso), brutal adolescence in a Jesuit mission and seminary, and escape to return to his village to undergo the initiation ritual of his people.

2147. Stoller, Paul. *Fusion of the Worlds: An Ethnography of Possession Among the Songhay of Niger*. Chicago: University of Chicago Press, 1989. A participant's account of possession cult activities among the Songhay from 1971 to 1987. Compelling reading.

Ghana

2148. Agawu, V. Kofi. "Music in the Funeral Traditions of the Akpafu." *Ethnomusicology* 32, 1 (1988): 75-105. A description of music in both Christian and non-Christian funeral traditions.

2149. Aning, Ben. "Atumpan Drums: An Object of Historical and Anthropological Study." In *Essays for a Humanist. An Offering to Klaus Wachsmann*, New York: The Town House Press, 1977. 58-72. See particularly pp. 66-70, on religious beliefs concerning the materials which go into the making of the drums.

2150. Chernoff, John. *African Rhythm and African Sensibility: Aesthetics and Social Action in African Musical Idioms*. Chicago: University of Chicago Press, Phoenix Books, 1981. See for comparisons of the African religious world, with its multiplicity of spirits, and music, with its multiplicity of rhythmic layers.

2151. Cudjoe, S.D. "The Techniques of Ewe Drumming and the Social Importance of Music in Africa." *Phylon* 14 (1953): 280-291. On Ewe drumming in general and on the religious dance in particular.

2152. Fiagbedzi, N. *The Music of the Anlo: Its Historical Background, Cultural Matrix, and Style*. Ph.D. diss., UCLA, 1977. Each Anlo diety has a corpus of sacred songs said to originate with the deity. Some of these require dance-drumming, some do not. Religious music is restricted to seasonal festivals. An initiation ceremony is described in detail with transcriptions of drumming at each stage of the rite. See especially pp. 170-230, Music and its Religious Matrix. Shows the radically differing policies of various Christian missions concerning the use of indigenous music—from the liberal policy of the 19th-century North German mission to the rigid policy of the Roman Catholic.

2153. Field, Margaret. "Spirit Possession in Ghana." In *Spirit Mediumship and Society in Africa*, Beattie and Middleton, ed. London: Routledge and Kegan Paul, 1969. 3-13. A study of the nature of spirit possession (dissociation), induction of dissociation (including music and dance), the possessing spirit (ghosts and Gods), the possessed person (lay or professional), and the social function of possession (confirmation of public opinion and morality).

2154. Hampton, Barbara L. "Music and Ritual Symbolism at the Ga Funeral." *YTM* 14 (1982): 75-105. A detailed description of a Ga funeral, including the music component, dance steps, songs texts, and the Ga belief system.

2155. Hampton, Barbara L. "The Role of Song in a Ga Ritual." In *Sacred Sound*, Joyce Irwin, ed. 1983. 11-26.

2156. Horton, Robin. "Types of Spirit Possession in Kalabari Religion." In *Spirit Mediumship and Society in Africa*, Beattie and Middleton, ed. London: Routledge and Kegan Paul, 1969. 14-49. A description of possession ritual dances involving spirits of the dead, founding heroes, and major and minor water spirits.

2157. Jones, Arthur Morris. *Studies in African Music*. 2 vols. London: Oxford University Press, 1959/repr. 1978. See Chap. 5 (93-127) on the music of the cult of Yeve, the God of Thunder.

2158. Kilson, Marion D. de B. *Kpele Lala: Ga Religious Songs and Symbols*. Cambridge: Cambridge University Press, 1971. An analysis of over 240 song texts of the ancestor cult of the Ga people of Ghana. Topics of song texts include Supreme Being, cosmogeny, cosmos, divine beings, and ritual.

2159. Kilson, Marion D. de B. "Twin Beliefs and Ceremony in Ga Culture." *Journal of Religion in Africa* 5, 3 (1973): 171-195. A study of the beliefs surrounding the birth of twins and the ceremonies required to establish a bond between the twins and the potentially disruptive spirits (bushcow) associated with them.

2160. Kubik, Gerard. "Àló—Yoruba Chantefables: An Integrated Approach Towards West African Music and Oral Literature." In *African Musicology: Current Trends, Volume I: A Festschrift Presented to J.H. Kwabena Nketia*, Jacqueline Djedje and William G. Carter, ed. Los Angeles: University of California Crossroads Press, 1989. 129-82.

2161. Nketia, J.H. Kwabena. *Drumming in Akan Communities of Ghana*. London and Edinburgh: Thomas Nelson and Sons LTD., for the University of Ghana, 1963. See pp. 90-102 for the religious associations of drumming.

2162. Nketia, J.H. Kwabena. "Historical Evidence in Ga Religious Music." In *The Historian in Tropical Africa*, Raymond Mauney, Jan Vansina, and L.V. Thomas, ed. London: Oxford University Press, 1964. 265-283. A study of song texts, instrumental forms, scale patterns, singing style, etc., to determine the source of Ga cult music and its relationship to the practice of neighboring tribes.

2163. Williams, Drid. "Sokodae: Come and Dance." *African Arts* 3, Spring (1970): 36-39, 80. Sokodae, one of the oldest dances found in Ghana, is danced to all of the gods of the three religious cults of the Ntwumuru and is at the call of the chief who can command it for special occasions such as funerals.

Nigeria

2164. Adegbite, Ademola. "The Drum and Its Role in Yoruba Religion." *Journal of Religion in Africa* 18, 1 (1988): 15-26. Drums are the bridge between the visible and invisible worlds. They accompany recitations, chants, and songs during religious ceremonies and festivals. During rituals, they facilitate the constant ecstatic communion of worshippers with their Orissa.

2165. Adewale, S.A. *The Religion of the Yoruba: A Phenomenological Analysis*. Ibadan, Nigeria: Department of Religious Studies, University of Ibadan, 1988. Topics include objects of worship, shrines, taboos, covenants, and rituals.

2166. Ajuwon, Bade. "Ogun's Iremoje: A Philosophy of Living and Dying." In *Africa's Ogun: Old World and New*, S. Barnes, ed. Bloomington, IN: Indiana University Press, 1989. 173-198. Funeral music in Yoruba religion.

2167. Ames, D.W. and A.V. King. *Glossary of Hausa Music and its Social Contexts*. Evanston, IL: Northwestern University Press, 1971. Consult English-Hausa index under religious celebrations and occasions, performance-possession dancers, and vocal music-possession songs and religious songs.

2168. Apter, Andrew Herman. *Rituals of Power: The Politics of Orisa Worship in Yoruba Society*. Ph.D. diss., Yale University Press, 1987.

2169. Babalola, Adeboye. "A Portrait of Ogun as Reflected in Ijala Chants." In *Africa's Ogun: Old World and New*, Sandra t. Barnes, ed. Bloomington, IN: Indiana University Press, 1989. 147-172.

2170. Barnes, Sandra T., ed. *Africa's Ogun: Old World and New*. African Systems of Thought, Bloomington, IN: Indiana University Press, 1989. Within this study of one of the primary deities in traditional African religions there is extensive documentation of the use and importance of dance and drum rhythms for addressing and experiencing the supernatural.

2171. Besmer, Fremont E. *Horses, Musicians and Gods: The Hausa Cult of Spirit Possession-Trance*. South Hadley, MA: Bergin and Garvey, 1983. An analytic study of the role of music and musicians in the Bori cult of affliction. Both physical and psycho-social conditions are either changed or regularized by means of medium-guided trance rituals.

2172. Carroll, Father K. "Yoruba Religious Chant." *African Music* 1, 3 (1956): 45-47. The similarities between indigenous Yoruba religious chant and plainchant are their solemnity, melodiousness and free rhythm. Their differences are the scales, the inflexible tonal inflections of the Yoruba language, and the necessity in Yoruba song for syllabic text setting.

2173. DjeDje, Jacqueline Cogdell. "Song Type and Performance Style in Hausa and Dagomba Possession (Bori) Music." *Black Perspective in Music* 12, 2 (1984): 166-82. An analysis of the function and role of the one-string fiddle, its performers, and the songs it accompanies reveals that there is no one prototype for the performance of possession songs among the Hausa and Dagomba; it also shows that music alone does not generate trance and that the ability to enter trance is culturally acquired, requiring initiation and other kinds of conditioning.

2174. Drewal, Henry John and Margaret T. Drewal. *Gèlèdé: Art and Female Power among the Yoruba*. Bloomington, Ind.: 1983. A description of masks and the rituals that honor the life-giving powers of women.

2175. Drewal, Margaret Thompson. "Symbols of Possession: A Study of Movement and Regalia in an Anago-Yoruba Ceremony." *Dance Research Journal* 7, 2/Spr.-Sum. (1975): 15-24. A discussion of the gods, the ritual process, stages in possession dance, drumming, and the role of regalia and gesture as symbols of possession.

2176. Drewel, Margaret Thompson. *Yoruba Ritual: Performers, Play, Agency*. African Systems of Thought, Bloomington, IN: Indiana University Press, 1992. This study of the dynamics of Yoruba ritual is particularly rewarding when read in conjunction with the accompanying video tape.

2177. Erlmann, Veit. *Music and the Islamic Reform in the Early Sokoto Empire: Sources, Idiology, Effects*. Abhandlungen für die Kunde des Morgenlandes, Bd. 48,1, Marburg: Deutsche Morgenlaendische Gesellschaft; Komissionsverlag Franz Steiner Wiesbaden, 1986. The *jihad* that took place in Nigeria in the early 19th century had only a moderate initial effect on the practice of music and possession, though later, attempts were made to effect more strenuous reforms. Relevant sections include 'Music and pre-Islamic Ritual' and 'Music, Islamic Ritual and Festivals.'

2178. Euba, Akin. "New Idioms of Music-Drama among the Yoruba: An Introductory Study." *YIFMC* 2 (1970): 92-107. The neo-traditional hymns in Yoruba music-drama observe in their melodies the speech tones of the Yoruba language, but still retain elements of European modality and equal temperament and are thus a synthesis of Yoruba and European traditions.

2179. Euba, Akin. "Ilu Esu (Drumming for Esu): Analysis of a Dundun Performance." In *Essays for a Humanist: An Offering to Klaus Wachsmann*, New York: The Town House Press, 1977. Nigeria. An analysis of the pitched drum music for the annual festival of Esu, one of the principal divinites of the Yoruba.

2180. Euba, Akin. "The Music of Yoruba Gods." In *Essays in Music*, Akin Euba, ed. Vol. 1. Bayreuth, Germany: IWALEWA-Haus, University of Bayreuth, 1988. 1-30. Topics: Yoruba divinities, the origin of music in Yoruba mythology, ensembles used for various divinities, and a description of some ceremonies. The article concludes with a summary of the roles of music: it announces religious events, creates a worshipful atmosphere, pleases divinities with their favorite music, indicates by its complexity the importance of the feted divinity, and induces a divinity to mount one or more of the devotees. Includes music transcription.

2181. Euba, Akin. *Yoruba Drumming: The Dundun Tradition*. Bayreuth African Studies Series, Vol. 21/22, Bayreuth, Germany: E. Breitinger, Bayreuth University, 1990. Pt. 1 deals with the social background of Dundun drumming and provides information on its religious significance. Pt. 2 describes drum ensemble construction and performance techniques. Pt. 3 covers the poetry and the music.

2182. Fagg, Bernard E.B. "The Discovery of Multiple Rock Gongs in Nigeria." *Man* 56, Febr. (1956): 17 ff. Repr. in *African Music* 1, no. 3, 6-9 (1956). Large slabs of rock, found in association with painted caves, are still used in religious ceremonies such as circumcision at initiation rites and communication with spirits.

2183. Hanna, Judith Lynne. "The Anthropology of Dance Ritual: Nigeria's Ubakala Nkwa Di Zche Iche." *DAI* 37, 3738-A (1976). A study of how social context allows dance pattern to communicate on cognitive and affective levels. Ph.D. diss., Columbia University.

2184. Harper, Peggy. "The Role of Dance in the Gelede Ceremonies of the Village Ijio." *ODU: A Journal of West African Studies* 4, October (1969): 67-

94. Dance is used to assure that women on whom mystic powers have been bestowed by the great mother apply their powers to the benefit of the community rather than to its destruction.

2185. Horn, A. "Ritual, Drama and the Theatrical: The Case of Bori Spirit Mediumship." *Nigeria Magazine* 136 (1981): 3-16. An examination of the Bori ritual-drama as an interface of religion and art.

2186. Ibitokun, Dr. Benedict. "Ritual and Entertainment, the Case of Gèlèdé in Egbado Ketu." *Nigeria* 136 (1981): 55-63. A description of a night performance of a women's fertility cult ritual-drama.

2187. King, Anthony. "A Report on the Use of Stone Clappers for the Accompaniment of Sacred Songs." *African Music* 2, 4 (1961): 64-71. A description of seven large, egg-shaped rocks worshipped as Gods. Includes transcription of music and text.

2188. King, Anthony. *Yoruba Sacred Music from Ekiti.* Ibadan, Nigeria: Caxton Press, 1961/repr. 1976. A brief study of Yoruba gods and of the central role of the dùndún family of drums in their worship. Mentioned specifically is music in honor of Sàngó, Ògún, and Ifá. Second half of book consists of transcriptions of drumming.

2189. King, Anthony. "Nigeria." In *Grove 6*, Vol. 13. 1980. 235-243.

2190. Kofoworola, Ziky and Yusef Lateef. *Hausa Performing Arts and Music.* Lagos, Nigeria: Department of Culture, Federal Ministry of Information and Culture, 1987. Of particular interest are Ch. 1 (pp. 1-24), on the religious sources of Hausa arts, and Ch. 11 (pp. 301-317), on spirit possession. Ch. 11 includes an interview with a Muslim musician who describes how possession takes place.

2191. Okoreaffia, C.O. "Igeri Ututu: An Igbo Folk Requiem Dance Ritual." In *The Performing Arts: Music and Dance*, et al. John Blacking, ed. The Hague/ New York: Mouton, 1979. 265-276. A description of a 4-day funeral ceremony for a man of wealth and of the music, which is performed by 5 men on 12 drums.

2192. Olbutboye, rOmrotbayrbo. *An Expository Analysis of Ujaamrersr Religious Chants of the Ekiti-Yoruba.* Ph.D. diss., University of Lagos, 1981, 1991.

2193. Olutoye, Omotayo. *Poetry in Religion: A Study of Chants and Songs in Olua Festivals.* Ikeja, Nigeria: Joe-Tolalu and Associates, 1991.

2194. Ottenberg, Simon. *Masked Rituals of Afikpo: The Context of an African Art.* Seattle, WA: Washington University. Henry Art Gallery, 1975. A description of the physical properties and symbolism of masks and of the roles they play in a variety of dances and dramas. Beautifully illustrated.

2195. Tremearne, Major A.J.N. *The Ban of the Bori: Demons and Demon-Dancing in West and North Africa.* London: Frank Cass and Co. Ltd, 1914/repr. 1968. According to Hausa belief, the *bori* are spirits, some of them potentially inimical, that belong or attach to each person. This account from the 1910s describes the elaborate and ongoing rites devoted to the propitiation and binding (*ban*) of these spirits, to prevent them from doing harm.

2196. Verger, Pierre. "Trance and Convention in Nago-Yoruba Spirit Mediumship." In *Spirit Mediumship and Society in Africa*, Beattie and Middleton, ed. London: Routledge and Kegan Paul, 1969. 50-66. A description of the initiation of a medium and his or her behavior when in trance, rites to Shango and Ogun, the social obligations of a medium, and the text of an Ogun ceremony.

2197. Vidal, A.O. *Oriki: Praise Chants of the Yoruba.* M.A. thesis, University of California at Los Angeles, 1971.

CENTRAL AFRICA

2198. Fernandez, J. *Bwiti: An Ethnography of the Religious Imagination in Africa.* Princeton: Princeton University Press, 1982. A thorough study of the capacity of an emergent religious culture—the Fang of Gabon—to create, from Christian and indigenous religious elements, its own realities. Consult index for numerous references to dances and music instruments.

2199. Roberts, Allen F. "Through the Bamboo Thicket: The Social Process of Tabwa Ritual Performance." *TDR: The Drama Review* 32, 2 (1988): 123-38. Zaire. A description of a Bulumbu spirit-possession ritual, a secret type of divination ritual that developed in response to Catholic missionary activity.

2200. Turnbull, Colin M. "Pygmy Music and Ceremonial." *Man* 55, February (1955): 23-24; 57, August (1957): 128. In contrast to their neighbors, the Bambuti have little indigenous religious ritual. Even the greatest of their religious festivals consist only of sung invocations to the bountiful God of the Forest.

EAST AFRICA

2201. Alpers, E.A. "Ordinary Household Chores: Ritual and Power in a Nineteenth-century Swahili Women's Spirit Possession Cult." *International Journal of African Historical Studies* 17, 4 (1984): 677-702. An analysis of and commentary on a possession cult in Zanzibar, originally described in 1869 by an Alsatian Catholic missionary. Possession is seen as women's response to their subordination to men during a time of social change.

2202. Beattie, John. "Spirit Mediumship in Bunyuro." In *Spirit Mediumship and Society in Africa*, Beattie and Middleton, ed. New York: Africana Publishing Corporation, 1969. 159-170. Western Uganda. Beattie distinguishes between spirit possession, spirit mediumship, and shamanism, describes a range of spirits available to a medium by the techniques of singing, shaking of gourd rattles, and drumming, and discusses cults persistance in spite of government and missionary opposition.

2203. Gieringer, Franz. "'To Praise the Sun': A Traditional Nyaturu Hymn of Praising God and Asking for His Blessing." *Anthropos* 85, 406 (1990): 518-23. Ukuta Yuva, sung primarily at betrothals, has an importance to the waNyaturu that is comparable to the importance of the Lord's Prayer to Christians. A brief study and full translation.

2204. Gray, Robert F. "The Shetani Cult among the Segeju of Tanzania." In *Spirit Mediumship and Society in Africa*, Beattie and Middleton, ed. London: Routledge and Kegan Paul, 1969. 171-187. A description of the exorcism of mischievous or malignant spirits (*shetani*) in a Muslim tribe.

2205. Loo, Joseph van de. *Guji Oromo Culture in Southern Ethiopia: Religious Capabilities in Rituals and Songs*. Collectanea Instituti Anthropos, Vol. 39, Berlin: Dietrich Reimer, 1991. With the collaboration of Bilow Kola. A study of Guji customs and symbol systems, with extensive analysis of song texts for various occasions. Chap. 5, Religious Songs and Traditional Values, explores 1) values in traditional rituals and songs [fertility, abundance, peace, a sense of identity, trust in God, ethics, and morality], 2) spirit possession songs, and 3) Christian songs (Catholic and Pentacostal).

2206. Middleton, John. "Spirit Possession among the Lugbara." In *Spirit Mediumship and Society in Africa*, Beattie and Middleton, ed. New York: Africana Publishing Corporation, 1969. 220-231. Possession is one way by which mediums, as diviners, prophets, or evangelist preachers, intercede with Spirit in the realm of chaos on behalf of humans, who inhabit the realm of order.

2207. Simon, Artur. "Musical Traditions, Islam and Cultural Identity in the Sudan." In *Perspectives on African Music*, Wolfgang Bender, ed. Bayreuth, Germany: Bayreuth University, 1989. 25-41.

2208. Southall, Aidan. "Spirit Possession and Mediumship among the Alur." In *Spirit Mediumship and Society in Africa*, Beattie and Middleton, ed. New York: Africana Publishing Corporation, 1969. 232-272. A personal account of possession among Roman Catholic diviners of the Alur. Drumming and dancing are central aspects of the events associated with *Jok* (spirit) possession. New manifestations of *Jok* in spirit possession represent profound changes that have taken place in Alur society.

SOUTH AFRICA

2209. Berliner, Paul. "Music and Spirit Possession at a Shona Bira." *African Music Society Journal* 5, 4 (1975-6): 130-139. A description of a formal religious ceremony in which family members come together to call upon a common ancestor for relief from misfortune. Three mbira, one hasho, and a singer provide the nucleus of the music ensemble.

2210. Berliner, Paul. *The Soul of Mbira: Music and Traditions of the Shona People of Zimbabwe*. Berkeley: University of California Press, 1978.

2211. Blacking, John. "The Context of Venda Possession Music: Reflections on the Effectiveness of Symbols." *YTM* 17 (1985): 64-87. An attempt to understand Venda music by locating the cognitive processes that generate it. The second part of the article deals with the cultural context of Venda possession dance, which sends only cult members in their own home, but not the musicians, into trance. A detailed study of the conditions that regulate if and how a Vendan responds to a possession ceremony and of the patterns of such a ceremony.

2212. Chilivumbo, A.B. "Vimbuza or Mashawe: A Mystic Therapy." *African Music* 5, 2 (1972): 6 ff. Under the direction of a healer, the communal Vimbuza dance is used to cure a person beset by social or psychological distress (*mashawe*) caused by evil spirits.

2213. Colson, Elizabeth. "Spirit Possession among the Tonga." In *Spirit Mediumship and Society in Africa*, Beattie and Middleton, ed. New York: Africana, 1969. 69-103. Zambia. A description of three types of spirit and their possession events: those concerned with community welfare; those concerned with their own desires; and ghosts whose intent is to kill. Colson also provides a history of possession among the Tongo and statistics concerning occurrences of possession.

2214. Faulkner, Laurel Birch. *Kasiyamaliro, Symbol and Sign: A Structural Analysis of Chewa Masked Dance*. M.A. thesis, Antioch University, 1991. Malawi.

2215. Friedson, Steven Michael. *The Dancing Prophets of Malawi: Music and Healing among the Tumbuka*. Ph.D. diss., University of Washington, 1991. The music and dance, *vimbuza*, and particularly drumming, are part of Malawi medical technology: they initiate and control the divination trance that allows the *nchimi* (healer) to diagnose his or her patients. A field-researcher's vivid and detailed account of Malawi divination and healing and the cultural, and especially the religious, framework within which it takes place. Forthcoming as a book entitled *The Dancing Prophets of Malawi: An Ethnography of Musical Experience*. University of Chicago Press.

2216. Friedson, Steven Michael, ed. *Musical Experience in Tumbuka Healing: The Vimbuza Complex*. Garland Encyclopedia of World Music, Hamden, CT: Garland Publishing, forthcoming.

2217. Garbett, G. Kingsley. "Spirit Mediums as Mediators in Valley Korekore Society." In *Spirit Mediumship and Society in Africa*, John Beattie and John Middleton, ed. New York: Africana Publishing Corporation, 1969. 104-127. A study of spirit-realms hierarchy, its mediums, and the ritual aspects of their services.

2218. Granquist, Raoul. *Culture in Africa: An Appeal for Pluralism*. Seminar Proceedings from the Scandinavian Institute of African Studies, Uppsala, Sweden: Nordiska Afrikainstitutet, 1993. Includes comment on church music in Zimbabwe.

2219. Jacobson-Widding, Anita. *Private Spirits and Ego: A Psychological Ethnography of Ancestor Cult and Spirit Possession among the Manyika of Zimbabwe*. Uppsala, Sweden: African Studies Programme, Dept. of Cultural Anthropology, University of Uppsala, 1987.

2220. Janzen, John M. "Doing 'ngoma': A Dominant Trope in African Religion and Healing." *Journal of Religion in Africa* 21, 4 (1991): 290-308. The term *ngoma* embraces drum, drumming, singing, dancing and associated behaviors and concepts. As a cult of affliction, *ngoma* attracts the ill, the dispossessed, the suffering. Through participating in *ndembu* performance, the afflicted regain a measure of control over their lives. This article attempts to construct a theory of how the system works. Verbalization in terms of both causative and healing spirits emerges as an important aspect of the theraputic process.

2221. Janzen, John M. *Ngoma: Discourses of Healing in Central and Southern Africa*. Berkeley: University of California Press, 1992.

2222. Johnston, Thomas F. *The Music of the Shangana-Tsonga*. Ph.D. diss., University of Witwatersrand, 1971.

2223. Johnston, Thomas F. "Possession Music of the Shangana-Tsonga." *African Music* 5, 2 (1972): 10-22. A description of exorcism rites, with text and transcription.

2224. Johnston, Thomas F. "Shangana-Tsonga Dance: Its Role in Exorcism, Initiation, and the Social Beer-Drink." *Anthropologie* 28, 1 (1990): 89-99.

2225. Kaemmer, John E. "Social Power and Musical Change Among the Shona." *Ethnomusicology* 33, 1 (1989): 31-46. Political change in a society brings about related changes in musical style and performance. One of the examples given is Christianization where new music complexes arose in the space once occupied by old rituals, yet with the new still resembling somewhat the old. Other political factors are examined including the move from a chief-based form of government, with its associated ritual, to a Europeanization of sorts in government.

2226. Katz, Richard. *Boiling Energy: Community Healing among the Kalahari !Kung*. Cambridge, MA: Harvard University Press, 1982.

2227. Katz, Richard. "The !Kung Approach to Healing: Spiritual Balance Through Dance." *Parabola* 18, 1 (1993): 72-81. Healing is an important unifying tradition in !Kung culture, and the all-night healing dance is the central event in this tradition. This article describes the dance, and the *num*, the healing spiritual energy that boils up from the belly and base of the spine to the base of the skull, resulting in *kia*, a state in which the healer sees what peoples' ailments are.

2228. Larlham, Peter. *Black Theater, Dance, and Ritual in South Africa*. Ann Arbor, MI: UMI Research Press, 1985. See chapters on traditional Zulu rites and ceremonies, Zionist Christian ritual, and Festivals of the Nazareth Baptist Church.

2229. Lee, Richard B. "The Sociology of Kung Bushman Trance Performances." In *Trance and Possession States*, R. Prince, ed. Montreal: Raymond M. Bucke Memorial Society, 1968. 35-54. Bushman trance dance events are cooperative, involve both men and women, protect all members of the community, and unite them in a common struggle against malevolent spirits of the dead.

2230. Lewis-Williams, David. "Rock Art and Changing Perceptions of Southern Africa's Past: Ezeljagdspoort." *Antiquity* 67, 255 (June, 1993): 273-291. On the close relationship between Bushman rock-art and shaman-artists' trance experiences.

2231. Malan, Jacques P., ed. *South African Music Encyclopedia*. 4 vols. Capetown: Oxford University Press, 1979-1986. See Vol. 2, 265-508, for an extensive article on indigenous musics.

2232. Mapoma, Isaiah Mwesa. "A Glimpse at the Use of Music in Traditional Medicine Among the Bantu: A Case of Healing Among the Bemba Speaking People of Zambia." *Mantu* 8 (1988): 117-23.

2233. Maraire, Dumisani Abraham. *The Position of Music in Shona Mudzimu (Ancestral Spirit) Possession*. Ph.D. diss., University of Washington, 1990. A Christian Shona man's encounter with traditional Shona possession. Maraire explains Shona spiritual categories and concepts: how one becomes an ancestor, how one gets possessed, Mudzimu ceremonies and possession, and the relationship of music to possession. Since a spirit can possess without music, since not all spirits possess, and since not all persons become possessed even when subjected to possession music, what is the role of music? Spirit possession is a family affair; it occurs when a family needs the guidance of an elder. Music is one of several final factors necessary to induce an ancestor to make himself known through a family member of his choice.

2234. Marshall, Lorna. "The Medicine Dance of the !Kung Bushmen." *Africa* 39 (1969): 347-381. The protection of health is the primary focus of !Kung ritual. The Medicine Dance, a curing ritual to protect the people from sickness and death, unites the community, reduces psychological stress, externalizes aggressions, and temporarily relieves the ever-present fear of death.

2235. Post, Laurens van der and Jane Taylor. *Testament to the Bushmen.* New York: Viking, 1984. Chap. 9, Dance, Trance and Medicine Men, includes a vivid description of a curing dance-trance, the central religious ritual of the Bushmen.

2236. Sacks, Kenneth. *The Dialectic of Shona Mbira DzaVadzimu.* MA thesis, UCLA, 1992.

2237. Soko, Boston J. *Traditional Forms of Instruction: The Case of the Jando Initiation Ceremony.* Catching Winged Words: Oral Tradition and Education, E.R. Sienaert and A.N. Bell, ed. Durban: Natal University Oral Documentation and Research Centre, 1988.

2238. Turner, Edith. "Zambia's Kankanga Dances: The Changing Life of Ritual." *Performing Arts Journal* 10, 3 (1987): 57-72. A comparison of six versions of a girls initiation ceremony, conducted between 1954 and 1985, shows that in spite of Christian missionaries and government interference, tribal rituals can adapt and retain their vibrancy and effectiveness.

2239. Turner, Edith. *The Spirit and the Drum.* Tucson: University of Arizona Press, 1987. The author's account of her fieldwork among the Ndembu of Zambia in the 1950s.

2240. Turner, Edith, with William Blodgett, Singleton Kahona, and Fideli Benwa. *Experiencing Ritual: A New Interpretation of African Healing.* Series in Contemporary Ethnography, Philadelphia: University of Pennsylvania Press, 1992. The author's personal account of a healing drum ceremony.

2241. Turner, Victor. *Chihamba, The White Spirit: A Ritual Drama of the Ndembu.* Manchester: Manchester University Press, 1962. A detailed description of the rituals of the most important of the cults of affliction. The study concludes with a cross-cultural comparison of characters like kavula, the spirit said to cause illness and ritually killed in Chihamba rites.

2242. Turner, Victor. *The Drums of Affliction: A Study of Religious Processes among the Ndembu of Zambia.* Oxford: Clarendon Press and International African Institute, 1968. A study of the cultural setting and structure of Ndemba rituals of affliction. Consult index for references to dance, drum, and singing.

2243. Wembah-Rashid, J.A.R. "'Isinyago and Midimu', Masked Dancers of Tanzania and Mozambique." *African Arts* 4, 2 (1971): 38 ff. A study of the face covers (*midimu*) and body covers that represent animal spirits (*isinyago*) and the initiation and other ceremonies of which they are a part. Beautifully illustrated.

CHRISTIAN MUSIC AND DANCE

2244. Abe, Gabriel Oyedele. "The Influence of Nigerian Music and Dance on Christianity." *Asia Journal of Theology* 5, Oct. (1991): 296-310. A study of the indigenization of worship in Nigeria and its effects on the Christian music of other countries and cultures.

2245. Agu, Daniel C.C. "Cultural Influence in Igbo Contemporary Choral Music." *International Council for Traditional Music United Kingdom Chapter Bulletin* 5 (1984): 4-13.

2246. Agu, Daniel C. C. "Youth Songs: A Type of Igbo Choral Music in Igbo Christian Worship." *African Music* 7, 2 (1992): 13-22. When Christianity came to Igboland in 1857, music for worship consisted of translated hymn texts set to European music. Beginning in 1953, with the birth of the youth fellowship, church music composers avoided the pitfalls of early Christian hymns by incorporating African instruments and observing Igbo language inflections. By being lively, easy to memorize, and familiar in idiom, music has once again become the center of Igbo Christian worship.

2247. Axelsson, Olof E. "Historical Notes on Neo-African Church Music." *Zambezia* 3, 2 (1974): 89-102. An excellent outline of the influence of Christian churches on the processes of musical acculturation that have taken place in southern Africa since the early 19th century.

2248. Balzer, Kirsten. "Music and Dance in Zionist Healing Ceremonies." In *Afro-Christian Religion and Healing in Southern Africa*, G. C. Oosthuizen and Irving Hexham, ed. African Studies, Lewiston, NY: E. Mellen Press, 1991. 172-183.

2249. Blacking, John. "Political and Musical Freedom in the Music of Some Black South African Churches." In *The Structure of Folk Models*, L. Holy and M. Stuchlik, ed. ASA Monograph no. 20, London: Academic Press, 1981. 35-62. The music Venda Zionists sing (indigenous psalms and hymns), the way they sing it (a slow call and response polyphony with hand clapping) and the resultant change during a performance to a more assertive affect reinforce the eschatological tone of the song texts and give expression on a non-verbal level to the political aspirations of a people who feel themselves socially and politically oppressed.

2250. Blacking, John. "Intention and Change in the Performance of European Hymns by Some Black South African Churches." In *Transplanted European*

Music Cultures, Geoffrey Moon, ed. Miscellanea Musicologica: Adelaide Studies in Musicology, Vol. 12, Adelaide: University of Adelaide, 1987. 193-200.

2251. Brooks, Christopher. "In Search of an Indigenous African Hymnody: The Aladura Churches among the Yoruba." *Black Sacred Music* 8, 2/Fall (1994): 30-42. A survey of the sources of hymn repertory used among the Aladura (separatist) Christian churches since the 1890s.

2252. Church Music. *African Music* 1, 3 (1956): 34-47. Brief articles on church music in East Africa, West Africa, the Yoruba of Nigeria, Nyasaland, and the Batetelu of the Belgian Congo. A factor common to those areas where tone languages are spoken is the impossibility of adapting texts in tone languages to western melodies.

2253. Cockrell, Dale. "Of Gospel Hymns, Minstrel Shows, and Jubilee Singers: Toward Some Black South African Musics." *American Music* 5, 4 (1987): 417-32. The Afro-American gospel hymn, minstrel show, and Jubilee choir were all known in late 19th-century South Africa and can still be detected in both white and black South African music today.

2254. Corbitt, John Nathan. *The History and Development of Music used in the Baptist Churches on the Coast of Kenya: The Development of an Indigenous Church Music, 1953-1984.* DMA, Southwestern Baptist Theological Seminary, 1985. Kenyan Baptist music comes in four musical styles including western mission music ('book' music) and music for hand clapping, dancing, and a variety of styles of chorus ('body' music). A study of historical influences, the character of the church and its life, the nature of the people and their environment, and an analysis of the four distinct musical styles.

2255. Corbitt, John Nathan. "Dynamism in African Christian Music: The Search for Identity and Self Expression." *Black Sacred Music* 8, 2/Fall (1994): 1-29. Across Africa, Christian music expresses and unifies each community through its mix of local culture, language, history, and Christian teachings. Includes a summary of earlier missionary traditions and of independent Christian churches.

2256. Dargie, David. "African Church Music and Liberation." In *Papers presented at the Third and Fourth Symposia on Ethnomusicology: Music Department, University of Natal, Durban 16th to 19 September 1982: Music Department, Rhodes University 7th to 8th October 1983*, Andrew Tracey, ed. Grahamstown: International Library of African Music, 1984. 9-14.

2257. Dargie, David. "Xhosa Church Music." In *Music and the Experience of God*, Collins, Power, and Burnim, ed. 1989. Concilium 202. 62-72. A historical look at Xhosa Christian Church music from its beginnings with Ntsikana's songs to Catholic Victorian style and its transformation back to using indigenous musical styles.

2258. Effa, Allan Louis. *Singing His Praises Among the Nations: The Role of Praise for African Missiology*. Th.M. diss., Fuller Theological Seminary, School of World Mission, 1991.

2259. Ekwueme, Lazarus Nnanyelu. "African Music in Christian Liturgy: The Igbo Experiment." *African Music* 5, 3 (1973-1974): 12-33. The Igbo have embraced Christianity more fully than has any other group in Africa. The author describes the conflict between Igbo tone-language and Christian hymn tunes and the difficulty of maintaining and adapting Igbo customs to Christian worship. He also describes the contributions of recent composers.

2260. Eúbà, Akin. "Yoruba Music in the Church: The Development of a Neo-African Art among the Yoruba of Nigeria." In *African Musicology: Current Trends*, J.C. DjeDje, ed. Vol. 2. Los Angeles: International Studies Oversears Program/The James S. Coleman African Studies Center University of California, Los Angeles, 1992. 45-64.

2261. Gory, Ronald William. *Singing as a Means of Communicating the Gospel: A Survey of Developments within the Methodist Chruch of Southern Africa, 1802-1980*. D.Th. diss., University of South Africa, 1987. During the long presence of Methodism in So. Africa, the singing of hymns, beginning with those of the Wesleys, has been of major importance in communicating the Christian faith and establishing missions in South Africa.

2262. Hastings, Adrian, ed. "African Hymnody: Christian and Traditional." *Journal of Religion in Africa* 20, June (1990): 118-224.

2263. James, Wendy. "Uduk Faith in a Five-note Scale: Mission Music and the Spread of the Gospel." In *Vernacular Christianity: Essays in the Social Anthropology of Religion, Presented to Godfrey Lienhardt*, W. James and D. Johnson, ed. New York, NY: Lilian Barber Press, 1988. 131-145. The hymns of the Uduk people in the Sudan.

2264. Jones, Arthur Morris. *African Hymnody in Christian Worship: A Contribution to the History of Its Development*. Mambo Occasional Papers, Missio-Pastoral Series, Vol. 8, Gwelo, Rhodesia: Mambo Press, 1976. A brief history of the first, difficult attempts to adapt Christian music to African tone languages.

2265. Jules-Rosette, Bennetta. *African Apostles: Ritual and Conversion in the Church of John Maranke*. Symbol, Myth and Ritual Series, Ithica NY: Cornell University Press, 1975. Conversion, Ritual Contexts and a Vision of Change as experienced and described by a member of the Church of the Apostles of John Maranke. In Song and Spirit, song is described as a managed event in ceremony and as an intentional act that provides a thematic unity for service worship. Ecstasy achieved through chant is interpreted as heaven on earth.

2266. Jules-Rosette, Bennetta. "Ecstatic Singing: Music and Social Integration in an African Church." In *More Than Drumming...*, Irene V. Jackson, ed. Westport, CT: Greenwood Press, 1985. 119-43. In Apostolic ceremonies that continuously alternate between sermon and song, the three types of singing are formal hymns, didactic songs, and ecstatic chants. The last two are used to invoke the immediate presence of the Holy Spirit. Ecstasy during trance functions to unify the congregation.

2267. Kiernan, J.P. "The Canticles of Zion: Song as Word and Action in Zulu Zionist Discourse." *Journal of Religion in Africa* 2, 2 (1990): 188-204. The singing of hymns plays a central role in Zionist meetings. A study of the texts reveals some predominant themes: deliverance, renewal, home, constitution, adversity, sin, and elitism.

2268. King, Roberta Rose. *Pathways in Christian Music Communication: The Case of the Senufo of Côte d'Ivoire*. Ed.D. diss., Fuller Theological Seminary, School of World Mission, 1989. The indigenous content in new songs makes a significant difference in effective communication of the Gospel within the African context. This content has four channels: linguistic, musical, kinesthetic, and performance. It allows for the integration of Senufo worldview with biblical teaching.

2269. Krabill, James R. "Dida Harrist Hymnody (1913-1990)." *Journal of Religion in Africa* 20, 2 (1990): 118-152. The Harrist religion, founded in 1913 In Ivory Coast, is a blend of basic Christian concepts with indigenous music, dance, and song. The author studies the oral hymn texts for clues to the teaching of the non-literate preachers of the religion and to its history and prayers.

2270. Lenherr, J. "Hymnody of the Mission Churches among the Shona and Ndebele." In *Christianity South of the Zambezi*, M. Bourdillon, ed. Vol. 2. Gwelo, Rhodesia (Zimbabwe): Mambo Press, 1977. 103-122.

2271. Londi, Boka di Mpasi. "Freedom of Bodily Expression in the African Liturgy." *Concilium* 132, 2 (1980): 53-64. In traditional African religion, bodily expression is the most sacred and communicative of acts: with reference to Vatican II, an argument for the inclusion of dance in the liturgy.

2272. Mapoma, Isaiah Mwesa. "The Use of Folk Music Among Some Bemba Church Congregations in Zambia." *YIFMC* 1 (1969): 72-88. Methodist and Anglican adaptations of folk tunes to religious texts reached a high point in the 1930's. The decline that followed was the result of objections by both clergy and congregation to the old fashioned repertory, to the songs' social origins, and other factors. By the 1960's, folks songs had been supplanted by translated Western hymns. Some churches (CMML) never adapted folk tunes because of their worldly, "pagan" origins. Attempts by Africans to create an indigenous liturgy have been more successful than White attempts.

2273. Martin, Stephen H. "African Church Music: The Genesis of an Acculturative Style." *Journal of Black Sacred Music* 2, 1 (Spring) (1988): 35-44. The development of indigenous Christian music took over a century, met much resistance, and has many regional variants.

2274. Mbunga, Stephen B. G. *Church Law and Bantu Music: Ecclestiastical Documents and Law on Sacred Music as Applied to Bantu Music.* Schoneck-Beckenried, Switzerland: Nouvelle Revue de Science Missionnaire, 1963. After providing a brief history of Bantu indigenous and Christian music, the author examines in detail §1264 of Canon Law, the repository of laws on sacred music, and the application of these laws to Bantu music. A valuable source for Roman Catholic church law on music.

2275. Merriam, Alan P. "Music Change in a Basongye Village (Zaire)." *Anthropos* 72 (1977): 806-46. Wherever music is tied to events, the music ceases when the events no longer occur: a study of the disappearance of traditional ritual music with the introduction of Christianity and a description of the indigenous Presbyterian church music.

2276. Methethwa, Bongani. "Music and Dance as Therapy in African Traditional Societies with Special Reference to the Blandla lamaNazaretha (the Church of the Nazarites)." In *Afro-Christian Religion and Healing in Southern Africa*, G. C. Oosthuizen, ed. Newiston, NY: E. Mellen Press, 1989. 241-256.

2277. Molyneux, Gordon. "The Place and Function of Hymns in the EJSCK (Église de Jésus-Christ sur terre par le Prophète Simon Kimbangu)." *Journal of Religion in Africa* 20, 2 (1990): 153-87. "Inspired" or "revealed" hymn creation has made a major contribution to the recent hymn repertory of the Kimbanguist Church of Bas-Zaire. The author studies the hymn texts as oral history and doctrine.

2278. Mthethwa, Bongani. "Western Elements in Shembe's Religious Dances." In *Papers presented at the Third and Fourth Symposia on Ethnomusicology: Music Department, University of Natal, Durban 16th to 19 September 1982: Music Department, Rhodes University 7th to 8th October 1983*, Andrew Tracey, ed. Grahamstown: International Library of African Music, 1984. 34-37. The majority of Nazareth Baptist Church songs are a mixture of African and European musical features. The rhythmic aspects in particular are African in character. Of two new religious dance forms, the earlier is based on an old Zulu religious dance, the more recent incorporates elements of urban dance and new church hymns.

2279. Mthethwa, Bongani. "Music and Dance in Zulu Christian Worship: Meaning of Religious Dances in the Shembe Church." *International Council for Traditional Music UK Chapter Bulletin* 9 (1985): 4-11. Isaiah Shembe, founder of the Nazareth Baptist Church in South Africa in 1911, composed song compositions and dance for his congregation. Most of these combine Western and indigenous Zulu musical practices. Whereas Western hymns are sung in passive worship contexts, *ukusina*, a traditional dance form introduced in 1920, is used in active worship.

2280. Mthethwa, B. N. "Music and Dance as Therapy in African Traditional Societies with Special Reference to the iBlandla lamaNazaretha (The Church of the Nazarites)." In *Afro-Christian Religion and Healing in Southern Africa*, G. C. Oosthuizen, ed. Lewiston, NY: E. Mellen Press, 1989. 241-256.

2281. Muirhead, Joan Marion. *The Religious Music of the Twentieth-century Charismatic Renewal in South Africa*. MMus diss., University of South Africa, 1983.

2282. Njoku, Johnston Akuma-Kalu. *Nature and Organizing Principles of African Music and the Emergence of Shona Catholic Mass Music in Zimbabwe*. Ph.D. diss., Indiana University, 1992.

2283. Nkinda, Masengo. "The Adaptation of Traditional Musical Instruments to Sacred Music: The Example of Zaire." *Musices Aptatio, Vatican*. 129-155. Traditional African religion includes singing, dancing, and the use of instruments. This is a study of various experiments in the inclusion of indigenous musical elements in worship since the Second Vatican Council.

2284. Olowola, Cornelius Abiodum. "An Introduction to Independent African Churches." *East Africa Journal of Evangelical Theology* 3, 2 (1984): 21-49. Includes discussion of the role of music in indigenous Christian worship.

2285. Olson, Howard. "African Music in Christian Worship." In *African Initiatives in Religion*, David Barret, ed. Nairobi: East African Publishing House, 1971. 61-72.

2286. Oosthuizen, Gerhardus Cornalis. *The Theology of a South African Messiah: An Analysis of the Hymnal of 'The Church of the Nazarites'*. Leiden: E.J. Brill, 1967. A study of the Nazarite hymnal from five standpoints: the Supreme Being, the Messiah, Man and the Supernatural World, the Community, and Eschatology.

2287. Oosthuizen, Gerhardus Cornalis et al., ed. *Afro-Christian Religion and Healing in Southern Africa*. African Studies, Lewiston, NY: E. Mellen Press, 1989. Consult index under dance, hymns, and possession.

2288. Oyer, Mary K. "Hymnody in the Context of World Mission." *The Hymnology Annual* 1 (1991): 51-75. Ed. by V. Wicker. Repr. from *IAH Bulletin*, 16, Jun., 1988, pp. 53-74. On African Christian music and hymns.

2289. Pailloux, R. *St. Clement's Hymnal (Inyimbo Shipya)*. Mansa, Zambia: Saint Clement's Sec. School, 1969.

2290. Seasoltz, R. Kevin. "The Dancing Church: An Appreciation." *Worship* 67, May (1993): 253-261. On the video *The Dancing Church: Video Impressions of the Church in Africa.*

2291. Steenbrink, Karel A. "Music in African and Asian Churches." *Exchange* 20, Apr. (1991): 1-45. Church music, liturgy and culture. Includes reprints from 2nd National Liturgical Conference, Jogjakarta, 1983.

2292. Thiel, Paul van. "Spontaneous Creativity and African Sacred Music." *AFER* 27, Ap. (1985): 80-86. Vatican II provides for and encourages the incorporation of indigenous singing and dancing in Catholic worship in Africa.

2293. Turkson, Adolphus R. "A Voice in the African Process of Crossing from the Traditional to Modernity: The Music of Ephraim Amu." *Ultimate Reality and Meaning* 10, Mar. (1987): 39-53.

2294. Warnock, Paul Willard. *Trends in African Church Music: A Historical Review.* M.A. thesis, UCLA, 1983. A valuable study and overview of musical and religious acculturation. Chapters cover five periods: Prelude (1419-1736), Foundation (1737-1850), Consolidation (1851-1918), Reassessment (1919-1957), and Re-orientation (1958-1982).

2295. Weman, Henry. *African Music and the Church in Africa.* Eric J. Sharpe, transl. Uppsala, Sweden: University Press Upsala, 1960. A study of the re-introduction of African elements into African church music. Topics include structure and forms of expression, music in African society, music in the African school, music in the Christian congregation, a new church music, the duty to identify the customs and thought-patterns of each indigenous group, and constructive proposals for a new church music.

2296. Whelan, Thomas R. "Liturgical Music and Ethnomusicology." *AFER* 25, June (1983): 172-181. An argument for the intrinsic necessity of a people to express their religious beliefs and aspirations in the musical language of their own culture. Although this thesis is universally accepted, it is not yet a universal reality in Africa.

28

North America: Euro-American and Afro-American Religious Music: General References

DICTIONARIES, ENCYCLOPEDIAS, AND GENERAL BIBLIOGRAPHIES

2297. Heintze, James R. *Early American Music: A Research and Information Guide*. New York: Garland, 1990. 1959 references, briefly annotated. Especially valuable for section on the music of ethnic or religious groups, 252-310. See index under hymnody, psalmody and sacred music, shape note, tune books, singing schools, etc.

2298. Hitchcock, H. Wiley. and Stanley Sadie, ed. *The New Grove Dictionary of American Music*. 4 vols. New York: Grove's Dictionaries of Music, 1986. Covers all aspects of American music. Consult under genres, personal names, denominations, and the entry under Notation.

2299. Horn, D. *Literature of American Music in Books and Folk Music Collections: A Fully Annotated Bibliography*. Metuchen, NJ: Scarecrow Press, 1977. Supplement, 1988, with Richard Jackson. The two volumes contain 2634 references.

2300. Jackson, Kenneth T. et al., ed. *Dictionary of American Biography*. 10 vols. New York: Charles Scribner's Sons, 1946-58/repr. 1995. With an index guide to the supplements.

2301. Kallman, Helmut, Gilles Potvin, and Kenneth Winters, ed. *Encyclopedia of Music in Canada*. 2nd ed., Toronto and Buffalo: University of Toronto Press, 1992.

2302. Krummel, D. W. "Bibliographies." In *NGDAM*, Vol. 1. 1986. 205-213. Discusses access by period, place, content, and form. Covers period from 1851 to 1985.

2303. Miller, Terry E. *Folk Music in America: A Reference Guide*. New York, NY: Garland, 1986. An annotated bibliography of available sources. This volume includes sections on American psalmody and hymnody, singing school and shape note traditions, and Afro-American religious and gospel music each with a discography.

2304. Proctor, George Alfred. *Sources in Canadian Music: A Bibliography of Bibliographies*. 2nd. ed., Sackville, New Brunswick: Ralph Pickard Bell Library. Mount Allison University, 1979.

HISTORICAL SURVEYS

2305. Ammer, Christine. *Unsung: A History of Women in American Music*. Westport CT: Greenwood Press, 1980. Ammer traces the works and influence of American female composers, instrumentalists, and vocalists from the colonial period through the 1970's. Includes information on women's musical involvement in Puritan worship (chap. 1) and sacred music composed by women in European and American idioms (chap. 6 and 7).

2306. Bohlman, Philip et al. "European-American Music." In *NGDAM*, 2. 1986. 64-86. A survey of the musical contributions, sacred and secular, of each European country to the musical life of the United States.

2307. Chase, Gilbert, ed. *The American Composer Speaks: A Historical Anthology, 1770-1965*. Baton Rouge: Louisiana State University Press, 1966.

2308. Chase, Gilbert. *America's Music: From the Pilgrims to the Present*. 3rd ed., Urbana, Il: University of Illinois, 1987/repr. 1992.

2309. Crawford, Richard. "A Historian's Introduction to Early American Music." In *Proceedings [of the American Antiquarian Society]*, 89. 1979. 261-98. Crawford writes for non-musical historians, introducing them to the issues and themes. Among these are the role of religious institutions in fostering musical education, the relationship between oral tradition and sacred music, and the influence of the Bay Psalm Book.

2310. Ellinwood, Leonard. "Religious Music in America." In *Religious Perspectives in American Culture*, W. Herbert, ed. Princeton, NJ: Princeton University Press, 1961. 289-359.

2311. Eskew, Harry and H. McElrath. *Sing with Understanding*. Nashville, TN: Broadman, 1980. Designed as a text for seminarians to be used in conjunction with a hymnal, this introduction looks at hymns in three contexts: 1) in relation to the arts and theology, 2) in relation to historical and cultural traditions, and 3) in Christian practice.

2312. Gleason, Harold and Warren Becker. *Early American Music: Music in America from 1620 to 1920.* 2nd ed., Music Literature Outlines, Series 3, Bloomington, IN: Frangipani Press, 1981. A history in outline form, with excellent bibliography at end of each chapter.

2313. Hamm, Charles. *Music in the New World.* New York: W. W. Norton, 1983.

2314. Hitchcock, H. Wiley. *Music in the United States: A Historical Introduction.* 2nd ed., Englewood Cliffs NJ: Prentice-Hall, 1974.

2315. Kallmann, H. *A History of Music in Canada, 1534-1919.* Toronto: 1960.

2316. Kingman, Daniel. *American Music: A Panorama.* 2nd ed., New York: Schirmer Books, 1990.

2317. McGee, Timothy J. *The Music of Canada.* New York: W.W. Norton, 1985. A section on religious music is included in three of the earlier periods covered by the book. The last chapter deals with music of the Canadian Indians and Inuit.

2318. Mellers, Wilfrid Howard. *Music in a New Found Land: Two Hundred Years of American Music.* New York: Stonehill Publishing Co., 1965/repr. 1975. 1965 ed. entitled *Music in a New Found Land: Themes and Developments in the History of American Music.*

CHURCH MUSIC: HISTORIES AND SURVEYS

2319. Bradshaw, Paul F. and Lawrence A. Hoffman, ed. *The Changing Face of Jewish and Christian Worship in North America.* Two Liturgical Traditions, Vol. 2. Notre Dame: University of Notre Dame Press, 1991. Sixteen essays in three groups: Liturgical Traditions and Theologies of 'The Other,' American Reform or Second Reformation?, and Critiquing Liturgical Reforms.

2320. Daniel, Ralph T. and Elwyn A. Wienandt. "Anthem." In *NGDAM*, Vol. 1. 1986. 55-57.

2321. Davison, Archibald. *Protestant Church Music in America.* New York NY: Gordon Press, 1933/repr. 1948.

2322. Dean, Talmage W. *A Survey of Twentieth-Century Protestant Church Music in America.* Nashville, TN: Broadman Press, 1988.

2323. Ellinwood, Leonard. *The History of American Church Music.* Music Reprint Series, New York: Da Capo Press, 1953/repr. 1970.

2324. Ferguson, Everett. *A Cappella Music in the Public Worship of the Church*. Way of Life Series, Abilene, TX: Abilene Christian University Press, 1972.

2325. Gebauer, V. E. "Problems in the History of American Church Music." *Hymn* 41, 4 (1990): 45-48. The topic of 20th-century church music is missing from all histories of American music. This article surveys the literature, proposes an outline for the historical treatment of 20th-century church music in all its diversity, and points to some inevitable tensions. He ends by arguing for a music that neither loses touch with tradition nor sacrifices vitality.

2326. Good, Edwin. "The Bible and American Music." In *The Bible and American Arts and Letters*, Giles Gunn, ed. Philadelphia, PA: Fortress Press; Chico, CA: Scholars Press, 1983. 131-158. A study of the use of the Bible in American religious music. Particular emphasis is on psalmody and the music of William Billings and Charles Ives.

2327. Lowens, Irving. *Music and Musicians in Early America*. New York: W.W. Norton, 1964. Reprints of articles written in the 1950s by one of the leading scholars in pre-Civil War American music.

2328. McDaniel, Stanley Robert. *Church Song and the Cultivated Tradition in New England and New York*. D.M.A. diss., University of Southern California, 1983. A study of the factors that transformed American church music from little more than recreational song singing, at the beginning of the 19th century, to a well-developed artistic undertaking by the end.

2329. Reid, Robert Addison. *Russian Sacred Choral Music and its Assimilation into and Impact on the American A Cappella Choir Movement*. D.M.A. thesis, University of Texas at Austin, 1983. Late-18th- and 19th-century unaccompanied choral music of the Russian Orthodox Church entered the United States, first through the Episcopal Church in America and subsequently in the American *a cappella* choir movement of the first half of this century. This study traces the infusion of Russian sacred choral music into the American *a cappella* repertory and discusses its impact on that movement.

2330. Routley, Erik. *Music Leadership in the Church: A Conversation Chiefly with my American Friends*. Nashville, TN: Abingdon Press, 1967. Originally presented before seminary audiences, the three pieces that make up the book compare English and American music leadership styles as they relate to Church history, the Bible, and Christian worship.

2331. Simmonds, Jim N. "Musical Theatre: A Prelude to the Gospel." *Crux* 21, 2/June (1985): 10-16. On the ethical aspects of musical theatre and its importance to evangelistic worship. Includes reply by M. Ertman, pp. 17-18.

2332. Smith, James G. and Thomas Brawley. "Choral Music." In *NGDAM*, Vol. 1. 1986. 430-436.

2333. Stevenson, Robert. *Protestant Church Music in America: A Short Survey of Men and Movements from 1564 to the Present*. New York: W.W. Norton, 1966.

2334. Topp, Dale. *Music in the Christian Community: Claiming Musical Power for Service and Worship*. Grand Rapids, MI: W.B. Eerdmans Publishing Co., 1976/repr.

2335. Westermeyer, Paul. "Twentieth-Century American Hymnody and Church Music: Essays in Honor of Martin E. Marty." In *New Dimensions in American Religious History*, Jay P. Dolan and James P. Wind, ed. Grand Rapids, MI: W. B. Eerdmans Publishing Co., 1993. 175-207. A survey of 20th-century church music from the standpoints of 1) the lack of historical analysis of 20th-century church music, 2) church music teachers and scholars, 3) 20th-century ecumenicity as shown in hymnals, 4) the new consensus of the 70s and 80s, and 5) the diversity of the 90s. Includes a long list of hymnals, chronologically arranged.

2336. Wienandt, Elwyn A. and Robert H. Young. *The Anthem in England and America*. New York: Free Press, 1970. The authors trace the history of the anthem beginning with the English anthems, especially the Non-Conformist anthem traditions, through the subsequent development of an American style.

PSALMODY AND HYMNODY: GENERAL HISTORIES AND SURVEYS

2337. Beckwith, John. *Sing Out the Glad News: Hymn Tunes in Canada*. Proceedings of the Conference Held in Toronto, February 7 and 8, 1986, Organized by the Institute for Canadian Music, Faculty of Music, University of Toronto: CanMus Documents 1, Toronto: Institute for Canadian Music, 1987. A collection of seven articles on hymnody among Anglo-Canadians, hymnody among native Canadians, and the singing school tradition.

2338. Christ-Janer, Albert, C.W. Hughes, and C. Sprague Smith, ed. *American Hymns Old and New: Notes on the Hymns and Biographies of the Authors and Composers*. 2 vols. New York: Columbia University Press, 1980. The most exhaustive study of this subject.

2339. Cooke, Nym. *American Psalmodists in Contact and Collaboration, 1770-1820*. Ph.D. diss., University of Michigan, 1990.

2340. Crawford, Richard, ed. *The Core Repertory of Early American Psalmody: First Line Index*. Recent Researches in American Music, nos. 11-12, Madison, WI: A-R Editions, 1984. Transcription of the 101 sacred compositions most frequently printed between 1698 and 1810. Crawford provides a wealth of information about and resources for the compositions including complete texts and music, biographies, and listings of additional references.

2341. Crawford, Richard. "Psalmody." In *NGDAM*, Vol. 3. 1986. 635-643. A revision of the author's article in *Grove 6*, Vol.15: 345-347.

2342. Echols, Paul C. "Hymnody." In *NGDAM*, Vol. 2. 1986. 446-455.

2343. Foote, Henry Wilder. *Three Centuries of American Hymnody*. Hamden CT: Archon Books, 1940/repr. 1968.

2344. Hinks, D.R. *Brethren Hymn Books and Hymnals, 1720-1884*. Gettysburg, PA: Brethren Heritage Press, 1986. A review of Brethren German and English hymn books highlighting changes in style, presentation, and content especially as they reflect concurrent changes in the life and agenda of the Brethren community. Includes an annotated bibliography of all relevant hymn books and hymnals.

2345. Hughes, C.W. *American Hymns Old and New: Notes on the Hymns and Biographies of the Authors and Composers*. New York: Columbia University Press, 1980.

2346. Richardson, Paul A., ed. "Theses and Dissertations Related to Hymnody." *Hymn* 42, Jan. (1991): 41.

2347. Rogal, S. *Sisters of Sacred Song: A Catalogue of British and American Women Hymnodists*. New York: 1981.

2348. Stigberg, D.K. *Congregational Psalmody in Eighteenth Century New England*. M.A. thesis, University of Illinois, 1970.

2349. Sydnor, James Rawlings. *The Hymn and Congregational Singing*. Richmond, VA: John Knox Press, 1960. Dedicated to the improvement of congregational hymn singing. On the structure and use of hymns, with helpful lists of hymns for different occasions and of different types.

2350. Sydnor, James Rawlings. *Introducing a New Hymnal: How to Improve Congregational Singing*. Chicago: G.I.A., 1989. A practical guide for successfully introducing a new hymnal into a congregation and improving congregational singing in Protestant worship.

2351. Temperley, Nicholas. "Psalms, Metrical." In *NGDAM*, Vol. 3. 1986. 643-648. Essentially the same article as that in *Grove 6*, Vol. 15, 376-381.

29

North America: Religious Music of Euro-American Origin

NEW ENGLAND

2352. Campbell, Donald Perry. *Puritan Belief and Musical Practices in the Sixteenth, Seventeenth, and Eighteenth Centuries.* D.M.A. thesis, Southwestern Baptist Theological Seminary, 1994.

2353. Crawford, Richard. "Massachusetts Musicians and the Core Repertory of Early American Psalmody. Vol. 2: Music in Homes and in Churches." In *Music in Colonial Massachusetts, 1630-1820*, B. Lambert, ed. Boston 1985. 583-630. Crawford indexes the 101 most frequently printed psalm settings in the US from 1698 to 1810, with a brief historical overview of the evolution in early American psalmody and biographical notes on composers.

2354. Crawford, Richard and D.W. Krummel. "Early American Music Printing and Publishing." In *Printing and Society in Early America*, W. Joyce et al., ed. Worcester, MA 1983. 186 ff., 215 ff.

2355. Davenport, Linda Gilbert. *Maine's Sacred Tunebooks, 1800-1830: Divine Song on the Northeast Frontier.* Ph.D. diss., University of Colorado, 1991.

2356. Davies, H. *The Worship of the American Puritans, 1629-1730.* New York: P. Lang, 1990. Chapter 6, entitled "Praises," describes the restricted role music and singing were allowed in Puritan worship.

2357. Dean, Talmadge W. *The Organ in Eighteenth Century English Colonial America.* Ph.D. diss., University of Southern California, 1960.

2358. Johnson, H. Earle. *Hallelujah, Amen! The Story of the Handel and Haydn Society of Boston.* New York: Da Capo Press, 1965/repr. 1981. New ed. with intro. by Richard Crawford.

NEW ENGLAND PSALMODY TO 1720

2359. Inserra, Lorraine and H. Wiley Hitchcock. *The Music of Henry Ainsworth's Psalter.* I.S.A.M. Monographs, No. 15, Brooklyn, NY: Institute for Studies in American Music, 1981. A facsimile and transcription of the influential psalter published in Amsterdam in 1612. Includes essay "Early Protestant Psalmody" and commentary on Henry Ainsworth and the text and music of his psalter.

2360. Lambert, Barbara. "The Musical Puritans." *Bulletin of the Society for the Preservation of New England Antiquities* 62 (1972): 66-75.

2361. Tallmadge, William. "Folk Organum: A Study of Origins." *American Music* 2, 3 (1984): 47-65. After reviewing the theories of the origins of organum, Tallmadge relates the earliest instance of organum to lining-out and the singing of psalm tunes in America in the *New England Courant* of 1724.

2362. Temperley, Nicholas. "The Old Way of Singing: Its Origins and Development." *JAMS* 34 (1981): 511-44. Writing with both a sympathetic and scholarly pen, Temperley traces the context and development of the "Old Way" or "Common" singing style and attempts to establish an organic explanation for its existence in European and American Protestant congregations. Attention is paid to concurrent theological and liturgical developments.

NEW ENGLAND PSALMODY, 1720-1770

2363. Becker, Laura L. "Ministers vs. Laymen: The Singing Controversy in Puritan New England, 1720-1740." *New England Quarterly* 55 (1982): 79-96. Documents the debate about the correct way to sing psalmody.

2364. Irwin, Joyce. "The Theology of 'Regular Singing,'" *New England Quarterly* 51 (1978): 176-192. Irwin reviews the primary theological positions put forth during the lengthy debates over regular singing in the 1720's with special attention to the challenge to Calvinist orthodoxy that such singing presented. Studies the sermons and writings of John Cotton, Cotton Mather, Thomas Symmes, and Thomas Walter.

2365. Osterhout, Paul R. "Note Reading and Regular Singing in Eighteenth-Century New England." *American Music* 4, 2, Summer (1986): 125-44. Challenging the assumption that Regular singing was synonymous with singing from written notation, Osterhout suggests that for the rural congregations of Massachusetts and Connecticut regular singing was used instead to describe the general musical practice of a given community. The author describes the evolution in singing style in Farmington, Hartford, Windsor, and East Windsor, CT.

2366. Owen, Barbara. "American Organ Music and Playing from 1700." *Organ Institute Quarterly* 10 (1963): 7-13. A brief history of the organ as it was introduced into Protestant worship in the 18th century and grew to acceptance and prominence in the mid-19th century. Includes information on influential composers, compositions, organists, and congregations.

SINGING SCHOOLS FROM BILLINGS TO THE 20TH CENTURY

2367. Bottoms, J.S. *The Singing School in Texas: 1971*. Ph.D. diss., University of Colorado, 1972.

2368. Britton, Allen P. "The Singing School Movement in the United States." In *IMSCR, VIII, New York 1961*, Jan LaRue, ed. Kassel and Basle 1961-2. 89 ff.

2369. Crawford, Richard. "Fuging-tune." In *NGDAM*, Vol. 2. 1986. 175-176.

2370. Crawford, Richard and David Warren Steel. "Singing School." In *NGDAM*, Vol. 4. 1986. 233-234.

2371. De Jong, Mary Gosselink. "'Both Pleasure and Profit': William Billings and the Uses of Music." *William and Mary Quarterly* 42, 1 (1985): 104-116. An examination of Billing's writings on music and the controversy over regular singing. Centers on his sermons and other writings, as well as on his fuging tunes.

2372. Graham, J.R. "Early Twentieth-Century Singing Schools in Kentucky Appalachia." *Journal of Research in Music Education* 19 (1971): 77. A profile of the teachers, methods and styles employed in the singing schools of Kentucky with attention to the shape note system.

2373. Kroeger, Karl. *The Worcester Collection of Sacred Harmony and Sacred Music in America, 1786-1803*. Ph.D. diss., Brown University, 1976. A comprehensive study of the Worcester Collection with reference to its general history, musical characteristics, hymns, fugue-tunes, and anthems.

2374. Kroeger, Karl. *The Complete Works of William Billings*. Boston: The American Musicological Society and The Colonial Society of Massechusetts, 1981. See Introduction, pp. 13-63.

2375. Kroeger, Karl. "William Billings and the Hymn-Tune." *Hymn* 37, 3 (1986): 19-26. On Billings and his tunebooks, his taste in texts, and performance practice.

2376. Kroeger, Karl. "The Music of William Billings: A Summary of Research." In *Report of Proceedings: Ph.D. in Music Symposium. April 5-7, 1985*, William Kearns and William Reeves, ed. Boulder, CO: University of Colorado, 1988. 131-133. Primarily on the republication of the complete works of Billings.

2377. Lowens, Irving. "The Origins of the American Fuging-Tune." In *Music and Musicians in Early America*, New York: W.W. Norton, 1964. 237-248. (*JAMS* 6, 1: 1953: 43-52) The American fuging-tune is not an attempt to create a fugue in the style of Bach; it is based, rather, on trends in English psalmody from the 16th to 18th centuries.

2378. Murray, Sterling. "Timothy Swan and Yankee Psalmody." *MQ* 61, 3, July (1975): 433-463. Murray focusses on the life and career of American psalmodist Swan (1758-1842) as a means of documenting and illuminating the influence and contributions of 18th and 19th century Yankee composers as a whole. The author cites excerpts from Swan's compositions.

2379. Nathan, Hans. *William Billings: Data & Documents*. Biographies in American Music, Detroit: Information Coordinators, Inc, 1976.

2380. Temperley, Nicholas and Charles G. Manns. *Fuging Tunes in the Eighteenth Century*. Detroit Studies in Music Bibliography, No. 49, Detroit MI: Information Coordinators, 1983. A comprehensive study and catalog of both British and American fuging tunes.

2381. Worst, J.W. *New England Psalmody 1760-1810: Analysis of an American Idiom*. Ph.D. diss., University of Michigan, 1974.

REVIVALS, AWAKENINGS, AND HYMNS

2382. Bruce, Dickson D., Jr. *And They All Sang Hallelujah: Plain-Folk Camp-Meeting Religion 1800-1845*. Knoxville TN: University of Tennessee Press, 1974.

2383. Catharine, Morgan. "Sacred Folk Song in America." *American Guild of Organists Quarterly* 12 (1967): 54-60.

2384. Crawford, Richard. "Watts for Singing: Metrical Poetry in American Sacred Tunebooks, 1761-1785." *Early American Literature* 11 (1976): 139.

2385. Downey, James Cecil. *The Music of American Revivalism, 1740-1800*. Ph.D. diss., Tulane University, 1968.

2386. Hammond, P. *Music in Urban Revivalism in the Northern United States, 1800-1835*. Ph.D. diss., Southern Baptist Theological Seminary, 1974.

2387. Hulan, Richard Huffman. "The American Revolution in Hymnody." *Hymn* 35, 4 (1984): 199-203. A brief chronicle of the impact of Cane Ridge (KY) camp meetings of the early 19th century on hymn writing.

2388. Hustad, D. "The Explosion of Popular Hymnody." *The Hymn* 33 (1982): 159 ff.

2389. Johnson, Charles Albert. *The Frontier Camp Meeting: Religion's Harvest Time.* Dallas: Southern Methodist University Press, 1955. Chapter 10 of this study covers the role music played in popularizing camp meeting religion with attention to the "unwritten music" of the Methodist camp meetings. Several surviving hymn texts are cited.

2390. Koskoff, Ellen. "The Joyful Sound: Women in the 19th-century United States Hymnody Tradition." In *Women and Music in Cross-cultural Perspective,* Ellen Koskoff, ed. New York: Greenwood Press, 1987. 177-194. The most popular, and disturbing, religious expression of 19th-century evangelical revivalism is made the more so by the increasingly active participation of women as lyricists, composers, performers, and journalists.

2391. Marini, Stephen. "Rehearsal for Revival: Sacred Singing and the Great Awakening in America [1734-1745]." In *Sacred Sound,* Joyce Erwin, ed. 1983. 71-91. On the importance of sacred singing to the Great Awakening and of the latter to the development by America's evangelical Calvinists of a distinctively American style of hymnody. (See bibliography for references to 18th century sources.)

2392. McKissick, M. *A Study of the Function of Music in the Major Religious Revivals in America since 1875.* MA thesis, University of Southern California, 1957.

2393. Rogal, Samuel J. *Sing Glory and Hallelujah! Historical and Biographical Guide to 'Gospel Hymns Nos. 1 to 6 Complete.'* Westport, CT: Greenwood Press, 1996.

2394. Rothenbusch, Esther Heidi. *The Role of 'Gospel Hymns Nos. 1 to 6' (1875-1894) in American Revivalism.* Ph.D. diss., University of Michigan, 1991. Compiled by musician Ira D. Sankey and used by evangelist Dwight L Moody, this collection of gospel hymns represents, more than does any other collection, the urban revivalism that was inspired by such music. After discussing the theological and musical origins of gospel hymnody in earlier American revivalism, the author analyzes the texts and musical styles in the Gospel Hymns repertory, documenting in the process the shift toward a more personal evangelical theology.

2395. Sallee, James. *A History of Evangelistic Hymnody.* Grand Rapids, MI: Baker Book House, 1978.

2396. Sizer, Sandra S. *Gospel Hymns and Social Religion: The Rhetoric of Nineteenth-Century Revivalism.* Philadelphia: Temple University Press, 1978. Employing a quantitative approach to metaphorical analysis, Sizer presents her studies of the strong correlation between 19th-century Revivalism and the rhetoric of hymns in use at the time. Emphasis is placed on the often conflicting understandings of passion.

2397. Weiss, Joanne Grayeski. *The Relationship Between the 'Great Awakening' and the Transitions from Psalmody to Hymnody in the New England Colonies*. D.A., Ball State University, 1988. The change in theology from a theocentric to an anthropocentric viewpoint characteristic of the Great Awakening is the single most important factor—both the rationale and the means—in the change from psalmody to hymnody. A study of the congregational song of the Congregationalists, Presbyterians and Baptists.

SHAPE-NOTE MUSIC; *THE SACRED HARP*

2398. Boyd, J.D. "Negro Sacred Harp Songsters in Mississippi." *Mississippi Folklore Register* 5 (1971): 60.

2399. Carnes, Jim. "White Sacred Harp Singing." In *Alabama Folklife: Collected Essays*, Stephen Martin, ed. Birmingham: University of Alabama, 1989. 45-51.

2400. Cobb, Buell E. *The Sacred Harp: A Tradition and Its Music*. Rev. ed., Athens, GA: University of Georgia Press, 1978/repr. 1989. The definitive work on the Sacred Harp movement and its traditional practice. The work continues to serve as the inspiration and reference for contemporary singings across the U.S. and is considered essential to the survival of Sacred Harp singing.

2401. Dyen, D.J. *The Role of Shape-note Singing in the Musical Culture of Black Communities in Southeast Alabama*. Ph.D. diss., University of Illinois, 1977.

2402. Ellington, Charles Linwood. *The Sacred Harp Tradition of the South: Its Origin and Evolution*. Ph.D. diss., Florida State University, 1969.

2403. Eskew, Harry. "'Christian Harmony' Singing in Alabama: Its Adaptation and Survival." *Inter-American Music Review* 10, 2/Spring-Summer (1989): 169-75. Presented in a unique form of 7-shape notation when first published (1883), the "Southern Harmony" was revised most recently in 1958. Changes include the omission of musical rudiments, the use of a widely accepted 7-shape notation, the removal of 179 unused songs (out of 532 from 1883) and the addition of 109 new songs. Due to the loss of leadership with the death of John Dearson, Sacred Harp singing is in decline.

2404. Eskew, Harry and James C. Downey. "Shape-note Hymnody." In *NGDAM*, Vol. 4. 1986. 201-205.

2405. Garber, Susan. *The Sacred Harp Revival in New England: Its Singers and Singings*. M.A. thesis, Wesleyan University, 1987.

2406. Hall, P.M. *The 'Musical Million': A Study and Analysis of the Periodical Promoting Music Reading through Shape-notes in North America from 1870 to 1914*. Ph.D. diss., Catholic University of America, 1970.

2407. Maney, Debbie, et al.,. "The Shape Note Singing Project." *Foxfire* 18, 4 (1984): 194-256. An introduction to the special issue on shape note and convention gospel singing.

2408. McKenzie, Wallace. "Anthems of the *Sacred Harp* Tunesmiths." *American Music* 6, 3 (1988): 247-63. After surveying the various, and sometimes conflicting, applications of the term 'anthem' in the late 18th and 19th centuries, the author considers anthems from three later periods. Changes include the addition of an alto voice to those a3, greater use of chromaticism, and passages of atypical expressiveness in their relationship to models included in "The Sacred Harp" of 1844.

2409. Perrin, Phil D. "Systems of Scale Notation in Nineteenth-Century American Tunebooks." *Journal of Research in Music Education* 18 (1970): 257-264.

2410. Sabol, Steven L. *Sacred Harp & Shape-note Music: Resources*. Fort Worth, TX: Hymn Society, 1994.

2411. Smith, Timothy Alan. *A Taxonomy of Pitch Formations, and an Implication-Realization Analysis of Folk-Hymn Melodies from the 'Repository of Sacred Music Part Second,' 'Kentucky Harmony,' 'Missouri Harmony,' 'Southern Harmony,' and 'Sacred Harp.'* DMA, University of Oregon, 1988.

2412. Stanislaw, Richard J. *A Checklist of Four-Shape Shape-Note Tunebooks*. (ISAM Monograph, 10), Brooklyn: Institute for Studies in American Music, 1978.

2413. Sutton, Brett. "Shape-Note Tune Books and Primitive Hymns." *Ethnomusicology* 26 (1982): 11-26. In this history of Primitive Baptist singing in the Blue Ridge region of Virginia and North Carolina, Sutton proposes that the formulation of the repertory occurred before the Civil War, that shape-note books informed the repertory, that once the church split into Black and White sectors, the Black's version of the music varied more from the original due to oral tradition, and that certain tunes resisted change more than others due to identification with social factors in the songs.

2414. Tadlock, P. "Shape-Note Singing in Mississippi." In *Discourse in Ethnomusicology: Essays in Honor of George List*, C. Card et al., ed. Bloomington, IN: University of Indiana, 1978.

2415. Willett, Henry. "Wiregrass Notes: Black Sacred Harp Singing from Southeast Alabama." In *Alabama Folklife: Collected Essays*, Stephen Martin, ed. Birmingham: University of Alabama, 1989. 52-56.

MORAVIANS AND OTHER GERMAN-AMERICAN SECTS

2416. Bohlman, Philip V. "Hymnody in the Rural German-American Community of the Upper Midwest." *Hymn* 35 (1984): 158-64. Bohlman focusses on the German-American hymn tradition both in its tenacity and adaptability over the past 150 years.

2417. Bower, Peter, ed. "Instrumental Music." *Reformed Liturgy and Music* 25, Sum. (1991): 111-135, 145-147. Ten articles on music and music instruments in worship in Reformed Churches.

2418. Bower, Peter C., ed. "Worship in the Global Congregation." *Reformed Liturgy and Music* 25, Fall (1991): 158-188, 201-203, 208-210. Nine articles on music and worship in Reformed Churches worldwide.

2419. Branstine, Wesley R. *The Moravian Church and its Trombone Choir in America.* D.M.A. diss., North Texas State University, 1984. On the musical heritage of the Moravian church and the trombone choir and its use in Bethlehem, PA.

2420. Caldwell, Alice May. *Music of the Moravian Liturgische Gesänge.* Ph.D. diss., New York University, 1987.

2421. Duncan, Timothy Paul. *The Role of the Organ in Moravian Sacred Music Between 1740-1840.* D.M.A., The University of North Carolina at Greensboro, 1989. Organ accompaniment was a vital part of all forms of congregational singing. A study of the music used in singing services and of the important role of the organ.

2422. Farlee, Lloyd Winfield. *A History of the Church Music of the Amana Society, the Community of True Inspiration.* Ph.D. diss., University of Iowa, 1966.

2423. Getz, Russell P. "Music in the Ephrata Cloister." *Communal Societies* 2 (1982): 27-38.

2424. Hartzell, Lawrence W. *Ohio Moravian Music.* Winston-Salem, NC: Moravian Music Foundation Press; London & Cranbury, NJ: Associated University Presses, 1988. The principal study of Moravian music in Ohio. Surveys music in the Ohio Indian missions between 1772 and 1823 and music in Moravian congregations between 1799 and 1842. Also discusses the music of principal composers.

2425. Ingram, Jeannine. "Moravians and Music in America." In *Southern Humanities Conference: Winston Salem, 1977*, W.E. Ray, ed. Winston-Salem, NC 1977. 54 ff.

2426. Ingram, Jeannine. "Music in American Moravian Communities: Transplanted Traditions in Indigenous Practices." *Communal Societies* 2, Autumn (1982): 39-51.

2427. Kroeger, Karl. "Moravian Music in 19th-century American Tunebooks." *Moravian Music Foundation Bulletin* 18, 1 (1973): 1 ff. Kroeger questions how much real impact Moravian music had on mainstream American music in light of its contributions to that music with attention to anthems, solo songs, and chorales.

2428. Kroeger, Karl. "The Moravian Choral Tradition: Yesterday and Today." *Choral Journal* 19, 5 (1979): 5-9, 12. A brief discussion of performance practice and modern editions.

2429. Kroeger, Karl. "On the Early Performance of Moravian Chorales." *Moravian Music Foundation Bulletin* 24, 2 (1979): 2 ff. Through a study of manuscripts of 18th and 19th-century chorale melodies, Kroeger attempts to tease out answers to questions about the chorales. Drawing heavily from primary sources, Kroeger addresses the use of organ for accompaniment, singing style and tempo.

2430. Martin, Betty Jean. *The Ephrata Cloister and Its Music, 1732-1785: The Cultural, Religious, and Bibliographical Background.* Ph.D. diss., University of Maryland, 1974. An excellent study of the music and musicians, hymns and choral works, and bibliography of the Ephrata Cloister. Analyses hymnals, music, and texts. With musical examples.

2431. Nolte, E.V. "Sacred Music in the Early American Moravian Communities." *Church Music* 2 (1971): 16-25. St. Louis. A brief look at the origins of the renewed Moravian Church in Germany in the 1720s, its composers and its choral music. Includes a list of published edd. of Moravian choral and solo vocal music. Reprinted by the Moravian Music Foundation, 1971.

2432. Old, Hughes Oliphant. *Worship That is Reformed According to Scripture.* Atlanta, GA: John Knox, 1984. On the liturgy of the Reformed Church.

2433. Polman, Bertus Frederick. *Church Music and Liturgy in the Christian Reformed Church of North America.* Ph.D. diss., University of Minnesota, 1980. On practices in the Christian Reformed Church from its 16th-century Dutch roots to the current trend of declining use of psalmody and increasing use of hymnody.

2434. Poole, Franklin Parker. *The Moravian Musical Heritage: Johann Christian Geisler's Music in America.* Thesis, George Peabody College for Teachers, 1971. A study of the anthems by Geisler performed in American Moravian settlements.

2435. Redway, Virginia Larkin. "James Parker and the 'Dutch Church.'" *MQ* 24 (1980): 481-500. A lively narrative of the life and times of Parker who is credited with printing an English language psalm book for the reformed Protestant Dutch church. Focuses on the shift from Dutch to English in Dutch church services.

2436. Rothrock, Donna. "Moravian Music Education: Forerunner to Public School Music." *Bulletin of Historical Research in Music Education* 8, 2 (1987): 63-82. An excellent introduction to Moravian practice of requiring the recitation of hymns and piano instruction as parts of a sound education.

2437. Vanderwel, David, ed. "Praise and Worship." *Reformed Worship* 20, June (1991): 2-41. Articles on worship in the Reformed Church movement.

2438. Westermeyer, Paul. "German Reformed Hymnody in the United States." *The Hymn* 31 (1980): 2: 89-94, 3: 200-204, 212. By 1780, there were more than 200 German Reformed Churches in Pennsylvania and environs. Westermeyer briefly surveys their history, liturgy, and response to revivalism, ecclesiastical civil war, and shift to the English language in the early 20th century.

2439. Wolf, Edward Christopher. "Two Divergent Traditions of German-American Hymnody in Maryland circa 1800." *American Music* 3, 3 (1985): 299. Wolf compares and contrasts the urban inclination to remain wholly faithful to the musical practices of German Lutheran hymnody and the rural departure from that model. Focuses on the pairing of German chorals with American tunes and the tunebooks of Adam Arnold.

THE MENNONITES, AMISH, AND DOUKHOBORS

2440. Bartel, Lee R. "The Tradition of the Amish in Music." *The Hymn* 37, 4 (1986): 20-26.

2441. Berg, Wesley. *From Russia with Music: A Study of the Mennonite Choral Singing Tradition in Canada.* Winnipeg: Hyperion Press, 1985. A detailed but readable study focusing on the Russian origins and history, religious context, primary leaders and musical qualities of Mennonite music.

2442. Hohmann, Rupert Karl. *The Church Music of the Old Order Amish of the United States.* Ph.D. diss., Northwestern University, Chicago, 1959.

2443. Klassen, Doreen Helen. *Singing Mennonite: Low German Songs among the Mennonites.* Winnipeg: University of Manitoba Press, 1989. Chapter 3 of this detailed study of various Mennonite song genres covers three types of religious songs: traditional, immigrant, and contemporary. Includes text, tune and commentary for 12 hymns.

2444. Klymasz, Robert B. "Tracking the 'Living Book': Doukhobor Song in Canada since 1899." *Canadian Folk Music Journal* 21 (1993): 40-44.

2445. Krahn, Cornelius, ed. *The Mennonite Encyclopedia. A Comprehensive Reference Work on the Anabaptist-Mennonite Movement.* Hillsboro, KS: Mennonite Brethren Publishing House; Newton, KS: Mennonite Publication Office; Scottdale, PA: Mennonite Publishing House, 1955-9/repr. 1969. See "Amish Division," "Ausbund," "Hymnology of the American Mennonites," "Hymnology of the Mennonites of West and East Prussia, Danzig, and Russia," "Music, Church," and "Old Order Amish."

2446. Martens, Helen. "The Music of Some Religious Minorities in Canada." *Ethnomusicology* 16, 3 (1972): 372-380. Music of the Mennonites, Hutterites, and Doukhobors.

2447. Mealing, Francis. *Our People's Way: A Study in the Doukhobor Hymnody and Folklife.* Philadelphia, PA: Mealing, 1972, 1978. Originally a Ph.D. diss., University of Pennsylvania.

2448. Oyer, Mary. *Exploring the Mennonite Hymnal: Essays.* Newton KS: Faith and Life Press; Scottsdale PA: Mennonite Publishing House, 1980.

2449. Peacock, Kenneth. *Songs of the Doukhobors: An Introductory Outline.* Ottawa: Queen's Printer for Canada, 1970. A songbook of religious and secular songs of a Russian Christian sect living in various Canadian provinces. Includes the text with translation and tunes for three psalms and 11 hymns.

2450. Penner, Larry. *Finding a Voice: A Discussion of Mennonite Music in Mennonite Culture.* Goshen, IN: Pinchpenny Press, 1992.

2451. Ressler, M.E. "A History of Mennonite Hymnody." *Journal of Church Music* 23 (1976): 2. A brief history of European and American Old Mennonite Church hymnody highlighting the 19th-century innovation of English language hymnody and the complementary use of tune books and singing schools.

2452. Schmidt, Orlando. *Church Music and Worship among the Mennonites.* Newton, KS: Faith and Life Press; Scottdale, PA: Mennonite Publishing House, 1981.

2453. Springer, Nelson and A. J. Klaussen. *Mennonite Bibliography, 1631-1961.* Scottdale, PA: Herald Press, 1977.

2454. Thomas, Dwight. "A Brief Introduction to the Hymnody and Musical Life of the Old Order River Brethren of Central Pennsylvania." *Hymn* 35, 2 (1984): 107-14. Thomas describes the dominant characteristics of the hymn style including slurs, lack of musical accompaniment, pitch, vocal quality, tempo and harmony.

THE SHAKERS

2455. Andrews, Edward Deming. *The Gift to be Simple. Songs, Dances and Rituals of the American Shakers*. New York: Dover Publications, 1940/repr. 1962. An authoritative account of the history, dance movements, and music of the Shakers.

2456. Andrews, Edward Deming. "The Dance in Shaker Ritual." *Dance Index* 1, April (1942): 56-67. A full description of Shaker religious dance.

2457. Bertolino-Green, Dianne Lyn. *Right-Brain Expressions of Religious Experience: A Bimodal Paradigm in Shaker Case Studies*. Ph.D. diss., The Southern Baptist Theological Seminary, 1987. Bimodal theory as applied to the expressions of religious experience of the Shakers—visions, glossolalia, dance, music, art, manufacture, and feminine equality—demonstrate well-being on the part of the participants, not pathology, according to the categories advanced. Explores implications of incorporating a balance of modes and feminine approaches to religious experience.

2458. Christenson, Donald E. *Music of the Shakers from Union Village, Ohio: A Repertory Study and Tune Index of the Manuscripts Originating in the 1840's*. Ph.D. diss., Ohio State University, 1988.

2459. Christenson, Donald E. "A History of the Early Shakers and Their Music." *Hymn* 39, 1 (1988): 17-22. On the founder of the sect, Ann Lee, and the establishment of communities in America.

2460. Cook, Harold. *Shaker Music: A Manifestation of American Folk Culture*. Lewisburg PA: Bucknell University Press, 1973. Diaries, correspondences, etc., as well as interviews with witnessess and participants, are used to constuct a picture of shaker music and musical culture, particularly notation, theory, and composition.

2461. Davies, J.G., P. Van Zyl, and F.M. Young. *A Shaker Dance Service Reconstructed*. Austin, TX: Sharing Co., 1984.

2462. Destoches, H. *The American Shakers*. Amherst, MA: University of Mass. Press, 1971. Within the context of an interdiscipilinary study of the Shakers, the author gives a sociological overview of the dance, music, and singing of Shaker communities drawing heavily from primary texts and the analysis of Edward Andrews.

2463. Fujie, Linda. "'Draw the Chord of Union Stronger': The Musical Life of the American Shakers." *The World of Music* 35, 3 (1993): 51-79. On Shaker history, the role of music in Shaker religious expression, and current song practice and repertory.

2464. Hall, Roger L. "Shaker Hymnody—An American Communal Tradition." *The Hymn* 27, 1 (1976): 22-29. Twenty Shaker hymnals were printed between 1813 and 1900. Hall groups these into three periods—1813-1847, 1852-1880, and 1875-1900—then compares three hymnals, one from each period, as to the number of hymns, notation, hymn origin, and settings. A transcription of a 19th-century dance song is included.

2465. Patterson, Daniel W. *The Shaker Spiritual.* Princeton: Princeton University Press, 1979. An outstanding study of this subject.

2466. Patterson, Daniel W. "Shaker Music." *Communal Societies* 2, Autumn (1982): 53-64.

2467. Patterson, Daniel W. *Gift Drawings and Gift Song. A Study of Two Forms of Shaker Inspiration.* Sabbathday Lake, MA: The United Society of Shakers, 1983.

2468. Richmond, Mary L. *Shaker Literature: A Bibliography.* 2 vols. Hancock, MA: Shaker Community, Inc. destr. by University Press of New England, 1977. Vol. 1: By the Shakers; Vol. 2, About the Shakers.

2469. Schaeffer, Vicki J. *An Historical Survey of Shaker Hymnody Expressing the Christian Virtues of Innocence and Simplicity.* D.M. diss., Indiana University, 1992. The large number of mid-19th-century hymn texts that stress innocence and simplicity and such related virtues as self-denial and battling against the flesh indicates the importance of these virtues to this communistic religious sect.

2470. Terri, Salli. "The Gift of Shaker Music." *Music Educator's Journal* 62, 1 (1975): 22-35. This survey includes facsimiles, musical examples, and other illustrations.

OTHER PROTESTANT SECTS OF EUROPEAN OR EURO-AMERICAN ORIGIN

General

2471. [American Religious Denominations, Music of]. In *New Grove's Dictionary of American Music*, 1986. See "Amish and Mennonite Music, "Baptist Church, music of the," "Church of Christ, Scientist, music of the," "Church of Jesus Christ of Latter-day Saints [Mormon Church], music of the," "Episcopal Church, music of the," "Lutheran Church, music of the," "Methodist Church, music of the," "Moravian Church, music of the," "Presbyterian Church, music of the," "Roman Catholic Church, music of the," "Shaker music," "Unitarian Universalist Church, music of the," and "United Church of Christ, music of the."

2472. Patterson, Daniel W. "Word, Song, And Motion: Instruments of Celebration among Protestant Radicals in Early Nineteenth-Century America." In *Celebrations: Studies in Festivity and Ritual*, Victor Turner, ed. Washington, D.C.: Smithsonian Institution, 1982. 220-230. Physical movement, heightened tonal and rhythmic speech, and patterned sacred song, rather than ceremonial objects, were the principal means through which early American Protestant radical sects expressed their religious experience. Motion, word, and song addressed the main concern of these sects: the transformation of personality and the formation of sacred community.

Baptist

2473. Drummond, Robert Paul. *A History of Music among Primitive Baptists since 1800*. D.A. thesis, University of Northern Colorado, 1986. The American folk hymns that have long constituted the most important worship music of the Primitive Baptists and have long resisted any attempts at modernization are now becoming a body of choral art music worthy of concert performance.

2474. Drummond, R. Paul. *A Portion for the Singers: A History of Music among Primitive Baptists since 1800*. Atwood, TN: The Christian Baptist Library & and Publishing Co., 1989. A historical study of the compilers, composers, and songs of the Primitive Baptists in the South and Southeast. Includes many music illustrations.

2475. Duncan, Curtis Daniel. *A Historical Survey of the Development of the Black Baptist Church in the United States as a Study of Performance Practices Associated with Dr. Watts Hymn Singing: A Source Book for Teachers*. Ed.D. diss., Washington University, 1979. On the history of lined hymn singing in the 17th and 18th centuries, and on the influence on 20th-century practice of life on plantations, survivals from African music, and characteristics of Black singing.

2476. Editors. *Church Music in Baptist History*. 19. 1984. Complete issue.

2477. Eskew, Harry L. "Southern Baptist Contributions to Hymnody." *Baptist History and Heritage* 19 (1984): 27-35.

2478. Gregory, David Louis. *Psalmody in the Mid-Nineteenth-Century Southern Baptist Tradition*. M.C.M., The Southern Baptist Theological Seminary, 1987. A study of the effect and continuing influence of psalmody upon the hymnody of early Southern Baptists.

2479. May, Lynn E. Jr., ed. "Shaping Influences on Baptist Church Music." *Baptist History and Heritage* 27, Apr. (1992): 3-41. A collection of four articles on Baptist hymnody.

2480. Measels, Donald Clark. *A Catalog of Source Readings in Southern Baptist Church Music: 1828-1890*. DMA, Southern Baptist Theological Seminary, 1986.

2481. Murrell, Irvin Henry, Jr. *An Examination of Southern Ante-bellum Baptist Hymnals and Tunebooks as Indicators of the Congregational Hymn and Tune Repertories of the Period with an Analysis of Representative Tunes*. D.M.A. diss., New Orleans Baptist Theological Seminary, 1984. A search for the hymns and tunes found in common in Southern ante-bellum Baptist hymnals and tunebooks and an examination of the common tune repertory to determine their common characteristics.

2482. Pass, David B. *Music and the Church*. Nashville, TN: Broadman Press, 1989. Church music from a Southern Baptist perspective.

2483. Peacock, James L. *Sound of the Dove: An Ethnography of Singing in Primitive Baptist Churches*. Ph.D. diss., University of North Carolina at Chapel Hill, 1989. A study of how a conservative style of singing expresses the self-understanding and the religious and social identity of a group of Primitive Baptists.

2484. Reynolds, William. *Companion to Baptist Hymnal*. Nashville, TN: Broadman Press, 1976. A three-part companion to the 1975 Baptist Hymnal covering the history of Baptist hymnody in America, the history of current hymns, and biographical notes on authors, composers, and sources.

2485. Reynolds, William. "Our Heritage of Baptist Hymnody in America." *Baptist History and Heritage* 11 (1976): 204.

2486. Tallmadge, W.H. "Baptist Monophonic and Heterophonic Hymnody in Southern Appalachia." *Yearbook of Inter-American Musical Research* 11 (1975): 105-136. Tallmadge provides commentary for his catalog of songs from the lining out tradition among Regular, Primitive, and United Baptists. Attention is paid to the historical and musical evolution of folk hymnody and the viability of lining out in the late 20th century. Includes seven songs with notation and an index of 302 folk hymns.

2487. Titon, Jeff Todd. "Stance, Role, and Identity in Fieldwork among Folk Baptists and Pentecostals." *American Music* 3 (1985): 16-24. The author uses personal experiences as a field researcher in both black and white church services to examine the various roles, stances, and identities he takes, or is assumed or forced to take, in these situations and the problems they present.

2488. Titon, Jeff Todd. "'God'll Just Bless You All Over the Place': Hymnody in a Blue Ridge Mountain Independent Baptist Church." *Appalachian Journal* 14, 4 (Summer) (1987): 348-58.

2489. Titon, Jeff Todd. *Powerhouse for God: Speech, Chant, and Song in an Appalachian Baptist Church*. Austin, TX: University of Texas, 1988. A multi-faceted study of a religious community, in two parts: 1) introduction and discussion of services, the community's religious roots, beliefs, and practices; 2) characteristic expressive forms including language, singing, prayer, teaching, preaching, testimony, and a life-story. Includes commentary of participants.

2490. Wicks, Sammie Ann. *Life and Meaning: Singing, Praying, and the Word among the Old Regular Baptists of Eastern Kentucky*. Ph.D. diss., University of Texas at Austin, 1983. Since its institution by the Westminster Assembly in 1644, lining hymnody of some form has been in continuous practice. This study documents the use of lining out on one region of Kentucky.

Congregational

2491. Goen, Clarence C. *Revivalism and Separatism in New England, 1740-1800: Strict Congregationalists and Separate Baptists in the Great Awakening*. Yale Publications in Religion, No. 2, New Haven: Yale University Press, 1962.

2492. Taylor, Phyllis J. *Non-keyboard Instrumental Music in the Worship of Certain Congregational Churches in Connecticut from 1636 to 1900*. Ph.D. diss., Graduate Theological Union, 1987. An exhaustively researched study of the progression from unaccompanied psalmody to the common use of organ accompaniment in Congregational worship, as well as of such instruments as bass viols. Attention is paid to the social and educational impact of changing the music of worship upon the wider community. Includes a 22 page bibliography.

Episcopal/Anglican

2493. Doran, Carol and William H. Peterson. *A History of Music in the Episcopal Church*. Little Rock, AR: Association of Anglican Musicians, 1991.

2494. Rasmussen, Jane. *Churchmen Concerned: Music in the Episcopal Church 1804-1859: A Study of Church Periodicals and Other Ecclesiastical Writings*. Ph.D. diss., University of Minnesota, 1983.

2495. Rasmussen, Jane. *Musical Taste as a Religious Question in Nineteenth-Century America*. Studies in American Religion, Vol. 20. Newiston, NY: E. Mellen Press, 1986. Nineteenth-century Episcopal clergy and laymen frequently voiced their dissatisfaction with the poor state of church music and the passiveness of the congregations. The author documents the various hard-fought attempts through the 1860s to promote a music that was both devotional and in good taste, attempts that culminated in the Canon on Church Music of 1874.

2496. Wilson, Ruth M. "Episcopal Music in America: The British Legacy." *Musical Times* 124, July (1983): 447-450. On Episcopal music between 1780-1820s.

2497. Wilson, Ruth Mack. *Anglican Chant and Chanting in England and America, 1660-1811*. Ph.D. diss., University of Illinois at Urbana-Champaign, 1988.

Evangelical

2498. Alexander, David Charles. *The Implications of Leo Tolstoy's 'What is Art?' for Music in the Evangelical Church*. Ed.D. diss., University of illinois at Urbana-Champaign, 1989. An attempt to determine if concepts of Tolstoy provide useful criteria for evaluating the role of music in the evangelical church. Part 1 presents the Tolstoyan theory of art in the form of six major themes. Part 2 examines works by Wolterstorff, Routley, Hustad, Johansson, and Berglund to determine the principles, aesthetic concerns, and current trends in evangelical church music. Part 3 proposes eight Tolstoy-based criteria to evaluate the issues raised in Parts 1 and 2.

2499. Gentry, Theodore. "The Origins of Evangelical Pianism." *American Music* 11, 1/Spring (1993): 90-111. A chronicle of the evangelical piano tradition that originated in the evangelical meeting and rose steadily to a position of popular acceptance during the early 20th century.

2500. Hustad, Donald P. *Jubilate II: Church Music in Worship and Renewal*. Carol Stream, IL: Hope Publishing Co., 1993. Rev. ed. of Jubilate: Church Music in the Evangelical Tradition. 1981.

2501. McCalister, Lonnie Kent. *Developing Aesthetic Standards for Choral Music in the Evangelical Church*. D.M.A., University of Oklahoma, 1987. The Bible itself provides the rationale for incorporating music of a high aesthetic standard in evangelical church music programs.

Lutheran

2502. Cartford, Gerhard Mailing. *Music in the Norwegian Lutheran Church: A Study of its Development in Norway and its Transfer to America, 1825-1917*. Ph.D. diss., University of Minnesota, 1961.

2503. Gudgeon, Richard G. *Martin Luther's Concept of Music as the Mistress or Governess of Human Emotions Leading One to All Virtues and Driving away Satan, the Instigator of All Sins, Is Still a Valid Form of Pastoral Care*. D. Min. diss., Colgate Rochester Divinity School/Bexley Hall/Crozer Theological Seminary, 1991. Includes *A Preface for All Good Hymnals* by Luther and *In*

Praise of the Noble Art of Music by Johan Walter Wittemberg, 1538, in the original German and in English translation.

2504. Horn, Henry E. *O Sing unto the Lord: Music in the Lutheran Church.* Philadelphia, PA: Fortress Press, 1956/repr. 1966.

2505. Stulken, M.K. *Hymnal Companion to the Lutheran Book of Worship.* Philadelphia: Fortress Press, 1981. This ambitious commentary includes a collection of essays on the international history of Lutheran hymnody, an annotated catalog of canticles and hymns, notes on authors and composers, and seven cross-referenced indexes.

2506. Susan, David J. "Some Parallel Emphases between Luther's Theology and his Thought about Music, and their Contemporary Significance." *Concordia Journal* 11, Jan. (1985): 10-14.

2507. Swanson, K.A. "Music of Two Finnish-Apostolic Lutheran Groups in Minnesota: The Heidemanians and the Pollarites." *Student Musicologists at Minnesota* 4 (1970-71): 1-35. An examination of 56 hymns and songs sung by two independent Apostalic groups originally from barren regions of Sweden and Finland. Singing is unaccompanied and transmitted orally.

2508. Warland, Dale. *The Music of Twentieth-Century Lutheran Hymnody in America.* DMA thesis, University of Southern California, 1965.

Methodist

2509. Baldridge, Terry L. *Evolving Tastes in Hymntunes of the Methodist Episcopal Church in the Nineteenth Century.* Ph.D. diss., University of Kansas, 1982. On changes to hymns and tunes of the 19th-century Methodist Episcopal Church due the the 'better music' movement and on the trends in the alterations in melody, harmony, rhythm, and meter.

2510. Joyner, F. Belton. *"All the Powers of Music Bring": Developing Resources for the Musically Untrained United Methodist Pastor for Strengthening Congregational Hymnody.* Ph.D. diss., Drew University, 1981.

2511. Kindley, Carolyn E. *Miriam's Timbrel: A Reflection of the Music of Wesleyan Methodism in America, 1843-1899.* D.A. thesis, Ball State University, 1985.

2512. Rice, William C. *A Century of Methodist Music, 1850-1950.* Ph.D. diss., State University of Iowa, 1953.

2513. Schwanz, Keith Duane. *The 'Wooden Brother': Instrumental Music Restricted in Free Methodist Worship, 1860-1955.* Ph.D. diss., Union Institute, 1991. Though not implicitly sinful, music instruments were considered an unhealthy accommodation to society and an unnecessary intrusion on that most acceptable means of grace, unaccompanied congregational singing. In terms of the three-component model of spiritual experience, expression, and Christian community, the Free Methodists emphasized the first and last, but severely limited the component of expression. Only after extensive effort and debate over several decades were instruments allowed.

2514. Warren, James I. *O for a Thousand Tongues: The History, Nature, and Influence of Music in the Methodist Tradition*. Grand Rapids, MI: F. Asbury Press, 1988. Making liberal use of primary texts, Warren chronicles the evolution of Methodist music by highlighting five major periods and a major musical figure representative of each period.

Mormon

2515. Arrington, Georganna Balif. "Dance in Mormonism: The Dancingest Denomination." In *Focus on Dance X: Religion and Dance*, Dennis Fallon et al., ed. Vol. 10. Reston, VA: American Alliance for Health, Physical Education, Recreation, and Dance, 1982.

2516. Cowan, Richard O. *The Doctrine and Covenants: Our Modern Scripture*. Rev. and enl. ed., Salt Lake City: Bookcraft, 1984. Mormonism and music. See esp. §25.

2517. Hatch, Verena Ursenbach. *Worship and Music in the Church of Jesus Christ of Latter-Day Saints*. Provo, UT: M.E.Hatch, 1968. The first seven chapters deal with various aspects of worship, theological architecture, and the LDS chapel. Chap. 8-15 cover church music history, role of church musicians, worship music, hymn text and tunes, music selection, and the church organ.

2518. Hicks, Michael. *Mormonism and Music: A History*. Urbana, IL: University of Illinois Press, 1989.

Pentecostal

2519. Alford, Delton L. *Music in the Pentecostal Church*. Cleveland, TN: Pathway Press, 1969.

2520. Duncan, Larry T. "Music among Early Pentecostals." *The Hymn* 38, 1 (1987): 11-15.

2521. Guthrie, Joseph Randall. *Pentecostal Hymnody: Historical, Theological, and Musical Influences*. D.M.A. thesis, Southwestern Baptist Theological Seminary, 1992. With its emphasis on praise, congregational participation, singing in the spirit, and the learning of songs by rote, present-day Pentecostal practice is a return to that of early Pentecostal revivals, around the beginning of this century.

2522. Hollenweger, Walter J. "Danced Documentaries: The Theological and Political Significance of Pentecostal Dancing." In *Worship and Dance*, J. D. Davies, ed. Birmingham, Eng.: University of Birmingham, 1975. 76-82. Includes a discussion of the dances and liturgy of black Pentacostal churches in the U.S.

2523. Spencer, Jon Michael. "The Heavenly Anthem: Holy Ghost Singing in the Primal Pentecostal Revival (1906-1909)." *Journal of Black Sacred Music* 1, 1 (Spring) (1987): 1-33. The author presents a theological and historical rationale for the specifically Pentecostal tradition of glossolalia or "tongue-singing." Spencer makes use of Pentecostal testimony as well as cross-cultural evidence. Includes the texts for 18 hymns.

Presbyterian

2524. Doughty, Gavin Lloyd. *The History and Development of Music in the United Presbyterian Church in the United States of America*. Ph.D. diss., University of Iowa, 1966. This study of the Presbyterian Church from 1800 includes a survey of the development of psalmody and hymnody and a discussion of American hymn and tune writers.

2525. Martin, R. *The Transition from Psalmody to Hymnody in Southern Presbyterianism, 1753-1901*. Ph.D. diss., Union Theological Seminary, 1963. A study of the struggle between psalmody and the hymnody that began with the introduction of Isaas Watts' psalm paraphrases and hymn to colonial America.

2526. Rightmyer, James Robert. *A Documentary History of the Music Program of Second Presbyterian Church, Louisville, Kentucky: 1830-1980*. DMA thesis, Southern Baptist Theological Seminary, 1980.

Unitarian

2527. Navias, Eugene B. *Singing our History: Tales, Texts and Tunes from Two Centuries of Unitarian and Universalist Hymns*. Boston: Unitarian Universalist Association, 1975.

Other Denominations and Groups

2528. Alford, Delton L. "The Sound and the Spirit." In *The Promise and the Power: Essays on the Motivations, Developments, and Prospects of the Ministries of the Church of God*, Charles W. Conn et al., ed. Cleveland, TN: Pathway Press, 1980. 201-224.

2529. Carroll, Kenneth L. "Singing in the Spirit in Early Quakerism." *Quaker History* 73, 1 (1984): 1-13. The author demonstrates that Quaker communities in New York and New England practiced singing, contrary to the popular conception that the Quakers did not allow singing.

2530. German, C. Dale. *An Inquiry in to the Relationship between Church Music and Wesleyan Doctrine as it Relates to the Church of the Nazarene: With Implications for a Ministry of Music*. D. Min. thesis, San Francisco Theological Seminary, 1984. The role music might play in the Church of the Nazarene with respect to Wesley's doctrine of holiness or Christian purification.

2531. Lockwood, George Frank. *Recent Developments in U.S. Hispanic and Latin American Protestant Church Music*. D.Min. diss., School of Theology at Claremont, 1981. The answers to 250 surveys sent out to church music leaders throughout the hemisphere reveals a widespread interest in new church music. The indigenization of hymnology is generally favored. Future work needs to chronicle, provide a theological rationale for, and disseminate information concerning new sacred music.

2532. Moore, J. Kenneth. "Socio-economic Double Entendre in the Songs of the Snake Handlers." *Hymn* 37, 2 (1986): 30-36. The Snake Handlers sect of West Virginia engages in continuous congregational dancing and singing to texts that mask condemnation of a system that keeps them in poverty.

2533. Rivard, Eugene Francis. *The Hymnody of the Christian and Missionary Alliance (1891-1978) as a Reflection of its Theology and Development*. D.M.A., Southwestern Baptist Theological Seminary, 1991. A study of the hymnals and other materials provide a history of the Missionary Alliance movement and an assessment of the extent to which the hymnals reflect the movement's theology. Recurrent themes are 'deeper life,' personal holiness, missions, and the 'fourfold Gospel'.

2534. Sikes, Walter W. "Worship among Disciples of Christ, 1809-1865." *Mid-Stream* 7, Sum. (1968): 5-32. A study of the music of Alexander Campbell and his use of the organ in commemorating the Lord's Supper.

MUSIC OF AMERICAN ROMAN CATHOLICISM

2535. Béhague, Gerard. "Hispanic-American Music (North America)." In *NGDAM*, Vol. 2. London 1986. 395-399.

2536. Britanyak, Thomas Paul. *The Historical Development of the Usage of Folk Music in the Catholic Church and Its Present Usage in the Churches of the Archdiocese of Seattle*. M.A., Seattle Pacific University, 1988.

2537. Damian, Ronald. *A Historical Study of the Caecilian Movement in the United States*. DMA diss., Catholic University of America, 1984. The most widespread and influential of efforts to reform Catholic church music during the 19th century, the Caecilian Movement reintroduced the *a cappella* style of the sixteenth century and Gregorian Chant in response to current Papal directives. The Movement provided a model for excellence for almost a century, until new Papal directives established guidelines that promoted the use of current styles of music.

2538. DjeDje, Jacqueline Cogdell. "An Expression of Black Identity: The Use of Gospel Music in a Los Angeles Catholic Church." *The Western Journal of Black Studies* 7, 3 (1983): 148-160.

2539. DjeDje, Jacqueline Cogdell. "Change and Differentiation: The Adoption of Black American Gospel Music in the Catholic Church." *Ethnomusicology* 30, 2 (1986): 223-52. An analysis of the impact, positive and negative, made by the introduction of gospel music in three South Central L.A. Catholic churches with attention to both the sociological and the musical factors.

2540. Foley, Edward. "When American Roman Catholics Sing." *Worship* 63 (1989): 98-112. Foley reports the relevant findings from the Notre Dame Study of Catholic Parish Life and then attempts his own analysis of the data, discussing the relationship of active parishioner participation to ritual and quality of composition.

2541. Grimes, Robert Raymond. *'How Shall We Sing in a Foreign Land?' Music of Catholic Immigrants in the Antebellum United States.* Ph.D. diss., University of Pittsburgh, 1992. A thorough study of the music of Irish immigrants in mid-19th-century northeastern U.S. Chapters five through seven investigate the music of canonical ritual, the popular music of ritual (the repertory of religious vernacular song), and the music of popular ritual.

2542. Higginson, J. Vincent. *History of American Catholic Hymnals: Survey and Background.* Springfield, OH: Hymn Society of America, 1982.

2543. Winter, Miriam Therese. *Vatican II in the Development of Criteria for the Use of Music in the Liturgy of the Roman Catholic Church in the United States and their Theological Bases.* Ph.D. diss., Princeton Theological Seminary, 1983. Two divergent theological orientations, two liturgical foci, and two streams of music both claim origin in the Sacrosanctum Concilium. The same document, however, provides the potential for theological and practical reconciliation: a theology of music, rooted in scripture and tradition, that would ensure that theological criteria, not aesthetic criteria, remain paramount.

2544. Winter, Miriam Therese. "Catholic Prophetic Sound after Vatican II." In *The Sacred Sound and Social Change: Liturgical Music in Jewish and Christian Experience*, Lawrence A. Hoffman and Janet Roland Walton, ed. Two Liturgical Traditions, Vol. 3. Notre Dame: University of Notre Dame Press, 1992. 150-173.

MISSION MUSIC

2545. Benson, N.A. "Music in the California Missions: 1602-1848." *Student Musicologists at Minnesota* 3 (1968-69): 128-167. 4 (1970-71): 104-125.

2546. Bienbar, Arthur, ed. *Mission Music of California*. Music Reprint Series, Owen F. Silva, transl. New York: Da Capo, 1941/repr. 1978. A collection of the texts and scores of hymns and masses sung in the Franciscan missions of Alta California. Includes biographical information on Franciscan musicians and commentary on musical styles and teaching methods.

2547. Crouch, M. with W. Summers and K. Lueck-Michaelson (eds). "An Annotated Bibliography and Commentary Concerning Mission Music of Alta California from 1769 to 1834: In Honor of the American Bicentennial." *Current Musicology* 22 (1976): 88-99.

2548. Da Silva, Owen, O.F.M. *Mission Music of California: A Collection of Old California Mission Hymns and Masses*. New York: Da Capo Press, 1941/repr. 1978. Printed music and a lengthy essay on mission music and musicians from a Franciscan point of view.

2549. Geiger, M.J. *Mission Santa Barbara 1792-1965*. Santa Barbara, CA: Franciscan Fathers of California, 1965. The roles and functions of music, sacred and secular, in mission life are described in several chapters, particularly Chapters 13, 28, and 34.

2550. Göllner, T. "Two Polyphonic Passions from California's Mission Period." *Yearbook for Inter-American Musical Research* 6 (1970): 67-76. Works from the latter part of the 18th century, with analysis of music and notation.

2551. Gormley, Regina Maria. *The Liturgical Music of the California Missions, 1769-1833*. DMA diss., Catholic University of America, 1992. Missionaries used music for development of the Indians both in worship and in education. The Juan Sancho mss. encompass music of diverse liturgical roles and include examples of monophony, simple polyphony, and more developed polyphony. The mss. are considered in light of Church tradition, particularly the Council of Trent, and of how a consideration of the factors that lead to the decline of mission music might shape directions for the future in keeping with the directives of Vatican II.

2552. Harshbarger, G.A. *The Mass in G by Ignacio Jerusalem and its Place in the California Mission Music Repertory*. Ph.D. diss., University of Washington, 1985.

2553. Ray, Sister Mary Dominic, O.P. and Jr. Joseph H. Engbeck. *Gloria Dei: The Story of California Mission Music*. State of California: Department of Parks and Recreation, 1974.

2554. Spiess, Lincoln Bunce. "Benavides and Church Music in New Mexico in the Early Seventeenth Century." *JAMS* 17 (1964): 144-156. A study of documents from the 1630s concerning the active musical life in New Mexico, and in particular, the performance of *canto de órgano*, church polyphony, before an impressed Navajo chief.

2555. Spiess, Lincoln Bunce. "Church Music in Seventeenth-century New Mexico." *New Mexico Historical Review* 40, 1 (1965): 5-21. An informative article on missionary music, instruments, and liturgical books including two missals from c.1690 and 1726.

2556. Spiess, Lincoln Bunce "Instruments in the Missions of New Mexico: 1598-1680." In *Essays in Musicology: A Birthday Offering for Willi Apel*, Hans Tischler, ed. Bloomington, IN: Indiana University, 1968. 131-136. A well-researched study of mission music in New Mexico.

2557. Summers, William J. "The Organs of Hispanic California." *Music (AGO-RCCO) Magazine* 10, 11 (1976): 50-51.

2558. Summers, William J. "Music of the California Missions: An Inventory and Discussion of Selected Printed Music Books Used in Hispanic California, 1769-1836." *Soundings, University of California Libraries, Santa Barbara* 9 (1977): 13.

2559. Summers, William J. "Santa Barbara Mission Archive Library." In *Resources of American Music History*, D.W. Krummel, ed. Urbana: University of Illinois Press, 1981. 41.

2560. Summers, William J. "Spanish Music in California, 1769-1840: A Reassessment." In *IMS12, 1977*, 1981. 360-379. On the music of Spanish Franciscan missionaries. Compositions range from 2-part works to extended masses. With many musical exx.

2561. Summers, William J. "The Spanish Origins of California Mission Music." In *Transplanted European Music Cultures*, Geoffrey Moon, ed. Miscellanea Musicologica: Adelaide Studies in Musicology, No. 12, Adelaide, Australia: University of Adelaide, 1987. 109-26.

2562. Warkentin, L. "The Rise and Fall of Indian Music in the California Missions." *Latin American Music Review* 2, 1 (1981): 45. A history of Native American music as it was first described by early missionaries through its incorporation into mission life and its subsequent decline. Covers period from 1769 to 1846. Includes an extensive bibliography.

2563. Whitinger, Julius Edward. *Hymnody of the Early American Indian Missions*. Ph.D. diss., The Catholic University of America, 1971. As part of their Indian missionary activity, Spanish Jesuits in the Southwest established music schools, choirs, and instrumental ensembles. French Jesuits in the Great Lakes basin also used music as an instructional aid.

REGIONAL RELIGIOUS MUSIC

2564. Adams, Linda Kinset. "Narrative Song as a Transitional Rhetorical Device in the Agape Church at Ellettsville, Indiana." *Folklore Forum* 24, 1 (1991): 36-50.

2565. Cansler, Loman D. "The Fiddle and Religion." *Missouri Folklore Society Journal* 13-14 (1991-92): 31-43.

2566. Downey, James C. "Joshua Leavitt's *The Christian Lyre* and the Beginning of the Popular Tradition in American Religious Song." *Latin American Music Review* 7, 2 (1986): 149-61. Downey traces the origin of Deavitt's song collection as the first to meld secular and sacred tunes into a religious popular music tradition. Attention is paid to the religious controversies the *Lyre* inspired among church musicians, composers and publishers.

2567. Fife, Austin E. and Alta Stephens Fife. *Heaven on Horseback: Revivalist Songs and Verse in the Cowboy Idiom*. Logan, UT: Utah State University Press, 1989. The authors discuss cowboy and revival songs as the "interplay between two mythic motifs" and document their mutual influence on one another with attention to hymns, prayers, and homeletic songs.

2568. Forrest, John. "The Devil Sits in the Choir." In *Diversities of Gifts: Field Studies in Southern Religion*, Ruel W. Tyson Jr. et al., ed. Urbana, IL: University of Illinois Press, 1988. 79-90.

2569. Miller, Terry E. "Voices from the Past: The Singing and Preaching at Otter Creek Church." *Journal of American Folklore* 88 (1975): 266. Vermont.

2570. Primiano, Leonard Norman. "Feminist Christian Songs: Occasions of Vernacular Religious Belief." *New Jersey Folklore* 10 (1985): 38-45.

2571. Scholten, J.W. *The Chapins: A Study of Men and Sacred Music West of the Alleghenies, 1795-1842*. Ph.D. diss., University of Michigan, 1972.

2572. Smith, Thérèse. *Moving in the Spirit: Music of Worship in Clear Creek, Mississippi, As an Expression of Worldview*. Ph.D. diss., Brown University, 1988.

2573. Sutton, Brett. "Speech, Chant, and Song: Patterns of Language and Action in a Southern Church." In *Diversities of Gifts: Field Studies in Southern Religion*, Ruel W. Tyson Jr. et al., ed. Urbana, IL: University of Illinois Press, 1988. 157-76.

30

North America: Afro-American Religious Music; Spirituals and Gospel; Contemporary Christian Music; Jewish and Asian-American Religious Music

AFRO-AMERICAN RELIGIOUS MUSIC: ENCYCLOPEDIAS, READINGS, AND BIBLIOGRAPHIES

2574. Brown, Marian Tally. *A Resource Manual on the Music of the Southern Fundamentalist Black Church*. Mus. Ed. D. thesis, Indiana University, 1974.

2575. Burnim, Mellonee. "Gospel Music Research." *Black Music Research Journal* 1 (1980): 63.

2576. Burnim, Mellonee. "Culture Bearer and Tradition Bearer: An Ethnomusicologist's Research on Gospel Music." *Ethnomusicology* 29, 3 (1985): 432-447. The author's account of her experience with Black church music as both an insider (an Afro-American and a gospel singer), and an outsider (a researcher). (Also in *The Garland Library of Readings in Ethnomusicology*, Vol. 7).

2577. Clifford, Mike et al., consultants. *The Illustrated Encyclopedia of Black Music*. New York: Harmony Books, 1982.

2578. Crawford, Richard. "On Two Traditions of Black Music Research." *Black Music Research Journal* (1986): 1-11. Tradition One: Within the tradition of music scholarship; distant, careful, precise. Black Music in the context of Western and American music-making. Tradition Two: A focus on Black music only and the experience and distinct perspective it reflects.

2579. De Lerma, Dominique-René. *Bibliography of Black Music*. 4 vols. Westport, CT: Greenwood Press, 1981-84. 1: Reference Materials (1981); 2: Afro-American Idioms (1981); 3: Geographical Studies (1982); 4: Theory, Education and Related Studies (1984).

2580. Floyd, Samuel A., Jr. "On Black Music Research." *Black Music Research Journal* (1983): 46. On the necessity for Black music-scholars and on nine specific areas in which further work needs to be done.

2581. Floyd, Samuel A., Jr. "Books on Black Music by Black Authors: A Bibliography." *Black Perspective on Music* 14, 3 (1986): 215-32. Includes a chronological list of black authors from 1828 to 1985.

2582. Floyd, Samuel A., Jr. *Black Music Biography: An Annotated Bibliography*. White Plains, N.Y.: Kraus International Publications, 1987.

2583. Floyd, Samuel A., Jr. and Marsha J. Reisser. *Black Music in the United States: An Annotated Bibliography of Selected Reference and Research Materials*. Milkwood, NY: Kraus International Publications, 1983.

2584. Jackson, Irene V. *Afro-American Religious Music: A Bibliography and a Catalogue of Gospel Music*. Westport, CT: Greenwood Press, 1979.

2585. Low, W.A. and Virgil A. Clift. *Encyclopedia of Black America*. New York: McGraw-Hill, 1981.

2586. Maultsby, Portia K. "Selective Bibliography: U.S. Black Music." *Ethnomusicology* 19 (1975): 421.

2587. Meadows, Eddie S. *Theses and Dissertations on Black American Music*. Beverly Hills, CA: Theodore Front Musical Literature, 1980.

2588. Southern, Eileen, ed. *Biographical Dictionary of Afro-American and African Musicians*. Westport, CT: Greenwood Press, 1982.

2589. Southern, Eileen. *Readings in Black American Music*. 2nd ed., New York: W.W. Norton & Company, 1983.

AFRICAN-AMERICAN MUSIC: GENERAL

2590. Brooks, T. *America's Black Musical Heritage*. Englewood Cliffs, NJ: Prentice-Hall, 1984.

2591. Burnim, Mellonee and Portia Maultsby. "From Backwoods to City Streets: The Afro-American Musical Journey." In *Expressively Black*, Geneva Gay and Willie Baber, ed. New York: Praeger, 1987. 109-135. The authors review African American musical history, both secular and sacred, with en eye to the "organizational principles, aesthetic concepts, and ideological premises" which they maintain have remained constant.

2592. De Lerma, Dominique-René, ed. *Reflections on Afro-American Music*. Kent, OH: 1973. Most of the essays in this wide-ranging collection refer to religious as well as secular music, with Chapter 14 devoted entirely to gospel music.

2593. Emery, Lynne Fauley. *Black Dance in the United States from 1619-1970.* Palo Alto: National Press Books, 1972. Chapters 1-3 provide a solid anthropological, historical and artistic review of religious dance among slaves in the Antebellum American South and vodun believers in the Caribbean.

2594. Haskins, James. *Black Music in America: A History through its People.* New York: Thomas Y. Crowell, 1987.

2595. Jackson, Irene V., ed. *More than Dancing: Essays on Afro-American Music and Musicians.* Contributions in Afro-American and African Studies 83, Westport, CT: Greenwood Press, 1985. A collection of essays that focus upon Afro-American music in the United States. Chapters 5, 8, and 9 directly address the subjects of music in African ritual settings, ecstatic singing in an African church and religious songs of the African diaspora, respectively, each with relevant discussions of music and religion.

2596. Kebede, Ashenafi. *Roots of Black Music: The Vocal, Instrumental and Dance Heritage of Africa and Black America.* Englewood Cliffs, NJ: Prentice-Hall, 1982.

2597. Lincoln, Charles Eric. *The Black Experience in Religion.* Garden City, NY: Anchor Press, 1974. Covering the full range of Black religious experience, the essays in this book are divided into five chapters. Chapter 1, concerned with mainline Christian practice, focuses extensively on the style and role of music. Chapter 4 covers music in cults and sects.

2598. Maultsby, Portia K. "Influences and Retentions of West African Musical Concepts in U.S. Black Music." *Western Journal of Black Studies* 3 (1979): 197. A scholarly study of the music of African Americans as it "exemplifies collective attitudes, values, philosophies and experiences" within the community while retaining a West African identity during each stage of development. Christian musical practice and style are discussed as part of each developmental stage.

2599. Maultsby, Portia K. "Africanisms in African-American Music." In *Africanisms in American Culture*, Joseph E. Holloway, ed. Bloomington and Indianapolis: Indiana University Press, 1990. 185-210.

2600. Roach, Hildred. *Black American Music: Past and Present [1976].* rev. ed., 2 vols. Malabar, FL: Robert E. Krieger Pub. Co., 1985. A musical history of African Americans in the US from the early 17th century through the 1970's. The book is in three parts: 1) The Beginning (1619-1870), 2) The Awakening (1870-1950's), and 3) Freedom Now (1950-1970's). Part 2 contains an extensive treatment of religious music with an eight-page list of readings and recordings.

2601. Roberts, John Storm. *Black Music of Two Worlds*. New York: Morrow Paperback Editions, 1972. A study of features of African music that appear in African-American music of different regions of the Western hemisphere.

2602. Skillman, Teri. *The Georgia Sea Island Singers*. Honolulu, HI: East-West Center, 1986.

2603. Small, Christopher. *Music of the Common Tongue: Survival and Celebration in Afro-American Music*. London/New York: John Calder/Riverrun Press, 1987. A study of African American music especially as it expresses philosophies of survival and celebration. Among the topics discussed are ritual performance, American psalmody and the blues as musical ritual and encounters between Euro- and African-American music styles.

2604. Southern, Eileen. *The Music of Black Americans: A History*. 2nd ed., New York: W.W. Norton & Company, 1983. The standard reference.

2605. Southern, Eileen. "Afro-American Music." In *NGDAM*, Vol. 1. 1986. 13-21.

AFRICAN-AMERICAN RELIGIOUS MUSIC

2606. Abbot, Lynn. "Wrapped up and Tangled Up in Jesus: The Story of Rev. Charlie Jackson." *Keskidee* 1 (1986): 4-7.

2607. Baer, Hans A. "An Overview of Ritual, Oratory and Music in Southern Black Religion." *Southern Quarterly* 23, 3 (1985): 5-14.

2608. Bailey, Ben E. "The Lined-Hymn Tradition in Black Mississippi Churches." *Black Perspective in Music* 6, 1, Spring (1978): 3-17. A study of the on-going practice of lining out hymns in rural and urban African American Protestant churches with attention to vocal qualities, pulse, cadence formula and context. Includes song texts.

2609. Baklanoff, Joy Driskell. "The Celebration of a Feast: Music, Dance, and Possession Trance in the Black Primitive Baptist Footwashing Ritual." *Ethnomusicology* 31, 3 (1987): 381-94. Sensory stimulation through music, body movements, sermons and alcoholic consumption induce an altered state of consciousness that reaffirms commitment to family, community, and church.

2610. Barton, W.E. "Old Plantation Hymns." In *The Social Implications of Early Negro Music in the United States*, Bernard Katz, ed. New York 1899/repr. 1969. Writing in the late 19th century, Barton analyzes both the musical qualities of and sources of inspiration for the religious songs and tunes of ante-bellum African Americans. The texts and tunes for over 25 songs representing common styles and themes are included.

2611. Boggs, B. "Some Aspects of Worship in a Holiness Church." *New York Folklore* 3 (1977): 29. Boggs employs frequent excerpts from interviews with congregation members to illustrate and explain various ritual and theological aspects of the worship service with an emphasis on the unifying force of singing during the services.

2612. Booker, Queen. "Congregational Music in a Pentacostal Church." *The Black Perspective in Music* 16, 1 (Spring) (1988): 31-44. Research, conversations, and personal experience document this historical study of music at St. Luke Church of God in Christ, a Black church in Tutwiler, Miss. Topics include call and response singing, the gradual acceptance of secular instruments, and periodic changes in the number and function of its choirs and in the order and content of the services.

2613. Boyer, Horace Clarence. *An Analysis of Black Church Music with Examples Drawn from Services in Rochester, New York*. Ph.D. diss., University of Rochester, 1973.

2614. Boyer, Horace Clarence. "Tracking the Tradition: New Orleans Sacred Music." *Black Music Research Journal* 8, 1 (1988): 135-47. Noting the rapid ascendancy of New Orleans as a gospel music center, the author attempts to give this development historical context. Attention is paid to the history of gospel quartets, accompanied gospel groups, gospel choirs and composers, publishers, and other promoters.

2615. Collins, Willie R. *Moaning and Prayer: A Musical and Contextual Analysis of Chants to Accompany Prayer in Two Afro-American Baptist Churches in Southeast Alabama*. Ph.D. diss., University of California, Los Angeles, 1988. Moans were one-sentence musical chants that were performed two to three times by a leader and congregation and that co-occurred with spoken or chanted prayers as a ritual occasion. They were used to support the prayer-sayer in louder and longer prayers, to elicit the Holy spirit, to convert sinners, and to support the preacher.

2616. Collins, Willie R. "An Ethnography of the Moan-and -Prayer Event in Two African American Baptist Churches in Southeast Alabama." In *African Musicology: Current Trends*, J.C. DjeDje, ed. Vol. 2. Los Angeles: International Studies Oversears Program/The James S. Coleman African Studies Center University of California, Los Angeles, 1992. 45-64.

2617. Cornelius, Steven. *The Convergence of Power: An Investigation into the Music Liturgy of Santería in New York City*. Ph.D. diss., University of California, Los Angeles, 1989. A demonstration of how musical sound mediates as celebration, communication, and invocation between the religious practitioner and *orishas* (forces of nature personified in various deities). A study of history, music instruments and structure, the musician's role within ritual, and two socially oriented case studies relating to spirit possession.

2618. Cornelius, Steven. "Encapsulating Power: Meaning and Taxonomy of the Musical Instruments of Santeria in New York City." *Selected Reports in Ethnomusicology/ Issues in Organology* Vol. 8 (1990): 125-142.

2619. Cornelius, Steven. "Drumming for the Orishas: Reconstruction of Tradition in New York City." In *Essays on Cuban Music*, Peter Manuel, ed. Lanham, MD: University Press of America, 1991. 137-155.

2620. Cornelius, Steven. "Personalizing Public Symbols through Music Ritual: Santaría's Presentation to Aña." *Latin American Music Review* 16, 1/Spring-Summer (1995): 42-57. On the central role the *batá* drums play in personalizing a relationship to the Yoruba *orisha* Aña.

2621. Crowder, William S. "Hymnsinging in the Black Church: A Lingering Tradition." *AME Zion Quarterly Review* 104, Oct. (1992): 16-20. On lined hymn singing.

2622. Dargan, William T. "Congregational Singing Traditions in South Carolina." *Black Music Research Journal* 15, 1/Spring (1995): 29-74. A comparison of seven regional sub-styles in terms of timbres, ornaments, density, tempi, cross-rhythms, body movement, and levels of spirit possession.

2623. DjeDje, Jacqueline Cogdell. *American Black Spiritual and Gospel Songs from Southeast Georgia: A Comparative Study*. Los Angeles, CA: Center for African-American Studies, University of California, 1978.

2624. Friedman, Robert. *Making an Abstract World Concrete: Knowledge, Competence and Structural Dimensions of Performance among Batá Drummers in New York City*. Ph.D. diss., Indiana University, 1982.

2625. Hawn, C. Michael. "A Survey of Trends in Recent Protestant Hymnals: African-American Spirituals, Hymns, and Gospel Songs." *Hymn* 43, Jan. (1992): 21-28.

2626. Hayes, Michael G. "The Theology of the Black Pentecostal Praise Song." *Black Sacred Music* 4, Fall (1990): 30-34. A brief exploration of the interdependent and meditative relationship between praise songs and the Pentecostal theological world view.

2627. Hemphill-Peoples, Jacquelyn Mary. *An Investigation of Factors that Have Influenced the Styles of Black Religious Music in Selected Black Churches of Buffalo, New York*. Ph.D. diss., SUNY, Buffalo, 1992. After a historical overview of the establishment of fifty-five black Baptist and Methodist Churches in Buffalo, N.Y., the author traces the development of music in three selected Buffalo churches from an initial similarity to white Protestant churches to distinctively black idioms. The greatest factor in this development was found to be the black preacher.

2628. Hovda, Robert W., ed. *This Far By Faith: American Black Worship and Its African Roots.* Washington, DC: The National Office for Black Catholics and The Liturgical Conference, 1977. A collection of reports and reflections written by an ecumenical panel of liturgists on Worship and Spirituality from the Black perspective. Relevant topics include the oral African tradition vs. the Ocular Western tradition, music in the Black Spiritual tradition, and a case study of liturgical practice in a Black parish.

2629. Jackson, Irene V., ed. *The African American Experience in Worship and the Arts.* New Haven, CT: Yale University Institute of Sacred Music, Worship, and the Arts, 1992. A collection of articles on various aspects of worship in African American churches. Includes articles on gospel, the spiritual, singing, song lyrics, theomusicology, music ministry in a racially diverse parish, and the dynamics of music in a worship event.

2630. Jackson, Joyce Marie. *The Performing Black Sacred Quartet: An Expression of Cultural Values and Aesthetics.* Ph.D. diss., Indiana University, 1988.

2631. Jackson, Irene V. "Afro-American Sacred Song in the Nineteenth Century: A Neglected Source." *Black Perspective in Music* 4 (1976): 22 ff.

2632. Jackson, Irene V. "Music among Blacks in the Episcopal Church: Some Preliminary Considerations [1980]." In *More than Dancing: Essays on Afro-American Music and Musicians,* Irene V. Jackson, ed. Westport, CT: Greenwood, 1985. 107-25. A history and description of the hymnal of Marshall W. Taylor, an African American minister. An extensive appendix includes a catalog of songs and composers and examples of six hymns.

2633. Johnson, Guy Benton. *Folk Culture on St. Helena Island, South Carolina.* Hatboro PA: Folklore Associates, 1930/repr. 1968. Part II of this study is concerned with the folk songs, and particularly the spirituals, of St. Helena and their kinship to and points of departure from Euro-American revival hymns. Repr. with foreword by Don Yoder.

2634. Jones, Marion Bernard. *Music in Liturgy: Enhancing the Quality of Worship in the AME Zion Church.* Ph.D. diss., Drew University, 1991. By carefully integrating music into the order of worship and making clear that the role of music is to worship God, the author demonstrated that the steady decline in church attendance, apparent since the 1960s, can be reversed.

2635. Katz, Bernard, ed. *The Social Implications of Early Negro Music in the United States, with over 150 of the Songs, Many of Them with Their Music.* New York: Arno Press, 1969. A collection of articles dealing with the cultural roles and social implications of various African-American musical styles with special attention given to the spirituals.

2636. Keister, Jay Davis. *Vodou Music and Spirit Possession in Washington, D.C.* M.A. thesis, UCLA, 1991.

2637. Leonard, Neil. *Jazz: Myth and Religion.* New York: Oxford University Press, 1987. A study of Jazz as divine and as diabolical.

2638. Lincoln, Charles Eric. *The Black Church in the African-American Experience.* Durham: Duke University Press, 1990.

2639. Mapson, Jesse Wendell. *Some Guidelines for the Use of Music in the Black Church.* Ph.D. diss., Eastern Baptist Theological Seminary, 1983. A re-examination of the historical and theological underpinnings of the Black church, for the purpose of helping black pastors and musicians to become more sensitive to issues related to the use of music.

2640. Mapson, Jesse Wendell. *The Ministry of Music in the Black Church.* Valley Forge, PA: Judson Press, 1984.

2641. Mason, John. *Orin Orisa.* New York: Yoruba Theological Press, 1992. On Santaría in the U.S.

2642. Maultsby, Portia K. *Afro-American Religious Music: 1619-1861.* Ph.D. diss., University of Wisconsin, 1974. Pt. 1, Historical Development; Pt. 2, Computer Analysis of One Hundred Spirituals.

2643. Maultsby, Portia K. "Music of Northern Independent Black Churches During the Ante-Bellum Period." *Ethnomusicology* 19 (1975): 401-420. During the 17th and 18th centuries, African Americans and European Americans attended the same churches. After the abolition of slavery, African Americans saw the need to develop their own church. From this separation, two distinctive styles of worship and singing arose: one, associated with educated, middle-class Blacks, resembled the White Protestant tradition; the other style, associated with uneducated, poor Blacks, was a form of spontaneous expression.

2644. Maultsby, Portia K. *Afro-American Religious Music: A Study in Musical Diversity.* The Papers of the Hymn Society of America, Vol. 35. Springfield, OH: Hymn Society of America, 1981. Revision of the author's Ph.D. diss. *Afro-American Religious Music 1619-1861.* 1974. On the influence of African culture on Afro-American music, including such topics as black preachers, music of the slaves, folk spirituals, and various performance practices.

2645. Maultsby, Portia K. "The Use and Performance of Hymnody, Spirituals, and Gospels in the Black Church." *The Western Journal of Black Studies* 7, 3 (1983): 161-71. Repr. in *Journal of the Interdenominational Theological Center.* 14, Fall/Spring (1987): 141-159.

2646. McCarthy, William B. "Evening Prayer Service at Mercy Mission." *Mid-America Folklore* 14, 2 (1986): 15-32. A record of a predominately Black and female congregation's religious expression with stress placed on the particularity of its concerns, anxieties and style. The roles, styles and choice of hymns and hymn leadership are discussed.

2647. Murphy, Joseph. *Working the Spirit: Ceremonies of the African Diaspora.* Boston: Beacon Press, 1994.

2648. Neeley, Bobby Joe. *Contemporary Afro-American Voodooism (Black Religion): The Retention and Adaptation of the Ancient African-Egyptian Mystery System.* Ph.D. diss., UC, Berkeley, 1988. Voodooism, with its symbolique of ritual, rite, myth, dance, language, music, song, behavior patterns, and communal participation, is the basis for all Afro-American religion. Aspects of African religion—dance, music, songs, magic, medicine, religious functionaries—are discussed relative to retentions in New Orleans.

2649. Nelson, Angela Spence. "Theology in the Hip-Hop of Public Enemy and Kool Moe Dee." *Journal of Black Sacred Music* 5, Spr. (1991): 51-59. Rap is theological when it addresses such issues as self-affirmation, truth, human liberation, love, hate, good, evil, and hope—issues through the examination of which a people is moved by the Divine Spirit toward unity and self determination.

2650. Nelson, Angela Spence. *A Theomusicological Approach to Rap: A Model Study for the Study of African American Popular and Folk Musics.* Ph.D. diss., Bowling Green State University, 1992.

2651. Osumare, Halifu. "Sacred Dance/Drumming: African Belief Systems in Oakland." In *African-American Traditional Arts and Folklife in Oakland and the East Bay,* W. R. Collins, ed. Oakland: Sagitarian Press, 1992. 17-21.

2652. Parrish, Lydia. *Slave Songs of the Georgia Sea Islands.* Hatboro PA: Folklore Associates, 1942/repr. 1965. The texts of African American shout songs and religious songs with background information. Includes a thematic bibliography. Music transcribed by Creighton Churchill and Robert MacGimsey. Reprint with an intro. by Olin Downes and a foreword by Bruce Jackson.

2653. Paul, J.D.B. *Music in Culture: Black Sacred Song Style—Slidell, Louisana, Chicago, Illinois.* Ph.D. diss., Northwestern University, 1973.

2654. Peasant, Julian Smith, Jr. *The Arts of the African Methodist Episcopal Church as Viewed in the Architecture, Music and Liturgy of the Nineteenth Century.* Ph.D. diss., Ohio University, 1993. The hymns of Watts, Wesley, and Newton were emphasized over spritual songs in an attempt to dampen musical expression and past cultural behaviors in favor of the appearance of being in the American mainstream.

2655. Pitts, Walter. "Like a Tree Planted by the Water: The Musical Cycle in the African-American Baptist Ritual." *Journal of American Folklore* 104, 413/Summer (1991): 318-340.

2656. Proctor, Henry Hugh. "The Theology of the Songs of the Southern Slave." *Journal of Black Sacred Music* 2, Spr. (1988): 51-64. The songs of the Southern slaves demonstrate the slaves' belief in God as revealed in nature, Christ as God's son and deliverer of mankind from sins, the Holy Spirit as God's felt presence, Angels as God's messengers, the Christian life as the ideal life, Satan as a personal devil and the enemy of all righteousness, and a future life in heaven or hell. Written in 1894.

2657. Raichelson, Richard M. *Black Religious Folksong: A Study in Generic and Social Change.* Ph.D. diss., University of Pennsylvania, 1975.

2658. Rosenberg, B.A. *The Art of the American Folk Preacher.* New York: Oxford University Press, 1970. An extensive study of the chanted sermon within African-American Christianity focusing on the common formulaic quality of such sermons, rhythmic tone as trigger for audience response, and antiphonal aspects of the service. Transcripts of 17 chanted sermons are included.

2659. Simpson, Robert. "The Shout and Shouting in Slave Religion of the United States." *Southern Quarterly* 23, 3 (1985): 34-47. On the shout as an African element in Afro-American religious expression and the role of the Great Awakening, with its camp meetings, emotional conversion, and vivid vocalism, in the integration of Protestantism with slave religion.

2660. Smith, Carl Henry. *The Lined Hymn Tradition in Selected Black Churches of Eastern Kentucky.* Ph.D. diss., University of Pittsburgh, 1987. A transcription and analysis of the performance of 24 hymns sung in the 'lined-out' tradition of black churches of eastern Kentucky.

2661. Smith, Timothy. "Chanted Prayer in Southern Black Churches." *Southern Quarterly* 23 (1985): 70-82.

2662. Southall, Geneva H. "Black Composers and Religious Music." *Black Perspective in Music* 2 (1974): 45 ff. Southall examines the roots of African American religious music with attention to its relationship to the Hebrew/Christian canon, slave life, African musical traditions and major composers.

2663. Southall, Geneva H. "Jubilee Singers, (Fisk)." In *NGDAM*, Vol. 4. 1986. 600.

2664. Southern, Eileen. "Musical Practices in Black Churches of Philadelphia and New York, ca. 1800-1844." *JAMS* 30 (1977): 296. The author traces the introduction of African American hymnals, spiritual songs, church music schools, and sacred music concerts in the rising independent African American urban churches.

2665. Southern, Eileen. "Hymnals of the Black Church." *The Black Perspective in Music* 17, 1-2 (1989): 153-70. Hymnals compiled expressly for the use of a Black congregation have been published since 1801. The first of these, *A Collection of Spiritual Songs and Hymns, Selected from Various Authors*, published by Richard Allen, a founder of AME, along with *Gospel Pearls* (1921), and *Songs of Zion* (1981) stand out, not just as anthologies of currently popular church music, but as histories of Black church music presented in the music itself.

2666. Spencer, Jon Michael. "The Heavenly Anthem: Holy Ghost Singing in the Primal Pentecostal Revival, 1906-1909." *Journal of Black Sacred Music* 1, Spr. (1987): 1-33.

2667. Spencer, Jon Michael. "Rhythm in Black Religion of the African Diaspora." *Journal of Religious Thought* 44, Wint/Spr. (1988): 67-82. Rhythm is the essential, perhaps the only, link that Afro-Americans have to Africa. Restricted by slave owners, rhythm—particularly the rhythm of drums—survived in North America in secular dance, hand-clapping, and especially in the ring shout. The two elements essential to all African religions, rhythm and dance, also survived in invisible slave churches, in the early Pentecostal-Holiness churches, where spirit possession was practiced, and in the spiritual, through whose freeing rhythmic movements the Holy Spirit delivered its unifying and liberating powers.

2668. Spencer, Jon Michael. "A Theology for the Blues." *Journal of Black Sacred Music* 2, 1 (Spring) (1988): 1-20. Stating that blues music was and is "sacred music," the author attempts to discern the heretofore unarticulated theology of blues singers and their music and place that theology in the context of black theology.

2669. Spencer, Jon Michael, ed. "The Theology of American Popular Music: A Special Issue of Black Sacred Music: A Journal of Theomusicology." *Black Sacred Music* 3, Fall (1989): 1-169. A collection of eleven articles on theological aspects of Afro-American popular music.

2670. Spencer, Jon Michael. "God in Secular Music Culture: The Theodicy of the Blues as the Paradigm of Proof." *Journal of Black Sacred Music* 3, Fall (1989): 17-49. A theodicy is an explanation for the existence of moral evil in a world created by an omnipotent, omniscient, and omnibenevolent God. Blues are theodical when they not only address evil and suffering, but devise provisional philosophical solutions to render these intelligible. Texts are examined for their representation of God, criticism of the church, and affirmation of true faith through atonement.

2671. Spencer, Jon Michael, ed. "Unsung Hymns by Black and Unknown Bards." *Journal of Black Sacred Music* 4, Spr. (1990): 1-171. A study of 100 hymns and music on the major events and topics relevant to Christianity.

2672. Spencer, Jon Michael. "The Hymnody of the African Methodist Episcopal Church." *American Music* 8, 3 (1990): 274-293. A study of the *Bicentennial Hymnal* as the culmination of the richest history of hymnology of any black religious denomination.

2673. Spencer, Jon Michael. "Black Denominational Hymnody and Growth toward Religious and Racial Maturity." *Hymn* 41, Oct. (1990): 41-45.

2674. Spencer, Jon Michael. *Protest and Praise: Sacred Music of Black Religion*. Minneapolis: Fortress Press, 1990. Divides African-American religious song texts into two groups: the protest song (inclucing spirituals, 19th-century hymns, etc.) and the praise song (including the ring shout, tongue song, gospel music, and chanted sermon).   Ch. 6, 'The Drum Deferred: Rhythm in Black Religion of the African Diaspora' turns to musical aspects of Afro-American religious music.

2675. Spencer, Jon Michael. "The Hymnology of Black Methodists." *Theology Today* 46, Jan. (1990): 373-385. "Songs of Zion and the new 1989 U[nited] M[ethodist] Hymnal."

2676. Spencer, Jon Michael, ed. "The R. Nathaniel Dett Reader: Essays on Black Sacred Music." *Black Sacred Music* 5, Fall (1991): vii-xiv, 1-138.

2677. Spencer, Jon Michael. *The Emergency of Black and the Emergence of Rap*. Durham, NC: Duke University Press, 1991. Whole issue of the *Journal of Black Sacred Music*. 5, 1, 1991. Includes articles on the relationship of Rap to prophecy, the ideology of the Nation of Islam, and the rapper as shaman.

2678. Spencer, Jon Michael, ed. "Sacred Music of the Secular City: From Blues to Rap." *Black Sacred Music* 6, Spr. (1992): 1-309. A collection of articles on the religious aspects of Afro-American music, including the blues, jazz, soul, rock, and rap.

2679. Spencer, Jon Michael. "'Sing a New Song': A Petition for a Visionary Black Hymnody." In *The Sacred Sound and Social Change: Liturgical Music in Jewish and Christian Experience*, Lawrence A. Hoffman and Janet Roland Walton, ed. Two Liturgical Traditions, Vol. 3. Notre Dame: University of Notre Dame Press, 1992. 300-313. A plea for a hymnody that reflects African history and scholarship and Afro-American values.

2680. Spencer, Jon Michael. *Black Hymnody: A Hymnological History of the African-American Church*. Knoxville, TN: University of Tennessee Press, 1992.

2681. Spencer, Jon Michael. *Blues and Evil*. Knoxville: University of Tennessee Press, 1993. A scholarly and poetically written study of the blues tracing three primary aspects of the religious cosmology of the blues: 1) methodology, 2) theology and 3) theodicy.

2682. Stone, S.M. *Song Composition, Transmission, and Performance Practice in an Urban Black Denomination, the Church of God and Saints of Christ.* Ph.D. diss., Kent State University, 1985. Founded in 1896, the CGSC has from its beginning fostered a repertory of 4-part songs composed by the members themselves and taught orally, rather than the more well-known spiritual, jubliee, quartet, hymn, or gospel song.

2683. Sutton, Brett. "Speech, Chant, and Song: Patterns of Language and Action in a Southern Church." In *Diversities of Gifts: Field Studies in Southern Religion*, Jr. Ruel Tyson, James Peacock, and Daniel Patterson, ed. Urbana, IL: University of Illinois Press, 1988. 157-176. A study of language patterns in the religious song of Black churches in the Blue Ridge Mountains.

2684. Turner, William C., Jr. "The Musicality of Black Preaching." *Journal of Black Sacred Music* 2, 1 (Spring) (1988): 21-34.

2685. Tyler, Mary Ann L. *The Music of Charles Henry Pace and its Relationship to the Afro-American Church Experience.* Ph.D. diss., University of Pittsburgh, 1981. Tyler uses Pace's song sheets to explore the African American aural-oral church experience with reference to tone patterns, grace notes, parallel harmonies, verbal interjections and other characteristics.

2686. Walker, Wyatt T. *"Somebody's Calling My Name." Black Sacred Music and Social Change.* Vally Forge, PA: Judson Press, 1979. A socio-historical introduction to the role of Black sacred music in building up the Black Church and fostering social protest. Discussion is limited to spirituals, Black "meta" music, hymns and gospel music; Pentecostal music and spirit possession is excluded .

2687. Walker, Wyatt T. *Spirits That Dwell in the Deep Woods: The Prayer and Praise Hymns of the Black Religious Experience.* New York: Martin Luther King Fellow Press, 1987.

2688. Whalum, Wendall. "Music in the Churches of Black Americans: A Critical Statement." *Black Perspective in Music* 14, 1 (1986): 13-20. Whalum cites inappropriate songs, incorrectly trained church musicians and faulty theological guidance among the primary problems of Afro-American church music.

2689. Wilcken, Lois E. *Vodon Music among Haitians living in New York City: a Symbolic Approach.* MA thesis, Hunter College, 1986. An attempt to identify the song structures, phrasing, rhythm, timbre and instrumentation in Vodun rites, discover their meanings, and show how they are bound together in an integrated system.

2690. Wilcken, Lois E. "Power, Ambivalence, and the Remaking of Haitian Vodoun Music in New York." *Latin American Music Review* 13, 1 (1992): 1-32. The ambivalence N.Y. Haitians feel about performance of vodoun as folk music lies in their experience of colonial class divisions, foreign cultural intervention, negative stereotyping of Haiti's neo-African culture, and negative feelings about their own African heritage.

2691. Williams, Robert. *Preservation of the Oral Tradition of Singing Hymns in Negro Religious Music*. Ph.D. diss., Florida State University, 1973.

2692. Williams-Jones, Pearl. "The Musical Quality of Black Religious Folk Ritual." *Spirit* 1 (1977): 21.

SPIRITUALS, BLACK AND WHITE

2693. Brown, Grayson W. "Music in the Black Spiritual Tradition." In *This Far by Faith: American Black Worship and its African Roots*, Rovert W. Hovda, ed. Washington, DC: The National Office for Black Catholics and the Liturgical Conference, 1977. 88-93.

2694. Brown, Joseph Augustine. *Harmonic Circles: Afro-American Religious Heritage and American Aesthetics*. Ph.D. diss., Yale University, 1984. A study of the raw materials and aesthetic principles available to composers and poets of spirituals. From Africa are the primacy of music and dance for communal artistic expression, multiple rhythms, ambiguity, and opportunities for improvisation and communal response. Other materials are Protestant theology, increased emphasis on mysticism, the assumption of a prophetic identity, and the political and moral constraints imposed upon both black and white Americans by slavery and the evolution of racism. Central to the study is the myth of Jacob.

2695. Cone, James. *The Spirituals and the Blues: An Interpretation*. Maryknoll, NY: Orbis Books, 1972/repr. 1991. Writing from a theological perspective, Cone asserts that the musical traditions of black spirituals and the blues share a common core of religious meaning and each has the power to foster survival within the African-American community. Cone sets both traditions within the context of Black religious thinking and historical experience. 1980 repr. Westport, CT: Greenwood Press.

2696. Cone, James. "Black Spirituals: A Theological Interpretation." In *Music and the Experience of God*, Collins, Power, and Burnim, ed. 1989. 41-51. On the subject of freedom in the theological foundations of black spirituals and laments, how the songs express the hope of liberation, affirm black beliefs and values, and assert the desire for human dignity.

2697. Dixon, Christa K. *Negro Spirituals: From Bible to Folk Song*. Philadelphia, PA: Fortress Press, 1976.

2698. DjeDje, Jacqueline Cogdell. *An Analytical Study of the Similarities and Differences in the American Black Spiritual and Gospel Song from the Southeast Region of Georgia*. M.A. thesis, UCLA, 1972.

2699. Downey, James C. and Paul Oliver. "Spiritual." In *NGDAM*, Vol. 4. 1986. 284-290. Except for the expanded bibliography in this article, it is essentially the same as "Spiritual" in *Grove 6*, Vol. 18, 1-7.

2700. Epstein, Dena. *Sinful Tunes and Spirituals: Black Folk Music to the Civil War*. Music in American Life Series, Urbana: University of Illinois Press, 1977/repr. 1981. Epstein points to the misuse of notated versions of Black spirituals to establish points of origin and influence without attention to other kinds of evidence as the cause for now largely discredited notions of musical development and influence.

2701. Epstein, Dena. "A White Origin for the Black Spiritual? An Invalid Theory and How it Grew." *American Music* 1, 2 (1983): 53-59. The theory that the spiritual was white in origin originated with Richard Wallaschek in 1893. A Viennese scholar who had never been to Africa or America, Wallaschek relied on printed slave and minstrel songs for his information. The theory received its strongest statement from George Pullman Jackson in various publications from the 1930s on. Although parallels between White and Black spirituals do exist, it is a mistake to rely solely on notated music and ignore how the music sounds and how it is performed.

2702. Epstein, Dena. "Black Spirituals: Their Emergence into Public Knowledge." *Black Music Research Journal* 10, 1 (Spring) (1990): 58-64. Spirituals first came into prominence from notated versions of spirituals sung by the Fisk Jubilee Singers in the 1870s. Most opinions concerning the spiritual were based on notated versions until rather recently when it became possible, through recordings, to distinguish between concert arrangements and performance in authentic folk style.

2703. Garst, John F. "Mutual Reinforcement and the Origins of Spirituals." *American Music* 4, 4 (Winter) (1986): 390-406. A balanced view regarding the white and black contributions to the spiritual.

2704. Hawley, Thomas Earl, Jr. *The Slave Tradition of Singing among the Gullah of Johns Island, South Carolina*. Ph.D. diss., University of Maryland, Baltimore County, 1993. A study of the musical and extra-musical elements of a style of spiritual whose roots in oral tradition date back over two centuries and whose existence is now threatened.

2705. Jackson, George Pullen. *White and Negro Spirituals: Their Life Span and Kinship, Tracing 200 Years of Untrammeled Song Making and Singing among our Country Folk, with 116 Songs as Sung by Both Races*. New York: Da Capo, 1944/repr. 1975. This book promotes a theory, first advanced by Wallaschek and since disproved, that the spiritual is white in origin.

2706. Jackson, George Pullen. "Spirituals." In *Grove 5*, 1954.

2707. Jackson, George Pullen. *White Spirituals in the Southern Uplands: The Story of the Fasola Folk, Their Songs, Singings, and "Buckwheat Notes"*. Hatboro, PA: Folklore Associates, 1964. Contains essay "Tunes of the White Man's Spirituals Preserved in the Negro's Religious Songs/White Man's and Negro's Spiritual Texts Compared," pp. 242-302. 1933 ed., /repr. 1965. New York: Dover. New ed. with an introduction by Don Yoder.

2708. Johnson, Hall. *Notes on the Negro Spiritual*. 2nd ed., Eileen Southern, New York: Norton, 1983. 273-80. Johnson takes the position that the African-American spiritual is little more than a variation on Euro-American folk music and lacks significant ties to African musical traditions. He presents a statistical comparison of the musical compositions of spirituals and revival camp songs.

2709. Johnson, Lonnel E. "Servant Imagery in African-American Spirituals." *Journal of Black Sacred Music* 2, 1 (Spring) (1988): 45-50.

2710. Jones, Arthur. *Wade in the Water: The Wisdom of the Spirituals*. Maryknoll, NY: Orbis Books, 1993. A six-part series of reflections on the primary themes of African-American spirituals: suffering and transformation, struggle and resistance, working spirituality, accountability, and hope and healing.

2711. Kirk-Duggan, Cheryl A. "African-American Spirituals: Confronting and Exorcising Evil through Song." In *A Troubling in My Soul: Womanist Perspectives on Evil and Suffering*, Maryknoll, NY: Orbis Books, 1993. 150-171. Through the combination of text and music, African American spirituals create an Afro-centric womanist, constructive concept of theodicy. In a racist, unjust world, the spiritual fashions a cosmology that proclaims an absolute faith in God and surrender to God's will, a life of praise and thanksgiving for everything in the knowledge that God judges and blesses all equally, and respect and love for self and others.

2712. Lorenz, E.J. *Glory Hallelujah! The Story of the Campmeeting Spiritual*. Nashville, TN: Abingdon Press, 1980. Beginning in Kentucky c1800 as part of the second Great Awakening, camp meetings quickly spread, and the new 'hymnody', the camp-meeting spiritual with its catchy, fervent melodies, conveyed the exhilaration, even the ecstasy, that newborn souls needed to express. This is a study of those songs, with many exx. of text and tune.

2713. Lovell, John, Jr. *Black Song: The Forge and the Flame: The Story of How the Afro-American Spiritual Was Hammered Out*. New York: Paragon House, 1972/repr. 1986. A thorough study of the texts of the spiritual, with emphasis on the black contribution to the spiritual. Part 1 discusses the African musical experience; Part 2 is a study of the slave song and its literary meaning; and Part 3 explores the development and spread of the spiritual from 1871.

2714. Maultsby, Portia K. "Black Spirituals: An Analysis of Textual Forms and Structures." *Black Perspective in Music* 4 (1976): 54. A description of spirituals from the first two published collections of African-American music to include music notation (1867, 1877). Spirituals with verse and chorus predominate (71%). Verses and choruses usually consist of alternations of new lines of text with recurring lines of text.

2715. McKenzie, Wallace. "E.A. McIlhenny's Black Spiritual Collection from Avery Island, Louisiana." *American Music* 8, 1 (Spring) (1990): 95-110. A study of *Befo' de War Spirituals: Words and Melodies*. Published in 1933, this collection of 120 Black spirituals includes 80 that appear in no other collections, making it a unique resource for local repertory.

2716. Peters, Erskine, ed. *Lyrics of the Afro-American Spiritual: A Documentary Collection*. Greenwood Encyclopedia of Black Music, Westport, CT: Greenwood Press, 1993.

2717. Robinson, Aminah Branda Lynn. *The Teachings: Drawn from African-American Spirituals*. New York: Harcourt Brace Jovanovich, 1992.

2718. Southern, Eileen. "An Origin for the Negro Spiritual." *Black Scholar* 3 (1972): 8 ff.

2719. Tallmadge, W.H. "The Black in Jackson's White Spirituals." *Black Perspective in Music* 9 (1981): 139. The author challenges Jackson's understanding of the origins and structures of camp-meeting songs by providing a detailed structural analysis of Jackson's 116 "white" melodies.

GOSPEL MUSIC, BLACK AND WHITE

2720. Allen, Ray. "Gospel Quartet Performance and Ritual in New York City's African-American Church Community." *Urban Resources* 4, 3 (Spring) (1987): 13-18.

2721. Allen, Ray. *Singing in the Spirit: An Ethnography of Gospel Performance in New York City's African-American Church Community*. Ph.D. diss., University of Pennsylvania, 1987.

2722. Allen, Ray. *Singing in the Spirit: African-American Sacred Quartets in New York City*. Philadelphia, PA: University of Pennsylvania Press, 1991. Publication of the American Folklore Society.

2723. Allen, Ray. "Shouting the Church: Narrative and Vocal Improvisation in African-American Gospel Quartet Performance." *Journal of American Folklore* 104, 413 (Sum.) (1991): 295-317.

2724. Allen, Ray. "Back Home: Southern Identity and African-American Gospel Quartet Performance." In *Mapping American Culture*, Wayne Franklin, ed. Iowa City: University of Iowa Press, 1992. 112-135. In Gospel song-texts, 'The South' functions for African Americans as an image of a sacred homeland

and as a place of hardship that was suffered and overcome—a metaphor for social, moral, and spiritual salvation. References to the South thus mediate between such polarities as secular and sacred, urban and rural, North and South, modern and traditional. Contemporary Gospel Quartets are seen to operate between these poles.

2725. Allgood, B. Dexter. *A Study of Selected Black Gospel Choirs in the Metropolitan New York Area.* Ph.D. diss., New York University, 1983.

2726. Allgood, B. Dexter. "Black Gospel Music in New York City." *The Black Perspective in Music* 18, 1-2 (1990): 101-15. A description of Black Gospel in New York from the 1920s to the 1980s. Included for mention are Rosetta Thorpe (1930s), Mahalia Jackson (1950s), Edwin Hawkins (1970s), and various Gospel groups.

2727. Anderson, Robert and Gail North. *Gospel Music Encyclopedia.* New York: Sterling Publishing Co., 1979.

2728. Blackwell, Lois S. *The Wings of the Dove: The Story of Gospel Music in America.* Norfolk, VA: Donning, 1978. Introduction by Brock Speer.

2729. Boyer, Horace Clarence. "Analysis of his Contributions: Thomas A. Dorsey: Father of Gospel Music." *Black World* 23 (1974): 20.

2730. Boyer, Horace Clarence. "Contemporary Gospel Music." *Black Perspective in Music* 7, 2, Spring (1979): 5, 22. and 1982, 2, 5 ff. In his two-part article Boyer first describes the sacred vs. secular debate surrounding the popularization of gospel music in the 1950's and 1960's. In Part Two he analyzes the characteristics and style of the music.

2731. Boyer, Horace Clarence. "Charles Albert Tindley: Progenitor of Black-American Gospel Music." *Black Perspective in Music* 11 (1983): 104 ff.

2732. Boyer, Horace Clarence. "A Comparative Analysis of Traditional and Contemporary Gospel Music." In *More Than Dancing*, Irene V. Jackson, ed. Westport CT: Greenwood, 1985. Boyer identifies nine musical elements for points of comparison between the two gospel styles: melody, harmony, form, rhythm, accompaniment, vocal timbre, vocal combinations, vocal background, and song texts. Also discussed are the tensions between the secularizing influence of popularization and the evangelistic mission of gospel music.

2733. Broughton, Viv. *Black Gospel: An Illustrated History of the Gospel Sound.* Poole, Dorset: Blandford Press; New York: Sterling Publishing Co., 1985.

2734. Burnim, Mellonee. *The Black Gospel Musical Tradition: Symbol of Ethnicity.* Ph.D. diss., Indiana University, 1980. An investigation that analyzes the meaning and significance of gospel music as a vehicle for expression among the majority of Black Americans through an examination of actual performance events at two churches in Indiana. The conclusion describes the many historical, ritual, and interactive factors by means of which gospel music symbolizes ethnicity among Black Americans.

2735. Burnim, Mellonee. "The Black Gospel Music Tradition: A Complex of Idiology, Aesthetic and Behavior." In *More Than Dancing*, Irene Jackson, ed. Westport, CT: Greenwood Press, 1985. 147-66.

2736. Burnim, Mellonee. "Functional Dimensions of Gospel Music Performance." *The Western Journal of Black Studies* 12, 2 (Summer) (1988): 112-21.

2737. Burnim, Mellonee. "The Performance of Black Gospel Music as Transformation." In *Music and the Experience of God*, Collins, Power, and Burnim, ed. 1989. 52-61. This article on black gospel music from a black standpoint proposes that participation in this 'ritual' leads to a transformation of the personae—through reception of the spiritual message and the experiencing of God—and a transformation of space: whatever space the event takes place in becomes a spiritual space.

2738. Casey, M.E. *The Contributions of the Reverend James Cleveland to Gospel Music and its Implications for Music Education*. M.A. thesis, Howard University, 1980.

2739. Cusic, Don. *The Sound of Light: A History of Gospel Music*. Bowling Green, OH: Bowling Green State University Popular Press, 1990. Writing to a lay Christian audience, Cusic covers the history of Christian music in broad strokes beginning with the early church through the Christian pop stars of the 1980's.

2740. Daniel, Wayne. "Making a Joyful Noise unto the Lord—The Gospel Roots of Bluegrass." *Bluegrass Unlimited* 19, 9 (1985): 58-62.

2741. Dargan, William Thomas. *Congregational Gospel Songs in a Black Holiness Church: A Musical and Textual Analysis*. Ph.D. diss., Wesleyan University, 1983. A study of the music of a holiness, 'sanctified,' or 'shouting' church and the influence of its style of music upon Black gospel music. The songs were interpreted as musical forms, ritual forms, and religious experience, and the interrelation of the three was examined.

2742. Dargan, William Thomas and Kathy White Bullock. "Willie Mae Ford Smith of St. Louis: A Shaping Influence upon Black Gospel Singing Style." *Black Music Research Journal* 9, 2 (Fall) (1989): 249-70.

2743. DjeDje, Jacqueline Cogdell. "Gospel Music in the Los Angeles Black Community: A Historical Overview." *Black Music Research Journal* 9, 1 (Spring) (1989): 35-79. A brief history of Gospel music in LA, 1930-1959, followed by a survey of the music and the publishing of it, and biographies of eleven prominent composers.

2744. DjeDje, Jacqueline Cogdell. "Los Angeles Composers of African American Gospel Music: The First Generations." *American Music* 11, 4/Winter (1993): 412-457.

2745. Downey, James C. "Mississippi Music: That Gospel Sound." In *Sense of Place: Mississippi*, Jackson, MS: University Press of Mississippi, 1979. Downey reflects on the sociological, religious, and geographic characteristics of Mississippi that have entered into the creation of gospel music and reviews the work of current Southern born artists in light of their ties to the gospel tradition.

2746. Duckett, A. "An Interview with Thomas A. Dorsey." *Black World* 23 (1974): 4. An extended interview with an innovative gospel composer and arranger tracing the origins and rise of the genre. Includes a history of the classic song, *Precious Lord*.

2747. Eskew, Harry et al. "Gospel music." In *NGDAM*, Vol. 2. 1986. 248-261. A reworking of "Gospel Music" in *Grove 6*, Vol. 7, 549-559.

2748. Feintuch, B. "A Noncommercial Black Gospel Group in Context: We Live the Life We Sing About." *Black Music Research Journal* 1 (1980): 37. Feintuch attempts to understand musical expression in light of social settings and lifestyle using a case study format.

2749. Franklin, Marion. *The Relationship of Black Preaching to Black Gospel Music*. Ph.D. diss., Drew University, 1982. A thesis project examining the links between Black preaching and gospel music and outlining a course of action for maintaining African American sacred music forms. Emphasis is placed on theological and liturgical context and function.

2750. George, Luvenia A. *Lucie E. Campbell and the Enduring Tradition of Gospel Hymnody*. Washington, DC: Smithsonian Institution, Program in Black American Culture, 1983.

2751. Harris, Michael W. *The Rise of Gospel Blues: The Music of Thomas Andrew Dorsey in the Urban Church*. New York and Oxford: Oxford University Press, 1992.

2752. Harvey, Louis Charles. "Black Gospel Music and Black Theology." *Journal of Religious Thought* 43, Fall/Winter (1987): 19-37.

2753. Haynes, Karima. "The Gospel Controversy: Are the New Songs too Jazzy and too Worldly." *Ebony* 47, 5 (March, 1992): 76-79. A broad overview of current tensions within the gospel industry between traditionalists and younger cross-over artists. Excerpts of interviews with a wide range of industry insiders, both performers and promoters, are included.

2754. Heilbut, A. "The Secularization of Black Gospel Music." In *Folk Music and Modern Sound*, William Ferris and Mary L. Hart, ed. Jackson MI 1982. 101-15. Heilbut documents the at-times confused integration of Gospel music with secular musical styles and political causes from the 1930's to the 1980's. Originally appeared as "New Signs on the Gospel Highway," *The Nation*, 230/18 (1980), 72.

2755. Heilbut, T. *The Gospel Sound: Good News and Bad Times*. 4th ed., New York: Limelight Editions, Harper and Row, 1992. Based on interview and personal observation, this study documents the origins and growth of gospel, the contributions of various individuals, quartets and groups, and a description of their singing techniques and performance characteristics.

2756. Hillsman, Joan R. *Gospel Music: An African American Art Form.* Washington, DC: Middle Atlantic Regional Press, 1990.

2757. Hinson, Glenn D. "Traveling Down that Gospel Highway: Carolina Traditions of Black Sacred Song." *Tar heel Junior Historian* 25, 2 (1986): 19-21.

2758. Hinson, Glenn D. *When the Words Roll and the Fire Flows: Spirit, Style and Experience in African American Gospel Performance*. Ph.D. diss., University of Pennsylvania, 1989.

2759. Jackson, Irene V. "Developments in Black Gospel Performance and Scholarship." *Black Music Research Journal* 10, 1 (Spring) (1990): 36-42. A report on the current literature available and scholarly work being done on the subject of gospel music. Reprinted from *Black Music Research Newsletter* 4/3 (1981).

2760. Lornell, Kip. *"Happy in the Service of the Lord" : Afro-American Gospel Quartets in Memphis*. Music in American Life Series, Urbana, IL: University of Illinois Press, 1988. This study places the development and importance of the Black American quartet tradition in their historical and cultural framework. Places special focus on Memphis as a locale and on the dissemination of the music in the mass media.

2761. Marks, Morton. "You Can't Sing Unless You're Saved: Reliving the Call in Gospel Music." In *African Religious Groups and Beliefs: Papers in Honor of William R. Bascom*, Simon Ottenberg, ed. Meerut, India: Archana Publications for Folklore Institute; Bloomington, IN: Folklore Institute, 1982. 305-331. An analysis of three gospel songs to illustrate the performance rules in operation in Afro-American fundamentalist churches. Includes song and sermon texts and compositions.

2762. McLemore, B.F. *Tracing the Roots of Southern Gospel Singers*. Jasper, TX: B.F. McLemore, 1988.

2763. Montell, William Lynwood. *Singing the Glory Down: Amateur Gospel Music in South Central Kentucky, 1900-1990*. Lexington, KY: University Press of Kentucky, 1991. Beginning with shape-note singing and the singing convention movement at the beginning of this century, this study moves through early gospel quartets, the shift to instrumental accompaniment, and the new era of quartet popularity (1950-90). Also describes individual singers and their Christian beliefs, performance aspects and text content, singing families, and the continuance of traditional gospel in southern harmony style, in spite of competition from newer styles.

2764. Oliver, Paul. "Spirituals/Gospel." In *The New Grove: Gospel, Blues and Jazz, with Spirituals and Ragtime*. New York & London: W.W. Norton & Co., 1986. Spiritual: 1-22; Gospel:189-222. These articles are expansions of articles in *Grove 6*.

2765. Peach, E., Jr. *The Gospel Song: Its Influences on Christian Hymnody*. Ph.D. diss., Wayne State University, 1960.

2766. Ricks, George R. *Some Aspects of the Religious Music of the United States Negro: An Ethnomusicological Study with Special Emphasis on the Gospel Tradition*. New York: Arno Press, 1960/repr. 1977. Reprint of 1960 Ph.D. diss. at Northwestern University. A socio-cultural, historical, and musico-theoretical study of Afro-American religious music in the U.S. during the period between c.1750 and 1959. Covers the three primary black religious musical genres—spiritual, the jubilee, and the gospel song—their origins in African music and musical values, and includes a description of Jubilee-style quartet singing, the influence of the Fisk Jubilee, and an analysis quartet style.

2767. Sankey, I.D. *My Life and the Story of the Gospel Hymns and of Sacred Songs and Solos*. New York and Philadelphia: Sunday School Times, 1907.

2768. Schwerin, Jules. *Got to Tell It: Mahalia Jackson, Queen of Gospel*. New York: Oxford University Press, 1992.

2769. Sizer, Sandra S. *Gospel Hymns and Social Religion: The Rhetoric of Nineteenth-Century Revivalism*. Philadelphia, PA: Temple University Press, 1979.

2770. Smucker, David. *Philip Paul Bliss and the Musical, Cultural and Religious Sources of the Gospel Music Tradition in the United States, 1850-1876*. Ph.D. diss., Boston University, 1981. The origins of gospel tune formation as seen through the life and works of Bliss. Among the sources are white minstrel songs, devotional hymns and revival songs; urban-industrialism; the congruence of romantic evangelicalism and the revivalist ethos; particular historical developments; and an interaction of religious and secular groups, urban and rural life styles, and cultivated and vernacular musical traditions.

2771. Stevenson, Robert M. "Ira D. Sankey and the Growth of 'Gospel Hymnody.'" In *Patterns of Protestant Church Music*, Durham, NC: Duke University Press, 1953/repr. 1957. Stevenson takes a utilitarian approach to gospel hymnody by judging the music by its impact on a congregation and its ability to influence converts.

2772. Tallmadge, W.H. "Dr. Watts and Mahalia Jackson—the Development, Decline and Survival of a Folk Style in America." *Ethnomusicology* 5 (1961): 95 ff. An examination of the tradition and on-going use of the lining-out technique, with attention to adaptations of the style as found in the gospel solos of Mahalia Jackson.

2773. Tallmadge, W.H. "The Responsorial and Antiphonal Practice in Gospel Song." *Ethnomusicology* 12 (1968): 219. Tallmadge reviews the three basic techniques of responsorial and antiphonal practice and traces their sources.

2774. Terrell, Bob. *The Music Men: The Story of Professional Gospel Quartet Singing*. Asheville, NC: B. Terrell Publisher, 1990.

2775. Warrick, Mancel et al. *The Progress of Gospel Music: From Spirituals to Contemporary Gospel*. New York: Vantage Press, 1977.

2776. Wilhoit, M.R. *A Guide to the Principal Authors and Composers of Gospel Song in the Nineteenth Century*. Ph.D. diss., Southern Baptist Theological Seminary, 1982.

2777. Williams-Jones, Pearl. "Afro-American Gospel Music: A Crystallization of the Black Aesthetic." *Ethnomusicology* 19, 3 (1975): 373-385. The indomitable spirit of the 'Black Aesthetic' permeates and informs Black gospel music, causing it to differ in form and content from Euro-centric models.

2778. Williams-Jones, Pearl. "Structure and Spirit: Improvisation Qualities of Black American Gospel Songs and Sermons." In *Improvisation in the Performing Arts: A Report of the Symposium of Improvisation in the Performing Arts, Held at the East-West Center July 10-23, 1983*, Ricardo D. Trimillos and William Feltz, ed. Honolulu, HI: East-West Center, Institute of Culture and Communication, 1985. 119-28.

2779. Williams-Jones, Pearl. "Washington, DC/Gospel Music City, USA: State of the Art." In *1987 Festival of American Folklife: Smithsonian Institution: National Park Service, June 24-28/July 1-5.*, Ed Brown, ed. Washington, DC: Smithsonian Institution, 1987. 16-21.

2780. Wolfe, Charles K. "Gospel Goes Uptown: White Gospel Music, 1945-1955." In *Folk Music and Modern Sound*, William Ferris and Mary L. Hart, ed. Jackson: University Press of Mississippi, 1982. Wolfe traces the impact of such factors as commercialization, the rapid growth of independent record companies, the sponsorship of publishers, and the decline of singing conventions on "white gospel music."

CONTEMPORARY CHRISTIAN MUSIC

2781. Ankerberg, John. *Rock Music's Powerful Messages*. Chattanooga, TN: Ankerberg Theological Research Institute, 1991.

2782. Aranza, Jacob. *Backward Masking Unmasked: Backward Satanic Messages of Rock and Roll Exposed*. Shreveport, LA: Huntington House, 1983.

2783. Are, Thomas L. *Faithsong: A New Look at the Ministry of Music*. Philadelphia, PA: Westminster Press, 1981.

2784. Baker, Paul. *Contemporary Christian Music: Where It Came from, Where It Is, Where It is Going*. rev. ed., Westchester, IL: Good News, 1985.

2785. Bangert, Mark P. "Music Criteria for Sound Worship." *Chicago Theological Seminary Register* 76, 2, Spr. (1986): 25-31.

2786. Barger, Eric. *From Rock to Rock: The Music of Darkness Exposed*. Lafayette, LA: Huntington House, 1990.

2787. Bauer, Sandra M. *Between Fire and Brimstones and Guitars: The Study of Worship as Recital*. D.Min. diss, Andover Newton Theological School (Newton Centre, MA), 1992. The author draws on the psychology of music, and especially Jungian theory, to examine the way in which the presence of God has been remembered and celebrated in community worship.

2788. Beyer, Huntley and Rebecca Parker Beyer. "Music Informing Spirit: A Commentary on the Theological Implications of Contemporary Music." *JAAR Thematic Studies* 49, 2 (1983): 7-17. An exploration of pan-historical (eclectic), indeterminate, and minimalist styles and their possibilities in expressing a contemporary vision of Christian redemption, love, and the incarnation through metaphysical and structural connections.

2789. Boe, D., L. R. Garrett, and M. Price. "Popular Culture and Sacred Music: The Impact of Popular Culture on Sacred Music." *NASM* 79 (1991): 131-143. Three articles on the subject.

2790. Cummings, Tony. "Christian Music in UK has Counterculture Buzz." *Billboard* 105, 14/April (1993): 2. On the marketing of UK Christian music in styles ranging from praise-worship to thrash metal.

2791. Drum, Gary Richard. *The Message in the Music: A Content Analysis of Contemporary Christian and Southern Gospel Song Lyrics*. Ph.D. diss., University of Tennessee, 1987.

2792. Edgar, William. "The Message of Rock Music." In *Art in Question*, Tim Dean and David Porter, ed. Basingstoke, England: Marshall Pickering, 1987. 28-51. On the theology of rock music.

2793. Ellsworth, Donald P. *Christian Music in Contemporary Witness: Historical Antecedents and Contemporary Practices.* Grand Rapids, MI: Baker Book House, 1980.

2794. English, Joan Pritcher. *Criteria for the Reform and Renewal of Contemporary Musical Forms in Christian Worship.* Ph.D. diss., Emory University, 1985. The insights of both Reformation and 20th-century ecumenical theologians (Hoon, Saliers, and White) with a purpose to finding common ground as well as meeting the needs of musical and cultural pluralism in contemporary congregations.

2795. Etzel, Crystal Lorinda. *The Evolution of Rhetorical Strategies: A Critical Essay on Contemporary Christian Music.* Ph.D. diss., The Pennsylvania State University, 1988. This study of rhetoric in Christian music from 1968 to 1988 focuses on five linguistic rhetorical strategies: relationship, antithetical construction, redundancy, metaphor, and image. These strategies were used for their persuasive appeal during the period 1968-1975, as vehicles of reinforcement, 1976-1982, and both, 1983-1988.

2796. Garcia, Guy. "Rock Finds Religion. Again. The Revived Spirituality of Today's Music is not a Call to Church but a Personal Appeal to the Divine." *The New York Times*, Jan. 2, 1994, Vol. 143, Sec. 2.

2797. Godwin, Jeff. *The Devil's Disciples: The Truth about Rock.* Chino, CA: Chick Publications, 1985.

2798. Godwin, Jeff. *Dancing with Demons: The Music's Real Master.* Chino, CA: Chick Publications, 1988.

2799. Godwin, Jeff. *What's Wrong with Christian Rock?* Chino, CA: Chick Publications, 1990.

2800. Hart, Lowell and Salem Kirban. *Satan's Music Exposed.* Chattanooga, TN: AMG Publishers, 1981.

2801. Haynes, Michael K. *The God of Rock: A Christian Perspective of Rock Music.* Lindale, TX: Priority Ministries and Publications, 1984.

2802. Howard, Jay R. "Contemporary Christian Music: Where Rock Meet Religion." *Journal of Popular Culture* 26, 1/Summer (1992): 123-130. From its modest beginnings in the late 1960s, Contemporary Christian Music has become a platform for seeking radical changes in church and society. Leading rock singers criticize the principles and culture of capitalist society and point at the irresponsible attitude of the Church in recognizing the needs of modern society.

2803. Hubley, Mary Oberle. "Some Reflections on "Contemporary" Hymns." In *Cum Angelis Canere*, R. Skeris, ed. 1990. 29-63. On what makes music sacred.

2804. Hunt, T.W. "Witnessing through Culture." In *Educating for Christian Missions*, A. Walker, ed. 1981. 137-153.

2805. Hustad, Donald P. "Doxology: A Biblical Triad." *Ex Auditu* 8 (1992): 1-16. A brief review of the relevant biblical and theological texts pertaining to the appropriateness of contemporary Christian praise songs and worship music. Includes an eight point approach for renewal of Christian liturgical musical practice. Reply by H. M. Best, pp. 17-21.

2806. Isaiah, Bettina Kuldell. *Christian Rock Music*. M.A. thesis, University of Maryland Baltimore County, 1988.

2807. Jasper, Tony. *Jesus and the Christian in a Pop Culture*. London: R. Royce, 1984.

2808. Middleton, J. Richard and Brian J. Walsh. "Theology at the Rim of a Broken Wheel: Bruce Cockburn and Christian Faith in a Postmodern World." *Grail* 9, June (1993): 14-39.

2809. Myra, Harold and Dean Merrill. *Rock, Bach and Superschlock*. Philadelphia, PA: A.J. Holman Company, 1972. A light-hearted chronicle of the conflicts and connections between popular music of the 1960's and '70's and evangelical Christian belief and practice. The authors advocate the adoption and adaptation of popular musical styles by Christian artists.

2810. Peck, Richard. *Rock: Making Musical Choices*. Greenville, SC. Bob Jones University Press, 1985.

2811. Romanowski, William David. *Rock'n Religion: A Sociocultural Analysis of the Contemporary Christian Music Industry*. Ph.D. diss., Bowling Green State University, 1990. Developing out of the Jesus Movement in the late 1960s, the CCM industry first used religious broadcasting stations and bookstores to create a marketing network modeled after the larger secular recording industry. Increasing commercialization was justified by expanding opportunities for evanglization of more young people, steering them and the industry ever more deeply into American consumerism. As tension between ministry and business developed, the industry reached a plateau in the late 1908s.

2812. Romanowski, Willian David. "Contemporary Christian Music: The Business of Music Ministry." In *American Evangelicals and the Mass Media: Perspectives on the Relationship between American Evangelicals and the Mass Media*, Quentin Schultze, ed. Grand Rapids, MI: Academie Books/Zondervan, 1990. 143-169.

2813. Romanowski, William David. "Roll over Beethoven, Tell Martin Luther the News: American Evangelicals and Rock Music." *Journal of American Culture* 15, 3/Fall (1992): 79-88. After a period in which the use of heavy-metal music and mannerisms to preach a Christian message alienated more traditional religious groups, Contemporary Christian Music has merged into the mainstream of the music industry.

2814. Ryken, Leland, ed. *The Christian Imagination: Essays on Literature and the Arts.* Grand Rapids, MI: Baker Book House, 1981. Contains several brief articles on the place of music in the Christian life.

2815. Seay, Davin, with Mary Neely. *Stairway to Heaven: The Spiritual Roots of Rock 'n' Roll, from the King and Little Richard to Prince and Amy Grant.* New York: Ballantine Books, 1986.

2816. Deleted

2817. Smith, James D. "Ancient Christian Trinitarian Metaphors and a Contemporary Analogy from Music." *Journal of the Evangelical Theological Society* 33, Spr. (1990): 353-357.

2818. Stefani, Wolfgang Hans Martin. *The Concept of God and Sacred Music Style: An Intercultural Exploration of Divine Transcendence/ Immanence as a Stylistic Determinant for Worship Music with Paradigmatic Implications for the Contemporary Christian Context.* Ph.D. diss., Andrews University, School of Graduate Studies, 1994.

2819. Swaggart, Jimmy. *Christian Rock and Roll.* Baton Rouge, LA: Jimmy Swaggart Ministries, 1986.

2820. Terrell, Janice. *The Growth of Contemporary Christian Music in the Last Ten Years (1973-1983).* M.A. thesis, American University, 1984. On the relationship of the music trade and popular music to the development of contemporary Christian music in the United States.

2821. Walsh, Brian J. "The Christian Worldview of Bruce Cockburn: Prophetic Art in a Dangerous Time." *Toronto Journal of Theology* 5, 2, Fall (1989): 170-187. An investigation of how Cockburn has translated his distinctive world view and life experiences as a Christian into the poetry and music of song.

2822. Whaley, Vernon M. *Trends in Gospel Music Publishing: 1940 to 1960.* Ph.D. diss., The University of Oklahoma, 1992. Dynamic individual publishers, evangelical theological tenets, charismatic performers, modern business practices, the resistance of the religious community to secular styles, and the willingness of gospel artists to use all styles are all factors.

2823. White, J.F. *Protestant Worship: Traditions in Transition.* Louisville, KY/Westminster: John Knox Press, 1989.

2824. Wolfe, Charles. "Bible Country: The Good Book in Country Music." In *The Bible and Popular Culture in America*, Allene Stuart Phy, ed. Philadelphia, PA: Fortress Press; Chico, CA: Scholars Press, 1985. 85-100. In sentimental country song over the last century, references to the Bible focused on mother ('My Mother's Bible'), the literal veracity of the Bible (especially the King James translation), patriotism, admonitions to read the Bible, and old-time values. The peak of Bible-song popularity was between 1945 and 1955.

2825. *What the Bible Has to Say about..."Contemporary Christian" Music: Ten Scriptural Reasons Why the "Rock Beat" Is Evil in Any Form.* rev. ed., Oak Brook, IL: Institute in Basic Life Principles, 1991, 1992.

2826. Yamin, George Y., Jr. "The Theology of Bruce Springsteen." *Journal of Religious Studies* 16, 1-2 (1990): 1-21. Springstein's songs constitute a contemporary theological epic that assimilates and reinterprets, in terms accessible to his listeners, many of the themes of the Judeo-Christian traditions. The author cites the titles to many songs and connects them to such themes as sacred time, sacred space, and the story of the fall and redemption of man through pain and suffering.

JEWISH RELIGIOUS MUSIC IN AMERICA

2827. Adler, Samuel. "Sacred Music in a Secular Age." In *Sacred Sound and Social Change. Liturgical Music in Jewish and Christian Experience*, Lawrence A Hoffman and Janet R. Walton, ed. Notre Dame, Indiana: Notre Dame Press, 1992. 289-299. Composers must begin to write music for the liturgy that is both contemporary in style and of quality if the trend in recent decades toward the banal and the "pseudo-Jewish, pseudo-pop-American and pseudo-Israeli" is to be reversed.

2828. Bradshaw, Paul F. and Lawrence A. Hoffman, ed. *The Changing Face of Jewish and Christian Worship in North America.* Two Liturgical Traditions, Vol. 2. Notre Dame: University of Notre Dame Press, 1991. Sixteen essays in three groups: Liturgical Traditions and Theologies of 'The Other,' American Reform or Second Reformation?, and Critiquing Liturgical Reforms.

2829. Davidson, Charles Stuart. *The Living Legacy of the American Hazzan: Max Wolberg, His Life and Works.* Ph.D. diss., The Jewish Theological Seminary of America, Cantors Institute, 1988.

2830. Hirshberg, Jehoash. "Preservation and Change in the Musical Tradition of the Karaite Jews in Israel and in the United States." *Journal of Synagogue Music* 16, 1 (1986): 21-29.

2831. Hoffman, Lawrence A. "Musical Traditions and Tensions in the American Synagogue." In *Music and the Experience of God*, Collins, Power, and Burnim, ed. Edinburgh: T. & T. Clark Ltd., 1989. 30-40. An article on the separation of rabbi and cantor in the modern performance of synagogue music. Poses a model of synergy to reconcile the issues of textual and musical relevance in the proper worship of God.

2832. Kligman, Mark. "Modes of Prayer: The Canonization of the Maqamat in the Prayers of the Syrian Jews in Brooklyn, New York." Proceedings of the Eleventh World Congress of Jewish Studies, June 22-29, 1993. Jerusalem: World Union of Jewish Studies, 1994. Division D, Vol. 2: 259-266. A study of three types of extra-musical associations with prayer modes: ethos, or character-istic emotion; theoretical, or the association of a specific mode with a particular book or section of the Bible; and song association, or the association of a new Hebrew text or a prayer with a particular Arabic melody or mode

2833. Kligman, Mark. *Modes of Prayer: Music in the Sabbath Morning Liturgy of Syrian Jews in Brooklyn.* Ph.D. diss., New York University, forthcoming.

2834. Koskoff, Ellen. *The Concept of Nigun Among Lubavitcher Hasidim in the United States.* Ph.D. diss., 1976.

2835. Koskoff, Ellen. *The Effect of Mysticism on the Nigunim of the Lubavitcher Hasidim.* Ph.D. diss., University of Pittsburgh, 1976.

2836. Koskoff, Ellen. "Contemporary Nigun Composition in an American Hasidic Community." In *Selected Reports in Ethnomusicology*, Vol. 3, No. 1. 1978. 153-74.

2837. Levine, Joseph A. *Emunat Abba, The Life and Works of Abba Yosef Weisgal (1885-1981), in Four Volumes. A Musical Compendium (I-II), Stylistic Analysis (III), and Biographical Study (IV).* DSM, The Jewish Theological Seminary of America, Cantors Institute, 1981. A study of the chanting of Weisgal reveals the syllabic, neumatic, and melismatic styles of traditional, unmetered Synagogue song and serves as a model for its restoration in America.

2838. Levine, Joseph A. "Last Chants for the Cantorate?" *Musica Judaica* 6, 1 (1983-84): 89-99. To save itself from creeping ineptitude, the American cantorate should return to the four sources of *hazzanut*: psalmody, Biblical cantillation, the prayer modes, and vocal shading and phrasing.

2839. Newhouse, Ruth Sragow. *Volume I: The Music of the Passover Seder from Notated Sources (1644-1945). Volume II: Ashkenazi Haggadah-Text Settings from Notated Sources (1644-1945).* Ph.D. diss., University of Maryland College Park, 1980. This study of over 750 versions and variant settings of approximately thirty-five texts, mostly from Ashkenazic sources, yields a number of melodic families both geographically and chronologically. Vol. II is a collection of over 300 settings.

2840. Rinder, Rose. *Music, Prayer and Religious Leadership, Temple Emanu-El, 1913-1969.* Berkeley, CA: University of California, Bancroft Library, 1971.

With an Introduction by Rabbi Louis I. Newman. An interview conducted by Malca Chall.

2841. Schiller, Benjie-Ellen. "The Hymnal as an Index of Musical Change in Reform Synagogues." In *The Sacred Sound and Social Change: Liturgical Music in Jewish and Christian Experience*, Lawrence A. Hoffman and Janet Roland Walton, ed. Two Liturgical Traditions, Vol. 3. Notre Dame: University of Notre Dame Press, 1992. 187-212.

2842. Shelemay, Kay Kaufman. "Music in the American Synagogue: A Case Study from Houston." In *The American Synagogue: A Sanctuary Transformed*, Jack Wertheimer, ed. Cambridge: Cambridge University Press, 1987.

2843. Slobin, Mark. *Chosen Voices: The Story of the American Cantorate*. Urbana, IL: University of Illinois Press, 1989.

2844. Slobin, Mark, D. Schiff, and I. J. Katz. "Jewish-American Music." In NGDAM , Vol. 2. 1986. 569-573.

2845. Summit, Jeffrey A. "'I'm a Yankee Doodle Dandy?': Identity and Melody at an American Simhat Torah Celebration." *Ethnomusicology* 37, 1 (1993): 41-62. For the Jewish community in Cambridge, MA, the combination of traditional dance and prayer and non-traditional music (including 'Take Me Out to the Ball Game' and 'Ol' Man River') seems to affirm the participants' identities as Americans and Jews and help the adaptation of ritual to contemporary life.

2846. Werner, Eric. "The Role of Tradition in the Music of the Synagogue." *Judaism* 13, Spr. (1964): 156-163.

2847. Werner, Eric. "What Function has Synagogue Music Today?" *Journal of the Central Conference of American Rabbis* 13 (1965/6): 35 ff.

ASIAN-AMERICAN RELIGIOUS MUSIC

2848. Asai, Susan. "Horaku: A Buddhist Tradition of Performing Arts and the Development of Taiko Drumming in the United States." *Selected Reports in Ethnomusicology* Vol. VI (1985): 163-172. Buddhist *taiko* drumming developed in the U.S. in the 1970s as a form of entertainment (*horaku*) designed to attract young people to Buddhist teachings. Includes description of *taiko* ensembles, drumming syllables, and notated examples.

2849. *Buddha Vandana: A Book of Buddhist Devotions*. Los Angeles: Dharma Vijaya Buddhist Vihara, 1990.

2850. *Chanting and Temple Rules*. Rev. ed., Cumberland, RI: Kwan Um Zen School, 1983.

2851. Freeman, Jan Ann. *The Ritual Music of Japanese Buddhism: A Study of the Hompa Hongwanji Tradition as Practiced in a Temple in Los Angeles*. MA thesis, UCLA, 1971. A study of the tradition-based ritual and chant of one of the 10 schools of the Jodo-Shinshu sect of Japanese Buddhism, performed at the Senshin Buddhist church in Los Angeles.

2852. Kodani, Masao. *Horaku*. Los Angeles: Kinnara, 1979. Horaku is a form of temple dance practiced in temples affiliated with the Jodo sect of Buddhism.

2853. Le Chan N. *Music Among Vietnamese Buddhists in Hartford, CT*. M.A. thesis, Wesleyan University, 1994.

2854. *The Liturgy of Nichiren Shoshu: [the Taisekiji version]*. Los Angeles: Nichiren Shoshu Temple, 1979. The prayer-books and devotions of the Buddhist sect. Text in Chinese, Hiragana, and English romanization.

2855. McNamer, Megan. "Musical Change and Change in Music: Implications for Hmong Identity." *Hmong World* 1 (1986): 137-63. Communal ritual songs and individuating secular songs exchange roles for Khmer in the U.S.

2856. Miller, Terry E. "The Survival of Lao Traditional Music in America." *Selected Reports in Ethnomusicology* Vol. 6 (1985): 99-109. Due to the lack of practicing monks, a loosely organized Buddhist religion, the conversion of many Laotians to Christianity, and the lack of community support, the survival of Laotian Buddhist music, and of Laotian village music in general, is in doubt.

2857. *Plum Village Chanting Book*. Berkeley, CA: Parallex Press, 1991.

2858. *The Shasta Abbey Psalter*. Mt. Shasta, CA: Shasta Abbey Press, 1979. Zen Buddhist prayer-book and devotions in English.

RELIGIOUS MUSIC OF OTHER NON-PROTESTANT GROUPS

2859. al-Faruqi, Lois Ibsen. "Islamic Music, American." In *NGDAM*, Vol. 2. 1986. 501-2.

2860. Foy, Janice Ann. *Croatian Sacred Musical Tradition in Los Angeles: History, Style, and Meaning*. Ph.D. diss., University of California, Los Angeles, 1990. This study of two southern California Croatian church communities and their music seeks to explore how music creates a sense of identity and cultural bonding in the communities. Emphasis is placed on music used in the context of mass and other religious rituals.

31

Central and South America and the West Indies: Latin American and Afro-American Religious Music

SURVEYS AND BIBLIOGRAPHIES

2861. Aretz, Isabel, Gérard Béhague, and Robert Stevenson. "Latin America." In *Grove 6*, Vol. 10. 1980. 505-534.

2862. Béhague, Gérard. *Music in Latin America: An Introduction.* Englewood Cliffs: Prentice Hall, 1979.

2863. Béhague, Gérard. "Folk and Traditional Music of Latin America: General Prospect and Research Problems." *The World of Music* 25, 2 (1982): 3-18

2864. Béhague, Gérard. *Resource Guide to Latin American Music.* Westport, CT: Greenwood Press, 1996.

2865. Cardinas, Julio Sanchez. "Santaría or Orisha Religions: An Old Religion in a New World." In *South and Meso-American Native Spirituality: From the Cult of the Feathered Serpent to the Theology of Liberation*, G. Gossen et al., ed. New York: Crossroad, 1993. 474-495. On the worldview and ceremonies of Santaría in Nigeria and the Western Hemisphere.

2866. Horowitz, M.M., ed. *Peoples and Cultures of the Caribbean.* New York: 1971.

2867. Jackson, Irene V., ed. *More than Drumming. Essays on African and Afro-Latin American Music and Musicians.* Contributions in Afro-American and African Studies, Westport, CT: Greenwood Press, 1985.

2868. Kirby, Diana Gonzalez and Sara Maria Sanchez. "Cuban Santería: A Guide to Bibliographic Sources." *Bulletin of Bibliography* 47, 2 (1990): 113-29.

2869. Kuss, Malena. "Current State of Bibliographic Research in Latin American Music." *Fontes Artis Musicae* 31, 4 (1984): 206-28. An apparaisal of what has been done, suggestions for the future, and three appendices with 149 entries.

2870. Kuss, Malena. "Toward a Comprehensive Approach to Latin American Music Bibliography: Theoretical Foundations for Reference Sources and Research Materials." In *Latin American Masses and Minorities...*, Dan C. Hazen, ed. 1987. 615-63.

2871. Murphy, Joseph M. *Waking in the Spirit. Ceremonies of the African Diaspora*. Boston, MA: Beacon Press, 1994. A sympathetic account of Haitian Vodou, Condomblé in Brazil, Cuban and Cuban-American Santaría, Revival Zion in Jamaica and the Black Church in the U.S. Concludes with observations on their commonalties.

2872. Schechter, John M. "Doctoral Dissertations in Latin American Ethnomusicology: 1965-1984." In *Latin American Masses and Minorities...*, Dan Hazen, ed. 1987. 673-78.

2873. Schechter, John M. "The Current State of Bibliographic Research in Latin American Ethnomusicology." In *Latin American Masses and Minorities: Their Images and Realities*, Vol. 1. Madison, WI 1987. 334-45.

2874. Tiemstra, Suzanne Spicer. *The Choral Music of Latin America: A Guide to Compositions and Research*. Westport, CT: Greenwood Press, 1992.

2875. Walker, Sheila S. *Ceremonial Spirit Possession in Africa and Afro-America: Forms, Meanings, and Functional Significance for Individuals and Social Groups*. Leiden: E.J. Brill, 1972 (1973). In this study of possession, Walker discusses the use of drum rhythms as well as singing and dancing to induce neurophysiological changes, thereby producing a trance state.

CENTRAL AMERICA

2876. Borg, Paul W. *The Polyphonic Music in the Guatemalan Music Manuscripts of the Lilly Library*. Ph.D. diss., Indiana University, 1985. Fifteen mss. of church music copied between 1582 and 1635 in northwest Guatamala consist of works in 16th-century European polyphonic style.

2877. Briggs, Charles L. "Hymns and Prayers." In *Competence in Performance: The Creativity of Tradition in Mexican Verbal Art*, Charles L. Briggs, ed. Philidelphia, PA: University of Pennsylvania Press, 1988. 289-339. Focusing on the relationship between textual and contextual elements, the author analyses the use of *alabados* hymns during Holy Week rituals. Includes extensive prayer and hymn texts.

2878. Duncan, Mary Elizabeth. *A Sixteenth-Century Mexican Chant Book: Pedro Ocharte's Psalterium, Antiphonarium Sanctorale cum Psalmis & Hymnis.* Ph.D. diss., University of Washington, 1975.

2879. Madsen, Wanda Jean. *Mexican Mission Music: A Descriptive Analysis and Comparison of Two Seventeenth Century Chant Books.* D.M.A. thesis, University of Oklahoma, 1984.

2880. Rosewall, Michael Paul. *Sacred Polyphony in New Spain: Performance Issues in the Choral Music of Mexico, 1550-1650.* D.M.A. thesis, Stanford University, 1992.

2881. Stevenson, Robert M. "European Music in Sixteenth-Century Guatamala." *MQ* 50, 3 (1964): 341-52. A chronicle of the enthusiastic reception European sacred music received from the indigenous people of Guatemala.

SOUTH AMERICA

2882. Alexandre, Antonio, ed. *Collection of Essays on the Sacred Music of Brazil.* Rome: Urbanania University, 1981. Nineteen articles in English, French, German, Portuguese, and Spanish. Major topics include church music history, sacred dance, and Gregorian chant.

2883. Béhague, Gérard. "Notes on Regional and National Trends in Afro-Brazilian Cult Music." In *Tradition and Renewal: Essays on Twentieth-Century Latin American Literature and Culture*, Merlin H. Forster, ed. Urbana, IL: University of Illinois Press, 1975. 68-80.

2884. Béhague, Gérard. "Some Liturgical Functions of Afro-Brailian Religious Music in Salvador, Bahia." *The World of Music* 19, 3/4 (1977): 4-23.

2885. Béhague, Gérard. "Brazil." In *Grove 6*, Vol. 3. 1980. 234-44.

2886. Béhague, Gérard. "Patterns of Condomblé Music Performance: An Afro-Brazilian Religious Setting." In *Performance Practice: Ethnomusicological Perspectives*, Gerard Béhague, ed. Westport, CT and London: Greenwood Press, 1984. 224-254. A synthesis of West African deities and ritual practices, the Condomblé of Bahia, Brazil, is examined in terms of its social organization, music, and the contexts of performance. Rituals, while allowing some latitude for individual competence, are tightly structured and prescribe specific ritual behavior. Music and dance are inseparable from this behavior and are the means through which religious fulfillment takes place.

2887. Brandt, M.H. *An Ethnomusicological Study of Three Afro-Venezuelan Drum Ensembles of Barlovento.* Ph.D. diss., Queen's University of Belfast, 1979.

2888. Carvalho, José Jorge de. *Ritual and Music of the Sango Cults of Recife [Brazil]*. Ph.D. diss., The Queen's University of Belfast, 1984.

2889. Carvalho, José Jorge de. "Music of African Origin in Brazil." In *Africa in Latin America: Essays on History, Culture, and Socialization*, Manuel Moreno Fraginals, ed. New York/Paris: Holmes & Meier/Unesco, 1984. 227-48. An informative overview of the distribution of African cultural groups in Brazil, the music of Afro-Brazilian cults, and a list of Brazilian deities.

2890. Carvalho, José Jorge de. "Aesthetics of Opacity and Transparence: Myth, Music and Ritual in the Xango-Cult and in the Western Art Tradition." *Latin American Music Review* 14, 2 (1993): 202-231. In a dense and stimulating article, the author differentiates between societies of ritual action, with their concern for insuring the continuing efficacy of existing ritual structures, from societies dominated by discourse, in which musical innovation is accompanied by self-conscious explication. Thus, a structure with three levels of meaning in Xango cult music serves a very different purpose than does a similar structure in Wagner's *Ring*.

2891. De Paula, Isodoro Lessa. *Early Hymnody in Brazilian Baptist Churches: Its Sources and Development*. D.M.A., Southwestern Baptist Theological Seminary, 1985. A study of the hymnal Cantor Cristao (Christian Singer) in editions from 1891 to 1971 shows the major body of hymn texts and tunes of Brazilian Baptist Hymnody to be Portuguese translations and adaptations of American gospel songs.

2892. Fox, Charles. *Candomblé and Community: Ritual and its Material Benefits at Casa Brance, a Candomblé Cult-house in Salvador, Bahia*. M.A. thesis, University of Florida, 1987.

2893. Herskovits, Melville J. "Drums and Drummers in Afro-Brazilian Cult Life." *MQ* 30, 4 (1944): 477-92. Repr. in M.J. Herskovits, ed.: *The New World Negro*, 1966/repr. 1969. 183 ff. An article relating the high religious position of drumming, the construction and power invested in the drums, rituals to keep the drums powerful, the power of rhythm, loaning practices, and father/son drumming tradition of Gêge, Ketu, and Jeshâ cults.

2894. Megenney, William W. "Sudanic/Bantu/Portuguese Syncretism in Selected Chants from Brazilian Unbanda and Candomblé." *Anthropos* Vol. 84, 4-6 (1989): 363-383. Also publ. in SEDOS Bulletin no. 9:306-310. Oct. 15, 1989.

2895. Merriam, Alan P. "Songs of the Ketu Cult of Bahia, Brazil." *African Music* 1, 3 and 4 (1956, 1957): 53-82; 73 ff. A study of the structure of the music of a Brazilian-based African cult with emphasis on problems of acculturation.

2896. Merriam, Alan P. "Songs of the Gege and Jesha Cults of Bahia, Brazil." *Jahrbuch für musikalische Volks-und Völkerkunde* 1 (1963): 100-135. An analysis of the music of two African-derived Brazilian cults with attention to range, melody, intervals, structure, ornamentation, instrumentation, and tempo. Includes a collection of Gege and Jesha compositions.

2897. Montiel, Naomi Woodfin. *The Use of Folk Idioms in Argentine Evangelical Music (1960-1990).* D.M.A., Southwestern Baptist Theological Seminary, 1992. A history of the use of folk music idioms, particularly the *carnavalito* and the *zamba*, within the evangelical church. Rhythmic features, textual mood and content, and to a lesser degree, scale content are retained; the original poet form is rarely used, and harmonic guidelines only when the essence of the style.

2898. Motta, Roberto Mauro Cortez. *Meat and Feast: The Xango Religion of Recife, Brazil.* Ph.D. diss., Columbia University, 1988. Xango ritual, with its animal sacrifice, singing, dancing, and trance, is a response to economic, nutritional, societal, and environmental pressures in the urban context. "Xango, therefore, is good to eat, good to organize, and good to think".

2899. Nawrot, Piotr. *Vespers Music in the Paraguay Reductions.* D.M.A. diss., Catholic University of America, 1993. A contribution to our knowledge of the teaching of music and the celebration of liturgical events in the Jesuit missions (*reductions*) in Paraguay between 1609 and 1767. Includes thematic catalog of newly discovered mss. and transcriptions.

2900. Pinto, Tiago de Oliveira. "'Making Ritual Drama': Dance, Music, and Representation in Brazilian *condomblé* and *umbanda*." *The World of Music* 33, 1 (1991): 70-88.

2901. Pressel, Esther. "Umbanda Trance and Possession in Sao Paulo, Brazil." In *Trance, Healing, and Hallucination: Three Field Studies in Religious Experience*, I.I. Zaretsky, ed. New York: Wiley Interscience, 1974. Chapter 4 of this field study of Umbanda religion describes the use of intense drumming and singing during possession rituals. Although Pressel provides examples of songs and documents the use of music to induce trance, she does not attempt to analyze the connection between such music and altered states of consciousness.

2902. Salter, Hal Christopher. *Sacred Rhythms in Afro-Brazilian Religions: An Outsider's Perspective and Impressions, via Transcriptional Analysis and Personal Experience.* M.A. thesis, UCLA, 1990. A study of rhythm in the religious music of Bahia, Brazil.

2903. Segato de Carvalho, Rita Laura. *A Folk Theory of Personality Types: Gods and Their Symbolic Representation by Members of the Sango Cult in Recife, Brazil.* Ph.D. diss., Queen's University of Belfast, 1984.

2904. Wafer, Jim. *The Taste of Blood: Spirit Possession in Brazilian Candomblé.* Series in Contemporary Ethnography, Philadelphia: University of Pennsylvania Press, 1991.

2905. Welch, David B. "A Yoruba/Nago 'Melotype' for Religious Songs in the African Diaspora: Continuity of West African Praise Song in the New World." In *More Than Drumming: Essays on African and Afro-Latin Music and Musicians*, Irene V. Jackson, ed. Westport, CT: Greenwood Press, 1985. 145-162. Melodic nuclei found in praise songs of the Shango cult of the Yoruba of Nigeria are also found in the Nago candomblé in Bahia and in cult music of Haiti.

WEST INDIES

2906. Ahyoung, Selwyn E. "The Music of the Shouter—Baptists of Trinidad, West Indies." *The Hymn* 37, 1 (1986): 19-24. The Shouter Baptists appear in a continuum of Trinidad religions, from African to European: Shango—Shango-Baptist—Shouter Baptist—Protestant/Catholic. The Shouter-Baptist share with the Shango religions the practice of possession, although possession is by the Holy Spirit only and is conscious, rather than by African deities, without consciousness or memory of possession. They differ by not practicing animal sacrifice and by singing what is basically Protestant hymnody, without the use of drums and African chants. Call and response in a strident, powerful tone is especially popular.

2907. Alcide, Marie-Jose. *Theatrical and Dramatic Elements of Haitian Voodoo.* Ph.D. diss., City University of New York, 1988. A study of Voodoo sacred rituals according to Aristotelian criteria reveals eight major theatrical elements and a model for a secular indigenous theatre.

2908. Amira, John and Steven Cornelius. *The Music of Santería: Traditional Rhythms of the Batha Drums.* Crown Point, IN: White Cliffs Media, 1992.

2909. Barad, Elizabeth. "Haiti Dances to a Different Drummer: A Country in Turmoil Turns to Ancient Folk Religion, with Rich Results for Dance." *Dance Magazine* 68, 8 (1994): 38-41.

2910. Bilby, Kenneth and Elliott Leib. "Kumina, the Howellite Church and the Emergence of Rastafarian Traditional Music in Jamaica." *Jamaica Journal* 19, 3 (1986): 22-28.

2911. Courlander, Harold. *The Drum and the Hoe: Life and Lore of the Haitian People.* Berkeley, CA: University of California Press, 1960. A broad anthropological study of dance and music in Haitian religious traditions with descriptions of death rites, dance dramas, drum rhythms and a wide range of song themes. Discusses regional variations and the theological and cosmological context for religious practice. Includes 186 transcr. by M. Kolinski.

2912. Davis, Martha Ellen. *Afro-Dominican Religious Brotherhoods: Structure, Ritual, and Music*. Ph.D. diss., University of Illinois, 1976.

2913. Deren, Maya. *Divine Horsemen: The Living Gods of Haiti*. New Paltz, NY: McPherson & Company, 1953/repr. 1984. A masterly and vivid explanation of the "metaphysical principles underlying the practices of voodoo." Dances are discribed within the context of the religion.

2914. Dobbin, Jay D. *The Jombee Dance of Montserrat: A Study of Trance Ritual in the West Indies*. Columbus, OH: Ohio State University Press, 1986. An anthropological and religious study of the central trance ritual on Montserrat. The trance, which involves possession by ancestors, is triggered by the Dance, and is a social and symbolic drama, the theme of which is the quest for the meaning of life. Modernized forms provide the entertainment, art, religion, therapy, and solidarity one symbolized in the ritual trance.

2915. Fleurant, Gerdès. *The Ethnomusicology of Yanvalou: A Study of the Rada Rite of Haiti*. Ph.D. diss., Tufts University, 1987. This study of the three principal dances of the Rada rite, the foundation of Vodun in Haiti, provides the correct order of invocation and a model for the ceremony. Examines drum rhythms and the song tunes and texts for the dances.

2916. Fleurant, Gerdès. "The Song of Freedom: Vodun, Conscientization and Popular Culture in Haiti." *Compost* 5 (1994).

2917. Fleurant, Gerdès. *Dancing Spirits: Rhythms and Rituals of Haitian Vodun*. Westport, CT: Greenwood Press, 1996.

2918. Friedman, Robert Alan. *Making Abstract World Concrete: Knowledge, Competence and Structural Dimensions of Performance among Batá Drummers in Santería*. Ph.D. diss., Indiana University, 1982.

2919. Gonzalez-Wippler, Migene. *The Santería Experience*. Englewood Cliffs, NJ: Prentice Hall, 1982. The author's account of her participation in the Santeria religion. Includes a description of ceremonial dances.

2920. Gonzalez-Wippler, Migene. *Santería: The Religion*. New York: Harmony, 1989.

2921. Guilbault, Jocelyne. "Fitness and Flexibility: Funeral Wakes in St. Lucia West Indes." *Ethnomusicology* 31 (1987): 273-99. A detailed ethnography of funeral wakes and an investigation of variation in the music activities. In a study of four performances, the author observes that music activities differ too much from one performance to the next to derive a summary generalization.

2922. Henney, Jeannette H. "Spirit-Possession Belief and Trance Behavior in Two Fundamentalist Groups in St. Vincent." In *Trance, Healing, and Hallucination: Three Field Studies in Religious Experience*, F.D. Goodman, J.H.

Henney, and E. Pressel, ed. New York: Wiley Interscience, 1974. 1-111. Henney considers the possibility that music and movement in Shaker ritual satisfies "aesthetic yearnings" as well as facilitates trance states. Henney also discusses the emphasis on breath work and group-imposed rhythm among Shakers and similar religious groups in the Lesser Antilles, Western Indies.

2923. Hernandez-Mergal, Luis A. *The Relationship between Music and Possession-Trance in Haitian Vodun*. M.A. thesis, UCLA, 1990.

2924. Hopkin, John Barton. "Music in the Jamaican Pentecostal Churches." *Jamaica Journal* 42 (1978): 22-40.

2925. Kolinski, Mieczyslaw. "Haiti." In *Grove 6*, Vol. 8. 1980. 33-37.

2926. Kurath, Gertrude P. "Stylistic Blends in Afro-American Dance Cults of Catholic Origin." *Papers Michigan Academy of Science, Arts and Letters* 48 (1962): 577-584. Kurath first sketches the history and characteristics of the dance dramas of Latin American Catholicism and then provides an interpretive analysis of the phenomenon.

2927. Laroche, Maximilien and Paulette Richards. "Music, Dance, Religion [Haiti: The Literature and Culture, A Special Issue, Part 2]." *Callaloo* 15, 3, Summer (1992): 797-810. On the relationship of music, dance, and religion to language. Music, dance and language communicate in ways that allow practitioners to express and receive messages. In Haitian Vodou, the drum is a voice, the body is a voice, and the ceremony is a multi-directional communication between officiants, supplicants, *lwa*, and spectators.

2928. Lewin, O. "Jamaica." In *Grove 6*, Vol. 9. 1980.

2929. Long, Joseph K. "Medical Anthropology, Dance and Trance in Jamaica." *Bulletin of the International Committee on Urgent Anthropological and Ethnological Research* 14 (1972): 17-23.

2930. Metraux, Alfred. *Voodoo in Haiti*. New York: Oxford University Press, 1959. An introduction to Haitian Voodoo theology and practice. Section 4, on ritual expression, includes a chapter on music and dance with emphasis on the role of drumming in ritual expression.

2931. Miller, Terry E. "Introductory Essay on H. Roberts's Spirituals or Revival Hymns." *Ethnomusicology* 33, 3 (Fall) (1989): 405-408. Provides ethnographic and historical information on the Revival Zion Church and on Christianity in Jamaica as background to Helen H. Roberts' previously unpublished 1921 essay on Jamaican music, "Spirituals or Revival Hymns of the Jamaica Negro" (see #2936).

2932. Moodie, Sylvia Maria. "Survival of Hispanic Religious Songs in Trinidad Folklore." *Caribbean Quarterly* 29, 1 (1986?): 1-31.

2933. Moore, Joseph. "Religious Syncretism in Jamaica." *Practical Anthropology* 12, 2/March-April (1965): 63-70. Includes a description of Cumina ritual dances.

2934. Moore, Joseph. "Music and Dance as Expressions of Religious Worship in Jamaica." In *The Performing Arts: Music and Dance*, Hague, Netherlands: Mouton, 1979. 293-318. Also publ. in *African Religious Groups and Beliefs: Papers in Honor of William R. Bascom,* ed. by S. Ottenberg. Meerut, India: Archana Publications for Folklore Institute. 1982. A study of the social, recreational, psychological and religious functions of the drumming and dancing of Kumina revival cults. Most cults employ possession by Christian spirits, though of distinctly non-Christian ancestry. Some also include Christian hymns.

2935. Nagashima, Yoshiko S. *Rastafarian Music in Contemporary Jamaica: A Study of Socioreligious Music of the Rastafarian Movement in Jamaica.* Performance in Culture, No. 3, Tokyo: Institute for the Study of Languages and Cultures of Asia and Africa, 1984.

2936. Roberts, Helen H. "Spirituals or Revival Hymns of the Jamaica Negro." *Ethnomusicology* 33, 3 (Fall) (1989): 409-74. The result of Roberts's first fieldwork, this previously unpublished article groups 46 hymns according to textual form (8 groups) and musical form. With transcriptions of rhythmic patterns, scale patterns, and entire songs.

2937. Scaramuzzo, Gene. "Zouk: Magic Music of the French Antilles." *Reggae & African Beat* 5, 4 (1986): 27-33.

2938. Schmidt, Cynthia E. *Shango Cult Music of Trinidad: The Annual Ceremony.* M.A. thesis, UCLA, 1974.

2939. Simpson, George Eaton. "Jamaican Revivalist Cults." *Social and Economic Studies* 5, 1-9 (1956): 321-42. Chapter 4, entitled "Religious and Magical Rituals in West Kingston Revivalism," devotes several pages to a description of religious services including the role of hymn singing, clapping, and music playing.

2940. Simpson, George Eaton. *Religious Cults of the Caribbean: Trinidad, Jamaica, and Haiti.* Rio Piedras, Puerto Rico: 1970. Discusses the dance and music of Caribbean religious cults as part of an anthropological and sociological study. Specifically mentioned are ceremonial dancing in Jamaica and Trinidad, ceremonial drumming in Trinidad, and the 'shouting' tradition among the baptists of Trinidad.

2941. Vega-Drouet, H. *Historical and Ethnological Survey on Probable African Origins of the Puerto Rico Bomba, Including a Description of Santiago Apostol Festivities at Loiza Aldea.* Ph.D. diss., Wesleyan University, 1979.

2942. Welch, David. "West African Cult Music Retentions in Haitian Urban Vaudou: A Preliminary Report." In *Essays for a Humanist: An Offering to Klaus Wachsmann*, New York: The Town House Press, 1977. 337-349.

2943. Wilcken, Lois. *The Drums of Vodou*. Performance in World Music Series, Vol. 7. Tempe, AZ: White Cliffs Media, 1992. Expert drumming is essential to the success of Haitian vodou ceremonies: a practical guide to drummers. Chapters cover social and historical context, the instruments, the rhythms (with notated examples), song and dance, and an interview with Frisner Augustin.

EAST INDIAN RELIGIOUS MUSIC OF THE WEST INDIES

2944. Arya, Usharbudh. *Ritual Songs and Folksongs of the Hindus of Surinam*. Leiden, Netherlands: E. J. Brill, 1968.

2945. Bissoondialsingh, Smt. Tara. "Indian Music in Trinidad." *Jyoti* 9 (1976): 1-5.

2946. Horowitz, M.M. "The Worship of South Indian Deities in Martinique." *Ethnology* 2 (1963): 339. The use of drums and bells in ritual celebration is discussed in this brief overview of south Indian religious practice as influenced by the surrounding Caribbean culture.

2947. Myers, Helen. "Trinidad and Tobago." In *Grove 6*, Vol. 19. 1980.

2948. Myers, Helen. *Felicity, Trinidad: The Musical Portrait of a Hindu Village*. Ph.D. diss., University Edinburgh, 1984.

2949. Myers, Helen. "Indian, East Indian, and West Indian Music in Felicity, Trinidad." In *Ethnomusicology and Modern Music History*, Blum, Bohlman, and Neuman, ed. Urbana, IL 1991. 231-241.

32

North American Indians: General References

MUSIC AND RELIGIONS OF THE INDIANS OF THE AMERICAS

2950. Collaer, Paul. *Music of the Americas*. New York: Praeger, 1973. A photographic study of the Indians of the Western hemisphere, with an extended introduction and a bibliography of 901 references.

2951. Harner, Michael. *The Way of the Shaman: A Guide to Power and Healing*. New York: Harper and Row, 1980. A study of the shamanic practices of the Indians of North and South America.

2952. Hultkrantz, Åke. *The Religions of the American Indians*. Monica Setterwall, transl. Berkeley and Los Angeles: University of California Press, 1979. German original, 1967. An informative and detailed study of Native American religious concepts and beliefs.

2953. Underhill, Ruth. *Red Man's Religion*. Chicago: University of Chicago Press, 1965. Contains chapters on Indian ceremonialism, the Sun Dance as prayer for the general welfare, and the role of the shaman.

NORTH AMERICAN INDIANS: BIBLIOGRAPHIES AND MULTI-VOLUME SETS

2954. Bradley, Ian L. and Patricia Bradley. *A Bibliography of Canadian Native Arts: Indian and Eskimo Arts, Craft, Dance and Music*. Agincourt, Ontario: GLC Publishers, 1977.

2955. Curtis, Edward S. *The North American Indian, Being a Series of Volumes Picturing and Describing the Indians of the United States, the Dominion of Canada, and Alaska*. 20 vols. Frederick Webb Hodge, ed. New York and

London: Johnson Reprint Corp., 1907-1930/repr. 1970. Each volume consists of descriptions of religion, ceremonials, history, mythology, and tales of tribes of a specific regional area. Covers approximately 70 tribes. A supplementary volume of illustrations accompanies each five volumes of text.

2956. Hirschfelder, Arlene B., Mary G. Byler, and Michael A. Dorris. *Guide to Research on North American Indians*. Chicago, IL: American Library Association, 1983.

2957. Hitchcock, H. Wiley and Stanley Sadie, ed. *The New Grove Dictionary of American Music*. 4 vols. New York: Grove's Dictionaries of Music, 1986. Consult under individual tribe names.

2958. Javitch, Gregory. *Selective Bibliography of Ceremonies, Dance, Music and Song of American Indians*. Montreal, Can: Osiris, 1974.

2959. La Barre, Weston. *The Peyote Cult*. 5th, enl. ed., Norman, OK: University of Oklahoma Press, 1989. Last half of book consists of five bibliographies—for the 1938, 1959, 1964, 1975 and 1989 editions—with bibliographical essays, "Peyote Studies," for the last four.

2960. Maguire, Marsha. *American Indian and Eskimo Music: A Selected Bibliography through 1981*. Washington, DC: Archive of Folk Culture, Library of Congress, 1983.

2961. Murdock, George Peter and Timothy J. O'Leary. *Ethnographic Bibliography of North America*. 5 vols. New Haven: Human Relations Area Files, 1975 & 1987. Contains c. 28,000 entries. No index. Martin, M. Marlene. 4th ed., *Supplement 1973-1987*. New Haven: Human Relations Area Files. 3 Vols. 1990. 25,058 new citations listed alphabetically by author. Consult index under dance and religious ceremonials.

2962. Ribeiro, Darcy. *Music of the American Indian*. 10 vols. Washington, DC: Library of Congress, 1954-55.

2963. Sturtevant, William C., ed. *Handbook of North American Indians*. 15 vols. Washington, DC: Smithsonian Institution, 1978-90. An impressive series of volumes on all aspects of the American Indian culture. Each volume has an extensive bibliography. The following volumes on specific areas are available to date: 5. Arctic (1984), 6. Subarctic (1981), 7. Northwest Coast (1990), 8. California (1978), 9 and 10. Southwest (1979, 1983), 11. Great Basin (1986), and 15. Northeast (1978).

RELIGION AND CULTURE

2964. Beck, Peggy V., Anna Lee Walters, and Nia Francisco. *The Sacred: Ways of Knowledge, Sources of Life*. Tsaile, AZ: Navajo Community College Press,

1992. A description of the "meaning, role, and function of sacred traditional practices and observances in the lives of The People, individually and collectively." Written by those with intimate knowledge of the traditional ways of the North American Indians and Eskimos.

2965. Brandon, William. *The American Heritage Book of the Indians*. New York: American Heritage Press, 1961. Among the dances mentioned or pictured are the Apache Mountain Spirit Dance, Shoshoni Ghost Dance, Hopi Snake Dance, Pueblo Rainbow Dance, and the Sun Dance.

2966. Driver, Harold E. *Indians of North America*. 2nd rev. ed., Chicago: University of Chicago Press, 1969. See Chapter 12, 'Music and Dance,' and the index under the terms 'dances,' 'rites,' 'shamans,' and 'singing' for numerous references.

2967. Erdoes, Richard. *Crying for a Dream: The World through Native American Eyes*. Sante Fe, NM: Bear and Company Publishing, 1990. Beautifully illustrated with color photographs, this text is concerned primarily with the spirituality and world-view of Native peoples with attention to spiritual practice including the Ghost Dance and sung prayer.

2968. Furst, Peter. "The Roots and Continuities of Shamanism." In *Arts-Canada*, 1973-1974. 184-187. Thirtieth Anniversary Issue, Stones, Bones and Skin: Ritual and Shamanic Art: 33-60.

2969. Kehoe, Alice B. *North American Indians: A Comprehensive Account*. 2nd ed., Englewood Cliffs, NJ: Prentice Hall, 1992.

2970. La Barre, Weston. *The Peyote Cult*. 5th, enl. ed., Norman, OK: University of Oklahoma Press, 1989. Covers more than 50 years of research into the religious use of Peyote. Contains the original essay of 1938, four subsequent bibliographical essays entitled "Peyote Studies" (copyright 1959, 1964, 1975 and 1989), and a concluding index to the entire volume.   See entries under dancing, music, singing, and songs.

2971. Park, Willard Z. *Shamanism in Western North America*. La Jolla, CA: Cooper Square Publications, 1938/repr. 1975. The source and power of shamans' songs are referred to and discussed throughout the text.

2972. Powers, William K. *Beyond the Vision: Essays on American Indian Culture*. Norman, OK: University of Oklahoma Press, 1987.

2973. Stewart, Omer C. *Peyote Religion: A History*. Norman, OK: Universtiy of Oklahoma Press, 1987. Authoritative work by a leading expert on the subject.

2974. Tedlock, Dennis and Barbara Tedlock, ed. *Teachings from the American Earth: Indian Religion and Philosophy*. New York: Liveright Publishing Corporation, 1975/repr. 1992. Contains numerous references to the use and significance of music, dance and song. Chapter 5: "The Doctrine of the Ghost Dance," by J. Mooney, is entirely dance related.

2975. Vecsey, Christopher. *Religion in Native North America*. Moscow, ID: University of Idaho Press, 1990.

MUSIC AND DANCE: GENERAL REFERENCES

2976. Baker, Theodore. *On the Music of the North American Indians*. Ann Buckley, transl. New York: Da Capo Press, 1882/repr. 1976, 1977, 1978.

2977. Crawford, D.E. "*The Jesuit Relations and Allied Documents*: Early Sources for an Ethnography of Music Among American Indians." *Ethnomusicology* 11 (1967): 199-206. A study of descriptions of music from the early 17th century, in two broad categories: 'The Medicine Man and his Music,' and 'Music by Groups and Other Individuals.'

2978. De Cesare, Ruth. *Myth, Music and Dance of the American Indian*. Sandy Feldstein, John O'Reilly, and Patrick Wilson, ed. Van Nuys, CA: Alfred Publishing Co., 1988.

2979. Densmore, Frances. *The American Indians and their Music*. New York: Johnson Reprint Corp., 1926/repr. 1970. Based on material in her many works for the Bureau of American Ethnology, this work begins with a description of social aspects including dances and ceremonies, then focuses on Indian music.

2980. Densmore, Frances. "The Study of Indian Music." In *Annual Report of the Smithsonian Institution for the Year Ended June 30. 1941*, Seattle, WA: Shorey Book Store, 1942/repr. 1966. 527. Densmore outlines her work in the field from the 1890s, placing special focus on her methods of recording Indian music and the equipment used.

2981. Herndon, Marcia. *Native American Music*. Darby, PA: Norwood Editions, 1980. A well-informed study of Native American music from topical, theoretical and historical points of view. Compares the Euro-American and Native American world views. Describes Indian music in terms of six music areas and discusses its use to secure power and in nativistic movements, ceremonials, and the life cycle.

2982. Heth, Charlotte, ed. *Native American Dance: Ceremonies and Social Traditions*. Washington, D.C.: National Museum of the American Indian, Smithsonian Institution, with Starwood Pub., 1992. 20 articles on current ceremonies of the Eskimo and the Native Americans of Canada, the U.S., and Mexico.

2983. Hofmann, Charles, ed. *Frances Densmore and American Indian Music: A Memorial Volume*. Contributions from the Museum of the American Indian, Heye Foundation, Vol. 23, New York: Heye Foundation, 1968. Lists 175 of

Densmore's books and articles on American Indian music, along with seven recordings and eight completed, unpublished mss.

2984. Howard, James. "Pan-Indianism in Native American Music and Dance." *Ethnomusicology* 27 (1983): 71-82. A definition of Pan-Indianism as the informal grafting of 'generalized' Native American ritual culture into one complex and a description of Pan-Indian ceremonial practices throughout the country.

2985. Jilek, Wolfgang. "Native Renaissance: The Survival and Revival of Indigenous Therapeutic Ceremonials among North American Indians." *Transcultural Psychiatric Research Review* 15 (1978): 117-47. A discussion of the therapeutic value of the ceremonies of various tribes, with attention to the Sun Dance and Winter Spirit Dance.

2986. Kealiinohomoku, Joann. "Ethnodance." In *The Religious Character of Native American Humanities*, Tempe, AZ: Department of Humanities and Religious Studies, 1977. 144-154.

2987. Keeling, Richard, ed. *Women in North American Indian Music: Six Essays*. Special Series, No. 6, Bloomington, IN: Society for Ethnomusicology/ University of Indiana Press, 1989.

2988. Keeling, Richard. "The Sources of Indian Music: An Introduction and Overview." *The World of Music* 34, 2 (1992): 3-21. An overview of Indian music: its non-professionalism, notions of inspiration, music as a medium used in maintaining spiritual contact, and a brief view of probable changes over five historical periods.

2989. Kurath, Gertrude Prokosch. "Indians, American, §II, 2: Dance." In *NGDAM*, Vol. 1. 1986. 474-479.

2990. Laubin, Reginald and Gladys. *Indian Dances of North America: Their Importance to Indian Life*. Norman and London: University of Oklahoma Press, 1977/repr. 1989. An extraordinary view of Native American dance by a dedicated non-Indian.

2991. Mills, Antonia Curtze. *The Beaver Indian Prophet Dance and Related Movements among North American Indians*. Ph.D. diss., Harvard University, 1982. The Prophet and Ghost Dance are one type of nativistic revitalization movement that began in the east and travelled west, parallel to contact with white settlers. They share a belief in a shamanic world view that is character-ized by the presence of shamans, rites designed to maintain world harmony, and a tradition that the world has been transformed many times.

2992. Nettl, Bruno et al. "Indians, American." In *NGDAM*, Vol. 1. 1986. 460-479.

2993. Rhodes, Willard et al. "North Ameirca, II. Indian and Eskimo Traditions." In *Grove 6*, Vol. 13. 1980. 295-320.

2994. Stevenson, Robert. "American Tribal Musics at Contact." *Inter-American Music Review* 14, 1 (1994): 1-44. A survey of journals, diaries and other documents by Europeans of the earliest observations of and about Native American music. Draws heavily on Theodore Baker's dissertation *Über die Musik der noramerikanischen Wilden* of 1882 [see #2976]. Covers period from 1496 to late 19th century.

2995. Thwaites, R.G., ed. *The Jesuit Relations and Allied Documents: Travels and Explorations of the Jesuit Missionaries in New France, 1610-1791.* New York: Pageant Book Co., 1896/repr. 1986.

2996. Young, Gloria Alese. *Powwow Power: Perspectives on Historic and Contemporary Intertribalism.* Ph.D. diss., Indiana University, 1981. The modern urban powwow in Oklahoma developed from the religious dances and intertribal ceremonies of the over thirty Oklahoma Indian tribes. The process of change involved innovation, cooperation and negotiation. The first of these, innovation, resulted from the introduction of ideas from individual dreams, visions and trances.

RELIGIOUS MUSIC AND DANCE

2997. Bierhorst, John, ed. *The Sacred Path: Spells, Prayers, and Power Songs of the American Indians.* New York: Morrow, William, & Co., 1984.

2998. Clark, Ella Elizabeth. *Guardian Spirit Quest.* Indian Culture Series, Billings, MT: Council for Indian Education, 1974/repr. 1987.

2999. Cloutier, David. *Spirit, Spirit: Shaman Songs, Incantations.* Providence, RI: Copper Beech Press, 1973. Versions based on texts recorded by anthropologists.

3000. Densmore, Frances. "The Use of Music in the Treatment of the Sick by the American Indians." *MQ* 13, 4, Pt. 1 (1927): 555-565. Densmore shows how rhythm and song are essential elements in the treatment of the sick. Important factors are the healer's confidence, a rattle, power songs, often communicated by a helping spirit, and, occasionally, herbs. Also in *Music and Medicine*, D.M. Schullian and M. Schoen, edds. New York: Henry Schuman. 1948.

3001. Densmore, Frances. "How the Indian Seeks Power through Dream Music." *Musical America*, 1927.

3002. Densmore, Frances. "The Influence of Hymns on the Form of Indian Songs." *American Anthropologist* 40 (1938): 175-177.

3003. Densmore, Frances. "The Belief of the Indians in a Connection Between Song and the Supernatural." *Anthropology Papers Bulletin* 151 (1953): 219 ff.

3004. Gill, Sam D. *Native American Religious Action: A Performance Approach to Religion.* Columbia, SC: University of South Carolina Press, 1987.

3005. Grim, John A. "Cosmogony and the Winter Dance: Native American Ethics in Transition." *Journal of Religious Ethics* 20, 2 (1992): 389-413.

3006. Hallowell, A.L. "Bear Ceremonialism in the Northern Hemisphere." *American Anthropologist* 28, 1 (1926): 1-175. A detailed study of the beliefs and ceremonies connected to the bear hunt in the Northern Hemisphere and Eurasia.

3007. Highwater, Jamake. *Ritual of the Wind: North American Indian Ceremonies, Music and Dance.* rev. ed., Toronto, Canada: Methuen Publications, 1977/repr. 1984. A testimony to the survival of Indians and Indian culture through an examination of Indian dance and ceremony, past and present. Gives special consideration to the Ghost Dance as what at one time was thought to be the end of Indian culture.

3008. Highwater, Jamake. *Dance: Rituals of Experience.* New York: A & W Publishing, 1978.

3009. Hofmann, Johanna Veronika. *Spirituality in the Inter-Tribal Native American Pow-wow.* M.A. thesis, UCLA, 1992.

3010. Howard, Joseph H. *Drums in the Americas.* New York: Oak Publications, 1967. Within this study of drum creation, style and purpose across cultural lines in the Americas, Howard describes the ritualized use of drums in North American and Canadian religious ceremonies. Includes an extensive bibliography.

3011. Hultkrantz, Åke. "Spirit Lodge, a North American Shamanistic Séance." In *Studies in Shamanism*, Carl-Martin Edsman, ed. Stockholm: Almqvist and Wiksell, 1967. 32-68. A detailed description of a ceremony among the Arapaho, the diffusion of the Spirit Lodge ceremony among Native American Indians, and the differences between Native American and Arctic Shamanism.

3012. Hultkrantz, Åke. *Shamanic Healing and Ritual Drama: Health and Medicine in Native North American Religious Traditions.* New York: The Crossroad Publishing Company, 1992. This general study of Native American concepts of healing contains descriptions of healing practice by region. The curative value of the Sun Dance and Ghost Dance is discussed in chapters 4 and 7 respectively.

3013. Jilek, Wolfgang. "Altered States of Consciousness in North American Indian Ceremonials." *Ethos* 10, 4 (1982): 326-343.

3014. Johnson, Willard. "A Recently Received Native American Shamanistic Myth of Little Spirits." *Western Folklore* 51, 2/April (1992): 207-213. A description of a myth received by Luciano Perez, a contemporary American shaman, during trance while performing a *yuwipi* ritual.

3015. Keeling, Richard, ed. *Music and Spiritual Power Among the Indians of North America*. The World of Music, 34, 2. Wilhelmshaven, Germany: Florian Noetzel, 1992. Entire issue.

3016. Kehoe, Alice B. *The Ghost Dance: Ethnohistory and Revitalization*. Case Studies in Cultural Anthropology, New York: Holt, Rinehart, and Winston, 1989.

3017. La Barre, Weston. *The Ghost Dance: Origins of Religion*. New York: Dell Publications, 1970/repr. 1979. An anthropological and psychological study of the phenomenon of religion.

3018. Lowie, Robert H. "Ceremonialism in North America." In *Anthropology in North America*, Frank Boas et al., ed. New York: Stechert, 1915. 229-258. A survey of the most important ceremonies in several cultural areas of the Northern Hemisphere, the myth and ritual, diffusion of ceremonies, ceremonial patterns, and the object of ceremonies.

3019. McAllester, David P. *Peyote Music*. Viking Fund Publications in Anthropology, Vol. 13. New York: Johnson Reprints, 1949/repr. 1971. Participants in a peyote ceremony spend more than half of their participating time in performing or listening to special peyote songs. McAllester undertakes a musicological and cultural study of the song-texts and melodies of the Peyote cult of the Comanche, along with an overview of the spread of the cult. Includes 84 song transcriptions from various tribes, with words.

3020. McAllester, David P. "Music and Religion in the Americas." In *The Encyclopedia of Religion*, Mircea Eliade, ed. Vol. 10. 1987. 178-182.

3021. Mooney, James. *The Ghost Dance Religion and the Sioux Outbreak of 1890*. Lincoln, NE: University of Nebraska Press, 1892-93/repr. 1991. An exhaustive survey of Ghost Dance history, theology, music and dance. Includes 100s of songs.

3022. Powers, William K. "Native American Religious Drama." In *Encyclopedia of Religion*, Mircea Eliade, ed. Vol. 4. 1987. 465-470.

3023. Schwarz, O. Douglas. *Plains Indian Theology: As Expressed in Myth and Ritual, and in the Ethics of the Culture*. Ph. D. diss., Fordham University, 1981. The goal of the Sweat Lodge, Vision Quest, and Sun Dance rites is the vision, the direct, personal experience of the Great Mystery. Through these rites, participants hope to discover, understand, and strengthen the sacred relationships that exist between the people, individually and collectively, and creation as a whole.

3024. Talamantez, Inés M. "Dance and Ritual in the Study of Native American Religious Traditions." *American Indian Quarterly* 6, 3-4 (1982): 338-57.

3025. Tijerina-Jim, Aleticia. "Three Native American Women Speak about the Significance of Ceremony." *Women and Therapy* 14, 1-2/Jan.-Feb. (1993): 33-39. Three women elders, from the Choctaw, Hopi, and Navajo, discuss the importance of ceremonial in their lives and in their culture.

THE SUN DANCE

3026. Amenta, Rosalyn Marie. *The Earth Mysticism of the Native American Tribal Peoples with Special Reference to the Circle Symbol and the Sioux Sun Dance Rite.* Ph.D. diss., Fordham University, 1987. Verbatim interviews with spiritually and philosophically gifted Native American leaders reveal that Plains Indians believe the earth with all its myriad phenomena to be the primary revelation of Sacred Reality. The Sioux Sun Dance Ceremony is reinterpreted from this standpoint—as the total immersion in all the phenomena of this Divine Reality.

3027. Amiotte, Arthur. "The Lakota Sun Dance: Historical and Contemporary Perspectives." In *Sioux Indian Religion: Tradition and Innovation*, Raymond J. DeMaillie and Douglas R. Parks, ed. Norman and London: University of Oklahoma Press, 1987. 75-90. A Lakota man reflects on the Sun Dance as observer and participant in light of the long history of the dance.

3028. Crummett, Michael. *Sun Dance: The Fiftieth Anniversary Crow Sun Dance.* Helena, MT: Falcon Press, 1993.

3029. Deloria, Ella C. "The Sun Dance of the Oglala Sioux." *Journal of American Folklore* 42 (1929): 354-413. A verbatim transcript with both free and literal translation of the ceremony.

3030. Detwiler, Frederick Emrey, Jr. *The Sun Dance of the Oglala: A Case Study in Religion, Ritual, and Ethics.* Ph.D. diss., Pennsylvania State University, 1983. The Oglala Sun Dance ritual takes place in four stages, which are analyzed in terms of religious phenomenology (van der Leeuw), ritual theories (Geertz and Turner), and a relational approach to ethics (Niebuhr). Among its various functions, the ritual complex appears to transform the social community into sacred community through encounter with the sacred powers.

3031. Dorsey, George Amos. *The Arapaho Sun Dance.* Chicago: Field Columbian Museum, 1903. A lengthy, day-by-day study of the Sun Dance of 1902. With many illustrations.

3032. Dorsey, George Amos. *The Arapaho Sun Dance: The Ceremony of the Offerings Lodge*. Chicago: Field Columbian Museum, 1903/repr. 1990. Also repr. Millwood, NY: Kraus Reprints 1968, 1973.

3033. Dorsey, George Amos. *The Sun Dance*. Chicago Anthropological Series, Vol. 9, No. 2. Glorieta, New Mexico: Rio Grande Press, 1905/repr. 1971. Vol. 2 of *The Cheyenne*. Orig. published by Field Columbian Museum, Chicago. 1905. A day-by-day study of the Sun Dance of 1902. With many illustrations.

3034. Feraca, S.E. *Wakinyan: Contemporary Teton Sioux Sun Dance*. Browning, MT: 1963. A study of the Sun Dance and ceremonial behavior associated with the Yuwipi and other cults.

3035. Hultkrantz, Åke. "Some Notes on the Arapaho Sun Dance." *Ethnos* 17 (1952): 24 ff. The author compares his observations of a 1949 Sun Dance to those of other ethnographers.

3036. Hultkrantz, Åke. "The Traditional Symbolism of the Sun Dance Lodge among the Wind River Shoshoni." *Scripta Instituti Donneriani Aboensis* 10 (1978): 70-95.

3037. Jorgensen, Joseph G. *The Sun Dance Religion: Power to the Powerless*. Chicago: University of Chicago Press, 1972. Conquest, dispossession, and redemption and the re-acquisition of power are the themes of this four-part study of the Sun Dance among the Utes and Shoshones. Covers tribal history, the context of the Sun Dance, religious acts, and on redemption as the religious context of the dance.

3038. Liberty, Margot. "The Sun Dance." In *Anthropology on the Great Plains*, W. Raymond Wood and Margot Liberty, ed. Lincoln, NE: University of Nebraska Press, 1980. 164-178. A brief survey of the literature and the current distribution and strength of the Sun Dance among 11 of the 19 tribes surveyed by L. Speier in 1921. Contains useful bibliography.

3039. Lincoln, Bruce. "A Lakota Sun Dance and the Problem of Sociocosmic Reunion." *History of Religions* 34, 1 (1994): 1-14. For many American Indian tribes, the Sun Dance is the central religious celebration of the year. Its function is to re-establish a connectedness to the powers that sustain the cosmos and to those who are part of one's social universe. But the admission of non-Indians, especially whites, into some of the rites has caused a rift among Indians as to who is a part of one's social universe.

3040. Linton, Ralph. "The Comanche Sun Dance." *American Anthropologist* 37 New Series (1935): 420-428. An account of the dance based on field observations made in 1933.

3041. Nevin, Arthur. "Two Summers with Blackfeet Indians in Montana." *Musical Quarterly* II (1916): 257-70. The author includes a lengthy eye-witness account of the Sun Dance ceremony as well as briefer accounts of religious dirges.

3042. O'Brodovich, Lloyd. "Plains Cree Sun Dance." *Western Canadian Journal of Anthropology* 1, 1 (1968): 71-87. Cree Studies Issue. Consists of a definition of the term 'sundance' and a description of the motivations, the ceremonies—the vow, the sacrifice, communications with the supernatural—and the acculturation process involved in the transition of the Cree to Plains culture.

3043. Opler, Marvin. "The Integration of the Sun Dance in Ute Religion." *American Anthropologist* 43 (1941): 550-72. An anslysis of the relationship between the ritual, the power, and responsibilities of the shamans, and cultural vitality. Includes a full description of the Sun Dance.

3044. Paige, Darcy. "George W. Hill's Account of the Sioux Sun Dance of 1866." *Plains Anthropologist* 24, May (1979): 99-112. One of the earliest published accounts of a Sioux Sun Dance.

3045. Potvin, Annette. *The Sun Dance Liturgy of the Blackfeet Indians*. MA, University of Ottawa, 1966.

3046. Schlesier, Karl. "Rethinking the Midewiwin and the Plains Ceremonial Called the Sun Dance." *Plains Anthropologist* 35, 127 (Feb.) (1990): 1-26.

3047. Voget, Fred. *The Shoshoni-Crow Sun Dance*. Norman, OK: University of Oklahoma Press, 1984. A lengthy study of the traditional Crow Sun Dance, the introduction of the Shoshoni Sun Dance to the Crow, the innovations of Pablo Juan Truhujo, the ceremony and symbolism of the Shoshoni-Crow Sun Dance, and its integration into Crow society and culture.

3048. Wissler, Clark, ed. *Sun Dance of the Plains Indians*. Anthropological Papers of the American Museum of Natural History, Vol. 16. New York: American Museum of Natural History, 1921.
    Part 1, 1915. Crow (Robert H. Lowie, 1-50).
    Part 2, 1917. Oglala Division of the Teton Dakota (J. R. Walker, 51-222).
    Part 3, 1918. Blackfoot (Wissler, 223-270).
    Part 4, 1919. Sarsi (Pliny Earl Goddard, 271-282) Plains-Cree (Alanson Skinner, 283-294) Cree in Alberta (Goddard, 295-310) Plains Ojibway (Skinner, 311-316) Canadian Dakota (W. D. Wallis, 317-380) Sisseton Dakota (Skinner, 381-385).
    Part 5, 1919. Wind River Shoshoni and Ute (Lowie, 387-410) Hidatsa (Lowie, 411-432).
    Part 6, 1921. Kiowa (Leslie Spier, 433-450).
    Part 7, 1921. Plains Indians: Development and Diffusion (of the Sun Dance) (Spier, 451-528).

33

North American Indians: Music and Dance by Region

NORTHEAST WOODLANDS AND EASTERN CANADA

3049. Barreiro, José and Carol Cornelius. *Knowledge of the Elders*. Ithaca, NY: Cornell University, Akwe:kon Press, 1991.

3050. Chafe, W.C. *Seneca Thanksgiving Rituals*. Bulletin 183 of the Bureau of American Ethnology, Washington, DC: U.S. Government Printing Office, 1961. A detailed report on the three parts of the Thanksgiving dance ritual, along with song texts and transcriptions. Includes a list of recorded versions of the ritual.

3051. Cornelius, Richard and Terence J. O'Grady. "Reclaiming a Tradition: The Soaring Eagles of Oneida." *Ethnomusicology* 31, 2 (1987): 261-272. The story of a revival of traditional Iroquois music and dance.

3052. Cronk, Maribeth Sam. *The Feather and Skin Dance Cycles: A Comparative Analysis of Iroquoian Sacred Music*. M.A., Institute of Canadian Studies, Carelton University, Canada, 1982.

3053. Fenton, William, N. and Gertrude Prokosch Kurath. "The Feast of the Dead, or Ghost Dance at Six Nations Reserve, Canada." In *Bureau of American Ethnology, Bulletin 149*, Washington, DC: Government Printing Office, 1951. 139-166.

3054. Fenton, William N. *An Outline of Seneca Ceremonies at Coldspring Longhouse*. Yale University Publications in Anthropology, No. 9, New Haven, CT: Yale University Press, 1936. An overview of the form and content of the cyclical rituals of the Longhouse with attention to differences in practice from other groups. HRAF.

3055. Fenton, William N. *Masked Medicine Societies of the Iroquois*. Smithsonian Institution Annual Report, Oshweken, Ontario: Iroqrafts, 1941/repr. 1984. Fenton describes the songs and dances performed in conservative Iroquois communities in New York as part of semi-annual masked healing rituals.

3056. Harrington, Mark R. *Religion and Ceremonies of the Lenape*. MAI Indian Notes and Monographs, Vol. 19, New York: AMS Press, 1921 (repr.). Harrington records the religious beliefs and accompanying ceremonial songs and dances of those Lenape living in Oklahoma, culled from his own field work and the archaeological work of others.

3057. Kurath, Gertrude P. "The Tutelo Fourth Night Spirit Release Singing." In *Midwest Folklore*, 4. Bloomington: Indiana University Press, 1954. 87-105. Kurath reviews the cultural content, melodic patterns, and tribal setting of the Tutelo ritual as it has come to be practiced by the Ontario Iroquois.

3058. Kurath, Gertrude P. *Iroquois Music and Dance: Ceremonial Arts of the Two Seneca Longhouses*. Bureau of American Ethnology, Bulletin 187, Washington, DC: Government Printing Office, 1964. Includes detailed description and analysis of Coldspring and Tonawanda music and dance of various types, including religious ritual.

3059. Kurath, Gertrude P. "The Tutelo Harvest Rite: A Musical and Choreographic Analysis." *Scientific Monthly* 76 (1953): 153 ff. A scientific analysis of the choreography used in the Four Nights Dance with attention to function and relationship to music.

3060. Kurath, Gertrude P. *Dance and Song Rituals of Six Nations Reserve, Ontario*. Vol. 220. Ottawa: National Museum of Canada, 1968. Kurath surveys and analyses a broad range of music and choreography associated with Canadian Longhouse ceremonies, drawing upon field work completed between 1948 and 1964.

3061. Kurath, Gertrude P. *Tutelo Rituals on Six Nations Reserve, Ontario*. Ann Arbor, MI: Society for Ethnomusicology, 1981. Part 1 contains song paraphrases and dance descriptions of three ceremonies. Part 2 is devoted to an analysis of their musical and cultural significance.

3062. Morgan, Lewis Henry. *League of the Ho-de-no-sau-nee or Iroquois*. New York: B. Franklin, 1851/repr. 1974. A new edition, with additional matter, edited and annotated by Herbert M. Lloyd. A sympathetic if paternalistic study of the tribe. Book 2 encompasses the various religious traditions of these communities, with Chap. 4 devoted entirely to religious dance.

3063. Rhodes, Willard. "Music of the North American Indian Shaker Religion." In *Studia Instrumentorum Popularia 3*, Gustaf Hilleston, ed. 1974. 180-84.

3064. Speck, Frank G. *A Study of the Delaware Indian Big House Ceremony: In Native Text Dictated by Witapanoxwe*. Publications of the Pennsylvania Historical Commission, New York: AMS Press, 1931/repr. A thorough discussion of Delaware religion as a whole and of ceremonial dance and song. Includes sample songs and a full description of the Mask Dance.

3065. Speck, Frank G. *The Tutelo Spirit Adoption Ceremony*. Harrisburg, PA: Pennsylvania Historical Commission, 1942. Contains 24 transcriptions by George Herzog.

3066. Speck, Frank G. *Midwinter Rites of the Cayuga Long House*. Lincoln, NE: University of Nebraska Press, 1949/repr. 1995. See Part 1, Chap. 4, for a discussion of the animal ceremonial dances and Part 2 for information about the Midwinter Dances. A sympathetic and empathic account of Cayuga prayers and myths.

3067. Sullivan, Lawrence E. "Multiple Levels of Religious Meaning in Culture: A New Look at Winnebago Sacred Texts." *Canadian Journal of Native Studies* 2, 2 (1982): 221-247.

3068. Tooker, Elizabeth. *The Iroquois Ceremonial of Midwinter*. Syracuse: Syracuse University Press, 1970. Part 1 is on the foundational principles of Iroquois rituals, Part 2, on the structure of the ceremonial in six branches of the Iroquois nation; and Part 3, on the historical development of the ceremonial.

3069. Tooker, Elisabeth, ed. *Native North American Spirituality of the Eastern Woodlands: Sacred Myths, Dreams, Vision Speeches, Healing Formulas, Rituals, and Ceremonials*. Classics of Western Spirituality Series, New York: Paulist Press, 1979. Chant, song, music, and dance are all discussed as part of chapters on the ceremonies of the Delaware, Winnebago, Menominee, Fox, and Iroquois and Southeastern healing formulas.

3070. Trigger, Bruce G., ed. *Northeast*. Handbook of North American Indians, Vol. 15. William D. Sturtevant, ed. Washington, DC: Smithsonian Institution, 1978. Includes an extensive bibliography.

3071. Whidden, Lynn. "The Cree Soundworld as Described by George Nelson, 1823." In *Ethnomusicology in Canada: Proceedings of the First Conference on Ethnomusicology in Canada/Premier congrès sur l'ethnomusicologie au Canada held in Toronto 13-15 May 1988*, Robert Witmer, ed. CanMus Documents, no. 5, Toronto: Institute for Canadian Music, 1990. 151-58. Drawing upon Nelson's letter, Widden examines three categories—use of silence, use of sound, use of organized sound—in Cree music with attention to the relationship between Cree religio-cultural values and music.

3072. Witthoft, J. "Green Corn Ceremonialism in the Eastern Woodlands." *Occasional Contributions from the Museum of Anthropology of the University of Michigan* (1949): 31-77.

SOUTHEAST WOODLANDS

3073. Capron, L. *The Medicine Bundles of the Florida Seminole and the Green Corn Dance*. Washington, DC: Government Printing Office, 1953.

3074. Densmore, Frances. *Choctaw Music*. Smithsonian Institution. Bureau of American Ethnology, Bulletin #136, New York: Da Capo, 1943/repr. 1972.

3075. Densmore, Frances. *Seminole Music*. Smithsonian Institution. Bureau of American Ethnology, Bulletin #161, New York: Da Capo, 1956/repr. 1972. A brief anthropological survey of Seminole life followed by a complete musicological analysis of social and sacred Seminole music.

3076. Draper, David E. "Breath in Music: Concept and Practice Among the Choctaw Indians." *Selected Reports in Ethnomusicology* Vol. 4 (1983): 285-300. An overview of the concept and uses of breath in the Judeo-Christian, yogic, and Native American traditions. Proposes that aspiration defines structural points in Choctaw singing and that a similar aspiration/hyperventilation technique may be used in attaining states of consciousness sanctioned in other religions.

3077. Draper, David E. "The Ritual Music of the Choctaw Stickball Game." *Louisiana Folklore Miscellany* 5, 4 (1984): 11-27. An ethnographic study of the music and dance that gives the game its religious quality.

3078. Galloway, Patricia, ed. *The Southeastern Ceremonial Complex*. Lincoln, NE: University of Nebraska Press, 1989.

3079. Herndon, Marcia. "Fox, Owl, and Raven." *Selected Reports in Ethnomusicology* Vol. III, 2 (1980): 175-192. A study of the Fox, Owl, and Raven as spirit messengers of ill omen and of those singing cures that the Cherokee could use to counteract their influence. Provides background on Cherokee cosmology and a description and analysis of the songs.

3080. Herndon, Marcia. "Sound, Danger, and Balanced Response." In *Explorations in Ethnomusicology. Essays in Honor of David P. McAllester*, Charlotte J. Frisbie, ed. Detroit Monographs in Musicology, Vol. 9. Detroit, MI: Detroit Information Coordinators, 1986. 129-138. Eastern Cherokees wrote down their sacred formulas in the decades following their removal from their ancestral lands in 1838. Performance takes place along a continuum that ranges from thought to muttering to speech to song. Texts that are sung are considered the most potent and are used only in cases of extreme danger. The author examines the melody and text of a Bruise Song and a Snakebite Song for the correlation of word, type of verbalization, melodic behavior, and healing action.

3081. Herndon, Marcia. "Insiders, Outsiders: Knowing our Limits, Limiting our Knowing." *The World of Music* 35, 1 (1993): 63-80. Herndon examines the insider/outsider dichotomy as a part-Cherokee and as a researcher with reference to songs of power.

3082. Howard, James H. *Shawnee!: The Ceremonialism of a Native Indian Tribe and its Cultural Background*. Athens, OH: Ohio University Press, 1981. An account of Shawnee history and culture based on personal observations, extensive scholarly research and the testimony of many informants. Three chapters are devoted exclusively to Shawnee ceremonialism.

3083. Howard, James H. and Willie Lena. *Oklahoma Seminoles: Medicines, Magic, and Religion*. The Civilization of the American Indian Series, Vol. 166, Norman, OK: University of Oklahoma Press, 1984. Ceremonialism is examined first in general terms (Chap. 5), then in two categories: the Green Corn Ceremony and the Nighttime Dances (Chaps. 6 & 7).

3084. Howard, James H. and Victoria Lindsay Levine. *Choctaw Music and Dance*. Norman, OK: University of Oklahoma Press, 1990. Documents the existing repertory of dance songs of the Mississippi and Oklahoma Choctaw in four chapters devoted to historical background, performance practice, dance choreography, and analysis. Includes transcriptions.

3085. Hudson, Charles M., ed. *Ethnology of the Southeastern Indians: A Source Book*. New York: Garland, 1985.

3086. Kilpatrick, Jack F. and Anna G. Kilpatrick. *Notebook of a Cherokee Shaman*. Washington, DC: Smithsonian Institution Press, 1970. A translation with commentary of a ms. from the 1930s containing healing chants for 50 ailments.

3087. Kurath, Gertrude P. "Effects of Environment on Cherokee-Iroqouis Ceremonialism, Music, and Dance." In *Symposium on Cherokee and Iroquois Culture, Bulletin 180 of the Bureau of American Ethnology*, Washington, DC: Government Printing Office, 1961. 173-95. Kurath posits that differences in Cherokee and Iroquois practice are caused by each tribe's natural and cultural environment. Includes several song transcriptions for comparison.

3088. Schupman, Edwin, Jr. *Current Musical Practices of the Creek Indians as Examined through the Green Corn Ceremonies of the Tulsa Cedar River and Fish Pond Stomp Grounds*. M.A. thesis, Miami University, Oxford, Ohio, 1984.

3089. Speck, Frank G. "Catawba Religious Beliefs, Mortuary Customs and Dances." In *Primitive Man*, Vol. 12. Washington, DC 1939. 21-57. Speck reports on information gleaned from an aged informant about the night dances no longer performed after 1875.

3090. Sturtevant, William C., ed. *A Seminole Source Book*. The North American Indian, New York: Garland Press, 1987. A collection of anthropological work published between 1896 and 1978.

3091. Sturtevant, William C., ed. *A Creek Source Book*. New York: Garland, 1987.

3092. Swanton, John R. *Indians of the Southeastern United States*. Bureau of American Ethnology, Bulletin 137, Washington, DC: Government Printing Office, 1946. Includes anthropological sketches of all tribes, chapters on musical instruments and ceremonial life and an extensive bibliography.

PRAIRIES

3093. Barrett, Samuel. "The Dream Dance of the Chippewa and Menominee Indians of Northern Wisconsin." *Bulletin of the Public Museum of the City of Milwaukee* 1 (1911): 251-406. Barrett compares the elements and style of the Dream Dance to those of the nine-day Ghost Dance ceremonial he observed in 1910.

3094. Beckwith, Martha W. *Myths and Ceremonies of the Mandan and Hidatsa*. American Folklore Society Memoirs Series, New York: Kraus Reprint, 1932/ repr. 1938. Beckwith transcribes the origin-tales of ritual and dance, including tales related to the Sun Dance.

3095. Bowers, Alfred W. *Hidatsa Social and Ceremonial Organization*. Lincoln: University of Nebraska, 1963/repr. 1992. A richly detailed documentary on the 19th-century lifeways of the Hidatsa. Presents extensive personal and ritual narratives by tribal elders. Includes descriptions of eight ceremonies with attention to ritual movement and singing.

3096. Callahan, A.A. *The Osage Ceremonial Dance I'n-Lon-Schka*. Norman, OK: University of Oklahoma Press, 1990. On ceremonial history, traditions, dance, music and dress. With music exx., dance steps, and drawings. Music and singing are described in Chap. 4 and dance with illustrative diagrams in Chap. 5.

3097. Catlin, G. *O-kee-pa: A Religious Ceremony and other Customs of the Mandan*. J.C. Ewers, ed. New Haven: Yale University Press, 1867/repr. 1967. Catlin gives a full account with illustrations of the ceremony.

3098. Densmore, Frances. *Chippewa Music*. 2 vols. Smithsonian Institution. Bureau of American Ethnology, Bulletin #45 & 53, New York: Da Capo, 1910, 1913/repr. 1972. The first of Ms. Densmore's monographs on Indian music. Densmore documents the beliefs, practices and songs of the Mide religion. Includes tabulated analysis of 90 Mide songs.

3099. Densmore, Frances. *Menominee Music*. Smithsonian Institution. Bureau of American Ethnology, Bulletin #102, New York: Da Capo, 1932/repr. 1972/repr. 1988. Among the songs catalogued and analyzed are dream religion songs, origin songs and medicine songs.

3100. Grim, John A. *The Shaman: Patterns of Siberian and Ojibway Healing.* Norman, OK.: University of Oklahoma Press, 1983. The use of drum, chant, and repetitive songs to evoke healing is discussed. See Chap. 6 and 7. Includes an extensive bibliography.

3101. Hoffman, Walter James. "The Midewiwin or 'Grand Medicine Society' of the Ojibwa." In *Seventh Annual Report of the Bureau of Ethnology, 1855-1886,* Washington, DC: Government Printing Office, 1891. 149-300. Music for the four degrees of initiation is discussed in the supplementary notes.

3102. Hoffman, Walter James. "Cult Societies and Ceremonies." *Fourteenth Annual Report of the Bureau of Ethnology* (1896): 66-160. On the Menomini Indians.

3103. Howard, James H. and Gertrude P. Kurath. "Ponca Dances, Ceremonies and Music." *Ethnomusicology* 3 (1959): 1-14. A description of three major types of dance—the Sun Dance, Wá-wa or Pipe Dance, and Hedúska or War Dance—the choreography and music of each, and elements apparently borrowed from other tribes and dances.

3104. Jenness, Diamond. *The Ojibwa Indians of Parry Island, Their Social and Religious Life.* National Museum of Canada Bulletin 78, Ottawa: J. O. Patenaude, 1935/repr. 1954, 1983. Ceremonial music and dance are mentioned in chapters five through eight which cover the supernatural world and shamanistic practices.

3105. Johnston, Basil. *Ojibway Ceremonies.* Lincoln, NE: University of Nebraska, 1990. A description by an Ojibway of important Ojibway rituals: the Naming Ceremony, the Marriage Ceremony, the Vision Quest, the War Path, and the Ritual of the Dead.

3106. Kurath, Gertrude P. "Chippewa Sacred Songs in Religious Metamorphosis." *Scientific Monthly* 79 (1954): 311-317.

3107. Landes, Ruth. *The Prarie Potawatomi: Tradition and Ritual in the Twentieth Century.* Madison, WI: University of Wisconsin Press, 1970. Sections on the history and power of the drum, drum rituals, and leaders are found in Chapter 5. Appendix B compares dance elements observed by Landes and those described by S.A. Barrett.

3108. McAllester, David P. "Menomini Peyote Music." In *Menomini Peyotism,* J.S. Slotkin, ed. Transactions of the American Philosophical Society, 42, Pt. 4. 1952. 681-700.

3109. Morinis, Alan. "Persistent Peregrination: From Sun Dance to Catholic Pilgrimage among the Canadian Prairie Indians." In *Sacred Journeys: The Anthropology of Pilgrimage,* Alan Morinis, ed. Westport, CT: Greenwood Press, 1992. 101-113.

3110. Murie, James R. *Ceremonies of the Pawnee*. 2 vols. Studies in the Anthropology of North American Indians, Douglas R. Parks, ed. Lincoln, NE: University of Nebraska Press, 1981/repr. 1989. Vol. 1: The Skiri, Vol. 2: The South Bands. Both volumes contain numerous song texts with English translation, dance ceremony diagrams, and commentary and background information on each ceremony.

3111. Parthun, Paul. *Ojibwe Music in Minnesota*. Ph.D. diss., University of Minnesota, 1976, 1985.

3112. Skinner, Alanson. "Songs of the Menomini Medicine Ceremony." *American Anthropologist* 27, NS (1925): 290-314. A collection of songs and medicine practices recorded in 1919 from some of the last remaining song leaders.

3113. Slotkin, J.S. "Menomini Peyotism." In *Transactions of the American Philosophical Society*, 42, pt. 4, New series. Philadelphia 1952. A full description of the theory, history and dogma of peyotism as well as its ceremonial aspects. Includes song and prayer texts.

3114. Vennum, Thomas, Jr. "Ojibwa Origin-Migration Songs of the Mitewiwin." *Journal of American Folklore* 91 (1978): 753-91. This article provides foundational background information on most Ojibwa sacred song.

3115. Vennum, Thomas, Jr. "A History of Ojibwa Song Form." *Selected Reports in Ethnomusicology* Vol. 3, 2 (1980): 43-75. A comparison of religious song forms between c1910 and 1980 as recorded on various media.

3116. Vennum, Thomas Jr. "Ojibway Drum Decor: Sources and Variations of Ritual Design." In *Circles of Tradition: Folk Arts in Minnesota*, St. Paul, MN: Minnesota Historical Society Press, 1989. 60-70. A study of the history, cultural value, and use of the Ojibwa shaman's drum. Written to accompany the film The Drummaker, which shows the creation and performance of the drum.

3117. Vilenskaya, Larissa. "The Sacred Fire: Healing among Cherokee Indians: A Personal Perspective." In *Proceedings of the Ninth International Conference on the Study of Shamanism and Alternate Modes of Healing*, Ruth-Inge Heinze, ed. Berkeley: Independent Scholars of Asia, 1992. 133-142. A description of the Sacred Fire Ceremony (Stomp Dance), its healing powers, its music, and a description of the dance itself.

GREAT PLAINS

3118. Boyd, Maurice. *Kiowa Voices: Ceremonial Dance, Ritual and Song, Vol. 1*. Fort Worth, TX: Texas Christian University Press, 1981. The knowledge and traditions of Kiowa elders are committed to print for the benefit of future generations.

3119. Densmore, Frances. *Pawnee Music*. Smithsonian Institution. Bureau of American Ethnology, Bulletin #93, New York: Da Capo, 1929/repr. 1972. Among the songs catalogued and analysed are the Ghost Dance songs and Morning Star ceremonial dance and ritual.

3120. Densmore, Frances. *Cheyenne and Arapaho Music*. Los Angeles, CA: Southwest Museum, 1936. Densmore gives musical analysis and commentary for the Ghost Dance, Sun Dance, medicine and peyote song traditions.

3121. Dieter-McArthur, Pat. *Dances of the Northern Plains*. Saskatoon, Saskatchawan: Saskatchawan Cultural Center, 1987.

3122. Dorsey, George Amos. *The Cheyenne [Ceremonial Organization]*. Fairfield, WA: Ye Galleon Press, 1905/repr. 1975. A reprint of Vol. 1. *Ceremonial Organization*, of *The Cheyenne*, publ. 1905 by Field Columbian Museum, Chicago. A description of the medicine arrows and various warrior societies. Both vols. (Vol. 2. *The Sun Dance*) were reprinted in Glorieta, NM: Rio Grande Press, 1971.

3123. Fletcher, Alice C. *A Study of Omaha Indian Music*. Lincoln, NE: University of Nebraska Press, 1893/repr. 1994. "Aided by Francis La Flesche, with a report of the peculiarities of the music by John Comfort Fillmore." Begun in 1883, this study of the Omaha is the first to arouse popular interest in American Indian music. Discusses the relationship of music to the life of the Plains Indians. Includes transcriptions and the native-language words for the songs.

3124. Fletcher, Alice C. *The Hako: A Pawnee Ceremony*. Twenty-Second Annual Report of the Bureau of American Ethnology, 1900-1901, Vol. 22, part 2. Washington, DC: Government Printing Office, 1904. Washington, DC. An exhaustive account of all aspects of the rituals connected with this prayer for children. The dance and songs of the prayer are listed throughout the text.

3125. Fletcher, Alice C. and Francis LaFlesche. *The Omaha Tribe*. Lincoln, NE: University of Nebraska Press, 1911/repr. 1992. Sacred songs are discussed in the context of child initiation, sweat lodge and maize rituals.

3126. Giglio, Virginia. *Southern Cheyenne Women's Songs*. Norman, OK: University of Oklahoma Press, 1994.

3127. Graber, David, ed. *Tsese-Ma'Heone-Nemeototse: Cheyenne Spiritual Songs*. Newton KS: Faith and Life Press, 1982.

3128. Herzog, George. "Plains Ghost Dance and Great Basin Music." *American Anthropologist* Vol. 37, July (1935): 403-419. A musicological study of the surprising stability of form shown by thirtyeight Plains Ghost Dance songs. (Also included in the *Garland Library of Readings in Ethnomusicology*, Vol. 7).

3129. Kracht, Benjamin Ray. *Kiowa Religion: An Ethnohistorical Analysis of Ritual Symbolism.* Ph.D. diss., Southern Methodist University, 1989. This three-part historical and anthropological study reconstructs Kiowa belief and ritual from 1832 to 1890, accounts for the dissappearance of the Sun Dance and other rituals and the appearance of syncretic religious cults between 1870 and 1940, and describes religious practices and cultural revivals since WWII.

3130. La Flesche, Francis. *The Osage Tribe: The Rite of Vigil.* Bureau of American Ethnology, Thirty-ninth Annual Report, 1917-1918, Vol. 39. Washington, DC: The Smithsonian Institution, 1929. 31-630. An exhaustive study of the ceremonies, music, and text of a rite that brings people in close touch with the Supernatural Power to which they appeal in times of distress. It is given in two versions, with texts for each given in a free translation, a transliteration of the original Osage, and a literal interlinear translation.

3131. La Flesche, Francis. *War Ceremony and Peace Ceremony.* Bureau of American Ethnology, Bulletin 101, Washington, DC: U.S. Govt. Printing Office, 1939. A detailed study, with texts and music.

3132. La Flesche, Francis. *The Osage and the Invisible World: From the Works of Francis La Flesche.* Norman, OK: University of Oklahoma Press, 1995.

3133. Lesser, Alexander. *The Pawnee Ghost Dance Hand Game: Ghost Dance Revival and Ethnic Identity.* Madison, WI: University of Wisconsin Press, 1933/repr. 1978.

3134. Lewis, Thomas H. "The Art and Iconology of the Dance in the Petroglyphs of the Northern Plains." *Northwest Anthropological Research Notes* Vol. 23, 1 (Spring) (1989): 109-23. The author studies 23 glyphs for information concerning ceremonial behavior in terms of myth, music, and organization of a prehistoric people.

3135. Linton, Ralph. *The Sacrifice to the Morning Star by the Skidi Pawnee.* Chicago, IL: Field Museum of Natural History, 1922. Contains excerpts of sacred songs. Information was compiled from the notes and articles of others.

3136. Linton, Ralph. *Annual Ceremony of the Pawnee Medicine Men.* Chicago, IL: Field Museum of Natural History, 1923. A ceremonial described from the unpublished notes of G. A. Dorsey.

3137. Lowie, Robert H. "Dances of Societies of the Plains Shoshone." In *American Museum of Natural History Anthropological Papers*, Vol. 11. New York: American Museum of Natural History, 1909. 803-35. Includes examples of sacred dances with illustrations of the Comanche, Wind River Shoshone and Ute tribes.

3138. Lowie, Robert H. *The Crow Indians.* Lincoln, NE: University of Nebraska Press, 1924/repr. 1983. Includes chapters on the Bear Song Dance,

Sacred Pipe Dance, and Sun Dance, with a glossary of terms. Considered a masterpiece of ethnography.

3139. Nettl, Bruno. "Musical Culture of the Arapaho." *Musical Quarterly* Vol. 41, 3 (1955): 325-331. An article on inspiration in creating songs and on the songs of the Peyote Cult and Ghost Dance religion.

3140. Powell, Peter J. *Sweet Medicine: The Continuing Role of the Sacred Arrows, the Sun Dance, and the Sacred Buffalo Hat in Northern Cheyenne History.* Norman, OK: University of Oklahoma Press, 1969. Beautifully written and well documented, this two volume work is a respectful, detailed study of sacred Cheyenne ceremonials and of their indispensible role in preserving Cheyenne culture. First-hand accounts, drawings, and photographs illustrate each aspect of Cheyenne religious dance and ritual.

3141. Powers, William K. "Plains Indian Music and Dance." In *Anthropology on the Great Plains*, Lincoln, NE: University of Nebraska, 1980. A survey of the literature, categories, diffusion, and contemporary Plains music and dance.

3142. Powers, William K. *War Dance: Plains Indian Musical Performance.* Tucson, AZ: University of Arizona Press, 1990. A collection of essays from 1968 to 1984 surveying Powers's experience with Plains Indian's music with special attention to the Powwow and War Dance.

3143. Schlesier, Karl H. *The Wolves of Heaven: Cheyenne Shamanism, Ceremonies, and Prehistoric Origins.* Norman, OK: University of Oklahoma Press, 1987. Though lacking in descriptions of shamanic song and dance, the author's detailed comparison of Northern Siberian and early Cheyenne shamanic cosmology shows them to be similar according to dozens of specific criteria. Also contains detailed description of shamanic ceremony pointedly excluding reference to song cycles.

3144. Thomas, Trudy Carter. *Crisis and Creativity: Visual Symbolism of the Ghost Dance Tradition.* Ph.D. diss., Columbia University, 1988. The symbol system found in the garments worn during the Ghost Dance rituals of the 1890's constitutes a composite of Plains values, encompassing themes of creation and world renewal, therewith providing a tangible formulation of the underlying orientations, themes and historical experience of Plains culture.

3145. Vander, Judith. *A View of Wind River Shoshone Music through Four Ceremonies.* Ph.D. diss., University of Michigan, 1978.

3146. Wiedman, Dennis. "Staff, Fan, Rattle & Drum: Spiritual and Artistic Expressions of Oklahoma Peyotists." *American Indian Art Magazine* Vol. 10, 3 (1985): 38-45.

3147. Wissler, Clark, ed. *Societies of the Plains Indians.* Vol. 11, part 10. New York: Museum of Natural History, 1915. Contains seventeen lengthy studies of the Societies and Dance Associations of the Plains Indians. Most include descriptions of a wide variety of dances. Authors are Wissler, Skinner, Goddard, Murie, and Lowie. Among the tribes whose dance and/or ceremonial associations are addressed are the Teton-Dakota, Eastern Dakota, Blackfoot, Sarsi, Ojibway, Cree, Ponca, and Shoshone.

3148. Wood, W. Raymond and Margot P. Liberty, ed. *Anthropology of the Great Plains*. Lincoln, NE: Univ. of Nebraska Press, 1980. Includes articles on the Sun Dance and Ghost Dance religion; see bibliography.

3149. Yellowtail, Thomas. *Yellowtail: Crow Medicine Man and Sun Dance Chief: An Autobiography*. Norman, OK: University of Oklahoma Press, 1991. Intended to allow the non-native insight into Native spirituality, this authobiography is rich with first-hand details of Crow ceremonial life. Recorded by Michael Oren Fitzgerald.

3150. Deleted.

Lakota/Sioux

3151. Berube, David Michael. *The Lakotan Ghost Dance of 1890: A Historical Performance Analysis*. Ph.D. diss., New York University, 1990.

3152. Black Bear, Ben, Sr. and R.D. Theisz. *Songs and Dances of the Lakota*. Rosebud, SD: Sinte Gleska College; Aberdeen, SD: North Plains Press, 1976. Although largely concerned with the social and contest dances, the authors provide a solid introduction to the importance of music and dance in ceremonial.

3153. Black Elk, Wallace and William S. Lyon. *Black Elk: The Sacred Ways of a Lakota*. San Francisco: Harper & Row, 1990. In two parts: 'The Making of a Shaman' and 'The Sacred Mystery Powers.' Contains numerous references to songs, drum, and ceremony. The story of a modern shaman, told in the first person.

3154. Brown, Joseph E., ed. *The Sacred Pipe: Black Elk's Account of the Seven Rites of Oglala Sioux*. Civilization of the American Indian Series, Norman OK: University of Oklahoma Press, 1953/repr. 1981. An explanation of the teachings, symbolism, and meaning of the sacred pipe—an alliance between humans and the Wakan-Tanka—by the only qualified shaman alive at the time of the recording. Shows how the sacredness of life is maintained by a variety of rites. Includes translation of song texts.

3155. Colby, L.W. "The Ghost Song of the Dakota." In *Proceedings and Collections of the Nebraska State Historical Society*, Lincoln, NE: The Society, 1895. Series 2, vol. I, 131-150. Includes the definitive 'Story of Ghost Dancing,' a written description by a young educated Oglala, Major George Sword. Includes nineteen stanzas from Ghost Dance songs, in both English and the original language, and one complete song, with music and text.

3156. Densmore, Frances. "Music in its Relation to the Religious Thought of the Teton Sioux." In *Holmes Anniversary Volume: Anthropological Essays Presented to William Henry Holmes in Honor of his Seventieth Birthday, Dec. 1, 1916*, F. W. Hodge, ed. New York: AMS Press, 1916/repr. 1977. 67 ff.

3157. Densmore, Frances. *Teton Sioux Music and Culture*. 1918/repr. 1992. Lincoln, NE: University of Nebraska. An analysis of Sioux songs with reference to their ceremonial, war-making, and social functions. A classic of descriptive ethnomusicology. Done in collaboration with Robert P. Higheagle.

3158. Fenton, William. *Sioux Music*. Saint Clair Shores, MI: Scholarly Press, Inc., 1991.

3159. Fletcher, Alice C. "The Elk Mystery of the Oglala." In *Peabody Museum Papers, 16th & 17th Annual Reports*, Vol. 3, Parts 2, 4. Cambridge, MA: Harvard University, 1884.

3160. Fletcher, Alice C. "The Shadow or Ghost Lodge: A Ceremony of the Oglala Sioux." In *Reports of the Peabody Museum of American Archaeology and Ethnology*, Cambridge, MA: Harvard University, 1884.

3161. Huenemann, Lynn F. "Dakota/Lakota Music and Dance: An Introduction." In *The Arts of South Dakota*, R. McIntyre and R. L. Bell, ed. Sioux Falls: Center for Western Studies, 1988.

3162. Johnson, Willard. "An Unusual Transmission of the Lakota Yuwipi Ritual." *Journal of Ritual Studies* Vol. 8 (1994): 96-124. In Nov., 1988, the Yuwipi ritual of the Lakota was transmitted to the American-born Mexican-Indian shaman, Luciano Perez. This article documents Perez' history and preparation for this event, the transmission ritual itself, and his subsequent life.

3163. Kemnitzer, Luis S. "The Cultural Provenance of Objects Used in Yuwipi: A Modern Teton Dakota Healing Ritual." *Ethnos* Vol. 1-4 (1970): 40-75.

3164. Kemnitzer, Luis S. "Structure, Content, and Cultural Meaning of *Yuwipi*: A Modern Lakota Healing Ritual." *American Ethnologist* Vol. 3 (1976): 261-280. Modern Lakota have access to modern medicine, Christian faith healing, and native religious and secular medical systems. After listing native categories of doctors, the author describes a healing sing (ceremonial) for which a *yuwipi* (a native healer who is tied and performs in a darkened room with the aid of pipe and helping spirits) presides.

3165. Lame Deer, Archie Fire, and Richard Erdoes. *Gift of Power: The Life and Teachings of a Lakota Medicine Man*. Sante Fe, NM: Bear and Co., 1992. The Story of Archie Fire Lame Deer and the long path he traveled to becoming a spiritual man and teacher of the Lakota way.

3166. Lewis, Thomas. *The Medicine Men: Oglala Sioux Ceremony and Healing.* Lincoln, NE: University of Nebraska Press, 1990. Topics include concepts of power, the Sun Dance, *Yuwipi* and other night songs, other medicines (inluding the Ghost Dance), and Heyuká (secret society). From the late 60s and early 70s.

3167. Mails, Thomas. *Sundancing at Rosebud and Pine Ridge.* Sioux Fall, SD: The Center for Western Studies, 1978.

3168. Mooney, James. *The Ghost-Dance Religion and the Sioux Outbreak of 1890.* rev. and abridged ed., Fourteenth Annual Report of the Bureau of American Ethnology, Smithsonian Institute, pt. 2, 1892-93, Chicago: University of Chicago Press, 1896/repr. 1965. 641-1136. The bulk of this volume is devoted to analysis of and commentary on the songs of the Ghost Dance with one chapter on the origin, diffusion and end of ceremony as a whole.

3169. Mooney, James. "Music in its Relationship to the Thought of the Teton Sioux." In *Holmes Anniversary Volume: Anthropological Essays Presented to William Henry Holmes in Honor of his Seventieth Birthday, Dec. 1, 1916,* F. W. Hodge, ed. New York: AMS Press, 1916/repr. 1977.

3170. Neihardt, John. *Black Elk Speaks: Being the Life Story of a Holy Man of the Oglala Sioux as Told through John G. Neihardt.* Lincoln, NB: University of Nebraska Press, 1932/repr. 1961. Focuses on the visionary aspects of Black Elk's shamanism.

3171. Paige, Harry W. *Songs of the Teton Sioux.* Los Angeles: Westernlore Press, 1970. A literary and cultural study of Sioux song texts, with no discussion of music. Chapter 5 deals with ceremonial songs and includes song texts with English translation and commentary.

3172. Powers, William K. "Contemporary Oglala Music and Dance: Pan-Indianism versus Pan-Tetonism." *Ethnomusicology* Vol. 12 (1968): 352-71. A comparison of the dominant Oklahoma pan-Indianism with North and South Dakota pan-Tetonism with special reference to the Oglala people. Discusses characteristic elements of both pan-complexes and shows that the Oglala hold a closer bond to pan-Tetonism than to pan-Indianism.

3173. Powers, William K. *Oglala Religion.* Lincoln, NB: University of Nebraska Press, 1977. Includes careful analysis of the myths and rites related to the Sun Dance.

3174. Powers, William K. "Oglala Song Terminology." *Selected Reports in Ethnomusicology* Vol. 3, 2 (1980): 23-41. Powers uses a structuralist-linguistic approach to analyse Oglala concepts of song, performance, composition, learning, and classification of instruments. He rejects the Euro-centric model of technical language about music and creates a space for Oglala terminology.

3175. Powers, William K. *Yuwipi: Vision and Experience in Oglala Ritual.* Lincoln, NB: University of Nebraska Press, 1982. A study of the inter-relationships between the Vision Quest, Sweat Lodge, and Yuwipi with respect to myth, ritual, and social organization. Primarily a description of the ritual itself. Includes an index and glossary of Lakota terms.

3176. Powers, William K. *Sacred Language: The Nature of Supernatural Discourse in Lakota.* Norman and London: University of Oklahoma Press, 1986. A study of the speech and song texts that are used to address supernatural beings and powers that inhabit and control the Lakota universe. Chapters cover incomprehensible terms, Oglala song terminology, song texts, containing the sacred, sacred numbers, naming the sacred, and shamans and priests.

3177. Powers, William K. "Text and Context in Lakota Music." In *Explorations in Ethnomusicology. Essays in Honor of David P. McAllester*, Charlotte J. Frisbie, ed. Detroit Monographs in Musicology, Vol. 9. Detroit, MI: Detroit Information Coordinators, 1986. An examination of the song texts and method of learning and performance of a contemporary curing ritual.

3178. Powers, William K. *Voices from the Spirit World: Lakota Ghost Dance Songs.* Kendall Park, NJ: Lakota Books, 1990.

3179. Severt Young Bear and R. D. Thiesz. *Standing in the Light: A Lakota Way of Seeing.* Lincoln, NE: University of Nebraska Press, 1994. A penetrating study of contemporary Lakota music and the profession of a singer.

3180. Walker, James R. *Lakota Belief and Ritual.* Lincoln, NE: University of Nebraska Press, 1991. A wealth of first-hand information on Lakota cosmology and ritual observances.

3181. White Hat, A., Sr., ed. *Lakota Ceremonial Songs.* Rosebud, SD: Sinte Gleska College, Inc., 1983.

GREAT BASIN

3182. D'Azevedo, Warren L., ed. *Handbook of North American Indians. Great Basin.* William C. Sturtevant, gen. ed. Vol. 11. Washington, DC: Smithsonian Institution; Berkeley, CA: California Indian Library Collections, 1986. Includes an extensive bibliography.

3183. Densmore, Frances. *Northern Ute Music.* Smithsonian Institution. Bureau of American Ethnology, Bulletin #75, New York: Da Capo, 1922/repr. 1972. A highly detailed account of the characteristics and plots (many with tabulated analysis) of Ute songs and dances. The Sun Dance and other ceremonially related pieces are described in full.

3184. Handelman, Don. "Transcultural Shamanic Healing: A Washo Example." *Ethnos* Vol. 32 (1967): 149-166.

3185. Hittman, Michael. *Wovoka and the Ghost Dance.* Yerington, NV: Yerington Paiute Tribe, 1990. Hittman's three part study of the movement and its founder is comprehensive. Part 3, section G, includes texts for nine Paiute Ghost Dance songs.

3186. Hittman, Michael. "The 1890 Ghost Dance in Nevada." *American Indian Culture and Research Journal* Vol. 16, 4 (1992): 123-166. One section of this lengthy article describes the ceremony. In another, Hittman raises the possibility of its being a round dance.

3187. Merriam, Alan P. and Warran L. d'Azevedo. "Washo Peyote Songs." *American Anthropologist* Vol. 59 (1957): 615-41. Merriman analyses song compositions, describes instruments and performance styles and provides a brief account of the movement's political and religious context.

3188. Reynolds, Mary Stephanie. *Dance Brings About Everything: Dance Power in the Ideologies of Northern Utes of the Uintah and Ouray Reservation and Predominantly Mormon Anglos of an Adjacent Uintah Basin Community.* 2 vols. Ph.D. diss., UC Irvine, 1990. A variety of analytic techniques reveal that Northern Utes and Anglo fine artists (only) attribute the greatest survival value, both personal and universal, to dance, ascribe transcendent, transformative religious attributes to dance (including interaction with specific spirits or vital forces), and consider dance to be vital.

3189. Vander, Judith. *Ghost Dance Songs and Religion of a Wind River Shoshone Woman.* Monograph Series in Ethnmusicology, Vol. 4. Los Angeles: University of California Press; Dept. of Music, UCLA, 1986. The author includes a brief introduction to the history and theology of the Naraya faith as well as musical and textual analysis of Naraya songs. Based on lengthy interviews with two Shoshone women. Analyses 17 Ghost Dance songs, musically and textually.

3190. Vander, Judith. *Songprints: The Musical Experience of Five Shoshone Women.* Urbana, IL: University of Illinois Press, 1988. These detailed and sensitive biographies include accounts of each woman's participation in the Ghost Dance, Sun Dance, Native American Church and other ceremonial dances.

3191. Vander, Judith. *Shoshone Ghost Dance Religion: Poetry, Songs and Great Basin Context.* Urbana, IL: University of Illinois Press, forthcoming.

3192. Vennum, Thomas, Jr. "Music." In *Great Basin*, W. d'Avevedo, ed. Handbook of North American Indians, Vol. 11. William C. Sturtevant, Washington, DC: Smithsonian Institute, 1986.

PLATEAU

3193. Dempsey, Hugh Aylmer. *The Blackfoot Ghost Dance.* Glenbow-Atlanta Institute Occasional Papers, Vol. 3. Calgary, Alberta: Glenbow-Atlanta Institute, 1968. The author concentrates on adaptations in meaning and function that have been made to the dance since the advent of reservation life.

3194. Duff, Wilson. *The Upper Stalo Indians of Fraser Valley, British Columbia.* Anthropology in British Columbia, Memoir #1, Victoria, B.C.: British Columbia Provincial Museum, Department of Education Victoria, 1952. The section on "Concepts of the Supernatural," pp. 97-122, describes several spirit songs and dances as well as the various ways in which a shaman acquires a spirit song.

3195. Johnson, Bryan R. *The Blackfeet: An Annotated Bibliography.* New York: Garland Publishing, 1988. An exhaustive bibliography on every aspect of Siksika Blackeet life.

3196. McClintock, Walter. *The Old North Trail or Life, Legends and Religion of the Blackfoot Indians.* Lincoln: University of Nebraska Press, 1968. The author was adopted into the tribe he reports on and thus gained access to many sacred ceremonies. Religious dance, chant and song are regular themes in the chapters of this thick volume.

3197. McLeod, Norma. "The Semantic Parameter in Music: The Blanket Rite of the Lower Kutenai." *Yearbook for Inter-American Musical Research* Vol. 7 (1971): 83-102. An investigation of the relationship between songs and vocables and the stages of a shaman's ceremony: the characteristics of the songs and vocables change as the ceremony progresses from the trance generating through the trance abating stages. Since the text consists entirely of vocables, the music itself becomes the semantic phenomenon.

3198. Merriam, Alan P. "Music and the Origin of the Flathead Indians: A Problem in Culture History." In *Inter-American Conference on Ethnomusicology: Bloomington, IN, 1965*, J. Orrego-Salas and G. List, ed. Bloomington, IN: University of Indiana Press, 1967. 129 ff.

3199. Merriam, Alan P. *Ethnomusicology of the Flathead Indians.* Viking Fund Publications in Anthropology, Vol. 44. Chicago, IL: Aldine Publishing Co., 1967/repr. Part 1 explores the Flathead concept of the spiritual origin of music, their musicianship, uses of music, and musical instruments. Part 2 studies songs and dances and sets up categories according to styles and substyles. Considered the first work to examine the music of a people in terms of its cultural context. Lengthy review by M. Kolinski, *Ethnomusicology*, 14, 1 (1970): 77-99.

3200. Miller, Jay. *Shamanic Odyssey: The Lushootseed Salish Journey to the Land of the Dead.* Menlo Park, CA: Ballena Press, 1988. Extended review by A. Hultkrantz in *Anthropos*, Vol. 85, No. 1-3: 251-262.

3201. Nettl, Bruno. *Blackfoot Musical Thought: Comparative Perspectives.* Kent, OH: Kent State University Press, 1989. Nettl undertakes a two-fold task: the presentation of issues for musical ethnography and the clarification of the conceptual and philosophical framework upon which Blackfoot music rests. Chapters cover the Blackfoot conception of the general character of music, Blackfoot beliefs about the origins of music, both with respect to culture and to repertories and individual songs, and the relationship of song to the rest of human life, human culture, specific activities, and to the supernatural. See bibliography for earlier works by the author on Blackfoot musical culture.

3202. Spier, Leslie. *The Prophet Dance of the Northwest and its Derivatives: The Source of the Ghost Dance.* Menasha: George Banta Publishing Company, 1935. On the Northwestern origin of the Ghost Dance, the Christianized form of the Prophet Dance (1820-1836), and syncretized versions in the Smohalla cult and the Shaker Religion. Contains descriptions of ceremonies in the 1800s.

3203. Teit, James A. "The Salishan Tribes of the Western Plateaus." In *H.W. Dorsey, Chief Clerk, Forth-Fifth Annual Report of the Bureau of American Ethnology...1927-1928*, Franz Boas, ed. Washington, DC: Government Printing Office, 1930. 23-396. A discussion of the religious dances of the Coeur d'Alene, Okanagon and Flathead groups.

3204. Wickwire, Wendy C. *Cultures in Contact: Music, the Plateau Indian, and the Western Encounter.* Ph.D. diss., Wesleyan University, 1982. The negative impact of Euro-American music on that of the Salishan Indians of British Columbia is used to point to the destruction on a larger scale of their socially and ecologically sustaining world views and practices.

3205. Wissler, Clark. *Social Organization and Ritualistic Ceremonies of the Blackfoot Indians; Ceremonial Bundles of the Blackfoot Indians.* American Museum of Natural History, Anthroplogical Papers, Vol. 7. New York: American Museum of Natural History, 1912. Section Four of Part Two includes a descriptive discussion of the dances and songs that accompany the medicine bundle ceremonies.

3206. Wissler, Clark. "Societies and Dance Associations of the Blackfoot Indians." In *Anthropological Papers of the American Museum of Natural History*, Vol. 11, Part 4. New York: American Museum of Natural History, 1912. 359-460. Sec. 3 describes a religious society, three religious dances and a ceremony.

SOUTHWEST

General References

3207. Bahti, Tom. *Southwestern Indian Ceremonials*. Flagstaff, AZ: KC Publications, 1982. A discussion of the religious symbolism and spiritual significance of ceremonial dances. Includes a calendar of ceremonial dances and other events for the entire Southwest (circa 1970) and color illustrations.

3208. Brown, Donald N. "The Distribution of Sound Instruments in the Prehistoric Southwestern United States." *Ethnomusicology* Vol. 11 (1967): 71-90. From archaeological evidence, Brown recreates the musical history of the Southwest, establishes its beginnings at 600AD and a proliferation around 1000AD, and gives descriptions of various instruments and their probable religious function.

3209. Collier, John and I. Moskowitz. *Patterns and Ceremonials of the Indians of the Southwest*. New York: Dutton, 1949. A descriptive account of Southwestern religious practice with nearly 100 pages of illustrations.

3210. Fergusson, Erna. *Dancing Gods: Indian Ceremonials of New Mexico and Arizona*. New York: Knopf, 1931. First-hand descriptions of the principal ceremonial dances of the Southwestern Indians.

3211. Frisbie, Charlotte J. *Music and Dance Research of Southwestern United States Indians: Past Trends, Present Activities, and Suggestions for Future Research*. Studies in Music Bibliography, No. 36, Detroit, MI: Information Coordinators, 1977. A critical review of research on native dance and music done between 1880 and 1976. Includes discographies and archive listings.

3212. McAllester, David P. *Indian Music in the Southwest*. Colorado Springs: Taylor Museum of the Colorado Springs Fine Arts Center, 1961. Reprinted in *Readings in Ethnomusicology*. Ed. by David P. McAllester, New York: Johnson Reprint Corp., 1971. An overview of the characteristics of the vocal music of the Pueblos, Apaches, and Navahos, with emphasis on ceremonial music.

3213. Underhill, Ruth. *Ceremonial Patterns of the Greater Southwest*. Monographs of the American Ethnological Society, Vol. 13, 14. New York: J. J. Augustin, 1948/repr. 1973.

Apache

3214. Basso, Keith H. "The Gift of Changing Woman." In *Anthropological Papers, #76*, Vol. 196. Washington, DC: Bureau of American Ethnology Bulletin, 1966. 113-73. See for analysis of Apache Sunrise Ceremony.

3215. Basso, Keith H. *The Cibecue Apache: Case Studies in Cultural Anthropology.* Prospect Heights, IL: Waveland Press, 1970/repr. 1986. Contains a comprehensive discussion and analysis of the Sunrise Ceremony. Includes informative sections on power and its uses, the acquisition of power, and the chants and the cost of acquiring power (sec. 3), curing ceremonials (sec. 4), and a girl's puberty ceremony (sec. 5).

3216. Basso, Kieth H. "Western Apache." In *Handbook of North American Indians: Southwest*, Alfonso Ortiz, ed. Vol. 10. Washington, DC: Smithsonian Institution, 1983. 477-480. The section on the religion and world view of the Western Apache discusses 'powers,' ceremonials, particularly curing ceremonials, and the central role of shamans in conducting them, and the sacred.

3217. Ganteaume, Cécile R. "White Mountain Apache Dance: Expressions of Spirituality." In *Native American Dance: Ceremonies and Social Traditions*, Charlotte Heth, ed. Washington, DC: National Museum of the American Indian, Smithsonian Institution, with Starwood Publishers, 1992. 65-76, 79-81. In the past, ceremonial dances were usually performed to cure illness. Now, though medicine may be used, dance still has a healing effect. Through dance the performers come into contact 'with the spiritual powers that created the universe and are manifest in nature.' White Mountain Appache religious ceremonies both invoke specific powers and recall the divine origins of the universe and the spiritual powers that sustain all life. The context and a general description are provided for the Sunrise Ceremony, the Crown Dance (including the story of its origin), the War Dance and the Hoop Dance.

3218. McAllester, David P. "The Role of Music in Western Apache Culture." In *Selected Papers of the Fifth International Congress of Anthropological and Ethnological Sciences*, Anthony F.C. Wallace, ed. 1960.

3219. Nicholas, D. "Mescalero Apache Girl's Puberty Ceremony." *El palacio* Vol. 46 (1939): 193 ff. A detailed description of all non-secret sacred elements including dances that make up the puberty rite.

3220. Shapiro, Anne Dhu and Inéz Talamantez. "The Mescalero Apache Girls' Puberty Ceremony: The Role of Music in Structuring Ritual Time." *Yearbook for Traditional Music* Vol. 18 (1986): 77-90. Music is used to structure time in order to sustain the experience of transcendence during an eight day ritual. Includes a breakdown of the time/music framework.

Hopi

3221. Black, R.A. *A Content-Anaylsis of Eighty-one Hopi Indian Chants.* Ph.D. diss., Indiana University, 1964.

3222. Fewkes, Jesse Walter. *The Snake Ceremonials at Walpi.* Vol. 4. New York: AMS Press, 1894/repr. 1977. A complete account of the 10-day ceremonial with descriptions and illustrations of many of the rituals and the sixteen songs of the ceremony.

3223. Fewkes, Jesse Walter. "Tusayan Snake Ceremonies: An Eyewitness Account." Vol. 16. Albuquerque, NM 1897/repr. 1986. 267-312. Fewkes reports on his discovery in the late 19th century of snake dances held in Cipaulove, Cunopavi, and Oraibi.

3224. Fewkes, Jesse Walter. "Tusayan Flute and Snake Ceremonies." United States Bureau of American Ethnology. Nineteenth Annual Report, 1897-98, Vol. 16, pt. 4. Washington, DC 1900. 957-1011. Eye-witness account of Hopi ceremonies.

3225. Frigout, Arlette. "Hopi Ceremonial Organization." In *Handbook of North American Indians: Southwest*, Alfonso Ortiz, ed. Vol. 9. Washington, DC: Smithsonian Institution, 1979. 564-576. A description of Hopi ceremonies, the calendar of events and cycles, and specific ceremonies such as Women's rites, initiation, Winter Solstice, and Kachinas.

3226. Hill, Stephen. *Kokopelli Ceremonies*. Sante Fe, NM: Kiva Publishing, Inc., 1995. A study of Kokopelli, the Humpbacked Flute Player, as he appears in rock art, legends, and ceremonials of the Hopi and Pueblo.

3227. Hodge, Frederick W. "Pueblo Snake Ceremonials." *American Anthropologist* Vol. 9, April (1896). Documentation of the Snake Ritual held outside the Hopi tribe of northeastern Arizona and the Jemez Valley of New Mexico.

3228. Humphreys, Paul. "Form as Cosmology: An Interpretation of the Structure in the Ceremonial Songs of the Pueblo." *Pacific Review of Ethnomusicology* Vol. 5 (1989): 61-88. A description of Pueblo cosmology in terms of concentric forms, and an analysis of a Hopi Katcina song in terms of the concentric model.

3229. Kealiinohomoku, Joann. "Music and Dance of the Hawaiian and Hopi Peoples." In *Art in Small-scale Societies: Contemporary Readings*, Richard L. Anderson and K. L. Field, ed. Englewood Cliffs, NJ: Prentice-Hall, 1993. 334-48. An investigation and comparison of the changes in the musical repertories of both cultures due to external influences. Good sections on the relationship of myths to Hawaiian music and of religion to Hopi music. Also in David P. McAllester, ed. *Becoming Human through Music*. 1985. 5-22.

3230. Kealiinohomoku, Joann W. "The Hopi Katsina Dance Event Doings." In *Seasons of the Kachina*, Lowell John Bean, ed. Hayward, CA: Ballena Press & California State University, 1989. 51-64. The author identifies and describes the elements that make up the 'doings' of Hopi dance, with attention to time, place, participants and dance activities.

3231. List, George. "The Hopi as Composer and Poet." In *Proceedings of the Centennial Workshop on Ethnomusicology Held at the University of British Columbia, Vancouver, June 19 to 23, 1967*, 3rd ed. P. Crossley-Holland, ed. Vancouver 1975. 43. Relying primarily upon Hopi sources the author examines music and dance as it feeds the ceremonial and spiritual life of the people.

3232. List, George. "Hopi Melodic Concepts." *JAMS* Vol. 38, 1 (1985): 143-52. Through a study of *kachina* dance songs and interviews with performers, List concludes that melodic contour rather than discreet pitches identify a melody.

3233. Rhodes, Willard. *Hopi Music and Dance*. Tsaile, AZ: Navajo Community College Press, 1977. A booklet covering both religious and secular ceremonial music.

3234. Sekaquaptewa, E. "Hopi Indian Ceremonies." In *Seeing with a Native Eye*, W.H. Capps, ed. New York: Harper and Row, 1976. An autobiographical account of experiences with the Kachina dances with attention to its modern relationship to ecology and spirituality.

3235. Udall, Sharyn R. "The Irresistible Other: Hopi Ritual Drama and Euro-American Audiences." *The Drama Review* Vol. 36, 2 (1992): 23-43. A study of the Snake Dance of the Hopi. The dance is ancient and has continued to be studied by Euro-Americans in an attempt to understand Hopi history and culture, though often in ethnocentric terms.

Navajo

3236. Aberle, David F. *The Peyote Religion among the Navaho*. Chicago: University of Chicago Press, 1966. Chapters 9 and 10 deal directly with the rituals of peyote religion and include photographs and diagrams of peyote ceremonies.

3237. Frisbie, Charlotte J. *Kinaalda, a Study of the Navaho Girls' Puberty Ceremony*. Middletown, CT: Wesleyan University Press, 1967. A meticulously detailed account of a Kinaaldá and its still vital link to Navaho religion in general. A model of anthropological method.

3238. Frisbie, Charlotte J. "The Navajo House Blessing Ceremonial." *El Palacio* Vol. 75, 3 (1968): 26-35. Frisbie discusses the types of Blessingway songs used in private and public house blessings.

3239. Frisbie, Charlotte J. "Ritual Drama in the Navajo Blessing Ceremony." In *Southwestern Indian Ritual Drama*, Charlotte Frisbie, ed. Albuquerque: University of New Mexico Press, 1980. 161-198. The use of song and dance is discussed in the last two sections of this essay while the overall focus is on the blessing as a dramatic whole.

3240. Frisbie, Charlotte J. "An Approach to the Ethnography of Navajo Ceremonial Performance." In *The Ethnography of Musical Performance*, Norma McLeod and Marcia Herndon, ed. Norwood, PA: Norwood Editions, 1980. 75-104. The author's attempt to record a rehearsal of some songs that were part of a curing ceremony was frustrated by the performer's position that such a rehearsal was not a performance, and that performance is only that which is used in conjunction with ceremony. Illustrates the point that what is considered performance in one culture, or by one person (such as a researcher), may not be so considered in or by another (such as a native).

3241. Frisbie, Charlotte J. "Vocables in Navajo Ceremonial Music." *Ethnomusicology* Vol. 24 (1980): 347-92. Introductory exploration of questions of vocable genesis, etic/emic typologies of linguistic transformation, and previous religious characteristics, functions, and construction.

3242. Frisbie, Charlotte J. *Navajo Medicine Bundles or Jish: Acquisition, Transmission, and Disposition in the Past and Present.* Albuquerque, NM: University of New Mexico, 1987. A study of the use of sacred 'medicine buldles' used by Chantway singers in Navajo ceremonies.

3243. Frisbie, Charlotte J. "Gender and Navajo Music: Unanswered Questions." In *Women in North American Indian Music*, R. Keeling, ed. Bloomington, IN: Society for Ethnomusicology, 1989. 22-38. A preliminary finding on the role gender plays in Navajo society and its musical traditions with attention to women's role in ceremonial singing.

3244. Frisbie, Charlotte J. and David P. McAllester, ed. *Navajo Blessingway Singer: The Autobiography of Frank Mitchell (1881-1967).* Tucson: University of Arizona Press, 1978. An authbiography of a religious leader as recorded by two anthropologists. The Blessingway Ceremony and Mitchell's role as spiritual musical leader is dealt with throughout the book.

3245. Gill, Sam D. *Sacred Words. A Study of Navajo Religion and Prayer.* Westport, CT: Greenwood Press, 1981. A classification and detailed study of Navajo prayer complexes.

3246. Haile, Berard. "Navaho Chantways and Ceremonials." In *American Anthropologist*, Vol. 40, New Series. Menasha 1938. 639-52. Haile identifies and defines the religious terms used by Navaho people to designate different types and styles of chantways.

3247. Haile, Berard. *The Navaho War Dance: A Brief Narrative of its Meaning and Practice.* Saint Michaels, AZ: St. Michaels Press, 1946. Haile focusses upon curative and therapeutic aspects in response to the trauma of the ritual.

3248. Haile, Berard. *The Navaho Fire Dance or Corral Dance: A Brief Account of its Practice and Meaning.* Saint Michaels, AZ: St. Michaels Press, 1946. A full account of the significance and practice of the Mountainway Ceremonial. Includes legends of the ceremonial's origins.

3249. Haile, Berard. *Prayerstick Cutting in a Five Night Ceremonial of the Male Branch of Shootingway*. Chicago: University of Chicago Press, 1947. After a lengthy introduction to Shootingway practice, the function and characteristics of the music are discussed in chapters two through six.

3250. Haile, Berard. *Head and Face Masks in Navaho Ceremonialism*. St. Michael's, AZ: St. Michaels Press, 1947. A day-by-day description of the masks and their uses in a Nightway ceremony. Includes extended discussion of the *ye-i* origins and traditions and the text of *acaleh*, the first dancers prayer-song, with interlinear English translation and a paraphrase.

3251. Klah, Hasteen. *Navajo Creation Myth: The Story of the Emergence*. Santa Fe, NM: Museum of Narajo Ceremonial Art, 1942. The creation myth as told by a Navajo medicine man. With translations of the texts of 30 ceremonial songs related to the myth.

3252. Kluckhohn, Clyde. "The Great Chants of the Navajo." *Theatre Arts Monthly* Vol. 17 (1933): 639-45. The nine-day Night Chants are understood by the author as a religious liturgy. Includes song texts.

3253. Kluckhohn, Clyde and Leland C. Wyman. *An Introduction to Navajo Chant Practice, with an Account of the Behaviors Observed in Four Chants*. Memoirs of the American Anthropological Association, Vol. 53. Menasha, Wis.: Kraus Reprints, 1940. A detailed study of Navajo sacred chant with attention to sociological and ceremonial factors.

3254. Lamphere, L. "Symbolic Elements in Navajo Ritual." *Southwestern Journal of Anthropology* Vol. 25, 3 (1969): 279-305. The symbolic objects and actions of the male Shootingway chant are analyzed in light of a natural/super-natural world model.

3255. Luckert, Karl W. *Navajo Mountain and Rainbow Bridge Religion*. Flagstaff, AZ: Museum of Northern Arizona, 1977. Written in response to the expanding waters of Lake Powell in 1971, this book provides in the Navajo's own words various viewpoints on the importance of Rainbow Bridge and the ceremonies attached to it. Includes translation of many prayer song texts.

3256. Luckert, Karl W. *A Navajo Bringing-Home Ceremony: The Claus Chee Sonny Version of Deerway Ajilee*. Flagstaff, AZ: Museum of Northern Arizona Press, 1978. A ceremonialist's account of a now extinct five-day healing ceremony.

3257. Luckert, Karl W. *Coyoteway: A Navajo Healing Ceremonial*. Tucson, AZ: University of Arizona Press, 1979. A nine-night ceremony described in three parts: the ceremonial and its priests, Coyoteway performed, and early records of Coyoteway.

3258. Matthews, Washington. "The Mountain Chant: A Navajo Ceremony." *Annual Report of the Bureau of American Ethnology* Vol. 5 (1887): 379-467. Provides full song and dance sequences with commentary as well as accounts of the myth of the ceremony's origin. Still considered the definitive account of this song ceremonial.

3259. Matthews, Washington. "Songs of Sequence of the Navajos." *Journal of American Folk-Lord* Vol. 7 (1894): 185-94. Matthews discusses methods used by singers to remember and present the correct sequence of song sets in ceremonies. Includes song texts.

3260. Matthews, Washington. *The Night Chant: A Navajo Ceremony. Memoirs.* American Museum of Natural History, Vol. 6, New York: AMS Press, 1902/repr. Includes detailed description of the rite, and the texts and translation of ritual songs.

3261. McAllester, David P. *Enemy Way Music: A Study of Social and Esthetic Values as Seen in Navaho Music.* Papers of Peabody Museum, Vol. 41, No. 3, Milwood, NY: Kraus Reprint, 1954/repr. 1973. An exemplary study of music in the context of Navaho cultural values. Special focus is placed on the Enemy Way ceremonial and how it expresses these values. Includes transcriptions and analyses of 75 Enemy Way songs.

3262. McAllester, David P. "A Paradigm of Navajo Dance." *Parabola* Vol. 4, 2 (1979): 28-35. In light of the breadth of dance traditions Navahos choose among, the author questions the advisability of narrow definitions of sacred dance.

3263. McAllester, David P. "Shootingway, an Epic Drama of the Navajos." In *Southwestern Indian Ritual Drama*, Charlotte Frisbie, ed. Albuquerque: University of New Mexico Press, 1980. 199-237. As both anthropological observer and active participant in the drama, McAllester recounts both the texts and contexts of songs sung with attention to the inter-relationship of the arts, mythology, blessing and relations with the outside world.

3264. McAllester, David P. "The War God's Horse Song: An Exegesis in Native American Humanities." *Selected Reports in Ethnomusicology* Vol. 3, 2 (1980): 1-21. An explication, new translation, and exhortation that Native American poetry be viewed not through Euro-American notions of poetry, but through the acknowledgement that poetic song texts both were and are composed according to different aesthetic standards.

3265. McAllester, David P. and S.W. McAllester. *Hogans: Navajo Houses and House Songs.* 2nd ed.,1995. In preparation. A collection of Navaho myths and house songs. Includes texts for the leader's house, Talking God's house, Sun's house and Changing Woman's songs. First ed., 1980, 1987.

3266. McAllester, David P. and Douglas F. Mitchell. "Navajo Music." In *Handbook of North American Indians: Southwest*, Alfonso Ortiz, ed. Vol. 10. Washington, DC: Smithsonian Institution, 1983. 605-623. An article on Navajo music in general, with sections on ceremonial songs, Christian hymns, Peyote songs, and transcriptions of 13 songs referred to in the text.

3267. Merkur, Daniel. "The Psychodynamics of the Navajo Coyoteway Ceremonial." *Journal of Mind and Behavior* Vol. 2, 3 (Autumn) (1981): 243-257. Merkur examines the curative and preventative aspects of hunter ritualism from a psychotherapeutic perspective with attention to the therapeutic role of singing.

3268. Reichard, Gladys A. *The Story of the Navajo Hail Chant*. New York: Reichard, 1944. Dictated by a Navaho ceremonial practitioner and presented in Navaho with English translation, with attention to ritual practice and content.

3269. Reichard, Gladys A. *Navaho Religion*. New York: Bollingen Foundation, 1950. Superb study of Navajo symbolism. Also published by Princeton University Press, Princeton, NJ.

3270. Wheelwright, Mary C. *The Hail and Water Chants*. Museum of Navajo Ceremonial Art: Navajo Religions Series, Santa Fe, NM: Museum of Navajo Ceremonial Art, 1946.

3271. Wheelwright, Mary C. *The Myth and Prayers of the Great Star Chant and the Myth of the Coyote Chant*. Santa Fe, NM: Museum of Navajo Ceremonial Art, 1956. Ed. with commentaries by David P. McAllester.

3272. Wyman, Leland C. "The Female Shooting Life Chant." In *American Anthropologist*, Vol. 38, New Series. Menasha 1936. 634-53. A first-hand account of a 'minor chant' service with attention to its place in the daily life and faith of Navaho people.

3273. Wyman, Leland C., ed. *Beautyway: A Navaho Ceremonial Recorded and Translated by Father Berard Haile*. Bollingen Series 53, New York: Pantheon Books, 1957. On the uses, mythology, songs, and geographical settings of Beautyway.

3274. Wyman, Leland C. *The Red Antway of the Navaho*. Sante Fe, NM: Museum of Navajo Ceremonial Art, 1965. A description of all aspects of a healing ceremony. Includes black and white and color photos of sand paintings.

3275. Wyman, Leland C. *Blessingway, With Three Versions of the Myth Recorded and Translated from the Navajo by Father Berard Haile, OFM*. Tucson, AZ: University of Arizona Press, 1970. A description of the religious context and meaning of Blessingway, followed by three detailed accounts of the ceremony. The first and largest provides English translation of numerous song texts.

3276. Wyman, Leland C. *The Mountainway of the Navajo, with a Myth of the Female Branch Recorded and Translated by Father Berard Haile, OFM.* Tucson, AZ: University of Arizona Press, 1975. Includes long sections on the history, theology, ceremonial procedure, sandpaintings, mythology, and song of Mountainway. With translation of texts.

3277. Wyman, Leland C. "Navajo Ceremonial System." In *Handbook of North American Indians: Southwest*, Alfonso Ortiz, ed. Vol. 10. Washington, DC: Smithsonian Institution, 1983. 536-557. An introduction to the Navajo ceremonial system and Navajo cosmology, a description of the Holyway chant complexes, Evilway ceremonies, and ceremonial organization.

3278. Wyman, Leland C. and Clyde Kluckhohn. *Navaho Classification of Their Song Ceremonials.* Memoirs of the American Anthropological Association, Vol. 50. New York: Kraus Reprint, 1938/repr. 1968, 1969. Describes six categories according to which song ceremonials are classified: Blessing Way, Holy Way, Life Way, Evil Way, War Ceremonial, and Game Way.

Papago and Pima

3279. Bahr, Donald, J. Giff, and M. Havier. "Piman Songs on Hunting." *Ethnomusicology* Vol. 23 (1979): 245-296. Bahr examines Piman hunting songs that function as cures for deer sickness, jimson weed sickness, and cow sickness. Advances the idea that the grouping of songs into multi-song sets results in a literary structure of great ritual power.

3280. Bahr, Donald, J. Gregoria, D. I. Lopez, and A. Alvarez. *Piman Shamanism and Staging Sickness [Kaicim Múmkidag].* Tucson, AZ: University of Arizona Press, 1974. A study of the use of song in divining, diagnosing, and curing an illness. Focus is on song texts and the role of song.

3281. Bahr, Donald and J. R. Haefer. "Songs of Piman Curing." *Ethnomusicology* Vol. 22 (1978): 89-122. A study of 'blowing' or curing songs performed in conjunction with jimson weed in terms of text, rhythm, melodic structure, and musical form, and as therapy.

3282. Chesky, J. *The Nature and Function of Papago Music.* Ph.D. diss., University of Arizona, 1943.

3283. Densmore, Frances. *Papago Music.* Smithsonian Institution. Bureau of American Ethnology, Bulletin No. 90, New York: Da Capo, 1929/repr. 1972. Chapters on 'Songs connected with ceremonies' and 'war songs' provide information about religiously themed musical traditions.

3284. Haefer, J. Richard. *Musical Thought in Papago Culture*. Ph.D. diss., University of Illinois, 1981. Propositional, perception, and discourse analyses of forty song texts on the subject of song and its creation. Haefer shows that it is in dreams that non-humans transmit songs to humans. Includes a glossary of Piman terms.

3285. Underhill, Ruth. *Singing for Power: The Song Magic of the Papago Indians of Southern Arizona*. Tucson, AZ: University of Arizona Press, 1938/repr. 1993. A descriptive account of the spirituality of the Papago people with attention to the importance of singing and songs in causing events to happen. Includes song texts.

3286. Underhill, Ruth. *Papago Indian Religion*. New York: AMS Press, 1946/repr. 1969. Underhill focuses upon communal, individual, shamanistic and modern ceremonial practice.

3287. Ware, Naomi. "Survival and Change in Pima Indian Music." *Ethnomusicology* Vol. 14, Jan. (1970): 100-13. In this overview of the musical situation of the Pima people, Ware observes that changes to the traditional repertory consist of the disappearance of songs and ceremonies, rather than the transformation of them, and the appearance of new genres of social music to take their place.

Pueblo

3288. Brown, Donald. "The Development of Taos Dance." *Ethnomusicology 5* Vol. 1 (1961): 33-41. An examination of indigenous Indian elements and non-Indian influences—those of Anglo-American and particularly Spanish-Catholic cultures—with special focus on the Winter Dances.

3289. Bunzel, Ruth L. "Zuñi Katcinas." *Annual Report of the Bureau of American Ethnology, No. 47* (1929-1930): 837 ff. Dance and song are described and analyzed in the first part of this lengthy study of the Katcina cult.

3290. Bunzel, Ruth L. *Introduction to Zuñi Ceremonialism*. Bureau of American Ethnology, Annual Report No. 47, 1929-1930, Washington, DC: Smithsonian Institution, 1932. 467-544. A presentation of Zuñi religious life, in particular ceremonial organization and ritual techniques. Includes a four-page section on singing and dancing.

3291. Champe, F.W. *The Matachines Dance of the Upper Rio Grande: History, Music, and Choreography*. Lincoln, NE: University of Nebraska Press, 1983. A description of the Matachines Dance of the Rio Grande Pueblos, performed primarily at San Ildefonso Pueblo. Based on observations over a 30 year period.

3292. Cushing, Frank Hamilton. *Outlines of Zuñi Creation Myths*. Thirteenth Annual Report of the Bureau of Ethnology, New York: AMS Press, 1896/repr.

1976. Some of the myth outlines include the mythological explanation for dance rituals such as the dance of the Corn Maidens and the Dance of the Flute.

3293. Densmore, Frances. *Music of the Santo Domingo Pueblo, New Mexico.* Southwest Museum Papers, No. 12, Los Angeles: Southwest Museum, 1938. Includes song texts and transcriptions for 15 ceremonial events.

3294. Densmore, Frances. *Music of Ancoma, Isleta, Cochiti, and Zuñi Pueblos.* Smithsonian Institution. Bureau of American Ethnology, Bulletin #165, New York: Da Capo, 1957/repr. 1972. A presentation of the compositions, texts, and context for a wide variety of social and ceremonial songs, with melodic and rhythmic analyses and cross-tribal comparison.

3295. Dozier, Edward P. "Rio Grande Pueblo Ceremonial Patterns." *New Mexico Quarterly* Vol. 27, 1 (1957): 27-34. Dozier discusses the dualism maintained between Spanish/Catholic customs and indigenous customs in ceremonial life.

3296. Dozier, Edward P. "Spanish-Catholic Influences on Rio Grande Pueblo Religion." *American Anthropology* Vol. 60, New Series, 3 (1957): 441-448. On the context of song, dance and chant among the Rio Grande Tewa Pueblos and the ceremonial system of the linguistically related Arizona Tewas.

3297. Dozier, Edward P. "Cultural Matrix of Singing and Chanting in Tewa Pueblos." *International Journal of American Linguistics* (1958).

3298. Fewkes, Jessie W. and Benjamin I. Gilman. *A Few Summer Ceremonials at Zuñi Pueblo: Zuñi Melodies, Reconnaissance of Ruins in or near the Zuñi Reservation.* A Journal of American Ethnology and Archaeology: Vol. 1, New York: AMS Press, 1891/repr.

3299. Garcia, A. and C. Garcia. "Ritual Preludes to Tewa Indian Dances." *Ethnomusicology* Vol. 12 (1968): 239-44. On the ritual customs that precede ceremonial dances, including announcement and summons, song preparations, song and dance rehearsals, preparation of paraphernalia, and special dance ceremonies on the eve of and meditation just preceeding the ceremony itself.

3300. Kurath, Gertrude P. "Motion Pictures of Tewa Ritual Dances." In *Southwestern Indian Ritual Drama*, Charlotte J. Frisbie, ed. Albuquerque, NM: University of New Mexico Press, 1980.

3301. Kurath, Gertrude P. and Antonio Garcia. *Music and Dance of the Tewa Pueblos.* Museum of New Mexico Research Records, No. 8, Mr. Smith, ed. Sante Fe: Museum of New Mexico Press, 1970. In Tewa ceremonial arts, beauty of form and execution, though essential, is secondary to communication with the unseen world and to promotion of social cohesion. Three aspects are discussed: ceremonial ecology, choreographic and musical patterns, and symbolic pageantry. Includes an extensive bibliography.

3302. Laski, Vera. *Seeking Life, The Raingod Ceremony of San Juan.* American Folklore Society Memoirs Vol. 50, Philadelphia, PA: American Folklore Society, 1958. A comprehensive account of the Pueblo Raingod Ceremony including background information, ceremony texts, and interpretive commentary.

3303. Ortiz, Alfonso. "Ritual Drama and Pueblo World View." In *New Perspectives on the Pueblos*, Alfonso Ortiz, ed. Albuquerque, NM: University of New Mexico Press, 1972. References to dance and music are made throughout this text on the mytho-poetic world view of the Tewas.

3304. Parsons, Elsie Clews. *The Scalp Ceremonial of Zuñi.* American Anthropological Memoirs #31, New York: Kraus Reprint, 1924/repr. 1964, 1974. After a brief introduction, Parsons compares the ceremony as she saw it in 1921 to what was reported by M. C. Stevenson in 1891.

3305. Parsons, Elsie Clews. *Pueblo Indian Religion.* 2 vols. Chicago: University of Chicago Press, 1939. Vol. 1 includes discussion of the ritual function of dancing and dance patterns and song. Vol. 2 contains full descriptions with commentary of various Pueblo ceremonies including initiations, curing ceremonies, Kachina dances and Saint's Day dances.

3306. Romero, Branda Mae. *The Matachines Music and Dance in San Juan Pueblo and Alcalde, New Mexico: Contexts and Meanings.* Ph.D. diss., UCLA, 1993. Matachines dance descended from Roman sword dances and rain rituals of Islamic North Africa and is related to the English Morris dance. Elements of this dance appear in traditional Pueblo ritual formats and in dances of Alcalde, New Mexico, a Chicano community. This study accounts for differences between the two in terms of their differing world views.

3307. Stewart, Dorothy N. *Handbook of Indian Dances: I. New Mexico Pueblos.* Sante Fe, NM: Museum of New Mexico, 1950/repr. 1952. Originally *American Indian Ceremonial Dances in the Southwest.*

3308. Sweet, Jill D. "Ritual and Theatre in Tewa Ceremonial Performances." *Ethnomusicology* Vol. 27 (1983): 253-269. On the changes made in Tewa ceremonial performances for a non-Tewa public. Though these public performances are more theatrical, the performers still view them as ritual, but keep the theatrical elements separate from the village ritual ceremonies. See also the author's Ph.D. diss., *Tewa Ceremonial Performances: The Effects of Tourism on an Ancient Pueblo Indian Dance and Music Tradition.* U. of N.M., 1981.

3309. Sweet, Jill D. *Dances of the Tewa Indians: Expressions of New Life.* Santa Fe: School of American Research Press, 1985. A simple introduction to the ceremonial, social and theatrical dances of the Tewas, beautifully illustrated with color photographs.

3310. Tedlock, B. "Songs of the Zuñi Kachina Society: Composition, Rehearsal, and Performance." In *Southwestern Indian Ritual Drama*, Charlotte J. Frisbie, ed. Prospects Heights, IL: Waveland Press, 1980/repr. 1989. 7. A detailed ethnomusicological analysis of 116 songs and 48 hours of interviews. Shows that native song classification system reveals full awareness of the process of composition.

3311. Yeh, N. "The Pogonshare Ceremony of the Tewa San Juan, New Mexico." *Selected Reports in Ethnomusicology* Vol. 3, 2 (1980): 100-45. General description of the Pogonshare—a ceremonial fertility dance—Tewa cosmology, the Pogonshare festival, and its music and dance. Includes transcription of festival music as well as the general model upon which new music is composed every year.

Other Tribes

3312. Bourke, John G. *The Snake Dance of the Moquis of Arizona: Being a Narrative of a Journey from Sante Fe, New Mexico, to Villages of the Moquis of Arizona [1884]*. Tucson, AZ: University of Arizona Press, 1884/repr. 1984. A 19th-century account of a Euro-American's travels through seven Moqui villages. Although judgmental in tone, the author provides detailed descriptions of the snake dance rites, placing them within the social and religious framework of the Moqui people.

3313. Densmore, Frances. *Yuman and Yaqui Music*. Smithsonian Institution. Bureau of American Ethnology, Bulletin #110, New York: Da Capo, 1932/repr. 1972.

3314. Du Bois, C.G. "Two Types or Styles of Diegueño Religious Dancing." In *Proceedings of the 15th International Congress of Americanists*, Vol. 2. 1906. 135-138.

3315. Hinton, Leanne. "Vocables in Havasupai Song." In *Southwestern Indian Ritual Drama*, Charlotte J. Frisbie, ed. Albuquerque, NM: University of New Mexico Press, 1980. 275-306. Shows that vocables are preferred to language when social solidarity and the sensation of spirituality are sought.

3316. Hinton, Leanne. *Havasupai Songs: A Linguistic Perspective*. Tübingen, Germany: G. Narr, 1984. An extremely detailed linguistic study of sacred, healing and social songs. Includes selected song texts.

3317. Opler, Marvin E. *The Character and Derivation of the Jicarilla Holiness Rites*. Albuquerque, NM: University of New Mexico Press, 1943. A study of the Jicarilla rite and comparison with the Ute Bear Dance.

3318. Sklar, Deidre. *Enacting Religious Belief: A Movement Ethnography of the Annual Fiesta of Tortugas, New Mexico*. Ph.D. diss., New York University,

1991. The hypothesis that movement embodies cultural knowledge and generates emotions is tested in this comparison of two major fiesta dances: the Danzante, a Matachine dance, and the Tigua. The first dance embodies the experience of conversion to Catholicism, the latter appears to embody self-concepts concerning Indian-ness. Movement description and participants' commentary are integrated into "thick description."

CALIFORNIA AND OREGON

3319. Barrett, S.A. "Ceremonies of the Pomo Indians." In *University of California Publications in American Archaeology and Ethnology*, Vol. 7. Berkeley 1917. 397-441. Barrett combines his own observations of dances with dance pattern diagrams and excerpts from the accounts of informants. Includes sections on the Ghost/Devil ceremony, Guksu ceremony, and the Messiah cult.

3320. Bean, Lowell John, ed. *California Indian Shamanism.* Menlo Park, CA: Ballena Press, 1992.

3321. De Angulo, Jaime. *The Music of the Indians of Northern California.* Peter Garland, ed. Sante Fe, NM: The Soundings Press, 1988. 9-31. A reprint from 1931, this brief survey of Indian regions in Northern California classifies and describes eight types of song, the first of which is shaman songs. Includes transcription of 28 songs with vocables.

3322. Densmore, Frances. *Music of the Maidu Indians of California.* Los Angeles: Southwest Museum, 1958. Pages 16-24 feature commentary on and description of songs of ceremonial dances. From research done in 1937.

3323. Devereux, G. "Dream Learning and Individual Ritual Differences in Mohave Shamanism." *American Anthropologist* Vol. 59, 6 (1957): 1036-1045. Devereux concludes that actual learning among Mohave singers takes place in a waking state and equates 'dream learning' with psychotic behavior.

3324. Dubois, C. "Wintu Ethnography." *University of California Publications in American Archeology and Ethnology* Vol. 36, 1 (1935): 1-148.

3325. Gifford, E.W. "Central Miwok Ceremonies." In *Anthropological Records*, Vol. 14. Berkeley 1931. This anthropological study includes detailed descriptions of over 20 sacred dances for the living.

3326. Hatch, J. "Tachi Yokuts Music." *Kroeber Anthropological Society* Vol. 19 (1958): 47-66.

3327. Heizer, Robert F., ed. *California.* Handbook of North American Indians, Vol. 8. William C. Sturtevant, ed. Washington, DC: Smithsonian Institution, 1978. Includes an extensive bibliography.

3328. Heizer, Robert F. and M.A. Whipple. *The California Indians: A Source Book*. 2nd ed., Berkeley, CA: University of California Press, 1971. References to dance and music are found throughout the essays in this collection. Includes a brief essay on the 1870 Ghost Dance.

3329. Keeling, Richard. *Songs of the Brush Dance and Their Basis in Oral-Expressive Magic: Music and Culture of the Yurok, Karok, and Hupa Indians of Northwestern California*. Ph.D. diss., UCLA, 1982. A study of the Brush Dance—a curing ritual—the unusual manner of vocal performance, and the world-view that influenced this way of performance. Focuses on characteristic vocal mannerisms and a pervasive microtonality.

3330. Keeling, Richard. "Musical Evidence of Female Spiritual Life among the Yurok." In *Women in North American Indian Music*, Richard Keeling, ed. Bloomington, IN: Society for Ethnomusicology, 1989. 67-78. Drawing upon archival recordings and narratives the author attempts to document the ritual and spiritual dimensions of Yurok women's lives. Includes song text and compositions for three women's songs.

3331. Keeling, Richard. *Cry for Luck. Sacred Song and Speech Among the Yurok, Hupa, and Karok Indians of Northwestern California*. Berkeley: University of California Press, 1992. Part 1 covers the basics of Northern California indigenous religious belief. Part 2 is devoted to ceremonial singing and dancing for the care of the world and human beings, Part 3, to medicine songs, and Part 4, to interpretations and musical analysis by the author.

3332. Keeling, Richard. "Music and Culture History Among the Yurok and Neighboring Tribes of Northwestern California." *Journal of Anthropological Research* Vol. 48, 1 (1992): 25-48.

3333. Kroeber, Alfred L. "The Religion of the Indians of California." In *University of California-Publications in American Archaeology and Ethnology*, Vol. 4, No. 6. Berkeley, CA: University of California Press, 1907. 319-356. An unsympathetic study of Native religious belief and practice. Touches on the use of dance and song in shamanistic individual and community ceremony.

3334. Kroeber, Alfred L. *Handbook of the Indians of California*. New York: Dover Publications, 1925/repr. 1976. Contains numerous references and descriptions of sacred dance and song. Lists the principal dances and ceremonies of the Kuksu system.

3335. Loeb, E. "Pomo Folkways." *University of California Publications in American Archaeology and Ethnography*, 2 (1926): 149-405. Vol. 19 describes the dances and ceremonies of the inland and coastal Kuksu, inland Pomo non-Kuksu dances, and the Ghost Ceremony religion.

3336. Magalousis, Nicholas M. "Music of the California Tribes, Past and Present." In *Early California Reflections: A Series of Lectures Held at the San*

Juan Capistrano Branch of the Orange County Public Library, Nicholas M. Magalousis, ed. San Juan Capistrano, CA: San Juan Capistrano Branch of the Orange County Public Library, 1987. The first in a collection of lectures on various aspects of early California culture.

3337. Meighan, Clement Woodward and Francis A. Riddell. *The Maru Cult of the Pomo Indians: A California Ghost Dance Survival.* Los Angeles: Southwest Museum, 1972. The Ghost Dance was spread by the Paiute prophets of the revivalist cults of the 1870s. It advocated a rejection of all white ways and a return to traditional Indian values and customs. This study is primarily a historical documentation of the Ghost Dance cult of the Pomo Indians including detailed descriptions of dance patterns, settings, costumes, and music. Only limited attempt is made at analyzing the meaning and significance of the rituals.

3338. Merriam, C.H. *Studies of California Indians.* Berkeley, CA: University of California Press, 1962. Contains three relevant ethnological accounts of the Western Wintoon Ceremony, the mourning ceremony of the Mewuk and the mortuary ceremony of the Tong-va of Tejon. Also includes illustrations of Pomo dance houses.

3339. Nomland, G. "A Bear River Shaman's Curative Dance." *American Anthropologist* Vol. 33 (1931): 38-41. An observers account of a female shaman's dance performed for the healing of tuberculosis.

3340. Painter, Muriel Thayer and E.B. Sayles. *Faith, Flowers and Fiestas: The Yaqui Indian Year: A Narrative of Ceremonial Events.* Tucson, AZ: University of Arizona Press, 1962. A description and illustration of traditional religious dances that have come under strong Catholic influence.

3341. Parkman, E. Breck. "Dancing on the Brink of the World: Deprivation and the Ghost Dance Religion." In *California Indian Shamanism*, Lowell John Bean, ed. Menlo Park, CA: Ballena Press, 1992. 163-183. Abandoned by the Missions in 1837 and subject to the cruelty of the miners during the Gold Rush, many California Indians embraced the Ghost Dance religion in the 1870s as a way to salvation and the restoration of their world. The author provides brief biographies of some of the leading Ghost Dance missionaries.

3342. Parrish, Vana. "Kashaya Pomo Dances." *Journal of California Anthropology* Vol. 2, Summer (1975): 34-37. On traditional religious dances.

3343. Roberts, Helen. *Form in Primitive Music: An Analytical and Comparative Study of the Melodic Form of Some Ancient Southern California Indian Songs.* American Library of Musicology, New York: W.W. Norton, 1933. A study of the structural features of 25 ceremonial songs of the Southern California Indians. Each is notated, translated, and described with respect to context and place in ritual.

3344. Steward, K.M. "Mojave Indian Shamanism." *Masterkey* Vol. 44 (1970): 15. This general description of Mojave conceptions of shamanism includes mention of the use of songs for curative purposes.

3345. Strong, W.D. "Aboriginal Society in Southern California." *American Archaeology and Ethnology* Vol. 29, 1 (1929): 1-358. Includes description of the dance ceremonies of six tribal groups: the Serrano, the Desert, Pass, and Mountain Cahuilla, the Cupeno, and the Luiseno.

3346. Thurston, Bertha P.A. "A Night in a Maidu Shaman's House." *The Masterkey* Vol. 7 (1933): 111. Los Angeles. Thurston describes her experience as both patient in and observer of a shaman healing ceremony.

3347. Thurston, Bertha P.A. "Maidu Medicine-man's Feast." *The Masterkey* Vol. 10 (1936): 16. Includes description of chanted farewell blessings and a song to the 'Night Spirit'.

3348. Wallace, William J. "Music and Musical Instruments." In *Handbook of North American Indians: California*, Robert Fleming Heizer, ed. Washington, DC: Smithsonian Institution, 1978. 642-648. A general article on the songs, most of which are religious, and instruments and their distribution among 39 California tribes.

3349. Waterman, T.T. "The Religious Practices of the Diegueño Indians." *University of California Publications in Archaeology and Ethnology* Vol. 8 (1910): 271-358. The author suggests a strong relationship between the mythology and song of the Diegueno. Includes a history of the people and descriptions of initiation and mourning ceremonies.

3350. Weaver, Roger. "Marie Norris's Interpretation of Fifty of Gatschet's Klamath Chants and Incantations." *American Indian Culture and Research Journal* Vol. 7, 3 (1983): 55-63. The author recounts an older Klamath woman's interpretation of the single line chants.

NORTHWEST COAST

3351. Amoss, Pamela. *Coast Salish Spirit Dancing: The Survival of an Ancestral Religion.* Seattle, WA: University of Washington Press, 1978.

3352. Barbeau, Marius. "Buddhist Dirges of the North Pacific Coast." *Journal of the International Folk Music Council* Vol. 14, Jan. (1962): 16-21. Correspondences between funeral dirges of the Pacific Coast Indians and Chinese and Mongolian Buddhism support the migration of native Americans across the Bering Strait.

3353. Boas, Franz. *The Social Organization and Secret Societies of the Kwakiutl Indians. Based on Personal Observations Notes Made by Mr. Grorge*

Hunt. Landmarks in Anthropology Series, New York: Johnson Reprint Corp, 1897 (repr.). See Chap. 8 for a lengthy discussion of the dances and music of the Kwakiutl Winter Ceremonial. Chaps. 11-13 discuss the ceremonial expression of other related tribes. Includes an appendix with song transcriptions and texts.

3354. Boas, Franz. "Kwakiutl Ethnography." Helen Codere, ed. Chicago: University of Chicago Press, 1966. An edition of the incomplete ms., based on observations in the 1890s. A major portion of the book is a detailed description of the winter ceremonial.

3355. Boas, Franz. "Dance and Music in the Life of the Northwest Coast Indians of North America." In *The Function of Dance in Human Society: A Seminar Directed by Franz Boas*, 2nd ed. New York: Dance Horizons, 1972. 7-18. Includes a detailed description of a Kwakiutl religious initiation ceremony.

3356. Budic, Caroline Mary. *Wolf Ritual Dances of the Northwest Coast Indians*. Ph.D. diss., UCLA, 1964.

3357. Collins, J.M. *Valley of the Spirits: The Upper Skagit Indians of Western Washington*. Vol. 56. Seattle, WA: Chapters 8 through 10, covering the potlatch ceremonies, the Spirit World, and the shaman respectively, contain information about musical practice.

3358. Dorsey, George A. "The Dwamish Indian Spirit Boat and Its Use." *Free Museum of Science and Art Bulletin* Vol. 3, 4 (1902): 227-238. Philadelphia

3359. Drucker, Philip. "Kwakiutl Dancing Societies." *Anthropological Records, University of California* Vol. 2, 6 (1940): 201-230. Drucker's survey covers secret initiatory rituals of Kwakiutl branches not covered by Boas' study.

3360. Emmons, George Thornton. *The Tlingit Indians*. Frederica de Laguna, ed. Seattle, WA: University of Washington Press, 1991. A work (by Emmons) written in the late 1880s is clarified, supplemented, and brought up-to-date by the editor.

3361. Ernst, Alice. *The Wolf Ritual of the Northwest Coast*. Eugene, OR: University of Oregon, 1952. A detailed study of the Wolf Ritual among the Makah, the Quillayute, and the Nootka. The aim of the ritual is the acquisition of the powers and knowledge, as well as the bravery and endurance, of the wolf for the purpose of ensuring the survival of the tribe.

3362. Goodman, Linda J. *Music and Dance in Northwest Coast Indian Life*. Tsaile, AZ: Navajo Community College Press, 1977. An introductory booklet with attention to the relationship between music, ceremony and healing among the Nootka and Kwakiutl. Includes song and dance texts.

3363. Goodman, Linda J. "Aspects of Spiritual and Political Power in Chiefs' Songs of the Makah Indians." *The World of Music* Vol. 34, 2 (1992): 23-42. In the past, song ownership provided spiritual and social status. Today, however, the songs have lost their inner meaning, have been 'stolen,' and new ones are not being created, resulting in a loss of identity in the Makah social and spiritual structures.

3364. Haeberlin, H.K. "SBeTeTDA'Q, A Shamanistic Performance of the Coast Salish." *American Anthropologist* Vol. 20, 3 (1918): 249-257. The author describes the songs and dance patterns of the ritual from the first hand accounts of informants with attention to differences in practice among Salish tribes.

3365. Halpern, Ida. "Music of the British Columbia Northwest Coast Indians." In *Proceedings of the Centennial Workshop in Ethnomusicology, Vancouver, 1967*, 3rd ed. Peter Crossley-Holland, ed. Victoria, Canada: The Government of the Province of British Columbia, 1968. 23-42. Includes a discussion of the potlatch and the bear, wolf and raven totems and the ceremonies and myths associated with them.

3366. Halpern, Ida. "On the Interpretation of 'Meaningless-Nonsensical Syllables' in the Music of the Pacific Northwest Indians." *Ethnomusicology* Vol. 20-71 (1976): 253. Through the study of various songs, Halpern proposes that 'nonsense syllables' fall into three categories of meaning: 1) syllables that have specific meanings or are abbreviations of words, 2) syllables that refer to totemic names of animals, or 3) syllables that imitate animal sounds.

3367. Holm, Bill. "Traditional and Contemporary Kwakiutl Winter Dance." *Artic Anthropology* Vol. 14 (1977): 5-24. A study of the Winter Ceremonial of the Southern Kwakiutl, a ceremonial that has survived often violent cultural change surprisingly intact.

3368. Jenness, Diamond. *The Faith of a Coast Salish Indian*. Anthropology of British Columbia. Memoir #3, Victoria, B.C.: Provincial Museum. Department of Education, 1955. An account of an extended interview with Old Pierre, a man of c75 from the Katzïe tribe of the Coast Salish. Chapters focus on the origin of the tribe, relationship of man to a supreme deity, winter dances, guardian spirits, medicine men, community rituals, and life cycle.

3369. Jilek, Wolfgang. *Indian Healing: Shamanic Ceremonialism in the Pacific North West Today*. Blaine, WA: Hancock House, 1982. After decades of suppression, the Guardian Spirit Ceremonial has been revived and is given here a detailed first-hand account. The ceremonial is a process through which an Indian alienated from his culture is able to re-identify with ancestral culture and obtain spiritual power.

3370. Jilek, Wolfgang G. "The Renaissance of Shamanic Dance in Indian Populations of North America." *Diogenes: Shamans and Shamanisms: On the Threshold of the Next Millennium*. Special vol., 158/Summer (1992): 87-100. Whereas the Salish Spirit Dance enacts a journey to the Land of the Dead, the Sun Dance focuses on the acquisition of shamanic power. These and similar dances are being revived throughout Amerindian culture in North America as both therapeutic and ideological movements.

3371. Johnston, Thomas F. "Tlingit Dance, Music, Society." *Acta Ethnographica Academiae Scientiarum Hungaricae* Vol. 34, 1-4 (1986-1988): 283-324. Covers the traditions, characteristics, genres, and themes of Tlingit music. Includes song texts and transcriptions as well as photographs of Tlingit dances. Also discusses Tlingit spiritual healing and religious dance.

3372. Johnston, Thomas F. "The Northwest Coast Tlinget Indian Musical Potlatch." *South African Journal of Musicology* Vol. 10 (1990): 77-97. A study of the social background and ceremonial structure of Tlinget potlaches. Topics include totems, crests, gift giving, symbolic behavior including artifacts and dance masks, music for healing and mediation, the role of the drum, and Tlinget musical style.

3373. Johnston, Thomas F. "The Socio-Mythic Contexts of Music in Tlingit Shamanism and Potlatch Ceremonials." *The World of Music* Vol. 34, 2 (1992): 43-71. A study of shamans' role in Tlingit society, their cosmological world-view, and their use of drums and music. Analyses seven songs, with a short section on polyphony.

3374. Johnston, Thomas F. "The Social Role of Alaskan Athabaskan Potlatch Dancing." In *Dance. Current Selected Research*, Lynette Y. Overby and James H. Humphrey, ed. Vol. 3. New York: AMS Press, 1992. 183-226. Potlatch dance provides symbolic resolution to the stresses specific to Athapascan life and particularly to the death of an individual and the redefinition of roles that death demands. Johnston looks at potlatch in terms of present and past practices, song, and dance movements and costumes, with special attention to the Lower Koyukon Athabascan Feast for the Dead, the major remaining traditional religious dance.

3375. Johnston, Thomas F. "The Ceremonial Roots of Tlingit Dance." *Dance: Current Select Research* Vol. 3 (1992): 227-98. The ceremonial potlatch and shaman's seance have been the two important contexts for traditional Tlinget dance. The latter has now been replaced by the civic or statewide socio-musical event. Johnston describes each in turn, including a vivid account of a shaman's powers.

3376. Jonaitis, Aldona. *Chiefly Feasts: The Enduring Kwakiutl Potlatch.* Seattle: University of Washington Press, 1991. References to dance and music of the potlatch are scattered throughout this sumptuously illustrated text.

3377. Kan, Sergei. "Shamanism and Christianity: Modern-Day Tlingit Elders Look at the Past." *Ethnohistory* Vol. 38, 4 (1991): 363-387.

3378. Kan, Sergei. "The Sacred and the Secular: Tlingit Potlach Songs Outside the Potlatch." *American Indian Quarterly* Vol. 14, Spr. (Fall, 1990): 355-367.

The author discusses the tension between the preservative value of secularizing dances and the spiritual value of maintaining their sacredness.

3379. Katzeek, David. *Celebration of Tlingit, Haida, and Tsimshian Culture.* Juneau, AK: Sealaska Heritage, 1992.

3380. Kew, J. E. Michael. "Central and Southern Coast Salish Ceremonies since 1900." In *Handbook of North American Indians: Northwest Coast,* Wayne Suttles, ed. Washington, DC: Smithsonian Institution, 1990. 476-480. On the initiation of a spirit dancer and the Spirit Dance, potlatches, funeral ceremonies, and the resurgence of the Spirit Dance in the late 20th century.

3381. Kolstee, Anton. *Bella Coola Indian Music: A Study of the Interaction Between Northwest Coast Indian Structures and their Functional Context.* National Museum of Man Mercury Series, Canadian Ethnology Service Paper no. 83, Ottawa: National Museums of Canada, 1982. Includes an attempt to correlate melody, action, and function in Bella Coola ceremonial music. Pt. 1, on songs in ethnographic context, covers situations, performance organizations, and two types of compositional processes. Pt. 2 is a study of the interrelationship of melodic structure, functions, and actions.

3382. Kolstee, Anton. "The Historical and Musical Significance of Northwest Coast Indian *hámáca* Songs." *Canadian Journal of Native Sttudies* Vol. 8, no. 2 (1988).

3383. Krause, Aurel. *The Tlingit Indians: Results of a Trip of the Northwest Coast of America and the Bering Straits.* Erna Gunther, transl. Vol. 15. Seattle: University of Washington Press for the American Ethnological Society, 1881-1882/repr. 1956. The dances of the Tlingit shaman are described in Chap. 11.

3384. Lane, B. *A Comparative and Analytic Study of Some Aspects of Northwest Coast Religion.* Ph.D. diss., University of Washington, 1953.

3385. Marr, Helen Hubbard. *Voices of the Ancestors: Music in the Life of the Northwest Coast Indians.* Greenwich, CT: The Bruce Museum, 1986.

3386. Padfield, Martha. "Cannibal Dances in the Kwakiutl World." *Canadian Folk Music Journal* Vol. 18 (1991): 14-19. Padfield uses the dance ritual to understand the larger mythic and cosmological patterns of Kwakiutl society. Covers music, masks, dance and poetry.

3387. Roberts, Helen and Morris Swadesh. "Songs of the Nootka Indians of Western Vancouver Island." *Transactions of the American Philosophical Society* Vol. 45, 3 (1955): 199-327. Philadelphia. Among the music analyzed for linguistic content, ethnology and musical components are songs associated with the Potlatch and Wolf Ritual.

3388. Suttles, W. "The Plateau Prophet Dance among the Coast Salish." *Southwestern Journal of Anthropology* Vol. 13 (1957): 352-96. Suttles summarizes the work of Spier, presents his own research and theorizes about the historical elements that contribute to the phenomenon. Although the focus is on the dance as historical, the dance itself is described.

3389. Suttles, Wayne, ed. *Northwest Coast*. Handbook of North American Indians, Vol. 7. William C. Sturtevant, ed. Washington, DC: Smithsonian Institution, 1990. Although lacking a chapter devoted solely to music and/or dance, this volume contains dozens of references to ceremonial and shamanistic dance and music throughout the text.

3390. Waterman, T.T. "The Paraphernalia of the Duwamish 'Spirit-Canoe' Ceremony." *Indian Notes, Museum of the American Indian* Vol. 7 (1930): 129-148; 295-312; 535-561.

3391. Wike, Joyce Annabel. *Modern Spirit Dancing of Northern Puget Sound*. M.A. thesis, University of Washington, 1941.

3392. Woodcock, George. *Peoples of the Coast. The Indians of the Pacific Northwest*. Bloomington, IN: Indiana University Press, 1977. The winter dances of the Kwakiutl are discussed in Chap. 9; other rituals are mentioned throughout the text.

WESTERN SUB-ARCTIC

3393. Beaudry, Nicole. "The Language of Dreams: Songs of the Dene Indians (Canada)." *The World of Music* Vol. 34, 2 (1992): 72-90. Shows the progression of spirituality from a spirit animal base to the Christianized prophet movement and the creation of the Tea Dance and the drum Dance to take the place of medicine dances.

3394. Honigmann, John J. "Expressive Aspects of Subarctic Indian Culture." In *Handbook of North American Indians: Subarctic*, June Helm, ed. Washington, DC: Smithsonian Institution, 1981. 718-732. An investigation of cognitive and contextual meanings in power, shamanism, values and ceremonials of pre-contact Athapaskan and Algonquian culture.

3395. Jenness, Diamond. *The Sarsee Indians of Alberta*. National Museum of Canada Bulletin, Vol. 90. Ottawa, Canada: J. O. Patenaude, 1938/repr. 1983. Based on research conducted in 1921. See pp. 47-57 for Sun Dance myth of origin and a description of the ceremony.

3396. Johnston, Thomas F. "Ancient Athabascan Ritual in Alaska." *Indian Historian* Vol. 8 (1975): 9-25, 46. The Hi'o Stick Dance, held in honor of the deceased husbands of a group of widows, is one of the last authentic and major musico-religious ceremonies of the Alaskan Athabascan Indians to survive.

3397. Johnston, Thomas F. "The History and Social Context of Athabascan Indian Music and Dance." *South African Journal of Musicology* Vol. 11 (1991): 9-35. Communal song and dance not only serve social obligations and functions but are thought to embody supernatural powers. Composers are accorded respect and social prominence.

3398. Lundstrîm, Hakan. "North Athabascan Story Songs and Dance Songs." In *The Alaska Seminar*, Anna Rirgitta Rooth, ed. Stockholm, Sweden: Acta Universitatis Upsaliensis, 1980. 126-164. Includes a study of songs used as spells by the Athapascan medicine man.

3399. Ridington, Robin. "Beaver Dreaming and Singing." *Anthropologica* Vol. 13, 12 (1971): 115. The author strives to understand the meaning of and relation between personal medicine and public shamanistic practice.

3400. Ridington, Robin. *Swan People: A Study of the Dunne-za Prophet Dance*. Mercury Series Publications, Vol. 38. Ottawa, Ontario: National Museums of Canada, 1978. A study of the Dunne-za (Beaver) Indian Prophet Dance and belief as a mosaic of meaning through which the people interpret their relationship to each other and their environment. Vol. 1 contains several chapters discussing the sources of song and the elements of the mytho-theological role of dance in the prophet tradition. Vol. 2. Texts.

3401. Speck, Frank. *Naskapi, the Savage Hunters of the Labrador Peninsula*. Norman, OK: University of Oklahoma Press, 1935. An important early study that focuses on the spirituality and conceptual framework of Labrador natives.

AMERICAN INDIAN CHRISTIAN MUSIC

3402. Cavanagh, Beverley. *Algonkian Indian Hymnody: Conflicts in Valuation as Determinants of a Tradition*. Paper presented at the 29th annual meeting of the Society for Ethnomusicology, Vancouver, Canada, 1985.

3403. Cavanagh, Beverley. "The Performance of Hymns in Eastern Woodlands Indian Communities." In *Sing Out the Glad News: Hymn Tunes in Canada*, John Beckwith, ed. CanMus Documents, Vol. 1. Toronto: Institute for Canadian Music, 1987. In most Indian and Inuit communities Christian worship merged with rather than replaced traditional religious practices. A brief survey of adaptations of hymn singing and other practices among the Iroquois, Micmac, and Naskapi-Montagnais.

3404. Cavanagh, Beverley. "The Transmission of Algonkian Indian Hymns: Between Orality and Literacy." In *Musical Canada: Words and Music Honouring Helmut Kallmann*, John Beckwith and Frederick A. Hall, ed. Toronto: University of Toronto Press, 1988. 3-28.

3405. Densmore, Frances. "Native Songs of Two Hybrid Ceremonies among the American Indians." *American Anthropologist* Vol. 43 (1941): 77-82. On the attempts by the Yaqui and the Native American Church (peyote cult) to combine their customs with Roman Catholic (the Yaqui) or Protestant beliefs. The Yaqui retained their old songs; the Native American Church adapted more Western-style music.

3406. Kirk, Martha Ann. *Dancing with Creation: Mexican and Native American Dance in Christian Worship and Education.* San Jose: Resource Publications, 1983. Kirk focuses on the prophetic and spiritual aspects of ethnic folk dance and suggests methods for incorporating such dance into Catholic worship. Also publ. by The Sharing Co.: Austin, TX, Doug Adams, ed., 1981.

3407. Kurath, Gertrude P. "Catholic Hymns of Michigan Indians." *Anthropological Quarterly* Vol. 30 (1957): 31-44. Washington. A study of the native language Catholic hymnody of the Michigan Algonquian. Emphasizes the positive aspects of acculturation.

3408. Larson, Paul E. "Mahican and Lenape Moravians and Moravian Music." *Unitas Fratrum* Vol. 21-22 (1988): 173-188.

3409. Painter, Muriel Thayer. *A Yaqui Easter.* Tucson, AZ: University of Arizona Press, 1971.

3410. Rhodes, Willard. "The Christian Hymnology of the North American Indians." *Men and Cultures: Selected Papers of the Fifth International Congress of the Anthropological and Ethnological Sciences, 1969* Vol. 5 (1960): 324-31. Philadelphia: University of Pennsylvania Press

3411. Spicer, Edward H. *Context of the Yaqui Easter Ceremony.* New Dimensions in Dance Research: Anthropology and Dance, Tamara Comstock, ed. New York: Committee on Research in Dance, 1974. An investigation of various aspects of the Yaqui Easter Ceremony including identity, history, and context.

3412. Spicer, Edward H. and Phyllis Balastrero. "Yaqui Easter Ceremonial." *Arizona Highways* Vol. 47, 3/March (1971). A vivid description of a 40-day dance ceremony with attention to traditional overtones added to the Christian story. Includes color photographs of the events.

3413. Stevenson, George W. *The Hymnody of the Choctaw Indians of Oklahoma.* Ph.D. diss., Southern Baptist Theological Seminary, Louisville, KY, 1977.

34

Central and South American Indians

GENERAL REFERENCES

3414. Aretz, Isabel. "Latin America I: Indian Music." In *Grove 6*, Vol. 7. 1980. 505-515.

3415. Howard, Pamela. "Dance and Dance-Drama of Latin American Indians." In *Theatrical Movement: A Bibliographical Anthology*, Bob Fleshman, ed. Metuchen, NY and London: Scarecrow, 1986. 692-717.

3416. Izikowitz, Karl Gustav. *Musical and Other Sound Instruments of the South American Indians*. Wakefield, Yorkshire: SR Publishers, 1935/repr. 1970. A detailed inventory of native instruments and description of their uses. See, e.g., comments on the religious aspects of kettle drum and bull-roarer.

3417. Lemmon, Alfred E. "Jesuit Chroniclers and Historians of Colonial Spanish America: Sources for the Ethnomusicologist." *Inter-American Music Review* 10, (Spring-Summer) (1989): 119-29. A survey of the chronicles of Jesuit institutions in Latin America from 1567, the time of the first permanent Jesuit institution in Spanish America, to the mid-eighteenth century, reveal that music and dance played an important role in the education of missionaries and local inhabitants.

3418. Olsen, Dale A. "Symbol and Function in South American Indian Music." In *Musics of Many Cultures: An Introduction*, Elizabeth May, ed. 1980. 363-385.

3419. Steward, Julian Haynes, ed. *Handbook of South American Indians*. 7 vols. Smithsonian Institution. Bureau of American Ethnology Bulletin 143, New York: Cooper Square Publishers, 1946-59/repr. 1963. Prepared in cooperation with the U.S. Dept. of State as a project of the interdepartmental Committee on

Scientific and Cultural Cooperation. Vol. 1. The Marginal Tribes. Vol. 2. The Andean Civilizations. Vol. 3. The Tropical Forest Tribes. Vol. 4. The Circum-Caribbean Tribes. Vol. 5. The Comparative Ethnology of South American Indians. Vol. 6. Physical Anthropology, Linguistics and Cultural Geography of South American. Vol. 7. Index.

3420. Sullivan, Lawrence E. *Icanchu's Drum: An Orientation to Meaning in South American Religions*. New York: Macmillan, 1988. A superb introduction to the religious world of the South American Indian. In Chapter 7, "Specialists," see 'Master of Song and Sound' for a survey of the religious use of song and instruments among various tribes.

CENTRAL AMERICA

3421. Bierhorst, John. *Cantares Mexicanos: Songs of the Aztecs*. Stanford: Stanford University Press, 1985.

3422. Boilés, Charles. *Cognitive Processes in Otomí Cult Music*. Ph.D. diss., Tulane University, 1969.

3423. Burton, Susan Sasse. *Malichi, the Flower Fawn: The Symbolism of the Yaqui Deer Dance*. M.A. thesis, Texas Woman's University, 1990. Two aspects of Laban Movement Analysis applied to the movement component of the Deer Dance demonstrate that the dominant theme is the powerful animal mimicry that enables the dancer to become the deer for the space of his ritual performance.

3424. Caceres, Abraham. *In Xochitl, in Cuicatl: Hallucinogens and Music in Mesoamerican Amerindian Thought*. Ph.D. diss., Indiana University, 1984.

3425. Carrasco, P. "Pagan Rituals and Beliefs Among the Chontal Indians of Oaxaca, Mexico." In *Anthropological Records*, Vol. 20. Berkeley, Los Angeles 1960. 87-117. Consists of the formulae (texts) and background for 18 rituals, followed by a description of the supernaturals to whom the offerings are addressed.

3426. Cashion, Susan Valerie. *Dance Ritual and Cultural Values in a Mexican Village: Festival of Santo Santiago*. Ph.D. diss., Stanford University, 1983.

3427. Chapin, Mac. "Losing the Way of the Great Father." *New Scientist* 131, August 10 (1991): 40-45. On the tradition of long narrative chants of the Cuna Indians of Panama.

3428. Constenla-Umaña, Adolfo. "The Language of the Bribri Ritual Songs." *Latin American Indian Literatures Journal* 6, 1 (Spring) (1990): 14-35. A linguistic analysis of Bribri ritual speech, a secret language, used only by shamans in dialog with supernatural beings. The texts are frozen, they deal with a limited number of topics and exhibit such features of exceptional language as simplification, clarification, and hybridization. Spectators have a general sense of what is said, but not a literal one (Costa Rica).

3429. Das, Prem. "Initiation by a Huichol Shaman." In *Art of the Huichol Indians*, Kathleen Berrin, ed. New York: Harry B. Abrams for the Fine Arts Museum of San Francisco, 1978. 129-142. This first-hand account of an initiation by a Huichol shaman describes the effects of ritual peyote use and how several nights of singing and dancing in alternation with meditation constituted the final phase of the initiation.

3430. Dow, James. *The Shaman's Touch: Otomi Indian Symbolic Healing*. Salt Lake City UT: University of Utah Press, 1986. This sympathetic investigation of the characteristics and functions of the Otomi shaman contains four pages on music as one of various aids used in healing. Includes extensive commentary and explanation by Don Antonio, the shaman.

3431. Franco Arce, Samuel. *Music of the Maya*. Guatemala: Casa K'ojom, 1991.

3432. Freidel, David, Linda Schele, and Joy Parker. *Maya Cosmos. 3000 Years on the Shamans Path*. New York: Morrow and Co, 1993. A detailed interpretation of Mayan art and architecture based on the recent discovery that ancient Mayan creation symbols represent a map of the night sky. See Chap. 6: Dancing Across the Abyss: Maya Festival and Pageant.

3433. Guerara-Berger, Marcos. "A Visit to a Bribri Shaman." In *South and Meso-American Native Spirituality: From the Cult of the Feathered Serpent to the Theology of Liberation*, G. Gossen et al., ed. New York: Crossroad, 1993. 371-390. A first-hand account of a healing ceremony among the Bribri of Costa Rica.

3434. Haddon, Alfred C. "The Secular and Ceremonial Dances of Torres Straits." *Internationales Archiv für Ethnographie* 6 (1893): 131-162. Whereas festive dances were 'secular' and sometimes allowed the participation of women, ceremonial dances were 'sacred' and were performed by men alone. These include initiation dances, the turtle procession, seasonal dances, and funeral ceremonies. Provides context for ritual dances from mythical references and other accounts.

3435. Hammond, N. "Classic Maya Music: Part 1, Maya Drums; Part 2: Shakers, Rattles, Raspers." *Archaeology* 25, 2 (1972): 124, 222.

3436. Hanna, Judith Lynne. "Dances of Anahuac—for God or Man? An Alternate Way of Thinking about Prehistory." *Dance Research Journal* 7, 1 (1975): 13-27.

3437. Marti, Samuel and Gertrude Prokosch Kurath. *Dances of Anahuac: The Choreography and Music of Precortesian Dances*. Viking Fund Publications in

Anthropology No. 38, New York: Wenner-Gren Foundation for Anthropological Research, 1964. A nicely-illustrated study of sacred and secular dance among the Mayans and Aztecs, in three parts: Sources (historical, social, and religious background of ceremonial and secular dances), Motions (Aztec ceremonial patterns derived from statues, painting engravings, etc.), and Branches (pre-Cortesian music and the symbolism of directions, numbers, and colors).

3438. Myerhoff, Barbara. *Peyote Hunt: The Sacred Journey of the Huichol Indians*. Ithaca, NY: Cornell University Press, 1978. Based on personal experience under the guidance of a shaman, the author draws a vivid picture of the rich complexities of the Huichol world view. Allows the shaman to tell his own story and interpret his culture's customs and symbols.

3439. O'Brien, Linda Lee. *Songs of the Face of the Earth: Ancestor Songs of the Tzutuhil-Maya of Santiago Atitlán, Guatemala*. Ph.D. diss., UCLA, 1975.

3440. O'Brien, Linda L. "Music in a Maya Cosmos." *The World of Music* 18, 3 (1976): 35-41. Sixteenth century Spanish influence has been absorbed by the Tzutuhil Mayan's into a cosmology in which all traditional music is ascribed to Tzutuhil ancestors. These Nawals still oversee from afar the performance of their music: communal celebration of calendric events and ritual observance of events in the life of the individual.

3441. Painter, Muriel T. *With Good Heart: Yaqui Beliefs and Ceremonies in Pascua, Village*. Edward H. Spicer and Wilma Kaemlein, ed. Tucson, AZ: University of Arizona Press, 1986. A vivid, detailed description in three parts: 1) Pre-Christian and Christian beliefs and practices, 2) Ceremonial organizations, and 3) Roman Catholic ceremonies. Most references to music and dance occur in Part 2 under "Native Dancers": the pascolar dancers and deer dancers, though major participants in Roman Catholic ceremonies, contain much that is pre-Christian in origin.

3442. Perez, Maria del Rosario. *Transformational Aspects of the Music of the Highland Tzeltal Maya*. Ph.D. diss., University of Washington, 1989. A semiotic approach to the role of music in the world view and ritual of six highland Tzeltal-Mayan communities.

3443. Rhodes, Willard A. "A Preliminary Study of the Mazatec Mushroom Ceremony." *Inter-American Bulletin* 50 (1965): 1-8. Also in *Primera Conferencia Inter-Americana de Ethnomusicologia, Cartagena de Indias, Colombia, 24- a 28 de Febrero de 1963, Trabajos Presentados*, 187-96. Washington, DC: Pan-American Union.

3444. Stevenson, Robert. *Music in Mexico: A Historical Survey*. New York: Thomas Y. Corwell, 1952. Still the most comprehensive history of music in Mexico, from early aboriginal music to mid-20th century.

3445. Stevenson, Robert M. *Music in Aztec and Inca Territory.* Berkeley and Los Angeles: University of California Press, 1968. A scholarly survey of the literature on Aztec music at contact and during the colonial phase, on Inca instruments and music teaching before and after conquest, and on literary and musical sources concerning Peruvian "folk music" 1500-1790.

3446. Stevenson, Robert M. "Maya music." In *Grove 6*, Vol. 11. 1980. 853-54.

3447. Stevenson, Robert M. "Aztec music." In *Grove 6*, Vol. 1. 1980. 760-61.

3448. Stone, Martha. *At the Sign of Midnight/The Concheros Dance Cult of Mexico.* Tucson, AZ: University of Arizona Press, 1975. An insider's account of life among a prominent group of central Mexican fiesta dancers.

SOUTH AMERICA

3449. Bartolomé, Miguel A. "Shamanism Among the Avá-Chiripá." In *Spirits, Shamans, and Stars: Perspectives from South America*, David L. Browman and Ronald A. Schwarz, ed. The Haghue: Mouton, 1979. Based on the criterion of power, the author distinguishes between several categories of Avá-Chiripá shamanic songs as well as songs that every tribal member may possess as personal. Shaman's songs are the most powerful and contain words that are completely unintelligible, perhaps vestiges of an archaic sacred language.

3450. Basso, Ellen. *A Musical View of the Universe: Kalapalo Myth and Ritual Performances.* Philadelphia: University of Pennsylvania Press, 1985. With an example of the mythical narrative of the Brazilian tribe as her starting point, Basso provides the context necessary to understand this form. She shows how meaning is constructed through performance, and explains narrative performance, myth, and sound as elements in a broad framework of discourse and symbolic and social meanings. Finally, Basso shows how the collective performance of music allows the Kalapalo to model themselves upon their images of powerful beings, and how, by experiencing the transformative powers inherent in human musicality, they feel the value of these models. Includes extended passages of mythological narrative.

3451. Basso, Ellen. "Musical Expression and Gender Identity in the Myth and Ritual of the Kalapalo of Central Brazil." In *Women and Music in Cross-Cultural Perspective*, Ellen Koskoff, ed. Urbana, IL: University of Illinois Press, 1987, 1989. 163-76. The genders reverse roles in rituals designed to assert and communicate the dangerous powers inherent in human sexuality and transform them. Exemplary as an interpretation of culture through the information contained in the performance of verbal and ritual art (i.e., music). Emphasis is on the symbolic content of sound(s) in Kalapalo rendering of myth and song. Enriched by numerous translated texts.

3452. Baumann, Max Peter. "Music, Dance, and Song of the Chipayas (Bolivia)." *Latin American Music Review* 2, 2 (1981): 171-222. Contains brief reference to church songs and ritual ceremony of these Christianized Indians.

3453. Baumann, Max Peter. "Music of the Indios in Bolivia's Andean Highlands (Survey)." *The World of Music* 25, 2 (1982): 80-96. A general survey of the religious music of a peasant group, a description of its aerophones and drums, musical groupings, and specific song forms.

3454. Béhague, Gérard. "Brazil." In *Grove 6*, Vol. 3. 1980. 230-234.

3455. Belzner, William. "Music, Modernization, and Westernization Among the Macuma Shuar." In *Cultural Transformations and Ethnicity in Ecuador*, Norman Whitten, ed. Urbana, IL: University of Illinois Press, 1981. 731-48.

3456. Boglár, Lajos. "Creative Process in Ritual Art: Piaroa Indians, Venezuela." In *Spirits, Shamans, and Stars: Perspectives from South America*, David L. Browman and Ronald A. Schwartz, ed. The Hague: Mouton, 1979. Among Piaroa, the shaman is also the head man of the local group. He sings his songs in the voices of the mythical narrators of the magic epic songs, thereby assuring his people of the continuing presence of the mythic characters in human affairs.

3457. Briggs, Charles L. "'Since I Am Woman, I Will Chastise My Relatives': Gender, Reported Speech, and the (Re)production of Social Relations in Warao Ritual Wailing." *American Ethnologist* 19, 2 (1992): 337-61. Ritual wailing provides the opportunity for Warao women, otherwise without public voice, to challenge the domination of male shamans and political leaders.

3458. Briggs, Charles L. "Personal Sentiments and Polyphonic Voices in Warao Women's Ritual Wailing: Music and Poetics in a Critical and Collective Discourse." *American Anthropologist* 95, 4 (1993): 929-58. The polyphonic and intertextual character of the funeral laments of the women of the Warao of Venezuala provide them with both individual and collective social power.

3459. Chaumeil, J. P. "Varieties of Amazonian Shamanism." *Diogenes*, 158 (1992): 101-113. From the outskirts of Amazonian megalopolises to the Amazonian jungles, shamanism is enjoying a period of renewal and revival. The article discusses its various traditional and syncretic forms.

3460. den Otter, E. *Music and Dance of Indians and Mestizos in an Andean Valley of Peru*. Delft: Eburon, 1985. Includes a description of religious music (hymns performed at mass; processions) and secular music (Chap. 2) and the contexts for such music (festivals of various kinds for religious music) (Chap. 4).

3461. Dole, Gertrude E. "Shamanism and Political Control among the Kuikuru." In *Peoples and Cultures of Native South America*, D.R. Gross, ed. Garden City: Doubleday/The Natural History Press, 1973.

3462. Donahue, George Rodney Jr. *A Contribution to the Ethnography of the Karaja Indians of Central Brazil*. Ph.D. diss., University of Virginia, 1982. This study of the Karaja Indians includes a description of important Karaja religious rituals, particularly the mask dance rites, which the Karaja perform throughout the year.

3463. Faron, Louis C. "The Mapuche of Chile: Their Religious Beliefs and Rituals." In *South and Meso-American Native Spirituality: From the Cult of the Feathered Serpent to the Theology of Liberation*, G. Gossen et al., ed. New York: Crossroad, 1993. 352-370. On Mapuche cosmology, shamanism and shaman's songs, and various ceremonies. The songs and ceremonies provide the sustained and responsible link between the living and the dead, a concept which is of central importance to Mapuche religious morality.

3464. Fock, Niels. *Waiwai: Religion and Society of an Amazonian Tribe*. Nationalmuseets Skrifter, Etnografiske Raekke, Vol. 8. Copenhagen: National Museum, 1963. A detailed account of Waiwai culture, including religious beliefs, myths and legends, cosmology, life cycle, and social and political organization. In shamanic chant, or 'magic blowing,' 'magic' refers to the coercive power exercised by certain songs when performed with the proper ritual. 'Blowing,' or ritual puffing, is performed with the mouth ('pu-pu') and is coupled with a magic song that can be used by lay persons and medicine men (shamans) alike, to kill or disable an enemy, cure the sick, avenge a death, avert supernatural dangers to which young children are subject, or dispel rain.

3465. Fuks, Victor. "Waiapi Musical Instruments: Classification, Symbols and Meaning." *Selected Reports in Ethnomusicology: Issues in Organology* Vol. 8 (1990): 143-174. A classification of the 68 instruments of the Waiapi of Brazil, with a discussion of their use and social context including ritual performances.

3466. Furst, Peter. "'I am a Black Jaguar!' Magical Spells and Shamanism of the Pemon of Southern Venezuela." In *South and Meso-American Native Spirituality: From the Cult of the Feathered Serpent to the Theology of Liberation*, G. Gossen et al., ed. New York: Crossroad, 1993. 393-413. A translation of a vivid account from the beginning of this century of the training and rituals of a Pemon shaman. Includes a translation of spells.

3467. Girard, Sharon Elizabeth. *Music of the Requiem in Venezuela: A Study of the Colonial Tradition and Its Background of Folk and Autochthonous Music of the Dead*. Ph.D. diss., UCLA, 1975.

3468. Grebe, M.E. *Generative Models, Symbolic Structures, and Acculturation in the Panpipe Music of the Aymara of Tarapaca, Chile*. Ph.D.diss., Queen's University of Belfast, 1980.

3469. Grim, John. "Cosmogony and the Winter Dance: Native American Ethics in Transition." *Journal of Religious Ethics* 20, 2 (Fall, 1992): 389-413. The Winter Dance ceremonial embodies the ethics of giving (as an expression of sacred power) and of empathy (expressed through guardian-spirit songs and spirit sickness). The ethics of giving prepare individuals for those spiritual encounters that engender the ethics of empathy.

3470. Hill, Jonathan David. "Kamayura Flute Music." *Ethnomusicology* 23, 3 (1979): 417-432. A study of *jaqui, tarawí,* and *uruá* flute music and how each is an element in a hierarchical system that integrates a style of music with a particular time of year, type of social relation, and mythological event.

3471. Hill, Jonathan David. *Wakuenai Society: A Processual-Structural Analysis of Indigenous Cultural Life in the Upper Rio Negro Region of Venezuela.* Ph.D. diss., Indiana University, 1983. According to Wakuenai belief, the performance of sacred musical sounds is able to classify, transform and restore a fully human, cultural order. The author studies the music in childbirth, initiation, curing rituals to illustrate how music performances both delineate and transcend the opposing processes of birth, growth, and death.

3472. Hill, Jonathan David. "Myth, Spirit-Naming, and the Art of Microtonal Rising: Childbirth Rituals of the Arawakan Wakuenai." *Latin American Music Review* 6, 1 (1985): 1-30. An explanation of the linguistic and musical structuring of a genre of sacred vocal music (málikai) preformed by ritual specialists.

3473. Hill, Jonathan David. "Wakuénai Ceremonial Exchange in the Venezuelan Northwest Amazon." *Journal of Latin American Lore* 13, 2 (1987): 183-224.

3474. Hill, Jonathan David. "Myth, Music, and History: Poetic Transformation of Narrative Discourse." *Journal of Folklore Research* 27, 1-2 (1990): 115-132.

3475. Hill, Jonathan David. "Metamorphosis: Mythic and Musical Modes of Exchange in the Northwest Amazon." In *A Universe of Music: A World History,* Malena Kuss, ed. Washington, DC: Smithsonian Institute Press, 1993.

3476. Hill, Jonathan David. *Keepers of the Sacred Chants: The Poetics of Ritual Power in an Amazonian Society.* Tucson, AZ: University of Arizona Press, 1993. A study of málikai—sacred chant—among the Wakuénai of Venezuela. Describes the two major and complementary functions of sacred chant as searching for names and heaping up names. Refers to songs and dance throughout. See in particular Chap. 5. 'Initiation into the Cult of Kuwái and the Musicalization of Mythic Speech.'

3477. Kauffman, Christopher Paul. *Variation in the Music, Song Texts and Instrumentation of the Papa Aysay Ceremony in Chinchero, an Indigenous Highland Community in Southern Peru.* Ph.D. diss., Indiana University, 1977.

3478. Langdon, E. Jean Matteson and Gerhard Baer, ed. *Portals of Power: Shamanism in South America.* Albuquerque, NM: University of New Mexico Press, 1992.

3479. Luna, Luis E. *Vegetalismo: Shamanism among the Mestizo Population of the Peruvian Amazon.* Stockholm Studies in Comparative Religion, Philadelphia PA: Coronet Books, 1986. Chapter 5, "The Gifts of the Spirits: The Magic Melodies and the Magic Phlegm" describes the process of learning magic songs (*icaros*) from various plant sources (*vegetales*), some of which songs empower the shaman with animal qualities needed to cure the ill.

3480. Olsen, Dale A. "Magical Protection Songs of the Warao Indians, Part I: Animals." *Latin American Music Review.* (1980/1981): 1, 2. Part 1 (131-151), 2, 1 Part 2 (1-10). Warao sing songs for protection against supernaturally transformed animals and other ferocious beasts and evil spirits that roam the jungle. These songs, which anyone can sing, involve correctly naming the *hoa* or threatening essence.

3481. Olsen, Dale A. *Music and Shamanism of the Winikina-Warao Indians of Venezuela: Music for Curing and Other Theurgy.* Ph.D. diss., UCLA, 1973.

3482. Olsen, Dale A. "The Function of Naming in the Curing Songs of the Warao Indians of Venezuela." *Anuario, Yearbook for Inter-American Musical Research* 10 (1974): 88-122. Melody and text work together to cure illness. Curing takes place when the shaman is able to name the essence (*hoa*) that is causing an illness. With textual illustrations. An analysis of 73 curing songs reveals that it is possible to determine, on the basis of melodic patterns, exactly what is taking place during an entire song cycle.

3483. Olsen, Dale A. "Music-Induced Altered States of Consciousness among Warao Shamans." *Journal of Latin American Lore* 1, 1 (1975): 19-33. Although inhalation of tobacco smoke is now used along with music to induce trance on some occasions, cultural conditioning is the 'deep structure' within which music—i.e., singing and the shaking of a large rattle—acts as a tool to achieve the deep trance necessary for curing. Provides transcriptions of music, with analysis. The shaman's view of the importance of music for the trance state is described.

3484. Overing, J. "The Shaman as a Maker of Worlds: Nelson Goodman in the Amazon." *Man* 25, 4 (1990): 602-619. Nelson Goodman's view of the cognitive process involved in world-making is used to understand the worlds of the 'before time' and 'today time' that the shaman creates through the language of his chant for curing illness. Focuses on the Piaroa, a tropical forest people of the Orinoco basin of Venezuela.

3485. Palavecino, Enrique. "The Magic World of the Mataco." *Latin American Indian Lore* 3, 2 (1979): 61-75. On the power of the shaman's curing song and instrument. This power is acquired gradually over time as he learns to communicate more effectively with beings in the spirit world.

3486. Perkins, John. *The World as You Dream It: Shamanic Teachings from the Amazon and Andes*. Rochester, VT: Destiny Books, 1994.

3487. Perrin, Michel. "Appendix: The Poetic Vision of Setuuma, Guajiro Shaman." *Diogenes*, 158/Summer (1992): 181-184. In this excerpt from a longer text, Guajiro shaman Setuuma Pushaina describes his experiences as a shaman, from the dream that began his life as a shaman to the spirits he works with in healing the ill.

3488. Poole, Deborah A. "Rituals of Movement, Rites of Transformation: Pilgrimage and Dance in the Highlands of Cuzco, Peru." In *Latin American Pilgrimage*, N. Ross Crumrine and E. Alan Morinis, ed. Westport, CT: Greenwood Publishing, 1989, 1991.

3489. Poole, Deborah A. "Accommodation and Resistance in Andean Ritual Dance." *Crama Review* 34, 2 (1990): 98-126. At the yearly festival *Qoyllur Rit'i*, pilgrims from all levels of society experience a cultural leveling, towns people assume temporary hierarchies in terms of their importance to the festival, and the dancers are the mediums through which the blessings of the White Christ Child are spread to the pilgrims' communities. This article examines the complicitous relationship between the Western spectator 'conquerors' and the Andean presenters as expressed in the latter's dances.

3490. Reichel-Dolmatoff, Gerardo. *Amazonian Cosmos: The Sexual and Religious Symbolism of the Tukano Indians*. Chicago: The University of Chicago Press, 1971. Originally published in Spanish in 1968. In Chapter 4 (Man and the Supernatural) and Chapter 5 (Society and the Supernatural), the shaman (*payé*) is discussed as mediator, particularly as regards the curing of disease.

3491. Reichel-Dolmatoff, G. *The Shaman and the Jaguar: A Study of Narcotic Drugs among the Indians of Colombia*. Philadelphia: Temple University Press, 1975. A first-hand study of the use of certain drugs among Colombian Indians and the closely related jaguar transformation complex. References to shamans, song, and dance occur throughout.

3492. Robertson-de Carbo, Carol E. "Tayil as Category and Communication among the Argentine Mapuche: A Methodological Suggestion." *YIFMC*. 8 (1976): 35-52. The Mapuche have no term for music; *tayil* is known only in terms of non-'musical' associations. Although each *tayil* is identifiable by a coincidence of a particular text and melodic contour, its significance lies in its use in marriage arangements and performance, in the burial of the dead, and in bridging the gap between present and past time. By limiting our definition and description of *tayil* to musical terminology because it resembles other sound complexes called music, we miss its more important non-musical components.

3493. Robertson-DeCarbo, Carol E. "Pulling the Ancestors: Performance Practice and Praxis in Mapuche Ordering." *Ethnomusicology* 23, 3 (1979): 395-416. On *entún kuifí*, or pulling the ancestors, reflecting the performance of *tayil* and the delineating between the real and the ideal, practice and praxis, in the Mapuche philosophical context.

3494. Schechter, J.M. *Music in a North Ecuadorian Highland Locus: Diatonic Harp, Genres, Harpists, and Their Ritual Junction in the Quehua Child's Wake.* Ph.D. diss., University of Texas, 1982.

3495. Seeger, Anthony. "What Can We Learn When They Sing? Vocal Genres of the Suya Indians of Central Brazil." *Ethnomusicology* 23 (1979): 373-94. An analysis of two genres—*akia* and *ngere*—and their social and cosmological significance:*akia* is linked to the individual and *ngere* to ceremonial groups.

3496. Seeger, Anthony. *Nature and Society in Central Brazil: The Suya Indians of Mato Grosso.* Cambridge, MA: Harvard University Press, 1981.

3497. Seeger, Anthony. "Oratory Is Spoken, Myth Is Told, and Song Is Sung, But They Are All Music to My Ears." In *Native South American Discourse*, Joel Sherzer and Greg Urban, ed. Amsterdam: Mouton de Gruyter, 1986. 59-82.

3498. Seeger, Anthony. *Why Suya Sing: A Musical Anthropology of an Amazonian People.* New York: Cambridge University Press, 1987. A detailed examination of how and why song holds a central position in Suyá society and the role it plays in myth telling, speech making, and a boy's initiation ceremony.

3499. Seeger, Anthony. "Voices, Flutes, and Shamans in Brazil." *The World of Music* 30, 2 (1988): 22-39. Examines three types of songs: Suyá songs that establish a set of relations between family, gender, and age, Xingu flute songs that mediate spiritual and human relations and link the past with the present, and Araweté shaman's songs that make audible the spiritual world.

3500. Seeger, Anthony. "When Music Makes History." In *Ethnomusicology and Modern Music History*, Blum, Bohlman, and Neuman, ed. Urbana & Chicago: University of Illinois Press, 1991. 23-34. How the Suya create their history through the performance of music. Exemplary as a study of a society from the prespective of musical performance and of a society's own understanding of its cultural forms. For an extended review, see Gerard Béhaque in *Latin American Music Review*, 9, 2, Fall/Winter 1988. 260-272.

3501. Sharon, Douglas G. *The Symbol System of a North Peruvian Shaman.* Ph.D. diss., UCLA, 1974.

3502. Sharon, Douglas G. *Wizard of the Four Winds: A Shaman's Story.* New York: Free Press, 1978. On Peruvian traditional medicine and shamanism.

3503. Siskind, Janet. *To Hunt in the Morning*. London and New York: Oxford University press, 1973. Songs are classified according to illness and are used in healing and in the transference of powers. A study of shamanism in lowland South American cultures.

3504. Siskind, Janet. "Visions and Cures Among the Sharanahua." In *Hallucinogens and Shamanism*, Michael J. Harner, ed. London: Oxford University Press, 1973. Includes references to songs sung at every stage of a curing ceremony. Peru.

3505. Smith, Richard Chase. *Deliverance from Chaos for a Song: A Social and Religious Interpretation of the Ritual Performance of Amuesha Music*. Ph.D. diss., Indiana University, 1977.

3506. Smith, Richard Chase. "The Language of Power: Music, Order, and Redemption." *Latin American Music Review* 5, 2 (1984): 129-60. Only the divinities have the power to create ritual songs. All such songs were revealed to the Amuesha by the divinities during vigils that involve deprivation as well as the use of psychoactive drugs. By singing the songs, the Amuesha share in their power over destructive forces.

3507. Stevenson, Robert. *The Music of Peru: Aboriginal and Viceroyal Epochs*. Washington, D.C.: Pan American Union Union, 1960. A meticulously documented historical survey with a 100-page musical supplement.

3508. Stevenson, Robert M. "Inca music." In *Grove 6*, Vol. 9. 1980. 56-57.

3509. Sullivan, Lawrence E. "Sacred Music and Sacred Time." *The World of Music* 26, 3 (1984): 33-51. Using examples of South American music, Sullivan explores the ways in which music reconstructs our notions of time in cosmogonic, cosmological, cultural, and eschatological terms.

3510. Sullivan, Lawrence E. "Watunna: An Orinoco Creation Cycle." *New Scholar* 10 (1986): 291-294.

3511. Townsley, G. "Song Paths: The Ways and Means of Yaminahua Shamanic Knowledge." *Homme* 33, Apr/Dec (1993): 449-468. Careful analysis of song texts, along with a shaman's own description of his visions, indicates that he investigates an illness and its precipitating spirit through metaphors that he creates in his songs, and thus with more safety than if he were to do so directly.

3512. Turino, Thomas. "The Charango and the Sirena: Music, Magic, and the Power of Love." *Revista de Música Latinoamericana/Latin American Music Review* 4, 1 (1983): 81-119.

3513. Turino, Thomas. Power Relations, Identity and Musical Choice: Music in a Peruvian Altiplano Village and Among Its Migrants in the Metropolis. Ph.D. diss., University of Texas, Austin, 1987.

3514. Turino, Thomas. "The Coherence of Social Style and Musical Creation among the Aymara in Southern Peru." *Ethnomusicology* 33 (1989): 1-30. Turnio examines the instruments and performance techniques, social and musical organization of ensembles, compositional processes, and musical form which he believes creates music as an icon of 'naturalness' or 'truth' for the Aymara.

3515. Urban, Greg. "Ceremonial Dialogues in South America." *American Anthropologist* 88, 2 (1986): 371-86.

3516. Wagley, Charles. "Tapirapé Indian Music in Central Brazil: A Memoir." In *Libraries, History, Diplomacy, and the Performing Arts: Essays in Honor of Carleton Sprague Smith*, Israel Katz, ed. Festschrift Series, No. 9, Stuyvesant, NY: Pendragon Press, 1991. 371-77. Includes a brief description of songs for harvest, for the arrival of spirits, and against the destructive spirit of thunder.

3517. Wright, Robin. "Guardians of the Cosmos: Baniwa Shamans and Prophets." *History of Religions* 32, 1/August (1992): 32-58 (Part 1). Part 2: 32, 2/Nov. (1992): 126-145. In order to practice curing, shamans enter trance through the use of snuff called 'parika.' Chant-owners, on the other hand, heal by the reciting of spells. A study of the 4-tiered cosmology, mythology, and idiology of Baniwa shamans and chant-owners, mediators between this flawed world and the primordial worlds from which cures and methods of beautification can be acquired.

3518. Zerries, Otto. "The Bullroarer Among South American Indians." *Revista do Museu Paulista* 7, New Series (1953): 275-309. São Paulo. The center of bull-roarer usage in funeral ceremonies (as the voice of the dead) and in boys' initiation rites is eastern Brazil. From here these uses spread northward and westward where the instrument is also linked to thunder, the voice of the jaguar, and children's toys.

35

Eskimo and Inuit Religious Music

GENERAL REFERENCES

3519. Cavanagh, Beverley A "Inuit." In *NGDAM*, Vol. 2. 1986. 494-497. A survey of Eskimo and Inuit music.

3520. Damas, David, ed. *Arctic. Handbook of North American Indians*, Vol. 5. William C. Sturtevant, ed. Washington, DC: Smithsonian Institution, 1984. Many of the 59 articles mention shamans, religion, ceremonies, and music. Includes a massive bibliography.

3521. Jenness, Stuart E., ed. *Arctic Odyssey: The Diary of Diamond Jenness, Ethnologist with the Canadian Arctic Expedition in Northern Alaska and Canada 1913-1916*. Hull, Quebec: Canada Museum of Civilization, 1991. This complete, detailed diary contains numerous references to shamans and shamic performance.

3522. Johnston, Thomas F. *Eskimo Music by Region: A Circumpolar Comparative Study*. Canadian Ethnology Services. Paper 32, p. 222, Ottawa: National Museums of Canada, 1976. A description, in 34 brief chapters, of the music of the arctic Eskimo shows that the Siberian and Alaskan Eskimo, along with the Eskimo of the Mackenzie Delta in Northwest Canada, form a music culture that is unified and distinct from that of the Inuit of Central and Eastern Canada and Greenland. Although the emphasis is on musical characteristics, context and associated behaviors are also mentioned, as is reference to ceremonial music whenever practiced.

ALASKAN ESKIMOS

3523. Binnington, Doreen and Liang Ming-Yueh. "Eskimo." In *Grove 6*, Vol. 13. 1980. 318-320.

3524. Crowell, Aron. "Postcontact Koniag Ceremonialism on Kodiak Island and the Alaska Peninsula: Evidence from the Fisher Collection." *Arctic Anthropology* 29, 1 (1992): 18-37. On the masks, head dresses and shamanic articles associated with ceremonies performed between 1879-1885.

3525. Fienup-Riordan, Ann. "The Mask: The Eye of the Dance." *Arctic Anthropology* 24, 2 (1987): 40-55. After decades of decline due initially to the influence of missionaries, ceremonial mask-making is experiencing a revival. Main themes are birth and rebirth. The various symbols and beliefs are explained.

3526. Fienup-Riordan, Ann. *The Real People and the Children of Thunder: The Yup'ik Eskimo Encounter with Moravian Missionaries John and Edith Kilbuck.* Norman, OK: University of Oklahoma Press, 1991.

3527. Fitzhugh, William and Aron Crowell, ed. *Crossroads of Continents. Cultures of Siberia and Alaska.* Washington, DC: Smithsonian Institution, 1988. Beautifully illustrated. Includes several articles on religion and dance.

3528. Fitzhugh, William and Susan A. Kaplan, ed. *Inua: Spirit World of the Bering Sea Eskimo.* Washington, DC: National Museum of Natural History/ Smithsonian Institution Press, 1982. Chapter entitled 'With the Spirits' deals with Inua mythology, the role of the shaman, dancing, and the Bladder Festival. Illustrated with over 350 representations of carvings, masks, etc.

3529. Hawkes, Ernest William. *The 'Inviting-In' Feast of the Alaskan Eskimo.* Department of Mines, memoir 45, no. 3, Ottawa: Government Printing Bureau, 1913. Held in 1911-1912, the festival is an appeal to the spirits represented by the masks, the totemic guardians of the performers, for future success in hunting.

3530. Hawkes, Ernest William. *The Dance Festivals of the Alaskan Eskimos.* University of Pennsylvania Anthropological Publications, Vol. 6, no. 2, Philadelphia: University of Pennsylvania, 1914. A description of five feasts, including the Bladder Feast and the Feast to the Dead, in the Bering Strait District.

3531. Holtved, Erik. "Eskimo Shamanism." In *Studies in Shamanism*, Carl-Martin Edsman, ed. Stockholm: Almqvist and Wiksell, 1967. A general survey of Eskimo and Inuit shamanism, including a description of its role, the use of drum, active and passive types, geographic distribution, and helping spirits.

3532. Johnston, Thomas F. "Alaskan Eskimo Dance in Cultural Context." *Dance Research Journal* 7, 2 (1975): 1-11. The three major contexts are feasting, gift-giving, and competitive athletic games. Johnston touches on related religious beliefs and the need to create an exciting sound and social togetherness as well as placate and forstall maleficent forces. He traces origins to the Amur River in Siberia and examines the physiological effect of drumming.

3533. Johnston, Thomas F. "A Historical Perspective on Alaskan Eskimo Music." *The Indian Historian* 7, 4 (1975): 17-26.

3534. Johnston, Thomas F. "Drum Rhythms of the Alaskan Eskimo." *Anthropologie* 26, 1 (1988): 75-82. Although rooted in shamanistic drumming practices of the past, contemporary drumming and singing accompanies mimetic dance. Most rhythms are in 5/8—short-long—patterns and change with changes in the story being danced. The box drum accompanies Messenger Feast dances as well as gift-giving ceremonies.

3535. Johnston, Thomas F. "Song Categories and Musical Style of the Yupik Eskimo." *Anthropos* 84, 4-6 (1989): 423-31.

3536. Johnston, Thomas F. "An Historical Survey of the Yupik Inviting-In Dance." In *Dance: Current Selected Research II*, Lynette Y. Overby and James H. Humphrey, ed. New York: AMS Press, 1990. 139-92.

3537. Johnston, Thomas F. "Context, Meaning, and Function in Inupiaq Dance." In *Dance: Current Selected Research II*, Lynnette Y. Overby and James H. Humphrey, ed. New York: AMS Press, 1990. 193-226.

3538. Johnston, Thomas F. "Contemporary Emphases in Northern Eskimo Dance." *International Review of the Aesthetics and Sociology of Music* 22, 1 (1991): 47-79. Includes a description of the shamanistic origins of many features in the modern Inupiaq re-enactment of the historic Eagle-Wolf Dance of the Messenger Feast. One of these is the drum-leader's movements that derive from the spirit-placation rites of the shaman drummer.

3539. Johnston, Thomas F. "A Historical View of Inupiat Eskimo Dance." *Anthropoplogie* 30, 3 (1992): 41-51. Missionary suppression, the demise of the traditional shaman drummer, language loss, and the rise of wage labor have all contributed to the loss of traditional dance. Religious connotations, such as spirit placation, have given way to affirmation of ethnicity, community solidarity, and other secular, social and psychological functions.

3540. Koranda, Lorraine D. "Some Traditional Songs of the Alaskan Eskimos." In *Anthropological Papers* 12, College, Alaska: University of Alaska, 1964. 17-32. A description of the Messenger Festival and its Wolf Dance, with reference to their shamanistic past.

3541. Koranda, Lorraine D. "Three Songs for the Bladder Festival, Hooper Bay." In *Anthropological Papers*, Vol. 14. College, Alaska: University of Alaska, 1968. 27-31. A brief description, with transcription, of songs sung to honor and appease the spirits of all the animals taken in hunt during the past season.

3542. Koranda, Lorraine D. "Music of the Alaskan Eskimos." In *Musics of Many Cultures*, Elizabeth May, ed. 1980. 332-359.

3543. Lantis, Margaret. *Alaskan Eskimo Ceremonial.* American Ethnological Society Monograph 11. Reissue, Seattle: University of Washington Press, 1939, 1947/repr. 1966. Originally a UCB dissertation. A first attempt to document the ceremonialism of all Alaskan Eskimos. Under two major headings: 1) The Rituals and their Distribution and 2) Ceremonial Elements or Complexes which Occur with Various Types of Ritual, and their Distribution. The latter includes discussion of the shaman's importance in ceremonialism, description of song and dance, and transcriptions of songs.

3544. Lantis, Margaret. "The Religion of the Eskimos." In *Forgotten Religions*, Vergilius Ferm, ed. New York: Philosophical Library, 1950. 309-339. A valuable summary of the main features of Eskimo religion: shamanism, cosmology, and the relationship of society to religion.

3545. Maguire, Marsha. *American Indian and Eskimo Music: A Selected Bibliography through 1981.* Washington, DC: Archive of Folk Culture, Library of Congress, 1983.

3546. McKennan, Robert A. *The Upper Tanana Indians.* New Haven: Yale University Press, 1959. Contains a short but informative section on shamanism and describes several shamanic healing seances that involve the singing of numerous songs. Central Alaska.

3547. Morrow, Phyllis. "It Is Time for Drumming: A Summary of Recent Research on Yup'ik Ceremonialism." *The Central Yup'ik Eskimos. Études/Inuit/Studies* 8 (Suppl. Issue) (1984): 113-40.

3548. Peacock, F.W. "Music of the Eskimo." *Them Days* 12, 2/Dec. (1986): 26-32.

3549. Ray, Dorothy Jean. *Eskimo Masks: Art and Ceremony.* Seattle: University of Washington Press, 1967. See Chap. 3: Masks in Dances and Festivals. The last half of the book consists of many illustrations of masks with explanitory comments.

3550. Riccio, Thomas. "A Message from Eagle Mother: The Messengers-Feast of the Inupiat Eskimo." *TDR—The Drama Review* 37, 1/Spring (1993): 115-146. A description of a Messenger Feast in January of 1988. Dances recounted traditional myths, particularly that of the Great Eagle Mother and her gift to the Inupiat after they danced and sang. The Feast thus reaffirmed Inupiat communal and cultural values.

3551. Spencer, Robert. *The North Alaskan Eskimo, A Study in Ecology and Society.* Bulletin 171, Washington: Smithsonian Institution, Bureau of Ethnology, 1959. Includes informative chapters on the supernatural, shamanism, and the animal cults with some description of associated songs. Arriving in the 1880's, Presbyterian missionaries were welcomed because they undermined the power of the feared shamans with both Christian ideology and medicine.

3552. Tennant, Edward A. and Joseph N. Bitar, ed. Yupik Lore. *Oral Traditions of an Eskimo People.* Bethel, AK: Lower Kuskokwim School District, 1981. A collection of accounts of various aspects of Yupik life. Includes several on shamanism and dance.

3553. Thuren, Hjalmar and William Thalbitzer. *The Eskimo Music.* Copenhagen: 1911.

3554. Turner, Edith. "Style and the Double Mind in Inupiat Eskimo Traditional Performance." *Performing Arts Journal,* 40/January (1992): 87-102. Secular and sacred dances each have their mode of consciousness. The 'Messenger Feast' ritual demonstrates how the release or climactic mode characteristic of sacred dance is generated from the obvious dancing mode of secular dance.

3555. Turner, Edith. "American Eskimos Celebrate the Whale. Structural Dichotomies and Spirit Identities Among the Inupiat of Alaska." *The Drama Review* 37, 1 (1993): 98-114. The annual celebration of the whale season is seen by the Inupiat not in terms of dichotomies and oppositions (Spring/ Summer, male/female, sea/air, etc.), but as a rejoicing for plenty, a giving of thanks to the spirit of the whale, and a reaffirming of cultural cohesion and identity.

3556. Voblov, I.K. "Eskimo Ceremonies." Charles Campbell Hughes, transl. *Anthropological Papers of the University of Alaska* 7, 2 (1958): 71-90. By the early 1930's, shamanic activities had largely been liquidated as a result, first of Russian Orthodox missionaries, then by Soviet Russian officials. Seven ceremonies that survived in some form are described in this account from 1934-1936.

3557. Wallen, Lynn Ager. *The Face of Dance: Yup'ik Eskimo Masks from Alaska.* Calgary, Can.: Glenbow Museum, 1990. A study of masks used in Yup'ik dance ceremonies until Christianization around the turn of the century. The author describes the role of dance masks in transmitting history and knowledge in ceremonial dances and in shamanic presentations, healing seances, and spirit communication. He also explains the differences in the materials and manufacture of sacred as opposed to secular masks.

3558. Weyer, Edward Moffat, Jr. *The Eskimos, Their Environment and Folkways.* Hamden, CT: Archon Books, 1932/repr. 1969. Chapters 14 through 26 provide a full presentation of all aspects of Eskimo religious life and belief, including festivals and Eskimo shamanism.

3559. Williams, Maria. "Contemporary Alaska Native Dance: The Spirit of Tradition." In *Native American Dance: Ceremonies and Social Traditions*, Charlotte Heth, ed. Washington, DC: National Museum of the American Indian, Smithsonian Institution, with Starwood Publishers, 1992. 149-154, 156-167. Suppressed in the earlier part of the century by missionaries and the U.S. Government, Eskimo dance has experienced a resurgence in recent decades. No longer tied to a shamanist past, revitalized, newly adapted dance serves to express gratitude and promote social cohesion and a new-found identity.

THE INUIT OF CANADA AND GREENLAND

3560. Cavanagh, Beverley. *Music of the Netsilik Eskimo: A Study of Stability and Change*. 2 vols. Ottawa: National Museums of Canada, 1982.

3561. Cavanagh, Beverley et al. "Native North Americans in Canada." In *Encyclopedia of Music in Canada*, H. Kallmann, G. Potvin, and K. Winters, ed. Toronto: University of Toronto Press, 1992. 923-935.

3562. Dewar, K. Patricia. *A Historical and Interpretive Study of Inuit Drum Dance in the Canadian Central Arctic: The Meaning Expressed in Dance, Culture, Performance*. Ph.D. diss., University of Alberta, 1990.

3563. Hauser, Michael. "Inuit Songs from Southwest Baffin Island in Cross-Cultural Context." *Etudes Inuit Studies*. 2, 1 (1978): 55-83 and 2, 2: 71-105.

3564. Lutz, Maija M. *The Effects of Acculturation on Eskimo Music of Cumberland Peninsula*. Ottawa: National Museums of Canada, 1978. See Chap. 5. 'Music and Religion: Shaman Activities Versus those of Christianity.' Due to thorough Christianization by Anglican missionaries, most religious music was Christian. Lutz relates some stories about shamans of the past and about the Sedna myth and (sea mammal) festival and the Caribou Festival, both of which included shamanic and other religious songs intended to invoke good spirits and drive away bad ones.

3565. Lutz, Maija M. *Musical Traditions of the Labrador Coast Inuit*. Ottawa: National Museums of Canada, 1982. A history of the conversion of the Inuit to Christianity by the Moravians during the late 18th and 19th centuries and a description of the current state of decline of Moravian church music.

3566. Merkur, Dan. *Becoming Half Hidden: Shamanism and Initiation Among the Inuit*. Hamden, CT: Garland Publishing, 1992. A study of shamanism, including command of spirits through hypnotic trances, from the perspective of shamans. Employs various criteria to show that shamans are expert in the religious uses of alternative psychic states. Compares data from all Inuit groups in Greenland, North America, and Siberia.

3567. Mol, Hans. "Religion and Eskimo Identity in Canada." *Native American Religion and Black Protestantism*, Martin E. Marty, ed. New York: 1993. 66-80. After an account, first observed by Rasmussen in 1923, of a shamanic séance intended to pacify the spirits responsible for a terrible snowstorm, the author describes the elements that make up Eskimo religion. He states that religion, and particularly taboo and shamanic ritual, helps to incorporate into a meaningful and consistent framework the harsh realities and unexpected crises of life. Includes a description of the elaborate death ritual.

3568. Petalaussie, Timanginak et al. "Music of the Inuit." *Musicworks* 23 (1983): 10-16. Toronto: Musicworks. Interviews with Inuit musicians on a variety of subjects, including throat games and the value of old chants.

3569. Rasmussen, Knud. *Intellectual Culture of the Copper Eskimos*. Report of the Fifth Thule Expedition, 1921-1924, Vol. 9, part 1, 1929; part 2, 1930. New York: AMS Press, 1929-1930/repr. 1976. Chapter 1 deals largely with the author's encounter with Copper Eskimo shamans and their explanation of their beliefs and roles. Chap. 7 includes the texts of several shaman songs presented in interlinear translation.

3570. Rasmussen, Knud. *Intellectual Culture of the Iglulik Eskimos*. Report of the Fifth Thule Expedition, 1921-1924, Vol. 7, 1. New York: AMS Press, 1929/ repr. 1976. An absorbing account of Iglulik life and beliefs about life. Includes a chapter on shamans and spirits, and a description of the ceremony for a shaman's journey to the sea spirit.

3571. Rasmussen, Knud. *Observations on the Intellectual Culture of the Caribou Eskimos*. Report of the Fifth Thule Expedition, 1921-1924, New York: AMS Press, 1930/repr. 1976.

3572. Rasmussen, Knud. *The Netsilik Eskimos: Social Life and Spiritual Culture*. W.E. Calvert, transl. Report of the Fifth Thule Expedition, 1921-1924, Vol. 9, no. 1-2. New York: AMS Press, 1931/repr. 1976.

3573. Thalbitzer, William. "The Ammassalik Eskimo." In *Contributions to the Ethnology of the East Greenland Natives*, Copenhagen: Bianco Luno, 1923. 279-290. Includes the texts of 12 religious drum songs (or angakok-shaman songs) with explanation. Most are songs of the shaman's assistant spirit.

3574. Thuren, Hjalmar. "On the Eskimo Music in Greenland." *Meddelelser om Grøland* 40, 1 (1914): 1-45. Also appears in William Thalbitzer, ed., The Ammassalik Eskimo II: Contributions to the Ethnology of the East Greenland Natives, Copenhagen, Denmark. 1914, 1941/repr. 1979 New York: AMS Press. 1-45.

3575. Turner, Lucien M. *Indians and Eskimos in the Quebec-Labrador Peninsula: Ethnology of the Ungava District*. Quebec: Presses Comeditex. 1979.

Reprint from 1894, 11th Annual Report of Bureau of Ethnology. Washington, DC: Smithsonian Institution. 167-350.

36

Oceania

GENERAL REFERENCES AND BIBLIOGRAPHIES

3576. Gourlay, Ken. *A Bibliography of Traditional Music in Papua New Guinea*. Port Moresby, Australia: Institute of Papua New Guinea Studies, 1974/repr. 1980.

3577. Kaeppler, Adrienne. "Bibliography: Hawaiian Hula Pahu." In *Dance—A Multicultural Perspective*, Janet Adshead, ed. Guildford, Surrey, England: National Resource Centre for Dance, University of Surrey, 1986. 49-53.

3578. Koch, G.E. "A Bibliography of Publications on Australian Aboriginal Music: 1975-1985." *Musicology Australia* 10 (1987): 58-70. 121 annotated entries. See index, p. 68, under music and belief.

3579. McLean, Mervyn. *An Annotated Bibliography of Oceanic Music and Dance*. Memoirs of the Polynesian Society, Vol. 41, Wellington, NZ: Polynesian Society, 1977. An extensive bibliography with no subject index.

3580. McLean, Mervyn. *Supplement: An Annotated Bibliography of Oceanic Music and Dance*. Auckland, NZ: Polynesian Society, 1981.

3581. Moyle, Alice M. "Source Materials: Aboriginal Music of Australia and New Guinea." *Ethnomusicology* 15, 1 (1971): 81.

3582. Moyle, Richard. "Music and Religion in Australia and Oceania." In *Encyclopedia of Religion*, Mircea Eliade, ed. Vol. 10. 1987. 176-178.

3583. Murphy, Kevin B., ed. "Music in the Pacific Islands." *Point* 2, 1 (1973): 1-162.

3584. Smith, Barbara B. and Adrienne L. Kaeppler. "Pacific Islands." In *Grove 6*, Vol. 14. 1980. 57-65.

3585. Stillman, Amy Ku'uleialoha. "Annotated Bibliography of Hula." In *The Hula*, J. Hopkins, ed. Hong Kong: APA Productions, 1982. 180.

3586. Stoneburner, B.C., comp. *Hawaiian Music: An Annotated Bibliography*. The Music Reference Collection, no. 10, Westport, CT: Greenwood Press, 1986.

3587. Swain, Tony. *Aboriginal Religions in Australia. A Bibliographical Survey*. Westport, CT: Greenwood Press, 1991. First three chapters review Western attitudes toward Aborigine religion, identify themes, and describe geographical areas. Remaining chapters present references by area. A superb bibliography, fully annotated.

ABORIGINES OF AUSTRALIA

3588. Appleton, Richard, et al. "Aborigines." In *The Australian Encyclopedia*, Terry Hills, NSW: Australian Geographical Society, 1988.

3589. Barwick, Linda. "Central Australian Women's Ritual Music: Knowing through Analysis Versus Knowing through Performance." *YTM* 22 (1990): 60-79. Without recourse to field experience, but fortified by various forms of indirect data, the author arrives at one kind of understanding of Aboriginal ritual music through analysis of text, melody and their intermeshing during the process of performance.

3590. Basedow, H. "Music and Dance." In *The Australian Aboriginal*, New York: AMS Press, 1925, 1929/repr. 1979. 371 ff.

3591. Berndt, Ronald M. "Other Creatures in Human Guise *and* Vice Versa: A Dilemma in Understanding." In *Songs of Aboriginal Australia*, Margaret Clunies Ross, Tamsin Donaldson, and Stephen A. Wild, ed. Sydney: University of Sydney, 1987.

3592. Berndt, Ronald M. and Catherine H. Berndt. *Arnhem Land: Its History and Its People*. Melbourne: F.W. Cheshire, 1954. Song-cycles, totems and rituals provide evidence for contact with pre-Macassans, Macassans, Europeans and Japanese. Contains an overview of religious practice.

3593. Berndt, Ronald M. and Catherine H. Berndt. *The World of the First Australians*. Sidney: Ure Smith, 1964. Chapter 11 on Art and Aesthetic Expression details the use of sacred songs, dance and drama in ritual as well as the selection and creative process behind song traditions. Includes numerous song texts and ritual accounts.

3594. Berndt, Ronald M. and Catherine H. Berndt. *The Australian Aboriginal Heritage: An Introduction through the Arts.* Sydney: Australian Society for Education through the Arts, 1973.

3595. Davies, E.H. "Paleolithic Music (Australia)." *Musical Times* 68 (1927): 691 ff. A study of the musical and anthropological qualities of music of the Aboriginees of Central Australia for totem and initiation rites. Includes transcripts of songs and descriptions of religious rites.

3596. Davies, E.H. "Music in Primitive Society." *Occasional Publications of the Anthropological Society of South Australia* Vol. 2 (1947).

3597. Elkin, A.P. *The Australian Aborigines: How To Understand Them.* 4th ed., Sidney: The University of Sydney, 1964. Within this classic anthropological study of Aboriginal peoples, Chapter 10, on Music and Dancing, provides both a descriptive and analytical study of sacred traditions. Chapter 9, a study of art and ritual by geographic area, provides nuanced contextual material on Aboriginal belief systems.

3598. Elkin, A.P. and T. Jones. *Arnhem Land Music, North Australia.* The Oceania Monographs, No. 9, Sydney: University of Sydney Press, 1957. In this two-part study, religious music is divided into two categories, sacred and secret, with the ritualistic distinction between the two described in some detail. Part One is concerned mainly with anthropological background, Part Two consists of musical analysis, transcripts and surveys. Originally appeared in *Oceania*, Vols. 24-26, 1953-56.

3599. Ellis, Catherine J. *Aboriginal Music Making. A Study of Central Australian Music.* Adelaide: Libraries Board of South Australia, 1964. Although the book consists primarily of a transcription of a group of sacred songs, it contains a brief but useful discription of the basic types of music making of which the most important and numerous is sacred and secret ceremonies.

3600. Ellis, Catherine J. "The Pitjantjara Kangaroo Song from Kariga." *Miscellanea Musicologica* 2 (1967): 171-267. A detailed, verse by verse analysis of a non-secret, pre-initiation song with reference to its relationship to and difference from the Dog Song. Includes a complete musical transcript.

3601. Ellis, Catherine J. "Structure and Significance in Aboriginal Song." *Mankind* 7, June (1969): 3-14. Ellis reviews the relevant musical theory as well as the structural qualities of Aboriginal songs in an attempt to answer what Aboriginal music communicates both within Aboriginal communities and to outsiders.

3602. Ellis, Catherine J. "The Role of the Ethnomusicologist in the Study of Andagarinja Women's Ceremonies." *Miscellanea Musicologica* 5 (1970): 76-208.

3603. Ellis, Catherine J. "Functions and Features of Central and South Australian Aboriginal Music." In *Autstralian Aboriginal Music*, J. Isaacs, ed. Sydney: Aboriginal Artists Agency, 1979. 23-26. A study of the role of songs in drawing on the spiritual and generative powers of the Dreaming. Also outlines the formal characteristics of the music.

3604. Ellis, Catherine J. "Australia, Folkmusic of: Aboriginal Music and Dance (south of the Tropic of Capricorn)." In *Grove 6*, Vol. 1. 1980.

3605. Ellis, Catherine J. "Time Consciousness of Aboriginal Performers." In *Problems and Solutions: Occasional Essays in Musicology Presented to Alice M. Moyle*, J.C. Kassler and J. Stubington, ed. Sydney, Australia: Hale and Iremonger, 1984. 149-185. Ellis considers the musical, anthropological and religio-philosophical factors in her study of "perfect time" among the Aborigines of northern South Australia, to support her theory that time structure is used to express "the timelessness of the Dreaming."

3606. Ellis, Catherine J. *Aboriginal Music: Education for Living: Cross-Cultural Experiences from South Australia*. St. Lucia: University of Queensland Press, 1985. Eliis presents a series of important issues for cross-cultural and inter-cultural living through her study of the music and performance of the Pitjantjatjara people. Chapter 2, on "Experience and Message." highlights the mythic, spiritual and religious aspects.

3607. Ellis, Catherine J. "Powerful Songs: Their Placement in Aboriginal Thought." *The World of Music* 36, 1 (1994): 3-20.

3608. Ellis, Catherine J., ed. *Power-Laden Australian Aboriginal Songs: Who Should Control the Research*. The World of Music, 36, 1. Wilhelmshaven, Germany: Florian Noetzel Edition, 1994. A series of articles on the problems and responsibilities that come into play when researchers are allowed into the religious world of the Aborigines.

3609. Genova, Vincent Anthony. *Torres Strait Island Music: A Cantometric Study*. Ph.D. diss., University of Pittsburgh, 1991.

3610. Jones, Trevor A. "Arnhem Land Music: A Musical Survey." *Oceania* 26 (1956): 252-339, part 2: 28 (1957): 1-30. Annotated transcript of songs, most of which are broadly religious in theme and/or have ritualistic purpose.

3611. Jones, Trevor A. "Australian Aboriginal Music: The Elkin Collection's Contribution toward an Overall Picture." In *Aboriginal Man in Australia*, R.M. and C.H. Berndt, ed. Sydney: Angus and Robertson, 1965. 283-374. An analysis of comparative tables of scalar material in the Elkin recordings with an eye to drawing conclusions about the overall style of Aboriginal music, both sacred and secular.

3612. Jones, Trevor A. "The Nature of Australian Aboriginal Music." *Australian Journal of Music Education* 2, April (1968): 9-13. A brief survey of the ethnomusicological research completed thus far with attention to melody, metre, rhythm, and the sacred role of the didjeridu.

3613. Jones, Trevor A. "The Traditional Music of the Australian Aborigines." In *Music of Many Cultures*, Elizabeth May, ed. 1980. 154-171.

3614. Kaberry, Phyllis M. "Death and Deferred Mourning Ceremonies in the Forest River Tribes, North-West Australia." *Oceania* 6, 1 (1935): 33-47. Provides a detailed description of mourning ceremonies, as well as of those who are in close contact with the spirits of the dead, who can detect the spirits that cause death, and who know the fate of the human spirit.

3615. Kassler, Jamie C. and Jill Stubington, ed. *Problems and Solutions: Occasional Essays in Musicology Presented to Alice M. Moyle*. Sidney: Hale and Iremonger, 1984. This collection of musicological studies of Aboriginal music includes several concerned with some aspect aboriginal musical culture broadly understood to be religious and/or ritualistic. Three articles of interest are Ellis' "Time Consciousness of Aboriginal Performers," Wild's "Walabiri Music and Culture," and Payne's "Residency and Ritual Rights."

3616. Keen, Ian. "Ambiguity in Yolngu Religious Language." *Canberra Anthropologist* 1, 1 (1977): 33-50. On the language of song and variation in interpretation as influenced by esoteric knowledge. Discusses Gunabibi songs in particular.

3617. Keen, Ian. "Images of Reproduction in the Yolngu Madayin Ceremony." *TAJA: The Australian Journal of Anthropology* 1, 2-3 (1990): 192-207.

3618. Kimber, Robert James. *Performance Space as Sacred Space in Aranda Corroboree—An Interpretation of the Organization and Use of Space as a Dramatic Element in the Performance of Selected Aboriginal Rituals in Central Australia*. Ph.D. diss., University of Colorado at Boulder, 1988. Concerning its use of space, aboriginal corroboree, or communal theatre, is compared to Ancient Greek theatre and to the environmental theatre of Richard Schechner. Corroboree as ritual is examined according to the theories of Mircea Eliade on the sacred and the centre, as well as of Victor Turner and Johathon Z. Smith.

3619. Lommel, Andreas. "Shamanism in Northwest Australia." *Oceania* 64, 4 (1994): 277-287. A memoir from 1938 concerning an encounter with a shaman-poet in the Kimberley Division, Western Australia. The author describes ceremonies he witnessed and recounts the shaman's explanation of how he learns songs and dances: while in trance, in the land of ancestral spirits. The memoir is followed by a discussion, in 1993, with one of the Ngarinyin people encountered in 1938, who describes how the power of nature, in this case certain snakes, was used to cure leprosy.

3620. Matthews, R.H. "Bull-roarers used by the Australian Aborigines." *Journal of the Royal Anthropological Institute of New Britain and Ireland* 27 (1898): 58 ff.

3621. May, Elizabeth and Stephen Wild. "Aboriginal Music on the Laverton Reservation." *Ethnomusicology* 11, May (1967): 207-17. This study of men's and women's songs at a Western Australia reservation includes descriptions of the men's sacred initiation songs.

3622. McCarthy, F.D. "The Dancers of Aurukun." *Australian Natural History* 14 (1964): 296 ff. McCarthy discusses the religious and totemistic beliefs as well as the practical inspiration behind Aboriginal dance, providing detailed accounts of several dances. Includes photographs of dances described.

3623. Morphy, Howard. "From Dull to Brilliant: The Aesthetics of Spiritual Power Among the Yolngu." *Man* 24, 1 (1989): 21-40. The quality of brilliance is associated in Yolngu art with Ancestral beings and their power and with beauty. A painting is considered both a manifestation of the being concerned and an icon (that which encodes meaning) of the Ancestral events depicted. Brilliant art and body painting, songs, dances, incantations, and ritual action combine to achieve the goals of ritual.

3624. Morton, John. "Singing Subjects and Sacred Objects: A Psycyhological Interpretation of the 'Transformation of Subjects into Objects' in Central Australian Myth." *Oceania* 59, 4/June (1989): 280-298. A study of the relationship between singing communication, the body, and the environment central to Aranda myth and rite, and of how various oppositions are realized and reconciled in Arandan myths.

3625. Moyle, Alice M. "Aboriginal Music on Cape York." *Musicology* 3 (1968): 3-20. A descriptive account of the music of Cape York Aborigines with reference to male cultic and initiation songs.

3626. Moyle, Alice M., ed. *Music and Dance of Aboriginal Australia and the South Pacific: The Effects of Documentation on the Living Tradition.* Oceania Monograph, Sydney, Australia: University of Sydney, 1992.

3627. Moyle, Alice M. and Catherine J. Ellis. "Australia II." In *Grove 6*, Vol. 1. 1980. 711-728.

3628. Moyle, Richard. *Songs of the Pintupi: Musical Life in a Central Australian Society.* Canberra: Australian Institute of Aboriginal Studies; Atlantic Highlands, NJ: Humanities Press, 1979. Song plays the central role in all Aboriginal ceremonies. Topics covered are categories of song (according to ceremony), music instruments, music ethnography (a description of performances) including issues of song origin and ownership, and musical analysis.

3629. Moyle, Richard. "Songs, Ceremonies and Sites: The Agharringa Case." In *Aborigines, Land and Land Rights*, N. Peterson and M. Langton, ed. Canberra: Australian Institute of Aboriginal Studies, 1983. 66-93. Individual songs are associated with ceremonies as well as with ancestral events that took place at specific locations. This article looks at the relationship between ceremony ownership and land ownership in Alyawarra territory. Includes issues related to routes of Dreaming lines.

3630. Moyle, Richard. *Alyawarra Music: Songs and Society in a Central Australian Community*. Canberra: Australian Institute of Aboriginal Studies, 1986. In this exemplary study, four song categories, with varying degrees of religious associations, are described and analysed in their ritual context. Includes a sound recording of the various song types. Done with the help of Slippery Morton, Alyawarra interpreter.

3631. Payne, Helen E. "The Integration of Music and Belief in Australian Aboriginal Culture." *Religious Traditions* 1, April (1978): 8-18. Ancestors can be felt or touched through the melodic line and interval structure unique to the songs of each ancestor. By re-actualizing Dreaming beings in this way, music is able to draw on supernatural forces at specific physical locations.

3632. Ross, Margaret Clunies, Tamsin Donaldson, and Stephen A. Wild, ed. *Songs of Aboriginal Australia*. Sydney: University of Sydney, 1987. Nine essays on the single most important form of Aboriginal music, accompanied song.

3633. Rudder, J. C. "The Song of the Turtle Rope." *Canberra Anthropologist* 3, 1 (1980): 37-47. An analysis of a Yolngu myth. Advocates a combined approach to the understanding of myth: links Aboriginal esoteric explication with structural and functional analysis of myth told by an elder of the Djambarrpuyngu clan.

3634. Stanner, W.E.H. *On Aboriginal Religion*. Sydney: University of Sydney, 1966. Although Stanner never focusses explicitly on the style and function of religious dance and music, reference to the ceremonial role of both is made throughout the text, especially in chapters one and two (Lineaments of Sacrifice and Sacrementalism; Rite and Myth).

3635. Strehlow, T.G.H. *Songs of Central Australia*. Sydney: Angus and Robertson, 1971. This lengthy, model study of Aboriginal culture includes explanation of the Dreaming as the source of Aboriginal song.

3636. Von Sturmer, John. "Aboriginal Singing and Notions of Power." In *Songs of Aboriginal Australia*, Margaret Clunies Ross, Tamsin Donaldson, and Stephen A. Wild, ed. Sydney: University of Sydney, 1987. 63-76. Discusses Aboriginal belief in the ability of ancient song forms to confer power, to call spirits into the presence of the song, and in the power of spirits to manipulate the environment.

3637. Waterman, Richard. "Music in Australian Aboriginal Culture: Sociological and Psychological Implications." *Journal of Music Therapy* 5 (1955). Also in *The Garland Library of Readings in Ethnomusicology*, Vol. 7.

3638. Watson, Eliot L.G. "The Sacred Dance: Corroboree of Natives of North-West Australia." *English Review* 38 (1924): 817-827. A description of the non-secret aspects of a pre-initiatory ceremony.

3639. Wild, Stephen A. *Walbiri Music and Dance in Their Social and Cultural Nexus*. Ph.D. diss., University of Indiana, 1975. Music and dance, the central focus of all Walbiri Aborigine rituals, express their belief in the supernatural power of their ancestors and their creation myths.

3640. Wild, Stephen A. "Men as Women: Female Dance Symbolism in Walbiri Men's Rituals." *Dance Research Journal* Vol. 10, 1 (1977): 14-22. A summary of work carried out at Lajamanu. Includes such topics as circumcision and Gadjari ritual, music and dance, and the symbolism of men dressed as women.

3641. Wild, Stephen A. "Primeval Music in Australia." *World Association for Christian Communication Journal* 26, 2 (1979): 15-17. A survey of the different genres of traditional music and the social and religious contexts in which it is performed.

3642. Wild, Stephen A. "Recreating the Jukurrpa: Adaptation and Innovation of Songs and Ceremonies in Walbiri." In *Songs of Aboriginal Australia*, Margaret Clunies Ross, Tamsin Donaldson, and Stephen A. Wild, ed. Sydney: University of Sydney, 1987. 97-120. Includes detailed examples of how new songs are learned from spirit familiars through dreams.

3643. Worms, E.A. "Australian Ghost Drums, Trumpets and Poles." *Anthropos* 48 (1953): 278 ff.

MELANESIA

3644. Mantovani, Ennio. "Celebrations of Cosmic Renewal." *Point Series*, No. 6 (1984): 147-168. A study of Melanesian regeneration mythology and associated rites.

3645. Read, W.J. "A Snake Dance of the Baining." *Oceania* 2 (1931): Melbourne. From the Toloi people of New Britain. See also Bateson, G., 'Further Notes on a Snake Dance of the Baining,' *Oceania*, 2 (1931-2); and Poole, J., 'Still Further Notes on a Snake Dance of the Baining,' *Oceania*, 13 (1942-43).

3646. Smith, Barbara B., et al. "Melanesia." In *Grove 6*, Vol. 12. 1980. 80-96.

3647. Wagner, Roy. "Ritual as Communication: Order, Meaning, and Secrecy in Melanesian Purification Rites." *Annual Review of Anthropology* 13 (1984): 143-155.

3648. Zemp, Hugo. "'Are'Are Classification of Musical Types and Instruments." *Ethnomusicology* 22, 1 (1978): 37-67. Sacred instruments, songs and ritual performance are discussed in relation to their role in classifying and ranking the four musical types among the 'Are 'Are people of the Solomon Islands.

Papua New Guinea

3649. Chenoweth, Vida. *The Usarufas and their Music*. Dallas, TX: Sil Museum of Anthropology, 1979. This systematic study of the music of a New Guinea tribe is divided between ethnography and musical analysis. It includes a few references to the ritual or magical use of music and dance.

3650. Feld, Steven. "Sound as Symbolic System: the Kaluli Drum." In *Explorations in Ethnomusicology: Essays in Honor of David P. McAllester*, Charlotte Frisbie, ed. Detroit: Detroit Monographs in Musicology, 9, 1986. 147-158. Papua, New Guinea.

3651. Feld, Steven. *Sound and Sentiment: Birds, Weeping, Poetics, and Song in Kaluli Expression*. 2nd ed., Philadelphia: University of Pennsylvania Press, 1990. According to Kaluli mythology, the spirits of the dead become birds in order to communicate with those they have left behind. Bird sounds are thus talk from the dead, song music and text represent bird cries and sound words, and weeping represents the song of a *muni* bird, a song that expresses the feelings of abandonment and loss of the dead. Kaluli are able to share in these feelings through song. A masterful achievement of embedding 'music' in its cultural context.

3652. Feld, Steven. "Aesthetics and Synesthesia in Kaluli Ceremonial Dance." *UCLA Journal of Dance Ethnology* 14 (1990): 1-16.

3653. Frisbie, Charlotte J. "Sound as a Symbolic System: The Kaluli Drum." In *Explorations in Ethnomusicology. Essays in Honor of David P. McAllester*, Charlotte J. Frisbie, ed. Detroit Monographs in Musicology, Vol. 9. Detroit, MI: Detroit Information Coordinators, 1986. 147-158. The Kaluli have invented an interpretive logic for hearing the correspondence between sounds and the deeply held sentiments they communicate: an examination of the artifact, sound, construction, play and performance, and 8 levels of metaphoric meaning of the Kaluli drum.

3654. Gell, Alfred. *Metamorphosis of the Cassowaries: Umeda Society, Language, and Ritual*. Monographs on social anthropology, Vol. 51. London: Athlone Press, 1975. On the ceremonies of the Umeda of Papua New Guinea.

3655. Glick, L.B. "Musical Instruments in Ritual." In *Encyclopedia of Papua and New Guinea*, P. Ryan, ed. Melbourne, Australia 1972.

3656. Hays, Terence E. "Sacred Flutes, Fertility, and Growth in the Papua New Guinea Highlands." *Anthropos* 81, 4-6 (1986): 435-53. Topics include distribution of the Highlands Sacred Flute Complex, native representations and public dogma—flute sounds as male spirits, as the voices of supernatural birds, of female or female-hostile spirits, of the ancestors, etc.—ceremonial contexts, sacred flutes and men's subjugation of women, and the central theme: male power over reproductive power expressed in male initiation ceremonies and pig festivals.

3657. Knapp, Bettina L. "Ceremonies and Rituals on the Trobriand Islands of Papua, New Guinea." *Arabesque* 11, 4 (1985): 4-7, 25. Part 2: 11, 5 (1986): 4-5, 17-18.

3658. Messner, Gerald Florian. "The Shark-Calling Ceremony in Paruai, New Ireland, Papua New Guinea." *The World of Music* 32, 1 (1990): 49-83. A study of the magico-religious performance of music in the shark-calling ceremony. Includes sections on the socio-mythic universe of shark callers, interviews, and analysis and transcription of songs.

3659. Moyle, Alice M. "Music (1) [Papua and New Guinea]." In *Encyclopedia of Papua and New Guinea*, P. Ryan, ed. Melbourne, Australia 1972.

3660. Niles, Don. "Spirits Given Substance through Sound: Men's Cult Usage of Voice Modifiers in Papua New Guinea." In *Tradition and its Future in Music*, Tokumaru Yoshiko et al., ed. Tokyo: Mita Press, 1991. 237-241. Gourd, bamboo, coconut shell, grass or leaf, bullroarer, and dried fruit husks are used to produce spirit voices.

3661. Pospisil, Leopold. *The Kapauku Papuans of West New Guinea*. New York: Holt, Reinhart and Winston, 1963, 1978. Part one of Chapter 4 includes references to the limited role and simple style of the religious music and dance of the Kapauku.

3662. Schieffelin, Edward L. *The End of Traditional Music, Dance, and Body Decoration in Basavi, Papua New Guinea*. Boroko: Institute of Papua New Guinea Studies, 1978. discussion paper, 30/31/32.

3663. Sheridan, R. J. "Music (2)." In *Encyclopedia of Papua and New Guinea*, Peter Ryan, ed. Melbourne, Australia: Melbourne University Press, 1972.

3664. Sillitoe, P. "A Ritual Response to Climatic Perturbations in the Highlands of Papua, New Guinea." *Ethnology* 32, 2 (Spring, 1993): 169-185.

3665. Tuzin, Donald F. *Sound, Ritual and 'Peak Experience.'* New York: Wenner-Gren Foundation for Anthropological Research, 1973.

3666. Williams, Francis E. *The Vailala Madness and the Destruction of Native Ceremonies in the Gulf Division.* Territory of Papua. Anthropological Report, Indianapolis, IN: Bobbs-Merrill, 1923/repr. 1960, 1969.

MICRONESIA

3667. Burrows, Edwin G. *Flower in My Ear: Arts and Ethos of Ifaluk Atoll.* Seattle, WA: University of Washington Press, 1963. The social, religious, and ceremonial functions of the dance, music and sung poetry of the Ifaluk are described in Part One, Chapters 2 and 3.

3668. Lawson, Mary Elizabeth. *Tradition, Change and Meaning in Kiribati Performance: An Ethnography of Music and Dance in a Micronesian Society.* Ph.D. diss., Brown University, 1989.

3669. Smith, Barbara B., et al. "Micronesia." In *Grove 6*, Vol. 12. 1980. 271-79.

3670. Yamaguchi, O. "Music as Behavior in Ancient Palau." In *Kikkawa Festschrift*, Tokyo, Japan 1973. 547 ff.

POLYNESIA

3671. Burrows, Edwin G. "Some Paumotu Chants." *Journal of the Polynesian Society* 12 (1903): 221 ff.

3672. Burrows, Edwin G. *Native Music of the Tuamotus.* Honolulu: Bishop Museum Bulletin 109, 1933. Burrows analyses the musical elements of 83 songs transcribed from the repertory of the various peoples of the Tuamotu Archipelago. Songs representing three specifically religious categories—solemn chants, laments, and incantational prayers—are presented.

3673. Burrows, Edwin G. "Music of the Tahaki Chants." In *The Legends of Mani and Tahaki*, Bulletin No. 127 of the Ber. F. Bishop Museum, Honolulu: Bishop Museum Bulletin 127, 1934.

3674. Burrows, Edwin G. "Polynesian Music and Dancing." *Journal of the Polynesian Society* 49, September (1940): 331-46. The two stated objectives of this article are to summarize the current data on Polynesian music and dance and to suggest avenues for further research. While stressing the recreational aspects of Polynesian music, Burrows does discuss much material with religious function and theme.

3675. Burrows, Edwin G. *Songs of Uvea and Futuna.* Honolulu: Bishop Museum Bulletin 183, 1945. In contrast to the Ethnologies of these two culture groups, in which the author divides their cultures into discrete categories with no attempt at integration or examination of cross relationships, Burrows here provides socio-historical background on religiously significant songs and dances, followed by detailed analysis of their musical characteristics.

3676. Emory, K. "Tuamotuan Chants and Songs from Napuka." In *Directions in Pacific Traditional Literature*, Adrienne L. Kaeppler, ed. Honolulu, HI: Bishop Museum Press, 1976.

3677. Firth, Raymond. *Tikopia Ritual and Belief*. London: Allen and Unwin; Boston: Beacon Press, 1967. Spirit possession and mediumship among Pacific islanders. See esp. Chap. 3.

3678. Firth, Raymond. *The Work of the Gods in Tikopia*. London School of Economic Monographs on Social Anthropology, Vol. 1-2. London: Althone, 1967. See Chap. 8 and 9 for detailed descriptions of pre-Christian religious songs. 1940 edition contains fuller vernacular texts.

3679. Firth, Raymond with Mervyn McLean. *Tikopia Songs: Poetic and Musical Art of a Polynesian People of the Solomon Islands*. Cambridge Studies in Oral and Literate Culture, New York: Cambridge University Press, 1990. A thorough and sensitive study of the full range of Tikopian songs, including sacred chants and dance songs, by Britain's most distinguished living anthropologist. The study is in three parts: 1) general, 2) musical analysis (provided by Mervyn McLean), and 3) song texts, translation and commentary on several dozen songs. Since the complete conversion of the Tikopia to Christianity in 1955, little remains of the pre-Christian religious song. The author groups what remains under the headings of major traditional pagan gods, lesser spiritual beings, and ancestors.

3680. Handy, E.S. Craighill and J.L. Winne. *Music in the Marquesas Islands*. Honolulu, HI: Bishop Museum Bulletin 17, 1925/repr. 1971. The authors present both the texts and musical analysis of two categories of song: *tapu* (sacred) music and non-*tapu* (recreational) music, along with historical background and description of rituals.

3681. Jeannette, Marie Mageo. "M'ai Aitu: The Cultural Logic of Possession in Samoa." *Ethos* 19, September (1991): 352-383. Possession in Samoa is used to cure a girl's spiritual sickness by replacing her conscious personality with that of Teine, the cultural ideal of the feminine. The ceremony includes song.

3682. Kaeppler, Adrienne L. "Folklore as Expressed in the Dance in Tonga." *Journal of American Folklore* 80, April-June (1967): 160-168. The author limits her study to dance forms that serve as accompaniment to *lakalaka* poetry. These dances aid in transmitting ideas of cosmology and sacredness as well as promoting the socio-political order.

3683. Kaeppler, Adrienne L. "Preservation and Evolution of Form and Function in Two Types of Tongan Dance." In *Polynesian Culture History*, G.A. Highland et al., ed. Honolulu: Bishop Museum, 1967. 503-536. The preservative impact of Catholic Christianity on the *me'etu'upaki* dance form is compared with the evolutionary impact of Wesleyan Christianity on the function of the *me'elaufola* dance on this group of islands south of Fiji and Samoa.

3684. Kaeppler, Adrienne L. *Tongan Musical Genres in Ethnoscientific and Ethnohistoric Perspective.* Paper Presented at the Annual Meeting of the Society for Ethnomusicology, Toronto, Toronto: 1972.

3685. Moyle, Richard. "Samoan Song Types." Studies in Music, Vol. 6. Nedlands: University of Western Australia Press, 1972. 55-67. Moyle examines seven of an estimated 32 song types in Samoan culture with attention to musical features specific to a particular style. The mythologically themed Tagi of the Fagono and the ritualistic Incantation songs are discussed with song texts and transcripts included for each.

3686. Moyle, Richard M. "Samoan Medicinal Incantations." *Journal of the Polynesian Society* 83 (1974): 155-179.

3687. Parsons, Claire D. F., ed. *Healing Practices in the South Pacific.* Honolulu: Institute for Polynesian Studies, 1985.

3688. Rabukawaga, Joshua. "The Little People: Early Fijian Music." *Point* 2, 1 (1973): 28-39. Includes a discussion of religious dance and spirit worship.

3689. Smith, Barbara B. "Music of Polynesia." In *Proceedings of the Centennial Worlshop in Ethnomusicology*, Peter Crossley-Holland, ed.: Government of the Province of British Columbia, 1968. 94-101. A discussion of the relation of Polynesian music to that of other cultures.

3690. Smith, Barbara B., et al. "Polynesia." In *Grove 6*, Vol. 15. 1980. 54-70.

Hawaii

3691. Beamer, Nona, ed. *Na Mele Hula, A Collection of Hawaiian Hula Chants.* Honolulu, HI: The Institute for Polynesian Studies, Brigham Young University—Hawaii Campus, 1987. A description, translation, and transcription of 33 chants divided into four groups: nature chants, chiefs chants, place chants, and volcano goddess chants.

3692. Donaldson, Beth Allegra Kahikina. *Ka makana hula: "The Gift of Hula", the Proclamation and Healing of the Hawaiian Hula.* M.A. thesis, Pacific School of Religion, 1991.

3693. Emerson, Nathaniel B. *Unwritten Literature of Hawaii. The Sacred Songs of the Hula.* St. Clair Shores, MI: Scholarly Press Inc, 1909/repr. 1965.

1906 ed. published by Bureau of Ethnology, Bulletin No. 38. Washington, DC: Smithsonian Institute.

3694. Hausman, Ruth L. *Hawaii: Music in Its History*. Rutland, VT: Charles E. Tuttle Co., 1968.

3695. Johnson, Rubellite K. *Kumulipo: The Hawaiian Hymn of Creation*. Honolulu, HI: Topgallant Publishing Co., 1981.

3696. Kaeppler, Adrienne L. "Music in Hawaii in the Nineteenth Century." In *Musikkulturen Asiens, Afrikas un Ozeaniens im 19. Jahrhundert*, Robert Günther, ed. Regensburg: Gustav Bosse Verlag, 1973. 331-38.

3697. Kaeppler, Adrienne L. "Acculturation in Hawaiian Dance." *YIFMC* 4 (1973): 38-46. The author traces the process of acculturation due to European Protestant influence as it changed Hawaiian dance from a sophisticated poetic form to a largely simplistic pantomine-based dance form.

3698. Kaeppler, Adrienne L. (Vol. 1) and Elizabeth Tatar (Vol. 2). *Hula Pahu: Hawaiian Drum Dances*. Honolulu, HI: Bishop Museum Press, 1993. Vol. 1. *Ha'a and Hula Pahu: Sacred Movements*. With Laba notation by Judy Van Zile. An attempt to discover and reconstruct the structured movements of indigenous Hawai'ian ritual dance. Vol. 2. *The Pahu: Sounds of Power*. With music notation ed. by Barbara B. Smith. A study of the Pahu (sacred drum), with rhythms in music notation and the spectral analysis of various drum sounds.

3699. Kahananui, Dorothy M. *Music of Ancient Hawaii, A Brief Survey*. Honolulu, HI: University of Hawaii, 1962 (1960).

3700. Kahananui, Dorothy M. "Influences on Hawaiian Music." In *The Kamehameha Schools 75th Anniversary Lectures*, Honolulu: The Kamehameha Schools Press, 1965. 117-37.

3701. Kanahele, George S., ed. *Hawaiian Music and Musicians: An Illustrated History*. Honolulu, HI: University of Hawaii Press, 1979. A well-written and illustrated encyclopedia of musical terms and influential musicians.

3702. Kealiinohomoku, Joann. "Music and Dance of the Hawaiian and Hopi Peoples." In *Art in Small-scale Societies: Contemporary Readings*, R. L. Anderson and K. L. Field, ed. Englewood Cliffs, NJ: Prentice-Hall, 1993. 334-48. An investigation and comparison of the changes in the musical repertories of both cultures due to external influences. Good sections on the relationship of myths to Hawaiian music and religion to Hopi music. Also in David P. McAllester, ed. *Becoming Human through Music*. 1985. 5-22.

3703. Marques, A. "Ancient Hawaiian Music." *Hawaiian Annual* (1914): 97-107.

3704. Roberts, Helen H. *Ancient Hawaiian Music*. New York: Dover, 1926/repr. 1967.

3705. Silva, Kalena. "Hawaiian Chant: Dynamic Cultural Link or Atrophied Relic?" *Journal of the Polynesian Society* 98, 1 (1989): 85-90. According to Hawai'ian tradition, skillfully chanted language possessed *mana*—power— derived from a spiritual source. In almost total decline by the 1960s, chanted Hawai'ian has been revived, particularly in conjunction with performance of *hâlau hula,* and may again be spoken with a spontaneity and fluency sufficient to make *mana* once again available to the individual speaker and to Hawai'ian culture.

3706. Tatar, Elizabeth. *Hawaiian Chant: Mode and Music*. Ph.D. diss., UCLA, 1978.

3707. Tatar, Elizabeth. *Nineteenth-Century Hawaiian Chant*. Anthropological Records 33, Honolulu, HI: Department of Anthropology, Bernice P. Bishop Museum, 1982. A study diagnosing what is Hawaiian in Hawaiian chants through cultural, linguistic, and acoustic analysis of 19th century chant and secondary sources. Characterized by meticulous research, excellent illustrations, and the exhaustive use of primary texts.

3708. Valeri, Valerio. *Kingship and Sacrifice: Ritual and Society in Ancient Hawaii*. Paula Wissing, transl. Chicago: University of Chicago Press, 1985.

3709. Wong, Kaupena. "Ancient Hawaiian Music." In *The Kamehameha Schools 75th Anniversary Lectures*, Honolulu: The Kamehameha Schools Press, 1965. 9-15.

Maori of New Zealand

3710. Andersen, Johannes C. *The Maori Tohunga and His Spirit World*. New York: AMS Press, 1948 (repr.).

3711. Barrow, Tul Terrence. *Traditional and Modern Music of the Maori*. Wellington, NZ: Seven Seas Publishing Co., 1965. Barrow chronicles the history of Maori music and dance as it changed from an art form with precise religious and social functions to a less strictly regulated form of entertainment.

3712. McLean, Mervyn and Margaret Orbell. *Traditional Songs of the Maori*. London: Oxford University Press, 1975/rev. repr. 1991.

3713. Youngerman, Suzanne. "Maori Dancing Since the Eighteenth Century." *Ethnomusicology* 18, January (1974): 75-100. A study of Maori ritual dances beginning with the first accounts in the journals of Captain James Cook.

CHRISTIAN MUSIC IN OCEANIA

3714. Cole, David R. *Music-making in the Contemporary Anglican Eucharistic Liturgy: A Theological and Practical Investigation, with Special Reference to the Liturgy of the Church in the Diocese of Newcastle, New South Wales, Australia.* D. Min. thesis, San Francisco Theological Seminary, 1990.

3715. Dawia, Alexander. "Indigenizing Christian Worship." *Point* 9, 1 (1980): 13-69. [Melanesian Association of Theological Schools Study Institute]. On the incorporation of indigenous dance in Christian worship in Melanesia.

3716. Iga, Carolyn Sanae. *A Study of the History of Hawaiian Music in Relation to the Development of the Christian Faith.* MCM, The Southern Baptist Theological Seminary, 1991. Hawaiian Protestantism in Hawaii and the history of Hawaiian music are traced in parallel in an attempt to present the vicissitudes in Hawaiian sacred music.

3717. Jones, Mary. *The History of Sacred and Biblically Inspired Dance in Australia.* Sydney: Christian Dance Fellowship of Australia, 1979.

3718. MacTavish, Shona. "Origins of the Religious Dance." *Silliman Journal* 21, 1 (1974): 116-124. To dance is to live. The controlled use of the whole body in dance is a natural form of religious expression to African and other tribal peoples and was once part of temple worship in Old Testament Judaism. The author took these observations to her native New Zealand where she successfully reintroduced dance, after centuries of religious repression, to Christian worship.

3719. McCredie, A.D. "Transplanted and Emergent Indigenous Liturgical Musics in East Asia, Australia and Oceania." In *Musica Indigena: Symposium Music-Ethnologicum: Roma 1975*, Rome, Italy 1975. 117-40.

3720. McLean, Mervyn. "Towards a Typology of Musical Change: Missionaries and Adjustive Response in Oceania." *The World of Music* 28, 1 (1986): 29-43. Widespread repression of native culture by missionaries during the 19th century resulted in the loss whole repertories and styles. European hymns were among the most important replacements. The author evaluates the current conflict between native and Euro-centric ways of hearing music. Includes a typology of native responses to the prohibitions.

3721. Murphy, Kevin B., ed. "Music in the Pacific Islands." *Point* 2, 1 (1973): 1-162. Includes an appendix: Something from Papua New Guinea (on liturgical music from New Guinea) pp. 145-162.

3722. Nichols, A. "Psalms and Hymns and Didgeridoos." *On Being* 11, 8 (1984): 22-26.

3723. Ole, Ronnie Tom. "Singing the Lord's Song in Our Land: Peroveta as Christian Religious Experience in Papua New Guinea." *Religious Education* 87 (1992): 182-90.

3724. Silva, Glenn. *A Comparative Study of the Hymnody of Two Hawaiian Protestant Denominations: Ho'omana Ia Iesu and Ho'omana Na'auao*. Ph.D diss., University of Washington, 1989. The hymns of two Protestant denominations on islands 320 miles apart are compared to determine the extent of traditional Hawaiian influences in this acculturated singing style.

3725. Stephens, Michael J. *The Function of Music in Black Churches on Oahu, Hawaii, as Illustrated at Trinity Missionary Baptist Church*. M.A. thesis, University of Honolulu, 1990. Large Black churches like Trinity more closely resemble mainland churches in choice of music, style of worship, and church membership than do smaller churches, where the influence of local culture and population is stronger.

3726. Stillman, Amy Ku'uleialoha. *Himene Tahiti: Ethnoscientific and Ethnohistorical Perspectives on Choral Singing and Protestant Hymnody in the Society Islands, French Polynesia*. 2 vols. Ph.D. diss., Harvard University, 1991.

3727. Stillman, Amy Ku'uleialoha. "Prelude to a Comparative Investigation of Protestant Hymnody in Polynesia." *YTM* 25 (1993): 89-99. Most of Polynesia was converted to Christianity by the end of the 19th century. Hymnody, which at first was rejected by many islanders, has come to be considered native, particularly in forms that exhibit indigenous features. A history needs to be written that shows not only the different styles of hymns, but the historical circumstances that engendered such a diversity of hymn-singing traditions.

3728. Suri, Ellison. *Music in Pacific Island Worship, with Special Reference to the Anglican Church in Lau, Malaita, Solomon Islands*. B.D. thesis, Pacific Theological college, 1976. An illustration of the use of Christian hymns in native languages.

Addendum

GENERAL REFERENCES AND STUDIES

3729.   Cooper, David A. "Invitation to the Soul." *Parabola* 19, 1 (1994): 6-11. This study of the 'sacred call' discusses the major role music played in the ancient mystery schools, the Indian sweat lodge ceremony, and among the Sikhs, Jews, and shamans and other spiritual healers.

3730.   Hill, Jackson. "Music and Mysticism: A Summary Overview." *Studia Mystica* 2, 4 (1979): 42-51. Surveys religious musical culture in Japan, China, Tibet, India, the West, and among the Sufis.

3731.   Holm, Jean, ed. *Worship*. London, New York: Pinter Publishers, 1994. A general introduction to the occasions for and forms and meaning of worship in Buddhism, Christianity, Hinduism, Islam, Sikhism, and Chinese and Japanese religions. Contains numerous references to chanting, dance, hymns, music, and singing.

3732.   Kim Tae-gon and Mihály Hoppál, ed. *Shamanism in Performing Arts*. Bibliotheca Shamanistica, 1. Budapest: Akadémiai Kiadó, 1995. Includes general articles on shamanic music and dance as well as studies of shamanic performance in Hungary, China, Korea, Manchuria, Siberia and Hawaii.

3733.   Lewis, Thomas P., ed. *The Pro/Am Book of Music and Mythology*. 2 vols. White Plains, NY:Pro/Am Music Resources, Inc., 1992. Vol. 1 consists of an alphabetical arrangement of 425 topic-entries related to music and mythology. Each entry is followed by often extended quotations from a variety of sources. Vol. 2 consists of two supplements (1990 and 1991) along with the list of sources and general index. An impressive and useful work.

3734.   Mahesh Yogi, Maharishi. *Maharishi Gandharva-ved: Creating Balance in Nature and Harmony in World Consciousness*. Maharishi Nagar: Maharishi

World Centre for Gandharva-Ved; Lancaster, MA: Maharishi Ayur-Veda Production International, 1991. On Gandharva-Ved music—music for sitar, flute, tabla, and voice—and its effects on participants and audiences.

3735.   McClenon, J. "The Experiential Foundations of Shamanic Healing." *Journal of Medicine and Philosophy* 18, 2 (1993): 107-127.

3736.   Raffe, Walter George. *Dictionary of the Dance.* New York: A. S. Barnes; London: Thomas Yoseloff, 1964/repr. 1975. A valuable resource.

3737.   Saxena, Madhu Baba. "Co-relation of Music with Spiritualism and Philosophy: An Analytical Study." *Sangeet Natak* 61-62, Jul-Dec (1981): 20-29.

3738.   Stewart, R. J. *The Spiritual Dimensions of Music: Altering Consciousness for Inner Development.* Rochester, VT: Destiny Books, 1990. Originally published as *Music and the Elemental Psyche.* Accompanied by five sound cassettes published by Readings for the Blind, Southfield, MI.

3739.   Stewart. Iris J. *Sacred Woman, Sacred Dance. Awakening Spirituality Through Dance and Ritual.* Rochester, VT: Inner Traditions, 1996. A study of women's sacred dance in Goddess-worshipping cultures and of the ways spiritual dance can be integrated into women's lives today.

3740.   Tagg, Philip. "'Universal' Music and the Case of Death." *CQ: Critical Quarterly* 35, 2 (1993): 54-85. Sec. 1. Death is universal. Music is said to be a universal language. Yet, when presented with music from eight different cultures, Swedish students did not recognize that, in spite of their very diverse styles and moods, all eight examples were of funeral music. Sec. 2 compares Ghanaian and North European treatments of death. Sec. 3 surveys the 'gloom and doom' connotations of the i-VI-i progression (from Chopin's *March Funebre*) as found in 70s and 80s rock music. Sec. 4 summarizes areas of intersubjective agreement concerning the opening survey and proposes possible universally practiced relationships between feeling states and specified features of music.

ASIA: GENERAL REFERENCES
EAST ASIA

3741.   Cheng Yingshi. "A Report on Chinese Research into the Dunhuang Music Manuscripts." Coralie Rockwell, transl. *Musica Asiatica* 6 (1991): 61-72.

3742.   De Vos Malan, Jacques. "K'ung, the Dragon of Emptiness." *South African Journal of Musicology* 2 (1982): 39-42. A study of music from the Zen concepts of emptiness, the unique moment, and spontaneous action and from the viewpoint that the purpose of music is to prepare the mind for the influence of the divine.

3743.   Falkenhausen, Lothar von. *Suspended Music: Chime-bells in the Culture of Bronze Age China*. Berkeley, CA: University of California Press, 1993. Revision of Ph.D. diss., Harvard University, 1988. A study of the ritual, political, and technical aspects of bronze chime-bell music from c.1700 to 221 BCE.

3744.   Gerson-Kiwi, Edith. "Melodic Patterns in Asiatic Rituals: The Quest for Sound Alienation." *Israel Studies in Musicology* 2 (1980): 27-31.

3745.   Hayman, Alan C. "Chak-Bup: The Buddhist Ceremonial Dance of Korea." *Journal of Korean Dance* 1, May (1982): 29-36.

3746.   Huhm, Halla Pai. *Kut: Korean Shamanist Rituals*. Seoul: Hollym International Corp., 1980.

3747.   Kim Seung-Nam. *A Contribution of Korean Traditional Theater to Liturgical Expression*. D.Min diss., Claremont School of Theology, 1992. A plea for the use of indigenous theatre and dance as means of achieving in Korean Christian worship an experience equivalent to that in Western Christian liturgy.

3748.   Picard, François. "Pu'an Zhou: The Musical Avatars of a Buddhist Spell." *Chime. Journal of the European Foundation for Chinese Music Research* 3 (1991): 32-37.

3749.   Pirazzoli-T'serstevens, Michele. "The Bronze Drums of Shizhai Shan, Their Social and Ritual Significance." In *Early South East Asia: Essays in Archaeology, History and Historical Geography*, R. B. Smith and W. Watson, ed. New York: Oxford University Press, 1979. 125-136.

3750.   Provine, Robert C., Jr. *Essays on Sino-Korean Musicology: Early Sources for Korean Ritual Music*. Traditional Korean Music, 2, Seoul: Il Ji Sa, 1988.

3751.   Schipper, Kristofer"A Study of Buxu: Taoist Liturgical Hymn and Dance." *Studies in Taoist Rituals and Music Today* (1989): 110-120.

3752.   Tamba, Akira. "Confluence of Spiritual and Aesthetic Research in Traditional Japanese Music." *The World of Music* 25, 1 (1983): 30-43. The influence of Buddhism on Noh drama is seen in the vocal cries and vowel modification in the actors' speech. The influence of Shinto is seen in the handling of time and the element of spontaniety or 'becoming.'

3753.   Zhu Jiajun. "An Approach to Music from the Cultural Symbolism of Chinese Characters: In the Case of Ritual Musics in East Asia." Jou, transl. *Journal of the Society for Research and Asiatic Music* 58 (1993): 3-4. A brief note on deciphering the hieroglyphic nature of Chinese characters associated with ritual music as a means of ferreting out knowledge of ancient culture.

TIBET AND BHUTAN

3754.   Aris, Michael. "Sacred Dances of Bhutan." *Natural History* 89, 3/Mar (1980): 38-47.

3755.   Cantwell, Catherine M. "A Tibetan Buddhist Ritual in a Refugee Monastery." *Tibet Journal* 10 (1985): 14-29.

3756.   Canzio, Ricardo. "The Place of Music and Chant in Tibetan Religious Culture." In *Tibetan Studies Presented at the Seminar of Young Tibetologists*, Martin Brauen and Per Kvaerne, ed. Zurich: Volkerkundemuseum der Universität Zurich, 1978. 65-74.

3757.   Canzio, Ricardo. *Sakya Pandita's 'Treatise on Music' and Its Relevance to Present Day Tibetan Liturgy*. Ph.D diss., University of London, 1979. The only study of the most important classical Tibetan theoretical work.

3758.   Canzio, Ricardo. "The Bonpo Tradition: Ritual Practices, Ceremonials, Protocol and Monastic Behavior." In *Zlos-gar: Performing Traditions of Tibet*, Jamyang Norbu, ed. Dharamsala, India: Library of Tibetan Works and Archives, 1986. 45-57. The only article of Bonpo monastic music based on fieldwork.

3759.   Crossley-Holland, Peter. "Discussion on Peter Crossley-Holland's 'The Religious Music of Tibet and its Cultural Background.'" In *Proceedings of the Centennial Workshop on Ethnomusicology*, Peter Crossley-Holland, ed. 2. Victoria: Department of Aural History, Provincial Archives, Province of British Columbia, 1978. 55-63. Also includes appendix of original article (see #228, above).

3760.   Draghi, Paul Alexander. "The Stag and the Hunting Dog: A Bhutanese Dance and its Tibetan Source." *Journal of Popular Culture* 16, 1 (1982): 169-75. On '*chams* by Milarepa as performed in Bhutan.

3761.   Egyed, Alice. "Notes on the Study of Variations in Rnying-ma-pa and Gsar-ma-pa 'Bskang-gso' Rituals and Their Music." In *Tibetan Studies: Proceedings of the International Association for Tibetan Studies*, Per Kvaerne, ed. Fagernes, Norway: International Association for Tibetan Studies, 1992.

3762.   Helffer, Mireille. "Preliminary Remarks Concerning the Use of Musical Notation in Tibet." In *Zlos-gar: Performing Traditions of Tibet*, Jamyang Norby, ed. Dharamsala, India: Library of Tibetan Works and Archives, 1986. 69-90.

3763.   Helffer, Mireille. "The '*Cham* of Padmasambhava in the Monastery of Hemis (Ladakh)." *The World of Music* 22, 1 (1980): 107-124. A general description of the masks worn and dances performed in celebration of Padmasambhava's birthday.

3764.   Helffer, Mireille. "The Musical Notation of the Hymn rTsa-brgyud-ma in the dGe-lugs-pa Tradition." In *Tibetan Studies in Honour of Hugh Richardson*, Michael Aris, ed. Proceedings of The International Seminar on Tibetan Studies, Oxford, 1979, Warminster, England: Aris and Phillips, 1976. 120-130.

3765.   Jaffrey, Madhur. "Buddhist Dance Spectacular in a Medieval Kingdom." *Asia* 2, 6/Mar-Apr (1980): 16-25.

3766.   Karmay, Samten G. "Three Sacred Bon Dances ('Cham)." In *Zlos-gar: Performing Traditions of Tibet*, Jamyang Norbu, ed. Dharamsala: India: Library of Tibetan Works and Archives, 1986. 58-68. The only English source on Bonpo music by a Bonpo author.

3767.   Large, John and Thomas Murry. "Observations on the Nature of Tibetan Chant." *Journal of Research in Singing* 5, 1 (1981): 22-28. Sonogram analyses of American singers performing Tibetan chant.

3768.   Lerner, Lin. "Two Tibetan Ritual Dances: A Comparative Study." *Tibet Journal* 8, 4/Winter (1983): 50-57.

3769.   Ronge, Veronika and G. Namgyal. "Casting Tibetan Bells." In *Tibetan Studies in Honour of Hugh Richardson*, Michael and Aung S. S. Kyi Aris, ed. Warminster, England: Aris and Phillips, 1980. 269-76.   A good study of instrument making.

3770.   Scheidegger, Daniel. *Tibetan Ritual Music: A General Survey with Special Reference to the Mindroling Tradition*. Opuscula Tibetana, 19. Rikon, Switzerland: Tibet-Institut, 1988. Emphasizes Nyingma tradition.   Surveys Tibetan music within a conceptual framework of Western notation and music-theory.

3771.   Stoddard, Heather. "A Note on Vajra-dance Choreography in the Snow in the Early 18th Century AD." In *Zlos-gar: Performing Traditions of Tibet*, Jamyang Norbu, ed. Dharamsala, India: Library of Tibetan Works and Archives, 1986. 125-131.

3772.   Vandor, Ivan. "Extra-musical Factors as Determinants in the Performance Practice of Tibetan Ritual Music: Some Considerations on Ethnomusicology." *National Centre for the Performing Arts Quarterly Journal* 11, 3-4/Sep-Dec (1982): 35-40.

SOUTHEAST ASIA

3773.   Cooler, Richard M. *The Karen Bronze Drums of Burma: Types, Iconography, Manufacture, and Use*. Studies in Asian Art and Archaeology, 16. Leiden; New York: E. J. Brill, 1995.

3774.   George, Kenneth M. "Lyric, History, and Allegory, or the End of Head-hunting Ritual in Upland Sulawesi." *American Ethnologist* 20, 4 (1993): 696-716.

3775.   Herbst, Ed. "Intrinsic Aesthetics in Balinese Artistic and Spiritual Practice." *Asian Music* 13, 1 (1981): 43-52. The distinction that scholars often make between efficacy and beauty is, with respect to Balinese ritual arts, a mis-leading one. No ritual occasion in Bali can be efficacious unless beauty and harmony are essential elements.

3776.   Schwörer-Kohl, Gretel. "Considering Gender Balance in Religion and Ritual Music among the Hmong and Lahu in Northern Thailand." In *Music, Gender, and Culture*, Herndon and Ziegler, ed. Wilhelmshaven: Florian Noetzel Verlag, 1990. 143-55. A comparison of the roles of women in Hmong and Lahu tribal rituals. Although both tribes are animistic, women play no role in Hmong ritual, but do play significant though varying roles among the Lahu subgroups.

3777.   Soedarsono. *'Wayang Wong' in the Yogyakarta Kraton: History, Ritual Aspects, Literary Aspects, and Characterization.* Ph.D. diss., University of Michigan, 1983.

SOUTH ASIA: INDIA AND NEPAL

3778.   Aiyar, P. K. Rajagopala. "Sama Veda and Sangita." *Journal of the Music Academy Madras* 52 (1981): 62-71.

3779.   Bailly, Constantine Rhodes. *Shaiva Devotional Songs of Kashmir: A Translation and Study of Utpaladeva's Shivastotravali.* Albany, NY: State University of New York Press, 1987. The spiritual diary of one of the masters of the *Pratyabhijna* school of Tantric Shaivism.

3780.   Flueckiger, Joyce Burkhalter. "*Bhojalî*: Song, Goddess, Friend: A Chhattisgarhi Women's Oral Tradition." *Asian Folklore Studies* 42, 1 (1983): 27-43.

3781.   Gupt, Bharat. "Origin of Dhruvapada and Krishna Bhakti in Brijabhasha." *Sangeet Natak* 64-65, Apr-Sep (1982): 55-63.

3782.   Iltis, Linda. "The Jala Pyâkhâ: A Classical Newar Dance Drama of Harasiddhi." In *Heritage of the Kathmandu Valley: Proceedings of an International Conference in Lübeck, June 1985*, Gutschow and Michaels, ed. Sankt Augustin, Germany: VGH Wissenschaftsverlag, 1987. 199-213. Nepal.

3783.   Nambiar, Balan. "Gods and Ghosts—Teyyam and Bhuta Rituals." *Marg* 34, 3/Jun (1981): 62-73.

3784.   Nijenhius, Emmie Te and Sanjukta Gupta. *Sacred Songs of India: Dîksitar's Cycle of Hymns to the Goddess Kamala.* 2 vols. Forum Ethnomusicologicum. Basler Studien zur Ethnomusikologie, Winterthur, Switzerland: Amadeus, 1987.

3785.   Oppitz, Michael. "Drawings on Shamanic Drums: Nepal." *Res: Anthropology and Aesthetics* 22 (1992): 62-81. An examination and interpretation of the chalk finger-drawings that decorate the drums of the tribal magic-healers of the Northern Mayar in the Himalayas of West-Central Nepal. Among all areas and groups is the use of drawings to depict those powers enlisted in healing trance.

3786.   Paintal, Ajit Singh. "Sikh Devotional Music—Its Main Traditions." *National Centre for the Performing Arts Quarterly Journal* 11, 2/June (1982): 17-24.

3787.   Wegner, Gert-Matthias. "Navadâphâ of Bhaktapur: Repertoire and Performance of the Ten Drums." In *Heritage of the Kathmandu Valley: Proceedings of an International Conference in Lübeck, June 1985*, Gutschow and Michaels, ed. Sankt Augustin, Germany: VGH Wissehchaftsverlag, 1987. 471-488. Nepal.

3788.   Wegner, Gert-Matthias. *The Nâykhìbâjâ of the Newar Butchers.* Studies in Newari Drumming II, Albrecht Wezler, ed. Stuttgart: Franz Steiner Verlag, 1988. A description of the ritual duties and processions in which Newar Butchers of Bhajpur, Nepal, participate.

3789.   Younger, Paul. "Singing the Tamil Hymnbook in the Tradition of Ramanuja: The *Adyayanotsava* Festival in Srirangam." *History of Religions* 20, 3/Feb (1982): 272-293.

ANCIENT NEAR EAST

3790.   Comotti, Giovanni. *Music in Greek and Roman Culture.* Rosaria V. Monson, transl. Baltimore, MD: Johns Hopkins University Press, 1989/1991. A translation of *La Musica nella Cultura Greca e Romana.*

3791.   Duchesne-Guillemin, Marcelle. "Music in Ancient Mesopotamia and Egypt." *World Archaeology* 12, 3/Feb. (1981): 287-297.

3792.   Furley, William. "Praise and Persuasion in Greek Hymns." *Journal of Hellenic Studies* 115 (1995): 29-36. Argues that Greek piety was based on a sense of the sacred and that hymns were sung, not only to prevent the gods from venting their wrath on the community, but to please them as well.

JUDAISM

3793.   Schwadron, Abraham A. *"Chad Gadya*: A Passover Song." *Selected Reports in Ethnomusicology* 4 (1983): 125-155. The *Chad Gadya* is the last of four sung texts to be added to the *Haggada* by Eastern European Jewry and is the culminating event of the seder proceedings. This essay examines its history, text, and music.

3794.   Seroussi, Edwin. *Old and New in the Singing of the 'Bakkashot' Among Morrocan Jews: Historical, Socio-cultural and Musical Aspects of the Tradition of Singing 'Bakkashot' According to the Book of 'Shir Yedidot' in Morocco and Israel.* M.A. thesis, Hebrew University of Jerusalem, 1981.

CHRISTIANITY:
GENERAL REFERENCES, HISTORY AND LITURGY

3795.   Baldovin, John F. *Liturgy in Ancient Jerusalem.* Grove Liturgical Study, 57. Bramcote, Nottingham, Eng.: Grove Books Ltd, 1989. Covers the period from 312 to 638 CE.

3796.   Brouwer, Frans and Robin A. Leaver, ed. *Ars et Musica in Liturgia: Essays Presented to Casper Honders on the Seventieth Birthday.* Studies in Liturgical Musicology, 1. Metuchen, NJ: Scarecrow Press, 1994. Includes articles on church music in 19th-century Iceland and the liturgical use of the organ in England and Germany.

3797.   Claghorn, Charles Eugene. *Women Composers and Hymnists: A Concise Biographical Dictionary.* Metuchen, NJ: Scarecrow Press, 1984.

3798.   Moody, Ivan, ed. *Contemporary Music and Religion.* Contemporary Music Review, 12, Pt. 2. Toronto, Canada: Harwood Academic Publishers, c/o International Publishers Distributor, Newark, NJ, 1995. Beginning with "Silence, Braying and Singing" by J. East, these eleven essays move on to discuss music as a sacred and timeless art, the music of Arvo Pärt, and other topics concerning both traditional and contemporary religious music.

3799.   Moore, James H. *Vespers at St. Mark's.* Studies in Musicology, 30, Ann Arbor, MI: UMI Research Press, 1981.

3800.   Music, David W. *Hymnology: A Collection of Source Readings.* Studies in Liturgical Musicology, 4. Lanham, MD: Scarecrow Press, 1996.

3801.   Payne, Randall Merle. *Christian Worship in Jerusalem in the Fourth and Fifth Centuries: The Development of the Lectionary, Calendar and Liturgy.* Ph.D. diss, Southern Baptist Theological Seminary, 1980.

3802.   Plank, Steven Eric. *'The Way to Heavens Doore': An Introduction to Liturgical Process and Musical Style*. Studies in Liturgical Musicology, 2. Metuchen, NJ: Scarecrow Press, 1994.

3803.   Reynolds, William J. and Milburn Price. *A Survey of Christian Hymnody*. rev. ed., Carol Stream, IL: Hope Publishing Co., 1987.

CHURCH OF ROME: MUSIC HISTORY AND LITURGY

3804.   Atlas, Allan W. *Music at the Aragonese Court of Naples*. Cambridge; New York: Cambridge University Press, 1985. A study of sacred and secular music at the court of 15th-century Naples.

3805.   Baldovin, John F. "Kyrie Eleison and the Entrance Rite of the Roman Eucharist." *Worship* 60 (1986): 334-347. The Kyrie is supplicational or penitential in character and processional in action. It was liturgically appropriate in the mass in the patristic past, but is too cumbersome in today's liturgy. For most occasions, the entrance rite might best consist of opening psalms or song, greeting, and opening prayer.

3806.   Banks, Jon. *The Motet as a Formal Type in Northern Italy, c. 1500*. 2 vols. Outstanding Dissertations in Music from British Universities, Hamden, CT: Garland Publishing, 1993. A revision of 1990 Ph.D. diss., University of Oxford. A study and identification of the diverse forms found in works entitled 'motet.'

3807.   Barbera, Charles André, ed. *Music Theory and Its Sources: Antiquity and the Middle Ages*. Notre Dame Conferences in Medieval Studies, Notre Dame, IN: University of Notre Dame Press, 1990. Essays based on conference held April 30-May 2, 1987.

3808.   Blackburn, Bonnie. "On Compositional Process in the 15th Century." *JAMS* 40 (1987): 210-284. This study of Aaron, Spataro, Zarlino, and Tinctoris demonstrates that there were two ways to compose polyphonic music during the 15th century: the contrapuntal way, in which voices were sung *super librum*—improvised over a given melody—or written successively, and the harmonic way, in which each voice was related to every other voice. Such a *res facta*—a term Tinctoris uses to specify a composition composed harmonically—could be composed either simultaneously or successively, provided a succession of consonances was the result. Dufay's *Nuper rosarum flores* (1437) is considered the first great representation of the second, new style.

3809.   Cutter, Paul F. *Musical Sources of the Old-Roman Mass: An Inventory of MS Rome, St. Cecilia Gradual 1071, MS Rome, Vaticanum Latinum 5319, San Pietro F22 and F11*. Neuhausen-Stuttgart, Germany: American Institute of Musicology: Hanssler-Verlag, 1979.

3810.   Doss, Mary Dugan. "Folk Ballads of Medieval Origin: A Sense of the Sacred." *Epiphany* 11, Spring (1991): 38-48. A survey of a wide selection of European Christian ballads with an eye to recovering a sense of wonder and the supernatural in modern life. Includes song texts with theological interpretations.

3811.   Duchesneau, Claude and Michel Veuthey. *Music and Liturgy: The U[niversa] L[aus] Document and Commentary.* Paul Inwood, transl. Washington, DC: Pastoral Press, 1992.

3812.   Foley, Edward. *Ritual Music: Studies in Liturgical Musicology.* Studies in Liturgy and Music, Beltsville, MD: Pastoral Press, 1995.

3813.   Funk, Virgil C., ed. *Sung Liturgy: Toward 2000 A.D.* Washington DC: Pastoral Press, 1991. Edward Foley and other major liturgists explore the social and religious trends that will influence worship and music in the years leading to the new millenium.

3814.   Kirkman, Andrew. *The Three-Voice Mass in the Later Fifteenth and Early Sixteenth Centuries: Style, Distribution, and Case Studies.* Outstanding Dissertations in Music from British Universities, Hamden, CT: Garland Publishing, 1995. Revision of 1992 dissertation from King's College University of London. A study of how the rise to prominence of the low countertenor in the part music of the 1460s and 1470s affected the 3-voice mass. Includes a detailed study of three works.

3815.   Nicholson, David, ed. *Liturgical Music in Benedictine Monasticism: A Post-Vatican II Survey.* St. Benedict, OR: Mount Angel Abbey, 1986.

3816.   Ongaro, Giulio. "Sixteenth-century Patronage at St. Mark's, Venice." *Studies In Medieval and Early Modern Music* 8 (1988): 81-155. On the complex system of patronage at the chapel of St. Marks from c1500 to the 1560s. Covers recruitment, training, and the economic and social status of the singers, including ways in which singers supplemented their modest income with work outside the basilica.

3817.   Prizer, William F. "Music and Ceremonial in the Low Countries: Philip the Fair and the Order of the Golden Fleece." *Studies in Medieval and Early Modern Music* 5 (1985): 113-153. Under the sovereignty of Philip the Fair (1478-1506), the Order had three functions: 1) to hold official meetings, 2) to conduct services at the Ste Chapelle at Dijon, the official chapel of the Order, and 3) to commission polyphonic music for grand ceremonial occasions at the archducal chapel. Josquin may have been one of those commissioned.

3818.   Reynolds, Stephen. "The Baltic Psaltery and Musical Instruments of Gods and Devils." *Journal of Baltic Studies* 14, 1/Spring (1983): 5-23.

3819.   Walters, Anne. "The Reconstruction of the Abbey Church at St. Denis (1231-1281): The Interplay of Music and Architecture and Politics." *Studies in Medieval and Early Modern Music* 5 (1985): 187-238.

3820.   Wattenbarger, Jonathan Roy. *Choral Settings of Principal Hymns of the Feast of Corpus Christi to 1600*. D.M.A., USC, 1986. A study of the origin and history of the feast of Corpus Christi and a survey of the choral music composed for it.

3821.   Winter, Miriam Therese. *Why Sing?: Toward a Theology of Catholic Church Music*. Washington DC: Pastoral Press, 1984.

RELIGIOUS MUSIC IN GREAT BRITAIN

3822.   Bowers, Roger. "New Sources of English Fifteenth- and Sixteenth-century Polyphony." *Early Music History* 4 (1984): 297-344.

3823.   Bowers, Roger. "New Sources of English Fourteenth- and Fifteenth-century Polyphony." *Early Music History* 3 (1983): 123-174.

3824.   Gatens, William J. *Victorian Cathedral Music in Theory and Practice*. London: Cambridge University Press, 1986.

3825.   Turbet, R. "The Great Service: Byrd, Tomkins and Their Contemporaries, and the Meaning of 'Great'." *Musical Times* 131 (1990): 275-277. There was no category of composition known as the 'Great Service' in Tudor and Stuart England. The only composition that deserves this title and to which it should be applied is Byrd's *Great Service*.

3826.   Warren, F. E. and Jane Stevenson, ed. *The Liturgy and Ritual of the Celtic Church*. 2nd ed., Woodbridge, Suffolk and Wolfeboro, NH: Boydell Press, 1987. Jane Stevenson's update of the 1881 work by Warren.

ORTHODOX AND PROTESTANT MUSIC
ON THE EUROPEAN CONTINENT

3827.   Hustad, Anne-Margrethe. "The North Russian Lament in the Light of the Religious Songs of the Old Believers." *Scando-Slavica* 27 (1981): 47-67.

3828.   Kerewsky-Halpern, Barbara. "Text and Context in Serbian Ritual Lament." *Canadian-American Slavic Studies* 15, 1/Spring (1981): 52-60.

3829.   Kligman, Gail. *Calus: Symbolic Transformation in Romanian Ritual*. Chicago: University of Chicago Press, 1981.

3830.   Mellers, Wilfrid Howard. *Bach and the Dance of God*. New York: Oxford University Press, 1981. A subjective yet illuminating interpretative analysis of Bach's music as a synthesis of the horizontal and the vertical, the linear and the harmonic, the metaphysical and the physical, the eternal and the temporal.

3831.   Smith, Charles Howard. *Scandinavian Hymnody from the Reformation to the Present*. Metuchen, NJ: American Theological Library Association: Scarecrow Press, 1987. A study of European free-church hymnody.

3832.   Suojanen, Päivikki. "What Does Hymn Singing Do To People." *Ethnologia Scandinavica* (1984): 79-97.

3833.   deleted

3834.   Tolbert, Elizabeth. "Magico-Religious Power and Gender in the Karelian Lament." In *Music, Gender, and Culture*, Herndon and Ziegler, ed. Wilhelmshaven: Florian Noetzel Verlag, 1990. 41-56. A study of the lament and the power it gives to women in a former Soviet state on the eastern border of Finland.

LITURGICAL DANCE AND DRAMA

3835.   Wallace, Robin. "The Role of Music in Liturgical Drama: A Revelation." *Music and Letters* 45 (1984): 219-28. Musicological scholarship and recordings stress the musical aspects of liturgical drama. The essence of liturgical drama, however, was in the drama and its religious message. Music played a secondary role; it was part of an attempt by the Catholic Church to achieve in the drama a kind of formalism and fixity. That sung drama was a temporary solution and a compromise is illustrated by the fact that during the 13th century, spoken vernacular mystery plays largely displaced the Latin sung drama.

3836.   Weyman, Gloria Gabriel, Lucien Deiss, Virgil Funk, et al. *Liturgical Dance*. Phoenix, AZ: North American Liturgy Resources/Epoch Universal Publications, Inc., 1984.

ISLAM

3837.   al-Faruqi, Isma'il Raji, ed. *Essays in Islamic and Comparative Studies: Papers Presented to the Islamic Studies Group of American Academy of Religion*. Washington, DC: International Institute of Islamic Thought, 1982.

3838.   Boyd, Alan William. *To Praise the Prophet: A Processual Symbolic Analysis of 'Maulidi,' a Muslim Ritual in Lamu, Kenya*. Ph.D. diss., Indiana University, 1981.

3839.   Danielson, Virginia. "The *Qur'an* and the *Qasidah*: Aspects of the Popularity of the Repertory Sung by Umm Kulthum." *Asian Music* 19, 1 (Fall/Winter) (1987): 26-45.

3840.   Dilley, Roy M. "Spirits, Islam and Ideology: A Study of a Tukulor Weavers' Song (Dillere)." *Journal of Religion in Africa* 17, 3 (1987): 245-79. Senegal.

3841.   Esposito, John L., ed. *Oxford Encyclopedia of the Modern Islamic World*. New York: Oxford University Press, 1995. See entries on 'Music' by Ali Jihad Racy and 'Devotional Music' by Virginia Danielson.

3842.   Gray, Laurel. "The Status of Music in Islamic Culture from Muhammad to Harun al-Rashid." *Viltis* 42, 4/Dec. (1982): 10-15.

3843.   Nelson, Kristina. "The Contribution of Musical Elements to the Ideals of Qur'anic Recitation." In *Essays in Islamic and Comparative Studies: Papers Presented to the Islamic Studies Group of American Academy of Religion*, Isma'il Raji al-Faruqi, ed. Washington, DC: International Institute of Islamic Thought, 1982. 101-107.

3844.   Tamadonfar, Mehran. "Political Activism and Quietism in Shi'a Rituals: Versatility in Paradox." In *The Cultures of Celebrations*, Ray B. Browne and Michael T. Marden, ed. Bowling Breen: Bowling Green State University Popular Press, 1994. 25-40.

SUB-SAHARAN AFRICA

3845.   Garfias, Robert. "The Role of Dreams and Spirit Possession in the *Mbira Dza Vadzimu* Music of the Shona People of Zimbabwe." *Journal of Altered States of Consciousness* 5, 3 (1979-1980): 211-234.

3846.   Johnston, Thomas F. "The Secret Music of the Nhanga Rites." *Anthropos* 77, 5-6 (1982): 755-774.

3847.   Modum, E. P. "Gods as Guests: Music and Festivals in African Traditional Societies." *Présence Africaine* 110, 2 (1979): 86-100.

3848.   Ottenberg, Simon, ed. *African Religious Groups and Beliefs: Papers in Honor of William R. Bascom*. Meerut, India: Archana Publications for Folklore Institute, 1982.

3849.   Waite, Gloria. "Spirit Possession Dance in Eastcentral Africa." *Journal of the Association of Graduate Dance Ethnologists* (1980): 31-38.

NORTH AMERICA:
EURO-AMERICAN AND AFRO-AMERICAN RELIGIOUS MUSIC

3850.   Bealle, John. "New Strings on the 'Old Harp:' The 1991 Revision of The Sacred Harp." *Tributaries: Journal of the Alabama Folklife Association* 1 (1994): 23-44.

3851.   Brown, C. H. *Instrumental Music in Christian Worship and Testimony: Has It a Scriptural Sanction?* Addison, IL: Bible Truth Publishers, 198-?

3852.   Cameron, Kenneth Walter, ed. *Early Anglican Church Music in America: Scarce Imprints of Hymns, Chants, Anthems, Psalms, Liturgical Tunes and Choral Pieces Used in the Episcopal Church Before and Immediately Following the Revolution: 1763-1830.* Hartford: Transcendental Books, 1983.

3853.   Hall, Susan Grove. "New Age Music, An Analysis of an Ecstasy." *Popular Music and Society* 18, 2 (1994): 23-33.

3854.   Jackson, Joyce Marie. "The Black American Folk Preacher and the Chanted Sermon: Parallels with a West African Tradition." In *Discourse in Ethnomusicology II: A Tribute to Alan P. Merriam,* Caroline Card et al., eds. Bloomington: Indiana University Press, 1981. 205-222.

3855.   Katz, Israel. "The Sacred and Secular Musical Traditions of the Sephardic Jews in the United States." *American Jewish Archives* 44, Spr/Sum. (1992): 331-356.

3856.   Krummel, Donald William. *Bibliographical Handbook of American Music.* Music in American Life, Urbana, IL: University of Illinois Press, 1987. An examination of over 750 bibliographies of books, periodicals, and other writings about American music from 1698 to the present. Includes lists of musical compositions and recordings.

3857.   Lau, Barbara A. "Religious Rituals and Cultural Cohesion: A Case Study: Shape-note Singing by Urban Black Americans in Four Midwestern Cities." *Mid-America Folklore* 10, 2-3/Fall-winter (1982): 27-57.

3858.   Maney, Debbie et al. "The Shape Note Singing Project." *Foxfire* 18, 4 (1984): 194-256. Introduction to a special issue on shape note and convention gospel singing.

3859.   Mauney, Richard Steadman. *The Development of Missionary Hymnody in the United States of America in the Nineteenth Century.* D.M.A., Southwestern Baptist Theological Seminary, 1993. A study of 60 hymn collections of the Congregationalists, Baptists, Presbyterians, and Methodists to determine the number of missionary hymns, their themes, scriptural foundations, and the ways in which the hymns reflect the theology of the missions movement.

3860. Owens, William A. "Anglo-Texan Spirituals." *Southwestern Historical Quarterly* 86, 1/July (1982): 31-48.

3861. Palmer, Robert. "The Church of the Sonic Guitar." *South Atlantic Quarterly* 90, 4 (1991): 649-73.

3862. Patterson, Daniel W. "Hunting for the American White Spiritual: A Survey of Scholarship, with Discography." In *The Bible in American Arts and Letters*, G.Gunn, ed. Philadelphia, PA 1983. 187-217.

3863. Robertson, Carol E., ed. *Musical Repercussions of 1492: Encounters in Text and Performance*. Washington DC: Smithsonian Institution Press, 1992.

3864. Rogal, Samuel J. *Guide to the Hymns and Tunes of American Methodism*. Westport, CT: Greenwood Press, 1986.

3865. Southern, Eileen. "Hymnals of the Black Church." *Journal of the Interdenominational Theological Center* 14, Fall/Spring (1987): 127-140.

3866. Spencer, Jon Michael. "The Emancipation of the Negro and the Negro Spirituals from the Racialist Legacy of Arthur de Gobineau." *Canadian Review of American Studies* 24, 1 (1994): 1-18.

3867. Spencer, Jon Michael. *Sing a New Song: Liberating Black Hymnody*. Minneapolis, MN: Fortress Press, 1995.

3868. Starks, George L., Jr. "Singing 'Bout a Good Time: Sea Island Religious Music." *Journal of Black Studies* 10, 4/June (1980): 437-444.

3869. Thornburg, Robert W. and Max Miller. "When Minister and Musician Meet." *Nexus* 24, 1-2 (1982): 23-35. A discussion of the principles of church music is illustrated with seven musical examples for chorus or congregation with organ accompaniment.

3870. Youngerman, Suzanne. *'Shaking is No Foolish Play:' An Anthropological Perspective on the American Shakers—Person, Time, Space and Dance-ritual*. Ph.D. diss., Columbia University, 1983.

CENTRAL AND SOUTH AMERICA AND THE WEST INDIES: AFRO-AMERICAN RELIGIOUS MUSIC

3871. Bourguignon, Erika. "Ritual and Myth in Haitian *Vodoun*." In *African Religious Groups and Beliefs*, Simon Ottenberg, ed. Meerut, India: Archana Publications for Folklore Institute, 1982. 305-331.

3872. Carvalho, José Jorge de. *Shango Cult in Recife, Brazil*. Rita Laura Segato, transl. Caracas, Venezuela: Fundef, Conac, OAS, 1992.

3873.   Carvalho, José Jorge de. *Studies of Afro-Brazilian Cults: A Critical and Historical Review of the Main Trends of Thought*. M.A. thesis, Queen's University of Belfast, 1978.

3874.   Fleurant, Gerdes. "The Music of Vodun." In *African and Oceanic Spirituality*. New York: Crossroad Press, forthcoming.

3875.   Tompkins, W. D. *The Musical Traditions of the Blacks of Coastal Peru*. Ph.D. dissertation, University of California, Los Angeles, 1981.

NORTH AMERICAN INDIANS: GENERAL REFERENCES

3876.   Davis, Mary B., ed. *Native America in the Twentieth Century: An Encyclopedia*. New York; London: Garland Press, 1994. See entries on 'Music' by Charlotte Heth and 'Dance' by Joann W. Kealiinohomoku.

3877.   Kurath, Gertrude Prokosch. "Masked Dances of Native North America." *The World of Music* 23, 3 (1981): 58-68. A brief look at the materials, purposes, and diffusion of masks. Masks depicting beasts, deities, or animals empower wearers in matters of survival. Use ranges from none in the Canadian interior to extensive in the Eastern Woodlands, Southwest, and the Pacific Northwest.

3878.   Martin, Joel W. "Before and Beyond the Sioux Ghost Dance: Native American Prophetic Movements and the Study of Religion." *Journal of the American Academy of Religion* 59, 4 (Winter, 1991): 677-701. Formed in response to colonialism, Native American prophetic movements functioned as collective initiations leading to the development of a pan-Native American identity. They provide material for comparison with other responses to colonialism, other American religions, and subsequent religious movements.

3879.   Osterreich, Shelly Anne, comp. *The American Indian Ghost Dance, 1870-1890: An Annotated Bibliography*. Bibliographies and Indexes in American History, No. 19, New York: Greenwood Press, 1991.

3880.   Paper, J. "Sweat-Lodge: A Northern Native American Ritual for Communal Shemanic Trance." *Temenos* 26 (1990): 85-94.

NORTH AMERICAN INDIANS:
MUSIC AND DANCE OF SPECIFIC TRIBES

3881.   Draper, David E. "Abba Isht Tuluwa: The Christian Hymns of the Mississippi Choctaws." *American Indian Culture and Research Journal* 6, 1 (1982): 43-61.

3882.   Frisbie, Charlotte J., ed. *Southwestern Indian Ritual Drama*. School of American Research Advanced Seminar Series, Prospect Heights, IL: Waveland Press, 1980/repr. 1989. A study of Southwest Indian ritual as a complex of music, theater, dance, literature, and other arts. Includes articles on Zuñi, Apache, Navajo, Hopi, Pueblo, Papago, Tewa, and Havasupai ritual dramas.

3883.   Geertz, Armin W. "The Sa'lakwmanayat Sacred Puppet Ceremonial Among the Hopi Indians in Arizona: A Preliminary Investigation." *Anthropos* 77, 1-2 (1982): 163-190.

3884.   Kettel, David. "Potlatching and Winter Dancing: The Dialectic of the Secular and Sacred in Northwest Coast Indian Social Formations." *Napao* 12, Oct (1982): 11-19.

3885.   Kolstee, Anton Frederik. *To Impersonate the Supernatural: Music and Ceremony of the Bella Bella/Heiltsuk Indians of British Columbia*. Ph.D. diss., University of Illinois at Urbana-Champaign, 1988.

3886.   Mansell, Maureen E. *By the Power of Their Dreams: Songs, Prayers, and Sacred Shields of the Plains Indians*. San Francisco: Chronicle Books, 1994.

3887.   Shimkin, D. B. "The Wind River Shoshone Sun Dance." *Bureau of American Ethnology Bulletin* 151, 41 (1953): 397-491.

3888.   White, R. C. "Two Surviving Luiseño Ceremonies." *American Anthropologist* (1953). Reprinted in *The Spanish Borderlands Sourcebooks*. David Hurst Thomas, ed. 4. *Ethnology of the Alta California Indians. Part II: Post Contact*. New York: Garland Publ., 1991.

CENTRAL AND SOUTH AMERICAN INDIANS

3889.   Bastien, J. W. "A Shamanistic Curing Ritual of the Bolivian Aymara." *Journal of Latin American Lore* 15, 1 (1989): 73-94.

3890.   Baudez, Claude-François. "The Maya Snake Dance: Ritual and Cosmology." *RES Anthropology and Aesthetics* 21 (1992): 37-52. A study and interpretation of the drawings on the piers of the architectural complex at Palenque.

3891.   Hill, Jonathan David. "Myth, Music, and History: Poetic Transformations of Narrative Discourse in an Amazonian Society." *Journal of Folklore Research* 27, 1-2 (Jan-Aug) (1990): 115-31.

OCEANIA

3892.   Johnson, Ragnar. "A Re-examination of the New Guinea Highlands Sacred Flute Complex: The Spirit Cries Played During *Ommura* Male Initiations." *Mankind* 13, 5/Dec (1982): 416-423.

3893.   McKnight, David. "Conflict, Healing, and Singing in an Australian Aboriginal Community." *Anthropos* 77, 3-4 (1982): 491-508.

3894.   McLean, Mervyn. "Dance and Music Learning in Oceania." *The World of Music* 32, 1 (1990): 5-27. A survey of various Oceanic locales regarding the roles that casual imitation, systematic rehearsal, and instruction play in the learning of dance and music. Rehearsal or instruction is most important for ritual occasions and initiation and whenever competition or group participation is involved.

3895.   Monberg, Torben. *Bellona Island Beliefs and Rituals*. Honolulu, HI: University of Hawaii Press, 1991. A reconstruction, based on interviews and actual performances of rituals, of the pre-Christian beliefs and related social structure of the natives of the Polynesian outlier islands of Bellona and Rennell.

3896.   Neuenfeldt, Karl W. "The Kyana Corroboree: Cultural Production of Indigenous Ethnogenesis." *Sociological Inquiry* 65, 1 (1995): 1-13.

Author Index

Fried, Morton 30
Friedland, Eric L. 921
Friedlander, Ira, ed. 2010
Friedman, Robert 2624, 2918
Friedson, Steven Michael 2215, 2216
Frigout, Arlette 3225
Frigyesi, Judit Laki 875, 876
Frisbie, Charlotte J. 3211, 3237-3244, 3653, 3882
Frishkopf, Michael 2011
Froehlich, Karlfried 1849
Fugler, Stephen Paul 1740
Fujie, Linda 2463
Fuks, Victor 3465
Fuller, Sarah Ann 1411-1415
Fung Yu-Lan 178
Funk, Virgil C. 1542, 1543, 3813, 3836
Funkhouser, Sara Ann 1454
Furley, William 3792
Furst, Peter 2968, 3466

Gagne, Ronald 1892
Gallaway, Craig 1771
Galles, D. L. C. M. 1741, 1772
Gallo, F. W. 1027
Galloway, Patricia, ed. 3078
Galpin, Francis William 760
Gamber, Klaus 1544
Gangwere, Blanche 1028, 1029
Ganteaume, Cécile R. 3217
Garber, Susan 2405
Garbett, G. Kingsley 2217
Garcia, A. 3299
Garcia, Guy 2796
Gardner, James Earl 1053
Gardner, Johann von 1659
Garfias, Robert 328, 3845
Garner, Edwin C. 332
Garrett, Clarke 102
Garside, Charles W 1800, 1801
Garst, John F. 2703
Gatens, William J. 3824
Gautam, .M. R. 498
Gautier, Daniel 2072
Gebauer, V. E. 2325
Gebr, Adela 1244
Geertz, Armin W. 3883
Geertz, Clifford 424
Geier, Martin 1825
Geiger, M. J. 2549
Gelineau, Joseph 1545-1549
Gell, Alfred 3654
Gellner, David N. 705
Genova, Vincent Anthony 3609
Gentes, Mary Josephine 649
Gentry, Theodore 2499
George, Kenneth M. 471-473, 3774
George, Luvenia A. 2750
Georgiades, Thrysbulos 1030
Gerbrandt, Carl 991
German, C. Dale 2530
Gérold, T. 1812
Gerson-Kiwi, Edith 31, 32, 877, 922, 1146, 1147, 3744
Gertsman, Evgenij V. 1625
Getz, Russell P. 2423

Gianturco, Carolyn 1467
Gibb, H. A. R. 1965
Gieringer, Franz 2203
Gifford, E. W. 3325
Giglio, Virginia 3126
Gilday, Edmund T. 346
Gill, Sam D. 3004, 3245
Gillen, Gerard 1742
Gillespie, John 1687, 1688
Gillingham, Bryan 1416, 4136
Ginn, Victoria 77
Girard, Sharon Elizabeth 3467
Gleason, Harold 2312
Glick, L. B. 3655
Goddard, P. E. 3048
Godwin, Jeff 2797-2799
Godwin, Joscelyn 33, 2032, 2073, 2085-2089
Goemanne, Noel 384
Goen, Clarence C. 2491
Goldberg, Clemens 1455
Goldberg, Geoffrey 878, 879, 923
Goldblatt, Elizabeth Ann 239
Goldschmidt, Ernst Daniel 924
Goldsworthy, David 474, 475
Göllner, T. 2550
Gomati, Viswanathan 611
Gonda, Jan 535
Gonzalez-Wippler, Migene 2919, 2920
Gonzálvez, Ramon 1363
Good, Edwin 2326
Goodman, Linda J. 3362, 3363
Gorali, Moshe 1031
Gorer, Geoffrey 2141
Gormley, Regina Maria 2551
Gory, Ronald William 2261
Gottlieb, Robert 693
Gough, Austin 1358
Gould, Ronald Lee 1826
Gourlay, Ken 3576
Govinda, Lama Anagarika 34, 240
Govindarajan, Hema 650
Graber, David 3127
Graceva, G. N. 154
Gradenwitz, Peter 843, 1245
Graham, J. R. 2372
Granquist, Raoul 2218
Gray, J. E. B. 536
Gray, John 2114
Gray, Laurel 3842
Gray, Robert F 2204
Grebe, M. E. 3468
Greene, David B. 1864
Gregory, David Louis 2478
Griaule, Marcel 2142
Grier, James 1477, 1478
Griffith, Ralph T. H. 527
Grim, John A. 155, 3005, 3100, 3469
Grimes, Robert Raymond 2541
Grimes, Ronald L. 12
Grindle, W. H. 1743
Grow, Mary Louise 398
Gruber, Mayer I. 826
Grund-Khaznader, Francoise 2124
Gudgeon, Richard G. 2503
Guerara-Berger, Marcos 3433

Subject Index

Cuicatl 3424
Cult of Affliction 2111, 2171, 2220, 2241, 2242
curing; *see* healing

Dagomba 2173
dance and religion 5, 11, 14, 22, 43, 56, 57, 61, 62, 73-93, 95, 106, 183, 3736, 3739
dance, by group: African American 2593, 2651; Asian 134-139; Christian 1000, 1043, 1080, 1148; Christian-Africa 2244, 2248, 2269, 2271, 2776, 2278-2280, 2287; Eskimo 3528, 3530, 3535-3559; Judaic 840, 846, 963, 974; Islamic 1990, 1998; Maya 3890; Mormon 2515; Pentecostal 2522; Sufi 2010, 2012, 2014, 2017-2020, 2022; women's 3739; *see also* Whirling Dervishes
dance, by location: Africa 2108, 2109, 2112-2114, 2121, 2124, 2125, 2177, 2129, 2141, 2143, 2151-2154, 2156, 2163, 2167, 2170, 2175, 2183, 2184, 2191, 2194, 2198, 2211, 2212, 2214, 2215, 2224, 2227-2229, 2233-2235, 2238, 2242, 2243; Bali 447, 448, 453, 455, 456, 458, 461, 462, 464-466, 469; Bhutan 3754, 3760, 3765; Central America 3890; China 183, 201, 213, 214; Greece 775, 777, 779; India 501, 507, 549, 572, 607, 608, 622, 625, 629, 637-673, 676, 679, 681, 683, 702, 704, 707-709, 711, 720, 722, 725, 730, 737, 743, 750; Indonesia 415, 475, 489; Japan 317-319, 322, 324, 326-330, 347; Java 419-421, 423, 430, 431, 438, 441, 443, 446; Korea 3745; Nepal 3782; Southeast Asia 363, 369-372, 390, 398; Tibet 238, 246, 247, 249, 251, 258, 3763, 3766, 3768, 3771; United States 2455-2457, 2461, 2462, 2464, 2515, 2522, 2532, 2593, 2596, 2609, 2648, 2651, 2667, 2693, 2768, 2845, 2852
dance in the Bible 818, 820, 824-828
Dance of Death 2100
dance, sacred 1000, 3739
dance; *see* liturgical dance; masked dance
Dattila[m] 517, 545
Dead Sea scrolls 822, 866
death 3740
Densmore, Frances 2983
Dervishes; *see* Whirling Dervishes
Dett, Nathaniel 2676
Devil and music 2656, 2797
dhikr 2003, 2007, 2008, 2011, 2015, 2021, 2019, 2023
dhrupad 3781
dictionaries and encyclopedias: Afro-America 2577, 2585, 2588; America 2298, 2300; Australia 3588; Bible 787, 798; Canada 2301; Catholic 1174; Christian Church 1010; church music 1014; Islam 1965, 3841; Judaism 832, 833, 835-837; liturgy and worship 1011, 1013, 1172, 1173; medieval France 1012; Mennonite

2445; Middle Ages 15; music 1, 9, 13; mythology and music 3733; Native America 3876; Papua and New Guinea 3663; Protestant church music 1810; religion 5, 7
Dida Harrist hymnody 2269
Didymus, the Blind (4th century CE) 1126
discant 1408, 1412, 1420, 1443
Disciples of Christ, church music; *see* church music, Disciples of Christ
divination-Africa 2139, 2199, 2208, 2215
Divine Names 2063
Djerba 944
Dominican chant 1247
Dorsey, Thomas A. 2729, 2746, 2751
Doukhobor music 2444, 2446, 2447, 2449
drama, religious: India 398; Noh 317-326; North American Indian 3012, 3022, 3235, 3239, 3263, 3300, 3303, 3310, 3315
Dreaming 3603, 3605, 3629, 3631, 3635
dreams, Aborigine 3642; Africa 3845; North American Indian 2996, 3001, 3069, 3093, 3099, 3284, 3323, 3393, 3399, 3886; South American Indian 3486, 3487
drumming/drums 5, 69, 70, 117; Africa 2109, 2111, 2120, 2126, 2128, 2131, 2138, 2149, 2151, 2152, 2161, 2164, 2170, 2175, 2179, 2181, 2188, 2191, 2202, 2208, 2215, 2220, 2239, 2240, 2242; Afro-American, North America 2619, 2620, 2624, 2651, 2667; Afro-American, South America 2875, 2887, 2893, 2901, 2906, 2908, 2909, 2911, 2915, 2918, 2927, 2930, 2934, 2940, 2943, 2946; Asian America 2848; Atumpan 2149; Cambodia 370; Carribbean 2943; Central Asia 360, 361; Eskimo 3531, 3532, 3534, 3538, 3539, 3547, 3562, 3573; Islam 1991; Japan 344; Korea 285; Laos 373; Malaysia 375; Mongolia 354; Nepal 3785, 3787, 3788; North American Indian 3010, 3107, 3116, 3146, 3153, 3372, 3373, 3393; Oceania 3650; Siberia/Lapland 149, 151, 153, 157, 159, 160-162, 166, 172, 173; South American Indian 3416, 3420, 3435, 3453; Sri Lanka 727, 729; Sumatra 491; Thailand 402; Tibet 225, 250
drums, kettle 365, 716
Drums of Affliction 2111; *see* Cult of Affliction
Druz 1993
Dufay, Guillaume 1395, 1448, 1453, 1463, 3808
Dundun drumming 2181
Dunhuang cave manuscripts 3741

Egypt 758, 763, 1683-1695, 3791
encyclopedias; *see* dictionaries and encyclopedias
entún kuifi 3493
Ephrata Cloister 2423, 2430

Rada rite 2915
Ramadan 2000
Ramanuja 3789
rangda 450
rap 2650, 2677, 2678
Rastafarian movement 2935
Recife, Brazil 2888
Reformation, Lutheran 1833, 1838
Reformation, Protestant, and music 1775, 1808, 1813
Reformed Church 2417, 2418, 2432, 2433, 2437, 2438
regular singing 2363-2365, 2371, 2486, 2490
Reims Cathedral 1441
requiem mass 1174, 1190, 3467
responsories 1262
Restoration cathedral music 1788
Revival Zion Church 2931
revivalism 2385, 2386, 2391, 2392, 2394, 2396, 2438, 2491, 2521, 2523, 2567, 2633, 2666, 2708, 2769, 2770
rhythm: Byzantine chant 1614, 1628; early polyphony 1410; rhythm, modal 1416, 1442; rhythm, plainchant 1275-1284, 1521
Rite of Jerusalem 1163, 1165, 1166, 1309
ritual and music 2, 12, 30, 40, 41, 43, 52, 53, 62, 64, 67, 68, 77, 78, 83, 84, 87, 90, 93, 106, 109, 110, 113, 114
ritual, by area: Africa 2119, 2120, 2121, 2124, 2125, 2127, 2135, 2140, 2141, 2143, 2146, 2154-2156, 2158, 2164, 2165, 2168, 2171, 2174-2177, 2183, 2185, 2186, 2191, 2194, 2199-2201, 2205, 2217, 2225, 2228, 2233, 2234, 2235, 2238, 2240-2242; Asia 130, 131, 138, 144, 3744, 3846; Bali 447, 449, 454, 456, 464-466, 468; Central/South America 2877, 2886, 2888, 2890, 2892, 2893, 2898, 2900, 2907, 2912, 2914, 2917, 2922, 2930, 2933, 2939, 2944, 2946; China 3753; Greece 779; India 504, 577, 579, 582, 584, 596, 610, 611, 613, 626, 633, 637, 640, 649, 650, 657, 661, 666; Indonesia: 470-473, 475, 483, 485, 486, 489, 490, 491; Japan 315 317, 322; Java 419, 425, 435, 445, 446; Korea 271, 275, 3750; Nepal 702, 705, 708-711, 716, 717; Romania 3829; Serbia 3828; Southeast Asia 370-372, 378-381, 382, 385, 387, 390, 395, 398, 400, 402, 403, 407, 411, 3774; Sri Lanka 724-726, 729; Thailand 3776
ritual, by group: Afro-American 2595, 2603, 2607, 2609, 2611, 2615, 2617, 2620, 2648, 2655, 2692, 2720, 2734, 2741 Central/South American Indian 3423, 3425, 3426, 3428, 3429, 3434, 3440, 3442, 3450-3452, 3456-3458, 3462-3466, 3471, 3472, 3476, 3488, 3489, 3494, 3505, 3506; Croatian-American 2860; Eskimo/Inuit 3543, 3554, 3567; Hmong-American 2855; North American Indian 2968, 2984,

3007, 3008, 3010, 3012, 3014, 3018, 3023, 3024, 3030, 3043, 3050, 3054, 3055, 3057, 3058, 3060, 3061, 3068, 3069, 3077, 3094, 3095, 3105, 3107, 3116, 3118, 3119, 3124, 3125, 3129, 3140, 3144, 3162, 3163, 3164, 3175, 3177, 3180, 3205, 3220, 3222, 3227, 3235, 3236, 3239, 3247, 3254, 3260, 3263, 3267, 3268, 3279, 3290, 3292, 3299, 3300, 3303, 3305, 3306, 3308, 3310, 3315, 3323, 3329, 3330, 3337, 3343, 3356, 3359, 3361, 3364, 3368, 3386, 3387, 3392, 3396; *see also* North American Indian Ceremonials, by Ceremonial
ritual, by religion:
  Bonpo 3756
  Buddhist: Asian America 2; China 205; Japan 335, 338, 339; Korea 286, 290, 292; Mongolia 356; Tibet 225, 228, 229, 236-239, 241, 245-248, 252-256, 259, 262, 3755, 3761, 3768, 3772
  Christian: African 2265, 2275; India 686; Western Europe 1107, 1211, 1331, 1391, 1397, 1403, 1404, 1411, 1518, 1530, 1534, 1569, 1576, 1578, 1591, 1592
  Confucian and Taoist: China 182, 184-186, 188-191, 194-197, 200-202, 3753; Korea 274, 275, 277-281
  Islamic/Muslim 1991, 1997, 1998, 2000, 2015, 2018, 2022, 2028, 3838, 3844; India/Pakistan 746, 750
  Judaic 899, 967, 975, 977; Judaic-American 2845
  Orthodox 1671, 1673
  shamanic: Central Asia 361 India 674, 675; Japan 347-349; Korea 294-296, 298, 299, 301-304, 306, 308, 3746; Mongolia 352; China 216; Siberia/Lapland 150, 152, 154, 163, 165, 174
  Shinto (Japan) 327-329
  Vedic-India 521, 530, 533, 539, 540, 545, 560, 561
  Zoroastrian 755
ritual drama, southwestern Indian 3882
Roberts, Helen H. 2931
rock and roll 2781, 2792, 2796-2802, 2806, 2809, 2810, 2811, 2813, 2815, 2819
rock gongs 2182, 2187
Roman Catholic church music; *see* church music, Roman Catholic
Roman Catholic church music, African American 2538, 2539, 2628
Roman Catholic Church, East Africa 2208
Roman de Fauvel 1905
Rome, ancient 1026, 3790
Routley, Erik 1061, 1070
Royal Chapel, France 1385
Rumi, Mevlana Jalau'ddin 2010
Ruzbahan Baqli 1967
Rwais (Morocco) 1998

3485; Orinoco 3510; Pemon 3466;
Piaroa 3456, 3484; Suya 3495-3500;
Tapirapé 3516; Tukano 3490; Waiapi
3465; Waiwai 3464; Wakuénai 3471-
3476; Warao 118, 3457, 3458, 3480-
3483; Yaminahua 3511; Xingu 3499
Southern Fundamentalist Black Church
2574
speculative music 2085
spell, Buddhist 3748
spirit-naming 3472, 3476, 3480, 3482
spiritualism 3737
spiritual, white 3862
spirituals 2465, 2623, 2625, 2628, 2629,
2633, 2635, 2642, 2644, 2645, 2664,
2665, 2667, 2682, 2686, 2693-2719,
2764, 2766, 2775, 2816, 3860, 3866
Springsteen, Bruce 2826
spruchmotette 1845
Stromata 2062
Sudan 2207
Sufi music and dance; *see* Islamic music
Sufi, Jewish 919
Surinam 2944
Swan, Timothy 2378
symbols/symbolism, by area or culture 4,
22, 51, 54, 55, 62, 63; Aborigine 3640;
Africa 2154, 2158, 2175, 2194, 2205,
2211, 2214; Afro-America (South
America) 2903, 2914; Afro-America
2734; Ancient Near East 760; Arctic
3525; Asia 129, 131, 138, 144; China
193; India 560, 577, 600, 658, , 693,
701, 711, 723, 729; Indonesia 415,
422, 437, 444, 464, 478, 481, 491; New
Guinea 3650, 3653; North American
Indian 3129, 3144, 3154, 3207, 3254,
3269, 3301, 3372, 3374; Philippines
389; South American Indian 3418,
3423, 3430, 3432, 3437, 3438, 3450,
3451, 3465, 3468, 3490, 3501;
Thailand 402; Tibet 254, 262
symbols/symbolism, by religion or topic:
Bach, J. S. 1852, 1856, 1857; Bible
800; Buddhist 144; Byzantium 1606;
Christian 1138, 1455, 2070, 2265
(Africa); Confucian 274; dance 92,
93, 138, 658, 689, 1897, 1900, 1924,
2914, 3144, 3207, 3423, 3437, 3640;
gospel music 2734; healing 3430;
instrument 68, 131, 153, 162, 164, 254,
262, 389, 402, 422, 481, 491, 729, 760,
800, 1138, 3465, 3468; Islam 1963,
1971; Judaic 856, 897; Kabbalah
2056; masks 2194, 2214, 3525; music
theory 129, 193, 689; notation 897;
number symbolism 1454, 1463, 1740,
2039; plainchant 1201, 1327
(notation); ritual 711, 2154, 2158,
3129, 3254, 3301; Roman Catholic
liturgy 1534, 1558, 1591; Santaría
2620, 2689; shamanism 49, 153, 162,
164, 166, 174, 299, 3430, 3438, 3490,
3501, 3785; Shinto 327; Sun Dance
3026, 3036, 3047; theatre 415, 437,

464, 2194; trance 118, 2175, 2211,
2914; Vedic 560
synagogue, ancient 1149
synagogue music 860, 862, 865, 871, 878,
887, 895, 896, 930, 931, 935, 952, 953,
963, 987, 2830-2833, 2837, 2838, 2841-
2843, 2846, 2847
Syrian Christian liturgical music-India 686
Syrian rite, music of the 1704-1706

Tabwa ritual 2199
Tallis, Thomas 1719
Talmud, music in 928
tantra 237, 568, 572, 573, 577
Taoism 182, 188, 191, 196, 197, 199-202,
3751
tariqat 2003
tayil 3492
Te Deum 1154
te'amim; *see* notation: Tiberian/Masoretic
accents
Temiar 379-381
Thanksgiving 3050
theodicy 2670, 2681, 2711
theology and music 61, 1048-1082, 1194-
1202, 1507-1595, 3821
Thoreau, Henry David 2095
Thyagaraja/Tyagaraja 570, 576, 582, 583,
596
Tibet 130, 133, 140, 142, 143, 144, 223-
263, 3754-3772
time 48, 417, 558, 3220
time consciousness, Aboriginal 3605
time, sacred 63
Tinctoris 3808
Tindley, Charles Albert 2731
Tonga 2213
trance 94, 95, 97, 99, 102, 113, 114, 118,
121, 126; Aborigine 3619; Africa
2109, 2110, 2114, 2115, 2125, 2137,
2138, 2140, 2141, 2147, 2153, 2156,
2167, 2171, 2173, 2175, 2177, 2190,
2196, 2199, 2201, 2202, 2205, 2206,
2208, 2209, 2211, 2213, 2215, 2217,
2219, 2223, 2229, 2230, 2233, 2235,
2266, 2287, 3845, 3849; Afro-
American, North America 2609, 2617,
2622, 2636, 2667, 2686; Afro-
American, Central/South America
2875, 2898, 2901, 2904, 2906, 2914,
2922, 2923, 2929, 2934; Central/South
American Indian 3483, 3517;
Indonesia 423, 433, 446, 447, 452, 453,
461, 466, 485; Islam 1986; North
American Indian 3011, 3013, 3880;
Siberia/Lapland 151, 166; South Asia
621, 632, 709; Southeast Asia 378, 381
Transcendentalism 2095
transmission, oral and literate 1303-1337,
1702, 1703
Trinidad 2939, 2940, 2945, 2947-2949
Trisagia 1617
tropes/troping: Byzantine 1640; Christian
Western Europe 1217, 1219, 1221,
1228, 1238, 1239, 1254, 1255, 1260,
1264, 1268, 1757; Judaic 886, 911

About the Author

E. GARDNER RUST is Professor of Music at Sonoma State University in California, where he has taught courses in world music for over twenty-five years. For the last decade, he has been developing a course on the music and dance of the world's religions. This book is an outgrowth of his interest in the subject.